Judah and the Judeans in the Persian Period

Judah and the Judeans
in the
Persian Period

edited by

ODED LIPSCHITS AND MANFRED OEMING

L.C.C.C. LIBRARY

Winona Lake, Indiana
EISENBRAUNS
2006

© Copyright 2006 by Eisenbrauns.
All rights reserved.
Printed in the United States of America.

www.eisenbrauns.com

Cataloging in Publication Data

Judah and the Judeans : in the Persian period / edited by Oded
Lipschits and Manfred Oeming.
    p. cm.
Includes bibliographical references and indexes.
  ISBN-13: 978-1-57506-104-7 (hardback : alk. paper)
  1. Judaea (Region)—History—Congresses. 2. Yehud (Persian
province)—Congresses. 3. Jews—History—586 B.C.–70 A.D.—
Congresses. 4. Judaism—History—Post-exilic period, 586 B.C.–
210 A.D.—Congresses. 5. Bible. O.T.—Criticism, interpretation,
etc.—Congresses. I. Lipschitz, Oded. II. Oeming, Manfred.
DS110.J78J83 2006
933′.03—dc22

2005037385

The paper used in this publication meets the minimum requirements of the
American National Standard for Information Sciences—Permanence of
Paper for Printed Library Materials, ANSI Z39.48-1984.♾™

Contents

PART 1
HISTORICAL, EPIGRAPHICAL, AND
ARCHAEOLOGICAL PERSPECTIVES

PART 2
BIBLICAL PERSPECTIVES

Introduction

This volume is the outcome of a conference, "Judah and the Judeans in the Achaemenid Period," that took place in Heidelberg on 15–18 July, 2003. The conference was sponsored jointly by the University of Heidelberg, the Hochschule für Jüdische Studien Heidelberg, and Tel Aviv University.

The topic of our symposium, "Judah and the Judeans in the Achaemenid Period," leads us into the realm of mystery. The word *mystery* evokes a twofold feeling of sadness and of hope: sadness, because we know so little and would like to know so much more; hope, because there is still much work to be done in this area. This realization can serve to invigorate our scholarly curiosity and enhance the intensity of our work. The Hebrew Bible contains very few passages that address Achaemenid rule over Judah and the Judeans (539–332 B.C.E.). Very few events are illuminated or given any kind of value judgment. Some of the texts speak to the beginning of the reign of Cyrus II (559–529) and the permission given to return and rebuild the temple (in Aramaic: Ezra 6:3–5; in Hebrew: Ezra 1:1–4; 2 Chr 36:22–23); a second group of texts provides a sketch of the building of the new temple (Haggai, Zechariah 1–8, Ezra 1–6); a third group addresses the events of the middle Persian era, including the introduction of the Torah, the prohibition of mixed marriages under Ezra, the rebuilding of the Jerusalem city wall, and several social reforms under Nehemiah (Ezra 7–10 and the Nehemiah Memoirs). We find the most detailed account in the book of Esther, a book with questionable historical reliability. Another matter of debate is which texts deal with the end of the Persian era in Judah (perhaps Zechariah 9; Daniel 11). The existing extrabiblical sources contain little or no reference to the Judeans or Judah. There are only a few archaeological and epigraphic finds. Thus, Herbert Donner justifiably refers to the Persian era as the "dark ages."

In addition to the scarcity of sources, there is a second reason that this era has not been at the forefront of scholarly endeavors: Haggai, Zechariah, Ezra, Nehemiah, and Chronicles, as well as Esther, are texts not found in the Christian lectionary. These books exist on the fringes of Christian biblical scholarship and of the interest of most congregations. This literature is often categorically denounced as deriving from the "era of law, of epigones, of paralysis." These prejudices have warped our view of these texts. In most textbooks dealing with the history of religion in Israel, the postexilic period suffers from severe neglect. The last 20 years, however, have seen an increased interest in this period. Accompanying this change is a process of radical reevaluation. A current textbook by Rainer Albertz summarizes the situation correctly:

> More recent research, which at many points has prompted critical questions about the customary early dating of many biblical texts, shows increasingly clearly that the post-exilic period, and especially the early post-exilic period (538–400), was one of the most productive eras in the history of Israelite religion. In the face of the challenge posed by the opportunity and the problems of rebuilding, at this time the foundations were laid which were normatively to shape later Jewish and Christian religion; at this time the course towards canonization was taken in the creation of a universally binding holy scripture; at this time the temple came to occupy the centre of religious life and became the central symbol of wide-ranging hopes; and at this time a horizon of eschatological expectation arose which increasingly clearly went beyond the limits of political history and human existence.
>
> The liveliness of the theological discourse, particularly in the post-exilic period, is evident from a multiplicity of "theological currents" which scholars have long detected in the texts of this period. Deuteronomistic, Priestly, Chronistic, wisdom, prophetic and psalms traditions clearly stand side by side and over against one another and often cross. Their variety is so great that even now it is difficult to give them their due place in the history of Israelite religion and the social history of the community.[1]

In all of this, the question of the degree of influence exerted by the Persian Empire on Israel's thought and belief remains a matter of great debate and disagreement. Did or did not the culture of this huge world empire influence the beginnings of Judaism and its literature? Answering this question necessitates a great deal of detective work. By weaving together the interdisciplinary insights of archaeology, epigraphy, military and economic history, the history of administrative organization, as well as biblical exegesis and theology, the contributors to this volume hope to shed more light on the mystery of the Achaemenid Period.

Part 1 of this book gathers together historical, epigraphic, and archaeological perspectives. It opens with an examination of one of the

---

1. Rainer Albertz, *A History of Israelite Religion in the Old Testament Period*, vol. 2: *From the Exile to the Maccabees* (trans. J. Bowden; OTL; Louisville: Westminster John Knox, 1994) 437–38.

central events of the Achaemenid Period, the return from Exile. The book of Ezra suggests that, soon after Cyrus's conquest of Babylon, the exiled Judahites were allowed to return to Jerusalem and its vicinity (Ezra 1:1). *Bob Becking* questions whether this return was a single event, as indicated by the book of Ezra. In Becking's view, the concept of the "mass return" should be construed as a historical myth. In contrast to religiohistorical myths, historical myth is defined by Becking as a *narratio* of the past that stands (partly) contrary to the available evidence. Historical myth constructs a past to serve specific ideological interests.

Oded Lipschits describes how the Shephelah and the hill country became the centers for rural communities, supplying mainly grain, wine, and olive oil. The "rural policy" of the Achaemenid regime in the Shephelah and hill country limited the development of the local population. For background on this settlement policy, he examines the descriptions of the rebuilding of Jerusalem in Ezra and Nehemiah, which reflect the unique fate of the city. A close inspection of the policies of the Achaemenid provincial authorities and the ongoing efforts of Judah's neighbors to prevent the building of the city walls may explain Jewish enthusiasm and the resurrection of national aspirations at that time from a fresh perspective.

Jon Berquist questions the assumptions that underlie the use of terms such as *Judeans, Jews, Yehudites, Jerusalemites, ha-golah,* and others to describe the populace of Persian Yehud. He shows how Yehudite society became an amalgamation of divergent forms and structures in which the various centers of power forced identity into hybridity. Berquist examines the way that multiple forces shaped identity—ethnic, religious, and political processes, as well as the dynamics of family life, education, economics, and resistance.

John Wright argues that the search for the borders of Yehud anachronistically presupposes the model of the modern Western nation-state and its colonial mapping of the world as normative for Yehud and the Achaemenid Empire. The borders of Yehud should be understood as permeable and interlacing, with various patronage systems making overlapping territorial claims, rather than circumscribing a unitary space controlled by a single sovereignty. Recently discovered Idumean inscriptions and the genealogies of the book of Chronicles provide positive evidence for remapping Yehud in this manner.

The Golah returnees were but one of several communities within the Persian Empire claiming some connection to the deity Yahweh. What kind of power relationship did the returnees have with these various groups and with the Persian imperial authorities? *John Kessler* examines the nature, self-definition, and functioning of ethnoreligious groups in the broader context of imperialism and colonialism. He proposes the model of the "Charter Group," a concept derived from the work of sociologist John Porter, as a heuristic vantage point from which to conceptualize the Golah returnees' power relationships within the context of the Empire.

Distinguishing the historical *ʿam hāʾāreṣ* from the people the redactor of Ezra–Nehemiah thought them to be, *Lisbeth Fried* argues that the disputes between the *ʿam hāʾāreṣ* and the *gôlâ* were a retrojection of later conflicts and thus not historical. She suggests that the *ʿam hāʾāreṣ* were Nehemiah's enemies, the empowered landed aristocracy. This group was Persian, comprising members of the dominant ethno-class, the satrapal officials. The policies revealed in Nehemiah's memoir reflect the contradictory attitudes of the Persian emperor toward this aristocratic class.

There are two possibilities for restoring the line of the city wall of Jerusalem as described by Nehemiah. According to the "minimalist" view, the city wall surrounded the City of David and the Temple Mount. According to the "maximalist" view, the city wall also encompassed the Southwest Hill. *David Ussishkin* argues for the maximalist position. It appears, however, that many parts of the larger city remained uninhabited. Jerusalem of the Persian Period can be compared with Byzantine Constantinople in the period before its conquest by the Ottomans in 1453 C.E.: a large, fortified—but half empty—metropolis.

The remarkable archaeological data collected from the excavations carried out at Lachish and the surveys around it warrant a creative analysis of the complex relationship between the archaeological reality and the biblical account. *Alexander Fantalkin* and *Oren Tal* argue that the establishment of the Achaemenid administrative center at Lachish in the early fourth century B.C.E. should be seen as a response to the changes that occurred in the area during this period. This is the background for Fantalkin and Tal's research on the reference to Lachish in Neh 11:30 and the creation of the border between Judah and Idumea.

In observations based entirely on archaeological data, *Ephraim Stern* observes that the abundance of local sanctuaries and clay figurines found all over the hill country (in both the kingdoms of Israel and Judah) from the eighth and seventh centuries B.C.E. stands in marked contrast to the complete lack of finds of that sort from the Persian Period. He concludes that the latest archaeological evidence clearly indicates that all the pagan popular religious elements had undergone purification during the Persian Period both in the province of Judah and in Samaria, and even the many smaller sanctuaries disappeared. In these two provinces there was only one central cult place during the Persian Period.

Diana Edelman explores the circumstances that gave rise to the settlement of Tyrian merchants in Jerusalem during the reign of Arta- xerxes I. She argues that they were granted a royal concession to con- duct trade in the *bîrâ* as a reward for the loyal long-term military service that Tyre had provided to Persia in naval battles, culminating in the 454 B.C.E. defeat of the Greek-Egyptian alliance during the revolt of Inaros in the Delta.

The archive of Jedoniah of Jeb (Elephantine) gives us a historical window into Egyptian Judaism that appears to be much closer to his- torical Israel of the pre- and postexilic periods in Palestine than the bib- lical version of Judaism. *Reinhard Kratz* examines the biblical sources for the rebuilding of the Second Temple in Jerusalem in light of the later events in Jeb. After asking what the primary sources from Elephantine contribute to the historical reconstruction of events in Jerusalem, he considers what conclusions follow from the Elephantine sources re- garding the authenticity and literary history of the biblical sources.

Gary Knoppers argues that recent studies of the material remains from Samaria warrant revisiting Judean-Samarian relations during the Persian Period. He concentrates on archaeological, epigraphic, and historical matters. Pertinent discoveries prompting discussion include the existence of a significant Samarian population during the Achae- menid era, a time when the community in Yehud was relatively small; the existence of monumental architecture on Mt. Gerizim at an earlier date than scholars had previously assumed; and material remains in- dicating significant cultural overlap between the Samarian and Judean communities.

Approximately 50 percent of the population of Yehud was of Israel- ite ancestry. *Ernst Axel Knauf* shows that Israelite influence can be traced in the language, literature, and religion of postexilic Judah: (1) Middle or Mishnaic Hebrew emerged during the Persian Period, traceable by its influence on Late Biblical Hebrew; (2) Israelite litera- ture merged into canonical tradition as late as the third century B.C.E.; (3) theologically, the influence of the Benjaminite region on biblical religion is attested by pro-Bethel texts and the concept of a peaceful "reunification" of Judah and Ephraim.

David Vanderhooft presents a comparative historiographical analysis of evidence regarding the entry of Cyrus II into Babylon in 539 B.C.E. He investigates the cuneiform, Greek, and biblical portrayals of the event and, more briefly, considers the archaeological correlates of these textual portraits. Vanderhooft clarifies the rationale for historiographic reconstruction in discrete Near Eastern traditions emanating from the sixth century, including traditions among the emerging Hebrew-speaking elite of the early Persian era.

Muhammad Dandamayev presents the limited information available on state administration in Mesopotamia during the Chaldean and Achaemenid Periods. He shows that the terminology of the Babylonian administration and the functions of various officials were essentially the same during Chaldean and Persian times. Dandamayev concludes that, even though local administrative traditions were not disrupted when Mesopotamia was conquered by the Persians in 539, we can observe significant gradual changes in the administrative structure as early as Cyrus's reign.

Laurie Pearce examines 3 Achaemenid-period documents published by Joannès and Lemaire as well as a corpus of some 90 soon-to-be-published texts. In addition to providing new geographical information, these documents increase our knowledge of the Judean population in Babylonia: (1) they increase the number of names that can be identified as Judean because of the presence of the Yahwistic element; (2) they offer evidence for the organization of Judeans into the typical Achaemenid socioeconomic organizational unit, the *ḫaṭru*; (3) they document the presence of Judeans in a town in southern Mesopotamia named āl-Yāhūdu and their participation in Babylonian economic activities as early as 572 B.C.E. Pearce provides a general introduction to the contents of these important documents and indicates areas that call for additional research.

Following the publication of new Aramaic ostraca from Arad and Beer-Sheba by J. Naveh, as well as of approximately 800 more Aramaic ostraca from the area of Khirbet el-Kôm/Makkedah, *André Lemaire* first presents an overview of the main historical issues involved in this often-neglected documentation and then the main problems connected with the historical interpretation of these generally short and cursive inscriptions. Lemaire also presents a sample of previously unpublished ostraca from the area of Khirbet el-Kôm/Makkedah.

Bezalel Porten and *Ada Yardeni* also examine the recently discovered Idumean Aramaic ostraca. Altogether, there are some 1,600 pieces, of which 1,400 are legible, scattered among numerous collectors and public institutions. In the search for natural groupings, or archives, scholars fall back upon the groupings as they came from the dealers' hands. Three of these collections have so far been isolated, each of about 50 documents. Eph'al and Naveh have published one group; the other 2 groups are from unpublished texts, one an archive of a storehouse director named Saadel and the second a collection that lists the names of workers. Using palaeography and prosopography, the authors address the question of the identity of the Alexander who appears in the date formulas.

Part 2 of the book assembles various biblical perspectives on the Persian era. Any discussion of the Persian era from a biblical point of view must address the issues evident in Ezra–Nehemiah. Two major problems facing a student of Ezra–Nehemiah are the work's unclear chronology and its apparently patchwork composition. Using the concept of historical periodization, *Sara Japhet* examines the abundant indications of time and references to dates in the text. She argues that historical periodization provides a system for structuring the entire work. The author of Ezra–Nehemiah organized the miscellaneous materials available to him according to topics and events related to the restoration of Judah and Jerusalem in analogy to the Exodus from Egypt. In conclusion, Japhet addresses the issue of "fact" and "fiction" in the context of her observations.

Tamara Cohn Eskenazi challenges the view that Persian and priestly interests were the driving force behind the missions of Ezra and Nehemiah. She suggests other ways to understand the nature and achievements of the two leaders and of Ezra–Nehemiah as a book. Her essay, "The Missions of Ezra and Nehemiah," focuses on (1) the redefinition of ethnic boundaries and national identity in the Persian Period; (2) the specific vocabulary used in Ezra–Nehemiah as a clue to the socio-economic issues regarding "foreign" wives; and (3) the relevance of reassessing information from classical Athens as a source for shedding light on Achaemenid Judah.

Within Ezra 1–6 there are a number of communications that are ostensibly from the Persian administration. If authentic, they are valuable resources for the history of the Persian Empire and Persian Yehud. However, if the Aramaic documents were to be discovered today without an archaeological or literary context, no one would date them to the Persian Period because of their language and orthography. Nevertheless, questioning their authenticity remains a minority view. *Lester Grabbe* examines the communications of Ezra in the light of the most recent information on language and orthography, epistolography, Persian history, and Achaemenid institutions.

The books of Ezra and Nehemiah regard the Persian government very highly; Nehemiah 9, on the other hand, presents a completely different perspective. Toward the end of this chapter, the attitude toward Persian authority seems completely negative (Neh 9:36ff.). Scholars have proposed several solutions to this problem, but all of these solutions presuppose that the book of Nehemiah is self-contradictory in one respect or another. *Manfred Oeming* presents a new translation of this passage. He argues that Nehemiah 9 is a theological interpretation of the history of Israel, containing a fundamental description of God and his relationship to Judah during the Achaemenid period. This fresh understanding opens the possibility of interpreting the whole book consistently.

The language used in the books of Ezra and Nehemiah reflects many features of the Judean speech community of the Persian Period. *Frank Polak* highlights aspects of the social and cultural complexity of this community by means of the language used and the way in which it is used. Even though the texts are written, it is possible to show that they reflect actual features of speech, which can be used to sketch a social and cultural profile of the language community. He addresses three main issues: (1) bilingualism and administration; (2) the status of written Hebrew; and (3) the Hebrew vernacular.

Insights into the Persian Period from a biblical perspective are not limited to the books of Ezra and Nehemiah, as the final few contributions below make clear. *Joseph Blenkinsopp* addresses the repristination of tribal consciousness, especially in evidence in Judahite–Benjaminite hostility subsequent to the fall of Jerusalem. This phenomenon suggests a new look at some familiar Benjaminite traditions, which appear to reflect the still very obscure situation during the first century of Persian rule. The most telling case is the tribal war of extermination led by Judah and directed against Benjamin in Judges 19–21. Blenkinsopp also briefly considers whether the uncertain archaeological record sheds light on this reading of the Benjaminite texts.

Yairah Amit compares the delicate balance in the characterization of Saul in the first book of Samuel with the explicit and implicit anti-Saul polemic and implicit pro-Saul polemic in the literature of the Persian Period. The existence of a polemic centered on Saul indicates that the issue of the preferred dynasty and the need to protect and to justify the choice of the House of David occupied the literature of the Persian Period. Amit also proposes that there was an attempt to rehabilitate the House of Saul during the Persian Period.

Because the Priestly Code (P) is generally dated within the Persian Period, a discussion of P nicely rounds out the discussions of biblical texts. *Hanna Liss* concentrates on the literary qualities of the Priestly

Code and attempts to understand these texts as literary artifacts. After developing criteria for the identification of a fictional text, she focuses on a close reading and literary exegesis of selected passages on the construction of the tabernacle. Liss concludes that P introduces cultic institutions as the only means for a meeting between Yahweh and Israel, while transferring them out of the natural ("historical") world into the realm of the text.

We would like to thank Mrs. Beitz from the Hochschule für Jüdische Studien, Eva Geissler, secretary in the Theological Faculty of the University of Heidelberg and the many assistants who worked hard in the background to ensure that this symposium ran smoothly.

We would also like to thank Jim Eisenbraun and his team for their cooperation and hard work in publishing this volume.

ODED LIPSCHITS   MANFRED OEMING
Tel Aviv University   University of Heidelberg

Abbreviations

General

A.	Louvre Museum siglum
Akk.	Akkadian
ANE	ancient Near East
AO	tablets in the collections of the Musée du Louvre
Aram.	Aramaic
BH	Biblical Hebrew
BM	tablets in the collections of the British Museum
BN	Bibliotheque Nationale
cstr.	construct
Dar.	Darius
DN	deity name
DH	Deuteronomistic Historian
frag(s).	fragment(s)
Heb.	Hebrew
IH	Israeli Hebrew
K	tablets in the Kouyunjik collection of the British Museum
LBH	Late Biblical Hebrew
LXX	Septuagint
MH	Mishnaic Hebrew
Mnmt	monument
mp	masculine plural
ms	masculine singular
MS(S)	manuscript(s)
MT	Masoretic Text
NA	Neo-Assyrian
NB	Neo-Babylonian
Nbk.	Nebuchadnezzar
Nbn.	Nabonidus
ND	field numbers of tablets excavated at Nimrud (Kalhu)
NinA	"Nineveh A," in R. Borger, *Die Inschriften Asarhaddons, Königs von Assyrien*. AfO Beiheft 9. Graz, Austria: Selbstverlag des Herausgebers, 1956
NJPSV	New Jewish Publication Society Version
NKJV	New King James Version
NRSV	New Revised Standard Version
obv.	obverse
OT	Old Testament
pl.	plural
PN	personal name
ptc.	participle
rev.	reverse
RN	royal name
Sam.	Samaritan

Sm.	tablets in the collections of the British Museum
suff.	suffix
SV	Subject-Verb word order
Syr.	Syriac
N	tablets from Nippur in the collections of the University Museum of the University of Pennsylvania, Philadelphia
Vulg.	Vulgate
WDSP	Wadi ed-Daliyeh Samaria Papyri

Reference Works

AASOR	Annual of the American Schools of Oriental Research
AB	Anchor Bible
ABD	Freedman, D. N. (editor). *The Anchor Bible Dictionary.* 6 vols. Garden City, N.Y.: Doubleday, 1992
ABL	Harper, R. F. (editor). *Assyrian and Babylonian Letters Belonging to the Kouyunjik Collections of the British Museum.* 14 vols. Chicago: University of Chicago Press, 1892–1914
ABRL	Anchor Bible Reference Library
ADAJ	*Annual of the Department of Antiquities of Jordan*
AfO	*Archiv für Orientforschung*
AfOB	Archiv für Orientforschung: Beiheft
AHw	Von Soden, W. *Akkadisches Handwörterbuch.* 3 vols. Wiesbaden: Harrassowitz, 1965–81
AJBA	*Australian Journal of Biblical Archaeology*
AJSL	*American Journal of Semitic Languages and Literatures*
ANET	Pritchard, J. B. (editor). *Ancient Near Eastern Texts Relating to the Old Testament.* 3d ed. Princeton: Princeton University Press, 1969
AnSt	*Anatolian Studies*
AOAT	Alter Orient und Altes Testament
AOS	American Oriental Series
AP	Cowley, A. E. (editor). *Aramaic Papyri of the Fifth Century* B.C. Oxford: Clarendon, 1923
AS	Assyriological Studies
ATD	Das Alte Testament Deutsch
AuOr	*Aula orientalis*
AUWE	Ausgrabungen in Uruk-Warka: Endberichte
BA	*Biblical Archaeologist*
BAR	*Biblical Archaeology Review*
BAR Int. Series	British Archaeological Reports, International Series
BASOR	*Bulletin of the American Schools of Oriental Research*
BBB	Bonner biblische Beiträge
BDB	Brown, F., S. R. Driver, and C. A. Briggs. *Hebrew and English Lexicon of the Old Testament.* Oxford: Clarendon, 1907
BEATAJ	Beiträge zur Erforschung des Alten Testaments und des antiken Judentum
BETL	Bibliotheca ephemeridum theologicarum lovaniensium
BHS	Elliger, K., and W. Rudolph (editors). *Biblia Hebraica Stuttgartensia.* Stuttgart: Deutsche Bibelgesellschaft, 1984
BIN	Babylonian Inscriptions in the Collection of James B. Nies
BJRL	*Bulletin of the John Rylands University Library of Manchester*

BJS	Brown Judaic Studies
BN	*Biblische Notizen*
BTAVO	Beihefte zum Tübinger Atlas des Vorderen Orients
BWANT	Beiträge zur Wissenschaft vom Alten und Neuen Testament
BZAW	Beihefte zur Zeitschrift für die Alttestamentliche Wissenschaft
CAD	Oppenheim, A. L., et al. (editors). *The Assyrian Dictionary of the Oriental Institute of the University of Chicago.* Chicago: The Oriental Institute of the University of Chicago, 1956–
CAH	*Cambridge Ancient History*
CahRB	Cahiers de la Revue biblique
CBQ	*Catholic Biblical Quarterly*
CHI	*Cambridge History of Iran.* Cambridge: Cambridge University Press, 1968–91
CHJ	Davies, W. D., and Louis Finkelstein (editors). *Cambridge History of Judaism.* 2 vols. Cambridge: Cambridge University Press, 1984–90
COS	Hallo, W. W. (editor). *The Context of Scripture.* 3 vols. Leiden: Brill, 1997–2003
CT	Cuneiform Texts from Babylonian Tablets in the British Museum
DDD	Toorn, K. van der, B. Becking, and P. W. van der Horst (editors). *Dictionary of Deities and Demons in the Bible.* Leiden: Brill, 1995
DJD	Discoveries in the Judaean Desert
DMOA	Documenta et Monumenta Orientis Antiqui
DNa	Inscription A from the tomb of Darius at Naqs-i Rustam
ErIsr	*Eretz-Israel*
EvT	*Evangelische Theologie*
FAT	Forschungen zum Alten Testament
FGH	Jacoby, F. (editor). *Die Fragmente der griechischen Historiker.* Leiden: Brill, 1954–64
FRLANT	Forschungen zur Religion und Literatur des Alten und Neuen Testaments
FuB	*Forschungen und Berichte*
GB	[Gesenius, Wilhelm, and] Gotthelf Bergsträsser. *Hebräische Grammatik.* 29th ed. 2 vols. Leipzig: Hinrichs, 1918–29. Reprinted, Hildesheim: Olms, 1962
GCCI	Dougherty, R. P. *Goucher College Cuneiform Inscriptions.* 2 vols. New Haven: Yale Unisveristy Press, 1923–33
GTA	Göttinger theologischer Arbeiten
HALAT	Koehler, L., and W. Baumgartner, et al. (editors). *Hebräisches und aramäisches Lexikon zum Alten Testament.* 4 vols. Leiden: Brill, 1967–90
HAR	*Hebrew Annual Review*
HAT	Handbuch zum Alten Testament
HdA	Handbuch der Altertumswissenschaften
HO	Handbuch der Orientalistik
HS	*Hebrew Studies*
HSM	Harvard Semitic Monographs
HSS	Harvard Semitic Studies
HTR	*Harvard Theological Review*
HUCA	*Hebrew Union College Annual*
ICC	International Critical Commentary
IEJ	*Israel Exploration Journal*

IOS	*Israel Oriental Studies*
JANES(CU)	*Journal of the Ancient Near Eastern Society (of Columbia University)*
JAOS	*Journal of the American Oriental Society*
JBL	*Journal of Biblical Literature*
JBTh	*Jahrbuch für biblische Theologie*
JCS	*Journal of Cuneiform Studies*
JESHO	*Journal of Economic and Social History of the Orient*
JJS	*Journal of Jewish Studies*
JNES	*Journal of Near Eastern Studies*
JNSL	*Journal of Northwest Semitic Languages*
JQR	*Jewish Quarterly Review*
JSJ	*Journal for the Study of Judaism*
JSJSup	Journal for the Study of Judaism, Supplement
JSOT	*Journal for the Study of the Old Testament*
JSOTSup	Journal for the Study of the Old Testament, Supplements
JSS	*Journal of Semitic Studies*
JTS	*Journal of Theological Studies*
JTVI	*Journal of the Transactions of the Victoria Institute*
KAI	Donner, H., and W. Röllig. *Kanaanäische und aramäische Inschriften.* Wiesbaden: Harrassowitz, 1962–64
KAT	Kommentar zum Alten Testament
KS	*Kirjath-Sepher*
LSJ	Liddell, H. G., and R. Scott. *Greek-English Lexicon.* Revised by H. S. Jones. Oxford: Clarendon, 1968
LTQ	*Lexington Theological Quarterly*
MDAIK	*Mitteilungen des deutschen archäologischen Instituts, Abteilung Kairo*
MdB	*Le Monde de la Bible*
NABU	*Nouvelles assyriologiques brèves et utilitaires*
Nbk.	Strassmaier, J. N. *Inschriften von Nabuchodonosor, König von Babylon (604–561 v. Chr.).* Leipzig: Pfeiffer, 1889
Nbn.	Strassmaier, J. N. *Inschriften von Nabonidus, König von Babylon (555–538 v. Chr.).* Leipzig: Pfeiffer, 1889
NCB	New Century Bible
NEAEHL	Stern, E. (editor). *New Encyclopaedia of Archaeological Excavations in the Holy Land.* 4 vols. Jerusalem: Israel Exploration Society and Carta / New York: Simon & Schuster, 1993
NEchtB	Neue Echter Bibel
OBO	Orbis biblicus et orientalis
OEANE	Meyers, E. M. (editor). *The Oxford Encyclopedia of Archaeology in the Near East.* 5 vols. New York: Oxford University Press, 1997
OLA	Orientalia Lovaniensia Analecta
Or	*Orientalia*
OrAnt	*Oriens antiquus*
OTL	Old Testament Library
OTS	*Oudtestamentische Studiën*
PEQ	*Palestine Exploration Quarterly*
PIHANS	Publications de l'Institut historique: Archéologique néerlandais de Stanboul
PJB	*Palästina-Jahrbuch*
RA	*Revue d'assyriologie et d'archéologie orientale*
RB	*Revue biblique*

RGTC	Répertoire géographique des textes cunéiformes
SBAW	Sitzungsberichte der Bayerischen Akademie der Wissenschaften
SBLABS	Society of Biblical Literature Archaeology and Biblical Studies
SBLDS	Society of Biblical Literature Dissertation Series
SBLMS	Society of Biblical Literature Monograph Series
SBLSymS	Society of Biblical Literature Symposium Series
Sem	_Semitica_
SHANE	Studies in the History of the Ancient Near East
STDJ	Studies on the Texts of the Desert of Judah
_TA_	_Tel Aviv_
TAD	Porten, B., and A. Yardeni. _Textbook of Aramaic Documents from Ancient Egypt._ 4 vols. Hebrew University Department of the History of the Jewish People, Texts and Studies for Students. Jerusalem: Academon, 1986–99
TAPA	_Transactions of the American Philological Association_
TCL	Textes cunéiformes du Louvre. Paris: Geuthner, 1910–
TDA	Tell Deir ʿAlla Balaam Inscription
TDOT	Botterweck, G. J., and H. Ringgren (editors). _Theological Dictionary of the Old Testament._ Grand Rapids, Mich.: Eerdmans, 1974–
Transeu	_Transeuphratène_
ThWAT	Botterweck, G. J., and H. Ringgren (editors). _Theologisches Wörterbuch zum Alten Testament._ Stuttgart: Kohlhammer, 1970–
TRE	Krause, G., and G. Müller (editors). _Theologische Realenzyklopädie._ Berlin: de Gruyter, 1977–
TRu	_Theologische Rundschau_
TUAT	Kaiser, Otto (editor). _Texte aus der Umwelt des Alten Testaments._ Gütersloh: Mohn, 1984–
TuM	Texte und Materialien der Frau Professor Hilprecht Collection of Babylonian Antiquities im Eigentum der Universität Jena
TynBul	_Tyndale Bulletin_
_UF_	_Ugarit-Forschungen_
VAB	Vorderasiatische Bibliothek
VS	Vorderasiatische Schriftdenkmäler
_VT_	_Vetus Testamentum_
VTSup	Vetus Testamentum Supplements
WBC	Word Biblical Commentary
WZKM	_Wiener Zeitschrift für die Kunde des Morgenlandes_
WHJP	World History of the Jewish People
WMANT	Wissenschaftliche Monographien zum Alten und Neuen Testament
_ZA_	_Zeitschrift für Assyriologie_
ZAH	_Zeitschrift für Althebräistik_
ZÄS	_Zeitschrift für ägyptische Sprache und Altertumskunde_
ZAW	_Zeitschrift für die Alttestamentliche Wissenschaft_
ZDPV	_Zeitschrift des deutschen Palästina-Vereins_
ZTK	_Zeitschrift für Theologie und Kirche_

PART 1

Historical, Epigraphical, and Archaeological Perspectives

"We All Returned as One!":
Critical Notes on the Myth of the Mass Return

BOB BECKING
Utrecht University

Introduction

In Ps 126 one reads:

1 When YHWH restored the fortunes of Zion,
  we were like those who dream.
2 Then our mouth was filled with laughter,
  and our tongue with shouts of joy;
  then it was said among the nations:
  "YHWH has done great things for them."
3 YHWH has done great things for us,
  and we rejoiced.

This psalm should be interpreted as a late retrospect of the return from Exile. The syntagma *b* + Infinitive in v. 1, *bšwb yhwh*, can only be construed as a reference to the past (Joüon and Muraoka 1991: §166 *l*). In this psalm, the return from Exile is seen as an unexpected intervention by YHWH in the course of history on behalf of the "we"-group. The remembrance of this earlier intervention functions as a ground to ask YHWH to intervene again in newly risen troubles.[1] The exact identity of the "we"-group cannot be established, but it seems clear—at least to me—that the use of this "we"-language indicates a religious idea by which this "we"-group construes itself as the descendants of and even identifies itself with "those who returned from Babylon." This implies that the return from exile is seen as a collective event in which Israel in its entirety was involved.

The book of Ezra suggests that, soon after Cyrus's conquest of Babylon, the exiled Judahites were allowed to return to Jerusalem and its vicinity (Ezra 5:1). The list of returnees in Ezra 2, when read at face

---

1. On the interpretation of Psalm 126, see, e.g., Beyerlin 1978; Mosis 1990; and the various commentaries on the book of Psalms.

value, gives the impression of a collective and massive return from exile. The elements from the book of Ezra seem to suggest that "We all returned as one." This image has yielded the view that the return was a single event to be dated in the early years of the Persian era. This view has been dominant in traditional descriptions of the history of ancient Israel by Jews and Christians alike (see Neusner 1987; Talmon 2001). This view is present in more-traditional "histories of Israel"[2] and can still be found in theological reflections on the Hebrew Bible (e.g., Brueggemann 1997). The view is present in retellings of the biblical stories for children and even in fine arts.[3]

Literary-Critical Objections

The historicity of this perception of the return from Exile has been challenged by scholars applying literary-critical methods. Charles Torrey already questioned the view. According to Torrey, Ezra never existed: the person is an invention of the tradition, and a return from Exile never took place.[4] The position of Torrey has recently been brought into the debate on the historicity of the exile (see, e.g., Carroll 1998). What strikes me is that the arguments in this debate are mostly of a restricted literary-critical nature. The pattern in this argument seems to be that (parts of the) book of Ezra should be dated late. An implicit assumption is the surmise that later texts seldom contain correct historical data. Archaeological data and written extrabiblical sources play only a minor part in the argument, if any. When assessing the authenticity of the material in the books of Ezra and Nehemiah, Old Testament scholars hold different positions. This will be clarified here by presenting two opposite positions.[5]

Baruch Halpern, in a very learned article (Halpern 1990), considers Ezra 1:1–4:3 as containing authentic material from the reign of Cyrus. Ezra 4:4–6:22 is, in his conception, written in a form comparable to the so-called "summary-inscriptions" of the Mesopotamian kings.[6] This implies that the material in the textual unit under consideration is not

---

2. Up to Sacchi 2000: 58–68.

3. Although a recent French novel toys with the idea of a twofold return: in 538 B.C.E. under Cyrus and in 522 B.C.E. under Darius (Banon 2003).

4. Torrey 1970: 285–335.

5. The discussion on the emergence and composition has not yet reached an end; see, e.g., Williamson 1987; Grabbe 1998; Becking 1998; Karrer 2000.

6. Halpern 1990: 111–12; note that Halpern is not giving a comprehensive description of this *Gattung* that differs from the Royal Annals.

ordered chronologically but geographically. Thus distorting the narrative order, Halpern claims that we have authentic material from different periods. This view has implications for the reconstruction of the Ezra episodes.

Lester Grabbe, on the other hand, has seriously reevaluated, if not discarded altogether, the authenticity of the sources underlying the book of Ezra (Grabbe 1991; Grabbe 1994: 30–41; Grabbe 1998: 125–53). Grabbe questions the authenticity of the Aramaic documents, the letters in Ezra 5–6, and the Ezra Memoir (Ezra 7–10). His main argument runs, as far as I can see, as follows: The comparative material by which to judge the authenticity of the "Archive material" is too small in number and of uncertain authenticity. We simply have too few contemporary letters and archival notes to conclude whether the Edict of Cyrus and the Aramaic letters in the book of Ezra are genuine or not.[7] Second, he argues that, even if the material in Ezra did go back to genuine documents, we do not possess these documents. He quite correctly remarks that we have the material embedded in the narratives and by implication in a reworked form. He even gives a few examples from Josephus for his thesis that "doctoring of documents to make them more pro-Jewish seems to have been a minor cottage industry," by which is meant that editorial intervention and embedding in a narrative can change the scope and the ideology of a document to such a degree that it is impossible to reconstruct the original text.[8] Grabbe's position can also be labeled "skeptical" or "minimalistic."[9]

Both Halpern and Grabbe, despite their different positions, apply about the same method: a literary-critical approach that seeks to distinguish between "authentic material" and "redactional reworkings" that are by implication of no historical value. Both make use of comparative material, Mesopotamian royal inscriptions, and Aramaic letters but only for comparing genres and not for providing independent data. Two remarks need to be made here in order to clarify the boundaries of literary criticism in a restricted discourse:

1. Although Halpern and Grabbe are aware of a world outside the text, they do not bring in historical evidence as part of their discourse.

---

7. An analysis of the letters by Schwiderski 2000, however, reinforces Grabbe's argument.

8. Grabbe 1991: 101–2.

9. Grabbe seems to have expected this kind of classification; cf. Grabbe 1991: 105–6.

2. The real weakness of literary criticism, however, is the lack of clear criteria by which to decide between "authentic" and "late"; between "tradition" and "redaction." This lack of clear criteria is in my view the basis for the divergence in the results of scholars who apply the same method.

My considerations, however, do not imply that the Hebrew Bible should be abandoned or set aside as not containing historical evidence at all. For an appreciation of the character of the historical narrative in the book of Ezra, as well as for a more reliable reconstruction, an investigation of the available evidence is needed. This external evidence consists in archaeological and epigraphic data and their interpretation.[10]

The Idea of a Historical Myth

Critical scholars label the book of Ezra, or parts of it, as a biased narrative about the past, as pure propaganda, or as ideological history. I prefer to construe Ezra 2 as the expression of a historical myth. The concept of *myth* in this context does not have a specific religiohistorical connotation. It is not meant in the same way as "a creation myth." *Myth* here is a historiographical category referring to a *narratio* on the past that stands (partly) contrary to the available evidence. A *historical myth* is a social construct that serves within a community or society. I here follow the definition of Jean-Jacques Wunenberger:

> In its most extensive definition, myth appears in a traditional society as a history concerning actions and individuals whose recollection is considered as an exemplary model because the story is a bearer of truth and meaning for those who are their intermediaries. . . . In short, myth is at the same time a message and a medium, a corpus of histories to decipher and a narrative of social practice. (Wunenberger 1994: 61; translated from French)

The historical myth quite often takes the form of a basic belief that things happened in a specific way. An example will be given: the myth of the mass resistance. Historical textbooks and other representations of the Netherlands during the Second World War have presented the view that the greatest part of the population was in one way or another involved in the resistance against the German occupation. Careful historical research made clear that this view was a myth. Participation in the resistance was surprisingly low. Nevertheless, during the 1950s and 1960s of the last century, this myth served as part of a proud public identity: "we resisted the Germans!" I would like to argue that the idea

---

10. See my remarks in Becking 2003.

"We returned as one from Exile" in the early years of the Persian hege-mony likewise was a historical myth. The following considerations are given as arguments for my position.

The Mass Return from Exile: History or Myth?

The answer to the question "myth or history?" cannot be given by literary-critical considerations only but requires an examination of the implications of the assumption that a mass return took place. If the concept of a mass return from Exile were correct, then (1) hints of it should be present in official Persian documents; (2) traces of it should be observable in the archaeological record of Persian-Period Yehud; and (3) a dramatic demographic decrease of Judeans in Mesopotamia should be traceable. These implications need to be compared with the extrabiblical evidence.

Empty Land and Mass Return

It should be kept in mind that the Myth of the Mass Return is par-tially based on the Myth of the Empty Land or, phrased otherwise: the idea that "we all returned from Exile" is connected to the idea that "we all went into Exile" (Knauf 1994: 167). Hans Barstad has discarded the view that during the Babylonian Exile Jerusalem and surrounding areas were almost completely depopulated and that the former Ju-deans were massively deported to Babylonia. His analysis of textual and archaeological data has informed the view that the "land was not empty." The territory of the former kingdom of Judah was populated, and this population contributed much to the books that now are part the Hebrew Bible (Barstad 1996). His view has been challenged by Da-vid Vanderhooft, who argued that the dating of the archaeological evi-dence on which Barstad builds his thesis should be treated with great care (Vanderhooft 1999). Bustenay Oded defends the thesis of radical discontinuity between the late monarchic and the Babylonian periods in Judah. His argument, however, is rather sloppy and far from con-vincing (Oded 2003). Lisbeth S. Fried agrees with Barstad that Judah was not a space empty of people during the "exilic" period, but she modifies his thesis by arguing that Judah was empty of its God (Fried 2003). Despite these remarks, Barstad's view is still valid (Carter 1999; Albertz 2001: 46–88; Barstad 2003).

This implies that any historical reconstruction of the transition to the Persian Period has to reckon with the fact that "Yahwists" inhab-ited the former territory of the kingdom of Judah during the Neo-Babylonian Period.

Persian Documents regarding a Return from Exile

If the mass return from Exile was a historical fact, then one might expect traces of it in official documents from Mesopotamia or Persia. The Cyrus cylinder[11] has been interpreted as showing a liberal policy of respect toward other religions—as showing that Cyrus's policy toward the descendants of the Judean exiles was not unique but fitted the pattern of his rule (e.g., Bickerman 1946; Ackroyd 1968: 140–41; Weinberg 1992: 40; Young 1992: 1231–32). Amelia Kuhrt, however, has made clear that the inscription is of a propagandistic and stereotypical nature (Kuhrt 1983). The text reflects the world view of the Marduk priests of the Esaĝila temple at Babylon. They present Cyrus as a "good prince" replacing the "bad prince" Nabonidus. The return of divine images and people related in Cyrus Cylinder 30–34, if not mere propaganda, refers to measures taken on a local scale. These were divine images from cities surrounding Babylon that were brought back to the shrines from which they had been exiled by Nabonidus.[12] This passage has nothing to do with Judeans, Jews, or Jerusalem (Kuhrt 1983: 87–88). The famous Behistun inscription of Darius[13] relates in its various versions his rebellion and rise to power but does not contain historical data on the return to Jerusalem or the rebuilding of the temple.[14]

The absence of evidence for a return of Israelites to Jerusalem and vicinity in the early parts of the Persian Period, however, should not be construed as evidence for the absence of such a massive migration. It should be noted that written evidence from the Achaemenid Empire is relatively scarce. Next to that, the absence of a reference to a migration to Jerusalem in the sources available should be taken as an indication that Judeans, or Yehudites, were of no great importance to the Persian administration.[15]

Archaeological Traces in Yehud

If the mass return from Exile was a historical fact, then one might expect archaeological traces of an increase in the population of Jeru-

---

11. See the most recent edition by Berger 1975; see also Lecoq 1997: 181–85; Cogan 2000.

12. Kuhrt 1983; see also Ahlström 1993: 814–16; Wiesehöfer 1994: 71–88; Nodet 1997: 20; Lecoq 1997: 73–82; Albertz 2001: 98–100.

13. Lecoq 1997: 187–217.

14. See, e.g., Ahlström 1993: 819–22; Wiesehöfer 1994: 33–43; Knauf 1994: 168; Lecoq 1997: 83–96; Albertz 2001: 100–102.

15. In the Persepolis inscription of Artaxerxes II (A²Pa), the Yehudites are not even mentioned as one of the peoples living in the Persian Empire; see Lecoq 1997: 271–72.

salem and vicinity in the early Persian Period. About 30 years ago, Kochavi argued that archaeological data hinted at an increase in the population of Judah/Yehud at the beginning of the Persian Period of some 25% (Kochavi 1972). His estimates have been rendered obsolete by recent excavations and surveys. More recent estimates, therefore, seem to be more accurate. It should be noted, however, that all estimates are quite rough in character, because all calculations are made using uncertain, approximate parameters. Scholars base estimates on different assumptions—for instance, the average number of people per dunam. Nevertheless, all recent estimates of demographic changes in Judah/Yehud show a similar pattern (Broshi 1978; Hoglund 1992a; Hoglund 1992b; Carter 1999; Hoglund 2002; Lipschits 2003):

- A decrease of the population is observable during the transition from the late monarchic or Iron IIC period to the Babylonian or Iron III period. A concentration of the population in the Bethel–Mizpah area is evident, indicating that "those who remained in the land" were concentrated in the Northern part of the former kingdom of Judah.
- A clear continuity between the Neo-Babylonian and the Persian I periods is evident. This implies that the land of Judah was not empty during the so-called exilic period and that a considerable part of the population of Yehud in the Persian I period consisted of the descendants of those who remained in the land.
- The population of Yehud in Persian I is estimated by Carter at 13,350 persons (Carter 1999: 201),[16] which is about 30% of the 42,000 persons cited in the list of returnees in Ezra 2 and Nehemiah 7. It is not easy to decide how many of these 13,350 persons should be construed as returning exiles. The archaeological record, however, supplies a few clues. The number of "New P sites," that is, sites that were inhabited for the first time in Persian I, in the various environmental niches of Yehud is 27% of the total inhabited sites during Persian I (if I understand Carter's charts correctly). Considering that not all returnees settled in new sites and that some of the descendants of those who remained in the land moved to these new sites, the number of

---

16. Lipschits (2003: 364) estimates the population of Yehud at 30,125 people. Note, however, that Lipschits posits a slightly larger territory for Yehud than Carter and that Lipschits does not distinguish between Persian I and Persian II. I construe his estimate as an indication of the population of greater Yehud during the fifth century B.C.E. It in fact is parallel to Carter's estimate for Persian II.

returnees in Persian I may be estimated at a maximum of 4,000 people.[17]

- Assuming that 4,000 individuals is the correct number, one should note that their return most likely took place during various waves of migration during Persian I.
- Carter and Hoglund have observed an increase in population in Yehud during the Persian II Period. Carter estimates the population of Yehud in this period at 20,650 persons (Carter 1999: 201). This increase, of course, may have been the result of a natural expansion of the population. The scale of the increase, however, is such that it more likely reflects an influx from outside. Hoglund makes a connection with the general political measures of the Persian Empire. In the middle of the fifth century B.C.E., the Persians seem to have stimulated trade in and with Yehud, and this led to new returnees and an increase of the population (Hoglund 1992a; Hoglund 1992b: esp. 57–59 and 63–64). He even argues that the missions of Ezra and Nehemiah should be construed as "an effort on the part of the Achaemenid Empire to create a web of economic and social relationship that would tie the community [in Yehud] more completely into the imperial system" (Hoglund 1992a: 244). This influx roughly coincides with the appearance of Nehemiah on the scene in Jerusalem and vicinity.

The general picture that emerges is that of a demographic decrease in the early sixth century B.C.E. followed by a very slow increase during the Persian Period. As Lipschits formulates: "the 'return to Zion' did not leave its imprint on the archaeological data, nor is there any demographic testimony of it" (Lipschits 2003: 365). The evidence available cannot be connected to a theory of mass return in the sixth century. It suggests waves of return that lasted throughout the course of a century (Weinberg 1992; Hoglund 1992b; Knauf 1994: 167; Carter 1999; Kinet 2001: 190–202).

"Jews in Iraq"

The heading of this subsection is anachronistic in two ways.[18] The territory of Mesopotamia was not yet called Iraq, and descendants of

17. Lipschits (2003: 365) suggests that "a few thousand of the nation's elite" returned at the beginning of the Persian Period. This number coincides with other estimates. His sociological conclusion that these returnees were the nation's elite is not supported by the archaeological evidence.

18. With a wink to Rejwan 1985.

the exiled Judeans were not yet called Jews. Nevertheless, some observations can be made because interesting pieces of evidence exist. The presence of "Jews in Iraq" in preclassical times is evident from the Murashu archives (Clay 1912) and is reflected in some late biblical books (Esther and Daniel). The Murashu archives date to the reign of Darius II. They contain a great number of Yahwistic theophoric names (Coogan 1976; Zadok 1979; Stolper 1985). It would be methodologically unsound to draw conclusions from this material about an earlier period. We simply do not know the provenance of these Yehudites/Jews in the Nippur region at the end of the fifth century B.C.E. The historical trustworthiness of Daniel and Esther is debated. Because both are Hellenistic books, they do not supply much insight into the whereabouts of Judeans/Yehudites during the fifth century B.C.E. In other words, both the Murashu archives and the late biblical books postdate the period of the assumed mass return from exile.

In an ideal world—in this case, a world with an abundance of evidence—patterns of ethnic movements are witnessed by major shifts in the percentage of personal names from that ethnic group in datable written documents. If we possessed documents from the Neo-Babylonian period in which about 5% of the personal names were "Israelite," next to documents from the early Achaemenid period in which this number decreased dramatically, then we would have evidence of a mass return. This evidence, unfortunately, does not exist.

We are not completely empty handed, however. Recently Joannès and Lemaire have published three cuneiform tablets that are relevant (Joannès and Lemaire 1999). All three documents are dated by remarks in their colophons. The first tablet is dated to Year 7 of Cyrus, 532 B.C.E. It documents Abda-Yahu's receipt of five sheqels of silver for the *ilku*-tax from Bunanitu, the widow of Aḥiqar, the governor. *Ab-da-ia-hu-ú* and his father, *ba-rak-ka-ia-ma*, clearly have Judahite names. Of the other 10 names in this document, 4 are Aramaic and 6 Akkadian. The provenance of the document has been established as URU *ša* Pna-*šar* 'the City-of-Nashar ["Eagleton"]', probably in the vicinity of Borsippa.[19] The second document is dated to the accession year of Cambyses (530/ 529 B.C.E.). It contains administrative dates. No West Semitic names are attested. The third document is of great importance. This document records the sale of a bovine by Hara, the daughter of Talimu, to *né-ri-ia-a-ma*, the son of ŠEŠ(*aḥi*)-*ia-a-qa-am*. The transaction took place in *al Ya-hu-du* 'the city of Judah', in Babylonia in 498 B.C.E. This reference to

---

19. Joannès and Lemaire 1999: 28.

"the city of Judah" reflects the Neo-Babylonian policy of bringing ex-iles together in ethnic communities. Evidence is available for commu-nities of people from, for example, Ashkelon, Gaza, Neirab, Qadeš, Qedar, and Tyre.[20] In this document from the reign of Darius I, 12 out of 18 names are Hebrew in character. Since this is only one document, we should be reluctant to draw conclusions, but the document under-scores the inference that not all exiles immediately returned to Yehud after Cyrus's conquest of Babylon.[21]

At the Heidelberg Symposium, Laurie Pearce gave a presentation that tallies with my conclusion that not all exiles returned to Yehud in the early decades of the Achaemenid rule over Babylonia (Pearce 2005). She is preparing the publication of some 100 cuneiform documents ap-parently from the same collection as the three texts already edited by Joannès and Lemaire. These new texts document transactions that took place at URU *ša* P*na-šar* 'the City-of-Nashar' as well as at *al Ya-hu-du* 'the city of Judah'. The documents date mainly to the early Achaemenid pe-riod, but some 10% of the texts are to be dated in the Neo-Babylonian period. In these documents, some 450 people are mentioned. Twenty-five percent of them bear West Semitic names. Sixty-four are Judeans or bear a name with a Yahwistic theophoric element. A dramatic decrease of the portion of Judeans/Yehudites in the transition from the Neo-Babylonian to the Persian Period is not observable in this archive. Al-though no further historical conclusions can be drawn prior to the publication of this archive, it should be noted that these texts likewise do not support the hypothesis of a mass return from exile.

Myth Rather Than History

In my view, the concept of the "mass return" should be construed as a historical myth. The historical evidence we have hints more at an on-going process, probably waves of returnees for more than a century. The idea should be regarded as a social construct that served certain interests. But whose? Here I would like to present a proposal.

Elsewhere, I have argued that the mission of Ezra should be dated to the reign of Artaxerxes II, that is, to the first years of the fourth cen-tury B.C.E. (Becking 1998). We can assume that around this time vari-ous factions were present in and around Jerusalem and that various forms of Yahwism/Judaism were in a way competing (Davies 1995). In

---

20. Joannès and Lemaire 1999: 24.
21. See also Albertz 2001: 88.

my view, the book of Ezra gives ideological support to one specific faction and to one form of Yahwism/Judaism (Becking 1999). This group is identified as stressing the celebration of the Passover festival and as stressing its construction of the "true Israel" as a restricted, religion-based ethnic group. Ezra 7–10 reports "events" from the mission of Ezra. The other parts of the book of Ezra are not likely to be historically trustworthy. Ackroyd argued that Ezra 1 should be interpreted as applying a "Cyrus-motif" to the prehistory of the Ezra community, using it for the author's ideological purposes, in order to show "imperial backing" for the Ezra group (Ackroyd 1991: 144). I would like to elaborate on his view with the following arguments:

- The return from Exile in the book of Ezra is presented as a fulfillment of prophecies by Jeremiah.[22] Whether or not we can identify the "source" of the prophecies (be it in Jer 25:12, 29:10; or 30–31) in the book of Ezra, this allusion to Jeremiah functions as a continuity theme. The "Ezra-group" construed itself as the continuation of preexilic Yahwism.
- The idea that "we all returned as one" plays an important role in this symbol system. This perception of past events, although incorrect in the eyes of the modern historian, helped the "Ezra-group" behind Ezra 9–10 and the "we"-group implied in Psalm 126 to safeguard this idea of continuity during the troublesome period of Exile and Return.
- The Persian king is portrayed as very friendly toward the Israelites in Exile and as supporting their return with financial gifts. No mention is made of a comparable policy toward other nations in exile. This motif indicates that the Ezra-group construed themselves as the elect.

Ezra 1 and 2 stress the imperial and divine support of this group (Becking 1999). They were the true Israel by divine election and royal command. This implies that politics and religion were merged in order to attain or defend a position of power both within the community and in connection with the central Persian rule. Thus, the "myth of the mass Return" functioned already around 400 B.C.E. as ideological support for this specific group at the cradle of Judaism.

---

22. Ezra 1:1.

Bibliography

Ackroyd, P. R.
1968   *Exile and Restoration: A Study on Hebrew Thought in the Sixth Century* B.C. London: SCM.
1991   *The Chronicler and His Age.* Journal for the Study of the Old Testament Supplement 101. Sheffield: Sheffield Academic Press.

Ahlström, G. W.
1993   *The History of Ancient Palestine from the Palaeolithic Period to Alexander's Conquest.* Journal for the Study of the Old Testament Supplement 146. Sheffield: Sheffield Academic Press.

Albertz, R.
2001   *Die Exilszeit 6. Jahrhundert v. Chr.* Biblische Enzyklopädie 7. Stuttgart: Kohlhammer.

Banon, P.
2003   *Etemenanki.* Paris: Flammarion.

Barstad, H. M.
1996   *The Myth of the Empty Land: A Study in the History and Archaeology of Judah during the 'Exilic' Period.* Symbolae Osloenses Fasciculus Suppletorius 28. Oslo: Scandinavian University Press.
2003   After the "Myth of the Empty Land": Major Challenges in the Study of Neo-Babylonian Judah. Pp. 3–20 in *Judah and the Judeans in the Neo-Babylonian Period,* ed. O. Lipschits and J. Blenkinsopp. Winona Lake, Indiana: Eisenbrauns.

Becking, B.
1998   Ezra on the Move: Trends and Perspectives on the Character and His Book. Pp. 154–79 in *Perspectives in the Study of the Old Testament and Early Judaism: A Symposium in Honour of Adam S. van der Woude on the Occassion of His 70th Birthday,* ed. F. García Martínez and E. Noort. Vetus Testamentum Supplement 73. Leiden: Brill.
1999   Continuity and Community: The Belief-System of the Book of Ezra. Pp. 256–75 in *The Crisis of the Israelite Religion: Transformation of Religious Traditions in Exilic and Post-Exilic Times,* ed. B. Becking and M. C. A. Korpel. Oudtestamentische Studiën 42. Leiden: Brill.
2003   Chronology: A Skeleton without Flesh? Sennacherib's Campaign as a Case-Study. Pp. 46–72 in *'Like a Bird in a Cage': The Invasion of Sennacherib in 701* BCE, ed. L. L. Grabbe. European Seminar in Historical Methodology 4 = Journal for the Study of the Old Testament Supplement 363. London: Continuum.

Berger, P.-R.
1975   Der Kyros-Zylinder mit dem Zusatzfragment BIN II Nr. 32 und die akkadische Personennamen im Danielbuch. *Zeitschrift für Assyriologie* 64: 192–234.

Beyerlin, W.
1978   *"Wir sind wie Träumende": Studien zum 126. Psalm.* Stuttgarter Bibelstudien 89. Stuttgart: Katholisches Bibelwerk.

Bickerman, E. J.
1946 The Edict of Cyrus in Ezra 1. *Journal of Biblical Literature* 65: 249–75.
Broshi, M.
1978 Estimating the Population of Ancient Jerusalem. *Biblical Archaeology Review* 4: 10–15.
Brueggemann, W.
1997 *Theology of the Old Testament: Testimony, Dispute, Advocacy.* Minneapolis: Fortress.
Carroll, R. P.
1998 Exile! What Exile? Deportations and the Discourse of Diaspora. Pp. 62–79 in *Leading Captivity Captive: 'The Exile' as History and Ideology*, ed. L. L. Grabbe. European Seminar in Historical Methodology 2 = Journal for the Study of the Old Testament Supplement 278. Sheffield: Sheffield Academic Press.
Carter, C. E.
1999 *The Emergence of Yehud in the Persian Period: A Social and Demographic Study.* Journal for the Study of the Old Testament Supplement 294. Sheffield: Sheffield Academic Press.
Clay, A. T.
1912 *Business Documents of Murashu Sons of Nippur Dated in the Reign of Darius II.* Philadelphia: The University Museum.
Cogan, M.
2000 Achaemenid Inscriptions. Pp. 314–16 in *The Context of Scripture II*, ed. W. W. Hallo et al. Leiden: Brill.
Coogan, M. D.
1976 *West Semitic Personal Names in the Murašû Documents.* Harvard Semitic Monographs 7. Atlanta: Scholars Press.
Davies, P. R.
1995 Scenes from the Early History of Judaism. Pp. 145–82 in *The Triumph of Elohim: From Yahwisms to Judaisms*, ed. D. V. Edelman. Contributions to Biblical Exegesis and Theology 13. Kampen: Kok Pharos.
Fried, L. S.
2003 The Land Lay Desolate: Conquest and Restoration in the Ancient Near East. Pp. 21–54 in *Judah and the Judeans in the Neo-Babylonian Period*, ed. O. Lipschits and J. Blenkinsopp. Winona Lake, Indiana: Eisenbrauns.
Grabbe, L. L.
1992 Reconstructing History from the Book of Ezra. Pp. 98–106 in *Second Temple Studies: 1. Persian Period*, ed. P. R. Davies. Journal for the Study of the Old Testament Supplement 117. Sheffield: Sheffield Academic Press.
1994 *Judaism from Cyrus to Hadrian.* London: SCM.
1998 *Ezra–Nehemiah.* Old Testament Readings. London: Routledge.
Halpern, B.
1990 A Historiographic Commentary on Ezra 1–6: Achronological Narrative and Dual Chronology in Israelite Historiography. Pp. 81–142 in *The Hebrew Bible and Its Interpreters*, ed. W. H. Propp, B. Halpern, and

D. N. Freedman. Biblical and Judaic Studies from the University of California, San Diego 1. Winona Lake, Indiana: Eisenbrauns.

Hoglund, K. G.

1992a *Achaemenid Imperial Administration in Syria–Palestine and the Missions of Ezra and Nehemiah.* Society of Biblical Literature Dissertation Series 125. Atlanta: Scholars Press.

1992b The Achaemenid Context. Pp. 54–72 in *Second Temple Studies: 1. Persian Period,* ed. P. R. Davies. Journal for the Study of the Old Testament Supplement 117. Sheffield: Sheffield Academic Press.

2002 The Material Culture of the Persian Period. Pp. 14–18 in *Second Temple Studies III: Studies in Politics, Class and Material Culture,* ed. P. R. Davies and J. M. Halligan. Journal for the Study of the Old Testament Supplement 340. London: Continuum.

Joannès, F., and Lemaire, A.

1999 Trois tablettes cunéiformes à onomastique ouest-sémitique, *Transeuphratène* 17: 17–34.

Joüon, P., and Muraoka, T.

1991 *A Grammar of Biblical Hebrew,* 2 vols. Subsidia Biblica 14/1–2. Rome: Pontifical Biblical Institute.

Karrer, C.

2000 *Ringen um die Verfassung Judas: Eine Studie zu den theologisch-politischen Vorstellungen im Esra-Nehemia-Buch.* Beihefte zur Zeitschrift für die Alttestamentliche Wissenschaft 308. Berlin: de Gruyter.

Kinet, D.

2001 *Geschichte Israels.* Die Neue Echter Bibel Ergänzungsband zum Alten Testament 2. Würzburg: Echter Verlag.

Knauf, E. A.

1994 *Die Umwelt des Alten Testaments.* Neuer Stuttgarter Kommentar: Altes Testament 29. Stuttgart: Katholisches Bibelwerk.

Kochavi, M.

1972 *Judea, Samaria and the Golan: Archaeological Survey, 1967–1968.* Jerusalem: The Survey of Israel. [Hebrew]

Kuhrt, A.

1983 The Cyrus Cylinder and Achaemenid Imperial Policy. *Journal for the Study of the Old Testament* 25: 83–97.

Lecoq, P.

1997 *Les inscriptions de la Perse achéménide.* Paris: Gallimard.

Lipschits, O.

2003 Demographic Changes in Judah between the Seventh and the Fifth Centuries B.C.E. Pp. 323–76 in *Judah and the Judeans in the Neo-Babylonian Period,* ed. O. Lipschits and J. Blenkinsopp. Winona Lake, Indiana: Eisenbrauns.

Mosis, R.

1990 "Mit Jauchzen werden sie ernten": Beobachtungen zu Psalm 126. Pp. 181–201 in *Die alttestamentliche Botschaft als Wegweisung* (FS Heinz Reinelt), ed. J. Zmijewski. Stuttgart: Katholische Bibelwerk.

Neusner, J.
1987   *Self-Fulfilling Prophecy: Exile and Return in the History of Judaism.* Boston: Beacon.
Nodet, E.
1997   *A Search for the Origins of Judaism.* Journal for the Study of the Old Testament Supplement 248. Sheffield: Sheffield Academic Press.
Oded, B.
2003   Where Is the "Myth of the Empty Land" to Be Found? History versus Myth. Pp. 55–74 in *Judah and the Judeans in the Neo-Babylonian Period*, ed. O. Lipschits and J. Blenkinsopp. Winona Lake, Indiana: Eisenbrauns.
Pearce, L. E.
2005   Judaeans in Babylonia. Pp. 399–411 in this volume.
Rejwan, N.
1985   *The Jews of Iraq: 3000 Years of History and Culture.* London: Weidenfeld and Nicholson.
Sacchi, P.
2000   *The History of the Second Temple Period*, Journal for the Study of the Old Testament Supplement 285. Sheffield: Sheffield Academic Press.
Schwiderski, D.
2000   *Handbuch des nordwestsemitischen Briefformulars: Ein Beitrag zur Echtheitsfrage der aramäischen Briefe des Esrabuches.* Beihefte zur Zeitschrift für die Alttestamentliche Wissenschaft 295. Berlin: de Gruyter.
Stolper, M. W.
1985   *Entrepreneurs and Empire: The Murashu Archive, the Murashu Firm and the Persian Rule in Babylonia.* Istanbul: Nederlands Historisch-Archeologisch Instituut.
Talmon, S.
2001   "Exile" and "Restoration" in the Conceptual World of Ancient Judaism. Pp. 107–46 in *Restoration: Old Testament, Jewish and Christian Perspectives*, ed. J. M. Scott. Supplements to the Journal for the Study of Judaism 72. Leiden: Brill.
Torrey, C. C.
1970   *Ezra Studies.* New York: Ktav.
Vanderhooft, D. S.
1999   *The Neo-Babylonian Empire and Babylon in the Latter Prophets.* Harvard Semitic Monographs 58. Atlanta: Scholars Press.
Weinberg, J. P.
1992   *The Citizen-Temple Community.* Journal for the Study of the Old Testament Supplement 151. Sheffield: Sheffield Academic Press.
Wiesehöfer, J.
1994   *Das antike Persien von 550 v. Chr bis 650 n. Chr.* Munich: Artemis & Winkler.
Williamson, H. G. M.
1987   *Ezra and Nehemiah.* Old Testament Guides. Sheffield: Sheffield Academic Press.

Wunenberger, J. J.
   1994   Mythophorie: Formes et transformations du mythe. *Religiologiques* 10:
          49–70.
Young, T. C.
   1992   Cyrus. Pp. 1231–32 in: *Anchor Bible Dictionary.* New York: Doubleday.
Zadok, R.
   1979   *The Jews in Babylonia during the Chaldean and Achaemenian Periods ac-
          cording to the Babylonian Sources.* Haifa: University of Haifa Press.

Achaemenid Imperial Policy, Settlement Processes in Palestine, and the Status of Jerusalem in the Middle of the Fifth Century B.C.E.

ODED LIPSCHITS

Tel Aviv University

Palestine in the Pre-Persian Period: The Geopolitical and Administrative Organization

Tiglath-pileser III's (745–727 B.C.E.) conquest of the Levant shaped its geopolitical and administrative character for generations to come. Tiglath-pileser conquered the strongest and largest kingdoms in the region, inflicting heavy damage. He deported large parts of the populations, replacing them with exiles from remote regions, and annexed their territory to Assyria, turning them into Assyrian provinces.[1] The

---

Author's note: This paper was written during my stay as a guest scholar at the Wissenschaftlich-Theologisches Seminar, Alttestamentliche Theologie, Universität Heidelberg (2002–2003). I would like to thank the Alexander von-Humboldt Stiftung for giving me the opportunity to conduct research in Heidelberg and Prof. Dr. Manfred Oeming for his generous hospitality and cooperation. I would like to thank Mr. Steffen Mahler and Mr. Joachim Vette for their assistance.

1. Five provinces were established by Tiglath-pileser III in northern Syria and on the Syrian coast after he conquered the region in the early years of his reign (740–738 B.C.E., Weippert 1982: 395–408; Hawkins 1995: 95–97; Naʾaman 1995: 105; and see the summary in Lipschits 2005: 4–5): Arpad (Arpadda); Kullanīa-Kalnē/Kinalūa; Ḫatarikka/Ḫadrāk; Ṣimirra (Ṣumur); and Manṣuāti. Three more provinces were established by Tiglath-pileser in central and southern Syria in the territories of Aram-Damascus, after it was conquered in 732 B.C.E.: Qarnīna (Qarnaim); Dimašqa; and Ṣūbat/Ṣūbite (Ṣôbā). At the same time, the Assyrian king established two provinces in the former kingdom of Israel: Dūʾru (Dôr) and Magidû (Megiddo). Many scholars assumed, with Emil Forrer (1920: 61) and Albrecht Alt (1929: 203–5), that another province existed in the northern part of Transjordan during the time of Tiglath-pileser: the province of Galʿad (Gilʿad/Gilead). However, there is no textual support for this assumption, and there is no concrete evidence regarding the Assyrian provincial system in the northern part of Transjordan. On this subject, see Oded 1970: 177–86; Naʾaman 1995: 107, with further literature. For a different opinion, see Ephʿal 1984; Stern 2001: 11–12, 43.

extent of Tiglath-pileser's success in annihilating the power of the Syrian kingdoms and abolishing the national distinctions of their populations is revealed by the fact that no independent political entity developed in the conquered Assyrian areas in the following centuries, nor was there any military threat to Egyptian, Babylonian, or Persian imperial rule from them. This state of affairs enabled the succeeding empires, and even the Seleucid dynasty, to control these regions and exploit their economic, commercial, and strategic potential.[2]

During the next 60 years, five more provinces were added to the array of provinces founded by Tiglath-pileser,[3] extending Assyrian direct rule over all the Levant. In addition to the provinces, a line of city-states was allowed to remain along the Phoenician and Palestinian coast, probably because they served the Assyrian interest, especially its maritime commerce, better as they were.[4] In the hill country east and west of the Jordan River, four small territorial kingdoms continued their existence under the Assyrian rule: Udūmu (Edom); Bīt-Ammān (Ammon); Māʾab (Moab), and Iaʾūdu (Judah). From the Assyrian point of view, these kingdoms were too small and too weak to be a threat, not to mention the fact that they served the Assyrian interests by supplying agricultural products and taking part in overland commerce, especially the Arab trade.

---

2. On this subject, from the Persian-Period perspective, see the review of Briant 2002: 1014–15, with further bibliography. On the persistence of the Assyrian geopolitical and administrative system at least until the third century B.C.E., see Limet 2000. See also Naʾaman 2000: 41–42.

3. Three of the new provinces were founded by Sargon II: Sāmerīna (720 B.C.E.; see Naʾaman 1995: 106–7; and fig. 1, p. 105; Stern 2001: 49–51); Ḥamāt (Amattu) (720 B.C.E.; see Hawkins 1995: 97; Naʾaman 1995: 107); Asdūdu (Ashdod; no later than 712 B.C.E.; see Tadmor 1964: 272–76; for a critique of Tadmor's proposal, see Naʾaman 1994: 9–11, with further literature). During the early days of Esarhaddon (680–669 B.C.E.), probably in 677/6 B.C.E., a new province was established south of Gubla (Byblos). Its capital was Kār-Esarhaddon, which had been built close to Ṣūdūnu (Ṣīdôn; Tadmor 1966: 98; Grayson 1991: 125; Redford 1992: 358; Naʾaman 1995: 17–19, and fig. 3 p. 108). The province of Ṣurru/Ṣūr (Tyre) was established in the last days of Esarhaddon or in the early days of Ashurbanipal (669–627 B.C.E.; see Grayson 1991: 126, 144–45; Naʾaman 1995: 107–9 and fig. 3).

4. Along the Phoenician coast, south of the two provinces created by Tiglath-pileser III (Kullanīa/Kalnē and Ṣimirra/Ṣumur), Gubla (Byblos) remained a vassal kingdom, apparently throughout the period of Assyrian rule (Parpola 1970: 135; Elat 1991: 26; Naʾaman 1994: 7). Neither the island of Tyre nor Samsimurūna or Arwāda, which extended to the north, were annexed. In Philistia, three small kingdoms survived: Isqalūna (Ašqelôn/Ashkelon; Naʾaman 1998: 222–25); Anqarrūna (Ekron; Dothan and Gitin 1994: 18–25; Gitin 1997; 1998: 274–78; Mazar 1994: 260–63); and Ḥazzat (Gaza; Tadmor 1964: 271; Katzenstein 1994: 37–38; Naʾaman 2004: 55–60).

During the last third of the seventh century B.C.E., the geopolitical and administrative situation of the Levant was totally different from the situation at the beginning of Tiglath-pileser's rule. Besides the geopolitical and administrative changes, the Assyrian conquest wreaked destruction in most of the urban centers and deported large parts of the population. We can assume that Assyrian policy was to retain fortifications only in provincial capitals (Stern 2001: 50) and to build forts and Assyrian economic and military centers in strategic places all over the country. In the former territories of the Israelite Kingdom, for example, except for the three capitals of the provinces,[5] there is not even one fortified settlement that can be dated to the seventh century B.C.E. (Tadmor 1973: 70–71).[6] Most of the major towns in this area were abandoned or only poorly rebuilt, and the total settled area in all cities was much smaller than before the Assyrian conquest. This archaeological phenomenon is descernible by the fact that most of the population in the Assyrian provinces, especially in the interior areas, lived on farms and in villages; there was a marked decline in urban life.

The geopolitical and administrative character of the Levant changed only slightly under Egyptian rule during the last third of the seventh century B.C.E.[7] During the short period of Egyptian rule, for which there is scant historical documentation, Egyptian economic and strategic interests were apparently concentrated primarily along the coast (from Philistia to Phoenicia).[8] It is not clear to what extent Egypt was

---

5. On Megiddo, see Lemon and Shipton 1939: 62, and see also figs. 71–73, 89; Na'aman 1993: 109–12; Finkelstein and Ussishkin 2000: 601; Peersmann 2000: 525–27, 532–33; Tappy 2001: 242–44. On Dor, see Stern 1990; 2001: 19, and on Samaria, see against the conclusions reached by Kenyon 1957: 199 (Crowfoot 1942; 1957a; Hoglund 1992: 85, 211, but see, however Kenyon 1942: 116, 117), the opinions of Tappy (2001: 223–26, 579) and Stern (1982: 50–51; 2001: 19–20).

6. See also the data from Zertal's survey (1990), and see the summary of Stern (2001: 49–50).

7. This is against the view expressed by Hoglund (1992: 16–17) that during the Egyptian imperial domination of the Levant there was a break with the previous Assyrian imperial system of administration, and as a result the Neo-Babylonians and Achaemenids could not maintain the previous Assyrian administrative patterns in the Levant. Aside from Tyre (perhaps; see below), there is no historical basis for Hoglund's conclusion that the various Levantine territories reverted to their own patterns of hereditary rule during Egyptian domination and that Egyptian overseers collaborated with these local rulers.

8. At a fairly early stage of Egyptian rule of the region, Egypt established its control all the way to Phoenicia, subjugating Tyre and apparently Arwad as well (Katzenstein 1973: 299 n. 24; 313 n. 100; Redford 1992: 442). It seems that Tyre was restored at this time to its status as a vassal kingdom and that the Egyptians established their foothold in Philistia immediately following the Assyrian retreat (Lipschits 2005: 28–29). The establishment of Egyptian dominion in this overland passageway to Egypt was rapid (Redford

interested in the hill country or what effort it invested in establishing its authority there. However, it seems that Egypt ruled the entire area and that Judah was subject to Egypt and unable to conduct its own foreign affairs, certainly not along the coast or in the Jezreel Valley.[9]

The Egyptians had no problem assuming control of the former Assyrian provinces in Syria and as far as the west bank of the Euphrates. However, the ease with which Syria fell into the hands of the Babylonians (summer 605 B.C.E.) and with which the Babylonians conquered all the rest of the Egyptian holdings to the Egyptian border in the following year is evidence that the Egyptians had not truly succeeded in establishing their control of the region and that they held the region more in the sense of filling the vacuum left behind by the Assyrian withdrawal (Lipschits 2005: 31–35).

In his military campaign conducted in Ḥatti-land between June 604 and January/February 603, Nabuchadrezzar conquered all of the Levant as far as Gaza.[10] According to the Babylonian Chronicle, none of the local kings dared to resist Nebuchadrezzar except for the king of Ashkelon. The Babylonian response was decisive, and the fate of that city served as an example to the other kingdoms in the region.[11] During this time, there is no reason to ascribe any other destruction layer in the archaeological record to the Babylonian army: most of the country was organized into provinces that dated back to the Assyrian Period. It appears that the Egyptian retreat left the country to the rule of Nebuchadrezzar, unopposed.

Babylonian policy in the region did not change even following Nebuchadrezzar's failed attempt to conquer Egypt and the subsequent temporary weakening of Babylonian rule in the region (Lipschits 1998: 472–80; 2005: 49–52). However, continued instability during the days

---

1992: 442); apparently, the Egyptians were required to fight only against Ashdod (Na᾽aman 1991: 39–40; James 1991: 714; Redford 1992: 441–42).

9. Necho's presence in Megiddo, the killing of Josiah (2 Kgs 23:29), the later deposing of Jehoahaz from the throne (v. 33), and the appointment of Eliakim-Jehoiakim (v. 34) all attest to Egypt's intention of ruling Judah.

10. On the background to the Babylonian military campaign, its main events, and consequences, see Lipschits 2005: 37–42, with further literature.

11. On the description of the destruction of Ashkelon in the Babylonian Chronicle (BM 21946, lines 18–20), see Wiseman 1956: 28, 68–69; Grayson 1975a: 20, 100. On the archaeological evidence for this destruction, see Stager 1996. It might have been at this time that the territory of Ashkelon was annexed to Ashdod. If this is the case, it is the single change that the Babylonians made in the geopolitical and administrative organization of the Levant during the first phase of their rule.

of Psammetichus II (595–589 B.C.E.), and even more during the first years of Hophra (589–570), and the increasing threat from Egypt caused Nebuchadrezzar to modify his policy (589 B.C.E.): during the following years he conquered the remaining small vassal kingdoms near the border with Egypt, annexed them, and turned them into provinces (Lipschits 1998: 482–87; 2005: 62–68). Judah was the first target of the Babylonians. Afterward, apparently in 585 B.C.E., they attacked Tyre and Sidon, setting up a siege on Tyre that lasted for 13 years (until 572 B.C.E.; Katzenstein 1973: 330; 1994: 186; Wiseman 1991: 235; Redford 1992: 465–66; Vanderhooft 1999: 100–102). Apparently during the years of the siege, the Babylonians also attacked Ammon and Moab (Lipschits 2004b) and established their control also over Gaza, Arwad, and Ashdod. It is very likely that the successful takeover of northern Arabia by Nabonidus and his move to Tema (553–543 B.C.E.) resulted in the disappearance of the kingdom of Edom and probably the integration of its territory with greater Arabia (Lemaire 2003: 290; and see also Briant 2002: 45).

During this phase of Babylonian rule in the Levant, the Babylonians displayed an attitude toward the kingdoms of Philistia and those on the Phoenician coast that differed from their Assyrian predecessors. The former were conquered and turned into Babylonian provinces. Although the fate of the latter is unclear, it appears that during most of the Babylonian rule, certainly during the Persian Period, they were ruled by kings (Katzenstein 1994: 46–48).[12] The new Babylonian policy was destructive to the southern part of Palestine as well as to the Transjordanian kingdoms[13] as Nebuchadrezzar went about creating a buffer zone between Babylon and Egypt out of devastated, diminished

---

12. It seems that the explanation for this change is Philistia's strategic importance as the gateway to Egypt and the necessity for Babylon to maintain control over the region. Likewise, the continued instability in Philistia, their close ties with and loyalty to Egypt, as well as intensive Egyptian activity that continued in the region throughout this period all required the Babylonians to tighten their control by conquering and subjugating the region. In contrast, Egypt was less of a threat to the Babylonians on the Phoenician coast, although Babylon's economic interests there were considerable. A generous measure of political and military autonomy was essential to maintaining commerce in the region, including trade with Egypt. A fine account dating to the fifth and sixth years of Nabonidus (551–550 B.C.E.) has been preserved regarding the commerce between Egypt and Babylon; see Oppenheim 1967; Brown 1969: 101; Katzenstein 1994: 48.

13. The Babylonians brought a harsh blow to all the urban centers in Judah and Philistia. However, contrary to the opinion of Stern (summarized in 2000; 2004), we have no archaeological or historical basis for the idea that all or even some of the former Assyrian and Egyptian provincial centers were also destroyed.

provinces.[14] There is no evidence that the Babylonians invested any kind of effort in economic development in this region; furthermore, it seems that Nebuchadrezzar used the destruction of the region as a lever for rebuilding the parts of Babylonia that had been damaged during the long years of war, devastation, and deportation inflicted by the Assyrians. Large groups of exiles from the ruling, economic, and religious elite of the local kingdoms were sent to Babylon and settled in the devastated areas to develop them. However, total devastation of the land was contrary to Babylonian interests, because the rural population was needed as the human nucleus for the new provinces they had established. The rural settlements all over the land survived, even if on a much smaller scale. The Babylonians had no reason to create a settlement vacuum, which would only have undermined stability in the region, making it more difficult to rule and exploit its economical potential. I would even surmise that it was in the Babylonians' interest to preserve the rural settlements in those areas in order to receive their wine, olive oil, grain, and other agricultural produce as taxes (Lipschits 2004a; 2004b; 2005: 212–61). However, because the Babylonians did not have a specific policy for developing and protecting the settlements, especially in the peripheral regions of the south, many changes occurred there, apparently as a side effect of the collapse of the central systems and the infiltration of seminomadic groups.[15]

This was the situation encountered by the Achaemenids when they inherited the Babylonian Empire. From that time on, settlement developed according to Achaemenid interests and needs.

The Geopolitical and Administrative Situation in Palestine during the Persian Period

When Cyrus II conquered Babylon (539 B.C.E.), he inherited a huge empire that included all of Mesopotamia, as well as the area Across the River.[16] During his time and at least from March 535 B.C.E. on, the territories of the Neo-Babylonian Empire were included in one satrapy

---

14. We have no information about any intended change to the borders of the old Assyrian array of provinces or to the former small kingdoms that became Babylonian provinces during the first half of the sixth century B.C.E. It appears that the former system of borders remained the same (Aharoni 1962: 313; Garelli and Nikiprowetzky 1974: 157–59; Hoglund 1992: 5–6; Na'aman 2000: 41–42; Lipschits 2005: 135–86).

15. On this historical process, see the summary by Lipschits 2005: 140–47; 227–40.

16. On the importance of this historical event, see Olmstead 1948: 59; Cook 1983: 32–33; 1985: 212 ;Frye 1984: 95; Briant 2002: 44–45. In light of this rapid change and the administrative continuity between Babylonian and Persian rule, we can understand why there is no marked change in the material culture in the area Across the River.

under the rule of Gūbaru, Governor of Babylonia and Across the River (Ebir Nāri) (Leuze 1935: 25–36; Rainey 1969: 52; Briant 2002: 64, 71, 74–75).[17] We can conclude that the former administrative system proceeded without any marked change, even after the conquest of Egypt by Cambyses II (525 B.C.E.),[18] when it was added to the Empire as a separate administrative unit (Olmstead 1948: 70–85; Graf 1993: 151; Hoglund 1992: 23; Briant 2002: 48–49). The first changes in the administrative system for the province Across the River followed the suppression of the wide-ranging revolts in various parts of the Empire following the accession of Darius I (522/521 B.C.E.). At this point, the Persians established a subdistrict named Across the River.[19] The province Babylonia and Across the River continued to function as a unit, and in March 520 a new governor, Uštānu, was installed (Rainey 1969: 52–53; Stolper 1989: 289; Briant 2002: 484).[20] More than 30 years later, in October 486, just two months before the death of Darius I and the accession of Xerxes, another governor with the same title appears in a Babylonian legal text (BM 74554), and this is the last time we hear of this large satrapy (Stolper 1989). It was not until after Xerxes suppressed the revolt in Babylon (482 B.C.E.; see Olmstead 1948: 237 n. 23), that the subdistrict of Across the River was separated from the province of Babylon and given independent and equal status (Olmstead 1948: 112, 115; Rainey 1969: 55–58; Eph'al 1998: 109).[21] This independent status was retained until the end of the Persian Period. This is also the picture reflected in Herodotus's description of the middle of the fifth century B.C.E. (Briant 2002: 951, with further literature).[22]

---

17. It is interesting to note that all of the texts mentioning this title came from Uruk, except for one that came from the area of Babylon. For the list of the texts and further bibliography, see Stolper 1989: 290, and note c; 292.

18. On the conquest of Egypt by Cambyses II, see Briant 2002: 55–61; Cruz-Uribe 2003, with further literature.

19. On the administrative system that was organized by Darius I, see Tuplin (1987: 111–13) and the more cautious reconstruction of Briant (2002: 487–90). On the extent of the satrapy and its inner structure, see Rainey 1969: 51–78.

20. Most scholars have based their reconstruction on the appearance of "Tattenai, the governor (satrap) of the province Across the River" in Jerusalem in the second year of Darius (Ezra 5:3, 6; 6:13) and his appearance with the same title in a tablet dated to 502 B.C.E. They interpret the data as if the region Across the River was at this time a subdivision of the larger satrapy and Tattenai (Tattannu) a subordinate of Uštānu (Olmstead 1948: 78–81; Rainey 1969: 52–55; Cook 1983: 42–43; Frye 1984: 114–15; Stolper 1989: 289–90, 293, and n. 7, n; Petit 1990: 189–90; Briant 2002: 487–88, 951, with further literature).

21. However, see the reservations raised by Stolper 1989: 293–303 (with further literature and various opinions on pp. 292–93, and nn. 9–12).

22. Many scholars have reconstructed the historical events according to the description of Herodotus in 3.88–95 (Leuze 1935: 226–29; for more literature, see Stolper 1989:

Urbanization along the Coast and Ruralism in the Hill Country at the Beginning of the Persian Period

During the long years of Persian rule in Palestine, many geopolitical changes occurred, along with administrative reorganization, particularly on the coast but also in the hill country and in the southern areas of Cis- and Transjordan. We can assume that, like the Assyrians, Egyptians, and Babylonians, the Achaemenids also tried to shape the political, social, and demographic systems in Palestine according to their own military, economic, and governmental interests. The main evidence for this can be found in the large, wealthy urban and commercial centers that were established at the very beginning of the Achaemenid period along the Mediterranean coast, most of them well built and planned, some according to the Hippodamian plan (Kenyon 1960: 311–12; Stern 1990; 2001: 461–64).[23] Each of these cities was surrounded by smaller sites, and between them were many forts and Achaemenid administrative centers.[24]

The Achaemenid regime had governmental, military, and economic reasons for establishing its base along the Mediterranean coast, stabilizing the political situation in this area, and encouraging maritime and overland trade. One of the major goals of the Persians was to secure the Via Maris, as well as the roads in southern Palestine, as part of the military, administrative, and economic effort to control the route to Egypt (Eph'al 1998: 117; Stern 2001: 371). Another need was to establish a strong political, military, and economic coalition vis-à-vis the Greeks. From the economic point of view, the Persian regime tried to develop and encourage the maritime trade that had been dominated by the Phoenicians (Briant 2002: 383, 489–90).[25]

Development of maritime trade was probably the main reason that the Achaemenids granted authority over all of the coastal area of Pal-

---

292 n. 9). However, Herodotus's list describes the Persian administrative organization during the time of Xerxes I or later, certainly not during the time of Darius I (Calmeyer 1990; Stern 2001: 368; Stolper 1989: 293 and n. 13).

23. For a detailed list of the cities along the Palestinian coast and for further literature, see Stern 2001: 380–407; Lipschits 2002a: 47.

24. On this settlement pattern along the coast, see Stern 2001: 380–407. On the settlement pattern along the Sharon Plain, see Tal 2000: 115–22.

25. This may explain why the Persians appointed a governor (who bore a Babylonian name) in Tyre already during the time of Darius (Dandamaev 1995: 29–31; but see Briant 2002: 952). Cruz-Uribe (2003: 16) has argued (in contrast to Wallinga 1987) that it may be that the Persians developed a sizable navy after the invasion of Egypt, when they gained control over significant numbers of ships.

estine (to the border of the province of Ashdod) to the kings of Tyre and Sidon at the end of the sixth or the very beginning of the fifth century B.C.E.[26] It appears that (under their patronage and under Phoenician rule) the Achaemenids allowed the coastal population a great degree of independence, at least in regard to internal, commercial, and economic affairs (Elayi 1980: 25; 1982; Stern 1990: 155 and n. 25; 1995: 433).[27] Many of the positions of authority on the local economic and political level had been filled by the Phoenicians after the deportations of locals by the Assyrians and the Babylonians, some as early as the end of the eighth century, and some only two generations previously.

From the archaeological point of view, there is a remarkable amount of Phoenician influence in evidence along the coast of Palestine from the beginning of the fifth century B.C.E.[28] The establishment of most settlements occurred during a period of less than 50 years, which implies that this was the result of some sort of official decision (Tal 2000: 121, and fig. 3, p. 125). Settlement activity culminated during the second half of the fifth and the beginning of the fourth centuries. By then many Phoenicians had already infiltrated the region (Lemaire 1990: 58–59; Tal 2000: 120–21, with further literature).

In contrast to the rich, well-developed cities found along the coast, very few building remains dating to the the Persian Period have been uncovered in the hill country—that is, within the province of Yehud or the province of Samaria (Lipschits 2002a). This is the case even at sites

---

26. The main source for this reconstruction is the inscription on the sarcophagus of Eshmunazor, king of Sidon, which says "the Lord of the Kings granted us Dor and Jaffa, the mighty lands of Dagan which are in the plain of Sharon" (Donner and Röllig 1962: no. 14, lines 18–19; 1964: no. 14, pp. 19–23. For an English translation, see Gibson 1982: 108). Despite many difficulties with reconstructing the chronology of the Sidonian kings and identifying the Persian king who is mentioned only as the "Lord of the Kings" (see Briant 2002: 490, and further literature on p. 952), it now appears that we can accept the chronological reconstruction of Elayi (2004) and date the delivery of the coastal area to the Phoenician kings to the end of the sixth or to the beginning of the fifth century B.C.E. According to Pseudo-Scylax, in the *Periplus*, neither the Tyrian nor the Sidonian territories were consolidated into a single large domain; instead, their territories were comprised of loosely associated smaller areas (Katzenstein 1979: 30–31; Elayi 1980: 17; 1987: 81–83; Gardiner 1991: 20; Stern 2001: 379–80, 386–87, 418). We may also accept the idea that in the early fifth century B.C.E. the Achaemenids granted Upper Galilee and the area east of Tyre to the Tyrians (Herbert and Berlin 2003: 46–48).

27. Compare with J. Lund's conclusion (1990: 32) about the northern coast of Syria: "if the ancient literary sources had not been preserved, forcing us to rely on the archaeological material alone, few would probably have dared to suggest that the northern coastline of Syria had ever been controlled by the Persians."

28. See Elgavish 1968: 42; 1994: 93–94; Stern 1984: 80–81; 2001: 379–407; Roll and Ayalon 1989: 34; Tal 2000: 120–22.

where an abundance of pottery vessels, seal impressions, and other typical Persian-Period finds have been found (Stern 2001: 424–27, 461–62; Lipschits 2002a: 45–46).

Albright and Kenyon claimed that the archaeological data reflect the cessation of town life in the Persian Period and the concentration of population in villages. Along the same lines, Aharoni and Kelso argued that the archaeological data reflect the fact that Persian-Period residences were built outside the limits of Iron Age cities, which is why they were not found in the excavations (Aharoni 1956: 108; 1964: 120; Kelso et al. 1968: 38). Stern, on the other hand (2001: 461–62), has claimed that the scarcity of building remains from this period does not reflect the reality of that time but is the outcome of incomplete archaeological data caused by three characteristic features of the Persian-Period strata: (1) many sites were abandoned after the Persian Period and never resettled, so the uppermost stratum was damaged (mainly by erosion); (2) at many sites, the Persian-Period occupation level was severely damaged by extensive building activities during the Hellenistic and Roman periods; (3) some sites were occupied by large palaces, forts, or administrative buildings, and the residential area was located at the edge of the site.

I agree with Stern's archaeological assessments in many respects. However, he does not distinguish between the coast and the hill country, and the situation in the coastal area is significantly different from the situation in the hill country. There, the absence of architectural remains is clear on both sides of the Jordan; furthermore, the contrast between the hill country and the coastal area is so sharp that one conclusion is clear: during the Persian Period, as in the Assyrian and Babylonian periods that preceded it, there was a marked process of attenuation of urban life in Judah, and to a lesser degree also in Samaria. This phenomenon contrasts with the continuation of rural settlements in Judah (especially in the northern part of the Judean Hills and in the region of Benjamin)[29] and Samaria.[30] The situation in Ammon and

---

29. See Carter 1994; 1999: 137–66; Lipschits 1999; 2003: 326–55; 2005: 240–61; Milevski 1996–1997: 7–29; Naʾaman 2000: 43.

30. See Finkelstein 1978: 64–74; 1981; Zertal 1990; Stern 2001: 424–28. The survey of Samaria revealed a large rural array, which means that during the Persian Period Samaria functioned as a center for production of olive oil and wine (Zertal 1990: 13–14; 1999). Excavations in this area have revealed Persian-Period strata (without building remains) only at Samaria and Shechem, while at Tell el-Farʿah (N) there were only scanty remains of a small village and at Tel Dothan there was no Persian-Period level at all. On this subject, see the comprehensive review by Stern 2001: 424–28.

Edom is comparable.[31] Exactly the same settlement pattern characterizes the northern coastline of Syria (Lund 1990)[32] and the western part
of Galilee, areas that served as the agricultural hinterland for the large
coastal towns between Achzib and the Acco plain (Stern 2001: 385).

The settlement pattern of the Persian Period was a continuation of
the process that began during the Babylonian Period, after the harsh
blow that the Babylonians dealt to the small kingdoms in the hill country west and east of the Jordan.[33] Neither the Babylonians nor the Persians had any interest in encouraging and developing urban centers in
the rural hilly regions on both sides of the Jordan. The function of those
regions as agricultural areas was much more important and as such
they were probably also easier to control.

Achaemenid Interests in the Hill Country
and Patterns of Settlement

As demonstrated above, the lack of local power structures (i.e., the
local dynasts, priesthood, the landed aristocracy, etc.) in Palestine at
the end of the sixth century was the result of the Assyrian and Babylonian onslaught and deportations. Along the coastal area, the Achaemenids allowed the Phoenicians to govern and develop the area in a
very early stage of their rule there; hence the rapid urbanization of the
area. And, of course, increased commerce enables new social and economic elites to develop quickly.

In the hill country, the economy was agricultural, and the social,
political, and demographic conditions were substantially different.
Furthermore, the area's importance to the Achaemenid regime was

---

31. On Ammon, see Sauer 1985: 213–14; 1986: 18; Herr 1995: 121; 1999: 227; LaBianca
and Younker 1995: 411; Lipschits 2004b. On Edom, see Bienkowski 2001b: 270.

32. Most of the important sites were near the coast, many with sheltered harbors,
and should be regarded as commercial centers of the coastal trade, while the small agricultural sites in the inner plains and the mountain areas served as the agricultural hinterland (Lund 1990: 28). Strabo (7, 16.2.9 [751–52]) described this situation with regard to
the Latakia region: "Then one comes to Laodicaea situated on the sea. . . . Its surrounding region . . . abounds in wine. Now this city furnishes most of the wine to the Alexan-
drians, because the whole of the mountain that lies above the city is covered with vines
almost as far as the summits."

33. On the "rural perspective" of sixth-century Judah, see Lipschits (2004a), in contrast to the opinion of Faust (2003: 37–53). In this regard, Hoglund's theory of a "Persian
policy" of ruralization (1991: 57–60) is debatable. Hoglund himself has admitted that his
argument is speculative and that the data can be explained in other ways. The problem
is that he was using very problematic archaeological data (Carter 1999: 247–48). In fact,
there is no archaeological evidence of demographic change or of any change in settlement pattern at the beginning of the Persian period (Lipschits 2003: 365).

not as great (Briant 2002: 976).[34] The Achaemenids, like the Babylonians that preceded them, were interested in maintaining the existing
rural settlements in the hill country, which were an important source
of agricultural goods, which were probably collected as tax. Exactly
the same situation obtained in the Negev and the southern Shephelah,
as we ascertain from the many ostraca from this region, most of them
published in recent years and dating to the fourth century B.C.E.[35]

Thus, the Achaemenids apparently had no interest in establishing
urban centers in the hill country or in developing new social, political,
and economic power structures on the local level. Their rule over the
hill country was different from their rule in the urban centers on the
coast: along the main roads and at strategic points, Achaemenid forts
and administrative centers were built. Garrison forces, mainly mercenaries, were stationed in the forts, and various economic and administrative functionaries were seated in the administrative centers, where
they managed the affairs of the province and were responsible for collecting the taxes, preparing the Achaemenid expeditions, and executing the orders of the central government. Even when the Achaemenids
had a specific commercial interest in the hill country, such as in the
unique products from 'En Gedi, they developed an isolated imperial
production center, without any cooperation from the local population.[36]

Samaria and Jerusalem:
When Did Jerusalem Become the Capital of Yehud?

Unlike Jerusalem, Samaria continued to exist without interruption
from the seventh to the fourth centuries as the political and administrative center of the province of Samaria. The city was able to develop
as an urban center long before Jerusalem (see Knoppers, in this volume

---

34. As an example of the difference between the coastal area and the hill regions,
compare the distributions of Greek pottery, as summarized in Lehmann 2000.

35. From the ostraca connected with taxes and tax collectors, we learn about the agricultural economy and understand the importance of this economy to the Persian regime. See Lemaire in this volume (pp. 413–456) for further literature and discussion.

36. The archaeological picture is very clear in this case: in contrast to the end of the
seventh century, when there were dozens of small Judahite settlement sites around 'En
Gedi and between it and the hill country, during the entire Achaemenid period the area
was empty and 'En Gedi was an isolated economic center. It may even have been a royal
estate. The absence of sites in the area of 'En Gedi and along the roads that connected it
with the hill area is a clear sign of the imperial monopoly on the production and transportation of goods that were produced there (Lipschits 2000: 37, and see also the list of
sites from the end of the Iron Age and from the Persian Period on pp. 40–42).

pp. 265–289). The fortifications from the eighth century probably survived until the end of the Persian Period and even into the Hellenistic and Roman periods (see above, n. 5). We know for certain that at the end of the fifth and during the fourth centuries there were local social and economic elites in this region, as the finds from Shechem and Wadi ed-Daliya and the Samarian coins may attest (see the summary of Stern 2001: 424–28). Some of the finds at Samaria dated to the Persian Period may point in the same direction: the imported Persian clay cup (Crowfoot 1957b: 216); the Attic ware (dated from the end of the sixth to the end of the fourth centuries; see Crowfoot 1957b: 213–16); three bronze fragments of an Achaemenid throne (Tadmor 1974: 37–43); the clay mold (dated to the Persian Period; see Resiner 1924: 24, pl. 64m; and cf. Tadmor 1974: 42 and n. 17); and the ostraca (especially in Paleo-Hebrew; see Birnbaum 1957: 11–25). Basing his conclusion on this material, Stern claimed that Samaria was one of the biggest urban centers in Palestine (2001: 424). Zertal has claimed that it was the biggest and most important city in Palestine (2003: 380). The very early date (the middle of the fifth century) of the first phase of the temple on Mt. Gerizim[37] may complete the picture. We can assume that the process of social and religious crystallization in Samaria took place much earlier than heretofore assumed, and it could be that the status of Samaria was enhanced as part of this process.[38]

There are no architectural or other finds that attest to Jerusalem as an urban center during the Persian Period.[39] Furthermore, there are no traces of rich tombs around the city during this period and no signs of rich material culture in or around the city. The absence of architectural remains may mean that Jerusalem was wretchedly poor, not just in the period after the Babylonian destruction but also at the height of the Persian Period (Kenyon 1967: 105; Weinberg 1970: 204; Lipschits 2003: 326–34).

---

37. See Magen 1993: 104–8; 2000; personal communication; Magen, Misgav and Tsfania 2004: 6; Stern and Magen 2000; 2002; Stern, personal communication.

38. This is not the subject of this paper (and cf. Knoppers' discussion in this volume), but if this is the case, then the term "Samarians," usually used for the pre–Mt. Gerizim Temple inhabitants of Samaria and thought to be an appropriate designation throughout the late Assyrian-Babylonian and early Achaemenid Periods (parallel to Bickerman's "Proto-Samaritans"), no longer should be extended quite so late, and we can start using the term "Samaritans" (Bickerman's "Samarians") for the population of the area following the foundation of the temple at a much earlier period than we heretofore thought. On these labels, see Macdonald 1972: 143–44. For further literature, see Bedford 2001: 13 n. 23.

39. See the summary of the archaeological evidence in Lipschits 2005: 214–16.

In light of this clear archaeological evidence, we should interpret the "Return to Zion" as a gradual process that did not leave its imprint on the archaeological data. After nearly a century of Persian rule, Jerusalem was small; the city itself was not larger than 60 dunams. According to the accepted demographic ratio, we should estimate the total number of Jerusalem residents at about 1,500,[40] probably the nation's elite—that is, priests and other temple servants, landed aristocracy, ruling social classes, and so on. There is no longer any room for theories regarding a "mass return" at the beginning of the Persian Period.[41]

Based on the interpretation of the archaeological material and the historical circumstances (Lipschits 2003; 2005: 123–26, 155–86, 261–74), we can reconstruct a very small return at the beginning of the Persian Period (probably accompanied by the temple vessels) and several small waves of return during the first hundred years of Persian rule (in the time of Cyrus II, Cambyses II, Darius I, Xerxes, and Artaxerxes I),[42] probably according to families.[43] If this is the case, we should also presume that most of the returnees were settled in Jerusalem and its surroundings.

We may compare this slow process to the biblical description of the three main "waves" of emigration from Babylon to Judah: the first at the very beginning of the Persian Period, after the conquest of Babylon by Cyrus (described in Ezra 1:9–11; 5:14–16—headed by Sheshbazzar); the second in the first days of Darius, after the death of Cambyses II (described in Ezra 2:1–2; cf. Hag 1:1; 2:2, 21—headed by Zerubbabel); and the third during the days of Artaxerxes I (Ezra 7–8).[44] The "list of

---

40. See Lipschits 2003: 364–65; 2005: 261–74; and cf. Carter 1999: 201; Becking, pp. 3–18 in this volume. Compare also Noth 1954: 308.

41. The very few, very late clues that we have regarding the first stage of the return to Zion attest to this limited immigration, both in number of people and in ability to found an urban center or even a cultic center. The prophecies of Haggai and Zechariah describe precisely these difficulties and economic problems (Meyers and Meyers 1987: xxxvii). The lack of Levites and Ezra's efforts to coerce some to join him on his way to Jerusalem (Ezra 8:15–20) may support this thesis.

42. See Hoglund 1992: 23; Kna'uf 1994: 167; Carter 1999: 199–201; Kinet 2001: 190–202; Lipschits 2005: 159–69.

43. On the importance of the family as the primary social entity in the exilic period, see Albertz 1992: 407–11; 2001: 135–36. Note also the evidence of the Neirab archive (Eph'al 1978: 84–87; see also Timm 1995). See, however, the remarks and reservations of Briant (2002: 885, with further literature).

44. In this essay, I will not deal with the chronological problems of Ezra and Nehemiah but merely state that I agree with the traditional chronology, accepted by most modern scholars. According to this chronology, Ezra arrived in Jerusalem in 458 (seventh year of Artaxerxes I, Ezra 7:7) and Nehemiah in 445 (twentieth year of the same Persian king, Neh 2:1).

returnees" in Ezra 2 and Nehemiah 7[45] also points in this direction.[46] It appears that the list is composed of two major sections, and it is plausible that these lists determined the affiliation of the residents of the province ("the whole community together," Ezra 2:64 and Neh 7:66), who, for the author/editor, are identical with "the people of the province who came up from among the captive exiles," that is, the legitimate continuation of the nation of Israel.[47]

We may conclude that there were no restrictions on Judeans who wished to return to Judah after the conquest of Babylon by Cyrus II. However, it is hard to believe that the Persian regime ordered or even encouraged Judeans to do so (Kuhrt 1983; van der Spek 1982; Hoglund 1992: 23). The existence of the temple was the main reason for priestly and Levitical families or other temple functionaries to come to Judah. The situation in Babylon may have been an important motivation for a

---

45. For a thorough comparison of the lists, see Batten 1913: 71–103; Galling 1951: 149–58; Allrik 1954. Modern scholarship has accepted the conclusion that the list in Ezra is later and secondary to the list in Nehemiah (Japhet 1982: 84; 1993: 112; Williamson 1983; Blenkinsopp 1988: 43–44; 86–87). For further literature, see Williamson 1985: 29–30.

46. Despite the fact that some scholars believe that the list reflects the waves of immigration that reached the province of Yehud at the beginning of the Return to Zion (cf. Galling 1951: 150–51; Myers 1965: 15–16), and despite the clear tendency among some scholars to assume that this was a summary list of several waves of immigration that had arrived before Nehemiah's time, I find it difficult to accept the idea that this was the list of those who actually returned from Babylon, whether at once or in several waves of immigration (Lipschits 2005: 159–69). Batten (1913: 72–73, 74–75), for example, proposed dating the list to the time of Ezra primarily on the basis of parallels between the names of those who immigrated with Ezra and the families of immigrants who appear on the list of the Returnees. Liver (1959: 117–19, and n. 40) attempted to establish this hypothesis on a historical basis, claiming it was during the early days of the Return to Zion that the major waves of immigration arrived and that they were joined by new waves at the beginning of Darius's reign, when the situation in Babylon worsened. On this subject, see also Myers 1965: 15–16; Schultz 1980; Williamson 1985: 31. Rudolph proposed seeing the list as a summary of immigration that took place within a relatively short period during the reign of Cyrus and the beginning of Darius's rule (1949: 17). This is, to a certain extent, an extension of Alt's proposal (1934: 24–25); Alt had postulated that this list was intended to regulate the rights of the returnees over the land. Williamson limits the date of the list to the time of Cyrus and Cambyses (1985: xxxiv, 31–32, with further literature). On this subject, see also Blenkinsopp 1988: 83. However, there is no supporting evidence in the archaeological and historical record for demographic changes to the extent of this list, either at the end of the sixth and beginning of the fifth centuries, or even during the course of the fifth century. Consequently, it is likely that the list of the returnees is a literary construction based on various lists, perhaps a census of all residents of the province made at various intervals.

47. See Gunneweg 1985: 53–66; Blenkinsopp 1988: 83; Albertz 2001: 127–28, and see in this direction the various ideas of Albright 1949: 87–88, 110–11; 1950: 64 n. 122; Bright 1959: 376–77.

few Judean families to move to Judah, especially the consequences of the revolts after the death of Cambyses II (522–521 B.C.E.; see Albertz 1992: 444) and after the death of Darius I (486–484; 483 B.C.E.; see Liver 1959: 117–19 and n. 40).[48] The unstable economic situation in Babylonia may have been another motivation for small groups of Judeans to move to Judah, while the developing coastal area in Palestine provided many possibilities for commerce and for integrating agricultural trade from the hill country with the coastal commerce. The stable situation in Samaria and Judah was a good foundation for developing agriculture and commerce in the area (Meyers 1987: 509–10).

The Status of Jerusalem during the Achaemenid Period: From Cultic Center to bîrâ

The real change in the history of Jerusalem occurred in the middle of the fifth century B.C.E., when the fortifications of Jerusalem were rebuilt. Along with scanty archaeological evidence,[49] we have a clear description of this event in the Nehemiah narrative.[50] The list of the builders of the wall (Nehemiah 3) that was combined with Nehemiah's Memoirs by a later editor (Lipschits in press) is another testimony to this event. Furthermore, the impression of this event as one of the most conspicuous, important events of the time led to enormous expectations for the renewed status of Jerusalem in the mind of the writer(s) of Nehemiah 11 (Lipschits 2002b; 2005: 423–40, with further literature).

The significance of this change in Jerusalem in the middle of the fifth century can only be interpreted in one way: Jerusalem became the capital of the province (*bîrâ*), replacing Mizpah. For the many scholars who have accepted Alt's theory (1931; 1934) that Judah was part of the province of Samaria until the days of Nehemiah, this conclusion is not new (and see in this direction the views of McEvenue 1981 and Bed-

---

48. Following Kuhrt and Sherwin-White (1987), we should be skeptical with regard to the various accounts of the harsh blow caused to Babylon by Xerxes. See also the very critical approach of Briant (2002: 114–16, 543–45) regarding the revolts in Babylon and the Achaemenid reaction. See Briant's survey of various scholars' opinions, with further literature on pp. 899–900, 962–63.

49. On the archaeological finds of the Persian Period city wall, as well as the other material from this period in Jerusalem, see the summary by Lipschits 2001; Stern 2001: 434–36; but see also the opinion of Ussishkin, pp. 147–166 in this volume.

50. On the Nehemiah source, see the summary of Reinmuth (2002: 335–36), who, in many respects following Williamson, argues that the story of the construction of the city wall ("Mauerbau-Erzählung") was composed during the governorship of Nehemiah and that it is a reliable contemporary source.

ford 2001: 45). However, Alt's hypothesis has no serious foundation, and most contemporary scholars do not support it.[51] Mizpah was probably the capital of Judah during the 141 years from the time of Gedaliah, the son of Ahikam (586 B.C.E.; Lipschits 2001) to the end of the Neo-Babylonian Period (Lemaire 2003: 292) and probably until the time of Nehemiah (445 B.C.E.; Blenkinsopp 1998: 42 n. 48; cf. Lemaire 1990: 39–40; 2003: 292).

As has been demonstrated very well by Lemaire and Lozachmeur (1987; 1995), in the Persian Period a provincial capital was called a *birtâ* (Akk. *birtū*, Heb. *bîrâ*), and the meaning was 'a fortified town', usually with a garrison in it (Neh 2:8; 7:2; cf. Hoglund 1992: 208–10; Fried 2002: 11–13). Because the fortifications of Jerusalem were destroyed by the Babylonians (cf. 2 Kgs 25:10), and because the first attempt to rebuild them without the permission of the Achaemenid authorities failed (as reported in Ezra 4; cf. Neh 1:3), it seems that, even if the temple had already been rebuilt in Jerusalem and even if the city had already been reestablished as the cultic center of the Judeans, it could not serve as a capital.

The main question remains: What changed in the middle of the fifth century B.C.E.? Why did Jerusalem become the capital of Yehud?

Why Did Jerusalem Become the Capital of Yehud in the Middle of the Fifth Century B.C.E.?

Assuming that the fortifications of Jerusalem were actually built during the first period of Nehemiah as governor in Yehud (Grabbe 2004: 301–2), the main question that may be asked is: What happened during the time when Artaxerxes I allowed the Judeans to build fortifications in Jerusalem? What was the reason for this change in Persian policy?

Most scholars have explained the building of Jerusalem's fortifications as the result of a Persian decision: it was a reward or perhaps even resulted from Persian interests or need. The emphasis has been placed on the active role of the Achaemenids. Most scholars have connected Achaemenid permission to build the fortifications of Jerusalem to political and military developments in the region: the pressure of the Delian League on the Mediterranean coast after 476; the revolt in Egypt (from winter 461/460 to 454); the unrest all along the coastal

---

51. See, e.g., Lemaire 1990: 32–36; Blenkinsopp 1998: 37; Lipschits 1998: 483; Mittmann 2000: 28–42, with further literature.

area of Palestine (including the reference to Dor in the Athenian tribute list from 454); and the revolt of Megabyzus (448). We do not have
to go as far as the theories of Morgenstern (1956; 1957; 1960) or Morton
Smith (1971: 127–29, 391–92);[52] sufficient rationales may be found in
the explanation put forward by Galling as the reason for the fundamental change in the Persian policy in the Levant and the mission of
Nehemiah (1937: 45–47); the many explanations by scholars for the
building of the fortifications in Jerusalem as an Achaemenid induce-
ment to loyalty;[53] or the theory that the Persian efforts to fortify Jerusalem, as well as the other actions of Nehemiah, were part of a much
larger imperial effort to control and integrate extensive areas into the
imperial system (Meyers 1987: 516; Hoglund 1992: 165–69, 207–12,
220–25; Fried 2002).

Most scholars reached their conclusions on this active Achaemenid
policy toward Judah on the basis of the Greek sources on the history of
this period, the book of Ezra–Nehemiah on the history of Judah and
the Judeans during this period, and a basic assumption regarding the
strategic importance of Judah.[54] However, it is questionable that there
was real danger to the rule of Artaxerxes I in the western part of his
empire as a result of the revolt in Egypt,[55] the pressure of the Delian
League,[56] and the alleged revolt of Megabyzus.[57] Did the Achae-

---

52. On the various theories of "the alleged disturbances at the end of the first quarter
of the fifth century," see Hoglund 1992: 61–64, 127–28 (and also add to these theories the
problematic suggestion made by Sowers 1996). See Hoglund's appropriate answer to
these theories (pp. 64–69), and compare with Briant 2002: 960.

53. See Olmstead 1948: 313–17; Rowley 1963: 237–38; Myers 1965: xxii–xxiii; Ackroyd
1968: 141; 1970: 175–76; Widengren 1977: 528–29; Bodi 2001: 69–86. On the various theories, see the review of Hoglund 1992: 86–92.

54. In addition to the basic studies by Hoglund and Carter and the literature cited
there, see also Meyers 1987: 511 and n. 13; Albertz 1992: 445–46; Yamauchi 2004: 9. I will
not treat here the various claims about the special benevolence of the Achaemenid kings
toward the Judeans and Judaism. See, against this, the note of Dandamaev and Lukonin
1989: 249.

55. See, for example, the historical reconstructions by Olmstead 1948: 289–90; Burn
1962: 5–16; and Cook 1983: 127; and compare the discussion of Bigwood 1976: 1–25 and
the discussion and concerns raised by Briant (2002: 573–78; 973–74, with further literature). It seems that the revolt was confined to the Delta and did not threaten Achaemenid control in other parts of the Empire.

56. Many historical reconstructions have been proposed, for example, on the basis of
the mention of Dor in the Athenian tribute list from 454 B.C.E.; but see, against this, the
note of Lemaire (1990: 56 n. 135).

57. There is good reason to doubt the reliability of the description of this revolt (it is
mentioned only by Ctesias, *Pers.* 68–70); compare Bigwood 1976; Hoglund 1992: 162–63;
Briant 1992: 577–79.

menids sense real danger? Was there any genuine change in the way the Achaemenids ruled the Levant?

Attempting to understand the segmented, literary-theological description in the Bible of the events in Jerusalem in the middle of the fifth century by using Greek literary sources, but without recourse to archaeological or any other evidence (such as Achaemenid sources), to explain Persian policy and action is, to say the least, methodologically problematic. The ubiquity of this problematic methodology was the reason for Hoglund's (1992) research into the efforts by the Achaemenid regime to control and integrate various areas into the imperial system. However, aside from the very problematic methodology[58] he utilized and problems with his archaeological data and conclusions,[59] the more basic problem of his widely cited thesis is the conclusion that the middle of the fifth century was the period when the Achaemenids expended much effort on controlling and integrating large territories of the Levant into the imperial system—and that Judah was an important objective of this effort.[60]

On this last point, I can easily agree with Briant's ironic amazement at the perceived importance of Judah for resolution of the Achaemenid problems along the coast and on the border with Egypt: "I have never understood what decisive strategic advantage against Egypt the small

---

58. This is not the place for a full criticism of the methodology at the base of Hoglund's thesis. However, aside from his decision to focus on the middle of the fifth century (pp. 163–64, 168–69, and see below), it is methodologically unacceptable to use architectural typology as an analytical tool for assessing possible increases in the garrisoning of imperial forces in the Levant as part of integrating large areas into the imperial system (pp. 165–205, and see esp. pp. 168–69), especially after nearly 300 years of Mesopotamian (Assyrian, Babylonian, and, later, Persian) rule in Palestine; there are many examples of Mesopotamian architecture and Persian reuse of Assyrian structures.

59. This is not the place to discuss the archaeological data presented by Hoglund, but in my opinion most (if not all) of Hoglund's fortresses are not to be dated to the middle of the fifth century. See the critique by Bienkowski (2001a: 358) regarding the date that Hoglund (1992: 172–75) assigned to Persian-Period structures at Tell es-Saʿidiyeh; see also Lemaire 1994. Compare this with Tuplin's explanation for the Achaemenid fortresses (1987).

60. Based on Hoglund's work, Carter (1999) suggests a new subdivision of the Persian Period: Persian Period A (from 539/8 to the mid-fifth century B.C.E.) and Persian Period B (from the mid-fifth century to 332). This division is problematic from almost every angle but especially in its attempt to define a material culture using (very problematic!) historical data (see the critique in Lipschits 2003: 359). The classification of the archaeological evidence into these two subdivisions does not stand the test of reality. Carter does not even try to substantiate the model that he presents. He lacks clearly defined assemblages of pottery that are stratigraphically distinguished and dated decisively in terms of chronology. To a large extent, his ideas remain a theoretical model that should not be adopted.

land of Judah could have had in the eyes of the Achaemenid central authority" (2002: 976, and see pp. 578–79, 974). Even more (in contrast to Hoglund's thesis), I doubt the relevance of a fortified city in the hill country for the Achaemenid military during the fifth and the fourth centuries; I doubt the importance of fortifications or even a garrison in Jerusalem for the continued conflict between the Persians and the Egyptians; and I doubt the need for such a substantial change in *modus operandi* in the middle of the fifth century. I also find no military motivation for strengthening the Persian holdings along the roads in the hill country and the Negev area during this period; however, the fact that Judah was situated between Persia and Egypt may explain the social, economic, and military processes that were at work at the end of the fifth and beginning of the fourth century, when the Egyptians freed themselves from the Persian yoke (preserving their independence until 343 B.C.E.). During this time, the Achaemenids may have thought that Palestine, especially the southern parts of it, had become a very important border area, making it a battlefield for the Persian army and many of its enemies. It may be that this period was the most important one in the history of this region after the Babylonian conquest and destruction at the end of the seventh and the beginning of the sixth century B.C.E. (Briant 2002: 646–55, 663–66, with further literature on pp. 991–92), and this probably was the time when the Achaemenids established their control and reorganized their administration and security along the roads in the southern parts of Palestine (the southern part of the coast area, the southern Shephelah, and along the Beer-sheba–Arad valleys). This is probably when the main administrative center at Lachish (Stratum I) was built (Tal and Fantalkin, pp. 167–197 in this volume); it was the period when most of the forts and administrative centers along the roads in the Negev area were built (Stern 2001: 420–21, 577–79); and it is the time from which come many unprovenanced Aramaic ostraca, as well as the ostraca from the Beer-sheba–Arad valleys. From all of these ostraca we learn about the importance of the southern Shephelah and this region to the Persian economy, military, and administration (see Lemaire, pp. 413–456 in this volume).

The answer to the question why Jerusalem became the capital of Yehud in the middle of the fifth century is found, in my opinion, in the internal Judean (or Jerusalemite) social, economic, political, and demographic process, which the Persians did not prevent, although they probably were aware of the risks they were taking and the fact that the process was to some extent not in their best interest.[61] At the center of this long process was the temple, not only as a cultic, literary, and theological center, but as a center for gathering taxes and carrying out other important fiscal tasks.[62]

This slow, gradual reestablishment of the local social, religious, and economic power around the temple personnel in Jerusalem occurred about two generations after the reestablishment of the city as the cultic center of Yehud. We cannot detect this process with archaeological tools, because the changes were too slow and too small. It is clear, however, that by the middle of the fifth century Jerusalem had arrived at a point of a change.[63]

If we accept the thesis that the Aramaic letters that were inserted into Ezra 4:7–24 reflect an attempt to build fortifications around Jerusalem during the reign of Artaxerxes I, before the arrival of Nehemiah,[64] we can see this as an attempt by local social powers to fortify Jerusalem without dependence on Achaemenid interests and even without the permission from the Achaemenid regime (vv. 12–16; cf. Williamson 1984: 82).[65] This attempt may explain the news that reached Nehemiah through Hanani, "one of my brothers" (Neh 1:2), who came from Judah and "said to me, 'Those who survived the exile and are back in the province are in great trouble and disgrace. The wall of Jerusalem is broken down, and its gates have been burned with fire'" (vv. 1, 3; Williamson 1984: 82; 1985: 56–57, 171; Blenkinsopp 1988: 113–14, 204). The news from Jerusalem stirred Nehemiah to seek permission from the king: "send me to the city in Judah where my fathers are buried so that I may

---

61. See the warnings in the letters cited in Ezra 4. For this case, it is not important if the Aramaic documents are authentic or not; see Williamson 1985: 62–63, as well as the discussion below.

62. On the importance of the temple as an instrument of Achaemenid fiscal administration, see Schaper 1995; cf. Schaper 1997.

63. Stern (2001: 581–82) worked with the same assumption, basing his view on the archaeological material, but he interpreted the cause and the results differently.

64. On the possible authenticity of the letters, see Stolper (1989: 300), as against the linguistic and stylistic arguments of Schwiderski (2000: 344–51; 354–80). However, the possibility that they are original documents that were edited and adapted to fit the frame of the editor's purposes should be considered (Williamson 1985: 59–60), as presented by Grabbe (in this volume), even if he is skeptical about the two documents discussed here. On the wall building, see Williamson 1984: 81–82; Yamauchi 1990: 270.

65. Blenkinsopp (1988: 113) has connected it with the mention of the גדר in Ezra's confessional prayer (Ezra 9:9). It is interesting to note, even if it is difficult to accept, the thesis of Morton Smith (1971: 122–24), who argued that with this event Ezra's mission ended in disgrace and he was recalled to the imperial court.

rebuild it" (2:5). This may also explain the description of the wall that Nehemiah inspected (Neh 2:13, 17; cf. 1:3) and the rapid completion of the building project, which focused on blocking the breaches in the wall and erecting gates (Williamson 1984: 82).

When Nehemiah arrived as the governor of the province, he found these local powers already established in Jerusalem. This is the first time that we have any reference to the problems of various social classes: commercial relations with the Phoenicians (Neh 13:16; see Williamson 1985: 395, and the discussion of Edelman, pp. 207–246 in this volume); the economic, social, and family relations with the upper classes and leaders in the neighboring provinces (Neh 6:17–19; 13:4, 23–28); the problem of marriage with foreign women (Ezra 9–10; Neh 13:27); and social conflicts between the rich families, nobles, and landowners and the poor families who had to sell their land and houses in order to pay their debts and heavy taxes (Neh 5:1–13; see Albertz 1992: 495–97, with further literature).

The agreement of the Persians to build fortifications in Jerusalem and to alter the status of the city to the capital of the province was the most dramatic change in the history of the city after the Babylonian destruction in 586. However, we know nothing about the reasons for this change. The most logical explanation is that the Persian authorities agreed to the request (of the Judeans/Jerusalemites/some representatives of the Judeans/Nehemiah?) when they realized that, besides its status as the ideological and literary center, Jerusalem had already become the fiscal center of the province (given the usual role of the temple in gathering taxes; see Schaper 1995; cf. Schaper 1997). It might be that the real Persian interest was in the fact that the governor of the province would as a result be as close as possible to the temple.

The importance of this change was understood by the compiler of the Nehemiah Memoirs and the editor of the book of Nehemiah as the beginning of a new period (Lipschits in press), with high expectations and national aspirations that the city would be renewed as of old, its military, material, and governing powers reestablished, and its status restored (Lipschits 2002b). However, in spite of attempts to repopulate the city, the poor archaeological remains in Jerusalem (at least in the narrow area of the city of David) show us that, even after the city wall had been rebuilt, the actual demographic and architectural situation in the city did not change dramatically. In fact, Jerusalem did not become a real urban center until the Hellenistic Period.

Bibliography

Ackroyd, P. R.
1968   *Exile and Restoration: A Study of Hebrew Thought of the Sixth Century* B.C. Philadelphia.
1970   *Israel under Babylon and Persia.* Oxford.

Aharoni, Y.
1956   Excavations at Ramath-Rahel, 1954 (Preliminary Report). *IEJ* 6: 102–11; 137–57.
1962   *The Land of Israel in Biblical Times: A Historical Geography.* Jerusalem. [Citations from the Hebrew revised edition, 1984]
1964   *Excavations at Ramat-Rahel, Seasons 1961 and 1962.* Rome.

Albertz, R.
1994   *A History of Israelite Religion in the Old Testament Period.* London. Translation by John Bowden of *Religionsgeschichte Israels in alttestamentlicher Zeit.* 2 vols. Göttingen, 1992.
2003   *Israel in Exile: The History and Literature of the Sixth Century* B.C.E. Atlanta. Translation by David Green of *Die Exilszeit: 6. Jahrhundert v. Chr.* Stuttgart, 2001.

Albright, W. F.
1949   *The Biblical Period from Abraham to Ezra.* New York.
1950   *The Biblical Period.* Pittsburgh.

Allrik, H. L.
1954   The Lists of Zerubbabel (Neh. 7 and Ezr. 2) and the Hebrew Numerical Notation. *BASOR* 136: 21–27.

Alt, A.
1929   Das System der assyrische Provinzen auf dem Boden des Reiches Israel. *ZDPV* 52: 220–42.
1931   Judas Nachbarn zur zeit Nehemias. *PJB* 27: 66–74. [Reprinted in *KS* 2 (1953): 338–45]
1934   Die Rolle Samarias bei der Entstehung des Judentums. Pp. 5–28 in *Festschrift Otto Procksch zum 60. Geburtstag.* Leipzig. [Reprinted in *KS* 2 (1953): 316–37]

Batten, L. W.
1913   *A Critical and Exegetical Commentary on the Books of Ezra and Nehemiah.* Edinburgh.

Bedford, P. R.
2001   *Temple Restoration in Early Achaemenid Judah.* Leiden.

Bienkowski, P.
2001a   The Persian Period. Pp. 347–65 in *The Archaeology of Jordan,* ed. B. MacDonald, R. Adams, and P. Bienkowski. Sheffield.
2001b   The Iron Age and Persian Periods in Jordan. Pp. 265–74 in *Studies in the History and Archaeology of Jordan 7.* Amman.

Bigwood, J. M.
1976   Ctesias' Account of the Revolt of Inarus. *Phoenix* 30: 1–25.

Birnbaum, S. A.
   1957   Inscriptions: Ostraca. Pp. 9–32 in *The Objects from Samaria*. Samaria–
          Sebaste Reports of the Work of the Joint Expedition in 1931–1933 and
          the British Expedition in 1935, No. 3, ed. J. W. Crowfoot, G. M. Crow-
          foot, and K. M. Kenyon. London.
Blenkinsopp, J.
   1988   *Ezra, Nehemiah*. OTL. Philadelphia.
   1998   The Judaean Priesthood during the Neo-Babylonian and Achaemenid
          Periods: A Hypothetical Reconstruction. *CBQ* 60: 25–43.
Bodi, D.
   2001   La clémence des Perses envers Néhémie et ses compatriotes: Faveur ou
          opportunism politique? *Transeu* 21: 69–86.
Briant, P.
   2002   *From Cyrus to Alexander: A History of the Persian Empire*, trans. Peter T.
          Daniels. Winona Lake, Indiana. [English translation of *Histoire de l'em-
          pire perse: De Cyrus à Alexandre*. Paris, 1996]
Bright, J.
   1959   *A History of Israel*. Philadelphia.
Brown, J. P.
   1969   *The Lebanon and Phoenicia: Ancient Texts Illustrating Their Physical Geog-
          raphy and Native Industries*. Beirut.
Burn, A. R.
   1962   *Persia and the Greeks: The Defense of the West, 546–478 B.C.* New York.
Calmeyer, P.
   1990   Die sogennante Fünfte Satrapie bei Herodot. *Transeu* 3: 109–29.
Carter, C. E.
   1994   The Province of Yehud in the Post-Exilic Period: Soundings in the Site
          Distribution and Demography. Pp. 106–45 in *Second Temple Studies 2:
          Temple and Community in the Persian Period*, ed. T. C. Eskenazi and K. H.
          Richards. JSOTSup 175. Sheffield.
   1999   *The Emergence of Yehud in the Persian Period: A Social and Demographic
          Study*. JSOTSup 294. Sheffield.
Cook, J. M.
   1983   *The Persian Empire*. London.
   1985   The Rise of the Achaemenides and Establishment of Their Empire.
          Pp. 200–291 in *The Median and Achaemenian Periods*, ed. I. Gershevitch.
          Vol. 2 of *Cambridge History of Iran*. Cambridge.
Crowfoot, J. W.
   1942   Buildings round and below the Summit. Pp. 5–20 in *The Buildings
          at Samaria*, ed. G. M. Crowfoot, K. M. Kenyon, and E. L. Sukenik.
          London.
   1957a Introduction. Pp. 1–8 in *The Objects from Samaria*, ed. J. W. Crowfoot,
          G. M. Crowfoot, and K. M. Kenyon. Samaria–Sebaste Reports of the
          Work of the Joint Expedition in 1931–1933 and the British Expedition
          in 1935, No. 3. London.

1957b Pottery: Imported Wares. Pp. 210–16 in *The Objects from Samaria*, ed. J. W. Crowfoot, G. M. Crowfoot, and K. M. Kenyon. Samaria–Sebaste Reports of the Work of the Joint Expedition in 1931–1933 and the British Expedition in 1935, No. 3. London.

Cruz-Uribe, E.
2003 The Invasion of Egypt by Cambyses. *Transeu* 25: 9–60.

Dandamaev, M. A.
1995 A Governor of Byblos in Sippar. Pp. 29–31 in *Immigration and Emigration within the Ancient Near East* (FS E. Lipiński), ed. K. van Lerberghe and A. Schoors. Leuven.

Dandamaev, M. A., and Lukonin, V. G.
1989 *The Culture and Social Institution of Ancient Iran.* Cambridge.

Donner, H., and Röllig, W.
1962 *Texte.* Vol. 1 of *Kanaanäische und Aramäische Inschriften mit einem Beitrag von O. Rössler.* Wiesbaden.
1964 *Kommentar.* Vol. 2 of *Kanaanäische und Aramäische Inschriften Mit einem Beitrag von O. Rössler.* Wiesbaden.

Dothan, T., and Gitin, S.
1994 Tel Miqne / Ekron: The Rise and Fall of a Philistine City. *Qadmoniot* 105–6: 2–28. [Hebrew]

Elat, M.
1991 Phoenician Overland Trade within the Mesopotamian Empires. Pp. 21–35 in *Ah, Assyria . . . : Studies in Assyrian History and Ancient Near Eastern Historiography Presented to Hayim Tadmor*, ed. M. Cogan and I. Eph'al. Jerusalem.

Elayi, J.
1980 The Phoenician Cities in the Persian Period. *JANES* 12: 13–28.
1982 Studies in Phoenician Geography during the Persian Period. *JNES* 41: 83–110.
1987 *Recherches sur les cités phéniciennes à l'époque perse.* Annali Istituto Universitario Orientale, Supp. 51. Naples.
2004 La chronologie de la dynastie sidonienne d'ʾEšmunʿazor. *Transeu* 27: 9–27.

Elgavish, Y.
1968 *Shiqmonah: The Strata from the Persian Period, Seasons 1963–1965.* Haifa. [Hebrew]
1994 *Shiqmonah: By the Coast of Carmel.* Tel Aviv.

Eph'al, I.
1978 The Western Minorities in Babylonia in the 6th–5th Centuries B.C.: Maintenance and Cohesion. *Or* n.s. 47: 74–90.
1984 Transjordan under Assyrian Rule. *IEJ* 4: 168–86.
1998 Changes in Palestine during the Persian Period in Light of Epigraphic Sources. *IEJ* 38: 106–19.

Faust, A.
2003 Judah in the Sixth Century B.C.E.: A Rural Perspective. *PEQ* 135: 37–53.

Finkelstein, I.
1978   *The Pattern of Settlement in the Yarkon Basin and the Mountain Area Border in the Israelite to Hellenistic Periods.* M.A. thesis. Tel Aviv University.
1981   Israelite and Hellenistic Farms in the Foothills and the Yarkon Basin. *ErIsr* 15 (Aharoni volume): 331–48. [Hebrew]
Finkelstein, I., and Ussishkin, D.
2000   Archaeological and Historical Conclusions. Pp. 576–605 in *Megiddo III: The 1992–1996 Seasons*, ed. I. Finkelstein, D. Ussishkin, and B. Halpern. Jerusalem.
Forrer, E.
1920   *Die Provinzeinteilung des assyrichen Reiches.* Leipzig.
Fried, L.
2002   The Political Struggle of Fifth Century Judah. *Transeu* 24: 9–21.
Frye, R. N.
1984   *The History of Ancient Iran.* Munich.
Galling, K.
1951   The "Gōlā-List" according to Ezra 2 // Nehemiah 7. *JBL* 70: 149–58.
Galling, K. (ed.)
1937   *Biblisches Reallexikon.* Tübingen.
Gardiner, J. D.
1991   *Hellenistic Phoenicia.* Oxford.
Garelli, P., and Nikiprowetzky, V.
1974   *Le Proche-orient asiatique: Les empires Mésopotamiens, Israel.* Paris.
Gibson, J. C. L.
1982   *Textbook of Syrian Semitic Inscriptions, III: Phoenician Inscriptions.* Oxford.
Gitin, S.
1997   The Neo-Assyrian Empire and Its Western Periphery: The Levant, with a Focus on Philistine Ekron. Pp. 77–104 in *Assyria 1995*, ed. S. Parpola and R. M. Whiting. Helsinki.
1998   The Philistines in the Prophetic Texts: An Archaeological Perspective. Pp. 273–90 in *Hesed ve-Emet: Studies in Honor of Ernest S. Frerichs*, ed. J. Magness and S. Gitin. BJS 320. Atlanta.
Grabbe, L. L.
1998   *Ezra and Nehemiah.* Old Testament Readings. London.
2004   *A History of the Jews and Judaism in the Second Temple Period, Vol. I: Yehud: A History of the Persian Province of Judah.* London.
Graf, D. F.
1993   The Persian Royal Road System in Syria–Palestine. *Transeu* 6: 149–68.
Graham, J. N.
1984   "Vinedressers and Plowmen": 2 Kings 25:12 and Jeremiah 52:16. *BA* 47/1: 55–58.
Grayson, A. K.
1975   *Assyrian and Babylonian Chronicles.* Locust Valley, New York. [Reprinted Winona Lake, Indiana, 2000]

1991   Assyria: Sennacherib and Esarhaddon (704–669 B.C.). Pp. 103–41 in *The Assyrian and Babylonian Empires and Other States of the Near East, from the Eighth to the Sixth Centuries B.C.* Vol. 3/2 of *CAH*. Cambridge.

Gunneweg, A. H. J.

1985   *Esra*. KAT 9/1. Gütersloh.

Hawkins, J. D.

1995   The Political Geography of North Syria and Southeast Anatolia in the Neo-Assyrian Period. Pp. 87–102 in *Neo-Assyrian Geography*, ed. M. Liverani. Rome.

Herbert, S. C., and Berlin, A. M.

2003   A New Administrative Center for Persian and Hellenistic Galilee: Preliminary Report of the University of Michigan / University of Minnesota Excavations at Kedesh. *BASOR* 329: 13–59.

Herr, L. G.

1995   Wine Production in the Hills of Southern Ammon and the Founding of Tall Al-ʿUmayrī in the Sixth Century BC. *ADAJ* 39: 121–25.

1999   The Ammonites in the Late Iron Age and Persian Period. Pp. 219–37 in *Ancient Ammon*, ed. B. MacDonald and R. W. Younker. Studies in the History and Culture of the Ancient Near East 17. Leiden.

Hoglund, K. G.

1991   The Achaemenid Context. Pp. 22–53 in *Second Temple Studies 1: Persian Period*, ed. P. R. Davies. JSOTSup 117. Sheffield.

1992   *Achaemenid Imperial Administration in Syria–Palestine and the Missions of Ezra and Nehemiah*. Atlanta.

James, T. G. H.

1991   Egypt: The Twenty-Fifth and Twenty-Sixth Dynasties. Pp. 677–747 in *The Assyrian and Babylonian Empires and Other States of the Near East, from the Eighth to the Sixth Centuries B.C.* Vol. 3/2 of *CAH*. Cambridge.

Japhet, S.

1982   Sheshbazzar and Zerubbabel. *ZAW* 94: 66–98.

1993   Composition and Chronology in the Book of Ezra–Nehemiah. *ErIsr* 24 (Malamat volume): 111–21. [Hebrew]

Katzenstein, H. J.

1973   *A History of Tyre*. Jerusalem.

1979   Tyre in the Early Persian Period (539–486 B.C.E.). *BA* 42/1: 23–34.

1994   Gaza in the Neo-Babylonian Period (626–539 B.C.E.). *Transeu* 7 : 35–49.

Kelso, J. L., et al.

1968   *The Excavation of Bethel 1934–1960*. AASOR 39. Cambridge.

Kenyon, K. M.

1942   The Summit Buildings and Constructions. Pp. 91–120 in *The Buildings at Samaria*, ed. G. M. Crowfoot, K. M. Kenyon, and E. L. Sukenik. London.

1957   Pottery: Early Bronze and Israelite. Pp. 91–209 in *The Objects from Samaria*. Samaria–Sebaste Reports of the Work of the Joint Expedition in 1931–1933 and the British Expedition in 1935, No. 3, ed. J. W. Crowfoot, G. M. Crowfoot, and K. M. Kenyon. London.

1960   *Archaeology in the Holy Land*. London. [4th ed., 1979]

1967 *Jerusalem: Excavating 3000 Years of History.* London.

Kienitz, F. K.
1953 *Die politische Geschichte Ägyptens vom 7. Bis zum 4. Jarhundert von der Zeitwende.* Berlin.

Kinet, D.
2001 *Geschichte Israels.* NEchtB 2. Würzburg.

Knauf, E. A.
1994 *Die Umwelt des Alten Testaments.* Neuer Stuttgarter Kommentar AT 29. Stuttgart.

Kreissig, H.
1973 *Die Sozialökonomische situation in Juda zur Achämenidenzeit.* Berlin.

Kuhrt, A.
1983 The Cyrus Cylinder and Achaemenid Imperial Policy. *JSOT* 25: 83–97.

Kuhrt, A., and Sherwin-White, S.
1987 Xerxes' Destruction of Babylonian Temples. Pp. 69–78 in *Achaemenid History II: The Greek Sources. Proceedings of the Groningen 1984 Achaemenid History Workshop*, ed. H. Sancisi-Weerdenburg and A. Kuhrt. Leiden.

LaBianca, Ø. S., and Younker, R. W.
1995 The Kingdoms of Ammon, Moab and Edom: The Archaeology of Society in Late Bronze/Iron Age Transjordan (ca. 1400–500 B.C.E.). Pp. 399–415 in *The Archaeology of Society in the Holy Land*, ed. T. E. Levy. New York.

Lehmann, G.
2000 East Greek or Levantine? Band-Decorated Pottery in the Levant during the Achaemenid Period. *Transeu* 19: 83–113.

Lemaire, A.
1990 Populations et territoires de Palestine à l'époque perse. *Transeu* 3: 31–74.
1994 Review of K. G. Hoglund, *Achaemenid Imperial Administration in Syria–Palestine and the Missions of Ezra and Nehemiah. Transeu* 8: 167–69.
2000 L'économie de l'Idumée d'apres les nouveaux ostraca araméens. *Transeu* 19: 131–43.
2003 Nabonidus in Arabia and Judah in the Neo-Babylonian Period. Pp. 285–98 in *Judah and the Judeans in the Neo-Babylonian Period*, ed. O. Lipschits and J. Blenkinsopp. Winona Lake, Indiana.

Lemaire, A., and Lozachmeur, H.
1987 *Bîrāh/Birtāh* en araméen. *Syria* 64: 261–66.
1995 La *birta* en Méditerranée orientale. *Sem* 43/44: 75–78.

Lemon, R. S., and Shipton, G. M.
1939 *Megiddo I.* Chicago.

Leuze, E.
1935 *Die Satrapieneinleitung in Syrien und im Zweistomlande von 520–320.* Halle.

Limet, H.
  2000   Les exploitations agricoles en Transeuphratène au Ier millénaire à la lumière des pratiques assyriennes. *Transeu* 19: 35–50.
Lipschits, O.
  1998   Nebuchadrezzar's Policy in Hattu-Land and the Fate of the Kingdom of Judah. *UF* 30: 467–87.
  1999   The History of the Benjamin Region under Babylonian Rule. *TA* 26: 155–90.
  2000   Was There a Royal Estate in Ein-Gedi by the End of the Iron Age and during the Persian Period? Pp. 31–42 in *Jerusalem and Eretz Israel (Arie Kindler Volume)*, ed. J. Schwartz, Z. Amar, and I. Ziffer. Tel Aviv. [Hebrew]
  2001   Judah, Jerusalem and the Temple (586–539 B.C.E.). *Transeu* 22: 129–42.
  2002a   The Policy of the Persian Empire and the Meager Architectonic Finds in the Province of Yehud. Pp. 45–76 in *New Studies in Jerusalem: Proceedings of the Seventh Conference*, ed. A. Faust and E. Baruch. Ramat-Gan. [Hebrew]
  2002b   Literary and Ideological Aspects in Nehemiah 11. *JBL* 121: 423–40.
  2003   Demographic Changes in Judah between the Seventh and Fifth Centuries B.C.E. Pp. 323–76 in *Judah and the Judeans in the Neo-Babylonian Period*, ed. O. Lipschits and J. Blenkinsopp. Winona Lake, Indiana.
  2004a   The Rural Settlement in Judah in the Sixth Century BCE: A Rejoinder. *PEQ* 136: 99–107.
  2004b   Ammon in Transition from Vassal Kingdom to Babylonian Province. *BASOR* 335: 37–52.
  2005   *The Fall and Rise of Jerusalem: The History of Judah under Babylonian Rule.* Winona Lake, Indiana.
  in press   Who Supported and Who Organized the Building of Jerusalem's Wall? The Sources of the List of "The Builders of the Walls" and the Biases of Its Settings. *Sara Japhet Festschrift.* [Hebrew]
Liver, J.
  1959   *The House of David from the Fall of the Kingdom of Judah to the Fall of the Second Commonwealth and After.* Jerusalem. [Hebrew]
Lund, J.
  1990   The Northern Coastline of Syria in the Persian Period: A Survey of the Archaeological Evidence. *Transeu* 2: 13–36.
Macdonald, J.
  1972   The Discovery of Samaritan Religion. *Religion: Journal of Religion and Religions* 2: 141–53.
Magen, Y.
  1993   Mount Gerizim and the Samaritans. Pp. 89–148 in *Early Christianity in Context*, ed. F. Manns and E. Alliata. Studium Biblicum Franciscanum: Collectio Maior 38. Jerusalem.
  2000   Mt. Gerizim: A Temple City. *Qadmoniot* 33/2: 74–118. [Hebrew]

Magen, Y.; Misgav, H.; and Tsfania, L.
2004   *Mount Gerizim Excavations, Volume I: The Aramaic, Hebrew and Samaritan Inscriptions.* Jerusalem.
Mazar, A.
1994   The Northern Shephelah in the Iron Age: Some Issues in Biblical History and Archaeology. Pp. 247–67 in *Scripture and Other Artifacts: Essays on the Bible and Archaeology in Honor of Philip J. King,* ed. M. D. Coogan, J. C. Exum, and L. E. Stager. Louisville.
McEvenue, S.
1981   The Political Structure in Judah from Cyrus to Nehemiah. *CBQ* 43: 353–64.
Meyers, C. L., and Meyers, E. M.
1987   *Haggai, Zechariah 1–8: A New Translation with Introduction and Commentary.* AB 25B. Garden City, New York.
Meyers, E. M.
1987   The Persian Period and the Judean Restoration: From Zerubbabel to Nehemiah. Pp. 509–21 in *Ancient Israelite Religion: Essays in Honor of Frank Moore Cross,* ed. P. D. Hanson, S. D. McBride, and P. D. Miller. Philadelphia.
Milevski, I.
1996–97 Settlement Patterns in Northern Judah during the Achaemenid Period according to the Hill Country of Benjamin and Jerusalem Survey. *Bulletin of the Anglo-Israel Archaeological Society* 15: 7–29.
Mittmann, S.
2000   Tobia, Sanballat und die persische Provinz Juda. *JNSL* 26/2: 1–50.
Morgenstern, J.
1956   Jerusalem—485 B.C. *HUCA* 27: 101–79.
1957   Jerusalem—485 B.C. *HUCA* 28: 15–47.
1960   Jerusalem—485 B.C. *HUCA* 31: 1–29.
Myers, J. M.
1965   *Ezra–Nehemiah.* AB 14. Garden City, New York.
Na'aman, N.
1991   The Kingdom of Judah under Josiah. *TA* 18: 3–71.
1993   Population Changes in Palestine following Assyrian Deportations. *TA* 20: 104–24.
1994   Ahaz's and Hezekiah's Policy towards Assyria in the Days of Sargon II and Sennacherib's Early Years. *Zion* 59: 5–30 [Hebrew]
1995   Province System and Settlement Pattern in Southern Syria and Palestine in the Neo-Assyrian Period. Pp. 103–15 in *Neo-Assyrian Geography,* ed. M. Liverani. Rome.
1998   Two Notes on the History of Ashkelon and Ekron in the Late Eighth–Seventh Century B.C.E. *TA* 25: 219–27.
2000   Royal Vassals or Governors? On the Status of Sheshbazzar and Zerubbabel in the Persian Empire. *Henoch* 22: 35–44.
2004   The Boundary System and Political Status of Gaza under Assyrian Empire. *ZDPV* 120: 55–72.

Noth, M.
1954   *Geschichte Israels.* Göttingen. ET: P. R. Ackroyd (trans.). *The History of Israel.* London, 1958.
Oded, B.
1970   Observations on Methods of Assyrian Rule in Transjordania after the Palestinian Campaign of Tiglath-pileser III. *JNES* 29: 177–86.
Olmstead, A. T.
1948   *History of the Persian Empire.* Chicago.
Oppenheim, A. L.
1967   Essay on Overland Trade in the First Millennium B.C. *JCS* 21: 236–54.
Otzen, B.
1964   *Studien über Deuterosacharja.* Copenhagen.
Parpola, S.
1970   *Neo-Asyyrian Toponyms.* Neukirchen-Vluyn.
Peersmann, J.
2000   Assyrian Megiddo: The Town Planning of Stratum III. Pp. 524–34 in *Megiddo III: The 1992–1996 Seasons,* ed. I. Finkelstein, D. Ussishkin, and B. Halpern. Jerusalem.
Petit, T.
1990   *Satrapes et Satrapies dans l'Empire achéménidede Cyrus le Grand à Xerxès Ier.* Liège.
Rainey, A. F.
1969   The Satrapy 'Beyond the River'. *AJBA* 1: 51–78.
Redford, D. B.
1992   *Egypt, Canaan, and Israel in Ancient Times.* Princeton.
Reinmuth, T.
2002   *Der Bericht Nehemias: Zur literarischen Eigenart, traditionsgeschichtlichen Prägung und innerbiblischen Rezeption des Ich-Berichts Nehemias.* OBO 183. Freiburg.
Resiner, G. A.
1924   *Harvard Excavations at Samaria.* Vol. 2. Cambridge, Massachusetts.
Roll, Y., and Ayalon, E.
1989   *Apollonia and the Southern Sharon.* Tel Aviv.
Rowley, H. H.
1963   *Men of God: Studies in Old Testament History and Prophecy.* London.
Rudolph, W.
1949   *Ezra und Nehemia.* Tübingen.
Sauer, J. A.
1985   Ammon, Moab and Edom. Pp. 206–14 in *Biblical Archaeology Today: Proceedings of the International Congress on Biblical Archaeologym Jerusalem, April 1984.* Jerusalem.
1986   Transjordan in the Bronze and Iron ages: A Critique of Nelson Glueck's Synthesis. *BASOR* 236: 1–26.
Schaper, J.
1995   The Jerusalem Temple as an Instrument of the Achaemenid Fiscal Administration. *VT* 45: 528–39.

1997 The Temple Treasury Committee in the Times of Nehemiah and Ezra. *VT* 47: 200–206.

Schultz, C.
1980 The Political Tensions Reflected in Ezra–Nehemiah. Pp. 221–44 in *Scripture in Context: Essays on the Comparative Method*, ed. C. D. Evans et al. Pittsburgh.

Schwiderski, D.
2000 *Handbuch des nordwestsemitischen Briefformulars: Ein Beitrag zur Echtheitsfrage der aramäischen Briefe des Esrabuches.* BZAW 295. Berlin.

Smith, M.
1971 *Palestinian Parties and Politics That Shaped the Old Testament.* New York.

Sowers, S. G.
1996 Did Xerxes Wage War on Jerusalem? *HUCA* 67: 43–53.

Spek, R. J. van der
1982 Did Cyrus the Great Introduce a New Policy towards Subdued Nations? Cyrus in Assyrian Perspective. *Persica* 10: 278–83.

Stager, L. E.
1996 Ashkelon and the Archaeology of Destruction: Kislev 604 B.C.E. *ErIsr* 25 (Aviram volume): 61*–74*.

Stern, E.
1982 *Material Culture of the Land of the Bible in the Persian Period, 538–332 B.C.* Warminster. [Hebrew original, 1973]
1984 The Persian Empire and the Political and Social History of Palestine in the Persian Period. Pp. 70–87 in *The Cambridge History of Judaism*, ed. W. D. Davies and L. Finkelstein. Cambridge.
1990 The Dor Province in the Persian Period in the Light of the Recent Excavations at Dor. *Transeu* 2: 147–55.
1995 Between Persia and Greece: Trade, Administration and Warfare in the Persian and Hellenistic Periods. Pp. 433–45 in *The Archaeology of Society in the Holy Land*, ed. T. E. Levy. London.
2000 The Babylonian Gap. *BAR* 26/6: 45—51; 76.
2001 *Archaeology of the Land of the Bible, Volume II: The Assyrian, Babylonian, and Persian Periods (732–332 B.C.E.).* New York.
2004 The Babylonian Gap: The Archaeological Reality. *JSOT* 28: 273–77.

Stern E., and Magen, Y.
2000 The First Phase of the Samaritan Temple on Mt. Gerizim: New Archaeological Evidence. *Qadmoniot* 33: 119–24. [Hebrew]
2002 Archaeological Evidence for the First Stage of the Samaritan Temple on Mount Gerizim. *IEJ* 52: 49–57.

Stolper, M. W.
1989 The Governor of Babylon and Across-the-River in 486 B.C. *JNES* 48: 283–305.

Tadmor, H.
1964 The Assyrian Campaigns to Philistia. Pp. 261–85 in *The Military History of the Land of Israel in Biblical Times*, ed. J. Liver. Tel Aviv. [Hebrew]
1966 Philistia under Assyrian Rule. *BA* 29: 86–102.

1973 On the History of Samaria in the Biblical Period. Pp. 67–74 in *Eretz Shomron: The Thirtieth Archaeological Convention, September 1972*, ed. J. Aviram. Jerusalem. [Hebrew]

Tadmor, M.
1974 Fragments of an Achaemenid Throne from Samaria. *IEJ* 24: 37–43.

Tal, O.
2000 Some Notes on the Settlement Patterns of the Persian Period Southern Sharon Plain in Light of Recent Excavations at Apollonia-Arsuf. *Transeu* 19: 115–25.

Tappy, R. E.
2001 *The Archaeology of Israelite Samaria, Volume II: The Eighth Century BCE.* HSS 50. Winona Lake, Indiana.

Timm, S.
1995 Die Bedeutung der spätbabylonischen Texte aus Nerab für die Rückkehr der Judäer aus dem Exil. Pp. 276–88 in *Meilenstein: Festgabe für Herbert Donner*, ed. M. Weippert and S. Timm. Wiesbaden.

Tuplin, C.
1987 The Administration of the Achaemenid Empire. Pp. 109–66 in *Coinage and Administration in the Athenian and Persian Empires*, ed. I. Carradice. BAR Int. Series 343. Oxford.

Vanderhooft, D. S.
1999 *The Neo-Babylonian Empire and Babylon in the Latter Prophets.* Atlanta.

Wallinga, H.
1987 The Ancient Persian Navy and Its Predecessors. Pp. 47–77 in *Achaemenid History I: Structures and Synthesis*, ed. H. Sancisi-Weerdenburg. Leiden.

Weinberg, S. S.
1970 Eretz Israel after the Destruction of the First Temple: Archaeological Report. Pp. 202–16 in vol. 4 of *Proceedings of the Israeli National Academy of Sciences*. [Hebrew]

Weippert, M.
1982 Zur Syrienpolitik Tiglathpileser III. Pp. 395–408 in vol. 2 of *Mesopotamien und seine Nachbarn. Politische und kulturelle Wechselbeziehungen im Alten Vorderasien vom 4. bis 1. Jahrtausend v. Chr.*, ed. H.-J. Nissen and J. Renger. Berlin.

Weisman, D. J.
1991 Babylonia 605–539 B.C. Pp. 229–51 in *The Assyrian and Babylonian Empires and Other States of the Near East, from the Eighth to the Sixth Centuries B.C.* 2nd ed. Vol. 3/2 of *CAH*. Cambridge.

Widengren, G.
1977 The Persian Period. Pp. 489–538 in *Israelite and Judaean History*, ed. J. H. Hayes and J. M. Miller. London.

Williamson, H. G. M.
1983 The Composition of Ezra i–vi. *JTS* 34: 1–30.
1984 Nehemiah's Walls Revisited. *PEQ* 116: 81–88.
1985 *Ezra–Nehemiah.* WBC 16. Waco, Texas.

Wiseman, D. J.
  1956   *Chronicles of Chaldeans Kings (626–556 B.C.) in the British Museum.*
         London.
Yamauchi, E. M.
  1990   *Persia and the Bible.* Grand Rapids.
  2004   The Reconstruction of Jewish Communities during the Persian Em-
         pire. *The Journal of the Historical Society* 4: 1–25.
Zertal, A.
  1990   The Pahwah of Samaria (Northern Israel) during the Persian Period:
         Types of Settlement, Economy, History and New Discoveries. *Transeu*
         3: 9–30.
  1999   The Province of Samaria during the Persian and Hellenistic Periods.
         Pp. 75–98 in *Michael: Historical, Epigraphical and Biblical Studies in Honor
         of Professor Michael Heltzer,* ed. Y. Avishur and R. Deutsch. Tel Aviv–
         Jaffa. [Hebrew]
  2003   The Province of Samaria (Assyrian *Samerina*) in the Late Iron Age
         (Iron Age III). Pp. 377–412 in *Judah and the Judeans in the Neo-Babylonian
         Period,* ed. O. Lipschits and J. Blenkinsopp. Winona Lake, Indiana.

Constructions of Identity in Postcolonial Yehud

JON L. BERQUIST
Westminster John Knox Press

This book's title explains its subject matter as *Judah and the Judeans in the Persian Period*, a phrase inhabited by three concepts. Studies of this sort have produced a clear understanding of the last of the concepts, *the Persian Period*, also called the Achaemenid Period, which refers to matters concerning an empire of southern and southwestern Asia during 539–333 B.C.E., whose emperors traced their lineage to the family of a certain Achemenes. However, the other terms are more problematic. Consider the term *Judah*. At times, scholars employ this term to define a geographic region, yet in other instances, *Judah* denotes a political entity. In either case, recent studies, including several in this volume, have problemized the precision of this term. Whether geographical or political, the extent and shape of Judah have proven difficult to determine, and I suggest that a significant number of scholarly differences reflect the diminishing common understanding of the term *Judah*. Now that studies of the Achaemenid Period are demonstrating the divergences in discerning what would mark a border or boundary of Judah, the disagreements between scholarly assessments of *Judah* are growing. Thus, we argue over Judah's population and demography,[1] sometimes without even recognizing that we fail to discern the limits of such a Judah.

The term *Judean* is just as problematic, if not more so. In our scholarship, we use the term, not as an adjective, but as a noun to indicate certain persons who, we assume, have something to do with "Judah" during "the Achaemenid Period."

Who, then, counts as a Judean? What criteria can we use to ascertain who is a Judean and who is not? What are the limits of this group, and what kind of group would they be? Scholarship on Achaemenid Judah

---

1. See Carter 1999 for a description of Judah's demography. Although his work is contested, Carter remains more precise in his delineation of Judean geographic boundaries than most of those who argue against his views.

(or Persian Yehud) has tended to ignore such questions, thus using the term without attention to the important assumptions about what it would mean "to be a Judean." Even if we set aside the emic/etic distinction (that is, the question of whether we should search for criteria of Judean-ness that make sense to us or that would make sense to Judeans themselves), there are still a variety of problems within scholarly usage of the term. Thus, we need to seek additional clarity about the identity of these Judeans. To examine this identity, we must focus on the scholarly uses of the concept of *identity*. Studies in ancient Judaism have rarely addressed this question (but see Mullen 1997; Cohen 1999; and Schwartz 2001), even though the larger field of cultural studies has concentrated on identity as a major problem for scholarship. Such studies recognize that arguments of identity base themselves in observed differences between groups (or at its base, between "us" and "them") and then provide theories to explain the differences (Lentricchia and McLaughlin [eds.] 1995; Rajchman [ed.] 1995; Hall and du Gay [eds.] 1996; Michael 1996). However, such explanations or theories are only relevant insofar as they explain the distribution of extant evidence.

In my attempt to untangle the competing assumptions about identity in Achaemenid Yehud, I will sketch five different modes of scholarship. These five modes do not represent a strict history of scholarship; rather, I intend them to reflect five different and continuing trends within scholarship. Within the discussion of each mode, I will briefly suggest some of the operative assumptions and will offer a few words of critique about the limits that these assumptions create. Finally, I will comment on some of the ramifications for our understanding of Judean identity within the Achaemenid Period.

Identity as Ethnicity

First, scholarship often uses *identity* to mean *ethnicity*. Judeans would therefore be members of an extended family, sharing lineage and descent, and measurable by genealogy. Such identity is objective; it is innate from birth. A person is Judean not because of anything she or he does but because of his/her parents. This ethnic identity is inherited, not enacted. Genealogy alone suffices to prove membership within the Judean populace, because every Judean is related to every other Judean through a family relationship that is precisely definable (in theory if not in actuality). This position has been the classic assumption of early and modern biblical scholarship.

As a theory of identity, ethnicity has several noticeable benefits. First, it reflects the biblical texts' interests in genealogy. Second, the theory of identity fits both the ancient and modern interests in telling history as a story of peoples, races, and *ethnoi*. Third, an ethnicity theory reflects the cross-generational aspects of the biblical representation of Judean identity. Lastly, this theory of ethnic identity creates a clear connection between the ancient biblical story and the contemporary world; the story of Judah is not just a story of ancient people but a story of ancestors and thus, for some people today, a story of their own ethnicity.[2]

Despite these advantages to an ethnic theory of identity, scholarship has often recognized the substantial problems with the categories of ethnicity. For instance, archaeologists have difficulty discerning the ethnicity of a given artifact's maker or user. Epigraphers know that they must speak of West Semitic name elements without making claims about the ethnicity of the persons called by those names. Historians find reconstructing ancient lineages to be problematic and uncertain. In the case of Persian Yehud, we know that there was significant mixed marriage, and so clear lines between different ethnic groups were increasingly problematic.

However, two problems with ethnic theories of identity run even deeper. First, ethnicity is essentially a modern concept and does not fit well with descriptions of the premodern world. Although moderns have constructed a history of the world dependent on separate races, ancient people would have been unlikely to recognize most of the modern ethnic distinctions and racial discourses as meaningful. At the very least, scholars should insist that ethnicity is not an objective category measurable through genealogy. Recent scholarship on ethnicity emphasizes the subjective character of ethnic boundaries; they are largely products of the mind and imagination (Cohen 1999: 6; Smith 1981: 66; Smith 1986: 32).

Second, such theories ignore too much of the biblical textual evidence. Racial and ethnic theories of identity assume a real, obvious, innate, and discernible difference between ethnic groups, but the texts of Persian Yehud recognize identity as unclear, inconsistent, and always contested. These texts are much more likely to use terms such as *hagolah* and *ʿam ha-ʾaretz* to signify identity while arguing about how these groups relate to each other. Nehemiah 5:7–8 depicts Nehemiah's perception that the deep divides between different groups in Judah were between kin; this argues against a primarily ethnic identity. The

---

2. This connects scholarship of the ancient period to questions of modern politics, as explored by works such as Whitelam 1996.

populace of Judah included identity groups that did not match the categories of genealogical or genetic proximity as much as affinities of language or location. A theory of identity that accurately reflects the biblical interests will emphasize that identity is problematic, unobvious, and highly contested.

Identity as Nationality

Ethnicity, however, has not been the only operative theory of identity. Scholars have also treated Judean identity as a matter of nationality or of connection to some other political organization. To be Judean was to be a member of this political entity. Judeans shared a certain administrative oversight or jurisdictional relationship. Frequently, this national authority was simplified into a geographical criterion—that is, all persons living within a certain region were Judeans. Again, this theory of identity is objective, but, in contrast to an ethnic theory, national identity was not innate (Ginsberg 1996). In this approach, a person could have become Judean or ceased being Judean. Furthermore, such national or geographic identities behave as social constructions produced by a number of competing social forces (Castoriadis 1987; Anderson 1991; Saper 1997).

A national or geographic theory of identity displays the advantage of an accord with much biblical evidence (or at least with its frequent interpretation). Furthermore, it allows for a simple understanding of the relationship between Persian identity and Judean identity; the latter is a subset of the former, since both are political terms. There was no such person as a non-Persian Judean during the Achaemenid period, because Judah existed only within the political borders and geographic boundaries of the Persian Empire.

John Wright's essay in this book discusses many of the problems inherent with the reduction of Judean identity to a geographical or political identity (2006). Although it explains the biblical evidence to a certain extent, this theory does not help in understanding the relationship of Achaemenid Judeans to people outside the territory immediately surrounding Jerusalem. Not only does such a theory of identity import assumptions about the modern nation-state and its theory of unitary sovereignty within measurable boundaries, it negates one of the things we know to be most significant about this period from the biblical and epigraphical records: identity was not restricted to the environs of Jerusalem but related to places such as Elephantine, Samaria, Babylon, and even al-Jahuda (Pearce 2005).

Identity as Religion

A third approach connects identity with religion; thus, to be Judean was to participate in a Yahwistic cult. Certainly, religion is a powerful force of identity, and traditional scholarship has asserted that during the Diaspora the Judean self-understanding as a people with a distinctive religion became increasingly prevalent. However, I would argue that we must understand Judean identity as something distinct from religion. The biblical texts portray the error of such an oversimplification, in that not all of the Judeans understood themselves as sharing a single religion. In fact, there was substantial disagreement about who was properly obedient to the faith. Furthermore, archaeology has shown us both non-Yahwistic religious practices within Judah and Yahwistic practices within the regions of Babylon and Egypt.

The religious theory of Judean identity is prominent among scholars and in the popular perception. The scholarly community has so long maintained that the Persian Period was the time when identity shifted from national to religious definitions. Professors and textbooks repeated the claim that, after the exile, the former Israelites and Judeans "became" Jews because their political-national affiliations vanished, leaving only religion to provide identity for the people (or evolved into the higher, religious form of identity, depending on one's perspective).

Furthermore, scholarship has long offered combinations of national and religious theories of identity. To be sure, this is in no small part a reflection of key Persian-Period biblical texts, such as Haggai, Zechariah, Ezra, and Nehemiah, which present Judeans as a people with two rulers, one secular (or national-political) and one religious (or priestly). This appears to be a significant way that a number of Judeans understood their own social organization. However, I am less convinced that this was an identity than that it was a polity.

Other combinations of politics and religion have prevailed in much recent scholarship, including different forms of temple-community (e.g., Weinberg 1992). These mixed theories attempt to work around the more obvious problems that limit each individual approach. As we have become increasingly aware in the last 20 years or so, the biblical evidence does not allow identity to be equivalent to geography or politics (due to the existence of other related communities outside the polity and geography of Jerusalem) or to religion (since there is no indication that every Judean was a member of same cult). These theories may have made sense before Elephantine and before Kuntillet ʿAjrud; now the facts reveal that such theories of identity are reductionistic and misleading. A theory that pulls together aspects of national and religious identity still has the problems of both.

I would argue that the national and religious theories of identity share a deeper problem, in that they are both top-down theories. As such, they develop easy criteria for our discernment about identity, but they are unlikely to reflect how ancient Judeans thought of themselves. These theories emphasize objective group membership and do not easily recognize that identity operates simultaneously as external, observable reality as well as internal, personal reality.

Identity as Role

A fourth approach provides a bottom-up model in contrast to the top-down models of nationality and religion. Sociologists developed role theory as a description of how individual people take on distinct roles in society, integrating functions and self-understandings. David L. Petersen's work on role theory and Israelite prophecy more than two decades ago introduced this type of analysis to biblical scholarship (1981). Ten years ago, Joseph Blenkinsopp (1995) and Lester L. Grabbe (1995) each published books that described the roles of leaders within Israel and Judah, such as priests, prophets, sages, and diviners. Although neither of their books focuses exclusively on the Achaemenid period, both their approaches and their results provide obvious implications for the question of identity in Persian Yehud. My own work in the second half of *Judaism in Persia's Shadow* attempted to describe different public roles within Achaemenid Judah (1995).

Role theory complicates the search for identity because of the multiplicity of roles. Thus, a social reconstruction that takes role theory seriously must account for the interaction of the various social roles. However, this becomes an infinite process. Role theory allows for the explanation of observed social behaviors, but the number of social roles is always too great to allow for the reconstruction of a society. Roles are scripts, not performances; potentialities, not actualities.

This is not to say that the study of roles should not be undertaken. On the contrary, the number of roles necessitates the expansion of this approach. We need to consider not only the formal named roles, but also the many roles that people live. More recently, I have focused on household and familial roles, which is one meager step in this direction (Berquist 2002). We need investigation into a multiplicity of roles, such as artisan, merchant, and farmer, as well as less-defined roles such as "follower of the law" and "singer of the psalms."

Role theory, despite its utility, also experiences several problems. The tendency to concentrate on public roles only is one of these limits. Additional study of diverse roles could help with this, although soon we would be unable to keep track of all of the roles and their interactions. However, this heuristic difficulty is minor when compared with two fundamental mistakes in a role-based theory of identity: essentialism and functionalism.

When I described the political roles of ancient Yehud, I tried consciously (and perhaps with some success) to avoid the essentialist mistake—the assumption that roles define all of life or render behavior definite and predictable, as if roles determined a person's essence (Berquist 1995: 241–55). In such a case, all prophets would act alike, since they were all acting as prophets. But since roles are scripts and not performances, a role indicates a nearly infinite number of possible actions.

Even if I have succeeded in avoiding essentialism, I have had much more trouble with the mistake of functionalism, which assumes that society is the sum total of the additive roles undertaken by its participants. Conflict theory has helped with that, and a class analysis was also useful; the political and anthropological theories of Eisenstadt, Price, Thapar, and others on secondary state formation were very valuable (Berquist 1995: 243–47; Coser 1956; Eisenstadt 1969; Price 1978; Thapar 1981). Yet even with these correctives, I never could quite connect the macro-forces of imperialism and the medium-scale constructions of secondary state formation to the public roles of individuals, much less the private roles. Role theory offered the promise of an integrative understanding of identity and social function across the various scales of analysis, but, even with complementary strategies, role theory does not escape the functionalist error.

Certainly role theory still has much to teach scholarship about life in Achaemenid Judah. However, a resistance to the functionalist error suggests that scholarship of Achaemenid Judah should ally itself with newer historiographic method, such as the postmodern direction that also seeks to avoid functionalism. Such a postmodern critique does not merely modify structural functionalism but begins from different assumptions, such as a basically chaotic system of nonrational human actions.

Postmodernism and the Mathematics of Chaos

Postmodern historiographies tend to emphasize the inherent instability of any system or society. All such systems are tenuous constructions. Likewise, Michel Foucault pointed out the ways that social

systems must deploy power and knowledge as tools toward constructing and controlling themselves as systems so that they maintain some
semblance of coerced stability even in the midst of their inherent disso-
lution (1980, 1982). There is a heuristic principle here: one studies the
places where society is about to fall apart in order to recognize the uses
of power to stabilize the society. Thus, Foucault studied prisons, mental hospitals, and other such heterotopia.

In particular, a postmodern approach to identity insists stridently
on what we already knew about role theory. Roles only describe partial
identity. In reality, roles are not only multiple in the sense that a society
requires a near infinite number of separate roles to operate; roles are
also multiple in the sense that each person has several roles. At most
moments, it is hardly possible to determine which role is being enacted. Each person's roles are not only overlapping but also contradictory. The combinations of possible role-scripts approach the infinite,
and the actualities for society are simply not predictable.

In this sense, the postmodern view of society is one of chaos, nonlin-
earity, and unpredictability. Yet observable patterns emerge. This fact
parallels the relationship that has developed between history and disciplines such as sociology and political anthropology. Whereas history
requires the location of discrete particulars (i.e., actual persons in history who performed specific actions in particular ways at definable moments and the observable effects of such actions on other persons over
time), these other disciplines focus on patterns rather than particulars.
Even when the particulars cannot be discerned or predicted, we may
still be able to observe the patterns. Moreover, the patterns may well
replicate themselves over time and in different situations and scales.
This is how I now understand what I wrote earlier when I combined
historical moments from Persian Yehud with individual roles (1995): I
used anthropological patterns (such as imperialism, core/periphery relations, secondary state formation, and so forth) in order to suggest
possible connections between the specific and the typical.

The development of chaos theory allows for new understandings of
complex systems, defined as systems in which simple, linear relationships of cause and effect cannot be discerned. At first, these systems
appear chaotic (or as a historian would argue, unique and not general-
izable). However, we may discern patterns within the chaotic random-
ness and the indeterminability of individual particles. Toward this end,
chaos theory's treatment of complex systems offers two significant concepts. One is the notion of fractal geometry, in which patterns replicate

on different levels. This allows for the analytical connection of different scales of observation and explanation within systems, recognizing that systems must be interpreted simultaneously with different scales if a description is to approach adequacy. Perhaps one of the more familiar implications of this multiplicity of interrelated scales is the so-called butterfly principle—a butterfly fluttering its wings in one place may change major weather systems across the globe. Thus, chaos theory recognizes systemic unpredictability as well as the need for impossible accuracy in determining initial state. The second notion from chaos theory is the idea of strange attractors. Despite various initial states and through the recursion of basic fractal patterns with the use of multiple scales, some patterns develop. Certain states appear more stable than others. Of course, this stability is only an illusion; in many cases, systems tend to approach one of a small set of almost-stable states, only to become more unstable and unpredictable upon approach. This chaotic principle seems to describe not only quantum behavior but also macroscopic social organization.

Thus, the search for patterns is warranted—but we must not confuse these patterns with categories into which we could place different types of societies or social situations. Patterns are themselves patterns of force, and the forces are vital to understanding the patterns. This moves our search for social patterns beyond the older categories of political anthropology and its theories of state formation. My concentration on secondary state formation recognized the relevant forces of imperialism and autonomy but still searched for a category into which to place Persian Yehud (1995). This was my error: obsessed with locating the right category, I failed to attend adequately to the forces themselves.

From Imperialism to Imperialization

Thus, scholarship must shift its focus from the categories of empire and imperialism (including the core/periphery dichotomy that I have found so useful) to the process of imperialization. Even in the modern world, imperialization has been poorly understood. In many ways, scholars have discerned the outlines of this process only after the fact, as empires have dissolved and given way to new forms around the globe. Although many of the numerous available studies of imperialism may prove helpful in our understanding of Achaemenid Judah, we would do well to search for the resources for understanding imperializing processes within the emerging discipline known as postcolonial studies.

The process of imperialization imprints an identity on people, including self-definitions as well as related mind-sets, orientations, beliefs, and roles (Memmi 1965). This process is a vast force within a society, and as such, it would have been a primary shaping force within the culture of Persian Yehud. However, the identities imposed by imperialization do not operate in a vacuum. Such imposed identities operate to displace other identities of autonomy. Such displacement fails; there is no cause-and-effect linearity at work within these processes of identity. The assumption of new identity obtains only where there is already humanity, identity, and agency. Thus, imperialization does not displace preimperial identity; the process is conflictual and transformative, as in any complex system. The rules of chaos apply. The interplay of imperialization and decolonization will continue, and this interplay will shape the society on large and small scales alike.

What I am calling *decolonization* could be described in different terms. Traditionally, we have called this *autonomy*—the desire for Yehud to be an independent state. I avoid this terminology, for several reasons. One is that it is easy to assume that such autonomy is a basic human need or desire. This way of thinking portrays autonomy as good and imperialization as evil (as in the "evil empire"), with autonomy being considered the eventual goal state.

Scholars more recently have termed this decolonization as *resistance*.[3] This term has been especially prevalent in feminist criticism and ideological criticism. I value this. However, I worry that it creates a problem opposite to that of the term *autonomy*. It is too easy to make imperialization (or oppression) the originating state that people then resist. It is not accurate to depict the conflicting forces within Yehud as primary and reactive; they came into being at the same time and they were deeply interactive.

For this reason, I do not wish to privilege either of the competing forces of imperialization and decolonization. These two processes cannot be separated into the simplistic dichotomies of past categories. The forces of imperialization and decolonization do not balance each other, nor do they move linearly one into the other through evolutionary paths of development. Instead, the society that this interplay produces approaches points of apparent stability without stabilizing itself at any of these points.

---

3. Two of the most influential works in this regard are Miller, Rowlands, and Tilley (eds.) 1989 and Scott 1990.

Processes of Identity Formation

This understanding of imperializing and decolonizing identity formation has great bearing upon the identity of Judeans in the Achaemenid Period. Simply put, the categorizing of identity as religious, national, or ethnic is a response to the wrong question. Identity refers to the pattern that multiple forces produce. Each point is fluid and changing, as a complex product of imperialization and decolonization. Religion, nationality, and ethnicity are all components of identity— and all of them are simultaneously both imperializing and decolonizing. Religion teaches people a place in the universe that supports the imperial status quo but also teaches the revolution of the status quo into a decolonized rejection of worldly imperial powers. National identity is both Persian and Yehudite; what this combination means to each individual is highly fluid and always a product of internal conflict. Ethnicity participates with pluralization as one element, and identity operates within a shifting complex consisting of family identity, clan identity, geographical identity, and imperial identity.

This approach transforms the previous questions about ethnicity, nationality, and religion as defining identity. No longer are such identities seen as fixed and static categories, but as continuing *processes*. We must speak not of identity but of identity formation.

Here, role theory returns as a helpful component of our discussion, because roles are necessarily learned (or at least inculcated). When we speak of prophets, sages, scribes, governors, priests, and other roles, we speak about how these roles are learned, developed, taught, transmitted, adapted, and individualized. Yet we do this with the realization that these roles are partial identities, as part of the hybridity that the imperializing and decolonizing process creates.

Our new focus on processes of identity formation will point us toward the sites (or in chaotic terms, the strange attractors) where these processes take shape and become most sharply contested (Hetherington 1998: 141–56). A partial list of such social sites of identity formation would include aesthetics, architecture, art, class, economics, education, entertainment, family, folktales, food, language, literacy, luxury goods, music, pilgrimage, proverbs, recreation, religion, rituals of the life cycle, sexuality, symbology, and transportation. Each of these will be both imperializing and decolonizing, and our task in understanding these processes of identity formation will be to discern the interplay of these forces. This investigation must not be static but must observe how identity develops over the human lifespan and throughout social change.

Implications

As an example, consider bilingualism. Although Ezra and Nehemiah's objections to mixed marriage are usually synchronized, Neh 13:24 has a concern that Ezra 9–10 does not overtly share. Nehemiah is appalled that some of the children do not speak the language of the people but instead speak various other languages. The loss of original language is seen as a key loss to identity. Yet Ezra–Nehemiah itself is a bilingual text, in which issues of translation are vital. Postcolonial studies highlight the role of language as a basic element of identity formation, maintenance, and transformation. The politics of language also plays itself out on national levels. Interactions between individuals who do not share core competencies in the same language or languages may well provide strong examples of identity development within society. We must look at monolingual as well as bilingual (and multilingual) people to see the identity issues within cultural patterns and note how imperialization and decolonization operate to shape language identity. Exploring the identity-formation issues within language may well lead to an understanding of other patterns that shape the larger society.

A second example is the canon, which is (in the language of chaos theory) a strange attractor. How does the canon form identity? The canon of Torah and Prophets available to Achaemenid Judeans contained (at least) two prime elements of identity formation. The first was a rejection of Egypt—to be Judean was to be someone who fled Egyptian slavery and who would do anything to avoid allegiance to Egypt in the future. The canon defined the identity of Judeans as those who are against Egypt. Imperializing and decolonizing forces combine in this theme. Second, the canon argued against autonomy, showing that Israelite and Judean monarchic self-rule was a mostly evil enterprise that ended badly and that God desired to curtail it, as seen most clearly in the Deuteronomistic History. The people rightly mistrusted every human leader and gave themselves over only to God's rule. Again, understanding the ways in which this ideology shaped identity requires a focus on imperialization and decolonization.

Understanding Judean identity formation involves a complex analysis of multiple social levels with attention to numerous processes in which people internalize the forces of imperialization and decolonization. As social agents, these self-identifying Judeans together constructed a story of the development of Judah during the Achaemenid Period, as they turned their role scripts into social action and deployed themselves in patterns of ethnicity, politics, and religion, as well as myriad other complex social patterns. Such attention to identity formation necessitates deeper and more critical understandings of the forces of imperialization and decolonization and the way that these forces shape identity and difference within societies.

Bibliography

Anderson, B.
1991   *Imagined Communities.* Rev. ed. London.
Berquist, J. L.
1981   *Judaism in Persia's Shadow: A Social and Historical Approach.* Minneapolis.
2002   *Controlling Corporeality: The Body and the Household in Ancient Israel.* New Brunswick.
Blenkinsopp, J.
1995   *Sage, Priest, Prophet: Religious and Intellectual Leadership in Ancient Israel.* Louisville.
Carter, C. E.
1999   *The Emergence of Yehud in the Persian Period: A Social and Demographic Study.* Sheffield.
Castoriadis, C.
1987   *The Imaginary Institution of Society.* Cambridge, Massachusetts.
Cohen, S. J. D.
1999   *The Beginnings of Jewishness: Boundaries, Varieties, Uncertainties.* Berkeley.
Coser, L. A.
1956   *The Functions of Social Conflict.* New York.
Eisenstadt, S. N.
1969   *The Political Systems of Empires: The Rise and Fall of the Historical Bureaucratic Societies.* Rev. ed. New York.
Foucault, M.
1980   *Power/Knowledge: Selected Interviews and Other Writings, 1972–1977.* New York.
1981   *The Archaeology of Knowledge, and the Discourse on Language.* 2nd ed. New York.
Ginsberg, E. (ed.)
1996   *Passing and the Fictions of Identity.* Durham, North Carolina.
Grabbe, L. L.
1995   *Priests, Prophets, Diviners, Sages: A Socio-Historical Study of Religious Specialists in Ancient Israel.* Valley Forge.
Hall, S., and du Gay, P. (eds.)
1996   *Questions of Cultural Identity.* London.
Hetherington, K.
1998   *Expressions of Identity: Space, Performance, Politics.* London.
Hobsbawm, E.
1983   Inventing Traditions. Pp. 1–14 in *The Invention of Tradition,* ed. E. Hobsbawm and T. Ranger. Cambridge.

Lentricchia, F., and McLaughlin, T. (eds.)
  1995   *Critical Terms for Literary Study.* 2nd edition. Chicago.
Memmi, A.
  1965   *The Colonizer and the Colonized.* New York.
Michael, M.
  1996   *Constructing Identities.* London.
Miller, D.; Rowlands, M.; and Tilley, C. (eds.)
  1989   *Domination and Resistance.* London.
Mullen, E. T., Jr.
  1997   *Ethnic Myths and Pentateuchal Foundations: A New Approach to the For-
          mation of the Pentateuch.* Atlanta.
Pearce, L. E.
  2006   New Evidence for Judeans in Babylonia. Pp. 399–411 in *Judah and the
          Judeans in the Persian Period,* ed. O. Lipschits and M. Oeming. Winona
          Lake, Indiana.
Petersen, D. L.
  1981   *The Roles of Israel's Prophets.* Sheffield.
Price, B. J.
  1978   Secondary State Formation: An Explanatory Model. Pp. 161–86 in *Ori-
          gins of the State: The Anthropology of Political Evolution,* ed. R. E. Cohen
          and E. R. Service. Philadelphia.
Rajchman, J. (ed.)
  1995   *The Identity in Question.* New York.
Saper, C. J.
  1997   *Artificial Mythologies: A Guide to Cultural Invention.* Minneapolis.
Schwartz, S.
  2001   *Imperialism and Jewish Society, 200 B.C.E. to 640 C.E.* Princeton.
Scott, J. C.
  1990   *Domination and the Arts of Resistance: Hidden Transcripts.* New Haven.
Smith, A. D.
  1981   *The Ethnic Revival.* Cambridge.
  1986   *The Ethnic Origins of Nations.* Oxford.
Sollors, W.
  1989   The Invention of Ethnicity. Pp. ix–xx in *The Invention of Ethnicity,* ed.
          W. Sollors. New York.
Thapar, R.
  1981   The State as Empire. Pp. 409–26 in *The Study of the State,* ed. H. J. M.
          Claessen and P. Skalník. The Hague.
Weinberg, J.
  1992   *Citizen-Temple Community.* Sheffield.
Whitelam, K. W.
  1996   *The Invention of Ancient Israel: The Silencing of Palestinian History.*
          London.
Wright, J. W.
  2004   Remapping Yehud: The Borders of Yehud and the Genealogies of
          Chronicles. Pp. 67–89 in *Judah and the Judeans in the Persian Period,*
          ed. O. Lipschits and M. Oeming. Winona Lake, Indiana.

Remapping Yehud:
The Borders of Yehud and
the Genealogies of Chronicles

JOHN W. WRIGHT

Point Loma Nazarene University, San Diego

A border dispute has plagued recent reconstructions of the social history of Judah. Scholars have encircled the maps of Palestine during Achaemenid hegemony with lines in order to create particular boundaries. These boundaries manufacture a territory that purportedly corresponds with a historical polity called "Yehud," a term found in texts and artifacts from Palestine from the sixth century through the fourth century B.C.E. Yet scholars have not been able to agree on common borders for this polity. As a result, estimations of its social, economic, and demographic resources radically differ.

It is the purpose of this essay to review and assess this border situa\of a unitary territory bounded by borders under one sovereignty anachronistically misconstrues the nature of this polity in terms of the modern nation-state. I will then argue that a kinship/patronage system structured the polity of Yehud. Such a system no doubt had territorial implications. Yet familial/patronage relationships would construct overlapping, permeable jurisdictions within a geographically confined area. I will argue that the genealogies of Judah and Benjamin in 1 Chronicles provide a glimpse into the geographical contours of Yehud in relationship to other familial/kinship groups under Achaemenid hegemony.

Shrinking Boundaries:
The Borders of Yehud in Recent Scholarship

Three scholars, Ephraim Stern (2001), Charles Carter (1999), and Oded Lipschits (2005), have recently devoted extensive discussions to the drawing of borders for Yehud. Each scholar has attempted to assess textual evidence found in the Hebrew Bible in conjunction with material evidence from the Persian Period in order to construct the boundaries of Yehud. The scholars agree upon the northern and eastern borders; substantial disagreement, however, exists on the location of the southern and western borders.

Ephraim Stern draws borders by correlating the overlap between the geographic locations of the lists of returnees/inhabitants of Judah in Ezra–Nehemiah with the dispersion of Yehud seals and Persian-Period coinage within Palestine.[1] A line of three fortresses in the Hebron highlands constitutes the southern border. Stern simply plots the towns to which both literary and material evidence refers and then encircles the whole area. A large Yehud results:

> The southern border of this area of distribution would appear to be at Beth-Zur; the northern limit is at Tell en-Nasbeh; the eastern limit is a line extending from Jericho to En-Gedi; in the west, some seal impressions were recovered at Gezer, which is definitely located in the district of Lod, and at Tel Harasim, which belonged to the Keilah district. Thus, the distribution of coins and impressions of the Judaean province encompasses the entire area mentioned in the Bible. (Stern 2001: 431)

Stern argues that the seals and coinage within this geographical area show that "the state of Judah and the rest of the country's provinces and major administrative units were established and became functional largely during the latter part of the Persian period" (2001: 582). However, the consistency of his concept is strained, especially regarding the southern border. He recognizes "that a large proportion of the population in this part of Palestine was already Edomite in the 4th century B.C.E." (2001: 447). Nonetheless, he suggests that "in this period Edomite settlement had not yet become consolidated into an independent administrative unit" (2001: 445). If so, this would exempt the area south of the border from the tributary system by which the Achaemenids controlled the whole region. Judah existed as a "state"; Idumea existed without a national government.

Charles Carter rejects the relevance of both the literary and material evidence by which Stern draws borders around Yehud. He argues that "the lists in Ezra and Nehemiah function either as indicators of the sites to which Jews had returned in the years after Cyrus's decree or sites in which returning exiles had real or fictional ancestral connections, whether or not they were within the borders of the province" (Carter 1999: 81). Carter follows Hoglund (1992) in arguing that the fortresses in the south do not mark borders but "represent an imperial concern to protect trade routes and communication lines necessary to

---

1. Stern here only lightly reworks his earlier material (Stern 1982: 245–50), material that was first published in Hebrew in 1973.

control the empire" (Carter 1999: 89). He further notes that the seal impressions "may indicate something of their economic function, and perhaps show intra-provincial relations, [but] they cannot demonstrate [a region's] inclusion within the province" (1999: 90).

What data, then, does one use to draw borders? Carter argues that "the complex issue of the boundaries of Yehud" is "perhaps best approached by considering the historical and geographic parameters" (1999: 90). He argues that "it is unlikely that a governing body with limited resources and limited autonomy, one that itself may have been undergoing internal conflict, would be able to extend its influence beyond certain topographical boundaries" (1999: 91). Therefore, Carter constructs borders so that "the province of Yehud excluded the Shephelah and . . . extended from just north of Bethel to just south of Hebron" (1999: 102). In the south, however, Carter includes areas that Stern places under Edomite control. Yet the significance of the borders remains unclear for Carter, except for a posited sovereignty over designated space. Carter writes, "Once again it is important to remember that according to my reconstruction loyal Judaeans would have lived outside the borders of Yehud. . . . Just as economic support for the temple and its operations may have flowed in to Yehud from beyond its borders, it is evident that other, non-cultic exchanges occurred as well" (1999: 292).

A final recent proposal is found in the work of Oded Lipschits (2005). Lipschits seeks to establish the borders of Yehud by comparing the borders of Judah under Assyrian and Egyptian rule to its area in the Hellenistic Period. According to Lipschits, "this research technique is possible because of the continuity that generally existed in regard to the borders of the territories and the stability of their populations and because the changes that characterized them occurred slowly" (2005: 135). Positing stable borders in the north and east from the Babylonian Period onward, he argues that Persian-Period boundaries "to the best of our knowledge, are identical to those that existed during the Hellenistic Period" (2005: 149). During the sixth through fourth centuries, "the Negev, the Hebron Mountains, and the southern and central Shephelah were separated from the province of Judah. These areas became the center of another national territorial unit: Idumea" (2005: 149). As with Carter, however, Lipschits's borders have a limited significance. "Notwithstanding this, sources contemporary with the Persian Period and later sources indicate that at least part of the Judean population remained in these areas" (2005: 182).

Lipschits's Yehud becomes smaller than the area drawn by Carter. Without the Shephelah, the southern border north of Hebron, Lipschits encloses an increasingly smaller area within the borders of this "national-territorial unit." Yehud continues to shrink. For all their differences, however, both reconstructions presuppose that the delimitation of a precise territory through drawing borders remains crucial to understanding the polity called Yehud. Even though, as Lipschits writes, "there is no information in the sources from the Persian Period about the boundaries of the province of Yehud" (2005: 154) and though "the information in the biblical sources is problematic, limited, and betrays a certain amount of confusion between the places where Judeans lived and the official limits of the province" (2005: 154), scholars persist in presupposing that Yehud had "official limits." It is precisely this presupposition that needs to be questioned. Borders themselves presuppose a certain type of polity—the modern nation-state—a polity that is anachronistic when applied to Yehud under the Achaemenids.

The State of Borders

Recent maps that depict Yehud as a precisely bounded territory belong to a tradition of map-making that originates as recently as 1718.[2] Borders are not ontologically real but are human constructs of the imagination. The concept of borders arises with the emergence of a particular form of polity—the modern nation-state. Depictions of borders for Yehud, therefore, anachronistically retroject a modernist, European polity onto the social realia of the sixth–fourth centuries B.C.E. The construction of borders for Yehud places it within an international polity that did not arise until the seventeenth century in Europe. It silently imposes a modernist notion of sovereignty on the description of Yehud under the Achaemenid King of Kings.

Perhaps it is not surprising that scholars would attempt to draw borders for Yehud, even though primary data resist such a depiction. As Daniel Philpott states, today "virtually all of the earth's land is par-

---

2. "It was primarily the wars and resultant congresses of the seventeenth and eighteenth centuries that rationalized frontiers into borders, although many boundaries were left untouched by these happenings. In the seventeenth century, for the first time, the practice of giving boundary populations an 'option' to belong to one state or another came into being. . . . The progression from frontiers to borders as mutually agreed lines on a map does not, however, appear until the eighteenth century: the first boundary literally drawn as a line seemingly being constructed only in the year 1718, as part of a treaty made in respect of Flanders in that year" (Giddens 1987: 90).

celed by lines, invisible lines that we call borders. Within these borders, supreme political authority typically lies in a single source—a liberal constitution, a military dictatorship, a theocracy, a communist regime" (2001: 3). Yet this political system is relatively recent in human history.[3] The modernist nation-state constructs a bounded territoriality that forms a unitary space over which the state rules supremely. Within the nation-state,

> territoriality is crucial. This is a principle that defines the set of people over whom the holder of sovereignty rules. They are to be identified, territoriality says, by virtue of their location within borders. The people within these borders may not necessarily conceive of themselves as a "people" or a "nation" with a common identity. . . . But their location within boundaries requires their allegiance to their sovereign. (Philpott 2001: 17)

Thus, the political scientist Anthony Giddens defines the modern nation-state through the particular relationship between sovereignty and territory: "The nation-state, which exists in a complex of other nation-states, is a set of institutional forms of governance maintaining an administrative monopoly over a territory with demarcated boundaries, its rule being sanctioned by law and direct control of the means of internal and external violence" (Giddens 1981: 190). Scholars have pointed to the Peace of Westphalia in 1648 as a crucial event for the establishment of this polity. As Philpott states, "Geographically, the Westphalian system was a European system. . . . But if the society of sovereign states' extent was European, its influence and implications were global. Europe's colonies in North America, South America, Africa, and Asia came under the control of sovereign states, making them effective extensions of the system" (Philpott 2001: 32). Borders historically originated in order to establish and enforce the power of a system of modernist nation-states.

This is not to deny the role that territoriality played within earlier polities, the various polities of traditional states. Yet within traditional states, borders per se did not demarcate, or create, a sole sovereign state; territoriality instead was bounded by the much more porous concept of frontiers. According to Giddens, within a traditional state, a "'frontier' refers to an era on the peripheral regions of a state (not necessarily adjoining another state) in which the political authority of the center is diffuse or thinly spread" (1987: 50). The difference is not

---

3. See Tilley 1975.

merely a boundary area rather than a boundary line. Frontiers indicate a different constellation of power from the single sovereignty over a unitary space that characterizes the modern nation-state. Thus, Giddens argues that

> the fact that such states have frontiers, including secondary settlement frontiers, rather than boundaries is indicative of their relatively weak level of system integration. It is essential to emphasize how different, as "social systems," traditional states are from modern ones. Because of their internal heterogeneity, a case can be made for regarding larger traditional states as "composed of numerous societies." (Giddens 1987: 53)

In traditional states, one does not have a homogeneous power exercised by virtue of sovereignty over a particular space; one instead has multiple powers that make various claims over particular bodies in different situations. These powers become increasingly diffuse and intermixed as one moves toward the periphery, the frontier, of a particular territory.

The difference between the polities of modern versus traditional states immediately impacts the interpretation of material remains from Yehud. As noted above, scholars such as Stern and Lipschits have constructed the southern border of Yehud according to the interpretation of the function of the series of fortresses found in a line to the north of Hebron.[4] Yet to do so is to respond to the wrong question. In traditional states, fortresses do not form a boundary, nor do they indicate the presence of a border. As Giddens writes, "It would be a mistake to suppose, even where the boundaries of traditional states are physically clearly marked by such [defensive] installations (something which is any case rare), that these are something akin to borders in the modern sense. . . . Rather, they formed the outer extension of an 'in-depth' defensive system" (1987: 51).[5] The fortresses suggest that the Hebron highlands formed a frontier area, an area of heterogeneous, interpermeable societies.

If the construction of borders imposes an anachronistic polity of the modern state upon Achaemenid Yehud, do we have any positive evi-

---

4. Hoglund (1992) carefully examines the fortresses and determines that they are not border outposts but are oriented in order to protect trade lines. Such an interpretation consistently follows Giddens's more general interpretation of such phenomena.

5. Giddens's interpretation corresponds entirely with the means by which the Achaemenids controlled their territory. Emphasis was not on the control of peripheries but on the surveillance of inner communication and transportation systems. See Briant 2002: 364–77.

dence for conceiving Yehud's territoriality? Whereas earlier scholarship has focused on the lists of returnees in Ezra/Nehemiah,[6] I would like to suggest that the Judah and Benjamin genealogies in 1 Chronicles present a glimpse into Yehud's territoriality and its polity. These genealogies present Yehud as a familial/patronage system. Yehud was not a state per se—definitely not a nation. The genealogies define the political formation of Yehud as an ethnos, with power distributed by real or fictitious familial/kinship ties. Persian-Period Yehud formed a polity that set the stage for the emergence of the polity of formative Judaisms in the Hellenistic and Roman eras, anchored in Jerusalem within the territory of Judah, yet reaching into various diaspora areas throughout the Mediterranean and Mespotamian worlds.

Geneaology as Geography: Kinship and Territoriality in the Genealogy of Judah in the Book of Chronicles

Achaemenid inscriptions bear witness to a great interest in genealogy. Genealogy provided legitimacy for authority. Genealogy provided the basis for Persian tribal structure, and familial ties provided by tribes had territorial implications. Pierre Briant writes, "the tribe is simultaneously a genealogical reality and a spatial reality: Maraphii and Pasargadae are both ethnonyms and toponyms. Each tribe and clan had a territory of its own. . . . This was a situation that was to obtain until the very end of the Achaemenid period" (Briant 2002: 18). In the country lists at Susa, Darius actually did not list countries, though the texts are often translated into English in this manner. "The word used in the inscriptions is *dahyu* 'people'" (Briant 2002: 177). The Great King was not a king over territories; he ruled over peoples; he was, as it were, the King of Kings. The Achaemenids conceived of their rule over particular territories through extended kinship structures (*ethnoi*) that had submitted to the great king. The administrative structure of the Empire was not primarily territorial. The Achaemenids consolidated their rule through patronage allegiances. Relationship to the king, not assignment to a particular territory, even characterized the satrapal system. As noted by Briant,

> At Behistun, when Darius names his two satraps, Vivāna in Arachosia and Dādarši in Bactria, he qualifies both as *bandaka*, a Persian term referring to a personal connection between the sovereign and the Persian aristocrats. In itself, the term connotes first and foremost the total loyalty

---

6. For the difficulty of using such data, see Lipschits 2002 and 2005.

to the king of the person described by it. In other words, the duty of a
satrap was not necessarily connected to a territory. Moreover, the term
satrapy . . . does not occur at Behistun: Vivāna and Dādarši are satraps *in*
Arachosia and *in* Bactria, respectively. (Briant 2001: 65)

A vast genealogical/kinship patronage structure supported Achaemenid hegemony over its vast territories. Genealogy merged into territory, and territory was recorded genealogically.

Given this conceptualization, it is not surprising that the Achaemenids envisioned the world as a huge circle of peoples in their royal
inscriptions, with the center being in areas of Achaemenid power.

A closed world, the world of the royal inscriptions was a circular world.
To the north, the Saka and Scythian peoples constituted a semicircle
from east to west; similarly, to the south the Libya–Ethiopia–Makran–
Karkā [departed Carians at the source of the Persian Gulf] group (attested in *DNa*) form another semicircle. . . . At the same time, this world
was organized around a center. In most of the inscriptions, it includes
Persia, Media, and Elam (not always listed in the same order), that is, the
countries where the sedentary centers of Achaemenid power were located: Pasargadae, Persepolis, Ecbatana, and Susa. (Briant 2001: 180)

People-groupings encircled the center of Achaemenid rule, forming a
depiction of the world through a geographical ordering of various
peoples. Geography implodes into genealogy, and genealogy is expressed through geography.

The Achaemenid merging of genealogy with geography provides an
interesting context for looking at the genealogies that begin the book
of Chronicles. The book of Chronicles also presents a genealogically/
geographically circular presentation of the world. As Magnar Kartveit
shows, 1 Chronicles 1 is "not only a genealogy, but also a *mappa mundi*,
perhaps even an *imago mundi*, where Israel lies in the middle" (1989:
116). Likewise, "the inner structure of chs. 2–8 is governed by a unique
ordering of the tribal units, encompassing groups of tribes recorded in
a geographical order. . . . The geographical circle ends in the center
where it started: after a general conclusion (9:1–2), it presents the inhabitants of Jerusalem" (Japhet 1993: 9). Just as people-groups from the
world encircle Israel geographically in chap. 1, the sons of Israel encircle Jerusalem geographically in chaps. 2–8. In the genealogies of
1 Chronicles, a genre of literature in which space withdraws from
view, geography nonetheless rules. The genealogies of Chronicles parallel the geographical/genealogical conceptions provided by Achaemenid domination.

If the above is accurate, perhaps it is worthwhile to examine the genealogies of Judah and Benjamin in 1 Chronicles 1–9 in order to conceive of the political territory of Yehud. Chronicles consistently pairs these tribes.[7] The traditional areas of these two tribes also mirror the chief settlement pattern as discovered in recent archaeological findings for the Persian Period (see Lipschits 2003). Finally, the two tribal genealogies form an inclusio, the first and the last, for the rest of the tribes of Israel in 1 Chronicles 1–9. They literarily encompass all Israel, with, as Japhet noted above, Jerusalem at their center. At the very least, Yehud included the kinship groupings of Judah and Benjamin.[8]

As scholarship has shown, these genealogies are extremely complex.[9] The genealogy's use of sources, literary structure, and ideological framing to narrate a certain conception of Israel and the world has received due and excellent attention. The genealogies merge ethnonyms and toponyms within the genealogical genre. Geography and genealogy merge, revealing a complex patronage system within a broader kinship/genealogical genre. It constructs a new type of polity, an ethnos. Such a polity possesses territorial dimensions but is not defined by that territoriality.

The territorial dimensions of the genealogies clearly appear within the genealogy of Judah (2:3–4:23). Topographical references within the genealogy of the sons of Judah occur at its fringes. Central genealogical lines are kept intact. Onomastics only become toponyms as the family lines reach their conclusions. Thus, the Davidic line in chap. 3 remains void of any topographic genealogical references—no names of villages occur as personal names. The same might be said concerning the beginning of the genealogy of Judah in chap. 2. The main genealogical lines of the house of Judah develop through the generations without any topographical allusions within personal names.

The first geographical reference in the genealogy of the sons of Judah appears in 2:21–24. This brief genealogy has proved problematic

---

7. On the relationship between Judah and Benjamin in the Persian Period, see Blenkinsopp in this volume (pp. 629–645).

8. While scholars currently contest whether Chronicles was composed in the Late Persian or Early Hellenistic Period, Williamson's argument for the mid-fourth century seems persuasive (1982: 15–17). Even if the work was composed in the Early Hellenistic Period, Alexander's conquests seemingly changed the internal organization or polity of Yehud very little.

9. The genealogies in Chronicles have recently received extensive scholarly attention. See the commentaries and, especially, Kartveit 1989, Oeming 1990; and Knoppers 2004, 2003, 2002, and 2001.

for interpreters and translators alike.[10] By focusing on the passage's internal coherence rather than its relationship to source materials, scholars have discovered a geopolitical story that maps out relationships between Judah and areas/people-groups east of the Jordan River.

The chronology of the story returns to Hezron, repeating story-time that the text previously developed in the genealogies of the sons of Ram and Caleb. Yet the chronology does not return to the leveled time of Jerahmeel, Ram, and Caleb. The recorded event occurs when Hezron was sixty years old, a time that grants a specificity to the ambiguity of the "after" that begins the passage. The text gives the lines of descent from two of the first three sons. Placed between Caleb and Jerahmeel, a fourth, unanticipated line appears.[11]

The NRSV reads v. 21 in a manner consistent with scholarly interpretation.[12] It highlights the sexual connotations of the passage, perhaps as a manner of forcing the genealogy to continue dealing with "private" matters. Yet the sexual connotations find their significance within the broader geopolitics of the text. A straightforward translation brings out these dynamics: "After Hezron came to the daughter of Machir, the father of Gilead, he married her. And he was sixty years old and she bore for him Segub." Marriage acquires geopolitical dynamics by the formation of an alliance between Hezron and Gilead, shown in Hezron's travel to the house of Machir. The wife of Hezron, Abijah (v. 24), is identified initially by the name of her father and her brother/place, Gilead. Through the descendants of Hezron and Abijah, "Judah" has an ancestral claim on 23 cities in the north of Israel within Gilead (v. 22). This ancestral claim occurs simultaneously with Gilead's ancestoral claim. Both Abijah and Gilead are the children of Machir; neither has a sole claim on the area. Judah's claim within the land of Gilead included 60 additional "cities" taken by Geshur and Aram (v. 23).

The geopolitical nature of the genealogy becomes clear in v. 23. "Geshur" and "Aram" are personalized geopolitical groups.[13] "Havvoth-jair" ("the life of Jair") localizes the descendants of Jair, the son of

---

10. Johnstone states that in v. 24, "the text is unfortunately, obscure" (1997: 50); Japhet states concerning vv. 18–24 that "these verses are heterogeneous and rather incoherent, and the text is corrupt at two crucial points—the opening and the conclusion" (Japhet 1993: 78).

11. Though the genealogical connection is loose, the passage seems to develop a line of Caleb.

12. "Afterward Hezron went in to the daughter of Machir father of Gilead, whom he married when he was sixty years old; and she bore him Sebub."

13. For Aram, see 1 Chr 1:17; for Geshur, see 1 Chr 3:2.

Segub. The "villages" of Kanath mentioned by the NRSV are literally its 'daughters' (בנות). A summary verse describes the list, not as the sons of Hezron, but as the "sons of Machir, the father of Gilead." The marriage merges the interests of the families of Hezron with the region of Gilead, the "sons of Machir." Marriage becomes the medium of mixing the allegiances of the families within a particular territory. Gilead is not part of Judah, but Judah has claims within certain families/villages of Gilead due to familial/kinship alliances.

Verse 24 presents difficulties if approached from the perspective of sources rather than its literary context. The text functions as an inclusio by synchronizing the descendants of Hezron through Abijah and those through Caleb his son. We may translate v. 24: "And after the death of Hezron, when Caleb came to Ephrath, the wife of Hezron was Abijah; she bore to him Ashhur, the father of Tekoa" (v. 24). The text draws a chronological simultaneity between the death of Hezron in Gilead and Caleb's marriage to Ephrath following the death of Azubah, mentioned earlier in v. 19. The verse ties the chronology of the disparate family lines of Hezron together, as well as producing a "posthumous" child of Hezron and Abijah. This descendant ties the family line to Tekoa, a village within the traditional region of Judah. The descendants of Hezron/Abijah embrace disparate territories both north and south, uniting them through descent from the same father and mother. Genealogies and marriages are not private affairs. They tell a story of the relationship of peoples and regions that map out allegiances and loyalties. Judah is a people in alliance with each other, not a unitary territory. The genealogy of Judah does not incorporate a continuous territory with common borders; it is a polity of allegiances that incorporates dispersed territories.

In a similar fashion, the genealogy of Judah has territorial dimensions in 2:42–50a and 50b–55. Here the sons of Judah reach far south of Jerusalem. The final genealogy(ies) of the sons of Judah given before the genealogy of David completes and then continues the genealogy of Caleb begun in 2:18–20. Whereas the first genealogy of Caleb introduced him as the "son of Hezron" (v. 18), the second introduces him as the "brother of Jerahmeel" (v. 42). The genealogy emphasizes its breadth, its inner-kin relations. The genealogy is structured chiastically. The passage begins with direct, legal descendants of Caleb (vv. 42–45), before giving descendants through Ephah, a concubine (v. 46). Though biologically related, these descendants are never described as Caleb's heirs, except in the summary statement (v. 50). The line of Jahdai, with no expressed relationship to Caleb, enters (v. 51),

followed by a line of Maacah, another concubine of Caleb, and the
naming of a daughter (vv. 48–49a). A summary statement sets these off
from the line of Hur that follows (v. 50). As the son of a wife of Caleb,
Hur completes the previous genealogy as well as extending it. The legitimate sons bracket those who are related but not legal heirs.[14]

The genealogy develops the story internally through repetition
rather than chronology. The time covered has been covered before.
More detail, however, enters the story. The genealogy ends with personal names transformed into designations for cities and people-
groups. The initial genealogy of the sons of Judah ends with a clearer
mapping of geopolitical relationships.

The genealogy begins with a textually contested verse (v. 42) that has
generated alternative readings.[15] However one reads v. 42, the genealogy quickly turns from personal names to names of particular places—
Ziph, Maresha, and Hebron (v. 42). The explicitly geopolitical nature
of the genealogy of Caleb continues in vv. 43–45 in the descendants of
the person/place Hebron.[16] As Knoppers states regarding vv. 43–45,
"many, but not all, of the names listed in these verses are to be associated with settlements" (2004: 312). The locations seem to continue to fill
out areas in the Hebron vicinity. The descendants of Caleb inhabit the
countryside of the southern Judean Hills. By the time the genealogy
reaches its deepest chronological descent in the sixth generation from
Caleb, the text abandons even the pretense of maintaining personal
names as designations for settlements. "Beth-zur" is named as the final
descendant of Caleb within this specific genealogy.

The next genealogies relate to Caleb (vv. 48–50a) but simultaneously
distance themselves from him, providing secondary genealogical lines
of descent. The genealogy also moves geographically farther away
from the territorial center of Judah. The names/towns move south, insofar as they are identifiable, into the Negev.[17] Familial ties loosen with
distance.

The text returns to Hur and his descendants in vv. 50b–55. As the
descendants of Caleb's legitimate sons in vv. 42–45 quickly moved to
geopolitical designations, so do the descendants of Hur. The pretense
of the genealogy quickly dissolves with names of settlements serving

---

14. For the chiastic structuring of the genealogy of Judah, see Williamson 1979.
15. As Japhet states, "the very unusually formulated second half-verse is probably
corrupt" (1993: 86).
16. See Curtis 1910: 95–96.
17. Curtis 1910: 96–97.

as personal names. Hur is the grandfather of Kiriath-jearim, Bethlehem, and Beth-gader (vv. 50b–51). The text even abandons the genealogical form momentarily in v. 53. Rather than genealogical descent, the text lists various clans associated with Keriath-jearim. When the text lists the "families (מִשְׁפָּחוֹת) of scribes at Jabez," the transition out of the genealogical genre has already occurred. Geography, not genealogy, now describes the patronage relationships within the text. As Knoppers states, "The sites involved range from Qiriath-jearim, Eshtaol, Manahath, and Zorah to the west of Jerusalem to Bethlehem and Netophah in the south" (2004: 314). Genealogy directly expresses geopolitical relationships within Judah.

A geographical pattern emerges at the end of the first account of the genealogy of Judah in vv. 42–55. The family of Judah is located in the Hebron area. As close genealogical connections dissolve, the kinship-group drifts to the south, only then to be bracketed by the north. The text maps out a normative geopolitical story for Judah. The family's territory has a locative center in the Hebron area, accompanied by dispersed, distant settlements.

Geography also plays a central role within 1 Chr 4:1–23. Geographical relationships replace direct genealogical ties. The text begins with a clear, formal genealogical structure. The two references to בְּנֵי יְהוּדָה (4:1; cf. 2:3) enclose the "sons of Hezron" and the Davidic family within the center of the descendants of Judah. Clear genealogical connections dissipate into disconnected names. As the genealogical relationships weaken, the emphasis on geography increases. The remaining sons of Judah are not bound together through familial ties but enter the family through patronage relations that have territorial specificity. Toponyms end up dominating the passage.

The genealogical genre organizes the beginning and the end of the passage, unifying the whole to the rest of the genealogy of Judah. Geographical references, however, provide stronger links to the previous genealogies of Judah than continuous lines of familial descent. Verse 2 alludes obliquely to geography by mentioning the Zorathites, a family related to Keriath-jearim.at the end of the first sons-of-Judah genealogy in 2:53. Verses 3–5 have toponyms that have been placed in the area of Bethlehem (Etham, Hushah, Tekoa), as well as farther south (Jezreel, Gedor).[18] Interestingly, the toponym Penuel is located in the Gilead area, maintaining a genealogical tie to the south in being the "father" of Gedor. Nor is it the only tie to the Gilead region in 4:1–23.

---

18. Curtis 1910: 105–6.

Asarel (v. 16) also seems to bear a geographical reference to this area.[19] The genealogical form only loosely sits over vv. 8–10. The toponyms move south with Anab and Jabez. Verses 18–19 have toponyms likewise in the area to the southwest (Eshtemoa, Gedor, Soco, Zanoah) and northwest of Hebron (Keilah).[20] Without direct genealogical ties, the sites nonetheless are located within the "sons of Judah." The toponyms tie the families into the same region as the Judean families found in chap. 2, even though they are not given close familial relationships within the genealogy of Judah. They are members of Judah, even if not directly genealogically related.

Not all the toponyms occur in areas previous tied genealogically to the "sons of Judah" in chap. 2. While the site of Beth-rapha is unknown, it seems that Ir-Nahash refers to a site at the northern end of the Arabah (v. 12).[21] Verse 14 gives toponyms, Ophrah, east of Bethel,[22] while Neh 11:35 associates Ge-Harashim with areas inhabited by Benjaminites. Perhaps most interestingly, the genealogy concludes with a series of toponyms associated with the southern Shephelah: Lecah (possibly Lachish), Mareshah, Beth-Ashbea, Chezib/Achzib (tied to Bethlehem through marriage), Netaim, and Gederah (vv. 21–23).[23] These sites exist outside the central territory of the sons of Judah. They are not integrated into the genealogy except in the loosest possible fashion. What is interesting is that all these sites/families are given specialized economic functions. Their inclusion in the sons of Judah, as stated in v. 23, seems to relate to the fact that they were "with the king in his service." They are included in the genealogy of Judah by economic specialization, not bloodline.

One final point highlights the different relationships that the text depicts within "the sons of Judah." Verses 13–15 bear a unique structure that isolates the genealogy of Kenaz within the family of Judah. The genealogy begins and ends with Kenaz, seemingly the same person. In order to accomplish this, of course, the genealogy must at some moment move away from Kenaz in order to return to its point of origin. This occurs in v. 15, when the text returns to Caleb, the son of Jephunneh The verses are hermetically sealed amidst the broader ge-

---

19. "Asriel (אשריאל) appears in some texts as a Manassite clan with connections to Gilead (Num 26:31; Josh 17:2; 1 Chr 7:14 [*Textual Note*]; cf. 1 Chr 25:2 אשראלה)" (Knoppers 2004: 349).

20. Curtis 1910: 111–12.

21. Aharoni 1979: 203.

22. Aharoni 1979: 121.

23. Curtis 1910: 113.

nealogy of Judah. No tie to others in the family of Judah exists. They belong only by virtue of their location within the broader Judean genealogy. Kenaz is both the origin and the destination, the *telos*, of this family.

Such a genealogical structure is unique in Chronicles. Yet it shows a process by which others outside the family of Judah are incorporated, to an extent, into the genealogy of Judah in the narrative world of Chronicles. The name *Kenaz* has previously appeared twice in the genealogies of Chronicles, both times in the genealogy of Edom/Esau (1:36, 52). The second reference is especially interesting. Here Kenaz is one of the 'clans' (מִשְׁפָּחֹת) of Edom, and "has strong links to southern Canaan" (Knoppers 2004: 346). The Judean genealogy of 1 Chronicles 4 places this family in the genealogy of Judah. It belongs both in Edom and in Judah. The text thinly veils the artificiality of the genealogy. Again, the group bears a specialized economic function within Judah. The descendants of Kenaz through the younger son, Seraiah, concludes with "Ge-Harashim," 'the valley of the artisans' (גֵּיא חֲרָשִׁים), "because they were artisans" (חֲרָשִׁים, 4:14). At least part of "Kenaz," the Edomite clan, now becomes loosely incorporated into the family of Judah. At least one of the "forefathers" of Kenaz may have Edomite connections as well.[24] By beginning and ending with Kenaz, the text incorporates a southern area/people associated with Edom into the family of Judah. Whereas earlier in the text genealogy served for geography, here geography serves for genealogy. Such persons stand only loosely affiliated with the family in contrast to others whose Judean bloodlines keep them not only related but connected.

The genealogy of the sons of Judah in 4:1–23 does not develop the familial lines of Judah, except in a most general, fictive manner. The members stand in Judah in a different relationship from those families mentioned in chap. 2 and extremely differently from the Davidic descendents in chap. 3. As genealogical relations weaken, geographic links strengthen, with specialized but subordinate relations of the families to Judah being emphasized.[25]

After this survey, we must here return to the question: Does the genealogy of Judah tell us anything about the territoriality of *Yehud*?

---

24. See 1 Chr 1:14.

25. Thus Knoppers correctly notes the ethnic diversity in the genealogy of Judah in Chronicles yet seemingly overstates the degree of the Chronicler's "inclusiveness" by not sufficiently recognizing the place in the genealogies where this ethnic diversity appears. See Knoppers 2001.

Seen from the perspective of drawing borders, the answer is obvious: No. As Gary Knoppers writes,

> Examination of the sites listed in the genealogy reveals that the Chronicler ascribes large areas to the tribe. . . . The writers, it seems, do not accept Yehud's circumscribed boundaries as normative for their people. . . . there is an idealistic aspect to the presentation in Chronicles. Extending the genealogy back to the time of the Ancestors, the authors stake a claim in the present. Current restrictions are not determinative in ascertaining Judah's legacy. (2004: 357–58)

However, a closer examination of the data, sensitive to the precise relationships drawn within the text, without importing an anachronistic polity upon Yehud, suggests that the genealogy may indeed describe *Yehud* under the Achaemenids.

First, the territory for the genealogically most-central families of Judah overlaps with the common area incorporated by recent scholars in their reconstruction of Yehud: from just south and west of Jerusalem, reaching south to the Hebron highlands. Perhaps the geography of the genealogies suggests that the area of the Hebron highlands itself was more in Yehud than Stern and Lipschits have argued. I have already argued that fortresses do not mark borders but serve other defensive functions within traditional states. East and west fade into frontiers, not borders, just as the density of Judean families lessens from the north–south, Bethlehem/Hebron axis. Such a view corresponds well with the material evidence from the fifth–fourth century B.C.E. in the same region.[26]

Yet the genealogies also reveal dispersed sites throughout the region. Sporadic geographical concentrations of Judah reach down into the Negev as well as northeast into Gilead. Other sites are scattered in the Arabah, not to mention the southern Shephelah. Areas in the north of Benjamin also occur. The genealogy of Judah, however, places these sites into different types of relationships to the central clans of Judah.

---

26. Lipschits estimates that the "Judean Hills" comprised 300 dunams of settlement during the Persian Period, 28% of the settled area. In contrast, the Jerusalem environs only contained 110 dunams, 10.3% of the settled area. See Lipschits (2005: 167). Such archaeological results differ greatly from the impression given in the resettlement lists in Ezra/Nehemiah (Lipschits 2005: 154–68). The correlation of the material remains with the Chronicles genealogies, therefore, suggests that the genealogies represent geographical data with less of an agenda than the list of the returnees. For other problems with reconstructing the territory of Persian-Period Yehud on the basis of the lists in Ezra and Nehemiah, see Lipschits 2002.

They relate to Judah through marriage alliances or economic functions or distant and loose kinship ties. Some are even simultaneously Edom-ite. Their presence amidst Judah does not mean that all the areas in which they lived or all their neighbors were Judean, nor were all the lands between them and the "Judean heartland." At times, they them-selves were not "Judean" but were subject to different types of author-ity. These families existed as part of Judah through patronage systems that were covered with the thin veneer of fictive kinship ties. The gene-alogies describe a particular ethnos with a territorial center, frontiers on its edges, and diaspora communities in areas away from its main territory. Perhaps the genealogy of Judah in Chronicles is not so much a flight of fancy as it is the actual description of the territorial implica-tions of a polity without borders—a polity of an ethnos, not a state.

A similar image appears within the genealogy of Benjamin. The sons of Benjamin receive their genealogical expression in three differ-ent genealogies in Chronicles. The first record comes amidst a military census of the seven Northern tribes (7:6–11); the second concludes the genealogy of the "sons of Israel" (8:1–40). The third (9:35–44) repeats a segment of this genealogy. This genealogy seemingly prepares for the narrative to follow in 10:1. For the purpose of this paper, the geneal-ogy of the "sons of Benjamin" in 8:1–40 will provide the focus for an investigation of topographical information within the Benjaminite genealogy.

As do all of the genealogies in 1 Chronicles 1–9, chap. 8 presents its own critical problems.[27] Strictly speaking, the chapter does not com-prise one genealogy but four separate ones.[28] Only the first has explicit genealogical ties to Benjamin as the ancestor of the tribe. Nonetheless, the conclusion of the chapter enfolds all its members into the Ben-jaminites: "All these were from the sons of Benjamin" (8:40). The "sons of Benjamin" appear as a conglomeration of different family groups. Each genealogical subsection has specific geographical dimensions.

The initial genealogy extends to six generations directly from Ben-jamin and seems devoid of toponyms masquerading as names. Ono-mastic toponyms are not necessary; the genealogy places its members within a specific locale. The passage describes the sons of Ehud as 'the heads of the inhabitants of Geba, and they resettled themselves in Manahat' (ראשי אבות ליושבי גבע ויגלום אל מנחת, v. 6). While scholars

---

27. See the discussion in Oeming 1990: 170–75.
28. 1 Chr 8:1–7; 8–12; 13–28; 29–40.

debate the precise location of this Geba, either way the town is to the northwest of Jerusalem in the traditional tribal land of Benjamin.[29] Manahat, however, most likely lies southwest of Jerusalem.[30] The text therefore depicts a migration of at least part of the "sons of Ehud" from the area to the north of Jerusalem to another area outside their traditional domain in Judah.[31]

The second genealogical segment has an even more interesting geographical pattern. The genealogy of Shaharaim begins following his divorce from his wives Hushim and Baara. Shaharaim sires children in the "fields of Moab," presumably from his wife Hodesh. The phrase seems to suggest a pastoral, migratory existence for this wing of the family of Shaharaim. Within a generation, however, the text designates Elpaal, Shaharaim's son through Hushim, as founder of Lod and Ono and their tributary villages (v. 12). Scholars locate these cities in the Shephelah, not far from Manahat, if it indeed was located in the Shephelah. The family of Shaharaim, affiliated with the sons of Benjamin, has a location to the east of the Jordan River and in the western Shephelah. The traditional area of Benjamin mediates between the two sites, though without specific identification with the region.

The third genealogical segment (vv. 13–28) begins with a geographical reference. The text designates Beriah and Shema as the familial heads of the inhabitants of Aijalon, a town northwest of Jerusalem (v. 13) on the western frontier of the traditional region of Benjamin.[32] The genealogy continues to connect Benjamin and the northern Shephelah. The text reports that the inhabitants of Aijalon complete a successful incursion toward Gath (v. 13). The genealogy, like the previous one, depicts this segment of the Benjaminites is pushing farther westward.

The names of the descendants of Beriah, Shema, Shashaq, Jeremoth, and Elpaal were apparently drawn from a myriad of sources.[33] Three names, however, stand out as toponyms. Two sons of Beriah, Arad and Eder, refer to a site(s) in the Arad Valley south of Judah (v. 15).[34] Anthothiah, a personal name related to the Benjamite site of

---

29. The site is identified with either Khirbet et-Tell (Aharoni 1979: 315) or a site that "rules the pass of Wadi Suweint" (Aharoni 1979: 379 n. 3).

30. Aharoni 1979: 346.

31. The root גלה does not necessarily involve an involuntary displacement but may indicate a voluntary migration and resettlement as well.

32. See Aharoni 1979: 346.

33. For the problems of vv. 13–14, see Japhet 1993: 93–95.

34. See the discussion in Aharoni 1979: 117.

Anathoth, appears as a son of Shashaq (v. 24). With the center in their traditional tribal area, the Benjaminites also have dispersed sites outside this region.

Verse 28 brings the genealogies of the descendants of Beriah, Shema, Elpaal, Shashaq, and Jeremoth to a close. It summarizes: "These are the heads of the father in reference to their genealogies, heads. These resided in Jerusalem" (v. 28). Commentators have expressed confusion about the supposed dual residency of these heads. Yet the text contains no contradiction. Verse 13 never assigns the dwelling place of these family heads to Aijalon. It does, however, clearly give them authority over the inhabitants there. The text depicts them as living in Jerusalem and exercising their authority in absentia from their town. Power moves from the center to the periphery via a kinship patronage system. Ties of family provide ties of jurisdiction that has territorial dimensions but is not defined by territory per se.

The final genealogical segment gives the descendants of Jeiel (vv. 29–40). The founding ancestor of this genealogical segment is not tied directly to Benjamin. Jeiel is identified as the founding father of the Benjaminite town of Gibeon to the northwest of Jerusalem (v. 29).[35] The first generation removed from Jeiel does not live in Gibeon, however, but in Jerusalem (v. 32). Again, commentators often express confusion over the phrase 'opposite their kinsmen' (נגד אחיהם). But within its narrative context, the text seems to refer to the characters given in v. 28. If so, the text depicts a "Benjaminite quarter" of Jerusalem in which elite families lived that maintained authority over kinship in towns in the traditional region of Benjamin.

In summary, the genealogy of Benjamin depicts a polity with shifting territorial dimensions. Benjamin remains within its traditional region but also migrates to outposts on the west into the Shephelah. It possesses a leadership based in Jerusalem, with dispersed familial groups scattered elsewhere. Delineated borders do not define the family of Benjamin. The genealogical relationships depict a traditional territorial center, an adjacent new territorial frontier, and scattered diaspora units. Such a depiction again correlates well with the current assessment of material remains in the area. "At the end of the sixth century B.C.E. and during the Persian period, the Benjaminite region went through a process of depopulation and settlement decline" (Lipschits 2003: 348). The northern Shephelah, however, witnessed demographic growth. Lipschits argues that "a decline in settlement in the

---

35. See Aharoni 1979: 417.

region of Benjamin was a major factor in renewed Judean settlement in the *northern Shephelah*, particularly in Ono–Lod Valley. We may reasonably conclude that settlement in the northern Shephelah, which was not within the borders of Yehud, gained momentum in the fifth century B.C.E. and attracted at least some residents who were abandoning the region of Benjamin" (Lipschits 2005: 167–68).[36] The topography of the Benjaminite genealogy quite possibly reflects the real territorial dispersion of the Benjaminite family in the fifth century B.C.E.

Conclusion

The modern nation-state has deeply, and negatively, affected the historical reconstruction of Palestine and the polities of Israel and Judah in the first millennium B.C.E. As Keith Whitelam has written, "The dominant model for the presentation of Israelite history has been, and continues to be, that of a unified national entity in search of a national territory struggling to maintain its national identity and land through the crises of history" (1996: 21). If the argument of this paper is persuasive, recent scholarly attempts to construct borders for Yehud also anachronistically project the polity of the modern nation-state back onto Judah and Judeans in the Achaemenid Period.

I have argued that we might base a different reconstruction, one more consistent with life under Achaemenid hegemony, on the genealogies of Judah and Benjamin in 1 Chr 2:3–4:23 and 8:1–40. Without denying the significance of territoriality, the genealogical/geographical data from this list generate a polity that is kinship- and patronage-based and that possesses frontiers and diaspora, anchored within central territories. Borders, per se, have no place in this polity.

This model is consistent with the material remains from the era. The genealogies of Judah and Benjamin reveal two territorial concentrations of settlements: (1) one to the south of Jerusalem from Bethlehem to Hebron; and (2) one to the north and west of Jerusalem, moving westward into the northern Shephelah. As in the material remains, Jerusalem itself stands in an area of relative demographic void that comprehends areas to its north and south.[37] As witnessed in the book of

---

36. Lipschits (2005: 167) states that these settlements took place "not within the borders" of Judah. Of course, if Judah was not defined by borders, such an argument is not germane. According to this paper, the "territory" of Yehud would have entailed property owned by a member of the clans of Judah and Benjamin.

37. As Lipschits concludes, "Most of the inhabitants of the province gathered in the region of Benjamin and in the environs of Bethlehem. Historical accounts of this appear

Nehemiah and in Malachi, the attempt to establish Jerusalem as the political center uniting these two areas must have entailed some struggle among the Persian-appointed authorities.

Epigraphic evidence also suggests a polity, not of borders, but of an ethnos. The Idumean ostraca published by Eph'al and Naveh display a predominance of Edomite names. Although their exact provenance is not known, the ostraca also include a minority of Judean names alongside the Edomite names.[38] It seems likely that those with the Yahwistic names (or at least their parents) sent their offerings and tithes (i.e., taxes) to the Temple in Jerusalem and thus, in some way, lived as Judeans even amidst the Edomites. Likewise, the members of the Judean colony in Elephantine could easily call themselves both "Syenians" and Judeans in such a polity, based on the contingencies of their documents.[39] Lipschits's fine analysis of *yhwd* seal impressions shows an administration centered in Judah, defined by the collection of goods there from a dispersed, scattered populace from which they were gathered (Lipschits 2005: 174–81). In such a familial/patronage-based polity, Judeans might be members of the Yehud polity even in areas not geographically controlled by Jerusalem but in areas where Judeans might live *qua* Judeans as a minority.

If this polity was as I have described it through the genealogies of Chronicles, it finally would explain the origins of a social system that carried the Judeans into the Hellenistic and Roman worlds and beyond. One problem with a small Yehud is the size of the Judean population in the Hellenistic and Roman worlds—human reproduction within this

in the two biblical narratives from the time of Gedaliah. From an archaeological standpoint, this region was less affected than others during the destruction of Jerusalem. Archaeological evidence from the Benjamin region covers the entire sixth century B.C.E. and reveals almost complete settlement continuity from the end of the Iron Age to the Babylonian and Persian Periods" (2005: 182).

38. The editors of the ostraca write, "Our ostraca do not contain any administrative or professional titles, and indicate nothing about state or regional administration. The socio-economic structure of certain groups mentioned in the ostraca is instructive: three documents refer to 'the House of PN' (PN = Ba'alrim, Yehokal, and 'Aliba'al), and 30 to the 'Sons of PN' (PN = Ba'alrim, Guru, Yehokal, Qosi, Rammarana, etc.). This feature clearly reflects a clan-tribal organization" (Eph'al and Naveh 1996: 15). Ironically, the editors miss the fact that these titles may themselves be administrative titles and therefore may indicate the "state or regional administration."

39. See, for instance, in Cowley 33 (A4.10), five men with Yahwistic names identify themselves as "Syenians" (סוכנן, line 6) when they petition to pay a local lord for permission to rebuild their Yahwistic Temple; yet in their request to Bagohi, governor of Judah, they identify themselves as "Jews all" (ויהודיא כל, verso line 22) Cowley 30 (A4.7). See Porten and Yardeni 1986: 78, 68–71.

territory and Hasmonean and Herodian conquests can only account for a certain percentage of growth. What we see in the genealogies of 1 Chronicles is a polity developed that keeps a territorial center (i.e., Jerusalem, the Judean Hill country, and the western area of Benjamin) with frontiers, expanding and contracting according to the military fortunes of the Hasmoneans and Herodians, that nonetheless already has political allegiances among populations who formerly were absorbed into the central territories, as well as having connections to diaspora communities, even as they spread throughout the Mediterranean and Mesopotamian worlds. This system, seen fully developed in the Roman era, has its origins, as so much else, in the years under the Achaemenids. The book of Chronicles attests to the early days of this social-historical development.

Bibliography

Aharoni, Y.
1979   *The Land of the Bible: A Historical Geography.* 2nd ed. Philadelphia.
Briant, P.
2002   *From Cyrus to Alexander: A History of the Persian Empire,* trans. P. T. Daniels. Winona Lake, Indiana.
Carter, C. E.
1999   *The Emergence of Yehud in the Persian Period: A Social and Demographic Study.* Journal for the Study of the Old Testament Supplement 294. Sheffield.
Curtis, E. L., and Madsen, A. A.
1910   *The Books of Chronicles.* International Critical Commentary. Edinburgh.
Eph'al, I., and Naveh, J.
1996   *Aramaic Ostraca of the Fourth Century BC from Idumaea.* Jerusalem.
Giddens, A.
1981   *Power, Property and the State.* Vol. 1 of *A Contemporary Critique of Historical Materialism.* Berkeley.
1987   *Contemporary Critique of Historical Materialism.* Vol. 2 of *The Nation-State and Violence.* Berkeley.
Hoglund, K. G.
1992   *Achaemenid Imperial Administration in Syria–Palestine and the Missions of Ezra and Nehemiah.* Atlanta.
Japhet, S.
1993   *I and II Chronicles: A Commentary.* Old Testament Library. Louisville.
Johnstone, W.
1997   *1 Chronicles 1–2 Chronicles 9: Israel's Place among the Nations.* Vol. 1 of *1 and 2 Chronicles.* Journal for the Study of the Old Testament Supplement 253. Sheffield.

Kartveit, M.
1989   *Motive und Schicten der Landtheologie in 1 Chronik 1–9.* Coniectanea Biblia: Old Testament Series 28. Stockholm.
Knoppers, G. N.
2001   Intermarriage, Social Complexity, and Ethnic Diversity in the Genealogy of Judah. *Journal of Biblical Literature* 120: 15–30.
2002   "Great among His Brothers," but Who Is He? Heterogeneity in the Composition of Judah. *Journal of Hebrew Scriptures* 3 (http:www.purl/org/jhs).
2003   Greek Historiography and the Chronicler's History: A Reexamination. *Journal of Biblical Literature* 122: 627–50.
2004   *1 Chronicles 1–9: A New Translation with Introduction and Commentary.* Anchor Bible 12. New York.
Lipschits, O.
2002   Literary and Ideological Aspects of Nehemiah 11. *Journal of Biblical Literature* 121: 423–40.
2003   Demographic Changes in Judah between the Seventh and Fifth Centuries B.C.E. Pp. 323–76 in *Judah and the Judeans in the Neo-Babylonian Period*, ed. Oded Lipschits and Joseph Blenkinsopp. Winona Lake, Indiana.
2005   *The Fall and Rise of Jerusalem: The History of Judah under Babylonian Rule.* Winona Lake, Indiana.
Oeming, M.
1990   *Das wahre Israel: Die 'genealogische Vorhalle' 1 Chronik 1–9.* Beiträge zur Wissenschaft vom Alten und Neuen Testament. Kohlhammer.
Philpott, D.
2001   *Revolutions in Sovereignty: How Ideas Shaped Modern International Relations.* Princeton and Oxford.
Porten, B., and Yardeni, A.
1986   *Letters.* Vol. 1 of *Textbook of Aramaic Documents from Ancient Egypt.* Jerusalem.
Stern, E.
1982   *Material Culture of the Land of the Bible in the Persian Period, 538–332 B.C.* Warminster.
2001   *The Assyrian, Babylonian, and Persian Periods (732–332 B.C.E.).* Vol. 2 of *Archaeology of the Land of the Bible.* New York.
Tilley, C.
1975   Reflections on the History of European State-Making. Pp. 3–43 in *The Formation of National States in Western Europe*, ed. Charles Tilley. Princeton.
Whitelam, K.
1996   *The Invention of Ancient Israel: The Silencing of Palestinian History.* Routledge.
Williamson, H. G. M.
1979   Sources and Redaction in the Chronicler's Genealogy of Judah. *Journal of Biblical Literature.* 98: 351–59.
1982   *1 and 2 Chronicles.* New Century Bible. Grand Rapids.

Persia's Loyal Yahwists:
Power Identity and Ethnicity
in Achaemenid Yehud

JOHN KESSLER
Tyndale Seminary, Toronto

Introduction

In contrast to the situation that obtained in scholarly circles 20 years ago, today the Persian Period is considered to be a crucial moment in the development of the literature of the Hebrew Bible and in the shape of the institutions and practices of Yahwistic worship both within and beyond the Persian province of Yehud. Thus, methodologically, in our current state of scholarly discourse, texts that overtly situate themselves in the Persian Period (such as Haggai, Ezra, or Nehemiah) and others that do not (such as Genesis or Hosea) are interpreted against the backdrop of the social realities of Persian Yehud.[1] The flow of the scholarly discussion generally follows one of two directions: either the biblical text is used to reconstruct the social world of Persian Yehud, or a reconstructed social world of Persian Yehud is used to illuminate the backdrop against which the words of an individual text are read. Sadly, however, in certain cases assertions are made about the Persian Period and its sociopolitical and religious struggles without reference to the extensive and rigorous body of literature that has emerged regarding the complex and variegated contours of life that obtained at that time.

Critical to our understanding of the religious and sociopolitical dynamics of Achaemenid Yehud is the issue of the nature, function, and influence of the Golah, or community of exiled and returned Judeans. Even the most superficial reading of the Hebrew Bible reveals the stamp that this group has left on the final form of the biblical text. In

---

1. Thus, for example, Ska (2001) views the dispute between the returnees and the non-exiled population as being reflected in the Abraham cycle. See also the discussion of "hidden polemics" in Amit 2003.

Ezek 11:1–21 and 33:23–29, this group's members are declared to be the true possessors of the land, while those who remained in the land are viewed as illegitimate usurpers. Similarly, in Jer 24:1–10, the exiles are viewed as good figs, and the remainees as bad ones. In Ezra and Nehemiah, virtually no mention is made of the remainees. Interest is focused on the Golah members, who represent the true Israel. Members of this group go into Exile and subsequently return to an empty land to reclaim their former dwellings, encountering and overcoming opposition from some so-called Yahwists of foreign origin in the land itself and from the North.

In contrast to this highly stylized portrait, a closer reading of the biblical text, as well as the available archaeological data, reveals a more nuanced picture, one in which the returnees find themselves in a variety of complex relationships with a great diversity of centers of power. The question that this paper will address, albeit in a preliminary way, is how the Golah returnees are best understood in this *pastiche* of complex relationships that characterized Yahwism in the Achaemenid Empire. I will address this question in three stages. First I will present a brief examination of the landscape of Yahwism in the Levant and Mesopotamia and some of the various questions raised with reference to it. Second, I will advance a sociological model or analogy—that of the "Charter Group"—as a heuristic point of departure for the discussion of Yahwistic power relations in the period. Third, I will briefly examine three elements of the Golah's role as a Charter Group, including matters of hegemony, empowerment, construction of identity, and issues of inclusion and exclusion.

Yahwism in the Empire: A Complex Phenomenon

In order to assess the role of the Golah returnees, we must situate this group in the broader context of Yahwism in the Empire. It is beyond the scope of this paper to discuss the debated transition from Yahwism to Judaism so often situated in the period (Edelman 1996; Becking and Korpel 1999; Albertz and Becking 2003), nor is my focus here specifically on the history of the former Southern Kingdom. Rather, my intent here is simply to present a brief sketch of the communities who identified themselves with the worship of Yahweh in our period.[2]

---

2. In 1983, S. Japhet presented a similar survey (1983). The present study updates her earlier one in the light of recent investigation.

Yehud

The former Kingdom of Judah, while severely depopulated and devastated, was not left completely empty.[3] Kings and Jeremiah suggest that the poor of the land were given some form of land tenure by the Babylonians (Jer 39:10; 2 Kgs 25:12; Jer 52:16; cf. Ezek 11:2–11, 14–18; 33:23–28). The term "people(s) of the land" (Ezra 4:4; 9:1, 2, 11; 10:11) likely includes a reference to nondeported Judeans (Grabbe 1998: 95; Barstad 1996: 44). Furthermore, archaeological research has revealed evidence of general demographic continuity in the Benjaminite territory to the north of Jerusalem and, by contrast, evidence of widespread destruction in the environs of Jerusalem and the Shephelah, and progressive collapse and depopulation in the Southern Highlands, Judean Desert, and the Jordan and Dead Sea regions (Milevski 1996; Lipschits 2003). Furthermore, biblical passages, specifically in Lamentations, Jeremiah, and the so-called "exilic" Psalms (44, 74, 79, 89, 102), may constitute evidence of the form of worship that persisted among this population during the exilic period (Janssen 1956: 19–22). There is ongoing debate about the degree of intervention that the Babylonians had in the administration of the region. Lipschits (1998; 1999; 2002; 2003) and Blenkinsopp (1998; 2000; 2003) have argued that the Babylonians established a provincial capital at Mizpah, possibly with some form of cult site. Vanderhooft (1999; 2003) by contrast argues for a more restrained view of Babylonian involvement.[4] He suggests, based on the dearth of Babylonian material evidence in the Levant and the absence of reverse deportations to the periphery of the Empire, that Babylon's primary interest was the elimination of Egyptian economic interests in the region and the occasional collection of tribute. Thus, no full-scale provincial structure was implemented.[5] However the case may be, it is generally accepted that some remnants of the former population were indeed left in place and that no external populations were brought in by the new rulers.

---

3. On the alternative reconstructions of this period, see Janssen (1956), Barstad (1996), and Carroll (1992), who favor minimal disruption. By contrast, Lipschits (2003) and Oded (2003), among many others, favor significant depopulation. For a fuller treatment of various aspects of Early Persian Yehud, see the survey in Kessler 2001.

4. See also Oded (2003: 68), who follows Vanderhooft.

5. Central to Vanderhooft's argument is his view that Assyrian control in the southern Levant diminished in the latter years of Assyrian rule, allowing the emergence of indigenous power structures. He thus challenges Graham's suggestion (1984) that the Babylonians inherited and perpetuated a fully functional provinical administrative system from the Assyrians. Kreissig (1973) also posits significant land redistribution in the Babylonian Period, with later repercussions in the Achaemenid era.

Samaria

A significant Yahwistic population existed in the province of Samaria, immediately to the north.[6] The existence of this community is evidenced in Jeremiah 41, Chronicles, Ezra–Nehemiah, as well as in onomastic evidence from the Wadi Dâliyeh Papyri and a variety of other epigraphic materials (Lemaire 1990; Ephʿal 1998; Tadmor 1983). The ethnic composition of this community has been the subject of significant debate; however, it is widely held that it contained both those who were descendants of the inhabitants of the former Northern Kingdom and those who were settled there by the Assyrians (Cogan 1988; Ephʿal 1998: 110; Zertal 1990; 2003: 405–6). Most significant for our purposes is the fact that the residents of this province, whose population was likely higher than that of Yehud (Zertal 1990), held an attachment to the worship of Yahweh, evident through their Yahwistic onomasticon (Lemaire 1994a: 41–46; 2001: 103–9), and a desire for political, economic, and religious influence and involvement in the re-emerging cultic and economic center in Jerusalem throughout most if not all of our period (Ezra 4:1–3; Neh 4:1–3; 6:10–19; 13:4–9).[7]

Egypt

As is well known, a significant Jewish community existed in Egypt beginning with the seventh century or earlier (cf. Isa 11:11; Jer 26:21–23, and 43–44; Porten 1984; 2003: 458). Despite areas of uncertainty such as the precise origins of the garrison at Elephantine,[8] the Egyptian Diaspora constituted a major center of Israelite and Judean population (Borgen 1992).[9] It is significant that, in the late sixth century, there is no evidence of a return to Yehud from Egypt, despite the fact that some evidence of the reverse has been cited (Porten 1984: 19 n. 69).

---

6. The bibliography on Samaria and Samaritan studies is immense. See Hjelm 2000 for a general survey and excellent historical examination of the development of Samaritan studies, and extensive bibliography. See also the contribution of G. Knoppers in this volume (pp. 265–289).

7. This is evident from the reference to Sanballat and Tobiah's interest and influence in Yehud (Neh 2:10; 4:1; 6:1; 13:5; etc.).

8. See the suggestions in Porten 2003; 1984: 378–83 and Knauf 2002.

9. In Jer 24:8, included among the "bad figs" are not only the Judeans who remained in the land but also those who fled to Egypt. This created a situation in which the Egyptian Diaspora, at a later period, had to be relegitimized. On this point see Bar-Kochva 1996; and de Pury and Römer 1995: esp. 34. The latter authors' important article stresses the potential conflict between the Egyptian and Babylonian Diaspora communities in the context of Judean politics during the seventh century, as well as the distinction between enforced exile, in one case, and voluntary flight, in the other.

Mesopotamia

The returnees were only a small portion of a much larger Yahwistic community in the east of the Empire, notably Elam and Babylonia. Evidence for the existence and life of this community is available in the cuneiform tablets published by Lemaire and Joannès[10] and may be glimpsed in biblical passages such as 2 Kgs 24:13–14; Jer 29:1–7; Ezek 20:1–2; Ezra 1:5; 4:3; 8:15–20.[11] Some data may also be inferred, with due critical caution, from Assyrian and Babylonian deportation and administrative policies (Oded 1995; and Dandamaev in the present volume, pp. 373–398), the later Murashu corpus (Cardascia 1951; Stolper 1985), and what we know of the Babylonian Jewish communities of later periods (Mantel 1973: 65–74).

Other Regions of the Levant

Finally, biblical and epigraphic evidence demonstrates that, from 587 onward, population with Yahwistic names and some attachment to Jerusalem (cf. Jeremiah 40–41) existed in the provinces and regions surrounding Yehud and Samaria. Included here would be Galilee (Freyne 1980: 24–25; Briend 1996; Lemaire 1994a: 40–41; 2001: 99; Eph'al 1998: 110),[12] Gaza (Lemaire 2001: 111 on the Yahwistic names in the Tell Jemmeh ostraca; Naveh 1992; Eph'al 1998: 114), Ashdod (Naveh 1971; Lemaire 2001: 110), the Idumean region to the south and southwest (Naveh 1985; Lemaire 1994a: 30; 2001: 11; Beit-Arieh 1996; Eph'al 1998: 11. Eph'al notes that the number of Yahwistic names on the ostraca from this region is very small), and the Transjordanian regions of Moab and Ammon (cf. Jer 40:10–14).[13] The current evidence from these latter regions is highly fragmentary, but increasing, and permits only the suggestion that former inhabitants of the Northern or Southern

---

10. Joannès and Lemaire 1999; see also the contribution of Pearce in this volume (pp. 399–411) and forthcoming.

11. For a survey of these, see Oded 1995.

12. Gal (1998) sees the region as having been almost completely depopulated in the eighth century. Chancey (2002: 45) is of a similar opinion but admits the ongoing presence of some remnants of the former Northern Kingdom. Lemaire cites the Yahwistic name 'Aqabyah on an ostracon from Tel Yoqneam (2001: 99). Freyne affirms significant continuity of Yahwistic population in this area, while Chancey opts for a quasi-total depopulation of the region from the Assyrian deportation to the Hellenistic Period, while admitting that some former Northerners may have persisted (2002: 45).

13. Lemaire (1994b: 19) cites three paleohebraic seals from Ammon; cf. also Lemaire 1994a: 48–51 with bibliography. He suggests the presence of an Israelite minority in the Ammonite region near the Jordan.

Kingdoms may have been resident there. In conclusion, one may summarize this complex Yahwistic tapestry as follows: (1) Golah returnees; (2) Golah remainees in Babylonia;[14] (3) Yehudite remainees; (4) Egyptian Yahwists; (5) Samarian Yahwists of diverse origins; and (6) other Yahwists in the Levant.

It is somewhat difficult to find an appropriate term to attach to these various groups of descendants of the habitants of the former Northern and Southern Kingdoms during our period. Geographical distribution, development, and independent religious expression made each distinct from the others. Although the terms *Judeans* or *Jews* were frequently used in the ancient world (Knauf 2002: 183; Neh 1:2; Esth 3:6; Porten and Yardeni 1986: A.4.7; Cowley 1923: 30; 22, 26; Aramaic *yhwdy'*, Hebrew *yhwdym*) and are current in modern discussions, they run the risk of homogenizing the disparate groups or anachronistically reading later understandings of Judaism back into them.[15] Thus, for the purposes of this study I propose viewing these groups as a *Yahwistic community* or *Yahwistic stakeholders*. The latter term, for example, is used in current parlance to denote the broadest grouping together of individuals connected with a particular institution or entity. Thus the stakeholders in a given educational institution would include not only the traditional "faculty, staff, and students" but also alumni, donors, neighbors, creditors, and the like. Thus this Yahwistic constituency or these stakeholders would consist of those who for one reason or another saw themselves as standing in some relationship to Yahweh or Jerusalem and being impacted by the emerging significance of that city with its newly reconstructed and rededicated temple (cf. Ezra 7:25–26).[16] Such an approach seeks to examine Yahwism or Judaism in a way that does not overly emphasize tightly drawn borders of separate provinces.[17]

---

14. The existence of other Yahwistic communities in the east is often speculated upon; see Smith-Christopher (2002: 71), who suggests that Judeans may have been conscripted for military service by Nabonidus and scattered in Arabia. See also Oded (1977: 481), who suggests that exiles from the former Northern Kingdom may have been included in the Babylonian-Elamite Jewish population.

15. See, for example, Knauf (2002), who, noting these variations, judiciously uses the term "pre-biblical Judaism" with reference to the Elephantine community, thus distinguishing it from its later Jerusalemite counterpart.

16. Such interest viewed from the perspective of the "other" is noted in Rappaport 1996: 966.

17. See here the insightful approaches of Wright (pp. 67–89), Berquist (53–66), and Fantalkin and Tal (167–197) in this volume, as well as Sapin 2003. All of the above authors raise questions regarding the drawing of boundaries in the Achaemenid Levant and the significance of such boundaries.

What was the status and role of the Golah returnees in the midst of this composite? Numerous studies have addressed diverse aspects of this issue. I will briefly indicate eight major lines of investigation.[18] First, various studies have sought to examine the nature and structure of the Golah community itself (Smith-Christopher 1989; 2002) either in its Yehudite (Weinberg 1992) or Babylonian manifestations (Eph'al 1978; Oded 1995; 2000; 2003). Second, a significant body of literature has attempted to define the Golah returnees' status vis-à-vis the Yehudite remainees and the degree of conflict that may have existed between the two groups.[19] A third group of studies examines the relationship between the returnees and the Yahwists in the province of Samaria (Hjelm 2000; Dexinger 1981; Tadmor 1983; Cogan 1988; Ben Zvi 1995), while a fourth approach enlarges the field to the analysis of the relationship between the community in Yehud vis-à-vis other communities in the Levant, specifically with reference to the role of Ezra in this context (Rappaport 1996; Knoppers 2001; North 1971; Mantel 1973; Williamson 1998). Thus Mantel (1973) sees all of the Diaspora communities as having been interrelated under the aegis of such figures as Ezra. In a similar vein, Knoppers (2001) sees the law as promulgated by Ezra as binding upon all the Yahwists of the Levant. Williamson (1998: 161) views the reconstructed temple as a center for the wider Diaspora, with Ezra's role as one of instructing faithful Yahwists on how to achieve a successful balance between obedience to Yahweh's Law and obedience to the Persian king. Fifth, several scholars have examined our period with its various forms of Yahwism from the perspective of the emergence of Jewish sectarianism (Mantel 1973; Blenkinsopp 1981; Talmon 1986; Rofé 1988; Williamson 1998), while a sixth approach looks at the emergence of Jewish identity (Japhet 1983; Hamilton 1995; Cohen 1999). Seventh, a large body of literature exists on the relationship between the events narrated in Ezra–Nehemiah, and Achaemenid imperial policy (Frei and Koch 1984; 2001; Fried 2001; 2002; Berquist 1995; Bodi 2001; Hoglund 1992; and the essays in Watts 2001). Eighth and finally, a few studies have sought to analyze some of the broader dynamics at play between these various Yahwistic groups. Thus Bedford (2002) has discussed the relationships that obtained between the Golah remainees

---

18. Due to the immense body of literature here, only a few representative works will be cited for each point.

19. The literature here is voluminous and the various positions too numerous to mention; see the detailed survey in Kessler 2001, with bibliography, and the critiques of the view of a conflict-ridden Yehud in Ben Zvi 1995: 109–10; and Williamson 1998: 159.

and Golah returnees. De Pury and Römer (1995) take up the conflict between the Egyptian and Babylonian Diasporas, and Rappaport (1996) surveys the relationship between the Yehudite Golah returnees and their neighbors.

A Proposed Model for the Study of the Golah:
The Charter Group

Despite the very great contribution of such studies, the current discussion is often characterized by a perhaps inevitable fragmentation, to the detriment of the larger picture. By this I mean that various aspects of Persian-Period Yahwism are treated in isolation from one another, while certain more overarching aspects of the question are insufficiently examined. Most important of these are the dual roles of ethnicity and distinctive beliefs and practices in the formation of group identity in the context of a multiethnic imperial/colonial administration. In an endeavor to advance the current debate, and to complement these more specialized studies, in the present essay I will propose a sociological analogy that I believe presents a useful heuristic paradigm for the study of the Golah.

Sociological models are frequently used with reference to a variety of issues and phenomena in the Old Testament (see for our period Hanson 1975; Fried 2002; Tollefson and Williamson 1992). However, as Carter (1996, with bibliography) notes, the use of the social sciences in biblical studies is fraught with difficulties, and the potential for superficial or erroneous conclusions is great. Conscious of such potential difficulties, especially the danger of anachronistic assumptions and the "reading" of one situation into another, this study will use a sociological model—that of the Charter Group—but only in a heuristic way. The interest of the model is in its ability to bring into focus some very specific key issues shared by communities facing challenges of a similar nature and then to observe the distinctive manner in which each group deals with such challenges.[20] Thus my use of the Charter Group analogy is intended merely to provide us with a vantage point from which to assess the data revealed by the more traditional methodologies of archaeology, biblical criticism, and historiography.[21]

---

20. A similar approach is taken by Smith (1989) in his comparison of the experience of the Golah with that of the other "Diasporic" populations.

21. There is no intent either to determine whether the biblical data conform to what the model would "predict" or to use the model as an all-encompassing grid into which all the data must be integrated.

The notion of a Charter Group is derived from the work of the Canadian sociologist John Porter, primarily his 1965 monograph, *The Vertical Mosaic*. Porter's study focused on the hegemonic status and functioning of the English and French elites in the emerging sociological context of Anglophone and Francophone Canada, respectively.

Porter's interest in Charter Groups must be understood in the broader context of his interest in the "sociology of power" (Porter 1965: 207). Defining power as the "recognized right to make effective decisions on behalf of a group of people" (p. 202), Porter notes that power is rarely purely political. Rather, it is found in all social institutions. He further observes that "differentiation of power roles emerges only as the scale of social development is ascended and population increases" (p. 204). Such development and differentiation may be found in a wide variety of societies, ancient and modern, preliterate and technologically advanced (pp. 204–5). Given this differentiation, Porter affirms that it is better to speak of "families of power" (i.e., elites) that stand in constant tension with one another and exert influence over the population under their charge. The sociology of power thus seeks to isolate the principal powers or decision-making roles in various systems and to investigate their functioning (p. 207). He notes that, since power always tends to grow and consolidate itself, thus encroaching on other areas of power, elites create a "floating equilibrium of compromise" (p. 210). Various circumstances may bring elites together or drive them apart (p. 208). Interdependence is necessitated by the need for expertise in various matters (p. 210). Conflict between elites is limited by some general agreement on ground rules (p. 210). Control over the incorporation of new members into the elite group is an extension of the power of the group itself. Such recruitment is often determined by kinship links and social background (p. 218).

Porter considers a Charter Group to be an elite (or composite of elites) with certain distinctive features. He defines a Charter Group as an ethnic elite that moves into a geographical region, establishes its power base, and creates a sociological and cultural structure distinct from the one already existing in that region. Thus, a Charter Group is "the first ethnic group to come into a previously unpopulated territory, as the effective possessor" (p. 60), noting as well that "a Charter Group may have to conquer an indigenous group to establish its claim" (p. 60 n. 1). The Charter Group may understand its own mission and purpose in the new land as a "Charter Myth" (p. 366). Members of a Charter Group frequently have a dual allegiance: they identify with their new land and emerging culture while at the same time retaining loyalty to their land and culture of origin (p. 71). Once established, the Charter Group comes to dominate the social, political, and religious institutions of the region.

It is the movement into a new situation from an external context, the seizure of control in the new situation, from which the group's members are ethnically and/or culturally distinct, and the exercise of that control, generally with the backing of a power base beyond the region itself that distinguishes the Charter Group from other "garden-variety" elites. Put another way, a Charter Group is a *non-indigenous, enfranchised elite.*[22] This ethnocultural position of dominance engenders several practical considerations and issues. The first is the issue of identity or *membership* in the Charter Group. Who is in and who is out?

A second issue is the possibility of admission to the group as full members. Frequently, additional resources or members of the labor force are needed. This need raises the question of whether "outsiders" may be admitted, and if so, on what basis. Are intermarriage and/or conversion permitted? May those who were not actually members of the Charter Group be allowed to participate in the broader socio-economic fabric of the region at some level (pp. 60–68)? According to Porter, those deemed eligible by the Charter Group might be assigned an "entrance status" (pp. 60–68) that is frequently ethnically or occupationally specific (pp. 65, 74). Once admitted, in some cases, the status of a group may change over time (p. 64). The discussion of the inclusion of outsiders frequently involves, to use Porter's words, "the mythology of race" (p. 61). As such, various groups are deemed most adept at certain skills and permitted to enter the realm to perform certain circumscribed functions.

A quotation from Porter summarizes his thinking here, and its applicability to the issue under study here is quite transparent. He states:

> In any society which has to seek members from outside there will be varying judgments about the extensive reservoirs of recruits that exist in

---

22. An interesting parallel here may be that of Liberia. There, as has frequently been noted, black settlers from the Unites States and West Indies came to dominate the nation's major sociopolitical institutions, despite the fact that they constituted only 4.5% of the population (Dollot 1981: 25; cf. Liebenow 1987: 3–7). Dollot (p. 34) comments, "One of the predominant characteristics of Liberian history is thus the persistent opposition between the tribal majority—itself quite divided, but rooted in the land, in some cases for centuries—and the tiny black and racially-mixed minority who monopolized the nation's power and wealth to its own exclusive benefit" (translation mine). While the specifics of the Liberian situation ought not to be read into Yehud or other contexts, it appears to be an excellent illustration of the phenomenon of an external, enfranchised elite described by Porter.

the world. In the process of this evaluation the first ethnic group to come into a previously unpopulated territory as the effective possessor, or who conquers an indigenous group, has the most to say. This group becomes the charter group of the society and among the many privileges and prerogatives which it retains are decisions about what other groups are to be let in, and what they will be permitted to do. . . . Also, the ethnic structure of a community in terms of its charter and non-charter groups is determined early and tends to be self-perpetuating. (1965: 60–61)

Porter then goes on to illustrate his point from writings of the period that contain various evaluations regarding the relative merits of such groups as Scandinavians, Bohemians, Slovaks, Italians, Syrians, and Armenians (p. 65).

We can summarize the critical elements of Porter's conception of a Charter Group as follows. A Charter Group is an ethnically defined elite that moves into a new geographical region, establishes its power base (if necessary, displacing the indigenous power bases), and creates a sociopolitical structure distinct from the one that already exists. The Charter Group comes to dominate the key political, economic, and religious institutions of the region. The group consists of its own inner diversity and retains a loyalty to its own milieu of origin. It may understand its own mission, purpose, and destiny in terms of a Charter Myth. Certain outsiders may be allowed to participate in the society dominated by the Charter Group. Admissibility is often determined on the basis of a mythology of race, whereby certain groups are said to possess desirable (or undesirable) characteristics. If admitted, these groups are sometimes given an entrance status that may be susceptible to change over time.

It is important to note that Porter's use of the term Charter Group is something of an aside, in that his purpose is not to construct a sociological model, based on a specific set of data. Rather, he employs the term as a description of certain aspects of the functioning of the elite groups he is studying. In this essay I have used Porter's suggestive comments to develop and nuance the meaning of the term and to suggest its potential value for the study of the Golah.

The Charter Group and the Sociology of Early Persian Yehud: Three Areas of Analysis

As noted above, a Charter Group may be understood as a transplanted, enfranchised elite, supported by external political structures. Given the realities of imperialism, colonialism, ethnic enclaves, and dominant elites in the Achaemenid Period, it is altogether apposite to bring this perspective to bear on the role of the Golah. Of particular interest are the unique, specific ways in which the Golah functioned as a Charter Group. In this study I will analyze three areas: (1) the nature and purpose of the Golah's geographic displacement and enfranchisement; (2) the Golah's control over key sociopolitical institutions; and (3) the Golah's ongoing struggle for self-definition and the inclusion and/or exclusion of outsiders.

Geographical Movement and Enfranchisement

The Golah returnees clearly constituted an identifiable group that moved from one geographical region to another. Texts such as Jeremiah, the DH, Ezra, Nehemiah, Chronicles, as well as Ezekiel take great pains to stress the notion of the movement out of the land of the people, the divine presence, and the temple vessels; then, at the appointed time, their return (Kalimi and Purvis 1994; Ackroyd 1972; Fried 2001: 50–52). In point of fact these sources reveal two perspectives here. Jeremiah, Ezekiel, and the DH view the movement of the exiles in the somber perspective of a forced departure from the land, as a result of unfaithfulness to the covenant. Ezra, Nehemiah, and to a certain degree, Chronicles, by contrast,[23] view the situation optimistically, as a new beginning. As Japhet (2003) states, there, "the history of Judah is seen from the perspective of those who left it and are now about to return." Thus a courageous few, supported by their co-religionists and the Persian throne, undertook a journey fraught with danger into the quasi-unknown to reconquer a territory in the name of their God. We note the clear sense of motion even in the self-designations of this group as those who "return" (שׁוּב, Ezra 2:1; 6:21; Neh 8:17), "come" (בוא, Ezra 3:8), or "come up" (עלה, Ezra 2:1; Neh 7:6, 61) from captivity. Thus from the perspective of Chronicles, Ezra, and Nehemiah, the Golah returnees' mission was, at least in part, to implant a "community of restoration" (cf. Bedford 2002: 154) in the former homeland, a community that would serve as an extension of the influence of the eastern Diaspora—a society that believed itself to have preserved the true Yahwistic faith during the exilic period.

Three highly distinctive features, however, relative to the Golah returnees as a Charter Group must be noted at this point. First, unlike the vast majority of colonists, ancient or modern, who have no traditional ethnic or religious ties to the land, the Golah returnees func-

---

23. On the difference in perspective between DtrH and Ezra–Nehemiah, see Japhet 2003.

tioned as a "refounding" Charter Group. As such they returned to a land to which they laid claim, whether through genealogical heritage, religious tradition, legal title to specific holdings, imperial allotment, or any combination of the above.[24] Furthermore, they claimed and believed themselves to be the sole legitimate heirs of the land, having had a long history in it. Thus at one level the Golah's discourse stresses their distinctiveness from the land's (indigenous) population (Ezra 4:1–3; 9:1–4). Yet at a deeper level it assumes that the local population is not the land's "true" inhabitants or legitimate possessors (Ezekiel 11, 33; Jeremiah 24).

Second, the Golah returnees had a bipartite allegiance, in that they are portrayed as being enfranchised by two distinct centers of power in the Babylonian heartland, rather than a single unified power. The first was the Persian Crown, which is described as appointing governors, authorizing immigration, and permitting temple reconstruction.[25] The second was the Golah remainees. This group possessed its own internal legal, religious, and social structure (Oded 1995; Eph'al 1978; Zadok 1979; Bickerman 1984; Beer 1992). The Golah returnees left the heartland as emissaries and members of this larger religious group (Bedford 2002). The roles and activities of Ezra and Nehemiah testify to the ongoing authority that the Golah remainee community held over the returnees. It is important to note that, in our sources, while a certain honor is attached to those who returned,[26] this granted them no special or autonomous authority vis-à-vis the Babylonian remainees. Thus, in Ezra 1:1–3 there is no critique of those who did not return. Furthermore, texts such as Esther appear to presuppose the ongoing legitimacy of the Diaspora quite apart from any immediate plans to return (see de Pury and Römer 1995).[27] It is also critical to note that the bipartite allegiance of the Golah returnees to the Golah remainees and to

---

24. On the issue of land tenure in Yehud, see Hoglund 1992; Ben Zvi 1995; Pastor 1997; and Rappaport et al. 1994.

25. The historicity of these elements has been and continues to be the subject of significant debate (see Grabbe in this volume, pp. 531–570). For the purposes of the present discussion, it is sufficient to note that some form of return seems likely to have occurred (Grabbe 1998). It is improbable that it could have occurred without Achaemenid authorization.

26. Japhet (2003: 84) sees the concluding words of Chronicles as "an expression of general blessing and encouragement."

27. It is beyond the scope of the present essay to address the issue of the tensions between the possibility of return, the realities of life in the land, the ongoing Diaspora, and the prophetic hope that one day all the exiles would return. However it is clear that Persian-Period Yahwism was able to hold both present and future in creative tension. This issue will be discussed below.

the Persian Crown is in itself complex. On one level it is hierarchical, flowing from the Empire to the Babylonian Golah remainees to the Golah returnees. Yet on another level the Jerusalem authorities could be approached independently. Thus the Persians could deal directly with their appointed governor, and other religious groups, such as the community at Elephantine, could communicate with the Jerusalemite or Samarian authorities on religious matters.

Third, unlike the quest for colonies in other contexts, which frequently grew out of a desire to access new raw materials, to engage in trade, to provide an outlet for excess population, or to enhance national prestige, the returnees' goals appear to have been far more limited. Yehud's reduced population and territory (thus Carter 1999; Lipschits 2003) and its limited economic potential severely restricted its viability and desirability as a locus of immigration. As Blenkinsopp observes with reference to the limited possibilities for a return to Yehud in our period, "most ex-Judeans lived elsewhere" (Blenkinsopp 2000: 129–34, esp. 33–34). Indeed the chronic shortage of resources and labor, and ongoing economic duress are themes running through Haggai, Ezra, and Nehemiah. Neither should Yehud's strategic importance (Briant 2000) or taxation potential be overestimated (see the population figures in Lipschits 2003). Thus the imperial administration's most foundational goal would have been the basic stability of the region. For the Babylonian Golah as a whole, I venture to suggest that the purpose of the reestablishment of a temple-centered community in Yehud was in large measure to provide a tangible anchor[28] for the exilic communities in the east. Such an anchor would provide a geographical center for a now multicentric Yahwism, and through that visible community, a link both to the traditions of the past and to the earlier eschatological hopes for the future. Thus, in many ways the Babylonian Golah's interest in Yehud was far less an economic or demographic venture than an attempt at ethnic, cultural, and religious identification with a geographic site deeply rooted in the community's historical and religious heritage.

Control of Key Sociopolitical Institutions

The Golah returnees dominated the major institutions of Yehud. A combination of circumstantial factors and Persian imperial decisions placed the members of this group in an especially advantageous position and gave them virtual hegemony over the province. The return-

---

28. Note the evocative image of the Jerusalem community as a 'nail' or 'tent peg' יתד in Ezra 9:8.

ees' "circumstantial" advantages, primarily related to their experience of exile, would have included the following: (1) genealogical connections to members of the former ruling elite, thus providing some claim to traditional legitimacy as power-holders (e.g., Sheshbazzar and Zerubbabel); (2) literacy on the part of some (cf. Oded 1995: 205, 208); (3) bilingualism, in an environment in which Aramaic constituted the lingua franca of politics and commerce;[29] (4) experience at self-organization and self-administration in the broader context of an ethnically and religiously diverse environment (Oded 1995; 2000; Eph'al 1978; Zadok 1979; Bickerman 1984; Beer 1992); (5) greater and more direct contact with the policies and practices of the imperial political and fiscal administration. As Briant notes, Persian rule was only progressively attained in the west, and the Golah returnees would have been at a distinct advantage as its effects were felt (Briant 1996: 1.59; Bianchi 1995: 17).

Even more significant were the advantages conferred upon the Golah returnees by the Persian throne. All the biblical sources view oversight in the nascent community at Jerusalem as having been bestowed upon the members of the Babylonian Jewish community who furnished the personnel and some of the finances to repopulate the area and to rebuild its temple (2 Chr 36:23; Ezra 1:1–6). Members of this group occupied the key political and religious institutions (Sheshbazzar: Ezra 1:8; 5:14; Zerubbabel: Ezra 3:2; Hag 1:1; Joshua: Hag 1:1; Ezra: Ezra 7:1–7; and Nehemiah: Neh 2:1–10). The historical likelihood of this portrait is suggested by the fact that such a policy was entirely in line with the so-called "dynastic model" employed by the Persians, whereby members of the former ruling elite, deposed by the Babylonians, were reinstated and served to further imperial interests (Briant 1982: 199–225; Bianchi 1994: 153–65). There is significant evidence from Sogdiana, Bactriana, Phoenicia, Cyprus, and Cilicia (cf. Lemaire 1996; Bianchi 1994, with bibliography; Briant 1982) to demonstrate the extent to which the Persians employed this model. Furthermore, the Golah returnees had the most direct access to and benefit from the subventions and fiscal support of both the Persian Crown and the Golah remainee community.[30]

---

29. As noted by Lemaire 1994a: 22. On the use of Hebrew in Yehud and Aramaic in the surrounding provinces and the Empire, see Lipiński 1990. On bilingualism in the Levant, see Lemaire 1996. See also the provocative discussion of bilingualism and Late Biblical Hebrew by F. Polak in the present volume, pp. 589–628.

30. On the fiscal role of the Jerusalemite Temple, see Schaper 1995; 1997. Briant (1996: 1.423) notes Persian support for local elites who collected taxes. Golah remainee and

Thus, the Babylonian Golah community, specifically through its delegated returnees, was entrusted with the direction of Yahwistic interests in Yehud. This status has been intuitively felt by historians of the period. In 1909, R. Kittel commented that Cyrus authorized the Babylonian community to rebuild the temple because these were "the only Jews he knew" (1909: 329). In 1954 Allrik (1954: 24) described the so-called Golah list in Ezra 2 as a "charter and a constitution." Galling (1951: 156–57) similarly saw the same list as having been compiled because legal authorization to participate in the temple rebuilding was limited to the Golah returnees. Similar lines of approach are followed by Talmon (1953) and Schultz (1980: 224, 234). Weisberg's evidence regarding guild structure during the reign of Cyrus (1967: chap. 2) suggests that certain groups could be given an exclusive "charter" (to use Weisberg's term) to undertake a given project. More recently, Briant, noting that relations between the Crown and local powers were regulated by contracts, has stated that the Judeans in Jerusalem received "une véritable Chartre" (Briant 1987: 6).

Thus the returnees were "Persia's Loyal Yahwists"—an ethnically defined group whose mission was to found (or in this case to reestablish) a community and central shrine around a shared version of the worship of Yahweh, in subjection to and with the support of the Persian Crown and their co-religionists in the east. Let me hasten, however, to nuance this assertion. D. L. Smith-Christopher (1989; 2002) has provided a helpful balance to this discussion. He appropriately stresses, first, the horrors of deportation and the rigors of exilic experience; second, the fact that resistance to foreign rule may be displayed in ways other than overt rebellion; and third, that the experience of the Golah returnees testified to the duress imposed on the community in Yehud due to Achaemenid taxation burdens. Indeed, I would add, the returnees' self-designation as "those who had escaped from the captivity" (שְׁבִי; cf. Ezra 2:1; Neh 1:3; 8:17) testified to their own conscious recognition of their dispossessed status. It is thus significant to understand the loyalty of the Golah to the Persians as provisional and limited, though nonetheless real. Persian initiatives, economic hardships notwithstanding, stood in general continuity with the aspirations and daily experience of the Golah remainees and returnees and, as an interim arrangement, it had much to commend itself (Kessler 1992: 74, 84; 2002: 259–61).

Achaemenid financial support for the political and cultic leadership in Yehud is a leitmotif running through Ezra–Nehemiah.

Furthermore, as Briant (1987: 15) has noted, Persian imperial policy specifically permitted the elites it installed to perpetuate their own traditions and sense of identity. He states, "a lively consciousness persisted in many territories, of belonging to an ethno-cultural community whose principles and goals were opposed to those of the Persians" (1987: 15).[31] What is more, the constraints involved in return to the land were such that a significant number of exiles were content to remain in Mesopotamia or Egypt (Blenkinsopp 2002; de Pury and Römer 1995). Thus, while the deleterious aspects of exile and foreign domination must not be unduly minimized, the viability of Jewish accommodation to Persian rule, whether in Yehud or the imperial heartland, must be kept squarely in view. Persian rule, generally speaking, worked toward the Golah's aspirations, rather than against them.

The returnees' status created a situation in which this group held a significant degree of power over elements of the Yahwistic constituency on two levels. The first was vis-à-vis the remainees within Yehud, where, as argued above, the returnees held the dominant position (Blenkinsopp 1991: 47; Lemaire 1994a: 22–23).[32] The second was with reference to the Yahwistic communities outside Yehud. Even if centers of Yahweh worship were to be found at other sites,[33] control of the Jerusalem Temple was no small endowment. However, despite its privileged position, the Golah did not exist in a demographic vacuum, nor could its members live in total isolation, as we have seen. Thus, questions of identity, inclusion, and exclusion become highly significant, and it is to this subject we now turn.

Identity, Inclusion and Exclusion:
The Golah and the Development of Jewish Identity

As noted above, group self-definition constitutes a critically important dimension of a Charter Group, since such elites by definition displace competing power bases and control the key institutions of a society. In Ezra–Nehemiah, three key elements serve to demarcate Golah members and differentiate them from other groups. The first is

---

31. Translation mine.

32. For the opposite view, see Ben Zvi (1995: 107), quoting Smith (1991).

33. See the contribution of Lemaire in the present volume, pp. 413–456. The question of the nature and function of other centers of Yahweh worship in our period is beyond the scope of this study.

genealogical/ethnic roots in the former Kingdom of Judah. This dimension is stressed by the extensive attention to genealogy in Ezra, Nehemiah, and Chronicles and the notion of the "holy seed" (Ezra 9:2, 8; cf. North 1971; Smith-Christopher 2002: 151–60).

The second is the experience of exile. This is evident both in the self-designations used for this group, such as הגולה ('Golah', Ezra 1:11; 9:4; 10:6; Neh 7:6; Esth 2:6) בני הגולה ('descendants of the Golah', Ezra 4:1; 6:19–20; 10:7; cf. Bedford 2001: 149), and the fact that the land is presented as empty. Furthermore, it is reinforced by the broader notion found in various prophetic texts that the Exile served as a purification for and punishment of the sins of the former kingdom (Gunneweg 1983). It is also implied by the understanding of the returnees as a remnant (Ezra 9:8; Hag 1:12, 14; 2:2; Zech 8:6). The third element is attachment to and acceptance of the specific form of Yahwism formulated by the Golah. Central to this formulation is adherence to the "Law of Moses," however defined[34] (on these three as defining elements, see Gunneweg 1983; Rappaport 1996).

Based upon this "neat and tidy" self-understanding, typified in Ezra and Nehemiah, the nature of Golah membership and its self-defined "charter mission" were clear. However life seldom accommodates itself easily to abstract, theoretical formulations. The experience of Charter Groups, both ancient and modern, must rise to a variety of challenges. Furthermore, as these challenges were confronted, divisions within the Charter Group itself appeared. The biblical texts reveal, both explicitly and unwittingly, the various questions faced by the Golah returnee community and the responses given. One critical issue here is the question of boundaries for membership and participation in the emerging Jerusalem community, especially in its cultic and economic life. Several factors made this question especially poignant: (1) the extent of the destruction of its temple and the need to maximize the potential labor pool;[35] (2) the highly reduced demographic levels in Yehud in general and Jerusalem in particular (Lipschits 2003; and Ussishkin in this volume, pp. 147–166); (3) the fact that the land was not empty, and some of the returnees found themselves to have kinship and religious ties with the resident population within and beyond Yehud (cf. independently Rappaport 1996: 966); (4) the existence of vari-

---

34. The themes of the return to Zion and the reconstruction of the temple were also highly significant but cannot be discussed here.

35. Lipschits (2003: 365) notes the difficulty of the returnees in finding adequate manpower and resources.

ous Yahweh worshipers of a diversity of genealogical origins and with divergent religious beliefs and practices who sought to have a stake in the rebuilding of the temple; and (5) the fact that, once the temple was rebuilt, it became a significant center of interest and power in the Yahwistic landscape of the period. Furthermore, it is essential to add that all of this was played out in the context of Persian military, strategic, and economic interests in the west.

It seems likely that the above-mentioned elements would produce movements in two opposite directions: inclusion and exclusion. Let us examine these in turn.

Movement toward Inclusion

A variety of factors would have militated in favor of an *inclusive* stance directed toward those who, strictly speaking, may not have met the aforementioned three criteria for membership in the Golah returnee group. These included the need for labor, the desire to increase the community's economic and demographic clout, kinship ties, and a shared desire to reconstruct the temple and to participate in its worship (cf. Rappaport 1996).

Evidence from our biblical sources bears witness to various strategies of inclusion employed. In the early period, the book of Haggai is inclusivistic in orientation, calling all without distinction to participate in the rebuilding project (2:1–5). The entire community, described as a remnant, is presented as acting in concert, in obedience to the prophet's words (1:12–15). To be sure, such a presentation is somewhat tendentious in light of the book's purpose as an apologia for Haggai and the importance of the prophetic role. Nevertheless, it is clear that the text excludes no one.[36] A similar inclusive stance is found at a much later period in Chronicles, which views those in the North as eligible for participation in the temple worship (Cogan 1988: 291; Braun 1977). Even the highly exclusivist text of Ezra–Nehemiah bears witness to subtle inclusivist strategies. In Ezra 2 and Nehemiah 7, the listing of returnees by place-names likely implies a technique whereby Yehudite remainees could be counted as Golah returnees (Japhet 1983: 114; Dyck 2000). A similar tactic is evidenced in Ezra 6:21, where participation in the Passover is open not only to the Golah group but to all who purify themselves from the uncleanness of the surrounding nations (Bedford

---

36. I do not accept the so-called "Samaritan hypothesis," whereby Hag 2:10–19 is a rejection of "foreign assistance." For a fuller discussion and bibliography, see Kessler 2002: 210–18.

2002: 150). Similarly, as Japhet (2003) suggests, Ezra 6:3–5 and Neh 1:3 may reflect conditions of an earlier period in which the non-exiled population was included with the returnees.

Such an inclusive policy would have served the interests of Golah returnee Charter Group, the Golah remainees, and the Persians in a number of ways. Most significant among these would be the speedy reconstruction of the temple, social cohesion under the leadership of the Golah returnees, and demographic and economic development.

Movement toward Exclusion

However, at the same time, such an inclusivist orientation would have generated forces of exclusion, specifically when it threatened to dislodge the Charter Group's hegemony over the social, political, and religious life of the province, or, perhaps more importantly, its own sense of identity rooted in the common shared historical experience of exile.

Thus, when exclusionary forces emerged, spurred on by a combination of the factors just mentioned, appeal could easily be made to the three boundary criteria of genealogical roots in the land, experience of exile, and adherence to the Law of Moses. The application of these exclusionary measures is abundantly clear in Ezra–Nehemiah. Northern Yahwists could be written off as having no genealogical history in the land (Ezra 4:1–2). The mere existence of nondeported Yehudite Yahwists could be obscured by the presentation of the land as empty. Adherence to the Law of Moses could be measured by conformity to practices of endogamy and Sabbath observance (Nehemiah 13; Ezra 10). Failure to comply could result in the forfeiture of property, economic privilege, or community membership (Ezra 7:26; 10:8). It is noteworthy that such measures could be applied both outwardly (toward non-exiled Yahwists) and inwardly, within the Golah returnee community, opening the way for sectarianism. Furthermore, as Blenkinsopp (1981) has suggested, sectarian tendencies in the Golah returnees could have been mimicked by other non-exiled communities.

The causes of this mid-fifth century contraction are debated. One group of studies view Persian imperial policy as highly significant. Thus Fried (2002) sees Nehemiah's exclusionary measures as a Persian-supported attempt to break local power bases. Bodi (2001: 85) takes a very similar position and stresses the Persian attachment to endogamy. Hoglund (1992: 236–40) similarly views the insistence on endogamy as a reflection of a Persian desire to tighten control in the west by keeping various land-based groups separate from one another.[37] A similar approach is followed by T. Eskenazi (1992), who views land tenure as a critical element. Thus the reaction against foreign wives was an attempt to prevent the transfer of land outside the kinship group.[38] Viewed from the perspective of the Golah as Charter Group, such insistence on endogamy (with its potential impact on land tenure) could be seen as but one element of the group's broader reaction to the perceived threat posed to its identity by a more inclusive stance.

One group especially sensitive to this inclusive stance would have been the Babylonian Golah remainees, who risked the loss of a significant measure of control over the life in Yehud. To borrow Bedford's (2002: 154) colorful terminology, there may have been a fear among the remainees in the east that the returnees were "going native." Ezra (Ezra 9:4–5; 10:10) and Nehemiah (Neh 13:23–27) may be seen to be representative of Golah remainees who were clearly threatened by the more open stance toward marriage with the peoples of the land practiced by the returnees. Similarly Nehemiah (Neh 13:4–9, 15–22, 28) stands opposed to the locals' willingness to accommodate the economic and religious practices of other non-Golah Yahwists who frequented the temple. After all, the Golah remainees had to face such assimilationist pressures at home. It was perhaps beyond their conceptual framework to conceive of the "others" surrounding the members of their group in Yehud not as Gentiles but as Yahwists of a different stripe, with differing interpretations of Yahwistic piety.

Furthermore, such openness also clearly threatened the interests of some within the Golah returnees, as well. Consequently, as Eskenazi (1989) has observed, much impetus for the exclusionary measures taken arose from within the community itself (Ezra 9:1–2; 10:2–5, 7–8). Several reasons may have prompted such a reaction: loyalty to the religious practices of the remainees in the east (the "old ways"), fear of the economic and political encroachment of the province to the North, and protection of priestly privilege.

---

37. Space does not permit the discussion of this approach here. The hypothesis of close Persian involvement in Yehud's internal affairs has been critiqued from a variety of angles. Briant (2002) raises the question of why Yehud, somewhat removed from the major trade routes, should receive such attention. From another perspective, Janzen (2000) views the political dimension of Ezra's mission as superimposed and extraneous. The essays in Watts (2001) deal with other aspects of the question.

38. Eskenazi does not stress the role of Persian policy.

Historically speaking, however, the high-water mark of the fifth-century exclusionary forces did not last. Rather, such forces yielded to a more inclusive stance, as evidenced in Ruth, Chronicles, and Judith (Rappaport 1996: 968). In such a context, the elements of genealogical roots in the Southern Kingdom and experience of exile were softened, and formal conversion and a dedication to adherence to normative Jewish practice were deemed sufficient for inclusion in the community of Yahweh. Various forces may have emerged in the late fourth century that favored a more inclusive policy. Included here are possibly the legitimization of the Diaspora communities, the weakening of Persian rule, the diminution of Samarian influence, or a desire to draw Yahwists of all stripes into the temple's orbit (cf. Rappaport 1996). Perhaps, however, we ought not to attempt to delimit one or another factor as decisive. Rather, it may be better to view the Charter itself as having outlived its functional usefulness. Thus the Charter—that feature of Persian Imperial policy that gave preferential status to the returnee community in Yehud—born in the late sixth and early fifth centuries, required a radical renegotiation in light of the political, sociological, demographic, and religious realities of the late fourth century. However that may be, one may, I suggest, affirm that in good measure the religious, social, and political dynamics of the community of Golah returnees in Yehud can be seen as the reflexes of contraction and expansion experienced by this Charter Group as it encountered the challenges of its environment.

In sum, then, we have seen that the Yahwistic landscape of the Persian Period is diverse, rich, and variegated and one fraught with a wide variety of power dynamics. The Golah returnees functioned as a Charter Group—that is, an elite who moved into a new territory, as representative both of the imperial Crown and the home religious community. Indeed, as Lipschits argues,[39] the installation and effective functioning of the Golah as an elite may have been a critical and decisive element in the emergence of Yehud as a center in the mid-fifth century. The Golah's role generated a number of dynamics, of which questions of identity and self-definition and the exclusion and inclusion of other groups and communities were an integral part. Viewing the Golah returnees as a Charter Group may indeed provide a valuable platform from which to assess and understand the sociopolitical dynamics at work in Persian Yehud.

---

39. See Lipschits in the present volume, pp. 19–52.

Bibliography

Ackroyd, P. R.
1972   The Temple Vessels: A Continuity Theme. Pp. 166–81 in Vetus Testamentum Supplement 22. *Congress Volume: Uppsala, 1971,* ed. H. Ringgren. Leiden.

Albertz, R., and Becking, B. (eds.)
2003   *Yahwism after the Exile: Perspectives on Israelite Religion in the Persian Era.* Assen.

Allrik, H. L.
1954   The Lists of Zerubbabel (Nehemiah 7 and Ezra 2) and the Hebrew Numeral Notation. *Bulletin of the American Schools of Oriental Research* 136: 21–27.

Amit, Y.
2003   Epoch and Genre: The Sixth Century and the Growth of Hidden Polemics. Pp. 135–52 in *Judah and the Judeans in the Neo-Babylonian Period,* ed. O. Lipschits and J. Blenkinsopp. Winona Lake, Indiana.

Bar-Kochva, B.
1996   *Pseudo-Hecataeus On the Jews.* Berkeley.

Barstad, H. M.
1996   *The Myth of the Empty Land: A Study in the History and Archaeology of Judah during the "Exilic" Period.* Symbolae Osloenses Supplement Series 28. Oslo.

Becking, B., and Korpel, M. C. A. (eds.)
1999   *The Crisis of Israelite Religion: Transformation of Religious Tradition in Exilic and Post-exilic Times.* Oudtestamentische Studiën. Leiden.

Bedford, P. R.
2001   *Temple Restoration in Early Achaemenid Judah.* Journal for the Study of Judaism in the Persian, Hellenistic, and Roman Periods Supplement Series 63. Leiden.
2002   Diaspora: Homeland Relations in Ezra–Nehemiah. *Vetus Testamentum* 52: 147–65.

Beer, M.
1992   Babylonian Judaism. Pp. 1076–83 in vol. 3 of *Anchor Bible Dictionary,* ed. D. N. Freedman. New York.

Beit-Arieh, I.
1996   Edomites Advance into Judah. *Biblical Archaeology Review* 22/6: 28–36.

Ben Zvi, E.
1995   Inclusion in and Exclusion from "Israel" in Post-monarchic Biblical Texts. Pp. 95–149 in *The Pitcher Is Broken,* ed. S. W. Holloway and L. K. Handy. Journal for the Study of the Old Testament Supplement 190. Sheffield.

Berquist, J. L.
1995   *Judaism in Persia's Shadow: A Social and Historical Approach.* Minneapolis.

Bianchi, F.
1994   Le rôle de Zorobabel et la dynastie davidique en Judée du VIe siècle au IIe siècle av. J.-C. *Transeuphratène* 7: 153–65.

1995   *I superstiti della deportazione sono là nella provincia (Neemia 1,3): Ricerche storico-bibliche sulla Giudea in età neobabilonese e achemenide (586 a.c.–442 a.c.).* Annali dell'Istituto Orientale di Napoli Supplement Series 82, agli Annali 55/1. Naples.

Bickerman, E. J.
1984   The Diaspora: The Babylonian Captivity. Pp. 342–57 in *Introduction: The Persian Period*, ed. W. D. Davies and L. Finkelstein. Vol. 1 of *The Cambridge History of Judaism*. Cambridge.

Blenkinsopp, J.
1981   Interpretation and the Tendency to Sectarianism: An Aspect of Second Temple History. Pp. 1–26 in vol. 2 of *Aspects of Judaism in the Graeco-Roman Period*, ed. A. Mendelson. Philadelphia.
1990   A Jewish Sect of the Persian Period. *Catholic Biblical Quarterly* 52: 5–20.
1991   Temple and Society in Achaemenid Judah. Pp. 22–53 in *Second Temple Studies 1: Persian Period*, ed. P. R. Davies. Journal for the Study of the Old Testament Supplement 117. Sheffield.
1998   The Judean Priesthood during the Neo-Babylonian and Achaemenid Periods: A Hypothetical Reconstruction. *Catholic Biblical Quarterly* 60: 25–43.
2000   A Case of Benign Imperial Neglect and Its Consequences. *Biblical Interpretation* 8: 129–36.
2002   The Bible, Archaeology and Politics; or The Empty Land Revisited. *Journal for the Study of the Old Testament* 27: 169–87.
2003   Bethel in the Neo-Babylonian Period. Pp. 93–108 in *Judah and the Judeans in the Neo-Babylonian Period*, ed. O. Lipschits and J. Blenkinsopp. Winona Lake, Indiana.

Bodi, D.
2001   La clémence des Perses envers Néhémie et ses compatriotes: Faveur ou opportunisme politique? *Transeuphratène* 21: 69–86.

Borgen, P.
1992   Judaism (Egypt). Pp. 1076–83 in vol. 3 of *Anchor Bible Dictionary*, ed. D. N. Freedman. New York.

Braun, R. L.
1977   A Reconsideration of the Chronicler's Attitude toward the North. *Journal of Biblical Literature* 96: 59–62.

Briant, P.
1982   Contrainte militaire, dépendance rurale et exploitation des territoires en Asie achéménide. Pp. 199–225 in *Rois, tributs et paysans: Études sur les formations tributaires du Moyen-Orient ancien.* Centre de Recherche d'Histoire Ancienne 43, Annales Littéraires de l'Université de Besançon 269. Paris.
1987   Pouvoir central et polycentrisme culturel dans l'empire achéménide: Quelques réflexions et suggestions. Pp. 1–31 in *Achaemenid History I: Sources, Structures and Synthesis*, ed. H. Sancisi-Weerdenberg. Leiden.
1996   *Histoire de l'empire perse de Cyrus à Alexandre.* 2 Vols. Achaemenid History 10. Leiden. English edition: *From Cyrus to Alexander: A History of the Persian Empire*, trans. P. T. Daniels. Winona Lake, Indiana, 2002.

2000   Histoire impériale et histoire régionale: A propos de l'histoire de Juda dans l'Empire achéménide. Pp. 235–45 in *Congress Volume: Oslo, 1998*, ed. A. Lemaire and M. Saebø. Vetus Testamentum Supplement 80. Leiden.

Briend, J.
1996   L'édit de Cyrus et sa valeur historique. *Transeuphratène* 11: 33–44.

Cardascia, G.
1951   *Les archives des Murasû*. Paris.

Carroll R., M. D.
1992   The Myth of the Empty Land. *Semeia* 59: 79–93.

Carter, C. E.
1996   A Discipline in Transition: The Contributions of the Social Sciences to the Study of the Hebrew Bible. Pp. 3–36 in *Community, Identity, and Ideology: Social Science Approaches to the Hebrew Bible*, ed. C. E. Carter and C. L. Meyers. Sources for Biblical and Theological Study 6. Winona Lake, Indiana.
1999   *The Emergence of Yehud in the Persian Period*. Journal for the Study of the Old Testament Supplement 294. Sheffield.

Chancey, M. A.
2002   *The Myth of a Gentile Galilee*. Society for New Testament Studies Monograph Series 118. Cambridge.

Cogan, M.
1988   For We, like You, Worship Your God. *Vetus Testamentum* 38: 286–92.

Cohen, S. J. D.
1999   *The Beginnings of Jewishness: Boundaries, Varieties, Uncertainties*. Hellenistic Culture and Society. Berkeley.

Cowley, A.
1923   *Aramaic Papyri of the Fifth Century B.C.* Oxford.

Dexinger, F.
1981   Limits of Tolerance in Judaism: The Samaritan Example. Pp. 88–114 in *Aspects of Judaism in the Graeco-Roman Period*, ed. E. P. Sanders, A. I. Baumgarten, and A. Mendelson. Philadelphia.

Dollot, L.
1981   *Le Libéria: Que Sais-Je?* Paris.

Dyck, J. E.
2000   Ezra 2 in Ideological Critical Perspective. Pp. 129–45 in *Rethinking Contexts, Rereading Texts*, ed. M. D. Carroll R. Journal for the Study of the Old Testament Supplement 299. Sheffield.

Edelman, D. V. (ed.)
1996   *The Triumph of Elohim: From Yahwisms to Judaisms*. Grand Rapids, Michigan.

Eph'al, I.
1978   The Western Minorities in Babylonia in the 6th–5th Centuries B.C. *Orientalia* 47: 74–80.
1998   Changes in Palestine during the Persian Period in Light of Epigraphic Sources. *Israel Exploration Journal* 48: 106–19.

Eskenazi, T. C.
1989   Ezra–Nehemiah: From Text to Actuality. Pp. 165–97 in _Signs and Wonders: Biblical Texts in Literary Focus_, ed. C. Exum. Atlanta.
1992   Out from the Shadows: Biblical Women in the Post-exilic Era. _Journal for the Study of the Old Testament_ 54: 25–43.
Frei, P.
2001   Persian Imperial Authorization: A Summary. Pp. 5–40 in _Persia and Torah: The Theory of Imperial Authorization of the Pentateuch_, ed. J. W. Watts. Society of Biblical Literature Symposium Series 17. Atlanta.
Frei, P., and Koch, K.
1984   _Reichsidee und Reichsorganisation im Perserreich._ Orbis biblicus et orientalis 55. Fribourg.
Freyne, S.
1980   _Galilee from Alexander the Great to Hadrian, 323 BCE to 135 CE: A Study of Second Temple Judaism._ Wilmington, Delaware.
Fried, L. S.
2001   "You Shall Appoint Judges": Ezra's Mission and the Rescript of Artaxerxes. Pp. 63–89 in _Persia and Torah: The Theory of Imperial Authorization of the Pentateuch_, ed. J. W. Watts. Society of Biblical Literature Symposium Series 17. Atlanta.
2002   The Political Struggle of Fifth Century Judah. _Transeuphratène_ 24: 9–21.
Gal, Z.
1998   Israel in Exile. _Biblical Archaeology Review_ 24: 48–53.
Galling, K.
1951   The "Gola-History" according to Ezra 2 and Nehemiah 7. _Journal of Biblical Literature_ 70: 149–58.
Grabbe, L. L.
1998   "The Exile" under the Theodolite: Historiography as Triangulation. Pp. 80–99 in _Leading Captivity Captive_, ed. L. L. Grabbe. Journal for the Study of the Old Testament Supplement 278. Sheffield.
Graham, J. N.
1984   Vinedressers and Ploughmen: 2 Kings 52:12 and Jeremiah 52:16. _Biblical Archaeologist_ 47: 55–58.
Gunneweg, A. H. J.
1983   עם הארץ: A Semantic Revolution. _Zeitschrift für die alttestamentliche Wissenschaft_ 95: 437–40.
Hamilton, M. W.
1995   Who Was a Jew? Jewish Ethnicity during the Achaemenid Period. _Restoration Quarterly_ 37: 102–17.
Hanson, P. D.
1975   _The Dawn of Apocalyptic._ Philadelphia.
Hjelm, I.
2000   _The Samaritans and Early Judaism: A Literary Analysis._ Journal for the Study of the Old Testament Supplement 303. Sheffield.

Hoglund, K. G.
1992 *Achaemenid Imperial Administration in Syria–Palestine and the Missions of Ezra and Nehemiah.* Society of Biblical Literature Dissertation Series 125. Atlanta.

Janssen, E.
1956 *Juda in der Exilszeit: Ein Beitrag zur Frage der Entstehung des Judentums.* Forschungen zur Religion und Literatur des Alten und Neuen Testaments 69. Göttingen.

Janzen, D.
2000 The "Mission" of Ezra and the Persian-Period Temple Community. *Journal of Biblical Literature* 119: 619–43.

Japhet, S.
1983 People and Land in the Restoration Period. Pp. 103–25 in *Das Land Israel in biblischer Zeit,* ed. G. Strecker. Göttingen.
2003 Periodization: Between History and Ideology—The Neo-Babylonian Period in Biblical Historiography. Pp. 75–89 in *Judah and the Judeans in the Neo-Babylonian Period,* ed. O. Lipschits and J. Blenkinsopp. Winona Lake, Indiana.

Joannès, F., and Lemaire, A.
1999 Trois tablettes cunéiformes à onomastique ouest-sémitique (collection Sh. Moussaïef). *Transeuphratène* 17: 17–34.

Kalimi, I., and Purvis, J. D.
1994 King Jehoiachin and the Vessels of the Lord's House in Biblical Literature. *Catholic Biblical Quarterly* 56: 449–57.

Kessler, J.
1992 The Second Year of Darius and the Prophet Haggai. *Transeuphratène* 5: 63–84.
2001 Reconstructing Haggai's Jerusalem: Demographic and Sociological Considerations and the Quest for an Adequate Methodological Point of Departure. Pp. 137–58 in *Every City Shall Be Forsaken.* Journal for the Study of the Old Testament Supplement 330, ed. L. L. Grabbe and R. D. Haak. Sheffield.
2002 *The Book of Haggai: Prophecy and Society in Early Persian Yehud.* Vetus Testamentum Supplement Series 91. Leiden.

Kittel, R.
1909 *Geschichte des Volkes Israel.* Gotha.

Knauf, E. A.
2002 Elephantine und das vor-biblische Judentum. *Religion und Religionskontakte im Zeitaler der Achämeniden,* ed. R. G. Kratz. Veröffenlichungen der Wissenschaftlichen Gesellschaft für Theologie 22. Gütersloh.

Knoppers, G. N.
2001 An Archaemenid Imperial Authorization of Torah in Yehud? Pp. 115–34 in *Persia and Torah: The Theory of Imperial Authorization of the Pentateuch,* ed. J. W. Watts. Society of Biblical Literature Symposium Series 17. Atlanta.

Kreissig, H.
  1973   *Die sozialökonomische Situation in Juda zur Achämenidzeit.* Schriften zur
         Geschichte und Kultur des Alten Orients 7. Berlin.
Lemaire, A.
  1990   Populations et territoires de la Palestine à l'époque perse. *Transeuphra-
         tène* 3: 31–74.
  1994a Histoire et administration de la Palestine à l'époque Perse. Pp. 11–53 in
         La Palestine à l'époque Perse, ed. E.-M. Laperrousaz and A. Lemaire.
         Paris.
  1994b Les transformations politiques et culturelles de la Transjordanie au
         VIᵉ siècle av. J.C. *Transeuphratène* 8: 9–27.
  1996   Zorobabel et la Judée à la lumière de l'épigraphie (fin du VIᵉ s. av.
         J.-C.). *Revue Biblique* 103: 48–57.
  2001   Épigraphie et religion en Palestine à l'époque achéménide. *Transeu-
         phratène* 22: 97–113.
Lemaire, A., and Lozachmeur, A.
  1996   Remarques sur le plurilinguisme en Asie Mineur à l'époque perse.
         Pp. 91–123 in *Mosaïque de langues, mosaïque culturelle: Le bilinguisme
         dans le Proche-Orient ancien,* ed. F. Briquel-Chatonnet. Antiquités sé-
         mitiques 1. Paris.
Liebenow, J. G.
  1987   *Liberia: The Quest for Democracy.* Bloomington, Indiana.
Lipiński, E.
  1990   Géographie linguistique de la Transeuphratène à l'époque achémé-
         nide. *Transeuphratène* 3: 95–107.
Lipschits, O.
  1998   Nebuchadnezzar's Policy in "Hattu-Land" and the Fate of the King-
         dom of Judah. *Ugarit-Forschungen* 30: 467–87.
  1999   The History of the Benjamin Region under Babylonian Rule. *Tel Aviv*
         26: 155–90.
  2002   Literary and Ideological Aspects of Nehemiah 11. *Journal of Biblical Lit-
         erature* 121: 423–40.
  2003   Demographic Changes in Judah between the Seventh and the Fifth
         Centuries B.C.E. Pp. 323–76 in *Judah and the Judeans in the Neo-Babylonian
         Period,* ed. O. Lipschits and J. Blenkinsopp. Winona Lake, Indiana.
Mantel, H. H. D.
  1973   The Dichotomy of Judaism during the Second Temple. *Hebrew Union
         College Annual* 44: 55–87.
Milevski, I.
  1996   Settlement Patterns in Northern Judah during the Achaemenid Pe-
         riod, According to the Hill Country of Benjamin and Jerusalem Sur-
         veys. *Bulletin of the Anglo-Israel Archaeological Society* 15: 7–29.
Naveh, J.
  1971   An Aramaic Ostracon from Ashdod. *ʾAtiqot* 9/10: 200–201.
  1985   Published and Unpublished Aramaic Ostraca. *ʾAtiqot* 17: 114–21.

1992   Aramaic Ostraca and Jar Inscription from Tell Jemmeh. *ʾAtiqot* 21: 49–53.

North, R.
1971   Civil Authority in Ezra. Pp. 377–404 in *Studi in onore di Edoardo Volterra*, ed. E. Volterra. Pubblicazioni della Facoltà di giurisprudenza dell'Università di Roma. Milan.

Oded, B.
1977   The Separate States of Israel and Judah. *Israelite and Judean History*, ed. J. H. Hayes and J. M. Miller. London.
1995   Observations on the Israelite/Judean Exiles in Mesopotamia during the Eight–Sixth Centuries BCE. Pp. 205–12 in *Immigration and Emigration in the Ancient Near East: Festschrift E. Lipiński*, ed. K. van Lerberge and A. Schoors. Leuven.
2000   The Settlements of the Israelite and Judean Exiles in Mesopotamia in the 8th–6th Centuries B.C.E. *Studies in Historical Geography and Biblical Historiography Presented to Zecharia Kallai*, ed. G. Galil and M. Weinfeld. Vetus Testamentum Supplement Series 81. Leiden.
2003   Where is the "Myth of the Empty Land" to be Found? Pp. 55–74 in *Judah and the Judeans in the Neo-Babylonian Period*, ed. J. Blenkinsopp. Winona Lake, Indiana.

Pastor, J.
1997   *Land and Economy in Ancient Palestine*. London.

Porten, B.
1984   The Diaspora: The Jews in Egypt. Pp. 372–400 in *Introduction: The Persian Period*, ed. W. D. Davies and L. Finkelstein. Vol. 1 in *The Cambridge History of Judaism*. Cambridge.
2003   Settlement of the Jews at Elephantine and the Arameans at Syene. Pp. 451–70 in *Judah and the Judeans in the Neo-Babylonian Period*, ed. O. Lipschits and J. Blenkinsopp. Winona Lake, Indiana.

Porten, B., and Yardeni, A.
1986   *Letters*. Vol. 1 of *Textbook of Aramaic Documents from Ancient Egypt*. Jerusalem.

Porter, J.
1965   *The Vertical Mosaic: A Study of Social Class and Power in Canada*. Toronto; Buffalo.

Pury, A. D. de, and Römer, T.
1995   Terres d'exil et terres d'accueil: Quelques réflexions sur le judaïsme postexilique face à la Perse et à l'Égypte. *Transeuphratène* 9: 25–34.

Rappaport, U.
1996   Les juifs et leurs voisins. *Annales-Histoire, Sciences Sociales* 51: 955–74.

Rappaport, U., et al.
1994   Land, Society and Culture in Judea. *Transeuphratène* 7: 73–82.

Rofé, A.
1988   The Onset of Sects in Postexilic Judaism: Neglected Evidence from the Septuagint, Trito-Isaiah, Ben Sira and Malachi. Pp. 39–49 in *The Social World of Formative Christianity and Judaism*, ed. J. Neusner. Philadelphia.

Sapin, J.
2003   Un rééquilibrage archéologique concernant la Judée à l'époque perse à propos d'un ouvrage récent. *Transeuphratène* 26: 121–41.

Schaper, J.
1995   The Jerusalem Temple as an Instrument of Achaemenid Fiscal Administration. *Vetus Testamentum* 45: 528–39.
1997   The Temple Treasury Committee in the Times of Nehemiah and Ezra. *Vetus Testamentum* 47: 200–206.

Schultz, C.
1980   The Political Tensions Reflected in Ezra–Nehemiah. Pp. 221–44 in *Scripture in Context: Essays in the Comparative Method*, ed. W. W. Hallo. Pittsburgh.

Ska, J. L.
2001   Essai sur la nature et la signification du cycle d'Abraham (Gn. 11,27–25,11). *Studies in the Book of Genesis: Literature, Redaction and History*, ed. A. Wénin. Leuven.

Smith, D. L.
1991   The Politics of Ezra: Sociological Indicators of Postexilic Judean Society. Pp. 73–97 in vol. 1 of *Second Temple Studies*, ed. P. R. Davies. Journal for the Study of the Old Testament Supplement 117. Sheffield.

Smith-Christopher, D. L.
1989   *The Religion of the Landless: The Social Context of the Babylonian Exile.* Bloomington, Indiana.
2002   *A Biblical Theology of Exile.* Overtures to Biblical Theology. Minneapolis.

Stolper, M. W.
1985   *Entrepreneurs and Empire: The Murāšu Archive, the Murāšu Firm, and Persian Rule in Babylonia.* Istanbul.

Tadmor, H.
1983   Some Aspects of the History of Samaria during the Biblical Period. *The Jerusalem Cathedra* 3: 1–11.

Talmon, S.
1953   The Sectarian *yhd*: A Biblical Noun. *Vetus Testamentum* 3: 133–40.
1986   The Emergence of Jewish Sectarianism in the Early Second Temple Period. Pp. 165–201 in *King, Cult and Calendar in Ancient Israel: Collected Studies.* Jerusalem.

Tollefson, K. D., and Williamson, H. G. M.
1992   Nehemiah as Cultural Revitalization: An Anthropological Perspective. *Journal for the Study of the Old Testament* 56: 41–68.

Vanderhooft, D. S.
1999   *The Neo-Babylonian Empire and Babylon in the Latter Prophets.* Harvard Semitic Monographs 59. Atlanta.
2003   Babylonian Strategies of Imperial Control in the West: Royal Practice and Rhetoric. Pp. 235–62 in *Judah and the Judeans in the Neo-Babylonian Period*, ed. O. Lipschits and J. Blenkinsopp. Winona Lake, Indiana.

Watts, J. W. (ed.)
2001 *Persia and Torah: The Theory of Imperial Authorization of the Pentateuch.* Society of Biblical Literature Symposium Series. Atlanta.
Weinberg, J.
1992 *The Citizen-Temple Community.* Journal for the Study of the Old Testament Supplement 151. Sheffield.
Weisberg, D. B.
1967 *Guild Structure and Political Allegiance in Early Achaemenid Mesopotamia.* Yale Near Eastern Studies. New Haven, Connecticut.
Williamson, H.
1998 Judah and the Jews. Pp. 145–63 in *Studies in Persian History: Essays in Memory of David M. Lewis,* ed. M. Brosius and A. Kuhrt. Achaemenid History XI. Leiden.
Zadok, R.
1979 *The Jews in Babylonia in the Chaldean and Achaemenian Periods in the Light of Babylonian Sources.* Haifa.
Zertal, A.
1990 The Pahwah of Samaria (Northern Israel) during the Persian Period: Types of Settlement, Economy, History and New Discoveries. *Transeuphratène* 3: 9–29.
2003 The Province of Samaria (Assyrian Samerina) in the Late Iron Age (Iron Age III). Pp. 377–412 in *Judah and the Judeans in the Neo-Babylonian Period,* ed. O. Lipschits and J. Blenkinsopp. Winona Lake, Indiana.

The ʿam hāʾāreṣ in Ezra 4:4 and Persian Imperial Administration

LISBETH S. FRIED

University of Michigan

According to Ezra 4:1–5, when the enemies of Judah and Benjamin heard that the returnees were building a Temple to YHWH, the God of Israel, they asked to participate with them in the building process. When prevented from doing so, these ʿam hāʾāreṣ discouraged the returning *gôlâ* community, made them afraid to build, and bribed officials to keep them from continuing the work:

> When the enemies of Judah and Benjamin heard that the returned exiles were building a temple to YHWH, the God of Israel, they approached Zerubbabel and the heads of fathers' [houses] and said to them, "Let us build with you, for we worship your God as you do, and we have been sacrificing to him ever since the days of King Esar-haddon of Assyria who brought us here." But Zerubbabel, Jeshua, and the rest of the heads of fathers' [houses] belonging to Israel said to them, "It is not yours but ours to build a house for our God. We alone will build to YHWH, the God of Israel, as King Cyrus of Persia has commanded us."
> So the ʿam hāʾāreṣ discouraged the people of Judah, and made them afraid to build, and they bribed officials to frustrate their plan throughout the reign of King Cyrus of Persia and until the reign of King Darius of Persia. (Ezra 4:1–5)

Who were these enemies of Judah and Benjamin? Who were the ʿam hāʾāreṣ who bribed the officials to make the Judahites afraid to build?

According to the redactor, the ʿam hāʾāreṣ were descended from those brought into the area by Assyrian kings (4:2, 10). Scholars, critical in their evaluation of other portions of the Bible, have accepted the redactor's viewpoint here with no discussion (e.g., Gunneweg 1983; Blenkinsopp 1988; Schaper 2000; Barstad 1996, 2003; Williamson 1985). They even include among the ʿam hāʾāreṣ the descendants of Judeans who

---

Author's note: This paper has benefited immensely from discussions at the Heidelberg conference and from comments by M. J. Boda, T. C. Eskenazi, A. Faust, V. (A.) Hurowitz, O. Lipschits, A. Schüle, and C. F. Thorpe on an earlier draft.

123

had escaped Babylonian captivity, which the redactor nowhere implies. They consider them to be poor, downtrodden, and newly disenfranchised by the returning *gôlâ*. Grabbe (1998: 138) puts the matter quite succinctly:

> The conclusion seems straightforward: the text [of Ezra–Nehemiah] simply refuses to admit that there were Jewish inhabitants of the land after the deportations under Nebuchadnezzar. Probably only a minority of the people were taken away, with the tens of thousands still left. These people continued to live in Judah, work the land, raise families, carry on their daily life. Presumably they would have quietly taken over any land abandoned because the owners had been killed in fighting or deported to Babylonia. There is no suggestion that any foreign peoples were brought in to replace those deported. Where are these people—Jews—in the books of Ezra and Nehemiah? They are absent. Instead we find references to the *ʿamê hāʾāreṣ*, 'peoples of the land,' who are identified as foreigners. One can only conclude that many, if not all, these 'peoples of the land' were the Jewish descendants of those who were not deported. In the eyes of the author of Ezra, these peoples were no longer kin; the only 'people of Israel' were those who had gone into captivity.[1]

Grabbe evidently believes that the conflicts between the returnees and the *ʿam hāʾāreṣ* are historical but that the redactor misrepresents them. These people who are treated as foreign outsiders by the returning community are descendants of those who never left. Other scholars (Williamson 1985; Bedford 2001) assert that these disputes in the early years of the return are not historical but simply a retrojection of later conflicts. While allowing for certain telling exceptions, Williamson (1985: 45) asserts that "it is both a mistake of method, and a misunderstanding of the writer's intention, to use this section [Ezra 3:1–4:5] primarily for the purpose of historical reconstruction." As Bedford has convincingly shown (2001), Haggai and Zechariah, dated securely to the early years of Darius I, know of no dissension in Judah or Jerusalem between returnees and local residents, either Judeans or non-Judeans. The dissension in Ezra that is set in the early years of the return between the *gôlâ* and the *ʿam hāʾāreṣ* is not historical. Williamson argues that the conflicts that the writer has set between the "people of Israel" and the "people of the land" are between Judeans and Samaritans but stem from the time of the redactor, the early Hellenistic Period, a time when relations between these two ethnic groups were strained.

---

1. Although stating this in the plural, Grabbe has both the singular and the plural forms in mind.

In this paper I seek the referent of the term ʿam hāʾāreṣ in Ezra 4:4. The phrase appears in the singular only this once in Ezra–Nehemiah, and exegesis is limited to this one verse.[2] Evidence suggests that the redactor uses the term in Ezra 4:4 exactly as it is used in the rest of the biblical corpus. The meaning does not change. As it does elsewhere, it refers to the landed aristocracy of an area. In the Persian empire, they were the satrapal officials who administered government. The redactor mistakenly assumes that these officials were descended from those brought into the area by Assyrian kings (4:3, 10). I discuss how he may have come to this view.

The ʿam hāʾāreṣ in the Biblical Corpus

In order to determine whether the redactor's application of the term ʿam hāʾāreṣ has changed from its use in the rest of the biblical corpus, it is necessary to consider how the term is used throughout the Bible.

The ʿam hāʾāreṣ in Preexilic and Exilic-Period Texts

In the Deuteronomistic History, the ʿam hāʾāreṣ are found participating in the revolt against Athalia (2 Kings 11); and they intervene after the assassinations of Amon (21:23–24) and Josiah (23:30) to elevate the next king to the throne. Würthwein (1936) concludes that they formed the state-supporting aristocracy of Judah, whereas de Vaux (1997: 70–72) argues that they included all the full citizens, the entire body of free men who enjoyed "civic rights." De Vaux contrasts Würthwein's "aristocracy" with his own "body of full citizens." In societies of the ancient world, however, the "full citizens" included only the landowners, so these definitions do not conflict. Gunneweg (1983) agrees that in the Deuteronomic History these men were "obviously . . . the landowning full citizens of the upper class." Dandamaev (1982: 40–41) discusses what it means not to be a full citizen in Babylon:

> Free-men deprived of civil rights consisted of . . . persons [who] did not own property within the city's lands, had no access to the Babylonian temples, and consequently could not become members of the popular assembly.

The ʿam hāʾāreṣ comprised the class of free, landowning, full citizens of preexilic Judah. They often owned others who did not belong to this

---

2. The term appears in various plural forms throughout the book of Ezra–Nehemiah. A discussion of the meaning of the plural forms is beyond the scope of the present paper but is forthcoming.

class. According to Jeremiah, the king cut a covenant with the officials of Judah, the officials of Jerusalem, the eunuchs (*śārisîm*, probably royal court officials; Tadmor 1995: 317–26), the priests, and the *'am hā'āreṣ*, who all promised to release their Hebrew male and female slaves (Jer 34:19).

Nicholson (1965: 59–66) argues nevertheless that the term *'am hā'āreṣ* has no fixed meaning but is context driven and sometimes simply refers to people in general. He cites Gen 42:6; Exod 5:5; and 2 Kgs 15:5; 16:15; and 25:3 as evidence. Gen 42:6 refers to the *'am hā'āreṣ* of the Egyptians to whom Joseph, in charge of Egypt's land, sells grain. However, if Joseph was believed to be in charge of grain production for all of Egypt, then he would have been seen as selling only to the heads of the landed estates in Egypt.[3] These free landowners would then have distributed it to their peasants and dependents. Joseph would not have been viewed as selling grain to every man or woman on the street who wanted it. Exod 5:5 also refers to Egyptians, and again the context does not make clear what the referent is. The text states that the Hebrews (slaves) were more numerous than the *'am hā'āreṣ* of Egypt. Since the Hebrews could not have been more numerous than the entire Egyptian population, the text must mean that these foreign slaves were more numerous than all the native landowners. These two stories have been assigned to the same author (E), who no doubt had the same group of people in mind.

Nicholson also cites 2 Kgs 15:5; 16:15; and 25:3 as evidence against a uniform interpretation of the term. According to 2 Kgs 15:5, the king was struck with leprosy and his son Jotham was over the house judging the *'am hā'āreṣ*. Nicholson assumes that the term refers here to all the people of Judah; Gray (1963) removes the phrase *hā'āreṣ*, with the Syriac; while Cogan and Tadmor (1988) argue that the same people are referred to here as in 2 Kings 11, 21, and 23—that is, the landed aristocracy of Judah. In agreement with Cogan and Tadmor, I think it seems likely that the Judean society, like other societies of the ancient Near East, was one in which the king judged the free landowners while the landowners judged any tenant farmers, slaves, women, and children who lived on their estates. In 2 Kgs 16:15, King Ahaz orders the priest Uriah to offer the king's burnt offering and grain offering plus the burnt offering of all the *'am hā'āreṣ*, their grain offering, and their liba-

---

3. For a discussion of the distributory role of the large estates in Egypt's economy, see the chapter on Egypt in Fried 2004.

tion offering on the great altar and orders that all the blood of the sacrifice be sprinkled on it. Cogan and Tadmor argue that the term refers to the same group of people active in 2 Kings 11; Gray again omits the term *hāʾāreṣ*, with the Greek, and again Nicholson interprets it as a reference to all the people of Judah. However, the payment of daily animal, grain, and drink offerings was a tax paid to the temple. Landowners and even the king paid such temple taxes in Babylon. Serfs and tenant farmers, in contrast, paid their rents and shares not to the temple directly but to the landowners from whom they leased their plots.[4] Slaves were not taxed of course, nor did they pay rent, nor did women and children. These categories of dependents would not have been obligated for these types of offerings.[5]

Nicholson finally cites 2 Kgs 25:3 as evidence for a variable, context-driven definition of the term. There it states that, in the final years of the monarchy, the siege of Jerusalem had gotten so bad that there was no longer any food for the *ʿam hāʾāreṣ*. Nicholson interprets this as a reference to all the people of Judah presently living in Jerusalem. Cogan and Tadmor translate it by saying that the famine was so severe that *even* the people of the land had no food to eat. In Mesopotamia, absentee landowners (members of the temple and the palace along with wealthy individuals) formed a prominent part of a city's population and were instrumental in bringing agricultural produce to urban dwellers (van de Mieroop 1997: 142–58; Hunt 1987: 161–92). If there was food to be had, it went to these absentee landowners first.

Nicholson does not mention 2 Kgs 25:19, which refers to "a commander of the army who musters the *ʿam hāʾāreṣ* [for the army]." Typically, it was the landowners who saw battle. A free class of small landowners constituted the backbone of any national army or militia. This is evident from Babylonian archives. Some of the land controlled by the Ebabbar and Eanna Temples in Babylon had been ceded to the temple by the king as a fief. Holders of these lands, called either *bīt ritti* ('hand land') or *bīt qašti* ('bow land'), were obligated to supply and equip either a foot soldier or an archer for the army (Cardascia 1958, 1977; Dandamaev and Lukonin 1989: 232–33). This practice of using fiefs to raise and equip soldiers and archers, well known from the time of Nabonidus, has recently been observed to have existed in Babylon in

---

4. See the chapter on Babylon in Fried 2004.
5. Women who brought a pigeon or turtledove to the priest after their monthly discharge brought it from the holdings of their husband. They brought the offering so that they would be available to their husbands again, not for themselves.

the 35th year of Nebuchadnezzar.[6] Evidence goes back to Hammurabi's Code (26–39) for the practice, if not the term itself. Under Hammurabi, the king leased land in exchange for military service (the *ilkum*; Postgate 1992). When the *ilkum*-land was inherited, the obligation for military service was inherited with it. Land not part of the *ilkum* was not encumbered in this way, so the *ilkum* would have been the major source of conscripts. Even if these soldiers did not join the aristocracy, they did become full citizens of the area, capable of sitting in the city's assembly; they joined the *ʿam hāʾāreṣ*.

Ezekiel, writing during the exile, seems to employ the same definition as the Deuteronomic Historian. According to Ezek 22:29, "the people of the land (*ʿam hāʾāreṣ*) have practiced extortion and committed robbery; they have oppressed the poor and needy, and have extorted from the alien without redress." They are thus not the poor and the disenfranchised but the powerful. In preexilic and exilic texts, therefore, the term *ʿam hāʾāreṣ* refers to the land-owning full citizens of an area.

The *ʿam hāʾāreṣ* in Postexilic Writings

Gunneweg (1983) argues that the term changed its meaning in the postexilic period: rather than being the powerful aristocracy, the *ʿam hāʾāreṣ* are now the poor, newly disenfranchised by the returnees. The Priestly writers, usually dated to the Persian Period, include several instances of the term in their writings (Lev 4:27; 20:2, 4; Gen 23:7, 12, 13; Num 14:9), making it possible to test this hypothesis.[7] In Lev 20:2, 4 the *ʿam hāʾāreṣ* are Israelite and responsible for executing those of Israel who consign their children to Molech. They seem to play the same role of the landed aristocracy that they play in E and in the Deuteronomic History. In Lev 4:27 they are required to bring a female goat or a sheep to the altar when they sin. This sacrifice would only be required of those owning herds of animals and thus able to afford it. It would not be demanded of someone who kept one goat outside his house for milk or of subsistence tenant farmers or sharecroppers,

---

6. M. Jursa (1998), although Postgate (1974: 223) notes a single Assyrian reference to a "bow field" (*ABL* 201:6). There appears little difference between the *ilku* service used by the Assyrian kings to obtain men and supplies for the army and the system used by the Persian kings described here.

7. For discussions of the date of P, see Milgrom (1991) and Levine (1993). Outside of P, uses of the term in the singular are rare and nondiagnostic in the postexilic period (Job 12:24; Hag 2:4; Zech 7:5; Dan 9:6). The appearances in Chronicles merely repeat those of Kings. Ezra 4:4, a diagnostic exception, is discussed in the following section.

slaves, women, or children. It would only have been required of the
ʿam hāʾāreṣ, the landowning full citizens of Judah.

In Genesis 23, a text also attributed to P, the ʿam hāʾāreṣ in Canaan
are not Israelite, but foreign. However, the meaning of the term is the
same. They are the landed aristocracy of the area: "And Abraham rose
and bowed to the ʿam hāʾāreṣ, the Hittites" (Gen 23:7). The ʿam hāʾāreṣ
are the Hittites who own land in Canaan. They are the men from
whom Abraham bought a section of a field in which to bury his wife.
These Hittite ʿam hāʾāreṣ sitting at the gate of the city evoke the image
of the elders deliberating at the gate in the book of Ruth. As elders,
they own land and participate in the administration of government.

In the P version of the story of the spies (Numbers 14) the ʿam hāʾāreṣ
are also foreign; yet, the term seems to refer to the same people as in
Gen 23:7. They are the foreign landowning aristocracy of Canaan (Levine 1993: 363–64). Joshua and Caleb admonish the Hebrews not to
fear them because they are "bread" for the Israelites. The people they
would have feared were the ones wielding the power, not their slaves,
tenant farmers, women, or children. P recognizes that some may dread
these foreigners who presently control the land, yet he is optimistic,
for their protection is removed from them. YHWH is with the Israelites
as long as they do not rebel against him (Num 14:9). For P, therefore,
writing in the Persian Period, the identity of the ʿam hāʾāreṣ does not
seem to have changed, except that now the ones who control the land
are foreign.

The ʿam hāʾāreṣ *in Ezra 4:4*

What is the meaning of the term in Ezra 4:4? The ʿam hāʾareṣ do not
seem to be the poor and disenfranchised but the powerful landed aristocracy who participate in the administration of government. Again,
according to the redactor's narrative:

> The enemies (ṣārê) of Judah and Benjamin heard that the returnees were
> building the temple to YHWH, the god of Israel, so they approached
> Zerubbabel and the heads of the fathers' [houses] and said to them, "Let
> us build with you, for like you we seek an oracle from your God, for we
> have been sacrificing to him from the days that Esarhaddon brought us
> up here." But Zerubbabel, Jeshua, and the rest of the heads of the fa-
> thers' [houses] of Israel said to them, "It is not for you but for us to build
> the house of our God for we alone will build to YHWH, the God of Israel,
> just as King Cyrus, king of Persia commanded us. Then the ʿam hāʾāreṣ
> discouraged the people of Judah and made them afraid to build. They
> hired officials against them to frustrate their plans all the days of Cyrus,
> king of Persia, until the reign of Darius, king of Persia. (Ezra 4:1–5)

The ʿam hāʾāreṣ, the enemies (ṣārê) of Judah and Benjamin, hired advisers to prevent the Jews from building. Thus, they were in a position to pay bureaucratic officials well enough to cause them to frustrate even the plans of Zerubbabel (the Persian-appointed governor of Judah) and Jeshua (the high priest). They were evidently not poor rural peasants but powerful, well-connected, and wealthy. Not only did they bribe officials to frustrate the Judeans' plans throughout the reign of Cyrus until the reign of King Darius of Persia (4:5), but they also wrote accusations against the Judeans to the Persian kings (4:6–10).

> In Xerxes' reign, in his accession year, they wrote an accusation against the inhabitants of Judah and Jerusalem. And in the days of Artaxerxes, Mithredates, Tabeel, and the rest of their associates wrote in peace[8] to Artaxerxes (the letter was written in Aramaic and translated). [The following is] Aramaic: (Reḥum the Chancellor and Shimshai the Secretary wrote a letter regarding Jerusalem to Artaxerxes the king, as follows): [From] Reḥum the Chancellor, Shimshai the Secretary, and the rest of their associates—the judges, the investigators, the Persian officials, the people of Erech, that is, the Babylonians, and the people of Susa, that is, the Elamites. (Ezra 4:6–9)

The ʿam hāʾāreṣ who wrote accusations to the kings against the Judeans were Persian satrapal officials! The writers were the chancellor, the scribe, the judges, and the official investigators of the satrapy Beyond the River. The redactor has glossed the list of officials with the phrase: "and the rest of the nations whom the great and noble Osnappar deported and settled in the cities of Samaria and in the rest of the province Beyond the River wrote" (Ezra 4:10). This gloss makes clear that to the redactor they are the same group of people whom he has labeled "enemies of the Judeans" (4:1) and ʿam hāʾāreṣ (4:4). Nevertheless, they are satrapal officials. The Iranian Mithredates, the Babylonian Tabeel, and the rest of their associates wrote the first letter to Artaxerxes (v. 7), and Reḥum the Chancellor (baʿal ṭēʿēm), Shimshai the secretary, and the rest of their associates—judges (dînaya), investigators (aparsatkāya), Persian officials (ṭarpelāya apārsāya), people of Uruk, that is the Babylonians, and people of Susa, that is, the Elamites, wrote the second letter (vv. 8 and 9).[9]

---

8. Probably not the personal name Bishlam.
9. Or, three letters could have been sent to Artaxerxes, one sent by Reḥum and Shimshai (v. 8) and another by Reḥum, Shimshai, and the rest of their associates (v. 9). For a discussion of the authenticity of the Aramaic letters in the book of Ezra, see Folmer

These letter-writers were the highest officials of the satrapy next to the satrap himself (Briant 1996; Fried 2004). First to sign was the chancellor. The title 'chancellor' (*baʿal ṭēʿēm*) is known from the letters of Arsames, satrap of Egypt during the reign of Darius II (423–405). ʿAnani, probably a Babylonian Jew, was chancellor (*baʿal ṭēʿēm*) of Egypt in Arsames' court. He seems to have acted as vice-satrap, equivalent to the Greek ὕπαρχ, hyparch, in charge of the Egyptian satrapy while Arsames was away (*TAD* A6.2:23). The Babylonian Jew Reḥum (Zadok 1979: 48) was the Achaemenid chancellor of Beyond the River under Artaxerxes. He served the same function as ʿAnani in Egypt. His seat of government was the city of Samaria (Ezra 4:17, 21, 23).[10]

Signing after the chancellor was the chancellery secretary, Shimshai. As in Egypt, he would have been native (*TAD* 6.1), since unlike other satrapal officials, the secretary was often required to interact with the local population (Fried 2004).

Signing after the satrapal secretary were the satrapal judges. As is clear from the Babylonian and Egyptian evidence, satrapal judges were appointed by the king or his agent (called judges of the king, *TAD* B5.1:3). Provincial judges, on the contrary (called judges of the province), were appointed by the satrap (*TAD* A5.2; Porten 1996: 136 n. 19). According to Herodotus (3.31), the royal or satrapal judges "are a body of Persian men picked [by the king] who hold office till death or till some injustice is detected in them." The judges who wrote the letter with Reḥum, the *baʿal ṭēʿēm*, functioned at the satrapal level, and so were Persian (and Babylonian) men appointed by the king himself, or by his imperial agent.[11] During the Achaemenid occupation of Babylon, for example, local judges were replaced by Persians (Dandamaev and Lukonin 1989: 122–23). The "judge of the canal of Sîn" was the Persian Ishtabuzanu; later his son, Humardātu, took over the post. A document on the receipt of a loan of 45 *mina* of silver by Marduk-naṣir-apli of the house of Egibi was registered in the presence of the Iranian judge Ammadātu. This was also true in Egypt. In both the Elephantine archives and the Arsames letters, every named judge was either Iranian or

---

(1995), Hensley (1977), Muraoka and Porten (1998), Porten (1978–79, 1983), and Schwiderski (2000).

10. The recognition that officials in Samaria held jurisdiction over Judah and Samaria led Alt (1953), Würthwein (1936), and others to conclude that Judah was not a separate province in the time of Cyrus. These scholars did not consider that officials operated between the satrap and the governor.

11. Ezra seems to have been one such imperial agent who appointed judges for the satrapy Beyond the River (Fried 2001).

Babylonian.[12] There were no Egyptian judges.[13] This was apparently the situation in Beyond the River. The judges, like the rest of the satrapal officials, were said to be from Susa and Uruk, central cities of power in the Achaemenid Empire.

The fourth title in the list, after chancellor, scribe, and judge, is the Persian title *aparsatkāya* ('investigator'). It is likely from the Old Persian root *u- 'well', *frasta 'questioned,' 'investigated', *ka 'the one who' + the plural Aramaic suffix āyē (Kent 1953: 176). The use of Persian titles demonstrates the Persian nature of the administrative system in the satrapies.

Much of our information on satrapal officials in the Persian Empire comes from Egypt (see Fried 2004). Except for the Egyptian scribes and accountants who interacted with the local population, officials in the Egyptian satrapy were from either Iran or Babylon. Pherendates, the satrap of Egypt under Darius I, and Arsames, Egypt's satrap under Darius II, were Persian. Their chief assistants were either Persian or Babylonian, as were the judges, heralds, provincial governors, garrison commanders, and the commanders of the separate military detachments. In fact, every official and every judge of Achaemenid Egypt whose names we know were either Persian or Babylonian or Jews from Babylon or Persia (Porten and Yardeni 1986; Briant, 1996; Fried 2004). For example, during Persian occupation, the Egyptian Khnemibre, chief of public works of Upper and Lower Egypt under the pharaohs, had been demoted. Under the Persians he reported to the Iranian Atiyvaya, *śariś* of Persia (Posener 1936: 117–30; Bongrani Fanfoni and Israel 1994). An early letter to Arsames (*TAD* A6.1) provides the titles of some officials in the satrapal hierarchy. The verso reads:

> [To] our lord Arsames [w]ho is in Egypt, [from] your servants Achaemenes and his colleagues the heralds, Ba[gadana and his colleagues] the

---

12. According to B. Porten (personal communication), the Aramaic Documents from Hermopolis and Elephantine reveal only one Egyptian who gave his son a Persian name: Bagadata, son of Psamshek (*TAD* B4.3:24; B4.4:20); one Aramean: Varyzata son of Bethelzabad (B3.9:11); and one Jew: Arvaratha son of Yehonatan (*TAD* B4.4:21). Also, if Ostanes is the physical brother of an ʿAnani in Judah (*TAD* A4.7/8:18), then a second Jew had an Iranian name. Besides these, Lozachmeur (1998) reports a graffiti on a stone block 3.5 m above the pavement of the funerary temple of Queen Mother Ankhesenpépy II, southwest of the monument of her husband, Pépy I. The inscription reads, לבגת בר חורי 'to Bagadāta son of Ḥori'. Thus, a second Egyptian gave his son a Persian name. This is out of thousands of names, strongly implying that those with Persian names were Persian.

13. Most situations which we would consider "legal" did not involve a judge. Sales and inheritances of goods, land, and offices were handled through contracts written by Egyptian or Aramean scribes writing in Aramaic (Muffs 1969; Seidl 1968).

judges, Peteisi and his colleagues the scribes of the province of Pamun-para/Nasunpara, Harudj and his colleagues the scribes of the province of. . . .

The name Bagadana is supplied from the recto. The herald, Achaemenes, and the judge, Bagadana, in the Egyptian satrapal court were both Iranian, as were probably their colleagues, the rest of the heralds and judges. The provincial scribes, Peteisi and Harudj, were Egyptian. Except for the scribes and the chief accountant, there were few Egyptians among the officials in the satrapal court in Egypt. The ones who held power in Achaemenid Egypt were primarily ethnic Iranians and Babylonians along with the occasional Babylonian Jew. They were not Egyptian. This was the pattern throughout the Empire. As elsewhere, the satrapal officials of Beyond the River who wrote the accusing letters to the king were Persians and Babylonians. Appointed by the king or his agent, they were sent to the satrapy Beyond the River to administer it.

The redactor refers to the foreign satrapal officials who wrote the accusing letters as *ʿam hāʾāreṣ*. This is clear from his use of the resumptive clause. He repeats the final clause of Ezra 4:5 in 4:24, the closing passage of this section. Both verses (4:5, 24) refer to King Darius of Persia. Ezra 4:4–5 states:

> Then the *ʿam hāʾāreṣ* undermined the resolve [lit., weakened the hands] of the people of Judah and made them afraid to build. They bribed ministers in order to thwart their plans all the years of Cyrus, king of Persia, and up to the reign of Darius, king of Persia.

Ezra 4:24 states:

> At that time, work on the House of God in Jerusalem stopped and remained in abeyance to the second year of the reign of Darius, king of Persia.

Commentators (Blenkinsopp 1988: 111; Williamson 1979; 1985: 57) point out that the repetition of the final phrase of 4:5 in 4:24 signals that the intervening material is a digression. A resumptive clause occurs when an author inserts material into a text and repeats the verse on either side of the inserted material to indicate the insertion. The resumption allows the reader to pick up where the text had left off. The intervening material is regarded as parenthetical and the repeated verses as a set of parentheses. Although Ezra 4:24 does not repeat 4:5 exactly, it still serves as a *Wiederaufnahmen*, a resumptive clause. Ezra 4:4–5 states that the *ʿam hāʾāreṣ* bribed officials and thus frustrated the plans of the Jews from the time of Cyrus up until the reign of Darius. Ezra 4:24 states that building began again in the second year of that same Darius. The intervening vv. 6–23, while parenthetical, are not irrelevant. They are meant to show exactly how these *'am hā'āreṣ* frustrated the plans of the Judeans during all these reigns: not only did they bribe officials, they wrote accusing letters to the kings, and we have those letters! Ezra 4:5–10 is a continuation of Ezra 1–4 (Grabbe 1998: 137). Foreigners bribe Persian officials in 4:5, they make an accusation in 4:6; now in 4:9–10 we learn that it is these same foreigners who have written the letters. The concluding verse, Ezra 4:24, then brings the narrative up to the second year of Darius, when the work was finally able to continue.

The letter that follows the final resumptive clause (4:24) is from Tattenai, Darius's governor of Beyond the River.[14] It brings the narrative up to the reign of that Darius under whom building resumed. Tattenai is shown in the letter as investigating the truth behind the accusations that the *'am hā'āreṣ* sent to King Artaxerxes. He talks to the Judeans themselves to learn about the matter, rather than relying on the letters. A favorable determination is rendered from the king. To the redactor, the Darius under whom work on the temple is completed can only be Darius II, not Darius I; that is, he can only be the Darius who reigned after Xerxes and after Artaxerxes.[15] The redactor provides the correct order of the kings in his list of those who give permission for the work to go ahead: Cyrus, Darius (I), Artaxerxes, and Darius (II; Ezra 6:15–16). Darius I is presumably included based on the writings of Haggai and Zechariah, while Artaxerxes is included because he finally relented and ordered Asaph to give Nehemiah wood to build the gate of the temple fortress (Neh 2:8).

The letters to and from the Achaemenid kings Xerxes and Artaxerxes that are enclosed between the resumptive clauses are meant to explain exactly how the satrapal officials, the *'am hā'āreṣ*, prevented the Jews from building the temple and city from the time of Cyrus up until the time of Darius. This is so, even though the events surrounding the activities of the *'am hā'āreṣ* (described in Ezra 4:1–5) are set in the time of the construction of the temple, whereas the letters that the redactor uses as evidence concern the wall around Jerusalem. To the redactor

---

14. Tattenai is known from a cuneiform text to have been governor of Beyond the River during the reign of Darius I under Ushtanni, satrap of Babylon and Across the River (Olmstead 1944; Ungnad 1940–41). His office was in Damascus. The redactor, writing in the Hellenistic Period, has confused the two Dariuses.

15. Even some modern scholars are convinced by this, for example, B. Becking (1998), who argues that the Second Temple was actually dedicated during the reign of Darius II, not I.

there is no discrepancy; the city and the temple are one (Eskenazi 1988). The confusion is apparent even in Nehemiah's memoir—Nehemiah's dedication of the city wall seems to include a dedication of the temple (Neh 12:31–44).

> Then I brought the leaders of Judah up onto the wall and appointed two great companies that gave thanks and went in procession. One went to the right on the wall to the Dung Gate. . . . The other company of those who gave thanks went to the left, and I followed them with half of the people on the wall. . . . and they came to a halt at the Gate of the Guard. So both companies of those who gave thanks stood in the house of God. . . . On that day men were appointed over the chambers for the stores.

Those that gave thanks during the dedication of the wall continued around the wall until they stood in the temple, the House of God (Neh 12:40). The temple appears to be part of the wall. Further, it was only then, after the wall-dedication ceremony, that men were appointed over the temple chambers and storerooms (12:44). It is no wonder that the redactor of Ezra 1–6, who surely had Nehemiah's memoir in front of him (Williamson 1977, 1983, 1985), assumed that the accusations to the king that delayed building the city wall also delayed the completion of the temple.

Nehemiah's memoir (set in the time of Artaxerxes) seems to have provided the redactor with the historical context for the accusing letter to that king. According to the memoir, enemies (*ṣārîm*) of the Jews attempted to prevent Nehemiah from rebuilding the city wall around Jerusalem (Neh 4:7–13[1–7]):

> When Sanballat heard that we were building the wall he became furious and greatly enraged and he mocked the Jews. And he said before his colleagues and the Samarian army, "What are these pathetic Jews doing?"
> And Tobiah the Ammonite was with him.
> So when Sanballat and Tobiah [and the Arabs, the Ammonites, and the Ashdodites] heard that the restoration of the wall of Jerusalem was progressing and that the breach was beginning to be closed, they became very angry. All of them conspired together to come to fight against Jerusalem and create a disturbance. We prayed to our god and mounted a guard against them day and night. But Judah said, "The strength of the porters falters and the rubble is great. We are not able to build the wall." And our *enemies* (*ṣārênû*) said, "They will not know and will not realize until we have come among them and have killed them and stopped the work."

According to Nehemiah's memoir, Sanballat (the governor of Samaria) backed up by his army, Tobiah (probably the governor of Ammon), and Geshem or Gašmu (king of the Arabic kingdom of Qedar) were the enemies of Nehemiah and of the Jews.[16] As royally appointed governors and rulers in their respective provinces, these three men formed much of the administrative apparatus in the southern provinces of Beyond the River. They were thus among the *ʿam hāʾāreṣ* of the area. According to Nehemiah, they were willing to kill to prevent a wall from being built around Jerusalem. This report in the memoir may have provided the redactor of Ezra 1–6 with his understanding of the historical context behind the letters between the satrapal officials and King Artaxerxes. Indeed, the letters in Ezra 4 concern wall-building, not temple-building.

Local governors such as Sanballat, Tobiah, and Gašmu would have had the connections, the power, and the resources required to bribe satrapal officials to frustrate the work. Nehemiah compares himself favorably to previous governors in Judah, stating that he alone did not acquire wealth or land during his tenure (Neh 5:15, 16). Most governors used their position to aggrandize wealth and power for themselves. Xenophon (*Hell.* 3.1.27–28) reveals the vast amount of land owned by Zenis of Dardanus, a provincial governor of the satrap Pharnabazus, in the years around 400. The personal wealth of this provincial governor was enough to provide nearly a year's pay to an army of 8,000 men! If local governors such as Sanballat, Tobiah, and Gashmû were the model for the *ʿam hāʾāreṣ*, then the definition of the term did not change in the Persian Period. These provincial governors as well as the satrapal officials over them formed the landed aristocracy who administered the southern provinces of Beyond the River. They were powerful, influential, wealthy—and foreign.

The Redactor's Misunderstanding

Likely taking his cue from Nehemiah, the redactor labels the satrapal officials who wrote the accusing letters to the Achaemenid rulers "enemies" of Judah and Benjamin (4:1). Ezra 4:1–5 belongs to the narrative context that the redactor constructs; it was not among his sources. Perhaps he creates the scene to explain the delay that he perceives in building the temple (Bedford 2001); more likely he writes it to explain the letters to and from the Achaemenid kings that he had at his disposal. To the list of satrapal officials, the redactor has glossed, "and the rest of the people whom the great and famous Osnappar deported and settled in the cities of Samaria and the rest of Beyond the River" (4:10).

---

16. See Fried 2002 for a proposed rationale for the conflict.

Why did the redactor assume that these satrapal officials were descendants of those brought into the area by Assyrian kings? The chancellor Reḥum was the primary letter-writer, and he had his seat of office in the city of Samaria (4:17). The redactor, writing in the Hellenistic Period,[17] assumed therefore that the letter-writers were Samaritan and (based on 2 Kings 17) that they had been brought into the area by Assyrian kings. This is not likely. The men listed as signatories were among the highest officials in the satrapal government of Beyond the River, "eating the salt of the palace" (Ezra 4:9). As such they would have been appointed by the king from his inner circle in Persia or Babylon and sent to the satrapy by the king himself. They would not have been the descendants of those deported into the area by the Assyrians. Few local dynasts governed satrapies. The Hecotomnids of Caria may be the lone exception to the general rule (Hornblower 1982; Ruzicka 1992). Even so, the use of the term ʿam hāʾāreṣ to refer to these satrapal officials is consistent with the meaning used throughout the biblical corpus. Satrapal officials, by definition, belonged to the landed aristocracy, and they administered the province of Beyond the River.

Persian Satrapal Officials:
The Ruling Aristocracy in Judah

Many scholars claim that imperially appointed satrapal officials simply collected money to send to Susa but had no real political power (most recently, Dandamaev 1999). They argue that real power lay in the hands of the local populace, the *gôlâ*, who administered themselves through their elders and through the local assembly (*qāhāl*). If this was true, then the meaning of the term ʿam hāʾāreṣ indeed had changed, and the application of the term to the satrapal officials is a misnomer. Power would have been in the hands of the *gôlâ*, not the ʿam hāʾāreṣ, the imperially appointed satrapal officials. However, Ezra 9 and 10 provide the only evidence offered for the power of elders or of the *qāhāl*. Ezra 9:1–2 states: "After these things were completed, some officials (*śārîm*) met with me and said that 'the people Israel, the priests, and the Levites have not separated themselves from the 'peoples of the lands.'. . . The officials (*śārîm*) and the prefects (*sĕgānîm*) are the first in this treachery." The complaint came not from the people, or the *qāhāl*, but

---

17. The list of high priests in Neh 12:22 has been shown to be complete up to Darius III (VanderKam 1991; 2004: 43–111; Fried 2003), thereby requiring a final redaction in the Hellenistic Period.

from the officials, the *śārîm*. When Ezra heard this he tore his garment and his cloak, pulled the hair from his head and beard, and sat desolate (9:3). As he wept and prayed before the temple a "very great assembly (*qāhāl*) of men, women, and children gathered to him weeping" (10:1). If this assembly included women and children, however, it was not a legislative body but a gathering.[18]

The passage continues:

> They sent out a herald (*qôl*) throughout all Judah and Jerusalem—to all the members of the *gôlâ* community—to gather in Jerusalem. All who would not come in three days according to the direction (*ʿăṣat*) of the officials (*hāśśārîm*) and the elders (*hazzĕqēnîm*) would have their property confiscated (*yāḥăram*) and would be separated from the assembly (*qĕhal*) of the *gôlâ* community. (Ezra 10:7–8)

The text does not say who the "they" were who sent out the herald. It has been assumed that it was the assembly, the *qāhāl*, that had the power to send out heralds, order attendance, confiscate property, and mandate divorces (Meyer 1965: 132–34; Widengren 1977: 522–33; Kaufmann 1977: 206–7; Blenkinsopp 1988: 175; Albertz 1994: 446–48). This would have given it quite a bit of power, suggesting a type of self-rule. However, it would not have been the *qāhāl*—consisting as noted above of men, women, and children—who had the authority. Nor would it even have been the elders in an officially constituted public assembly. Power in the Achaemenid Empire lay not in the hands of either assemblies or local elders but with the imperially appointed Iranian and Babylonian officials (*hāśśārîm*). Assemblies held no real power in the Achaemenid Empire. A search among the Neo-Babylonian- and Persian-Period instances of the word *puḫru* ('assembly') and *paḫāru* ('to assemble') reveals the nature of this institution. A *puḫru* was called for judicial decisions: a sheep stolen or land needing to be reassigned. (No legislative sessions are recorded.[19]) The parties to the transaction spoke

---

18. The Akkadian word *puḫru* also has this double connotation. It can refer to a casual gathering or to a group of men called for a specific purpose (*CAD* P, unpublished manuscript). See Fried 2002, 2004 for a discussion of the rationale behind the order to against intermarriage. Discussion of these issues is beyond the scope of the present paper.

19. Van de Mieroop (1997: 120) argues this is an accident of scribal practices. Mesopotamian records are primarily concerned with the transfer of property, and no exchanges took place between government and citizenry. However, this cannot be the whole story. Ultimate decision-making powers belonged to the king. Whether or not citizens advised, the responsibility was the king's or the king's surrogates. If citizens advised, this advice was not given publicly in assembly but in private audience and not recorded. The only evidence offered for exceptions to this comes from literary texts (van de Mieroop 1997: 118–41, with bibliography; 1999; Bloom 1992).

before judges, who gave their opinion, and the scribe drew up the case. The witnesses listed agreed that the matter occurred and the decision was rendered as described. Those called to testify during the proceedings were not the same ones who are listed as the witnesses to them, although the same term is used (*mukinnu*). The 20 or 30 men listed as witnesses to the trial and to the ultimate decision formed the *puḫru*. These members (*mār banī*) of the assembly (*puḫru*) did not speak. The royally appointed official—the provincial governor, mayor, judge, or temple leader—announced the verdict. Although the decisions were rendered in the name of the assembly, rather than in the name of the specific official who led it, the assembled *mār banī* simply witnessed the decisions. They did not contribute to the decision-making process.[20] The purpose of trials before an assembly of respected citizens was only so that trials would be open and transparent, with decisions rendered in full view of the public. Dandamaev (1982; 1995) has studied the role of assemblies and the elders in Neo-Babylonian- and Persian-Period cuneiform texts. His evidence confirms the nonparticipatory role of the elders. As Dandamaev makes clear, the centuries-old rivalry between the royal court and the popular assembly of the city had already ended under the Chaldaean kings, with the defeat of the assembly. There were no legislative assemblies, no vehicle for local control in Babylon under either Nabonidus or the Achaemenids.

Nor was Persian control over affairs at Syene/Elephantine restricted by local assemblies. Tuplin (1987: 111) suggests that the Jewish community assembly at Elephantine was a judicial body that adjudicated land disputes. Yet every land dispute mentioned in the papyri was resolved by a judicial proceeding before the imperially appointed Iranian or Babylonian judges, not in assembly. The cases that Tuplin brings to bear (*TAD* B2.6, B3.3, and B3.8) are marriage and divorce proceedings in which a party proclaims in front of an assembly that a couple is divorced, or in which one party announces before an assembly that he will fulfill an obligation if a divorce does occur. The assembly itself

---

20. Pace M. A. Dandamaev 1976, 1979, 1982, 1995; and Dandamaev and Lukonin 1989: 361. In all these works, Dandamaev states that "the most important questions [of temple administration] were resolved by an assembly of the citizens of the temple district in question." He should have said "before" an assembly. . . . The evidence he adduces only indicates that the *mār banī* served as witnesses to the decision that was made by the judges or ranking officials. There is no indication they spoke, voted, or gave assent. Athenian trials cannot be used as a model of Mesopotamian trials. In Athens, where a trial could be before hundreds of citizens, there were no judges, few witnesses, and the verdict was rendered according to the majority vote of the assembled. This was not the case in Mesopotamia under the Persians.

made no decision and did not contribute. As everywhere else in the Achaemenid Empire, assemblies served as witness to the transactions only.

Besides observing legal cases, assemblies sometimes convened to hear important instructions from high-ranking officials (Dandamaev 1982: 40).[21] The situation in Achaemenid Judah was no different. Nehemiah, the Persian governor, reports in his memoir that he called an assembly to announce his decision regarding usury and the return of property and persons offered as pledges for loans (Neh 5:7b–8). The men of the assembly said "Amen," acknowledging the decision (Neh 5:13). They did not participate in any deliberations.

Nor did local elders by themselves hold political power in the Persian Empire. In the book of Ezra, the Aramaic term שְׂבַיָּא 'elders' occurs in the introduction to Tattenai's letter (Ezra 5:5); in the body of the letter (5:9); in Darius's response to it (6:7, 8); and in the result of the response, the dedication of the temple (6:14). These elders are not shown having real power, however. Japhet (1982: 82) asks how likely it would have been for Tattenai, Darius's newly appointed *hyparch* of Beyond the River, to negotiate directly with the elders of the Judeans over the rebuilding of the temple (Ezra 5:3, 4, 9). Would he not have negotiated with his own subordinate, Zerubbabel, the governor of Yehud, rather than with the Judahite elders? Indeed, he would not have negotiated with the elders or Zerubbabel, but negotiation is not portrayed here, only an investigation of the facts behind the Jerusalem Temple building project.

Besides Tattenai's letter and the response, references to elders occur in Ezra 10:8 and 14. The first records a decision of the assembly. As in Babylon and elsewhere throughout the Achaemenid Empire, the elders would have witnessed the announcement, but they would not have participated in it. Elders are also recorded in connection with the enforced divorces. There too they would have been involved in their normal role as witnesses to the proceedings only. As in Babylon, Egypt, and elsewhere, reference to the elders does not imply their active participation. Both the instigation for the divorces as well as the sanctions imposed for those failing to comply would have been by order of imperially appointed provincial officials, the *śarîm* (9:1; 10:7).

Local Judeans—the *gôlâ*—had no more political power in Judah than did local Egyptians in Egypt. The satrapies and provinces were tightly

---

21. This role for the elders is also exhibited in Ruth 4:1–6. Elders were called to serve as witnesses to the transaction, but they did not participate directly in it.

administered as fiefdoms for the king by their Persian and Babylonian overlords. There was no local self-rule anywhere in the Persian Empire and no vehicle for it (Fried 2004). Local assemblies did not hold political power. Persia was not a democracy. Those with political power in the provinces were the officials whom the king or his satraps and imperial agents appointed.

Conclusion

The people who wrote accusing letters against the Judeans, whom the redactor labels ʿam hāʾāreṣ, were the satrapal officials who administered the government of Beyond the River. They included the chancellor, the satrapal scribe, the judges, the investigators, and the rest of their colleagues, the Persian officials from Susa in Elam and from Uruk in Babylon—all who ate the salt of the palace. These satrapal officials held the real political power in the Empire, and as such they formed the landed aristocracy of the satrapy. The meaning of the term did not change, but the people who had previously been designated by the phrase were no longer designated by it. The Judean ʿam hāʾāreṣ, the Judean aristocracy who had controlled Judah before the exile, were not in charge of Judah anymore. The land was now in the control of strangers. The Persian and Babylonian officials of the satrapy Beyond the River were the new ʿam hāʾāreṣ. They were the ones who administered Judah, and they were foreign.

Bibliography

Albertz, R.
1994   *From the Exile to the Maccabees*, trans. J. Bowden. Vol. 2 of *A History of Israelite Religion in the Old Testament Period*. OTL. Louisville.
Alt, A.
1953   Die Rolle Samarias bei der Enstehung des Judentums. Pp. 316–37 in vol. 2 of *Kleine Schriften zur Geschichte des Volkes Israel*. Munich.
Barstad, H.
1996   *The Myth of the Empty Land: A Study in the History and Archaeology of Judah during the "Exilic" Period*. Symbolae Osloenses: Fasc. supplet 28. Oslo.
2003   After the "Myth of the Empty Land": Major Challenges in the Study of Neo-Babylonian Judah. Pp. 3–20 in *Judah and the Judeans in the Neo-Babylonian Period*, ed. O. Lipschits and J. Blenkinsopp. Winona Lake, Indiana.

Becking, B.
1998   Ezra's Re-enactment of the Exile. Pp. 40–61 in *Leading Captivity Captive: "The Exile" as History and Ideology*, ed. L. L. Grabbe. JSOTSup 278. Sheffield.

Bedford, P.
2001   *Temple Restoration in Early Achaemenid Judah*. Leiden.

Blenkinsopp, J.
1988   *Ezra–Nehemiah*. OTL. Philadelphia.

Bloom, J. A.
1992   *Ancient Near Eastern Temple Assemblies*. Ph.D. dissertation. Annenberg Research Institute. Philadelphia.

Bongrani Fanfoni, L., and Israel, F.
1994   Documenti achemenidi nel deserto orientale egiziano (Gebel Abu Queh–Wadi Hammamat). *Transeuphratène* 8: 75–93.

Cardascia, G.
1958   Le fief dans la Babylonie achéménide. *Recueils de la societé Jean Bodin*, 1²: Les liens de vassalités et les immunités: 55–88.
1976   Armée et fiscalité dans la Babylonie achéménide. *Armées et fiscalités dans le monde antique* 25: 1–11.

Cogan, M., and Tadmor, H.
1988   *II Kings*. AB 11. Garden City, New York.

Dandamaev, M.
1976   Social Stratification in Babylonia (7th–4th Centuries B.C.). Pp. 433–44 in *Wirtschaft und Gesellschaft im alten Vorderasien*, ed. J. Harmatta and G. Komoróczy. Budapest.
1979   State and Temple in Babylonia in the First Millennium B.C. Pp. 589–96 in vol. 2 of *State and Temple Economy in the Ancient Near East*, ed. E. Lipiński. Leuven.
1982   The Neo-Babylonian Elders. Pp. 38–41 in *Societies and Languages of the Ancient Near East: Studies in Honour of I. M. Diakonoff*. Warminster.
1995   Babylonian Popular Assemblies in the First Millennium B.C. *The Canadian Society for Mesopotamian Studies Bulletin* 30: 23–29.
1999   Achaemenid Imperial Policies and Provinical Governments. *Iranica Antiqua* 34: 269–82.

Dandamaev, M., and Lukonin, V.
1989   *The Culture and Social Institutions of Ancient Iran*, trans. P. Kohl and D. Dadson. Cambridge.

Eskenazi, T. C.
1988   *In an Age of Prose: A Literary Approach to Ezra–Nehemiah*. SBLMS 36. Atlanta.

Folmer, M. L.
1995   *The Aramaic Language in the Achaemenid Period*. Orientalia Lovaniensia Analecta 68. Leuven.

Fried, L. S.
2001   You Shall Appoint Judges: Ezra's Mission and the Rescript of Artaxerxes. Pp. 63–89 in *Persia and Torah: The Theory of Imperial Authorization of the Pentateuch*, ed. J. W. Watts. SBLSymS 17. Atlanta.

2002 The Political Struggle of Fifth-Century Judah. *Transeuphratène* 24: 61–73.
2003 A Silver Coin of Yoḥanan Hakkôkēn. *Transeuphratène* 25: 47–67, pls. 2–5.
2004 *The Priest and the Great King: Temple-Palace Relations in the Persian Empire.* Biblical and Judaic Studies from the University of California, San Diego 10. Winona Lake, Indiana.
forthcoming From Zeno-philia to Phobia: Encounters with the Other in Fifth-Century Judah.
Grabbe, L. L.
1992 The Authenticity of the Persian "Documents" in Ezra. Paper read to the Aramaic Section of the Society of Biblical Literature Annual Meeting, San Fransisco.
1998 *Ezra–Nehemiah.* Old Testament Readings. London.
Gray, J.
1963 *I and II Kings.* OTL. Philadelphia.
Gunneweg, A. H. J.
1983 'AM HA'AREṢ: A Semantic Revolution. *ZAW* 95: 437–40.
Harris, R.
1961 On the Process of Secularization under Hammurapi. *JCS* 15: 117–20.
Hensley, L. V.
1977 *The Official Persian Documents in the Book of Ezra.* Ph.D. dissertation. University of Liverpool.
Hornblower, S.
1982 *Mausolus.* Oxford.
Hunt, R. C.
1987 The Role of Bureaucracy in the Provisioning of Cities: A Framework for Analysis of the Ancient Near East. Pp. 161–92 in *The Organization of Power: Aspects of Bureaucracy in the Ancient Near East,* ed. M. Gibson and R. D. Biggs. Chicago.
Japhet, S.
1982 Sheshbazzar and Zerubbabel against the Background of the Historical and Religious Tendencies of Ezra–Nehemiah. *ZAW* 94: 66–98.
Jursa, M.
1998 Bogenland schon unter Nebukadnezar II. *NABU:* 124.
Kaufmann, Y.
1977 *From the Babylonian Captivity to the End of Prophecy,* trans. C. W. Efroymson. Vol. 4 of *History of the Religion of Israel.* New York.
Kent, R. G.
1953 *Old Persian: Grammar, Texts, Lexicon.* AOS 33. New Haven, Connecticut.
Levine, B. A.
1993 *Numbers 1–20.* AB 4. New York.
Lozachmeur, H.
1998 Un nouveau graffito araméen provenant de Saqqâra. *Semitica* 48: 147–49.
Meyer, E.
1965 *Die Entstehung des Judentums.* Hildesheim. [orig., 1896]

Mieroop, M. van de
1997 *The Ancient Mesopotamian City*. Oxford.
1999 The Government of the Ancient Mesopotamian City: What We Know and Why We Know So Little. Pp. 139–61 in *Priests and Officials in the Ancient Near East*, ed. K. Watanabe. Heidelberg.

Milgrom, J.
1991 *Leviticus 1–16*. AB 3. New York.

Muffs, Y.
1969 *Studies in the Aramaic Legal Papyri from Elephantine*. Leiden.

Muraoka, T., and Porten, B.
1998 *A Grammar of Egyptian Aramaic*. New York.

Nicholson, E. W.
1965 The Meaning of the Expression *ʿam haʾarez* in the Old Testament. *JSS* 10: 59–66.

Olmstead, A. T.
1944 Tattenai, Governor of "Across the River." *JNES* 3: 46.

Porten, B.
1978–79 The Documents in the Book of Ezra and the Mission of Ezra. *Shnaton* 3: 174–96. [Hebrew]
1983 The Address Formulae in Aramaic Letters: A New Collation of Cowley 17. *RB* 90: 396–415.
1996 *The Elephantine Papyri in English: Three Millennia of Cross-Cultural Continuity and Change*. New York.

Porten, B., and Yardeni, A.
1986 *Textbook of Aramaic Documents from Ancient Egypt, 1: Letters*. Jerusalem.

Posener, G.
1936 *La première domination perse en Égypt*. Cairo.

Postgate, J. N.
1974 *Taxation and Conscription in the Assyrian Empire*. Rome.
1992 *Early Mesopotamia: Society and Economy at the Dawn of History*. London.

Ruzicka, S.
1992 *Politics of a Persian Dynasty: The Hecatomnids in the Fourth Century B.C.* Norman, Oklahoma.

Schaper, J.
2000 *Priester und Leviten im achämenidischen Juda*. FAT 31. Tübingen.

Schwiderski, D.
2000 *Handbuch des nordwestsemitischen Briefformulars: Ein Beitrag zur Echtheitsfrage der aramäischen Briefe des Esrabuches*. BZAW 295. Berlin.

Seidl, E.
1968 *Ägyptische Rechtsgeschichte der Saiten- und Perserzeit*. Glückstadt.

Tadmor, H.
1995 Was the Biblical *sārîs* a Eunuch? Pp. 317–26 in *Solving Riddles and Untying Knots: Biblical, Epigraphic, and Semitic Studies in Honor of Jonas C. Greenfield*, ed. Z. Zevit, S. Gitin, and M. Sokoloff. Winona Lake, Indiana.

Tuplin, C.
1987 The Administration of the Achaemenid Empire. Pp. 109–66 in *Coinage and Administration in the Athenian and Persian Empires*, ed. I. Carradice. BAR International Series 343. Oxford.

Ungnad, A.
1940–41 Keilinschriftliche Beiträge zum Buch Esra und Ester. *ZAW* 58: 240–44.

VanderKam, J. C.
1991 Jewish High Priests of the Persian Period: Is the List Complete? Pp. 67–91 in *Priesthood and Cult in Ancient Israel*, ed. G. A. Anderson and S. M. Olyan. Sheffield.
2004 *From Joshua to Caiaphas: High Priests after the Exile*. Minneapolis.

Vaux, R. de
1997 *Ancient Israel: Its Life and Institutions*. The Biblical Resource Series. Grand Rapids.

Widengren, G.
1977 The Persian Period. Pp. 489–538 in *Israelite and Judean History*, ed. J. Hayes and J. Maxwell Miller. Philadelphia.

Williamson, H. G. M.
1977 *Israel in the Books of Chronicles*. Cambridge.
1983 The Composition of Ezra I–IV. *JTS* 34: 2–30.
1985 *Ezra, Nehemiah*. WBC 16. Waco, Texas.

Würthwein, E.
1936 *Der ʿam haʾaretz im Alten Testament*. BWANT 17. Stuttgart.

Zadok, R.
1979 *The Jews of Babylonia during the Chaldean and Achaemenian Periods according to the Babylonian Sources*. Haifa.

The Borders and De Facto *Size of Jerusalem* in the Persian Period

DAVID USSISHKIN

Tel Aviv University

The borders and the size of Jerusalem in the Persian Period have been discussed and debated by many scholars since modern research of Jerusalem began in the nineteenth century C.E. The borders of the city—as generally agreed upon—were marked by the course of its city walls, which according to the biblical text had been restored by Nehemiah. Hence, the reconstruction of the course of the the city wall has formed the focal point of the scholarly discussion on the size of Jerusalem during that period.

The essence of the problem is, in fact, whether the city wall of the Persian Period surrounded only the City of David and the Temple Mount, as advocated by the "minimalists," or surrounded also the Southwest Hill, as suggested by the "maximalists." Among the "minimalists" are Michael Avi-Yonah (1954; 1956), Yoram Tzafrir (1977), Hugh Williamson (1984), Hanan Eshel (2000), and Ephraim Stern (2001: 434–36). Among the "maximalists" are Père Hugh Vincent (Vincent and Stève 1954: 237–59, pl. 61), Jan Simons (1952: 437–58), and Meir Ben-Dov (2002: 84–87).

The debate on this question is based on sources of two kinds. On the one hand, the written biblical sources, in particular the book of Nehemiah, include much information on the city wall and its course and on the topography of Jerusalem. Indirect data are also to be found in the descriptions of Josephus. On the other hand are the archaeological data accumulated during 150 years of continuous field research.

In my view, the corpus of archaeological data should be the starting point for the study of Jerusalem, its borders, history, and material culture in the biblical period. This source of information should take precedence, whenever possible, over the written sources, which are largely

---

Author's note: This essay is based on the lecture given at the symposium on Judah and Judaeans in the Achaemenid Period on 16 July 2003, with minor changes and the addition of references.

147

biased, incomplete, and open to different interpretations. This rule should apply also to the issue under discussion here. First, we have to evaluate the archaeological evidence relevant to the questions of the borders and size of Jerusalem, and then, as a second step, we should evaluate the written sources. The present essay is dedicated in the main to an analysis of the archaeological data, which in my view are sufficient to clarify the problem and to draw immediate conclusions.

The study of the borders of Jerusalem in the Persian Period from an *archaeological* perspective, in other words, the reconstruction of the line of the city wall described in the book of Nehemiah on the basis of the *archaeological* evidence, relies on a reconstruction of the city wall during the First Temple Period. This starting point for the study of Nehemiah's wall was well defined by Avi-Yonah: "It is generally agreed that the line of the city wall at the time of Nehemiah is identical to that during the end of the Monarchy Period. Nehemiah himself defines his task as repair rather than rebuilding of the wall. . . . We can therefore rely on the description of Nehemiah for the reconstruction of the wall as a continuation from the period before the First Destruction" (Avi-Yonah 1956: 160).

However, the starting point for the study of the borders and walls of Jerusalem in the First Temple Period is the reconstruction of the borders and walls of Jerusalem in the second millennium B.C.E. We have, therefore, to begin by examining the borders of Jerusalem and the line of its city walls in the periods that predate the Persian Period.

The first fortified settlement dates to the Middle Bronze II Period, in the first half of the second millennium B.C.E., and it extended along the Southeast Hill, that is, the City of David. Figure 1 shows the borders of the settlement as reconstructed by Kathleen Kenyon (1974: 90–94). On the eastern side, and probably also on the western side, the topography determined the borders of the settlement. On the northern side, the boundary of the settlement was arbitrarily restored, and possibly it extended along a more northerly line. The fortifications of the city are well known on the eastern side of the hill that is on the western slope of the Kidron Valley. Segments of a city wall and possibly a segment of a tower were uncovered in the excavations of Kenyon (1974: 82–84, pls. 19–20, 24; Steiner 2001: 10–23) and those of Yigal Shiloh (1984: 12, 26). Two massive towers were recently discovered by Roni Reich and Eli Shukrun near the Gihon Spring (Reich and Shukrun 1998; 1999). It appears that the famous water system known as the Warren Shaft also dates to this period and was incorporated in the fortifications (Reich and Shukrun 1998; 1999). The city wall must have surrounded the

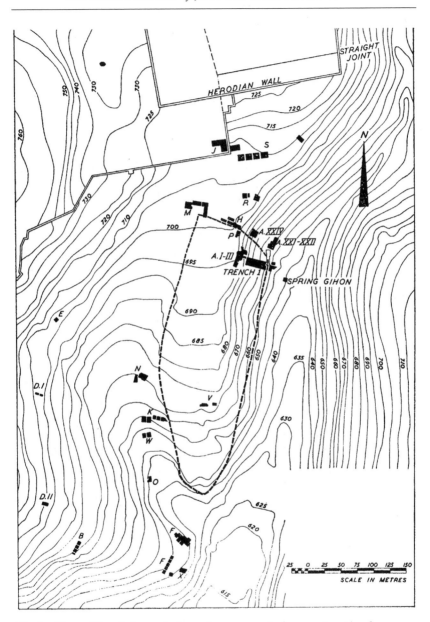

Fig. 1. Plan of Pre-Solomonic Jerusalem, suggested reconstruction by Kenyon (after Kenyon 1974: fig. 18).

settlement; therefore, we can safely assume that it also extended along the western side of the City of David, that is, along the eastern side of the Central Valley, termed by Josephus the "Tyropoeon Valley" (fig. 2:3). Few excavations have been conducted here, and hopefully segments of this wall will be discovered in future digs.

The second fortified settlement in biblical Jerusalem is the large city of the later part of the First Temple Period (fig. 2). This city was destroyed and burned by the Babylonian army in 586 B.C.E. The pottery data from the excavations in the City of David and the Southwest Hill indicate that the large city and its fortifications already existed in the later part of the eighth century and that this was the walled city challenged by Sennacherib's task force in 701 B.C.E. This city extended over the City of David and the Southwest Hill, as well as the Temple Mount, where the royal acropolis, which included the king's palace and the temple, was located. Strong fortifications surrounded the city. Segments of city walls and towers, in which more than one construction phase could be discerned, have been uncovered along the eastern slope of the City of David by Kenyon (Steiner 2001: 89–92), Shiloh (1984: 8–10, 28; figs. 30, 33), and Reich and Shukrun (2000; see also Shanks 1999); on the so-called Ophel by Eilat Mazar (Mazar and Mazar 1989: 1–48); in the Western Quarter by Avigad (1983: 46–60; Avigad and Geva 2000; Geva and Avigad 2000), and possibly also on Hagai Street by Amos Kloner (1984) and in the Ottoman citadel near Jaffa Gate (Geva 1979; 1983: 56–58).

During the long interim period between these two fortified settlements, that is, between the end of the Middle Bronze Age in the sixteenth century and the eighth century B.C.E., settlement in Jerusalem continued, apparently uninterrupted, in the central part of the City of David, in the general region above the Gihon Spring. This is indicated by the archaeological finds—remains of structures, floors, pottery, and burials.

In my view this settlement was unfortified, and there is no city wall that can be assigned to this period. The lines of the city walls uncovered along the eastern slope of the City of David, the earlier one as well as the later ones, built in some areas one on top of the stump of the other, indicate that no other city wall was erected here during the interim period between the time of these two walls. Contrary to Kenyon (1963: 9–10; 1964: 8; 1968: 105–6; 1974: 81–83, 89–91) and Jane Cahill (2003: 21–23), it seems that the Middle Bronze Age city wall fell into disuse or was even destroyed at the end of the period. Naturally, its terraced remains and still-standing huge towers protecting the Gihon

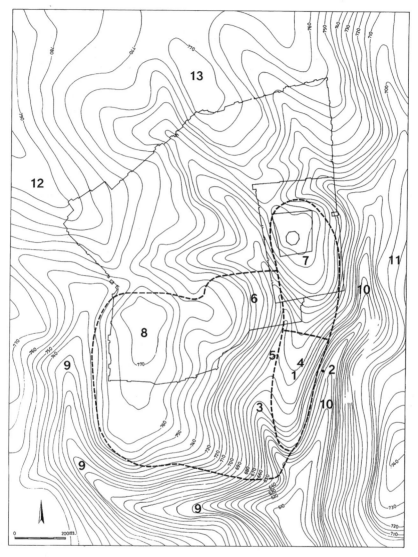

Fig. 2. Jerusalem of the First Temple Period. (1) the City of David; (2) the Gihon Spring; (3) the Central Valley; (4) the place of the "Stepped Structure"; (5) the place of Crowfoot's excavations; (6) the "tombs" uncovered in Mazar's excavations; (7) the Temple Mount; (8) the Southwest Hill; (9) the Hinnom Valley; (10) the Kidron Valley; (11) the Mount of Olives; (12) the Northwest hill; (13) the Northeast hill.

Spring were reused by builders of the fortifications of the Judean city in the eighth century and incorporated by them, but this does not prove that the former were in use and functioning during the "interim period." Two parallel wall segments uncovered in a single square at the top of the slope were identified by Kenyon (Kenyon 1974: 114–15, pl. 37) and by Margreet Steiner (2001: 48–50) as parts of a tenth–ninth-century casemate wall, but the factual evidence hardly supports such a conclusion.

The poor character of the settlement in the interim period is illustrated in the area of the Gihon Spring, the most sensitive point in the City of David: fortifications and water systems were constructed both in the Middle Bronze II and the late First Temple Periods; however, during the in-between period, hardly any indications of human activity have been discerned here.

To this interim period belongs the problematic complex known as the "stepped stone structure" and the underlying terraces (fig. 2:4; see Shiloh 1984: 16–18, 29, figs. 16–19; Steiner 2001: 36–39, 43–52; 2003; Cahill 2003: 33–54). Its date and function are unclear. I am inclined to agree with Steiner and Israel Finkelstein that the complex is relatively late in date, built perhaps in the first quarter of the first millennium, because its construction phase contains red-burnished pottery (Steiner 2001: 50–52; 2003: 357–59; Finkelstein 2003: 84–86). The function of the "stepped stone structure" is unclear, and possibly it supported the wall of a fortress or some monumental compound built on the summit of the hill. However, the problem is complex and irrelevant to our subject.

A few words may be stated here on the period of the United Monarchy. According to the generally accepted view, based in its entirety on biblical evidence, Jerusalem was built by King Solomon as a magnificent capital (see, e.g., A. Mazar 1990: 375–79; Shanks 1995: 47–77). According to this view (illustrated in the reconstruction reproduced here in fig. 3), Solomonic Jerusalem (as well as the ninth-century city) was sausage-shaped and included the City of David and the Temple Mount. This city is always reconstructed as being surrounded by a city wall, based on 1 Kgs 9:15: "This is the record of the forced labour which King Solomon conscripted to build the House of the Lord, his own palace, the Millo, the wall of Jerusalem, and Hazor, Megiddo and Gezer."

I have expressed my opinion on other occasions that the reconstruction of Solomonic Jerusalem as a magnificent, fortified city contradicts the archaeological evidence, which in my view should be the starting point for the research (Ussishkin 2003a; 2003b). The archaeological evidence is clear and comprehensive, and it is unlikely that the picture

Fig. 3. Suggested reconstruction of Solomonic Jerusalem (after Shanks 1995: 74–75).

will drastically change in the future. It appears that during the reign of Solomon, as in the entire period between the end of the Middle Bronze Age and the eighth century B.C.E., only a relatively small settlement, not protected by a city wall, existed in the central part of the City of David (see summary of the archaeological evidence, reaching entirely different conclusions, in Cahill 2003).

The reconstruction of the development of Jerusalem in the biblical era as presented above leads to the unavoidable conclusion that a city wall was not built along the western slope of the City of David during the First Temple Period. It appears, as explained above, that the city wall of the Middle Bronze II settlement must have been extended here because it surrounded the settlement of the time. The large city of the eighth and seventh centuries was also protected by a city wall. However, this city included the City of David, the Temple Mount, and the Southwest Hill. This city wall surrounded the entire settlement of the time; there was no need or reason to build a defense wall that separated the City of David and the Southwest Hill, and we can safely assume that a city wall was not built here after the Middle Bronze Age.

The archaeological evidence from the northwest end of the City of David, from the areas bordering on the southwest corner of the Haram esh-Sharif, supports this view. The entire area was excavated down to bedrock by Benjamin Mazar, and no remains of a First Temple Period city wall were detected. Several rock-cut caves, possibly tombs or cisterns, were discovered by Mazar on the eastern slope of the Southwest Hill (fig. 2:6; see B. Mazar 1971: 22–23; E. Mazar and B. Mazar

1989: 49–55). He raised the possibility that this was a cemetery dating to the earlier part of the First Temple Period, to the time when this area had still been situated outside the boundaries of the settlement. Theoretically, a graveyard would indeed have implied that the boundary of the city extended at that time along the western side of the City of David, but the factual data are vague and problematic. It is not clear whether these caves were originally cut as tombs (Barkay 1985: 474–75), or what their date is, so we cannot use these data in our evaluation.

The archaeological evidence from the western section of the City of David is partial, and in fact only one single systematic excavation was carried out here. In 1927 J. W. Crowfoot excavated a wide trench, oriented from east to west, across the Central Valley (fig. 2:5; Crowfoot and Fitzgerald 1929). A massive structure was uncovered at the lower edge of the western slope of the City of David (1929: 12–26; frontispiece, pls. 1–4). Crowfoot identified it as a gatehouse constructed in the Bronze Age and used until the Roman Period. Ever since its discovery, scholars have generally agreed that this structure was a gatehouse in the western wall of the City of David, and it plays a prominent part in all suggested reconstructions of biblical Jerusalem and its fortifications. A detailed description, ground plan, section, and several photographs were published by Crowfoot. In my view, analysis of these data indicates that this is probably a massive substructure of a large edifice that was not preserved. The construction of such a substructure was necessary because of the steep slope and the narrowness of the ravine at this spot. It appears that the structure postdates the Persian Period.

Figure 4 presents the ground plan and section of the excavated remains. Two structures oriented to the northwest belong to the uppermost level and date to the Byzantine Period; hence they are irrelevant to us. The underlying "gatehouse" comprises two "gate towers" and is based on bedrock. The "gate passage" can be observed between the "gate towers"; it is oriented from west to east and is ca. 3.5 m wide. Crowfoot uncovered the back corner of the northern "gate tower" beneath the overlying Byzantine building; the "gate tower" is thus ca. 8.5 m thick. All of the 19-m-long façade of the southern "gate tower" was exposed, but its back side remained unexcavated. Adjacent to the façade of the "gatehouse" were found other, narrower walls, termed here "additional walls." They were built against the walls of the "gatehouse" and include a wall blocking the "gate passage" and a long wall built parallel to the façade of the "gate towers." The "additional walls," also based on bedrock, rise as high as the walls of the "gatehouse," that is, about 7 m or more, and their orientation also fits that of the "gate-

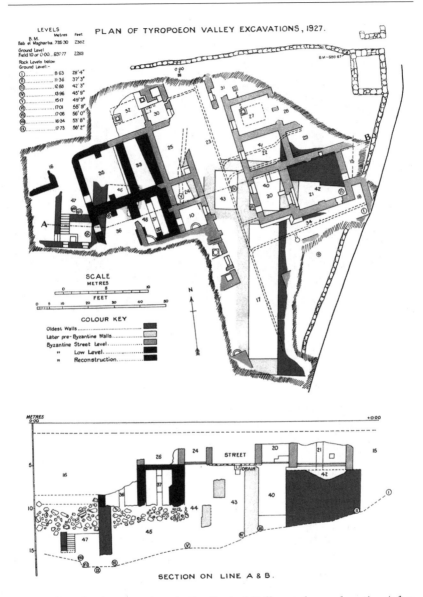

Fig. 4. Crowfoot's excavations in the Central Valley—plan and section (after Crowfoot and Fitzgerald 1929: pl. 22).

house" exactly. However, their style of construction is different from that of the "gatehouse." Crowfoot believed that the "additional walls" were added in the Late Roman Period.

Fig. 5. The "gatehouse" uncovered by Crowfoot: the gate passage and north-ern tower, from southwest (after Crowfoot and Fitzgerald 1929: pl. 1).

The accompanying section (fig. 4) extends across the Central Valley from side to side, facing north. Bedrock is shown at the bottom by broken lines. The northern "gate tower" is shown at right, and parallel to it, the "additional" wall. Both structures are based on the sloping bedrock and were preserved to a height of 6–7 m, reaching the same elevation; the overlying Byzantine building is shown above them.

Figure 5 shows the front corner of the northern "gate tower," which contained large, square-shaped blocks, some of which measure more than 1.30 m. On the right side the sloping bedrock in the "gate passage" can be seen. In the wall of the "gate tower" to the left of the standing man, the entire upper course of stones projects from the line of the wall into the "gate passage."

Figure 6 shows the "gate passage" between the two "gate towers" after the removal of the "additional wall" that blocked it. On the right can be seen one of the "additional walls" built against the corner of the "gate tower." This "additional wall" exactly fits the corner and the orientation of the "gate tower"; both of them were preserved to the same height, but their style of construction differs.

Fig. 6. The "gatehouse" uncovered by Crowfoot, after the removal of the "additional" wall built across the "gate passage"; from northwest (after Crowfoot and Fitzgerald 1929: frontispiece).

Already before the beginning of the excavation, Crowfoot assumed that the city wall of the ancient periods must have passed here. Thus, he wrote in the introduction to the report: "it was hoped that in the course of this excavation we might find traces of the west wall of David's city" (Crowfoot and Fitzgerald 1929: 3).

Based on this assumption, he reached the following conclusions on the structure he uncovered:

At first . . . we were inclined to attribute the towers to the Maccabaean Period, but it soon became obvious that though the towers contained Maccabaean work, the plan of the gate was very much more ancient. The masonry of different parts of the walls varies . . . and it is plain that they have been patched and repaired in the course of time, like most other city walls; but the mere dimensions prove . . . that our walls belong in origin to a much earlier age. . . . Walls like ours which measure more than 27 feet (i.e., *ca.* 9 m.) in thickness are characteristic of the very early days before lime-mortar was used. . . . If a gateway of this type had been found on a hill where nothing else of the Bronze Age was known to exist, few archaeologists would have hesitated to refer it to this period, or, at latest, to the Early Iron Age. (Crowfoot and Fitzgerald 1929: 17; see also Crowfoot 1927: 183)

The gatehouse type characteristic of the Bronze and Iron Ages is well known today, and this model has nothing in common with Crowfoot's so-called gate. The position of the structure at the bottom of the steep slope of the City of David, inside the deep ravine, also lacks any topographical logic for the location of a city gate.

Several data indicate that the so-called gatehouse was in fact a substructure mostly covered by a constructional fill from the time of its construction. One can also assume that the "additional walls" belong to the original structure, although their style of construction differs. The "gate towers" and the "additional walls" were preserved to the unusual height of ca. 6 m or more, the bedrock in the "gate passage" slopes, the wall of the "gate tower" with its projecting stone blocks is badly constructed, all units created by the "gate towers" and the "additional walls" lack any floors or openings—all of these are indications that the so-called gatehouse was merely a substructure.

On the other hand, one datum contradicts the conclusion that the entire fill was laid at the time when the structure was built. A hoard containing 319 coins, mostly dated to the time of Alexander Jannaeus, was discovered in the earthen fill in front of the southern "gate tower" (Crowfoot and Fitzgerald 1929: 15, 19, 103–5). This hoard appears to be a cache, although no container in which the coins had been placed was discovered and although not all the coins were found together. Crowfoot states (1929: 19) that "the greater part" of the coins (hence not all of them) were found "close to the south wall of Room 40," which is one of the "additional walls" built against the southern "gate tower" (fig. 4). The "cache" was found at an elevation 10.8 m below the surface (1929: 15), that is, 1.5–2 m above bedrock. However, the preliminary excavation report states that the coins were uncovered "a little more than a metre above the rock" (Crowfoot 1927: 180).

One can assume that the cache (if indeed it was a cache) was buried not deeper than 1 m from the surface of the time. It would follow, on the basis of this datum, that the floor surface of the time in front of the "gatehouse" extended at 2–3 m above bedrock. However, such a conclusion contradicts all other data, as discussed above.

It is difficult to determine the character of the structure conclusively. It seems that the so-called gatehouse and the "additional walls" were concurrently constructed in the deep ravine as a substructure for a building that was not preserved. One way or another, it seems clear that the structure was not a gatehouse, as suggested by Crowfoot.

The report on the pottery and other finds was prepared by G. M. Fitzgerald. The pottery and finds from the fills above the elevation of the top of the gatehouse walls date to the Late Roman, Byzantine, and later periods (Crowfoot and Fitzgerald 1929: 73–101, pls. 13-17). The lower part of the fills contained Iron Age pottery from the eighth and seventh centuries B.C.E., of the types typical to Lachish Levels III and II; a few fragmentary figurines from this period; as well as Hellenistic pottery (1929: 66–72, pls. 11-12). The Iron Age pottery was possibly embedded in the fills of the structure, but it could also have belonged to the debris antedating the fills that rested at the bottom of the ravine, accumulated here when this area was part of the eighth- and seventh-century city. Both the Hellenistic pottery and the Alexander Jannaeus coins cache hint that these fills, and therefore the adjoining walls of the structure, date to no earlier than the first century B.C.E. or first century C.E.

To end the discussion on the question of a possible city wall that extended along the western side of the City of David: it seems clear that when the large city that emerged in the eighth century B.C.E. was surrounded by a wall, this wall extended around the settled area. There was no need to build a separate wall around the City of David (which at that time was merely one quarter in a large city), and we can safely assume that no city wall was built along the eastern slope of the Central Valley after the end of the Middle Bronze Age. The archaeological evidence is incomplete because most of this region has not been excavated. Nevertheless, the finds from the two fields thus far excavated fit the above conclusion.

When Nehemiah restored the city wall destroyed by the Babylonians in 586 B.C.E., it is clear, in view of all the above, that he restored the city wall that encompassed the Southwest Hill, as suggested by the "maximalists." The theory that Nehemiah restored a Middle Bronze wall that went into disuse many hundreds of years earlier does not make sense.

Based on her excavations, Kenyon suggested that Nehemiah's wall deviated from the line of the eighth–seventh-century city wall along the eastern side of the City of David. Kenyon believed that Nehemiah abandoned the line of the city wall extending along the lower part of the slope and built a new line nearer to the summit (Kenyon 1974: 181–87, fig. 28). This suggestion was adopted by Shiloh (1984: 29) and others (e.g., Stern 2001: 435). In my view it can be assumed that here, too, Nehemiah restored the line of the existing wall extending along the lower slope, on which we now know much more due to the work of Reich and Shukrun (2000; see also Shanks 1999). In the excavation of Area G on the lower part of the slope, Shiloh discovered remains of the Persian Period—pottery and seal impressions. These remains probably belonged to the intramural settlement rather than to an extramural suburb, as he assumed (Shiloh 1984: 20, 29).

At this point, and based on the above conclusions, we must evaluate the written sources, first and foremost the descriptions of the wall in the book of Nehemiah. A full discussion of theses sources is beyond the scope of this paper; let me touch on only two points.

First, in following the identification by Crowfoot in 1927 of the "gatehouse" situated in the Central Valley (see above) this "city gate" was identified by Albright (1930–31: 167) as the 'Dung Gate' (*Sha'ar Ha'ashpoth*) and by Albrecht Alt (1928) as the 'Valley Gate' (*Sha'ar Haggai*), both mentioned in Nehemiah's descriptions. While Albright's suggestion has almost been forgotten, Alt's identification of this structure with *Sha'ar Haggai* has generally been accepted by the "minimalists," for example, Avi-Yonah (1954: 244–45; 1956: 162, map 9), Tzafrir (1977: 39), and Eshel (2000: 333 and n. 30, fig. 1). However, once it is accepted that the structure excavated by Crowfoot is not a gatehouse, this identification falls through. Significantly, the name of this gate also makes it difficult to locate it in the Central Valley. The sole valley in the Jerusalem area defined as *Gai* is *Gei Ben-Hinnom*, the 'Hinnom Valley', which is generally identified with the ravine encompassing eighth–seventh-century Jerusalem along the southern and southwestern border (fig. 2:9). It makes much more sense, therefore, to reconstruct the Valley Gate along the Hinnom Valley, as suggested by the "maximalists," for example, Simons (1952: 443, fig. 56) and Vincent (Vincent and Stève 1954: pl. 61).

The second issue, raised by Ben-Dov (2002: 84–87) relates to the position and number of the city gates. In every walled city, the city gate forms a weak point in the defense line. Hence, the smaller cities of the biblical period, such as Megiddo and Lachish, had only one city gate.

The larger cities, such as Bronze Age Hazor and Ebla, naturally had several city gates located along various parts of the city wall. Jerusalem of the eighth–seventh centuries B.C.E., spread across several hills, must have had a few city gates situated in different parts of the city wall at a fair distance from one another.

This problem becomes evident in the reconstructions of the city based on the "minimalist" concept, for example, Tzafrir's reconstruction, reproduced here in fig. 7. About ten city gates are mentioned in the book of Nehemiah. They are marked in the reconstruction, and their proximity to one another strikes the eye. Such a great number of city gates would better fit a larger city, as suggested by the "maximalists," because the gates would then be located at a considerable distance from one another.

Finally, we must discuss the question of the de facto size of the inhabited city: it appears that the area of urban settlement in Persian Jerusalem did not necessarily parallel the area encompassed by the contemporary city walls.

A cardinal argument raised by the "minimalists" in recent years is that very few remains of the Persian Period have been uncovered in the various excavations carried out in different

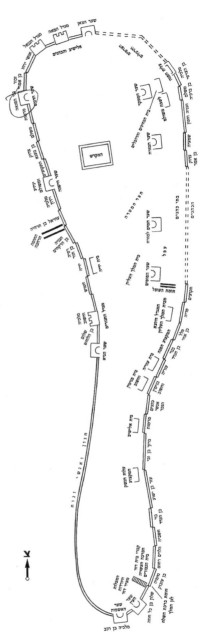

Fig. 7. Suggested reconstruction of Jerusalem in the Persian Period (after Tzafrir 1977: fig. 4).

parts of the Southwest Hill (the present-day Jewish Quarter, Armenian Quarter, Mount Zion, and the Ottoman Citadel). According to the "minimalists," this datum indicates that the Southwest Hill was not included in the settled area during the Persian Period. Their view was well expressed by Avigad:

> In the other, more significant matter, our excavations in the Jewish Quarter supplied unequivocal data, although of a completely negative nature. In all our excavations at many different spots, it has become clear beyond any doubt that the Western Hill was entirely unoccupied during the Persian Period, the period of the Return from Exile. We have discovered here neither structures of this period nor pottery (except for a few isolated sherds). Further, in the excavations conducted within the citadel, in the Armenian Quarter, and on Mount Zion, the only evidence from the Persian period which has come to light is a single *Yehud* coin of the 4th century B.C.
>
> This conclusion is not especially surprising, and can readily be explained by the fact that the relatively few exiles returning were not capable of repopulating and restoring the extensive, desolate quarter on the Western Hill. The smaller City of David was more than sufficient for their needs. . . . From all the above we can conclude that the minimalist view of the settlement in Jerusalem in the period of the Return to Zion is correct—that is, that it was limited to the narrow confines of the City of David, and that the *Mishneh* on the Western Hill remained desolate and uninhabited. (Avigad 1983: 62)

As argued above, it seems clear to me that the entire area surrounded by the eighth–seventh-century city wall was included in the walled settlement of the Persian Period. The archaeological data indicate that the large city contained many unsettled areas and that the populated part of the settlement was situated in the City of David and the area of the Temple Mount. The acute shortage of population in Jerusalem is expressed in Neh 7:4: "The city was large and spacious; there were few people in it and no houses had yet been rebuilt." This is the background to the attempts to resettle the large city, as told in Neh 11:1–2: "The leaders of the people settled in Jerusalem; and the rest of the people cast lots to bring one in every ten to live in Jerusalem, the holy city, while the remaining nine lived in other towns. And the people were grateful to all those who volunteered to live in Jerusalem."

Jerusalem in the Persian Period is not the only case of a large city with many unsettled areas, surrounded by a strong city wall. The situation was similar, for instance, in Constantinople, the capital of the Byzantine Empire, in the period before its conquest by the Ottomans in 1453 C.E. (fig. 8). Runciman vividly describes the situation in Constantinople at that time:

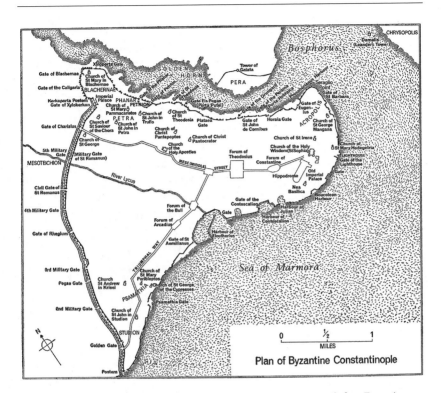

Fig. 8. Map of Constantinople in the fifteenth century C.E. (after Runciman 1965: illustration on p. 88).

The city itself, within its fourteen miles of encircling walls, had even in its greatest days been full of parks and gardens, dividing the various quarters. But now many quarters had disappeared, and fields and orchards separated those that remained. The traveller Ibn Battuta in the mid-fourteenth century counted thirteen distinct townlets within the walls. To Gonzales de Clavijo, in the first years of the fifteenth century, it was astounding that so huge a city should be so full of ruins; and Bertrandon de la Broquière a few years later was aghast at its emptiness. . . . In many districts you would have thought that you were in the open countryside, with wild roses blooming in the hedgerows in spring and nightingales singing in the copses. (Runciman 1965: 9–10)

The case of Constantinople illustrates the case of Jerusalem: a magnificent metropolis, heavily fortified, which due to tragic historical circumstances was emptied of the majority of its population, while the walled area remained as large as it had been before.

One can summarize the history of the city of Jerusalem in the Persian Period as follows. Following the Babylonian conquest of 586 B.C.E., the city was largely destroyed and its population depleted. Nehemiah found the city largely abandoned with its old, massive city walls still standing but partly damaged or destroyed. In an effort to revive Jerusalem, he first turned to restoring the city walls. This action (as pointed out to me by Axel Knauf) was first and foremost a symbolic, national, political act rather than a purely military act. Following this, attempts were made to settle the vast intramural areas, but these attempts largely failed. Large regions of the walled city remained uninhabited, while the population concentrated around the City of David and the area of the Temple Mount. This was probably the appearance of the city encountered by Alexander the Great in 332 B.C.E., and it remained so until its period of renewed prosperity, which began in the Late Hellenistic Period, in the second century B.C.E.

Bibliography

Albright, W. F.
  1930–31 Excavations at Jerusalem. *Jewish Quarterly Review* 21: 163–68.
Alt, A.
  1928 Das Taltor von Jerusalem. *Palästinajahrbuch* 24: 74–98.
Avigad, N.
  1983 *Discovering Jerusalem*. Nashville: Thomas Nelson.
Avigad, N., and Geva, H.
  2000 Iron Age Strata 9–7. Pp. 44–82 in *Architecture and Stratigraphy: Areas A, W and X-2, Final Report*, ed. H. Geva. Vol. 1 of *Jewish Quarter Excavations in the Old City of Jerusalem*. Jerusalem: Israel Exploration Society.
Avi-Yonah, M.
  1954 The Walls of Nehemiah: A Minimalist View. *Israel Exploration Journal* 4: 239–48.
  1956 Topography. Pp. 156–68 in vol. 1 of *Sepher Yerushalayim* (The Book of Jerusalem), ed. Avi-Yonah. Jerusalem: Bialik Institute / Tel Aviv: Dvir. [Hebrew]
Barkay, G.
  1985 *Northern and Western Jerusalem in the End of the Iron Age*. Ph.D. dissertation. Tel Aviv University. [Hebrew]
Ben-Dov, M.
  2002 *Historical Atlas of Jerusalem*. New York: Continuum.
Cahill, J. M.
  2003 Jerusalem at the Time of the United Monarchy: The Archaeological Evidence. Pp. 13–80 in *Jerusalem in Bible and Archaeology: The First Temple Period*, ed. A. G. Vaughn and A. E. Killebrew. Society of Biblical Literature Symposium Series 18. Atlanta: Society of Biblical Literature.

Crowfoot, J. W.
1927   Second Report of the Excavations in the Tyropoeon Valley. *Palestine Exploration Fund Quarterly Statement*: 178–83.
Crowfoot, J. W., and Fitzgerald, G. M.
1929   *Excavations in the Tyropoeon Valley: Jerusalem 1927.* Palestine Exploration Fund Annual 1927. London: Palestine Exploration Fund.
Eshel, H.
2000   Jerusalem under Persian Rule: The City's Layout and the Historical Background. Pp. 327–43 in *The History of Jerusalem: The Biblical Period*, ed. S. Aḥituv and A. Mazar. Jerusalem: Yad Izhak Ben-Zvi. [Hebrew]
Finkelstein, I.
2003   The Rise of Jerusalem and Judah: The Missing Link. Pp. 81–101 in *Jerusalem in Bible and Archaeology: The First Temple Period*, ed. A. G. Vaughn and A. E. Killebrew. Society of Biblical Literature Symposium Series 18. Atlanta: Society of Biblical Literature.
Geva, H.
1979   The Western Boundary of Jerusalem at the End of the Monarchy. *Israel Exploration Journal* 29: 84–91.
1983   Excavations in the Citadel of Jerusalem, 1979–1980. *Israel Exploration Journal* 33: 55–71.
Geva, H., and Avigad, N.
2000   Area W: Stratigraphy and Architecture. Pp. 131–97 in *Architecture and Stratigraphy: Areas A, W and X-2, Final Report*, ed. H. Geva. Vol. 1 of *Jewish Quarter Excavations in the Old City of Jerusalem*. Jerusalem: Israel Exploration Society.
Kenyon, K. M.
1963   Excavations in Jerusalem, 1962. *Palestine Exploration Quarterly* 95: 7–21.
1964   Excavations in Jerusalem, 1963. *Palestine Exploration Quarterly* 96: 7–18.
1968   Excavations in Jerusalem, 1967. *Palestine Exploration Quarterly* 100: 97–109.
1974   *Digging Up Jerusalem.* London: Ernest Benn.
Kloner, A.
1984   Reḥov Hagay. *Excavations and Surveys in Israel* 3: 57–59.
Mazar, A.
1990   *Archaeology of the Land of the Bible, 10,000–586 B.C.E.* New York: Doubleday.
Mazar, B.
1971   The Excavations in the Old City of Jerusalem near the Temple Mount: Second Preliminary Report, 1969–70 Seasons. *Eretz-Israel* 10 (Shazar volume): 1–33. [Hebrew]
Mazar, E., and Mazar, B.
1989   *Excavations in the South of the Temple Mount. The Ophel of Biblical Jerusalem.* Qedem 29. Jerusalem: The Hebrew University, Institute of Archaeology.
Reich, R., and Shukrun, E.
1998   Jerusalem: The Giḥon Spring. *Excavations and Surveys in Israel* 20: 99*–100*.

1999   Jerusalem: The Gihon Spring. *Hadashot Arkheologiyot: Excavations and Surveys in Israel* 109: 77*–78*.

2000   Jerusalem: City of David. *Hadashot Arkheologiyot: Excavations and Surveys in Israel* 112: 82*–83*.

Runciman, S.

1965   *The Fall of Constantinople, 1453.* Cambridge: Cambridge University Press.

Shanks, H.

1995   *Jerusalem: An Archaeological Biography.* New York: Random House.

1999   Everything You Ever Knew about Jerusalem Is Wrong (Well, Almost). *Biblical Archaeology Review* 25/6: 20–29.

Shiloh, Y.

1984   *Excavations at the City of David I. 1978–1982: Interim Report of the First Five Seasons.* Qedem 19. Jerusalem: Hebrew University, Institute of Archaeology.

Simons, J.

1952   *Jerusalem in the Old Testament: Researches and Theories.* Leiden: Brill.

Steiner, M. L.

2001   *The Settlement in the Bronze and Iron Ages.* Vol. 3 of *Excavations by Kathleen M. Kenyon in Jerusalem, 1961–1967.* Copenhagen International Series 9. Sheffield: Sheffield Academic Press.

2003   The Evidence from Kenyon's Excavations in Jerusalem: A Response Essay. Pp. 347–63 in *Jerusalem in Bible and Archaeology: The First Temple Period*, ed. A. G. Vaughn and A. E. Killebrew. Society of Biblical Literature Symposium Series 18. Atlanta: Society of Biblical Literature.

Stern, E.

2001   *The Assyrian, Babylonian and Persian Periods 732–332 B.C.E.* Vol. 2 of *Archaeology of the Land of the Bible.* New York: Doubleday.

Tzafrir, Y.

1977   The Walls of Jerusalem in the Period of Nehemiah. *Cathedra* 4: 31–42. [Hebrew]

Ussishkin, D.

2003a   Solomon's Jerusalem: The Text and the Facts on the Ground. Pp. 103–15 in *Jerusalem in Bible and Archaeology: The First Temple Period*, ed. A. G. Vaughn and A. E. Killebrew. Society of Biblical Literature Symposium Series 18. Atlanta: Society of Biblical Literature.

2003b   Jerusalem as a Royal and Cultic Center in the 10th–8th Centuries B.C.E. Pp. 529–38 in *Symbiosis, Symbolism, and the Power of the Past: Canaan, Ancient Israel, and Their Neighbors from the Late Bronze Age through Roman Palaestina*, ed. W. G. Dever and S. Gitin. Winona Lake, Indiana: Eisenbrauns.

Vincent, H., and Stève, A.

1954   *Jérusalem de l'Ancien Testament: Recherches d'archéologie et d'histoire.* Paris: Gabalda.

Williamson, H. G. M.

1984   Nehemiah's Walls Revisited. *Palestine Exploration Quarterly* 116: 81–88.

Redating Lachish Level I:
Identifying Achaemenid Imperial Policy at the
Southern Frontier of the Fifth Satrapy

ALEXANDER FANTALKIN AND OREN TAL
Tel Aviv University

The extensive archaeological excavations carried out at Lachish (Tell ed-Duweir) have uncovered substantial architectural remains and pottery finds attributed to Level I. Both the British excavations on behalf of the Wellcome-Marston Archaeological Research Expedition to the Near East, under the direction of J. L. Starkey (Tufnell 1953), and the renewed excavations on behalf of the Institute of Archaeology of Tel Aviv University, under the direction of D. Ussishkin (2004), have produced remarkable archaeological data. These data together with the results of surveys in the areas surrounding Lachish (Dagan 1992; 2000) enable us to revise previous interpretations of the finds from Level I (fig. 1). Following our revision, we shall argue that the construction of the Residency of Lachish Level I, and a number of other structures, should be dated to ca. 400 B.C.E., in sharp contrast to the previously suggested date of ca. 450 B.C.E. Our revised chronology for Level I, combined with a reassessment of other sites in southern Palestine, demands a fresh look at a wide range of issues related to the Achaemenid imperial policy in the region. It seems that the establishment of the fortified administrative center at Lachish around 400 B.C.E. and of other Persian centers in southern Palestine at that time became necessary when Persian domination over Egypt came to an end in 404–400/398. Consequently, southern Palestine became an extremely sensitive *frontier* of the Persian Empire, all of which paved the way to a higher level of direct imperial involvement in the local administration.

Author's note: We are grateful to O. Lipschits and M. Oeming for their kind invitation to attend the conference Judah and the Judeans in the Persian Period; D. Ussishkin for placing at our disposal his renewed stratigraphic analysis of the Persian Period occupation at Lachish before its publication; J. N. Tubb and A. Villing for their help in our research at the British Museum, London; and D. Edelman, A. Kuhrt, E. Lytle, and O. Lipschits for commenting on the manuscript.

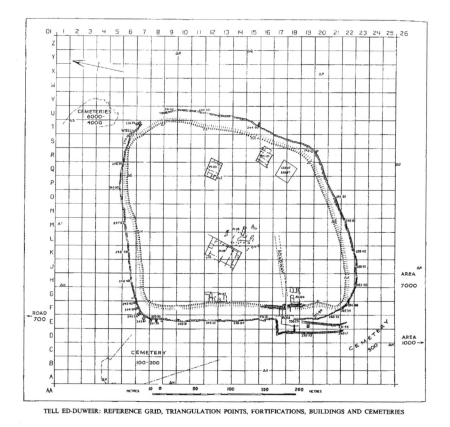

TELL ED-DUWEIR: REFERENCE GRID, TRIANGULATION POINTS, FORTIFICATIONS, BUILDINGS AND CEMETERIES

Fig. 1. Site plan. Reprinted from O. Tufnell, Lachish III: The Iron Age *(London, 1953) pl. 108. Used courtesy of the Wellcome Library, London.*

Archaeological Synopsis of Level I and Its Dating

Lachish is located on a major road leading from the Coastal Plain to the Hebron hills, bordering the Judean foothills (the Shephelah in the local idiom), some 30 km southeast of Ashkelon. According to the archaeological evidence, both the Residency and fortifications (the city wall and the gate) were constructed according to a preconceived plan. These architectural components suggest a Persian governmental center. The Residency was erected on the highest point of the mound upon the podium of the destroyed Judean palace-fort of the Late Iron Age. It was thus located close to the center of the mound, with its back wall facing the city gate. The ground plan of the Residency reflects the com-

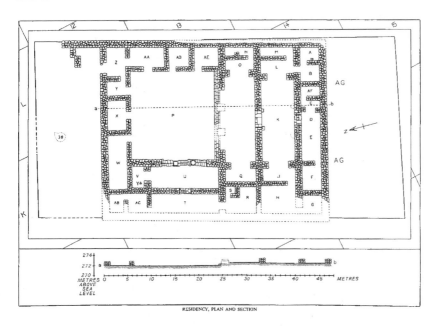

RESIDENCY, PLAN AND SECTION

Fig. 2. Residency. Reprinted from O. Tufnell, Lachish III: The Iron Age
(London, 1953) pl. 119. Used courtesy of the Wellcome Library, London.

bination of an Assyrian building with central courtyard, evident by
the open court in its northern part, and a Syrian *bīt-ḫilāni,* evident by
the portico in the west part of the courtyard (fig. 2).[1] Columns of the
porticoes were made of well-cut drums standing on round column
bases above a square, stepped plinth. The presence of characteristic
dressed stones indicates that some of the rooms were roofed by barrel
vaulting.[2]

---

1. On the Assyrian open courtyard, see in general Amiran and Dunayevsky 1958;
Aharoni 1975: 33–40; Reich 1992a. On the Syrian *bīt-ḫilāni,* see in general Frankfort 1952;
Reich 1992a; Arav and Bernett 2000.
2. The well-cut drums found in the Residency at Lachish are the earliest stone-made
examples documented in Palestine (see Fischer and Tal 2003: 21, 29). In earlier periods,
they were most likely preceded by wooden columns, such as those reconstructed in the
megara-styled Late Bronze Age buildings of cultic nature. A similar process is evident in
the dressed-stone barrel vaulting, which likely replaced a similar technique in mud
brick, for which we have examples in the monumental architecture of Palestine from the
Middle Bronze Age, such as the mud-brick city gates at Tel Dan (*NEAEHL* 1.324–26) and
Ashkelon (*NEAEHL* 1.106–7); and from the Late Iron Age, such as the Assyrian vaulted
mud-brick building at Tell Jemmeh (*NEAEHL* 2.670–72).

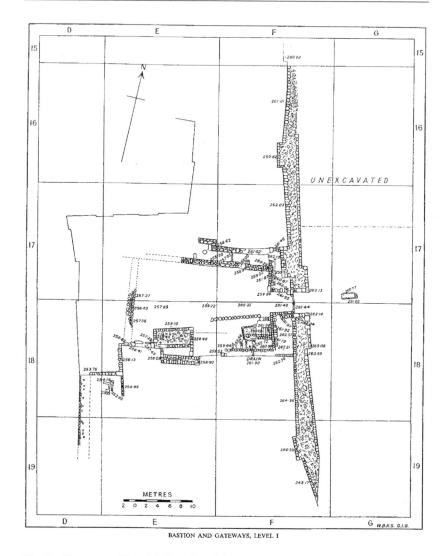

Fig. 3. *City gate of Level I. Reprinted from O. Tufnell,* Lachish III: The Iron
Age *(London, 1953) pl. 112. Used courtesy of the Wellcome Library, London.*

The city wall and the city gate reused the ruined fortifications of the
Late Iron Age Level II, while preserving their contour and method of
construction (fig. 3). By contrast, the Residency was built on pits and
debris layers, which contained Persian-Period pottery predating its

construction, as shown in the renewed excavations (Ussishkin 2004: 96, 842). There is also evidence for its reuse during a subsequent Late Persian or Early Hellenistic stage: the drums of dismantled columns were found in a secondary context (Tufnell 1953: 133 and pl. 22:7).

Based on renewed stratigraphic analysis (Ussishkin 2004: 95–97, 840–46), we may conclude that Level I consisted of three phases:

- The first phase is designated by us Level IA, which is characterized by Early Persian pits.
- The second phase is designated Level IB, which is characterized by massive Late Persian construction. This included the Residency, fortifications, and a number of other structures and corresponds to Lachish's role as a regional administrative center.
- The third phase is designated Level IC, which is characterized by a Late Persian and/or Early Hellenistic occupation, corresponding to the reuse of both the Residency and the building next to the Great Shaft, and the erecting of the Solar Shrine.

In the process of studying local and imported pottery from the renewed excavations of Level I, we were able to establish a more accurate dating for each of these phases (Fantalkin and Tal 2004). The assemblage of Level I consists of common, semifine and imported fine wares. The vast majority of common and semifine ware is definitely local, though there is a single example of an Egyptian ware bowl and few examples of East Greek amphoras from Chios. The common ware includes bowls and heavy bowls, as well as kraters, cooking pots, jugs, juglets, flasks, storage jars, amphoras, and lamps. The semifine ware includes bowls, juglets, and amphoras. The fine ware, for which we have a considerable number of fragments, is restricted to Attic imports. The pottery finds are mostly of Persian date and came from pits and fills that represent occupation layers. The difficulty in distinguishing typological developments in common and semifine ware pottery types of the fifth and fourth centuries B.C.E., forced us to regard the Attic imports as the best anchor in establishing a chronological frame for the occupational periods of Level I.

The bulk of Attic imports retrieved in the renewed excavations must be placed in the first half of the fourth century B.C.E., with several transitional late-fifth/early-fourth-century B.C.E. types (Fantalkin and Tal 2004: 2187–88). The same holds true for the vast majority of Attic imports retrieved during earlier British excavations at the site. This pottery is cursorily described in *Lachish III* but has never been fully published.[3] Despite the difficulties in distinguishing between common and semifine ware from the fifth and fourth centuries B.C.E., the general impression is that a majority of the local pottery is datable to the first half of the fourth century B.C.E. This impression is based on the appearance of so-called "coastal" types at the site and the high occurrence of various pottery types of different wares. These characteristics may point to the fourth century B.C.E., when the regional frontiers of material culture (and especially pottery) were blurred. Unlike the frequency of imports on the Coastal Plain, the diffusion of Attic imports in inland regions such as the Judean foothills and the central mountain ridge is low. Therefore, when encountered in assemblages, Attic imports are typically connected to major administrative centers (as in the case of Samaria). It appears most logical to attribute the bulk of Attic ware retrieved from the site to the Residency—in other words, our Level IB.[4]

In 1953, Olga Tufnell, in her *Lachish III*, dated the foundation of the Residency to ca. 450 B.C.E. (Tufnell 1953: 58–59). This date was based on the Attic imports and the mention of Lachish in Neh 11:30.[5] This date has been subsequently accepted in the archaeological literature as an undisputed fact, the most recent studies not excluded (cf., e.g., Hoglund 1992: 140; Carter 1999: 170; Stern 2001: 447–50; Lipschits 2003: 342). However, since the publication of *Lachish III*, significant progress

3. The present whereabouts of many of these sherds is unknown. However, we located and inspected more than two dozen fragments in the storerooms of the British Museum. The vast majority of these newly rediscovered sherds can be dated to the first half of the fourth century B.C.E., a date consistent with that of the Attic ware retrieved during the more recent excavations.

4. See Tufnell's observation: "At the time of excavations Starkey was of the opinion that the temporary resettlement of the ruined Residency took place in the middle of the fifth century B.C., on the evidence of the Black Glazed and Black Figured Attic sherds, which J. H. Iliffe dated to 475–425 B.C. Further investigation of the position of sherds in relation to the Residency floor levels, however, does not preclude the possibility that the good quality Attic imports were used by the original inhabitants of the building, for there were Attic sherds lying on or close to the original floor surfaces in several rooms" (1953: 133).

5. "Taking into consideration Sir J. D. Beazley's remarks on the Red Figured sherds, Miss du Plat Taylor noted an equal proportion of fifth- and fourth-century types, which limits the time range more closely to the last half of the fifth century, continuing into the fourth century B.C. . . . The contents of the floors and fillings of the Residency rooms were consistent. Characteristic Attic sherds provided the best comparisons to dated pottery from other sites, ranging from the mid-fifth to mid-fourth century B.C. . . . A date for occupation of the Residency from about 450–350 B.C. is in close agreement with the historical evidence, for Lachish is mentioned as one of the villages in which the children of Judah dwelt after Nehemiah's return about 445 B.C." (Tufnell 1953: 133, 135).

has been achieved in the study of plain Attic ware and painted Black and Red Figure ware.[6] Based on studies that have appeared since the publication of *Lachish III*, du Plat Taylor's observation regarding an equal proportion of fifth- and fourth-century types (see n. 4) appears to be inaccurate. Consequently, the bulk of imported pottery should be placed in the first half of the fourth century B.C.E. Tufnell's date for the establishment of the Residency, ca. 450 B.C.E., is irreconcilable with ours. Her argument rests on a miniscule proportion of Attic sherds datable to the late fifth century B.C.E. We believe, however, that these sherds are better explained as heirlooms than as constituting a chronological anchor for the establishment of the Residency.

Most of the pits from Level IA clearly predate the construction of the Residency.[7] Indeed, unlike the Residency, the Attic pottery from these pits includes mostly fifth-century B.C.E. types, such as a few earlier forms of Attic Type A skyphoi.[8] It seems that the "pit settlement"

---

6. It will suffice to cite the publications of the Athenian Agora (namely, Sparkes and Talcott 1970), as well as the series of articles and monographs of B. B. Shefton (2000, with earlier bibliography), among others. We should add that in many instances the dating of a given assemblage in the Athenian Agora are based (in whole or in part) on the recovery of Athenian tetradrachms currently dated to circa 450s–404 B.C. (cf. Kroll 1993: 6–7), and that, more often than not, the higher dating (the 450s) was assumed while establishing a date for any given context. The chronology of the Athenian Agora deposits was criticized by Francis and Vickers (1988) as a part of their approach in lowering the dates of all late Archaic Greek art by roughly 50 years (cf. Francis and Vickers 1985). In this regard, one should mention Bowden's attempt to lower the chronology of Greek painted pottery by roughly 40 years (1991). In both cases, the suggested low chronology for the Greek pottery should be rejected (for a general critique of Francis and Vickers's low chronology, see Cook 1989; for rejecting their lower date for the Athenian Agora deposits, see Shear 1993; for rejecting their lower date for the Near Eastern sites, such as Meẓad Ḥashavyahu, see Waldbaum and Magness 1997: 39–40; Fantalkin 2001a: 128–29; for the improbability of significant lowering of accepted Aegean Iron Age absolute chronology and related problems, see Fantalkin 2001b, with earlier references). Most recently, James has reopened the debate (2003), modifying Bowden's earlier study (1991).

7. The renewed excavations demonstrate that the Residency was erected above pits and debris layers containing typical Persian-Period pottery (Ussishkin 2004: 96). Moreover, more pits were uncovered in the Iron Age courtyard, and C. H. Inge suggested (in a field report dated February 1938) that they also predate the Residency (cited in Tufnell 1953: 151). The Level I city was fortified by a city wall and a city gate built over the ruined fortifications of Level II (Tufnell 1953: 98–99, pl. 112). In Area S of the renewed excavations, it was observed that a Level I pit (Locus 5508) had been cut in a place where the city wall, not preserved at this point, must have passed. According to the excavator, it indicates that the fortifications were also built in our Level IB (Ussishkin 2004: 97, 463, fig. 9.41).

8. It is worth noting that, according to registration files in the British Museum, a fragment of an early-fourth-century B.C.E. Attic glazed bowl (BM/1980,1214.9758) was found in the burnt brick debris, below the level of one of the Residency's rooms. If this is

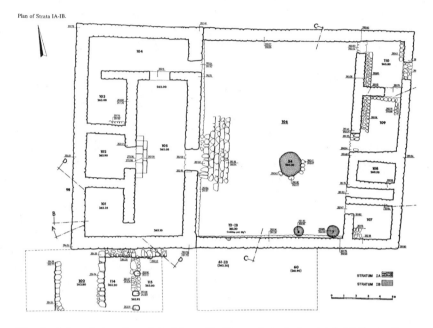

Plan of Strata IA-IB.

Fig. 4. Solar shrine. Reprinted from Y. Aharoni et al., Lachish V: Investigations at Lachish: The Sanctuary and the Residency *(Tel Aviv, 1975)*
pl. 56. Used by permission of the Institute of Archaeology, Tel Aviv University.

of Level IA, preceding the massive construction activities of Level IB,
may be generally dated to the fifth century B.C.E.[9]

Level IC is attributed to the Late Persian and Early Hellenistic occupation of the site. The finds retrieved from the Residency reflect no
definite Hellenistic use. It may be assumed, therefore, that the Residency was reused before the end of the Persian Period and abandoned

---

indeed the case, this sherd may serve as further evidence for placing the Residency
within the first half of the fourth century B.C.E., as suggested by the vast majority of the
finds from the Residency's floors and fills.

9. We tend to consider this phase sporadic, because not all the pits of Level I are necessary connected to Level IA. Moreover, the possibility of the existence of earlier pre–
Level I occupations at the site cannot be completely rejected. There are a few vessels of
possible late-sixth-century B.C. date that were retrieved in the renewed excavations;
among them are an Egyptian bowl (cf. Fantalkin and Tal 2004: fig. 30.7: 1) that is dated
according to comparative material to the Late Saite and Persian Period; and two fragments of Chian amphoras (cf. Fantalkin and Tal 2004: figs. 30.2: 1; 30.3: 16) that can be
dated to the late sixth century B.C.E. In both cases, however, a much later date appears to
be possible.

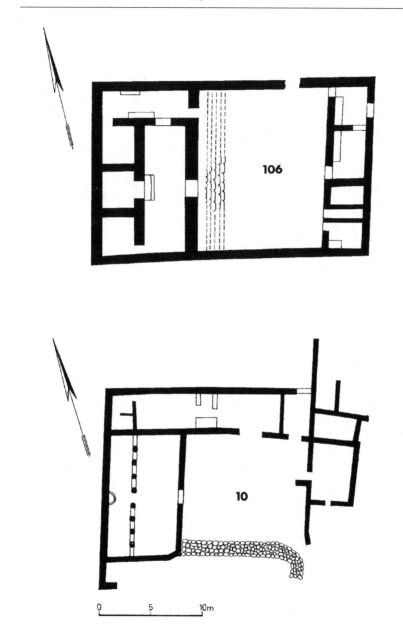

Fig. 5. Solar shrine (top) and building in grid squares R/Q/S.15/16: 10–21 (bottom). Reprinted from Y. Aharoni et al., Lachish V: Investigations at Lachish: The Sanctuary and the Residency *(Tel Aviv, 1975) fig. 3. Used by permission of the Institute of Archaeology, Tel Aviv University.*

during Late Persian times. The ceramic evidence does not clarify the nature of this later phase, and the reasons for the site's abandonment during the Hellenistic Period cannot be determined. The Solar Shrine appears to be the only building of a secure Hellenistic date (fig. 4). Following Aharoni's suggestion, it may be reconstructed as a Yahwistic shrine serving nearby rural, and possibly urban, inhabitants of Jewish faith during the Early Hellenistic Period. We have a dedication altar with a possible Yahwistic name incised upon it found in Cave 534 southwest of the city gate (Tufnell 1953: 226, no. 534, pls. 49:3, 68:1; and see also pp. 383–84; for its reading, Dupont-Sommer in Tufnell 1953: 358–59; and Aharoni 1975: 5–7, fig. 1, with discussion).[10]

This altar formed part of an assemblage found in a number of caves southwest of the city gate (506, 515, 522, 534; cf. Tufnell 1953: 220–21, 224–26) and was probably cultic in nature. The recovery of Persian and Hellenistic pottery in Pit 34 below the floor in the center of the temple's courtyard strongly suggests a Hellenistic date for its foundation. According to Ussishkin (2004: 96 n. 9), this data is not reliable: only a few Hellenistic sherds were uncovered in Pit 34, their stratigraphy is unclear, and a single fragment was uncovered deep beneath the floor of the antechamber. However, if we accept Aharoni's stratigraphic attribution of Building 100 to the Hellenistic Period and contemporaneous stratigraphic relation to the Solar Shrine (Aharoni 1975: 5), we see no possibility for an earlier dating. Moreover, none of the finds recovered in the Solar Shrine is of Persian date. The same holds true for the Hellenistic pottery recovered during Aharoni's excavations but never presented in the report. This pottery is at present in the Israel Antiquities Authority storehouses.

Some reference must be given to another building (fig. 5, bottom) still in use during this phase and discovered to the north of the Great Shaft (Grid Squares R/Q/S.15/16: 10–21). According to Tufnell (1953: 147), "Nearly all the pottery fragments were found on or in the floor levels of the building and can be associated with it." She adds, ". . . there are enough fourth- to third-century forms in the rooms to show that the house was in use at that time" (1953: 148).[11] Aharoni's sugges-

---

10. Starkey's identification of its cult as an intrusive one, "introduced during the Persian regime" (Tufnell 1953: 141 [*PEQ* October (1935) 203]), supported by Ussishkin in light of his reconstruction of the Solar Shrine as a cultic Persian governmental center (2004: 96–97), can be rejected due to the late date of the finds (third and second centuries B.C.E.).

11. Tufnell misread, however, the cooking-pot fragments that are of Early Roman date (cf. 1953: pls. 104, 692) and may well correspond to the two Roman coins found minted at Ashkelon (cf. 1953: 413, nos. 56a and 56b).

tion, based on their similar building plan, orientation, and a limestone altar imitating a shrine (1975: 9–11, fig. 3), that this building served as the fourth- to third-century B.C.E. forerunner of the Solar Shrine is reasonable. It seems that both the Solar Shrine and the building in Grid Squares R/Q/S.15/16: 10–21 were abandoned sometime during the second half of the second century B.C.E.[12]

A Reorganization of the Southern Frontier of the Fifth Satrapy

The Arrangement of Boundaries

Our reevaluation of the archaeological data and the revised chronology for Level I force us to reconsider a range of issues related to Achaemenid imperial policy in southern Palestine.

First, we have to address the question of "Lachish and its fields" mentioned in Neh 11:30. One could suggest that our "pit settlement" (Level IA) is a reflection of the settlement's renewal, which can be connected to Judean settlers returning from the Exile. Likewise, the establishment of the fortified center with the Residency (Level IB) could have been initiated by the Achaemenid government in response to changes occurring in the Judean foothills at the time (cf. Tufnell 1953: 58–59). However, does the present state of research permit us to take literally the passage in Nehemiah 11? Much of the scholarship regarding this particular chapter has recently been summarized and reevaluated by O. Lipschits (2002). According to Lipschits, although a few scholars accept the list's historicity despite historical and textual problems, the vast majority suggest different interpretations. According to some, this list represents settlements where Judeans resided before the Exile, although certain parts of the region were no longer within the boundaries of the province of Yehud. Others suggest that these are the settlements that were not destroyed by the Babylonians and, as such, continued to be settled by Judeans, even though they were subjected to Edomite/Arab influence. It has even been proposed that the list reflects the reality of the end of the First Temple Period or even the Hasmonean Period (see Lipschits 2002, with earlier references). The majority of scholars, however, follow the view of Gerhard von Rad (1930: 21–25), who saw the list in Nehemiah as an ideal vision and not an actual reflection of the borders of Yehud. According to this view, it is a utopian

---

12. According to Finkielsztejn (1999: 48 n. 6), Hellenistic Lachish was destroyed by John Hyrcanus in the course of his campaign in Edom. We cannot support such a claim, however. No Hellenistic destruction is documented at the site, and none of the Hellenistic finds attests to an exclusive Edomite presence.

outlook, based on perceptions of the remote past and on hopes for the future, after the building of the walls of Jerusalem.

What can be said from an archaeological perspective? The establishment of the Persian fortified administrative center around 400 B.C.E. is definitely preceded by the "pit settlement." A special term appears in Neh 11:30 for the hinterland of Lachish—שדתיה, that is, its fields. It seems that the author had an intimate knowledge of Lachish's area and thus deliberately labeled it in a different manner as an agricultural hinterland. In the survey map of Lachish, eleven settlements from the Persian Period were documented (Dagan 1992: 17*). Given the nature of material collected in the surveys, it is virtually impossible to establish their precise chronological setting within the Persian Period. Generally, they could be attributed to a fifth and fourth centuries B.C.E. chronological horizon. It seems to us, however, that given the existence of the "pit settlement" at Lachish already in the fifth century B.C.E. (Level IA), it is more than probable that some of the sites discovered in the survey are of the same date. The establishment of the Persian fortified administrative center around 400 B.C.E. (Level IB) can be seen as a response to the changes occurring in the area. Who were these new settlers? Were they Judeans, Edomites/Arabs, or both? Based on the archaeological data, we find it virtually impossible to answer this question in a satisfactory manner. It should be noted, however, that even many of those who follow von Rad's view admit that, although Nehemiah 11 is an ideal vision, there is no dismissing the possibility that Judeans continued to live in the towns of the Negev and the Judean foothills during the sixth and fifth centuries B.C.E., after the Babylonian destruction (cf. Lipschits 2002). It seems that, even if some Judeans did indeed remain in this region, a larger number of Edomites/Arabs expanded toward the north, gaining control over lands of questionable Judean control. Epigraphic evidence suggests that, by at least the second half of the fourth century, a majority of Edomites/Arabs inhabited the region side by side with a minority of Judeans (Zadok 1998: 792–804; Lemaire 2002: 218–23, 231–33, 264–83, 284–85). The resettlement in the area surrounding Lachish during the fifth century B.C.E., either by Judeans, Edomites, or both may have created potential territorial quarrels between the inhabitants of the area. The establishment of the administrative center at Lachish (bordering Judah and Edom) could have played a significant role in preventing any further territorial disputes in an area where borders are flexible. This new reality required a new policy in which a Persian official, or officials, most likely with a garrison, were stationed permanently at Lachish in order to protect the political, economic, and social interests of the Empire in the region.

This new interpretation of the archaeological data from Lachish forces us to reconsider the previous scholarly consensus regarding the boundaries of the province of Yehud. Those who believe that the list in Nehemiah 11 is wishful thinking have stated that such a utopia can be explained by the fact that most of the settlements appearing in the list are in areas that are not within the boundaries of the province at the time of Return, whereas the actual areas of settlement are hardly represented. What do we really know about the boundaries of the province at the time of Return, that is, the fifth century B.C.E.? Can the existence of these boundaries during the Early Persian Period really be assumed?

The boundaries of Yehud are one of the most debated issues in the study of the Persian Period in the region of Israel. According to most scholars, after the Neo-Babylonian destruction, Lachish never reverted to being a part of Judah, and it likely served as the center of the province of Edom (see, most recently, Lipschits 2003: 342). However, there are still numerous questions concerning the boundaries of both provinces, Yehud and Edom, during the Persian Period (see Carter 1999: 75–113, 288–94, with earlier references). The insufficiency of biblical testimony and the fragility of the archaeological interpretations have led some to apply Christaller's "Central Place Theory" (1933) to the analysis of the boundaries of Yehud. This theory is based on the logical assumption that the socioeconomic relationship between larger, central sites and smaller, "satellite" sites is best represented graphically, through a series of interconnected hexagons, a spatial organization that is similar to the geographical organization implemented in southern Germany during the 1930s. This model was subsequently applied to other geographical settings, while political, economic, and social aspects of a settlement were reconstructed according to a pattern of "Site Hierarchy" (cf. Lösch 1954; Haggett 1965: especially pp. 121–25). Later scholars such as Johnson (1972), who suggests that a rhomboid pattern is preferable to a hexagonal one, modify the model without contradicting its basic premises (see in general Jansen 2001: 42–44). Scholars who have tried to apply this theory to the boundaries of Yehud have drawn a series of circles or ellipses with radii of approximately 20 km surrounding Jerusalem, Lachish, and Gezer (cf., e.g., Carter 1999: 93–97, fig. 7). Both Lachish and Gezer, at least according to general scholarly consensus, have architectural remains that can be interpreted as governmental complexes. It is postulated that the spheres of influence of these sites intersect at the border of the Judean foothills and the hill country. The Judean foothills were therefore outside the province of Yehud.

It is definitely not our intention to embark here on taking theoretical models from the exact sciences and applying them to a complicated human past. What appears to be quite certain, however, is that the new archaeological evidence from Lachish undermines previously proposed reconstructions of the boundaries of the provinces of Yehud and Edom, based as they are on the Central Place Theory. These reconstructions assumed the establishment of Lachish Phase IB as a major administrative center by at least 450 B.C.E. (i.e., Tufnell's dating), in stark contrast to the foundation date closer to 400 B.C.E. that is suggested here. It seems to us that, given the contested nature of the region's periphery (cf. Berquist 1996; M. J. Allen 1997), the final settlement of its boundaries, including those of Yehud, is better seen as part of a flexible process that was finally accomplished no earlier than the fourth century B.C.E. In this regard, it is worthwhile to remember that the creation of an Idumean provincial district cannot be traced before the fourth century B.C.E. (cf. de Geus 1979–80: 62; Eph'al 1984: 199; Graf 1990: 139–43). The same holds true for Yehud. This is not to suggest that Judah was not an autonomous entity with a series of governors already in the beginning of the Achaemenid Period (Williamson 1998) and perhaps even earlier (Na'aman 2000). But signs of autonomy such as the minting of Yehud coins and standardized Aramaic stamp-seal impressions on local storage-jar handles, whether connected to the Judahite administrative authority or more likely simply to be explained as potter's marks (Ariel and Shoham 2000: 138–39), probably did not appear before the fourth century B.C.E.[13] The same holds true for a few thousand Aramaic ostraca (Lemaire 1996; 2002; Eph'al and Naveh 1996, all with further bibliography) and a "dated" ostracon discovered earlier that actually dates to 363 B.C.E., all allegedly from the site of Khirbet el-Kom and its immediate environs in the Judean foothills (Edom). It thus seems that southern Palestine experienced a significant transformation in its political organization sometime around 400 B.C.E. This transformation suggests a higher level of direct imperial involvement in the local administration. What one can observe here is a completely different

13. On the chronology of the Yehud coins, see the recently published summary by Ariel on the coins discovered during "Operation Scroll" in the caves of the northern Judean Desert: dates of "early" coin types are lowered on the basis of their contexts (2002: 287–94, with further references). On the Aramic stamp-seal impressions, see the recently published summary by Ariel and Shoham (2000), where Persian types are differentiated from Hellenistic counterparts on the basis of contexts, comparisons, and paleography.

level of Achaemenid involvement in local affairs that most likely included a fixed arrangement of district boundaries, garrisoning of the frontiers, and, most of all, tight Achaemenid control and investment, witnessed by the unprecedented construction at the sites in southern Palestine briefly and selectively described below.

A New Architectural Landscape

Tell Jemmeh in the southeastern Coastal Plain should be considered another example of Achaemenid governmental presence. The site, located some 10 km south of Gaza, was excavated during the 1920s, first by W. J. Phythian-Adams (1923) and, more thoroughly, by W. M. F. Petrie (1928). In accordance with Stern's thorough analysis of Petrie's stratigraphic conclusions (1982: 22–25), Persian remains at the site should be divided into three stratigraphic phases: the first, probably of mid-fifth-century B.C.E. date—Building A—a central courtyard fortress with dimensions of ca. 38 × 29 m; the second, probably of late-fifth/early-fourth-century B.C.E. date—Building B—a Residency (or "Palace") composed of two separate units of the central courtyard house type; and the third, probably of late-fourth- to third-century B.C.E. date—storehouse and granaries—scattered on the mound. This theory may be strengthened by the limited number of published Attic fragments and vessels from Petrie's excavations (1928: pl. 46; but see also Iliffe 1933: nos. 8–11, 13–14, 16–19, 21, 23, 25–27, 29–31, 33–36, and relevant plates; and Shefton 2000: 76 n. 4). It would, however, be extremely intriguing to recheck these data in light of the recent excavations carried out at the site (cf. Van Beek 1983; 1993; *NEAEHL* 2.667–74).[14]

---

14. It is worth quoting some of Van Beek's observations regarding the date of the Persian remains at Tell Jemmeh: "Petrie's historical biases led to strange interpretations as, for example, his haste to have granaries built by 457 B.C.E. so that they might serve as grain depots to feed a Persian army during its invasion of Egypt in 455 B.C.E. The key evidence here is the large red-figured lekythos in the Rockefeller Museum, which was found beneath one of the granaries [Petrie 1928: pl. 46: 4]. This lekythos was reluctantly dated to 460 B.C.E. by Gardiner, as against his preferred date of 450 B.C.E.; but for Petrie, a date of 450 was seven years too late to get it under a granary. Indeed, the lekythos may well have been *in situ* in the pre-granary layers, rather than having been thrown in the foundation hole just prior to construction of the granary, as Petrie assumed. According to Beazley, the lekythos is by the Phiale Painter, a pupil of the Achilles Painter, both of whom were active between 450 and 420 B.C.E. On this evidence alone, the granaries could hardly be dated much before the end of the 5th or early 4th centuries B.C.E. Thus, Petrie's lack of interest in late periods and his historical biases led to a cavalier treatment of archaeological deposits from the granary periods" (Van Beek 1993: 577–78, with earlier references). Bearing in mind this quotation, Tufnell's comparisons with dated pottery from other sites, chiefly with Tell Jemmeh's 457 B.C.E. dating (1953: 135; see above, n. 5), further undermines her dating of the Residency.

Persian remains at Tel Seraᶜ are quite similar to those discovered at Tell Jemmeh. The site is located in the western Negev desert on Naḥal Gerar, some 20 km to the east of Tell Jemmeh. Judging from the short report published by the excavator, Persian-Period Tel Seraᶜ (Stratum III) consisted of the same elements discovered at Tell Jemmeh: a brick-lined granary (ca. 5 m in diameter) in Area A on the south part of the mound and the remains of a citadel and courtyard building in Area D on the north part of the mound (*NEAEHL* 4.1334).

The same applies to the remains discovered at Tel Haror located in the western Negev desert on Naḥal Gerar, located midway between Tell Jemmeh and Tel Seraᶜ. The excavator's brief report concludes that there are one or two Persian-Period settlement phases at the site (i.e., Stratum G1), represented in Area G on the southern part of the upper mound by a large building, cobbled floors, and grain and refuse pits (*NEAEHL* 2.584). It is thus tempting to see both Tel Seraᶜ and Tel Haror in a similar stratigraphic context to the one suggested in Tell Jemmeh, since both sites not only share similar architectural elements but also yielded numerous Greek ware fragments, Aramaic ostraca, and other finds that may point to a governmental role.

To the above sites, we are inclined to add Tel Ḥalif, located some 15 km to the east of Tel Seraᶜ. Excavations in Stratum V, which, according to the excavators, belongs to the Persian Period, uncovered elements of a large building with walls one meter thick in Field II and pits and bins scattered in Fields I and III and Area F6 (*NEAEHL* 2.558). Furthermore, the excavators of Tell el Ḥesi, some 20 km to the north of Tel Seraᶜ, conclude that the Persian-Period settlement at this site ceased to exist by the end of the fifth century B.C.E. (Bennett and Blakely 1989). Therefore, one may presume a southward shift in the settlement process of the western Negev desert region at this time. Needless to say, without the full analysis and publication of the finds from these sites, our argument is largely theoretical. However, the architectural elements discovered in the excavations of Tell Jemmeh, Tel Haror, Tel Seraᶜ, and Tel Ḥalif, as well as their location along the same latitude line and their placement at somewhat fixed intervals of 10–15 km on the southernmost inhabited Lowlands regions of southwestern Palestine, doubtless had an Egyptian-oriented raison d'être.

The location of governmental sites in the Highlands (the central mountain ridge) was dictated by other factors, among which topography and the immediate environs seem to have played a significant role.

Reich's reconstruction of the Beth-Zur II Citadel as a Persian Residency on the basis of its similarity to Lachish (in dimensions and building plan) is worth noting (1992b). The site is located some 30 km south of Jerusalem in the hill country of Judah. Whether we accept or reject his reconstruction (and see Carter's counterarguments, 1999: 154–57), the fact remains that the pottery finds and coins (Sellers 1933; Sellers et al. 1957) show that, during the late fifth or early fourth century B.C.E., Beth-Zur experienced a change in its settlement history. At this time a fortress or, perhaps, a residency was erected at the site.

The same is perhaps true of the meager architectural remains discovered at Ramat Raḥel (Stratum IVb), which include the sections of a wall (1.2 m thick) in the eastern part of the excavated area, following the course of an earlier Iron-Age citadel's outer wall. According to the excavator, it served as part of a defensive wall enclosing a large courtyard and a complex of three rooms (two adjoining and a larger to the south) with a passageway between (Aharoni 1964: 17–19). Aharoni dated the material from Stratum IVb, especially the material discovered in the foundation trench of the defensive wall, to a transitional Persian–Hellenistic date—that is, the late fourth century B.C.E. This date, however, is disputed by Stern (1982: 35–36), who suggests a fifth-century B.C.E. date on the basis of the recovered Attic and east Greek ware. However, the few published Attic fragments (Aharoni 1956: pl. 13C) may easily attest a fourth-century B.C.E. date. Furthermore, Naʾaman has recently suggested that, during the period of the Neo-Assyrian domination over Palestine (Stratum Vb), Ramat Raḥel's citadel served the seat of an Assyrian official appointed to supervise Jerusalem's affairs (2001). It seems that the site was abandoned (or destroyed) sometime during the last quarter of the seventh century B.C.E. (Stratum Va). Naʾaman suggests that during the fifth century B.C.E., after Jerusalem was established as the center of the province of Yehud, the Achaemenid authorities resettled Ramat Raḥel (Stratum IVb), making it their center of government, similar to that of the Neo-Assyrians. In any case, none of the published finds from the excavations at Ramat Raḥel attests an exclusively fifth-century B.C.E. date.

ʿEn Gedi (Tel Goren) on the western shore of the Dead Sea is another worthy example. Here as well one may suggest a governmental function for the site as a royal estate during the Iron Age and the Persian Period (cf. Lipschits 2000; 2003: 340). The excavators postulate a fifth- and fourth-century B.C.E. occupation date, based on the main feature of the Persian Period at the site, Building 234 (Mazar, Dothan, and Dunayevsky 1966: 38–39; but especially Mazar and Dunayevsky 1967: 134–40). According to the excavators, Building 234 was in use during the last three-quarters of the fifth century B.C.E. and was destroyed in ca. 400 B.C.E. Judging from the Attic ware distribution within Building 234, the excavators conclude that the western part of the building was cleared of debris and reused as a dwelling by the surviving inhabitants of the site for half a century or more (the first half of the fourth century B.C.E.) until this too was destroyed by nomadic (possibly Nabatean) raiders (Mazar and Dunayevsky 1967: 138). The finds from this later phase, such as glass pendants in the shape of human heads and a relief-ware rhyton, are not consistent, however, with the proposed lateral domestic function assigned by the excavators to this later phase. Excavations at the site were published in a preliminary form, and it is thus difficult to verify their conclusions. As it stands, there is a consensus that some construction activity occurred in ca. 400 B.C.E.

There is certainly an extensive amount of site hierarchy among the above-mentioned governmental sites, and a few suspected others that are beyond the scope of this study. In our opinion, however, Lachish ranked fairly high on our proposed hierarchical ladder.

With the above outline of the southern governmental Palestinian sites of the inhabited land in mind, we can now briefly address the question of the Negev desert fortresses (and suspected fortresses), which yield some indications of Persian-Period occupation. Among them are Ḥorvat Rogem (Cohen and Cohen-Amin 2004: 160–72); Ḥorvat Ritma (Meshel 1977; Cohen and Cohen-Amin 2004: 185), Meṣad Naḥal HaRoʿa (Cohen 1980: 71–72; 1986: 112–13; Cohen and Cohen-Amin 2004: 176–85), Ḥorvat Mesora (Cohen 1980: 70; 1986: 113; Cohen and Cohen-Amin 2004: 172–75), as well as the suspected fortresses located at Arad (Aharoni 1981: 8; Herzog 1997: 245–49; *NEAEHL* 1.85), Beer-sheba (Aharoni 1973: 7–8; *NEAEHL* 1.172), and perhaps also at Tell el Farʿah (S), where tombs with varied finds of the period were excavated (Stern 1982: 75–76). Surprisingly, the location of these fortresses on the same latitude line suggests a linear setting. We have Ḥorvat Rogem, Arad, Beer-sheba, and possibly Tell el Farʿah (S) arranged in linear fashion on the edge of the inhabited territory and Meṣad Naḥal Ha-Roʿa, Ḥorvat Ritma, and Ḥorvat Mesora in another somewhat linear pattern some 30 km to the south of the former. We further suggest that Kadesh-barnea (Cohen 1980: 72–74, 78; but especially 1983: 12–13) and ʿEn Ḥazeva (biblical Tamar; Cohen and Yisrael 1996; but see Naʾaman 1997, who suggests that the Stratum 4 fortress is of Persian date) were the southernmost defensive line against the south (i.e., Egypt), although Persian finds at Kadesh-barnea were attributed by the excavator to an unwalled domestic settlement and at ʿEn Ḥazeva are merely absent. Evidently, all suspected fortresses were located on main routes,

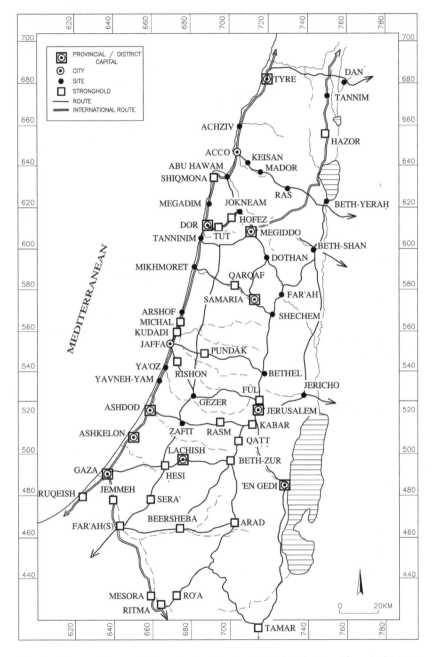

Fig. 6. Sites and suggested routes in Persian-Period Palestine (from Tal 2005: fig. 1).

with the aim of protecting the southern Arabian trade and alerting the Persians to an approaching Egyptian army (fig. 6). The preliminary form of some publications on these fortresses and suspected fortresses as well as the reported character of the finds make it difficult to reach a conclusion on the precise date within the Persian Period for each foundation—the more so, because the finds shown in the recent final publication of the Negev highlands Persian-Period fortresses (namely Ḥorvat Rogem, Ḥorvat Ritma, Meṣad Naḥal HaRoʿa, and Ḥorvat Mesora; Cohen and Cohen-Amin 2004: 159–201) point to a late Persian rather than an early Persian date, although the finds are quite scant and the quantity of imported ware is very small. One thing is clear, however: the careful pattern of their arrangement indicates that most (if not all) were contemporaneous with each other. What is the best explanation for this new settlement pattern?

*The Rationale behind the Achaemenid Imperial Policy at the
Southern Frontier of the Fifth Satrapy*

What occurred in the region that triggered the Achaemenid authorities to act in the way they did? A broader look, beyond the borders of southern Palestine, shows that in 404–400/398? B.C.E. Persian domination over Egypt, in effect since 525 B.C.E. (almost continuously), came to an end.[15] It seems that the end of Persian domination in Egypt and the establishment of the fortified administrative center at Lachish, both around 400 B.C.E., as well as the establishment of other Persian centers in southern Palestine at that time are not just coincidental. In this case, the establishment of Persian fortified administrative centers at Lachish, Tell Jemmeh, Tel Haror, Tel Seraʿ and Tel Ḥalif, Beth-Zur, Ramat Raḥel, and ʿEn Gedi must be seen, not just as a response to the changes occurring in the region during the fifth century B.C.E., but mainly as a response to a new political reality: Egypt is no longer a part of the Persian Empire or subject to Achaemenid rule. Graf's suggestion that garrisons strung between Gaza and the southern end of the Dead Sea protecting the southern frontier during the period of Egypt's independence between 404–343 B.C.E. (1993: 160) may fit well with such a

---

15. Due to the fact that one of the documents in the Elephantine archive, from September 400 B.C.E., refers to Year 5 of King Amyrtaeus (most likely a grandson of Amyrtaeus I), he must have been proclaimed Pharaoh during 404 B.C.E. Based on the Elephantine documents, it may be safely assumed that, though between 404 and 400 B.C.E. Upper Egypt still remained under Persian control, Amyrtaeus had already dominated all or part of the Delta (Briant 2002: 619, 987, with earlier references).

reconstruction, especially when one observes the linear arrangement of the fortresses listed above.

Lowering the dating of the establishment of the Residency at Lachish to around 400 B.C.E. may have additional significance. More than a decade ago, Hoglund proposed that the Inarus Rebellion in ca. 464–454 B.C.E. was an extremely significant event due to Delian League involvement. He argues that this is the reason for the establishing of a network of Persian fortresses of a distinctive type (central courtyard) in Palestine, dating to the mid-fifth century B.C.E. (Hoglund 1992: 137–205). This theory was adopted in another extensive summary published by Carter (1999) and most recently by Betlyon (2004). In all cases, the ca. 450 B.C.E. date is seen as a clear-cut line in the history of Persian-Period Palestine. Tufnell's dating of the Residency at Lachish to ca. 450 B.C.E. may have served as key evidence for both Hoglund and Carter. Based on Hoglund's work, Carter suggests a new subdivision for the Persian Period: Persian Period I lasts from 538 to 450 B.C.E. and Persian Period II from 450 to 332 B.C.E. Those reconstructions, however, find no echoes in the archaeological record (see critique on Carter's method in Lipschits 2003: 359; but more extensively, Sapin 2003; and on Hoglund's method, Sapin 2004: 112–24). In fact, *not a single site* in Hoglund's list of fortresses can be dated with any degree of certainty to around 450 B.C.E. The same holds true for Hoglund's list of sites in Transjordan.[16] From the data presented above, it is clear that both Hoglund's and Carter's theories must be rejected.

The Inarus Rebellion was just another event in a series of upheavals in the long period of Persian rule over Palestine and Egypt (cf., e.g., Tal 1999: table 4.13, with relevance to the southern Sharon Plain). This event, with no trace of rebellion anywhere but in the Nile Delta (Briant 2002: 575–77, 973), was not significant enough to motivate a new policy regarding the political reorganization of Palestine. The events that had

---

16. Thus, Hoglund amends Pritchard's date of 420 B.C.E. for Tell es-Saʿidiyeh's Persian-Period building, placing it in the mid-fifth century B.C.E. However, the recent excavations at Tell es-Saʿidiyeh have demonstrated that Prichard's Stratum III square building must be seen as the climax of a renovation process above a number of earlier levels of a courtyard building that started sometime in the Persian Period or even earlier (Tubb and Dorrell 1994: 52–59). Therefore, as Bienkowski points out, "these earlier levels may not fit into Hoglund's suggested chronology, or his proposed construction specification for a garrison" (2001: 358). Moreover, Bienkowski offers an additional example of a Persian-Period administrative building discovered at al-ʿUmayri (cf. Herr 1993), which continues from the Neo-Babylonian period, "suggesting that such administrative buildings simply reused existing structures" (Bienkowski 2001: 358).

followed the year 404 B.C.E., on the other hand, seem to be on a completely different scale. We believe that the situation in Egypt and the new reality in southern Palestine triggered the Persian authorities to establish an impressive administrative center at Lachish. The establishment of the Residency was accompanied by additional architectural features (see above) and reflected a new political reality that apparently demanded a new "imperial landscape" (cf. DeMarrais, Castillo, and Earle 1996). We have to realize that, for the first time in more than a century of Persian rule, southern Palestine became *the frontier* of the Persian Empire. This frontier was an extremely sensitive one, not only bordering on recently rebellious Egypt, but also subject to external influences from the west (Berquist 1996). It is no longer plausible to speculate that, after the Persian conquest, Egyptian civilization continued just as before, virtually unaffected. New discoveries have shown that Egypt was an integrated and extremely important part of the Achaemenid Empire (Briant 2001, with earlier references). One has to recognize the significance of this new situation for both Persian and Egyptian affairs, especially during the first half of the fourth century B.C.E. (Briant 2002: 664–66, 991–92). As Ray has pointed out, "the entire history of Egypt in the fourth century was dominated, and perhaps even determined, by the presence of Persia, a power which doubtless never recognized Egyptian independence, and which was always anxious to reverse the insult it had received from its rebellious province" (Ray 1987: 84). With southern Palestine as the southern frontier of the Persian Empire, the region must have been organized differently. From an archaeological point of view, it looks as though the Persian authorities expended significant energy organizing their newly created buffer zone with Egypt ca. 400 B.C.E. We are suggesting that only after this date should one look for established boundaries for the provinces of Yehud or Edom. It seems that before this date, during the fifth century B.C.E., the Persian authorities deliberately permitted a certain degree of independence with regard to the resettlement of the area: first they let the newly established rural communities organize themselves and, thereafter, they included them within a rigid taxation system. The organization and spatial distribution of these newly established rural communities may be seen as an internal creation, due to the "self-organization process,"[17]

---

17. For a definition and theoretical framework for the "self-organization" paradigm, see Nicolis and Prigogine 1977; Prigogine and Stengers 1984; Haken 1985; McGlade and van der Leeuw 1997. For methodological implications, see Allen 1982; 1997; cf. also Schloen 2001: 57–58. In terms of the "self-organization" approach, the arrival of the Golah

and without strict imperial intervention at any time during the fifth century B.C.E.[18]

The ethnic diversity in the area discussed—Judeans, Idumeans, Samaritans, descendants of the Philistines, which included a strong Phoenician element and even Greeks (cf. Eph'al 1998)—may be seen as an additional component that triggered the immediate need for the intervention of imperial authority in the newly established frontier, resulting in roads,[19] fortresses, and royal residences.[20]

The Effects of the Achaemenid Reconquest of Egypt on Southern Palestine

Persian domination over Egypt was reestablished for a short period, between 343 and 332 B.C.E., prior to the Macedonian conquest.[21] As a result, the frontier shifted once more, leaving Palestine deep in Achaemenid territory. It is thus tempting to connect the 343 B.C.E. date with the archaeologically attested abandonment of the Residency, which was then reused by local inhabitants during the late years of Persian rule.[22] In this context, for levels attributed to the Late Persian Period, it

---

returnees, who may be considered a "Charter Group" (see Kessler, in this volume, pp. 91–121), doubtless creates a new paradigm. This new pattern suggests that the Golah returnees may be identified as creating an "order parameter" that "enslaved" a previous unsteady system and brought it into a new steady state. This transformation took place during the fifth century B.C.E. as a result of "self-organization" and without strict Achaemenid intervention. However, the imperial Achaemenid authority, doubtless stood behind the initial decision-making, that is, in letting the groups of people return. In this regard one should look for a delicate combination of the so-called "positive-pull factors" and the "negative-push factors" that make any migration possible (cf. Antony 1990; Burmeister 2000).

18. Perhaps with the exception of Stratum IVb at Ramat Raḥel, which may be considered the sole center of Persian government during the fifth century B.C.E. However, even this attribution is uncertain due to the fact that none of the published finds from the excavations at Ramat Raḥel attests to an exclusive fifth-century B.C.E. date (see above).

19. For the political reasoning behind the construction and maintenance of formal road systems, see Earle 1991. For the social complexity inherent in the establishment of a road system, see Hassig 1991.

20. For somewhat similar cases of organizing a frontier, see Smith 1999; 2000 (for Urartu); and Parker 1997; 2001; 2002; Gitin 1997 (for Neo-Assyria). For suggested reorganization of the Achaemenid Cilician frontier at the beginning of the fourth century B.C.E., see Casabonne 1999.

21. For the reconquest of Egypt in 343/342 B.C.E., see, in general, Briant 2002: 685–88, with earlier references.

22. Here, some reference must be made to the Tennes Rebellion; it was Barag (1966) who first suggested that destruction (and abandonment) evident in more than a few

is abandonment rather than destruction that we are witnessing in the above-listed governmental sites of southern Palestine, with the exception of the alleged destruction at ʿEn Gedi. Some of these sites were never resettled after this abandonment, while others were occupied during the Hellenistic Period, a few of which preserved the governmental character of their Achaemenid predecessors.

sites in Palestine, the Coastal Plain, Galilee, and Judah, including Lachish and ʿEn Gedi (1966: 11 and n. 31) are the result of this event. Stern on the other hand partially relates this event to several sites along the coast of Palestine (1982: 243; 1995: 274). The extent of this rebellion and its exact dating are still questionable (Elayi 1990: 182–84; Briant 2002: 683–84, 1004). Our reconstruction tends to support Stern's view and other minimalists.

Bibliography

Aharoni, Y.
 1956 Excavations at Ramat Raḥel, 1954: Preliminary Report. _Israel Exploration Journal_ 6: 102–11, 137–57.
 1964 _Excavations at Ramat Raḥel: Seasons 1961 and 1962._ Rome.
 1981 _Arad Inscriptions._ Jerusalem.
Aharoni, Y. (ed.)
 1973 _Beer-Sheba I: Excavations at Tel Beer-Sheba, 1969–1971 Seasons._ Tel Aviv University Publications of the Institute of Archaeology 2. Tel Aviv.
Aharoni, Y., et al.
 1975 _Lachish V: Investigations at Lachish: The Sanctuary and the Residency._ Tel Aviv University Publications of the Institute of Archaeology 4. Tel Aviv.
Allen, M. J.
 1997 _Contested Peripheries: Philistia in the Neo-Assyrian World-System._ Ph.D. dissertation, University of California, Los Angeles.
Allen, P. M.
 1982 The Genesis of Structure in Social System: The Paradigm of Self-Organization. Pp. 347–74 in _Theory and Explanation in Archaeology,_ ed. C. Renfrew, M. J. Rowlands, and B. A. Segraves. New York.
 1997 Models of Creativity: Toward a New Science of History. Pp. 39–56 in _Time, Process and Structured Transformation in Archaeology,_ ed. S. E. van der Leeuw and J. McGlade. One World Archaeology 26. London and New York.
Amiran, R., and Dunayevsky, I.
 1958 The Assyrian Open-Court Building and Its Palestinian Derivatives. _Bulletin of the American Schools of Oriental Research_ 149: 25–32.
Antony, D. W.
 1990 Migration in Archaeology: The Baby and the Bathwater. _American Anthropologist_ 92: 895–914.

Arav, R., and Bernett, M.
2000 The *bīt-ḫilāni* at Bethsaida: Its Place in Aramaean/Neo-Hittite and Is-
raelite Palace Architecture in the Iron Age II. *Israel Exploration Journal*
50: 47–81.
Ariel, D. T.
2002 The Coins from the Surveys and Excavations of Caves in the Northern
Judean Desert. *ʿAtiqot* 41: 281–304.
Ariel, D. T., and Shoham, Y.
2000 Locally Stamped Handles and Associated Body Fragments of the
Persian and Hellenistic Periods. Pp. 137–71 in *Inscriptions*. Vol. 6 of
Excavations at the City of David, 1978–1985, ed. D. T. Ariel. Qedem 41.
Jerusalem.
Barag, D.
1966 The Effects of the Tennes Rebellion on Palestine. *Bulletin of the American Schools of Oriental Research* 183: 6–12.
Bennett, W. J. Jr., and Blakely, J. A.
1989 *Tell el-Hesi: The Persian Period (Stratum V)*. Winona Lake, Indiana.
Berquist, J.
1995 The Shifting Frontier: The Achaemenid Empire's Treatment of West-
ern Colonies. *Journal of World-System Research* 1. [http://jwsr.ucr.edu/
archive/vol1/v1_nh.php]
Betlyon, J. W.
2004 Egypt and Phoenicia in the Persian Period: Partners in Trade and Rebellion. Pp. 455–77 in *Egypt, Israel, and the Ancient Mediterranean World:
Studies in Honor of Donald B. Redford*, ed. G. N. Knoppers and A. Hirsch.
Probleme der Ägyptologie 20. Leiden.
Bienkowski, P.
2001 The Persian Period. Pp. 347–65 in *The Archaeology of Jordan*, ed. B. Mac-
Donald, R. Adams, and P. Bienkowski. Levantine Archaeology 1. Sheffield.
Bowden, H.
1991 The Chronology of Greek Painted Pottery: Some Observations. *He-
phaistos* 10: 49–59.
Briant, P.
2001 New Trends in Achaemenid History. *Noruz Lecture Foundation for Iranian Studies Washington D.C.: March 23, 2001*. [http://www.fis-iran.org/
achemenid.htm]
2002 *From Cyrus to Alexander: A History of the Persian Empire*. Trans. P. T.
Daniels. Winona Lake, Indiana.
Burmeister, S.
2000 Archaeology and Migration: Approaches to an Archaeological Proof
of Migration. *Current Anthropology* 41: 539–67.
Carter, C. E.
1999 *The Emergence of Yehud in the Persian Period: A Social and Demographic
Study*. Journal for the Study of the Old Testament Supplement 294.
Sheffield.

Casabonne, O.
1999   Local Powers and Persian Model in Achaemenid Cilicia: A Reassessment. *Olba* 2: 57–66.
Christaller, W.
1933   *Die zentralen Orte in Süddeutschland: Eine ökonomisch-geographische Untersuchung über die Gesetzmässigkeit der Verbreitung und Entwicklung der Siedlungen mit städtischen Funktionen.* Jena.
Cohen, R.
1980   The Iron Age Fortresses in the Central Negev. *Bulletin of the American Schools of Oriental Research* 236: 61–79.
1983   Excavations at Kadesh-Barnea, 1976–1982. *Qadmoniot* 61: 2–14. [Hebrew]
1986   Notes and News: Negev Emergency Project, 1984–1985. *Israel Exploration Journal* 36: 111–15.
Cohen, R., and Cohen-Amin, R.
2004   *Ancient Settlements of the Negev Highlands II: The Iron Age and the Persian Period.* Israel Antiquties Authority Report 20. Jerusalem.
Cohen, R., and Yisrael, Y.
1996   The Excavations at ʿEin Ḥaẓeva / Israelite and Roman Tamar. *Qadmoniot* 112: 78–92. [Hebrew]
Cook, R. M.
1989   The Francis-Vickers Chronology. *Journal of Hellenic Studies* 109: 164–70.
Dagan, Y.
1992   *Archaeological Survey of Israel: Map of Lakhish (98).* Jerusalem.
2000   *The Settlement in the Judean Shephelah in the Second and First Millennium* B.C.: *A Test-Case of Settlement Processes in a Geographical Region.* Ph.D. dissertation. Tel Aviv University. [Hebrew]
DeMarrais, E.; Castillo, L. J.; and Earle, T.
1996   Ideology, Materialization, and Power Strategies. *Current Anthropology* 37: 15–31.
Earle, T.
1991   Paths and Roads in Evolutionary Perspective. Pp. 10–16 in *Ancient Road Networks and Settlement Hierarchies in the New World,* ed. C. D. Trombold. Cambridge.
Elayi, J.
1990   *Sidon: Cité autonome de l'Empire perse.* 2nd ed. Paris.
Ephʿal, I.
1984   *The Ancient Arabs: Nomads on the Borders of the Fertile Crescent, 9th–5th Centuries* B.C. Jerusalem.
1998   Changes in Palestine during the Persian Period in Light of Epigraphic Sources. *Israel Exploration Journal* 48: 106–19.
Ephʿal, I., and Naveh, J.
1996   *Aramaic Ostraca of the Fourth Century* BC *from Idumaea.* Jerusalem.
Fantalkin, A.
2001a Meẓad Ḥashavyahu: Its Material Culture and Historical Background. *Tel Aviv* 28: 3–165.

2001b Low Chronology and Greek Protogeometric and Geometric Pottery in the Southern Levant. *Levant* 33: 117–25.

Fantalkin, A., and Tal, O.

2004 The Persian and Hellenistic Pottery of Level I. Pp. 2174–94 in *The Renewed Archaeological Excavations at Lachish, 1973–1994*, ed. D. Ussishkin. 5 volumes. Tel Aviv University Monograph Series of the Institute of Archaeology 21. Tel Aviv.

Finkielsztejn, G.

1999 More Evidence on John Hyrcanus I's Conquests: Lead Weights and Rhodian Amphora Stamps. *Bulletin of the Anglo-Israel Archaeological Society* 16: 33–63.

Fischer, M., and Tal, O.

2003 Architectural Decoration in Ancient Israel in Hellenistic Times: Some Aspects of Hellenization. *Zeitschrift des Deutschen Palästina-Vereins* 119: 19–37.

Francis, E. D., and Vickers, M. E.

1985 Greek Geometric Pottery at Hama and Its Implications for Near Eastern Chronology. *Levant* 17: 131–38.

1988 The Agora Revisited: Athenian Chronology c. 500–450 B.C. *The Annual of the British School at Athens* 83: 143–67.

Frankfort, H.

1952 The Origin of Bit Hilani. *Iraq* 14: 120–31.

Geus, C. H. J. de

1979–80 Idumaea. *Jaarbericht van het Vooraziatisch-Egyptisch Genootschap ex Oriente Lux* 26: 53–72.

Gitin, S.

1997 The Neo-Assyrian Empire and Its Western Periphery: The Levant, with a Focus on Philistine Ekron. Pp. 77–103 in *Assyria 1995: Proceedings of the 10th Anniversary Symposium of the Neo-Assyrian Text Corpus Project*, ed. S. Parpola and R. M. Whiting. Helsinki.

Graf, D. F.

1990 Arabia during Achaemenid Times. Pp. 131–48 in *Centre and Periphery: Proceedings of the Groningen 1986 Achaemenid History Workshop*, ed. H. Sancisi-Weerdenburg and A. Kuhrt. Leiden.

1993 The Persian Royal Road System in Syria–Palestine. *Transeuphratène* 6: 149–66.

Haggett, P.

1965 *Locational Analysis in Human Geography.* London.

Haken, H.

1985 Synergetics: An Interdisciplinary Approach to the Phenomena of Self-Organization. Pp. 205–11 in *Links between the Natural and Social Sciences*, ed. J. Portugali. Special Theme Issue of *Geoforum* 16/2. Oxford.

Hassig, R.

1991 Roads, Routes, and Ties that Bind. Pp. 17–27 in *Ancient Road Networks and Settlement Hierarchies in the New World*, ed. C. D. Trombold. Cambridge.

Herr, L. G.
1993 What Ever Happened to the Ammonites? *Biblical Archaeology Review* 19/6: 26–35, 68.

Herzog, Z.
1997 The Arad Fortresses. Pp. 111–256 in *Arad*. Tel Aviv. [Hebrew]

Hoglund, K. G.
1992 *Achaemenid Imperial Administration in Syria–Palestine and the Missions of Ezra and Nehemiah*. Society of Biblical Literature Dissertation Series 125. Atlanta.

Iliffe, J. H.
1933 Pre-Hellenistic Greek Pottery in Palestine. *Quarterly of the Department of Antiquities in Palestine* 2: 15–26.

James, P.
2003 Naukratis Revisited. *Hyperboreus: Studia Classica* 9: 235–64.

Jansen, H.
2001 *The Construction of Urban Past: Narrative and System in Urban History*, trans. F. de Jong. Oxford and New York.

Johnson, G. A.
1972 A Test of the Utility of the Central Place Theory in Archaeology. Pp. 769–85 in *Man, Settlement and Urbanism*, ed. P. J. Ucko, R. Tringham, and G. W. Dimbleby. Cambridge.

Kroll, J. H.
1993 *The Athenian Agora XXVI: The Greek Coins*. New Jersey.

Lemaire, A.
1996 *Nouvelles inscriptions araméennes d'Idumée au Musée d'Israël*. Supplément 3 à Transeuphratène. Paris.
2002 Vol. 2 of *Nouveaux ostraca araméens d'Idumée et probleme d'interpretation*. Supplément 9 à Transeuphratène. Paris.

Lipschits, O.
2000 Was There a Royal Estate in En-Gedi by the End of the Iron Age and during the Persian Period? Pp. 31–42 in *Jerusalem and Eretz Israel (Arie Kindler Volume)*, ed. J. Schwartz, Z. Amar, and I. Ziffer. Ramat Gan. [Hebrew: English abstract, p. 101*]
2002 Literary and Ideological Aspects of Nehemiah 11. *Journal of Biblical Literature* 121: 423–40.
2003 Demographic Changes in Judah between the Seventh and the Fifth Centuries B.C.E. Pp. 323–76 in *Judah and the Judeans in the Neo-Babylonian Period*, ed. O. Lipschits and J. Blenkinsopp. Winona Lake, Indiana.

Lösch, A.
1954 *The Economics of Location*. New Haven, Connecticut.

Mazar, B.; Dothan, T.; and Dunayevsky, I.
1966 *En-Gedi: The First and Second Seasons of Excavations, 1961–1962*. ʿAtiqot 5. Jerusalem.

Mazar, B., and Dunayevsky, I.
1967 En-Gedi: Fourth and Fifth Seasons of Excavations, Preliminary Report. *Israel Exploration Journal* 17: 133–43.

McGlade, J., and van der Leeuw, S. E.

1997   Introduction: Archaeology and Non-linear Dynamics: New Approaches to Long-Term Change. Pp. 1–31 in *Time, Process and Structured Transformation in Archaeology*, ed. S. E. van der Leeuw and J. McGlade. London and New York.

Meshel, Z.

1977   Horvat Ritma: An Iron Age Fortress in the Negev Highlands. *Tel Aviv* 4: 110–35.

Naʾaman, N.

1997   Notes on the Excavations at ʿEin Hazeva. *Qadmoniot* 113: 60. [Hebrew]

2000   Royal Vassals or Governors? On the Status of Sheshbazzar and Zerubbabel in the Persian Empire. *Henoch* 22/1: 35–44.

2001   An Assyrian Residence at Ramat Rahel? *Tel Aviv* 28: 260–80.

Nicolis, G., and Prigogine, I.

1977   *Self-Organization in Non-equilibrium Systems*. New York.

Parker, B. J.

1997   Garrisoning the Empire: Aspects of the Construction and Maintenance of Forts on the Assyrian Frontier. *Iraq* 59: 77–87.

2001   *The Mechanics of Empire: The Northern Frontier of Assyria as a Case Study in Imperial Dynamics*. Helsinki.

2002   At the Edge of Empire: Conceptualizing Assyria's Anatolian Frontier ca. 700 BC. *Journal of Anthropological Archaeology* 21: 371–95.

Petrie, W. M. F.

1928   *Gerar*. London.

Phythian-Adams, W. J.

1923   Report on Soundings at Tell Jemmeh. *Palestine Exploration Fund* 1923: 140–46.

Prigogine, I., and Stengers, I.

1984   *Order out of Chaos*. New York.

Rad, G. von

1930   *Das Geschichtsbild des chronistischen Werkes*. Stuttgart.

Ray, J. D.

1987   Egypt: Dependence and Independence (425–343 B.C.). Pp. 79–95 in *Sources, Structures and Synthesis: Proceedings of the Groningen 1983 Achaemenid History Workshop*, ed. H. Sancisi-Weerdenburg. Achaemenid History 1. Leiden.

Reich, R.

1992a Palaces and Residences in the Iron Age. Pp. 202–22 in *The Architecture of Ancient Israel*, ed. A. Kempinski and R. Reich. Jerusalem.

1992b The Beth-Zur Citadel II: A Persian Residency? *Tel Aviv* 19: 113–23.

Sapin, J.

2003   Notes et Discussions. Un rééquilibrage archéologique concernant la Judée à l'époque perse: À propos d'un ouvrage récent. *Transeuphratène* 26: 121–42.

2004   La "frontière" judéo-iduméenne au IVᵉ s. av. J.-C. *Transeuphratène* 27: 109–54.

Schloen, J. D.
2001 *The House of the Father as Fact and Symbol: Patrimonialism in Ugarit and the Ancient Near East.* Studies in the Archaeology and History of the Levant 2. Winona Lake, Indiana.

Sellers, O. R.
1933 *The Citadel of Beth-Zur.* Philadelphia.

Sellers, O. R., et al.
1968 *The 1957 Excavations of Beth-Zur.* Annual of the American Schools of Oriental Research 38. Cambridge, Massachusetts.

Shear, T. L. Jr.
1993 The Persian Destruction of Athens: Evidence from Agora Deposits. *Hesperia* 62: 383–482.

Shefton, B. B.
2000 Reflections on the Presence of Attic Pottery at the Eastern End of the Mediterranean during the Persian Period. *Transeuphratène* 19: 75–82.

Smith, A. T.
1999 The Making of an Urartian Landscape in Southern Transcaucasia: A Study of Political Architectonics. *American Journal of Archaeology* 103: 45–71.
2000 Rendering the Political Aesthetic: Political Legitimacy in Urartian Representations of the Built Environment. *Journal of Anthropological Archaeology* 19: 131–63.

Sparkes, B. A., and Talcott, L.
1970 *The Athenian Agora XII: Black and Plain Pottery of the 6th, 5th and 4th Centuries* B.C. Princeton.

Stern, E.
1982 *Material Culture of the Land of the Bible in the Persian Period, 538–332* B.C. Warminster and Jerusalem.
1995 Historical Conclusions. Pp. 271–83 in *Excavations at Dor: Final Report Volume I A. Areas A and C: Introduction and Stratigraphy,* by E. Stern. Jerusalem.
2001 *Archaeology of the Land of the Bible II: The Assyrian, Babylonian and Persian Periods 722–332* B.C.E. New York.

Tal, O.
1999 The Persian Period. Pp. 83–222 in *Apollonia-Arsuf: Final Report of the Excavations I: The Persian and Hellenistic Periods (with Appendices on the Chalcolithic and Iron Age II Remains),* by I. Roll and O. Tal. Tel Aviv University Monograph Series of the Institute of Archaeology 16. Tel Aviv.
2005 Some Remarks on the Coastal Plain of Palestine under Achaemenid Rule: An Archaeological Synopsis. *Persika* 6: 71–96.

Tubb, J. N., and Dorrell, P. G.
1994 Tell es-Saʾidiyeh 1993: Interim Report on the Seventh Season of Renewed Excavations. *Palestine Exploration Quarterly* 126: 52–67.

Tufnell, O.
1953 *Lachish III: The Iron Age.* London.

Ussishkin, D. (ed.)
2004   *The Renewed Archaeological Excavations at Lachish, 1973–1994.* 5 volumes. Tel Aviv.
Van Beek, G. W.
1983   Digging up Tell Jemmeh. *Archaeology* 36/1: 12–19.
1993   The Reexcavations of Sites: Tell Jemmeh. Pp. 575–80 in *Biblical Archaeology Today, 1990: Proceedings of the Second International Congress on Biblical Archaeology. Jerusalem, June–July 1990,* ed. A. Biran and J. Aviram. Jerusalem.
Waldbaum, J. C., and Magness, J.
1997   The Chronology of Early Greek Pottery: New Evidence from Seventh-Century B.C. Destruction Levels in Israel. *American Journal of Archaeology* 101: 23–40.
Williamson, H.
1998   Judah and the Jews. Pp. 145–63 in *Studies in Persian History: Essays in Memory of David M. Lewis,* ed. M. Brosius and A. Kuhrt. Achaemenid History 11. Leiden.
Zadok, R.
1998   A Prosopography of Samaria and Edom/Idumea. *Ugarit-Forschungen* 30: 781–828.

The Religious Revolution in Persian-Period Judah

EPHRAIM STERN

The Hebrew University

The following remarks are based in their entirety on archaeological finds and are therefore limited to the presentation of these data. I realize that my interpretation of these finds may be oversimplified. Nevertheless, I believe that the issue is of singular importance because it belongs to the Persian Period and as such is worthy of our attention.

I will begin with a discussion of the period preceding the Persian Period. During the seventh century B.C.E., the last century of the independent Judean Kingdom, no fewer than eight nations were settled in Palestine. These include the Arameans of the kingdom of Geshur, who lived on the northeastern border of Israel; the Phoenicians, who inhabited the northern coast and the Galilee; the Samaritans, who replaced the people of the destroyed Israelite Kingdom in the province of Samaria; the late Philistines, who prospered in their four cities, Ashdod, Ashkelon, Gaza, and Ekron; the three nations of east Jordan, the Ammonites, the Moabites and the Edomites; and finally, the Judeans (Stern 2001: 3–300).

In this period, each of these nations had its own independent cult, consisting of the worship of a pair of major deities. Each of the male gods of these nations had its own distinct name: the Arameans had Haddad as their chief deity; the Phoenicians had Baʿal; Dagan or Baʿal Shmem was the chief god of the Philistines; Milcom of the Ammonites; Chemosh of the Moabites; Qos of the Edomites; and YHWH of the Judeans and the Samaritans. It is interesting to observe that among all of them, including the Philistines and even the Judeans, the chief female deity was Ashtoret (Ashtart) or Asherah (Stern 1999).

Each of these nations created the images of its gods in a form different from those of the others. By the seventh century B.C.E., the representation of the various deities had been consolidated, and it is easy for any expert in ancient art to attribute a figurine to an Aramean, Phoenician (Stern 2001: 54–55, 77–87), Edomite (Beit-Arieh 1995), or even

Moabite cult (Daviau and Dion 2002), or to that of the Israelites and the Judeans. At the same time, the various nations used the same cult objects, the same types of stone and clay incense altars, bronze and clay censers, cult stands and incense burners, chalices, goblets and bronze and ivory rods adorned with pomegranates, and so forth.

We may also assume, on the basis of recent archaeological finds, that in Israel and Judah—as in all other Palestinian states—many sanctuaries dedicated to the national deity had presumably been erected in all the important settlements of the country. The Bible itself testifies to the existence of sanctuaries at Dan, Shechem, Bethel, Shilo, and Beersheba, while many others were recovered in excavations at Dan, Mesad-Michmash, Vered Jericho, Uza, Radum, and Beer-sheba. The best known of them all is the sanctuary at Arad (Stern 2001: 200–212).

It can also be assumed that a sanctuary of YHWH existed in Lachish, the second city in importance in Judah, just as in the Lachish relief at Nineveh a pair of large cultic stands is depicted as spoils of war looted by Sennacherib's soldiers after they sacked the city (Ussishkin 1982: 84–85).

A sanctuary called "a house of Yahweh" is mentioned in many inscriptions of that period. In one of the Arad ostraca, for example, it is said of someone that "he sits in the house of YHWH" (Aharoni 1981: 35–39), and an inscription inscribed on a small ivory pomegranate reads: "Sacred to the priests of the house of YHWH" (Avigad 1989). And there is also the seal of "Miqnayahu servant of YHWH" (Avigad and Sass 1997: 59), which indicates that Miqnayahu served in the cult of one of the many YHWH temples. In fact, the pagan cult unique to Judah is represented by a rich assemblage of clay figurines dating from the late eighth century down to the beginning of the sixth century B.C.E. These figurines are distributed all over Judah, from the Benjamin region in the North, at Bethel, Tell en-Nasbeh, Gibeon, Ramot, and Moza to Jerusalem, Ramat Rahel, Beth-Zur, and Tel Rabud on the mountain ridge, to Jericho and Ein-Gedi in the east and Gezer, Beth-shemesh, Batash, Azekah, Tell Judeideh, Tell ʿErani, Tel Halif, Tel Lachish, Tell Beit Mirsim and others in the west. In the southern part of the country they are found at Tel Sheba, Tel Masos, Tel ʿIra, ʿAroer, and Arad. They appear in large settlements and in small fortresses such as Khirbet Abu Tuwein. In short, they occur in all parts of Judah.

Raz Kletter, who studied this particular Judean find, concluded that, "If we adopt the heartland of Judah concept, then ca. 96% of them were found within this area. This figure is so high that there is only one possible conclusion: *these pottery figurines are Judean"* (Kletter 1996; Stern 1999).

To sum up: the discovery of hundreds of clay figurines typical of Judah alone, as well as the remains of local sanctuaries may point to the practice of a local "national Judean paganism," and the material remains discovered in archaeological excavations belong mainly to this cult.

From the archaeological point of view, we know almost nothing about the cult of the following Babylonian Period, which lasted from the destruction of the First Temple in the year 586 B.C.E. down to 539 B.C.E. I do not intend to deal with this period here but wish to stress my conclusion that this period can be defined as a definite vacuum. The Babylonians destroyed not only Judah but the rest of the country as well. They exiled the Philistines, who never returned, and completely devastated many regions of the country, including the previously prosperous sea coast, while Edomites moved to occupy the southern part of Judah up to Beth-Zur and including the territories of Lachish and Maresha (Stern 2000).

At the beginning of the Persian Period, when the curtain is lifted again, a completely different situation is encountered. Instead of separate national religions in all parts of the country that are unique to each of the individual nations, new types of clay figurines appear that differ from the earlier figurines in two aspects. (1) They have completely lost their individual national characteristics and have become part of the Mediterranean koine. (2) They are henceforth produced in two styles: (a) the Phoenician style that preserves eastern elements, and (b) the western Greek style that becomes increasingly dominant throughout pagan Palestine (in the areas outside of Judah and Samaria) and lacks nearly all regional or local characteristics.

A great number of assemblages of cultic figurines were found in the territories of the "new Idumea," the former Philistia, Phoenicia, and the Galilee, that is, in the parts of the country still under pagan domination. In these areas have been found dozens of favissae full of clay figurines and stone statuettes, most of them along the coastal region (Stern 1982: 182–98; 2001: 478–510).

In the areas of the country inhabited by Jews during the Persian Period, on the other hand, not a single cultic figurine or sanctuary has been found! This, in spite of the many excavations and surveys that have been conducted, and the same is true of Samaria. Archaeologists have also failed to locate any sanctuaries for this period within Judah and Samaria, while many have been found outside their borders, with two exceptions: the new Temple of Jerusalem, which was never excavated, and the Samaritan Temple on Mount Gerizim.

No actual details are known about the structure of the Jerusalem Temple. The centrality of the Temple of Jerusalem and its function are attested, among other things, by several Yehud coins bearing names of priests, such as the well-known coin of Yohanan the priest and that of Jadoa, and others. These coins attest that at least some of them were struck by the priesthood for the benefit of the Temple and it can be assumed that Jerusalem and its Temple fulfilled a decisive role not only in the religious life of the country but also in its economy (Spaer 1986–87; Barag 1986–87).

We may be able to glean some information about the Temple of Jerusalem from a comparison with the contemporary Samaritan Temple on Mount Gerizim (a large part of which has been unearthed in recent years by Yitzhak Magen), which played a similar role. According to the latest excavation results, this temple was built at the end of the fifth or beginning of the fourth century B.C.E.—in all events, after the establishment of the province of Judah, for among the large number of Samaritan coins discovered there were some Judean coins (which may indicate the existence of contacts between them and perhaps also visits by Jewish pilgrims to Mount Gerizim). In any case, the plan of this temple, in the opinion of the excavator, resembles that of the Temple of Jerusalem as described in the book of Ezekiel (Magen 2000).

More than 300 monumental stone-carved inscriptions of different periods, which have not yet been published, were uncovered that had once been inscribed on the outer wall surrounding the temple. From these inscriptions we know that the Temple on Mount Gerizim, like the Temple of Jerusalem, was known to worshipers as "the House of YHWH" (Magen, Tsfania, and Misgav 2000: 131, no. 14).

The changes undergone by the Samaritan cult on Mount Gerizim apparently parallel those of Judah and Jerusalem. In the seventh century B.C.E., at the time that the first foreign exiles were sent to Samaria, the mountain still served as a pagan cult center. Proof of this is provided, in my opinion, by the discovery of three unique limestone capitals found on the mount (not in situ), which bear the common motifs of the "tree of life" and cobra snakes (uraei) widespread in both Israel and Judah in the First Temple period. In my opinion, these capitals attest to an early pagan phase of the Temple on Mount Gerizim, before it became a center of monotheistic religion in the Persian Period (Stern and Magen 2002).

The importance of the temple and the new Jewish center in Jerusalem for the Jews of Palestine and the two diasporas—Babylonia and Egypt—in which they were concentrated in the Persian Period can perhaps be examined on the basis of another archaeological find. And here I wish to present a theory that seems completely plausible to me, but with which I am not sure the reader will agree.

As is well known, the Jewish community in the Persian Period was dispersed in three areas. In addition to the Jewish center in Jerusalem and Yehud, Jews also lived in the Babylonian diaspora (where the new Jewish religion was developed) and in the Egyptian diaspora, which because of the different composition of the Jewish exiles settled there— former soldiers and officials of the Judean Kingdom, some of whom had sought refuge there even before the destruction of the temple— continued the pagan tradition of the kingdom and built at Elephantine the "Temple of the God Yahu," which was also known as the "Altar House of the God of Heaven." Some members of this community even bore pagan names, such as Anat, and so on. During the Persian Period, however, it is possible that this community began accepting "innovations" from Jerusalem, which may be how the famous Passover Letter should be interpreted (Porten and Yardeni 1986: 54–55, 68–71, 76–77).

Especially important in this matter are three archaeological finds that have been uncovered recently. Up to now many scores of seal impressions of the Persian province of Yehud have been discovered, all of them without exception from the area of Judah (Stern 1982: 202–6; Christoph 1993). This is clearly the case also for the finds from an unidentified site known as "Tell Harasim," recently excavated on the western border of the province. Two Yehud seal impressions were found there. One bears the name "Yehud Yeho'ezer PHW" (similar to seal impressions from Ramat Rahel and the City of David) and the other, "Hanuna Yehud." This is the first time that Yehud seals have been found in the northern part of the southwestern Shephelah, and they confirmed what we had already conjectured many years ago, namely, that this area of the country also belonged to the province of Yehud (Keilah district). According to Joseph Naveh, an identical seal impression was found a century ago in the German excavations at Babylon! This seal impression is today in Berlin (Naveh 1996).

A third Yehud seal impression discovered outside of Judah was uncovered in Rudolf Cohen's excavations at Kadesh-barnea in northern

Sinai. This site, too, is situated far from the borders of Persian Judah, but it undoubtedly served as a station on the shortest route from Judah to Egypt and had already done so toward the end of the Judean Kingdom (Cohen 1983: 28, fig. 22).

There is no doubt that these impressions were imprinted on wine jars, but, in my opinion, it seems completely irrational to transport by land over great distances this type of fragile pottery jar filled with wine only for the purpose of paying taxes (when we also know that the Persians demanded and received taxes from remote areas only in silver and gold). I therefore wish to propose here that it was the Jews in the Egyptian and Babylonian diasporas who imported the wine from Judah for religious purposes, wine that was in no danger of having been touched by heathen hands.

If my hypothesis is correct, it can serve as additional evidence of the centrality of the Temple of Jerusalem, of its priests and of Judah in general in the life of the Jewish people during the Persian Period.

In summary, we can state that, in contrast to the cult prevailing among the inhabitants of Judah at the end of the period of the monarchy, the latest archaeological evidence clearly indicates that all the pagan-popular elements had undergone purification during the Persian Period (and also in the Samaritan cult that replaced the Israelite). And this, of course, raises the important question: where did the Jews of Palestine pray in the Persian Period during the times that they were not on pilgrimages to Jerusalem?

Bibliography

Aharoni, Y.
1981   *The Arad Inscriptions.* Jerusalem: Israel Exploration Society.
Avigad, N.
1989   The Inscribed Pomegranate from the "House of the Lord." *Israel Museum Journal* 8: 7–16.
Avigad, N., and Sass, B.
1997   *Corpus of West Semitic Seals.* Jerusalem: Israel Academy of Sciences and Humanities, Israel Exploration Society, and Institute of Archaeology, Hebrew University.
Barag, D.
1986–87 A Silver Coin of Yohanan the High Priest and the Coinage of Judaea in the Fourth Century BC. *Israel Numismatic Journal* 9: 4–21.
Beit-Arieh, I.
1995   *Horvat Qitmit: An Edomite Shrine in the Biblical Negev.* Institute of Archaeology Monograph 11. Tel Aviv: Tel Aviv University Press.

Christoph, J. R.
1993   *The Yehud Stamped Jar-Handles Corpus: Implications for the History of Post-exilic Palestine.* Ph.D. dissertation, University of Michigan.
Cohen, R.
1983   *Kadesh Barnea: A Fortress from the Time of the Judaean Kingdom.* Jerusalem: Israel Museum.
Daviau, P. M. M., and Dion, P. E.
2002   Moab Comes to Life. *Biblical Archaeology Review* 28/1: 38–43, 46–49.
Kletter, R.
1996   *The Judaean Pillar-Figurines and the Archaeology of the Asherah.* Oxford: BAR.
Magen, Y.
2000   Mt. Gerizim: A Temple City. *Qadmoniot* 33/2 (120): 74–118. [Hebrew]
Magen, Y.; Tsfania, L.; and Misgav, H.
2000   The Hebrew and Aramaic Inscriptions from Mt. Gerizim. *Qadmoniot* 33/2 (120): 125–32. [Hebrew]
Naveh, J.
1996   Gleanings of Some Pottery Inscriptions. *Israel Exploration Journal* 46: 44–47.
Porten, B., and Yardeni, A.
1986   *Letters.* Vol. 1 of *Textbook of Aramaic Documents from Ancient Egypt.* Jerusalem: Hebrew University.
Spaer, A.
1986–87   Jaddua the High Priest. *Israel Numismatic Journal* 9: 1–3.
Stern, E.
1982   *Material Culture of the Land of the Bible in the Persian Period 538–332 BCE.* Warminster: Aris and Phillips.
1999   Religion in Palestine in the Assyrian and Persian Periods. Pp. 245–55 in *The Crisis of Israelite Religion: Transformation of Religious Tradition in Exilic and Post-exilic Times,* ed. B. Becking and M. C. A. Korpel. Leiden: Brill.
2000   The Babylonian Gap. *Biblical Archaeology Review* 26/6: 45–51, 76.
Stern, E. (ed.)
2001   *The Assyrian, Babylonian and Persian Periods, 732–332 BCE.* Vol. 2 of *Archaeology of the Land of the Bible.* New York: Doubleday.
Stern, E., and Magen, Y.
2002   Archaeological Evidence for the First Stage of the Samaritan Temple on Mount Gerizim. *Israel Exploration Journal* 52: 49–57.
Ussishkin, D.
1982   *The Conquest of Lachish by Sennacherib.* Tel Aviv: Tel Aviv University.

Tyrian Trade in Yehud under Artaxerxes I: Real or Fictional? Independent or Crown Endorsed?

DIANA EDELMAN
University of Sheffield

Neh 13:16 contains the brief but important claim that, during Nehe-miah's lifetime, men of Tyre lived in the city of Jerusalem. They im-ported fish and all kinds of merchandise and were selling them on Shabbat to the people of Judah and Jerusalem. At the very least, this statement reflects a general knowledge of the spread of Phoenician trade during the Persian Period from the coast to inland markets in southern Eberi-Nari. But the comment raises a number of specific rhe-torical and historical issues that need further examination to determine whether the information contained in the verse reflects only general knowledge or specific knowledge of conditions in Jerusalem during the reign of Artaxerxes I. Three main issues will be addressed in this article. (1) Are the Tyrians being used as an object lesson to show how *gērîm* or, perhaps more narrowly, members of a trading enclave in Jerusalem must live by Torah? Or, is the lesson more generalized—that any *gērîm* anywhere within a Jewish community must follow Torah? (2) Does the verse reflect actual conditions in the time of Artaxerxes I or actual con-ditions in Jerusalem at the time of the author, who may have lived as late as the Hellenistic period? Alternatively, is it loosely based on the dominance of inland trade by the Phoenicians at the time of the author? (3) Were these Tyrian merchants private entrepreneurs who settled in Jerusalem under their own initiative, or were they private entrepre-neurs who were there as a result of a trading concession granted by the imperial court, forming a resident trading enclave?

The text relates that these merchants of Tyre[1] physically lived within Jerusalem, which was a *bîrâ* or fortified settlement with a Persian garri-son and a civilian population (Neh 1:8; 7:2; Lemaire and Lozachmeur

---

1. The proposed emendation of *haṣṣōrîm* to *haṣṣayyādîm* has no textual basis; the text makes sense as it stands in all traditions and should not be emended.

1987). H. Kreissig has suggested that Tyre was not their actual homeland; rather, the label "Tyrian," like "Canaanite" earlier, was a synonym
for traders from the coastal cities (1973: 69). He cites no evidence to
support this view, however, and his position might have been more
logical if the more general term, *Phoenicia*, had been used instead of the
specific term *Tyre*. In the Persian Period, Sidon was the preeminent city
of Phoenicia, so his argument also would primarily reflect the reality of
the first half of the sixth century B.C.E. and earlier, when Tyre was preeminent. One would then need to suppose that the term was not subsequently adjusted to reflect the changed situation. In addition, the
Tyrians and Sidonians were known to have created a number of trading
colonies all around the Mediterranean, so there is little reason to doubt
their physical presence in Jerusalem and Yehud.

The merchants were not itinerant traders but resident aliens (so, e.g.,
Salles 1994: 212) or, alternatively, members of a resident trading enclave
(so, e.g., Williamson 1985: 395). In the first case, they may have had limited legal rights as nonnatives living in Yehud. However, it is possible
that they may have had full rights under Torah as fellow Persian citizens, if they held that status in the Persian Empire. In the second case,
they might have lived under their own code of law, as members of a
recognized, self-regulating trading colony.[2] In both cases, they would
have secured their merchandise from family members or business partners back home in Tyre.

Their clients included not just residents of the *bîrâ* but also the
people of Judah. The *waw* in the Hebrew phrase *libnê yĕhûdâ ûbîrû-
šāláyim*, if construed as a *waw copulativum*, signals a clear distinction
being made between the two listed items. If construed as a *waw expli-
cativum*, it could be seen to claim that the people of Judah were those
specifically living in Jerusalem. However, no *waw* would have been
needed to express this latter idea and the result is also illogical; Jerusalem was not coextensive with the entire province. Since the same
thought could have been conveyed by placing the two phrases side by
side in apposition, the presence of the *waw* is more logically understood as creating a list of two sets of clients. Thus, these merchants resided in the *bîrâ* and sold to others stationed and living there but also
had a wider circle of clientele within the larger province. This means
either that they traveled from the city to outlying local markets as well

---

2. This was the case in the Old Assyrian trading colony established in the Hittite city
of Kanesh. For details, see discussion below. While there is a huge time gap between this
colony and the Persian Period, it is likely that practices that were found to work would
have continued in use over time.

(so, e.g., Kreissig 1973: 69), that they supplied goods to others who lived in or serviced these outlying markets, or that Yehudites from the countryside traveled to Jerusalem to buy from the Tyrian merchants resident there.

Finally, these merchants sold fish specifically but also a wider range of goods: *dā'g wĕkol-meker*. A letter from Sennacherib to his father, Sargon II, records the distribution of tribute and audience gifts to members of the court that includes fish stored in two types of containers, whose size, weight, or design is described by the nouns *maqartu* and *lattu* (Martin 1936: 44; Postgate 1974: 283–84; Parpola 1987: 35; K956/ABL 568, lines 3–4, 8, 9–10, 19).[3] The text is broken, but at the end of the section, the name of Azuri, king of Ashdod, appears, suggesting that he was sending the tribute that included the fish in the containers.

Both types of container occur once more in ND 2672, a fragmentary administrative text from Nimrud that also probably dates to the time of Sargon II. Three *maqartu*-containers appear in line 9, and 20 *lattu*-containers appear in line 10. They are part of the tribute payment, along with fish, linen, and cloth, that appear to have accompanied a shipment of horses from Ashkelon to an official named Addu-Hati (Postgate 1974: 388–89). By inference, the tribute items also originated in Ashkelon.

S. Parpola has linked the first type of container with the Aramaic term *mqarta*, meaning 'cooling' (1987: 35 n. 9), although if this derivation is correct, it is of no help in understanding how the container was designed or how it functioned. In the *CAD* both terms for the containers are thought to be measurements of volume, with one *maqartu* holding more than 20 *lattu*.

It seems as though this particular way of packing fish in containers of two different sizes or weights was unique to the Philistines, although M. Elat has suggested these might have been Egyptian products imported by the Philistines (1978: 32). Martin wonders if the containers might have held a fish bread mentioned by Herodotus (1.200; Martin 1936: 49). If the Tyrian traders were selling fish packed in *lattu*- or *maqartu*-containers in the market in Jerusalem, they would have purchased it from producers in Ashdod, Ashkelon, or possibly Gaza and sold it on.[4] The fish undoubtedly was a delicacy consumed

---

3. I am indebted to Nadav Naʾaman for calling my attention to these particular texts and to Stephanie Dalley for helping to clarify whether *maqartu* and *lattu* are nouns designating types of container or types of fish.

4. For the existence of such trade already well established in the Assyrian Period, see Master 2003: 56–61.

by the elite rather than a dietary staple of the general population, which would have eaten little animal protein because of the cost.

Fresh-water fish from the Nile was also exported from Egypt. Excavations at Kition Bamboula in Cyprus have found imported Egyptian fish in a stratum dating to the third century B.C.E. (Salles 1994: 199), but it is likely that such fish would have been exported in earlier periods as well. Thus, the Phoenicians may have been offering their customers in Jerusalem Egyptian fish along with or instead of Philistine fish and/or salt-water fish caught and processed in Tyre. The Hebrew uses a generic term that does not allow firm conclusions to be drawn about the ultimate source of origin of the product(s).

Persian-era fish bones have been uncovered in Jerusalem in Area E1 of the City of David excavations. They belong to the gilt-head sea bream (*sparidae sparus aurata*), a salt-water fish that inhabits Mediterranean coastal waters. This type of fish was recovered from 24 loci in the City of David from levels belonging to Middle Bronze II, Iron II, and also the Hellenistic Period, showing it had been a staple in the local diet for a long time (Lernau and Lernau 1992: 132–33, 137). This species accounts for 44.9% of all excavated fish bones in the City of David, which comprise ten total fish families. Lernau and Lernau suggest that the fish were caught either in the littoral lagoon of Bardawil off the northern Sinai Peninsula or along the coast of Gaza (1992: 133). However, it seems arbitrary to limit their origin to these two areas when they could have been found in any shallow coastal water along the length of the western Levantine coast.

The presence of Tyrian merchants in Jerusalem may not seem surprising in light of the apparent presence of people from many adjoining regions, evidenced by the fact that the returnees supposedly divorced women of various origins at Nehemiah's instigation (Neh 13:23). However, the town may not have been the melting pot that it appears at first glance. The merchants were males residing in the city because of business, some undoubtedly with families. The other foreigners listed in the book of Ezra, by contrast, were female and were brides of members of the Yehudite elite. Their presence was the result of marriage contracts that need not have required the presence of enclaves or isolated families from these various ethnic groups in the *bîrâ*. In traditional arranged marriages, equal social status is an important concern, so most of these brides would have been daughters of the elite in the adjoining regions.

Some of the soldiers stationed in the fortress may have been non-Yehudite, and so there may have been some ethnic enclaves in the town, as at the Egyptian *bîrâ* at Elephantine, for example, but we can-

not be certain of this. Neh 7:2 claims that the local police chief was a Yehudite named Hananiah, and the soldiers may well have been drawn
from the local population as well. The garrison commander would have
been Persian, however. We cannot know, so we need to be careful not to
extrapolate the presence of Ammonite, Moabite, and Ashdodite enclaves in Jerusalem from the list of foreign wives in Neh 13:23.[5]

While the presence of a Tyrian enclave is signaled by the description
in the text, there is no indication that the parents of these women also
lived in Jerusalem or facilitated the arrangement of such marriages
through personal familiarity with neighboring women and their families. The specific references to Ammon and Moab in this context, as in
13:1, may have been ideological constructs designed to create ethnic
boundaries to separate Yehud from these nearby groups after the loss
of political independence in the region. Thus, while it would be unrealistic to assert that the Tyrian merchants were the only *gērîm* with an
enclave in the *bîrâ*, it is equally unrealistic to view the *bîrâ* as a melting
pot similar to most Western urban centers today.

The Rhetorical Function of Nehemiah 13:16

In the narrative world of Nehemiah, the settlement of Tyrian traders
in Jerusalem was a development that had taken place after his initial
governorship had ended and he had returned to Susa. He discovered
both their presence and their abuse of Shabbat after his return to the
city, sometime after the 32nd year of Artaxerxes I (434 B.C.E.; Neh 13:6–
7). However, because the book focuses on tensions between the returning *gôlâ* and the non-*gôlâ* factions in Jerusalem and Yehud, even in the
narrative world, the lack of mention of these merchants prior to 13:16

---

5. If some of the fish being sold by the Tyrian merchants in Jerusalem was fish in
lattu- and *maqartu*-containers that had been acquired from Ashdod, this would tend to
indicate in turn that there were no resident Ashdodite traders with families. Instead, the
Tyrians were acting as middlemen in securing this product. Thus, these women would
not have been the daughters of resident Ashdodite merchants. It should also be observed
that in Africa, marriages within the Hausa trading diasporas in Yorubaland are always
endogamous (Cohen 1971: 271) as a way of maintaining tight membership and group
loyalty. If ancient trading diasporas used the same mechanism as one way of maintaining solidarity and loyalty, then no offspring of any member of a resident trading colony
in Jerusalem would have intermarried with the local community. However, the texts
from Kārum Kanesh indicate that some traders resident in Kanesh took second wives
from the native population to tend to their needs while they were away from Assur,
where their primary wives remained with their families (Lewy 1956: 3–10). These men
clearly were traveling back and forth on a regular basis, however.

need not preclude their residence throughout the period of time covered in the entire narrative.

Chapter 13 deals with reforms that were made after the reading of the book of Moses to the people on the day that the city walls were dedicated. The setting assumes that Jerusalem became an official settlement at this time. Its residents were now protected by the completed walls, and the city was, by inference from Neh 1:8 and 7:2, a functioning fort. The residents were also to be bound by the Torah for their legal code.

Existing violations were corrected immediately. These included evicting Ammonite and Moabite men from the assembly (13:1–9),[6] giving the Levites their due portions (13:10–13), not allowing the sale of goods on Shabbat by either local merchants or resident Tyrian traders (13:15–22), and placing men who had married Ammonite, Moabite, or Ashdodite women under oath not to marry their children to foreigners (13:23–29). The section detailing the correction of Torah violations is framed by issues arising from marriages to foreigners, especially Ammonites and Moabites, and the summary in v. 30 also highlights this point: "I cleansed them from everything foreign."

The statement concerning the Tyrian traders is not a specific example of cleansing Jerusalem from foreign influence; the issue at stake is not primarily their foreign origin, and they were not evicted, as were the Ammonite, Moabite, and Ashdodite spouses. Rather, the issue is Shabbat transgression. This is emphasized by the shutting down of local merchants as well as the Tyrian merchants on Shabbat. Nevertheless, the action taken against them illustrates the need for resident foreigners in Jerusalem to be bound by Torah and so continues the theme of dealing with non-Jews who were living or would live in the newly rebuilt *bîrâ*, which also served as the provincial capital.

The statement in Neh 13:16 does not condemn the presence of Tyrian merchants as residents within the city confines; rather, it condemns business transactions on Shabbat. So why did the writer name Tyrian merchants specifically as transgressors? His purpose could not have been to lessen the wrongdoing by having non-Jews make the first mistake because v. 15 includes Jewish merchants alongside the Tyrian merchants in the transgression. Similarly, his purpose was not just having

---

6. Since only males were counted as full-fledged members of political and religious assemblies, the issue at stake here involves foreign males, who by implication would have married women of Jerusalem, become locally resident, and so gained membership in the local assembly as heads of tax-paying family units.

the first reported instigators of Shabbat transgression be resident foreigners who, nevertheless, were bound by Torah; local merchants were said to have been as guilty as the Tyrians. Thus, it seems that he wanted to send an important message to both the native and the *gēr* in Jerusalem and Yehud concerning the sanctity of Shabbat.

In the narrative world, the marriages to foreigners preceded both the pledge by members of the Yehudite assembly to be bound by Torah in Nehemiah 10 and the reinforcement of this pledge in 13:1 that required action after the city's dedication. The correction of the nonpayment of the levitical portions likewise required action once the city was officially constituted. But the Shabbat transgressions were not a preexisting condition like the others. They had developed during Nehemiah's absence and were being initiated by citizens of Jerusalem and by resident foreigners. In the former case, Shabbat legislation would have been binding. In the latter case, if the Tyrians were resident aliens, whether Persian citizens or Phoenician citizens, they would have been bound by Torah as the local law. However, if they were part of an officially endorsed trading colony, they may have been exempt from local law.

The status of the Tyrian traders thus affects the underlying rhetoric of the passage. If they were presumed to be members of a trading colony, the writer would be asserting that, contrary to custom, such traders were bound by the laws of Torah concerning Shabbat while they were resident in Jerusalem and were trading in the *bîrâ* or the wider province. If the traders merely had the status of resident aliens, however, they would automatically have been subject to the local laws, so the rhetorical message would be slightly different. As private entrepreneurs who had taken up residence in the *bîrâ*, they, like the native-born merchants who were selling surplus agricultural goods from local estates in the surrounding region, would have been breaking the laws of Shabbat, by which all civilian residents in the *bîrâ* were bound. The writer would have been chastizing those who were subject to the Torah for transgression of its Shabbat regulations.

The Tyrian Traders as Independent Private Entrepeneurs or Imperially Sponsored Private Entrepreneurs

To resolve whether the writer was envisioning an official enclave or a group of resident aliens, it is necessary to determine the likely status of any historical Tyrian traders who might have been considered Jerusalemite residents in the eyes of the Persian court. They would have been private entrepreneurs in either case; but would they have arrived under their own initiative as Persian citizens or vassals, or would they have been members of a trading enclave that had received imperial endorsement? Any who had arrived on their own initiative would not have been entitled to any sort of special status or exemption from the local laws. They either would have had the legal status of *gērîm* and been subject to the prevailing laws of Yehud while receiving limited protection against wrongs done by citizens with full rights, or they would have had full rights under the local laws as Persian citizens. Those who arrived as private traders with the official endorsement of the Persian crown, however, may have been exempted from local law and subject to their home laws, the laws of Tyre in this case, if Persia continued Assyria's earlier practice of granting special privileges to resident merchant enclaves in foreign lands.

Unfortunately, the mechanics of long-distance trade in the ancient Levant during any pre-Roman period are still not well understood. Although a number of studies have appeared in recent decades (so, e.g., Cohen 1971: 266–81; Veenhof 1972; Adams 1974; Lamberg-Karlovsky 1975; Curtin 1984; Salles 1991; Salles 1994; Parkins and Smith 1998; Holladay 2001), the lack of detailed, relevant evidence continues to hamper a clear understanding of the various options and practices in the various empires that controlled the region—the Assyrian, Neo-Babylonian, and, of particular interest in this study, the Persian. Thus, it is not possible to resolve the status of the Tyrian merchants definitively. Nevertheless, various observations can be made that indicate that, while these merchants were private entrepreneurs, they probably were not able to settle in Jerusalem without imperial endorsement.

The existence of local markets where individuals traded their surplus products and goods for other desirable products and goods or sold commodities for metal *specie* is widely assumed. What is not known, however, is whether or not the local government received a percentage of the profits earned from these transactions—for example, by charging a fee or percentage of the saleable wares to bring goods into the marketplace.[7]

The description in Neh 13:15–16 suggests that Jerusalem was perceived as functioning in the narrative world not merely as a local mar-

---

7. Another important question is whether a network of trade conducted from houses existed on the local level, which might have substituted for, or minimized the importance of, any local markets. For a discussion of the function of such networks in Africa, see Hill 1971.

ket but as a regional marketplace, in addition to being a fort, the provincial administrative seat of Yehud, and a civilian settlement. Goods that arrived via long-distance trade were for sale alongside local agricultural produce. Thus, the situation envisioned in vv. 15–22 is not a local market but a regional market. The clients include not just the residents of Jerusalem itself but the people of Yehud, the wider province. This raises the possibility that Jerusalem was envisioned to be serving as a central trading place, with outlying stations being supplied from it.

The earliest, well-documented example of foreign traders residing in a city where they were not citizens is provided by the Assyrian trading enclave (*kārum*) in the commercial quarter of the Hittite city of Kanesh, from ca. 1910–1830 B.C.E. (Level II). Kanesh served as a sort of mother enclave that then supplied other commercial quarters in outlying cities, including Durhumit and Burushhaddum, the centers for the production of copper and silver, and smaller *wabartum*-posts (Larsen 2000: 80, 85; Veenhof 1995: 866–67). In order to appeal to the capital in Assur, their representatives had to go through the Kanesh authorities (Larsen 2002: xiii).

The Assyrian traders who took up residence in Anatolia were private entrepreneurs. Business was often family-based, with the father in Assur and the oldest son in Kanesh, and other sons, brothers, and nephews in various towns in Anatolia (Veenhof 1995: 869; Larsen 2002: xiii). The traders based in Kanesh were under the jurisdiction and control of the City Assembly of Assur, which had two "Envoys" residing in Kanesh at all times to represent the city and its assembly (Larsen 2000: 85). In addition, however, it should be noted that the king of Assur sent letters himself to the authorities of the Kanesh *kārum*, and oaths were sworn there by both "the life of the city" and "the life of the city and the king" (Larsen 2000: 83). As chairman of the city assembly, the king was responsible for implementing decisions taken by the body (Larsen 2000: 82).

Three specific examples of how the traders remained under the jurisdiction and control of their home city, Assur, are found among the extant texts. One includes an order delivered to the *kārum* by "envoys of the city" to contribute to the costs of the fortification of Assur (Veenhof 1995: 867). A second prohibits the merchants from trading in certain Anatolian products that might harm Assyrian interests (Veenhof 1995: 867), and there is one example of merchants who broke this rule by trading *sapdinnum* and *pirikannum* textiles and were fined (Dercksen 2000: 137). Finally, a ruling was made in Assur that no more than one-third of the capital raised to buy goods could be spent on tin (Dercksen 2000: 137).

The rights of trading enclaves in Kanesh and other satellite towns and posts in the region were guaranteed by local Anatolian rulers, who had to swear an oath in the presence of an envoy of the city assembly and representatives of the *kārum* in Kanesh. Although only one fragmentary example of these oaths from Kanesh has been published so far (Çeçen and Hecker 1995), M. T. Larsen reports that two texts were discovered in a house in Kanesh in 2000 (2002: xiii). They contain treaties made with the king of Kanesh and with the ruler of Hahhum, a major town on the Upper Euphrates. Once published, they should confirm the information already known from the other fragmentary example from Kültepe and the draft of an oath found in an Assyrian *kāru* in Apum (Tell Leilan), dating to ca. 1750 B.C.E. (Eidem 1991).

In addition to indicating who represented Assur at the oath ceremony, the two texts show that the local rulers agreed to guarantee safe passage of all Assyrian caravans through their land. In return, they received taxes on goods that were transported, even in times of unrest when the roads were impassable. Assyrians had extraterritorial rights, forming their own social, political, and legal system independent of the local foreign palaces. In a guarantee of noncompetition, the local rulers agreed not to allow Akkadian traders to enter their land and agreed to hand over any who arrived to the Assyrian authorities, who would put them to death (Eidem 1991; Çeçen and Hecker 1995; Dercksen 2000: 146).

The oaths were necessary because the cities involved in each case were independent polities. The suggestion by J. Lewy to see the Hittite region as part of an early Assyrian Empire (1956: 51–53) has been rejected since the thousands of Kanesh texts and other Middle Assyrian texts have been studied more thoroughly and the political situation has become clearer. Permission to allow foreign traders to take up residence in a city that was not their home was a calculated risk that required concessions, especially the granting of independent legal jurisdiction that might create problems if disputes arose with locals. However, permission also afforded large financial returns from transport taxes and access to foreign goods.

Even though the palaces or their representatives were the contracting parties and overseers of the formal agreements that allowed Assyrian traders to create enclaves in Anatolia, the trading that was conducted was private, not palace owned or palace controlled. *Naruqqu* contracts named investors and specified the percentage of profits that each would receive from his investment (Larsen 1977: 123–45). Prices fluctuated according to the availability of goods, weather, and war; they were not fixed by the crown (Veenhof 1972: 88; Adams 1974: 246). Silver was used as a standard of exchange, functioning effectively as money (Veenhof 1972: 349–52). In addition, markets existed in which the goods could be sold by merchants or their agents (Veenhof 1972: 351–57).[8] Thus, the suggestion by K. Polanyi (1957; 1975) that the traders were government officials, that no markets existed, and that the system was based on barter rather than on monetary exchange is incorrect and has now been widely rejected (so, e.g., Veenhof 1972: xxiii, 348–52; Adams 1974: 246; Lamberg-Karlovsky 1975: 350; Cartledge 1983: 6–7; Dercksen 2000: 150–51).

Once treaties were negotiated, however, each sponsoring royal court benefited from the private trade through the receipt of various fees levied upon the goods as they left one realm and entered another. Expenses and fees involved in caravan transport included (1) 1/19 of the top packs on the donkeys to be paid to the caravaneer; (2) 1/10 of the value of the goods for road tolls and traveling expenses for fodder, food, possibly grazing rights, lodging additional personnel such as porters, additional donkeys, payments to messengers, guides, the costs of military protection and gifts to local dignitaries en route and in the foreign host country; (3) 1/20 of the value of the sealed goods, paid in silver, to the House of the Eponym/City Hall in Assur; and (4) 2/65 of the value of the tin of the sealed load or 1/20 of the value of the textiles, paid in tin, at the palace of the destination city, when the packs were unsealed; (5) a head tax levied on all members of the caravan, costing between 10 and 15 shekels in tin per person. Finally, the palace of the destination city retained the right to purchase up to 10% of all shipments of quality textiles. All in all, costs may have run as high as 20–25% of the value of the shipment, which left room to turn a tidy profit (Holladay 2001: 186–88). The royal courts at the points of origin and destination, however, received a steady stream of revenue and goods and only had to secure the roads and rivers in their own territories,

---

8. Many of the contracts refer to goods being sold in the house of PN. While this has been construed to refer to a business firm that is organized on analogy with a family, the possibility needs to be considered that, as in Africa, trade was being conducted in actual houses rather than in open marketplaces. However, unlike in Africa, the Assyrian merchants in Kanesh would not have been resident guests in the houses of local landlords who arranged for the sale of goods on their behalf and received a percentage (Hill 1966: 349–66). These traders had their own residential quarters and could have conducted trade from their own homes.

which they would have done anyway to guarantee the passage of their own messengers and personnel.

This model of long-distance trade, including modes of transport, taxes and tolls, and resident trading enclaves, apparently did not die out in the Middle Bronze period (contra Elat 1978: 27); kings of the Neo-Assyrian empire established *kāru*-trading settlements and *bīt kāri*-custom houses in tributary lands throughout their expanding empire. Once trade was in place, long-distance trading diasporas would inevitably have followed. Even though the political situation had changed in the Neo-Assyrian Period from the situation evidenced in the Middle Assyrian Kanesh texts, the need to protect trading enclaves in cities that lay outside the direct legal control of the Assyrian king remained. The Assyrian kings now had more power than the assembly of Assur and were negotiating with vassal kings and rulers of city-states, territorial states, and tribes, not with rulers who had equal political status, even if they were from a less advanced polity. Vassals who were recalcitrant and repeatedly rebelled against their vassal treaties eventually were deposed and their land was turned into an Assyrian province.

In the first instance, trading enclaves were established in existing cities, such as took place in Anatolia. In the second case, however, former *kāru*-enclaves came under the direct control and jurisdiction of the Assyrian king, and all the residents became Assyrians, effectively eliminating the definition of a *kāru* as a foreign-resident enclave. The existing traders in a given city probably continued their routes as before and may even have expanded into new markets. Now, however, there would only have been a single *bīt kāri*–customs house in the settlement to collect transport taxes belonging to the Assyrian king. The former local palace was gone, eliminating the need to pay two sets of taxes to different rulers.

It is not surprising, then, that after the territory of some vassals was converted into provinces, certain cities located on strategic roads were renamed, with the first element of the new name being *kār*, or 'trading center'. Often they had new population groups transported from elsewhere in the Empire. While the new citizens were all Assyrian, it is unclear whether the Assyrians imposed a single set of laws across the Empire or left regional legal systems in place to be administered locally. In the new cities named *kār*-RN or DN, it is possible that Assyrian law became the norm, but what happened if there was a dispute between resident merchants and their suppliers back in a former home region that had maintained its traditional legal system is not known.

According to a stone slab in the Nabu Temple at Calah, Shalmaneser III (858–24 B.C.E.) conquered Til Barsip on the east bank of the Euphrates in Aramean territory, renamed it Kār-Shalmaneser 'trading center of Shalmaneser', and settled Assyrians in it (Grayson 1996: 19; A.O.102.2.30–35). It was now fully within the control of the Assyrian administration, and its newly settled occupants were full citizens of Assyria.

Tiglath-pileser III (744–727 B.C.E.) set up one *bīt kāri* or customs house somewhere on the coast of Syria or Lebanon (Iran stele II.B.13; Tadmor 1994: 104–5) and another one in Gaza (summary inscription 4:8–14; 8:14–18; 9:13–16; Tadmor 1994: 140–41; 176–79, 188–89). In these cases, he was establishing points in existing cities of his vassal kings for the collection of Assyrian tolls and taxes on long-distance trade goods. It is likely, therefore, that Assyrian trading enclaves were also established shortly thereafter in both sites, although this was not a necessary corollary to the setting up of each *bīt kāri*. In theory, the custom house would simply have collected a newly imposed set of Assyrian taxes on the existing trade, cutting into the profits that had formerly been realized by the traders when taxes were paid only to the local palace.

A letter sent to Tiglath-pileser III at Calah (Nimrud) from an unnamed official in an undisclosed location states that he executed the king's command "to be kind to" the ruler of Tyre.

> All the *karrani* are open to him and his subjects enter and leave the *bīt karrani* as they wish and sell and buy. Mt. Lebanon is at his disposal and they go up and down as they wish and bring the wood. I levy taxes (*mikse*) on anyone who brings down the wood and I have appointed tax-collectors (*makisani*) over the *karrani* of all Mt. Lebanon. . . . I told them they could bring down the wood and do their work with it but that they were not to sell it to the Egyptians or the Philistines, or I would not allow them to go up to the mountain. (Postgate 1974: 390–91, ND 2715; Saggs 2001: 155–58)[9]

The letter details certain terms of a vassal treaty, evidenced by the use of the idiom "show kindness to." The Assyrian king has established trading enclaves or trade centers inland in Lebanon and custom houses as well, probably one in Tyre itself. Tyrian merchants are free to trade in Assyrian trading centers as long as they pay the new set of taxes

---

9. This letter is written in Assyrian rather than Babylonian, accounting for the difference in spellings of the term *kāru*. I thank Dr. Stephanie Dalley for clarifying this point for me.

being levied, in addition to whatever other local taxes might still be due. No timber can be traded with Philistia or Egypt, however. The same letter mentions that the Sidonians had chased off the tax collector *(makisu)* whom the official had put "over those who come to the *karrani* in Sidon." He solved this problem by sending the Itu'aeans to Mt. Lebanon, who made the people grovel to the point that they reinstated the tax collector in Sidon. The context suggests that the same offer had been made to the king of Sidon as to the king of Tyre concerning access to timber in Lebanon. The Sidonians, however, were refusing to pay Assyrian taxes that had been levied on timber cut in Mt. Lebanon and moved into Sidon. It is likely that they, like the Tyrians, had been restrained from selling timber to the Egyptians and the Philistines, unless Tiglath-pileser had designated Sidon to be the sole dealer in long-distance timber exchange and had made Tyre the local dealer within Assyrian holdings.

Sargon II (721–705 B.C.E.) actively built up trading centers, *kāru*, within his Empire. The Khorsabad inscriptions mention six newly established trading centers, all in Mannean territory. In his sixth year Sargon captured the city of Harhar, resettled recently defeated peoples in it, set his governor over them, and renamed the city Kār-Sharrukin—'trading center of Sargon'. The newly established province administered from Kār-Sharrukin included the upper canal of the land of Aranzeshu, the canal of Bit-Ramatua, and the lands of Urikatu, Sikris, Shaparda, and Uriakku. At the same time, he turned Kisheshim into Kār-Nergal, which became the seat of the governor of a new province that included the newly conquered lands of Bit-Sagbat, Bit-Hirmami, Bit-Urmargi, and the cities of Harhubarban (?), Kilambati, and Armangu (Luckenbill 1927: 5–6; Fuchs 1994: 442). The following year he captured the four cities of Kisheshlu, Kindau, Anzaria, and Bit-Gabia along the main Khorasan Road. He rebuilt them and renamed them Kār-Nabu, Kār-Sîn, Kār-Adad, and Kār-Ishtar. All four appear to have been assigned to the province administered from Kār-Sharrukin (Levine 1977: 149; Fuchs 1994: 442; Luckenbill 1927: 6–7). Apparently at some point in his reign he prohibited the sale of humans in *kāru* centers (Lanfranchi and Parpola 1990: 114; K 1897; CT 53 59).

Smugglers were actively hunted down and put out of business because they cut into royal profits by avoiding customs and other taxes. N III 3158/TCL 9 67 is a letter from Ashur-resuwa to the king concerning six Kummean smugglers who were operating illegally, securing Assyrian goods in the town of Aira, ruled over by Saniye. They were somehow transporting them to Urartu to sell and then transporting other goods from Urartu to Kumme to sell (Lanfranchi and Parpola 1990: 79–80). The king is told that he needs to order Saniye to arrest these men and get details of their operation, including where they buy and sell their goods, who "receives them from their hand," and "who lets them pass (the border)." The concern is to determine how they are circumventing official channels to avoid paying the various tolls and custom taxes. Additional letters detail attempts to track these men and the eventual capture of one of them (Lanfranchi and Parpola 1990: K1111/ABL 590, 81; K1224/CT 53 170, 91; K1862/CT 53 194, 136).

A letter from Crown Prince Sennacherib to his father, Sargon II, shows that private trade caravans could move alongside or as part of official caravans bearing tribute. He reports that envoys from Kumme had arrived with the tribute and seven teams of mules and wants to know if these should be sent on to Babylon or received there. He then reports that they also brought dyed wool and that the envoys have insisted that the royal weavers are to select the wool they want before the merchants are allowed to buy any of it. Sennacherib is asking for clarification regarding who should have the right of first selection (Parpola 1987: 33–35; K 125; ABL 196).

The crown prince must have been aware of the palace's right of first selection of merchandise from foreign traders, which, in the trading enclave at Kanesh in the Middle Bronze Age, amounted to up to 10% of the goods. Thus, his request for clarification is hard to understand. Nevertheless, he may be pointing out that the Kummeans, some of whom had recently been taken to task for smuggling, were now making a point of following the letter of the law and showing their incorruptibility. The letter reveals that the pecking order for foreign wares—palace first and then private traders—had not changed, and caravans could include official tribute in kind as well as private wares that would be sold for profit.

After a rebellion in Gaza and the defeat of their Egyptians allies in battle at Raphia in 716, Sargon II "opened the sealed *kāru*" near the Brook of Egypt in order to "mix" Egyptian and Assyrian traders. The text is found on lines 46–48 of Fragment D of the Nimrud Prism (Gadd 1954: 179–80; Tadmor 1958: 34). The word *kāru* is partially restored (Tadmor 1958: 34) but is probable. The somewhat cryptic reference seems to be to a specific port or commercial town that had been closed down, with seals placed over the closed doors of the houses or the custom house (*bīt kāri*) perhaps (Malamat 1986), but was now reopened.

It is unfortunate that we do not know where this specific *kāru* was located (Tadmor 1966: 2; Elat 1978: 26–27; Naʾaman 1979: 80–86; Ephʿal

1982: 101–5; Reich 1984; Ahlström 1993: 675–76), which king had authorized its establishment, or what had led to its possible closure.[10] It is logical to assume, however, that it was one of the sites near the Wadi Besor (Na'aman 1979: 74–77) that had been built after Tiglath-pileser III had made Idibi'ilu the 'gate-keeper' (*atûtu*) of the region south of Gaza and north of Egypt. The *kāru* would have been placed there to obtain revenue from the Arabian trade that might have been diverted to this newly settled region instead of moving into Gaza. When Sargon reopened the site, some sort of official agreement would have been negotiated with the Egyptian authority to allow the creation of a resident trading diaspora there. Though recently defeated in battle, Egypt still lay outside the Empire or was at most a vassal, so a trading agreement would have been necessary.

The progress of Assyrian control over trade within the western part of the Empire is evident in the treaty between Esarhaddon (680–669 B.C.E.) and Baal, king of Tyre. Large sections of the text are broken, but fortunately for the present discussion, some of the stipulations concerning trade are intact.[11]

> These are the *kāru*-centers and the caravan routes which Esarhaddon, king of Assyria, [entrusted] to his servant Baal: to Akko, Dor, to the entire district of the Philistines, and to all the cities within the territory on the seacoast, and to Byblos, the Lebanon, all the cities in the mountains, all [these] cities being cities of Esarhaddon, king of Assyria. (Parpola and Watanabe 1988: 25, K3500 + K10235 [+] Sm. 964 [unpub.] lines 18–26)

As was the case under Tiglath-pileser and the then-contemporary monarch of Tyre, so still, Tyrian traders were allowed to use roads and official trading centers that permitted the appointed agents of the Assyrian king to collect tolls and taxes on all merchandise being transported and on personnel involved in trade. Now that the Philistine coast had been subdued and incorporated into the Assyrian trading network, the former prohibition on selling wood there had been overturned. However, trade with Egypt was still outside of the terms of the

---

10. Ahlström has suggested that Sargon may have been reversing the earlier policy of Tiglath-pileser III that had prohibited the sale of timber to Eygpt (1993: 676). In this case, the trading center would have predated that prohibition and would have been shut down by the order of Tiglath-pileser III. I think it more likely, however, that the center would only have been established after Sargon's campaigns in this region, beginning in 720 B.C.E., and his creation of the *bīt kāri* in Gaza.

11. In a broken section that follows this one, lines 27–30, there is mention of the people of Sidon, but the context is too incoherent to be informative.

treaty, as was trade with Cyprus and other Aegean islands or with Anatolian ports. All of these lay beyond direct Assyrian control.

When the Sidonian king Abdu-Milkutti entered into an alliance with Sanduarri, the king of Kundu and Sissu in Cilicia, Esarhaddon captured Sidon and executed its king in 677–76 B.C.E. (Borger 1956: 49–50, Nin A III: 32–38). It seems that the trading restrictions that had been placed on Baal of Tyre had similarly been imposed on the king of Sidon. By entering into an alliance with an Anatolian king, he would have been breaking the terms of his treaty with the king of Assyria. Esarhaddon then built an Assyrian trading center, named after himself, Kār-Ashshur-ahu-iddina, which perhaps was to serve as the central place of exchange and the customs collection point in Phoenicia. His plan seems to have been to guarantee that he received his due share of imposts and taxes from maritime trade conducted by his Phoenician subjects. All Phoenician ships would have been required to dock there to offload and pay taxes on incoming goods or to pay taxes on outgoing goods.[12]

Letter K1281/ABL 992 from Itti-Shamash-balatu, a customs official who appears to have been stationed in Arwad, to Esarhaddon may shed additional light on the motives behind the creation of Kār-Esarhaddon. In this letter Itti-Shamash-balatu reports that Ikkilu of Arwad is turning all of the boat trade for himself, providing for anyone who goes to him but killing anyone who docks at the Assyrian *kāru*. In his defense, he claims that the palace has written, "Do only what is good for you." Itti-Shamash-balatu asks for permission from Esarhaddon to arrest Ikkilu, informing his majesty that many in his royal entourage have invested silver in Ikkilu's house and that they and the merchants are intimidating him. He also pleads for a re-posting to the capital, apparently in the hopes of escaping the threats being made against him (Luukko and van Buylaere 2002: 113–14).

This letter shows that Assyrian courtiers were making private investments in trading ventures, just as had occurred during the era that Kārum Kanesh had been in operation. To maximize profits, they had cut a deal with the local king to pay taxes only to him at the port of entry and exit, trying to avoid a second Assyrian tax there, because they already had paid taxes to the Assyrian king as the goods arrived at and exited from their home city. They were trying to pay only one set of

---

12. For the suggestion that he wanted to eliminate the Phoenician ports as intermediaries, see Tadmor 1966: 98. I am uncertain what the implications of this statement are. Ahlström has proposed that the new city, located on the mainland, was meant to replace the destroyed city of Sidon (1993: 743).

taxes to the Assyrian king instead of two. It may have been in the aftermath of this complaint and the disobedience of the king of Sidon that Sargon decided to establish Kār-Esarhaddon as the single (?) authorized trading center along the Phoenician coast to oversee the flow of goods in and out of the area and ensure the collection of taxes and tolls into Assyrian coffers.

Finally, after Esarhaddon captured Memphis in Egypt in 671 B.C.E. and installed tax collectors and Assyrian officials in the region (Borger 1956: 98–99, Mnmt A), he apparently set up a *kāru* named Kār-Baniti near the Mediterranean coast as well. His successor, Ashurbanipal (668–631 or 627 B.C.E.), had his troops camp near it in 668 as they marched eastward toward Memphis to regain control of that city and subjugate the ruler, Taharqa, who had taken it in revolt shortly before (Luckenbill 1927: 293, Rassam cylinder A). It is likely that the trade restrictions that had been placed on Phoenician merchants were lifted at the end of Esarhaddon's reign once this *kāru* had been established and the Delta region had been placed under Assyrian control. Long-distance trade would have added even greater tax and toll revenues to the Assyrian coffers than those that would have been collected from local trade.

The trade center or *kāru* of Naukratis was established in the Delta region of Egypt by 625 B.C.E. at the latest. Its status as an Assyrian initiative or an Egyptian initiative is hard to determine based on the limited evidence available. Herodotus (2.154) and Diodorus (1.66–67) state that the Saite pharaoh Psammetichus I (664–610 B.C.E.) founded Naukratis. Between them, the two historians supply two possible sets of circumstances that could have prompted the settlement of Naukratis. First, Diodorus claims that, in his early days, Psammetichus was one of twelve kings in Egypt. His domain bordered the Mediterranean coast in the Delta region, and he was engaged in trade with Phoenicians and Greeks (1.66). Naukratis could have been set up as a trading post at this early date, prior to the reunification of Egypt and the establishment of Memphis as the capital.

A second possibility for the founding is suggested slightly later in his reign, after he had united Egypt and become its sole ruler in Memphis. Both Herodotus and Diodorus report that Psammetichus had used mercenaries from Caria and Ionia to gain control of Egypt. Herodotus claims that the mercenary Carians and Ionians who helped him unite Egypt first arrived on Egyptian soil as pirates/plunderers that were forced ashore under circumstances unspecified (2.152). Both writers agree that after his success he gave these mercenaries the region called "The Camps" in which to live, apportioning much land in the region downstream from Memphis and slightly inland from the Pelusiac mouth, south of Bubastis. Psammetichus continued to use Greek mercenaries to maintain control over Egypt throughout his reign (Diodorus 1.67; Herodotus 2.154). Naukratis could have been one of these two camps or another settlement in the same region assigned to the Carians and Ionians.

R. D. Sullivan argues that Diodorus's claim that Psammetichus I founded the city is consistent with the finding of scarabs on the site that bears this name as well as the presence of seventh-century pottery from Rhodes and Chios (1996: 187, 190). It appears, however, that the scarabs bear the name of Psammetichus II (595–589 B.C.E.) instead (Boardman 1999: 121), so they are of no use for establishing the founding date of the site. Boardman gives a date of ca. 600 B.C.E. for the earliest Chian pottery but reports that the earliest datable pottery found so far on site is a sherd of Corinthian "Traditional" ware, datable to 630–620 B.C.E. (Boardman 1999: 119, 121). Other "Early Corinthian" pottery dates to the last decade of the seventh century and the beginning of the sixth century B.C.E., as do Athenian vases and Rhodian or Rhodian-style vases (Boardman 1999: 121–22, 125). Thus, a date in the last quarter of the seventh century seems assured for the beginnings of trade on site, at least, which supports the claim of both Herodotus and Diodorus that it was founded during the reign of Psammetichus I. However, the pottery suggests a date later than either scenario sketched in Diodorus concerning its possible origin.

The founding date becomes important because of the implications its bears for possible Assyrian involvement in encouraging the opening of new trading centers in the vassal territory of Egypt. If Naukratis was established while Psammetichus was an Assyrian vassal, then the Assyrian royal court would have benefited financially from the trade as well as the Memphite court, setting up its own *bīt kāri* in the new towns that were designated as trading centers. If the city was founded after Psammetichus threw off his Assyrian vassalship, then it would have been an undertaking by Egypt that put money into its coffers alone. Even if Diodorus's claim that Psammetichus had been actively involved in trade with Greece and Phoenicia while he was a local kinglet is historically unreliable and reflects instead the situation that he created only after becoming king of Egypt, it nevertheless shows that tradition remembered him as having a strong interest in international trade.

A survey of the eastern Delta region between the Suez Canal and Gaza has uncovered 45 sites dating to the Saite period, most of which were temporary encampments and stations (Oren 1984: 28). However, 4 were surrounded by inset–outset walls measuring about 200 m long on each side and 15–20 m thick. They include Migdol, Naukratis, Tel Defenneh, and Tell el-Maskhuta (Oren 1984: 10–13). The first three sites have evidence of metal-working in bronze and copper, with slag, crucibles, arrowheads, spearheads, armor scales, and weights found in situ (Oren 1984: 28). Combining this information with the defensive nature of the walls, we can say that these sites almost certainly were forts and probably also housed families of the soldiers, as did the forts at Syene and Elephantine.

Unlike Kār-Baniti, then, which was built by Esarhaddon somewhere in the Delta region, Naukratis was likely built by Psammetichus as a fort for resident Greek mercenaries. It secondarily became a trading center, undoubtedly with a customs house that brought in wares predominantly from the home territories of the soldiers living there; Ionia and Caria, but also Corinth and Attica. However, the possibility cannot be excluded that the site had housed a small trading post prior to its expansion into a fort.

The pottery evidence found so far suggests a founding date of about 630 B.C.E., which would have been well after Psammetichus had unified Egypt, casting doubt on both reasons for its founding deduced from Herodotus and Diodorus. By this date, Psammetichus's rebellion against Assyrian vassalship had been resolved (Luckenbill 1927: 298; Rassam A), and Psammetichus was cooperating again with the Assyrians as they fought for survival against a takeover by the Neo-Babylonians. It is unclear if he was their ally or a nominal vassal again, but in the latter scenario, Assyria almost certainly would have reaped financial rewards from the trade conducted at Naukratis, placing an agent there to collect its rightful share of tolls.

The mechanics of long-distance trade under the Achaemenids are not well known, due to the paucity of private archives and official records to shed light on the subject. It is likely that most of the long-established Assyrian trading networks and practices continued during the short-lived Neo-Babylonian Empire and were left in place or adopted by the Persians. This would include custom houses in cities and stations along the roads to collect transport tolls and taxes; and trading centers, possibly with resident trading enclaves, where merchants from various parts of the Empire could exchange goods. New routes and markets would have opened up as the Empire expanded, however.

Given the Persian tendency to use local law codes for the various subject peoples in various parts of its Empire (so, e.g., Dandamaev and

Lukonin 1989: 116–30; Briant 2002: 510–11), a question about foreign resident trading enclaves in cities with a *bīt kāri* or cities that had the status of a *kāru* needs to be considered: even if such cities were within the confines of the Empire and part of the provincial administration, would resident foreign merchants have been allowed to form self-regulating communities in which the laws of their home community were followed rather than the local laws? Since there was not a single overarching legal system, the older practice of granting resident merchant groups the right to live according to their home laws may well have been adapted for use in the Persian Empire. The king would no longer have negotiated with his counterpart in an independent polity, but Persian representatives in the local *bīt kāri* may have entered into formal agreements on behalf of the king to grant certain rights to trading enclaves, who would have had their own representatives in the enclave. There may even have been a representative from the home city also involved to guarantee the extradition of law-breakers back home and their prosecution.

In most instances, laws would not have varied too drastically within parts of the Empire, as can be seen by comparing written examples that have been recovered from digs at various sites from varying time periods in the ancient Near East. It appears that important types of sales (e.g., real estate, slaves) as well as loans and funding agreements were documented; consequently, a judge could easily have ruled on the specific terms contained in writing, regardless of the ethnic origin of the parties involved or his own background. For lesser transactions based on oral agreement, a judge would have had to rule according to the claims of each party and the credibility of their witnesses or of their own accounts of the events. Here again, the case would have had to involve specific agreements between two individuals that would not give rise to further disputes based on potential differences in law among ethnic groups within the Empire.

Various sources provide a glimpse into the mechanics of long-distance trade in the Persian Period. Babylonian records demonstrate that goods that moved by water along the rivers and canals within the territory of Babylonia were taxed just as if they had been transported over the road systems. In addition, fees were paid to men to pilot the boats carrying the goods (Briant 2002: 380–81) Satraps were charged with the safety of roads within their provinces and with punishing robbers (Dandamaev and Lukonin 1989: 210).

By this time, the Akkadian term *kāru* had also become a designation for a transport tax levied on goods that were being transported locally as well as over longer distances. A *bīt kāri* was a local office where a number of taxes were collected by a *rab kāri*—not just transport tolls but also rent due on land that had been leased from the king (van Driel 2002: 274–82). Because we have so few private archives from the Assyrian and Neo-Babylonian Periods that would allow us to learn more about the names of specific transport taxes, it is difficult to tell whether this meaning of *kāru* was a Persian development or a meaning that already had evolved earlier and was merely adopted by the Persians.

An excerpt has survived from a ledger written during the reign of Xerxes, ca. 475 B.C.E., at an unspecified custom house (*bīt kāri*) in the Delta area (Yardeni 1994) that provides useful information about taxation on long-distance sea trade involving Phoenician and Ionian vessels. It indicates that every merchant boat entering Egypt was taxed at a rate of 20% of the value of its cargo. Ionian ships paid this assessment (*mndtʾ*) in silver and also paid with part of the cargo as well. Phoenician ships likewise paid a levy (*mʾsr*) in silver and in kind.[13] In addition, every boat paid a tax known as "silver of the men," which seems to have corresponded to the head tax that had been assessed on traders for millennia (Yardeni 1994: 70). Exit taxes for export to the sea and head taxes were paid by all ships except one type of Phoenician vessel. Ionian ships also paid an export tax on natron, which they took on as outbound cargo (Yardeni 1994: 72).

While the ledger discussed above confirms the long-standing range of taxes paid to the governing bodies, it sheds no light on the existence or operations of long-distance trading diasporas. In fact, it allows for the possibility that some long-distance trade may have been conducted without resident traders from the home countries in place in Egypt to receive the goods. Merchandise could have been sold off to local interested merchants once it had cleared customs and the right of first selection of merchandise by "palace" representatives had been exercised or waived. On the other hand, the ledger does not rule out the existence of resident enclaves to receive the goods either.

Herodotus may provide evidence of a resident Tyrian enclave in Egypt at Memphis, the capital of the Delta region. He mentions the existence of a commercial area in Memphis called the "camp of the Tyrians" (2.112). It was located all around the sacred precinct of the king, which lay south of the great Temple of Hephaestus(/Ptah), the patron

---

13. Yardeni 1994: 70, contra Briant 2002: 380–81, who says the tax was 10% and that the Phoenicians only paid in kind.

god of artisans. He states that Phoenicians from Tyre lived there. This appears to have been an area of permanent residences occupied by Tyrian merchants and tradesmen and not simply an area where Tyrian sailors could stay temporarily as the goods from their ships were off-loaded and processed, before returning home.

The correspondence of the Egibi firm in Babylonia provides additional, vital information about another Persian-era trading diaspora. Six letters indicate that there was a resident Babylonian trading enclave in the city of Humadeshu in Persia during the reigns of Cyrus and Cambyses (Zadok 1976: 67–76). One of the Egibi brothers, Idinna, was resident in the latter city, as head of the local branch, and another relative or employee, Nabu-zera-iqisha, appears to have married a local wife, who bore him a son named Baga'pada. He also worked for the firm when he grew up (Zadok 1976: 93).

There were other Babylonian merchants in Humadeshu, and all were under the jurisdiction of a *rab tamkarī* official named Artarushu, who appears as a witness in two documents (CT 384/BM 30704; BM 30682). This individual bore an Iranian name, implying that he was either a local appointee of the city or that he was a royal Persian appointee who oversaw all the trade in the city, local and long-distance. He resolved a dispute over the sale of two Iranian female slaves by two Iranian merchants or owners to the Babylonian merchant Idinna in Humadeshu (Dandamaev and Lukonin 1989: 219). The same letter, CT 384, mentions a scribe of the house of the treasurers in Humadeshu as well (*tupšarru ša bīt kāṣirāni*).

Caution must be used in drawing conclusions from the use of Babylonian titles for officials in Humadeshu. Records kept by Babylonians may have used familiar titles rather than Persian equivalents, or the Persians may simply have adopted these working titles that had become standard in the Assyrian and Neo-Babylonian trading network. Even if both officials were part of the Persian administration or the local city administration, their presence does not rule out the possibility that the Babylonian trading enclave established there was self-regulating and followed practices and the laws of the home city of Babylon. The rules for interaction among different ethnic traders may have changed over time and, in the situation of a multiethnic Empire, may have required disputes to be taken to an appointed *rab tamkarī* for resolution or the use of Persian scribes to record transactions and payments made to the Persian royal coffers. In the end, however, the letters do not help us to know whether resident trading enclaves in various parts of the Empire were self-regulating, employing the laws of their home territories, within the Empire; whether they were under local law; or whether they were under Persian court law.

A letter from Sippar, dated 503 B.C.E., indicates that an Egyptian trader was resident in that city, selling Egyptian linen (CT 2 2) to personnel at the Ebabbara Temple. Unfortunately, it is unclear from this isolated reference whether he was an independent, private entrepreneur who had managed to establish good supply networks from the homeland and simply lived in the city as a resident alien under local Babylonian law, or whether he was part of an Egyptian trading enclave established there that regularly sold good quality linen to priests and others (Dandamaev 1999: 371). In the latter scenario, we do not know whether he would have been under Babylonian law, Persian law, or Egyptian law.

The limited information about long-distance trade in the Achaemenid Empire is insufficient for us to know with certainty whether or not a group of Tyrian traders could have established a mercantile quarter in Jerusalem under their own initiative by simply moving into the town and setting up shop, receiving merchandise from family members and other established contacts. The existence of the resident Tyrian trading enclave in Memphis in the Persian Period could be used to argue for a similar arrangement in Jerusalem, but only with great care. The trading quarter in Memphis apparently was established by Psammetichus I during the Assyrian Period and would have involved an official agreement between the two polities, both of whom were vassals or a vassal and an ally of Assyria. The agreement would have required permission from the Assyrian king. The one in Jerusalem, by contrast, would have been established by the king of Persia with his Phoenician client king in a subprovincial administrative center. But it is not certain that the Tyrian merchants actually formed a trading enclave in Jerusalem, so the latter point is hypothetical only.

The official status of Tyre and Sidon within the Persian Empire is disputed. It is uncertain whether their territories were annexed to the Empire and counted as constituent subregions of provinces in which the rulers functioned as governors under the satrap (so, e.g., Cook 1983: 174–75; Briant 2002: 411) or whether their lands remained outside the provincial system as vassal states (so, e.g., Frye 1984: 110). This point is crucial for understanding the official status of the Tyrian merchants resident in Jerusalem. If the kings of Tyre and Sidon were vassals rather than subprovincial governors, they would have needed to negotiate a trade agreement directly with the Persian court to allow their private traders to become residents within the provincial territory of the Empire. In this case, it is likely that the enclave would have been self-regulating, following Tyrian home law.

As noted above, the existence of different legal systems within the Empire may have led to self-regulating trade enclaves in trading centers in which all the traders were citizens of the Empire but were from different ethnic groups with different legal practices. On the other hand, it is possible that in cities that were not official *kāru*-centers, all nonnative merchants who took up residence were simply expected to live under the local law code. In this case, however, one must ask whether they would have been extended full rights under the local code as Persian citizens or whether they would have been considered *gērîm*, resident aliens.

The Historical Accuracy of Nehemiah 13:15 and Concomitant Historical Implications

The rhetorical analysis above has not yielded definitive information that can help with issues of historicity, although it has raised the possibility that the Tyrian merchants may be assumed to have constituted a resident enclave with an official status, akin to a *kāru*. The brief review of long-distance trade in the ancient Near East, including the era of the Persian Empire, has failed to provide a firm answer about whether or not the Tyrian traders resident in Yehud, though private entrepreneurs, would have needed an official trading concession granted by the Persian court to operate within the *bîrâ*. Also unresolved is the issue of whether or not they would have constituted a resident foreign enclave with the right to administer law among its residents according to its home legal traditions.

Three main options, each with a range of variations, exist for understanding the nature of reality reflected in Neh 13:16: (1) the text reflects actual conditions during the reign of Artaxerxes I; (2) it reflects actual conditions in Jerusalem at the time that the author or a subsequent editor composed the verse as part of chap. 13, which may have been any time during the reign of Artaxerxes I or later; or (3) it does not reflect actual historical conditions in Jerusalem at any period but derives from the writer/editor's general awareness that in the Persian Period or his own day, Persian or Hellenistic, the Phoenicians expanded their trading influence to inland markets in the western Levant. The last two options do not preclude the actual existence of such a colony in Jerusalem under Artaxerxes I but presume that the author did not know that this was the case.

Decisions concerning the availability and reliability of the sources used to compose Nehemiah 13, its integral or secondary nature in the book, or the dates when the book was initially composed or possibly secondarily expanded or edited will lead individuals to argue for one of the three options over the other two (for convenient summaries of options, see, e.g., Myers 1965: xxxviii–liii; Kellermann 1967; Williamson 1985: xiii–xxxvi; Blenkinsopp 1988: 70–72; Grabbe 1998: 154–58). Without additional evidence, however, there is no way to rule out one or more options or to favor one over another.

A few personal comments on some of the above issues will be offered. There is a chronological incongruency in Nehemiah 13 involving Eliashib the priest, who, according to vv. 4 and 5, had prepared one of the large temple storerooms for Tobiah the Ammonite at some point before the reading of the law in v. 1. Yet Tobiah's use of it was unaltered until Nehemiah's return in Year 32 of Artaxerxes, instead of being remedied immediately, despite the command to remove the Ammonites and Moabites from the congregation. According to v. 3, the command had otherwise been executed before Nehemiah's departure. Furthermore, Eliashib is not designated "high priest" here, even though he served in that capacity during Nehemiah's term in office (3:1, 20), beginning with the time of his arrival. Yet 12:26 claims that Eliashib's father, Joiakim, was high priest at some point during Nehemiah's governorship. One or more of these statements is unreliable.

The presence of this chronological inconsistency does not mean that the entire chapter has been added. However, it is curious that chap. 13 is designed to show the fulfillment of the covenant oaths sworn in chap. 10, which specifically mention no intermarriage (v. 30), no selling on shabbat (v. 31), payment of an annual temple tax (vv. 32–33), provision of wood for the altar (v. 34), and the delivery of firstfruits to temple storehouses (vv. 35–37) as well as the tithes of produce designated for the Levites (vv. 37–39). Chapter 13 addresses the giving of Levites their due portions (vv. 10–13), no selling on Shabbat (vv. 15–22), and no intermarriage (vv. 23–29), dealing with the main oaths in reverse order. It omits only the temple tax; the provision of wood for the altar and the firstfruits are mentioned together briefly in the closing v. 31. What is to be made of this? Were both chapters part of the original design of the book to show statement and fulfillment? Or, was one original and the other added secondarily to demonstrate fulfillment? And finally, are one or both chapters original, showing Nehemiah to have enacted legal reforms in the newly established *bîrâ* of Jerusalem? Or, has one or both chapters been added secondarily by someone who wanted to counter the claims that Ezra established the law in Jerusalem, not Nehemiah?

Let us return to the three possible historical scenarios that can be based on Neh 13:16. Option 3 has few historical implications beyond general observations made already: the Tyrians, as one of the two main Phoenician cities, developed inland markets in the Persian and/or Hellenistic Period. The passage does not help identify a more specific time frame or a specific location of one of these markets, unless one were to suppose that the decision to assign the merchants Tyrian rather than Sidonian identity was influenced by a predominance of Tyrian trade at the time of writing. It can be noted that Sidon was the preeminent Phoenician state during the reign of Artaxerxes I. It had achieved this status by the early fifth century B.C.E. and continued to hold it until the closing years of the Persian era (Markoe 2000: 51–52). The impact of this first option on understanding the imperial or local trading policy during a specific portion of the Persian or Hellenistic Period is nil.

Option 2 allows the historian to identify Jerusalem as a specific Tyrian inland market and, possibly, Yehud as a larger trading zone during the Persian or Hellenistic Period. However, without being able to identify the specific king under whom such a trading enclave was established, this verse can be of limited help in understanding imperial policy in Yehud. It need not reflect the political supremacy of Tyre over Sidon, which would provide a clue to the possible times of composition. We cannot infer that the establishment of Tyrian versus Sidonian traders in Jerusalem was a direct result of Tyre's ascendancy over its neighbor. As a relatively unimportant backwater area of the Persian and Greek Empires, the weaker of the two powers may have expanded into this area by default; the other city was not interested because it expected little return.

Option 1 allows the historian to identify Jerusalem as a specific Tyrian inland market and Yehud as a larger trading zone that was established during the reign of Artaxerxes I. This, in turn, opens up the possibility for exploring the reasons that Artaxerxes I would have granted Tyre a trading concession in Jerusalem and Yehud or that Phoenician traders would have settled in Jerusalem at this time and developed localized, inland markets.

It appears that Artaxerxes I was the Persian monarch who was responsible for the rebuilding of Jerusalem. He decided to move the provincial seat from Mizpah, which had served in that capacity since 586 B.C.E., back to Jerusalem, the capital of the former nation of Judah. This move appears to have been the result of the more strategic location of Jerusalem. It lay at a major juncture between the north–south main road in the central highlands and one of the main east–west roads that gave access from the coast to the Jordan Valley. Mizpah, by contrast, lay only beside the north–south main road. In addition, water was perennially available in Jerusalem from the Gihon Spring; in Mizpah, the town was dependent on cisterns or had to draw water from the closest perennial source, which lay 0.5 km away as the crow flies. For purposes of communication, troop movement, trade, and water access, Jerusalem was better located.

Neh 2:8 notes that a *bîrâ* or fortress stood near the temple in the city, while 7:2 claims that an individual named Hananiah, possibly the son of Zerubbabel, had already been appointed as chief of police for the larger settlement (*śar habbîrâ*) when Nehemiah arrived. Nehemiah claims to have confirmed the latter in his post and to have made him responsible for security over the city gates once they were in place, the walls had been repaired, and a civilian population had been settled inside the walls, beside the fortress.

These circumstantial clues tend to suggest that, in the opinion of the author of the book of Nehemiah, the purpose of Nehemiah's mission was to complete Jerusalem's establishment as a fortress city. The first stage had been the construction of the fortress, which had taken place under his immediate predecessor, earlier in the reign of Artaxerxes I. Only the gates remained to be installed from that phase of work. Nehemiah claims that he was accompanied by army and cavalry officers when he arrived (Neh 2:9), some of whom would have been put in charge of the newly completed garrison.

Even if the autobiographical format of the book of Nehemiah stems from a later writer who chose to use the name to give his story a ring of authenticity, the details he has given suggest that Nehemiah's commission would have been to implement plans to incorporate the fortress into a larger walled settlement, which was to become the seat of the local provincial government. To accomplish this task, he would have had to have an official commission to rebuild the old city walls and gates and to establish a civilian population inside the walls, as the author of Nehemiah was well aware (Neh 2:5, 8).

According to the dates supplied in the book of Nehemiah, this final stage of work on Jerusalem began in the 20th year of Artaxerxes (I), or 445/444 B.C.E. Whether it lasted the entire 12 years of his governorship, after which he was allegedly recalled by the Persian king,[14] is uncer-

---

14. Note the odd description of Artaxerxes as "king of Babylon" and not of Persia, in 13:6.

tain. The historicity of the claims that the walls were repaired in 52 days (6:15) is hard to judge but seems like an exaggeration. Regardless, no mention is made of the length of time it took to install all the new gates or for the civilian population to build their homes inside the walls after they were completed. Undoubtedly, other government buildings would have been built beside the fortress on the acropolis, as well as houses for officials.

Jerusalem's establishment as the new Persian *bîrâ* and provincial seat in Yehud coincides in general with the period of Inaros's revolt, which probably began in 460 B.C.E., shortly after the death of Xerxes, and was quelled in 454 but with ongoing repercussions until about 450 B.C.E. The initial construction of the fortress could have begun before the revolt, during the revolt, or shortly after its suppression. If it began before the revolt, Xerxes would have ordered its construction, but Artaxerxes I would have seen its completion.

If construction began sometime at the end of Xerxes' reign, its purpose would have been to integrate Yehud more fully into the Persian road, postal, military, and economic network. This could have been done for a number of reasons. The aim may simply have been to boost the region's tax potential, particularly due to its location adjoining the coastal plains. Food supplies would have been needed to feed the workmen who were building triremes in the port cities and to feed crews and soldiers on campaign. A desire to have forts and food supplies available on the northern border of Egypt may also have been deemed desirable in the event of future unrest. Additionally, if Idumea had not yet been set up as a separate subprovince,[15] the ability to provide food and protection to Arab traders who were moving goods across the Beer-sheba Valley to Gaza may have been a further consideration.

If construction began soon after the outbreak of the revolt, Artaxerxes I logically would have desired to use Yehud either as a staging ground for sending soldiers overland into Egypt or as a breadbasket to help generate food supplies for both naval and land-based troops en route to the Delta region. There was a ten-year gap between the beginning of the revolt and its final quashing (Briant 2002: 573–77). This lengthy response time may have been the result of a need to secure Yehud by developing its forts and roads and installing a population

---

15. The date of the establishment of Idumea as a separate administrative unit is uncertain. The earliest reference to it derives from Greek sources. I favor a date of establishment of ca. 400 B.C.E., after Egypt successfully overturned its status as a Persian province and became an independent nation once again.

base in underdeveloped areas to begin food production (Hoglund 1992: 165–69, 242–44).

If construction only commenced in the wake of the revolt's quelling, it would likely have been part of a larger plan by Artaxerxes I to create a stronger Persian presence in the northern border regions of Egypt in the case of future trouble. By integrating the administrative districts in Yehud (and perhaps simultaneously in Samerina) more completely into the Persian road, military, and economic systems, the Persian monarch would have been able to facilitate the presence of troops within the region in newly established forts and fortress cities (*bîrôt*). At the same time, he could have facilitated the movement of additional troops through the region along newly established Persian roads that had appropriately spaced stations to supply postal agents and fortresses. The forts would have been able to supply rations as necessary from a newly established tax base, with taxes derived from farmsteads set up throughout these regions.

The "return" of the *gôlâ* community[16] to Yehud would have been an integral part of any of the three plans sketched above. Regardless of which theoretical scenario was the actual case, all would have supplied badly needed human resources within the underdeveloped parts of Yehud, particularly in the Judean highlands south of Jerusalem and in the Shephelah, which had never fully recovered its population after 701 B.C.E. when its territory had been ceded to Philistine control. The easiest way to accomplish this task would have been to resettle people in these regions, and it seems as though it would have been a simple matter to identify descendants of the Judahite exiles who had been settled in Babylonia in 592 and 586 B.C.E. Some of the Babylonian villages mentioned in the Murashu documents bear ethnic labels,[17] and a recent corpus of documents, probably from the region near Borsippa, comprises documents that refer to a place called the "town of the Judahites."[18] It

---

16. This is the term used in the books of Ezra and Nehemiah to designate the descendants of the elite who had been exiled to Babylonia in 592 and 586 B.C.E., who returned to their homeland, now the Persian subprovince of Yehud, reportedly in various waves under Cyrus, Darius, and Artaxerxes I.

17. Stolper 1985: 73–79. Ethnic groups whose names were attached to *hatru* settlements include people from Arum, people from Assa, Carians, Cimmerians, people from the suburbs of Nippur, people from Der, people from Melitene, people from Sharrabanu, people from Shumutkunu, Urartians, Arabs, Tyrians, Indians, Phrygians, Sardinians, and people of Hamqadua.

18. Joannès and Lemaire 1999: 17–27. There are 93 documents in a new corpus that has been entrusted for publication to Dr. Laurie Pearce at the University of California at Berkeley. She informs me that 30 of the 93 texts were composed in âl-Jahûdu and another

is likely that there were a number of non-Jews who were also included in the project, because the Persians would have been more interested in having the desired number of settlers than in matters of "ethnic purity."[19] But it seems that the returning leadership included a number of priests, who may well have tried to convince the authorities that the bulk of the settlers needed to be Yhwh-worshipers. Since this was the deity's traditional territory, he would only bless the land if he were properly honored on a regular basis.

The decision to grant Tyrian traders rights within the provincial capital may have been part of the larger general plan for the redevelopment of Jerusalem, or perhaps, was a secondary development that took place as the city was being rebuilt. If one favors a date for the beginning of the project after the quelling of Inaros's revolt, then the first option is likely. However, if the construction of the fortress had already begun before or during the revolt, then the second option is also possible. In either case, it would have come as part of the larger economic strategy for the development of this region, in addition to its military development.

Rewarding the preeminent Phoenician city-states, Tyre and Sidon, by giving them trading rights in certain inland territories of Cisjordan would have had a beneficial effect on the development of local economies. The possession of a range of imported goods would have allowed the native and foreign soldiers stationed in the newly built *bîrôt*, along with other administrative appointees of the crown and the emerging elite, to purchase what they needed and wanted with their salaries. At the same time, it would have reinforced the Phoenician's role as duly authorized private trading agents of the crown, preventing inroads by Greek traders, thereby punishing them for their ongoing anti-Persian hostilities.[20]

---

4 texts, written elsewhere, mention the town (private correspondence). See her essay in this volume, pp. 399–411.

19. So Thompson 1992: 418. His claim that none of the immigrants was a descendant of those exiled is unlikely unless he also would argue that the non-*gôlâ* priesthood was responsible for the development of early Judaism, controlled the temple after it was rebuilt, and then forced its new religion on the local population, the majority of whom had never heard of the deity Yhwh and would have seen no benefit in abandoning their traditional gods to worship a single supreme deity. It can be noted that the alleged list of returnees included Persians (Bigvai) and Elamites (Neh 7:7, 12, 19).

20. J.-F. Salles has noted that no traces of Cypriote pottery have been found in Jerusalem in the Persian Period and wonders if this might be evidence of an exclusive agreement between Jerusalem and Tyre "forbidding" the importation of olive oil that was not Judean (1991: 228). It more likely is evidence of not needing additional olive oil. Neh 13:15

Farmers living in the newly established network of rural agrarian villages and farmsteads in Yehud may have bartered excess produce or frills in the years of good harvests. Neh 13:16 seems to distinguish between the citizens of Jerusalem proper and those living in the province at large, possibly suggesting that Tyre had been granted a trading license within the confines of the entire province. This, however, was not the same as giving Tyre direct political control over Jerusalem or Yehud. Rather, they would have had a preferential market outlet and region of economic exchange in the Cisjordanian hinterland, which remained under the direct control of the Persian crown and a provincial governor.

Two motives can be postulated as underlying Artaxerxes' decision to establish a Phoenician trading colony in Jerusalem. The first may have been a desire to reward the king of Tyre for playing a crucial role in turning the tide in the revolt of Inaros in Egypt by granting him a trading concession in the newly established *bîrâ*. Phoenician contingents were among the naval forces that broke the blockade against Memphis and then defeated an additional Athenian squadron that had been sent to the rebels as reinforcements. These two exploits were the turning points that allowed the Persians to gain the upper hand and suppress the rebels soon thereafter (Herodotus 1.104; 3.12; 7.7; Diodorus 11.74.1–5; Thucydides 1.109.1–2; Briant 2002: 573–77).

Herodotus gives a number of examples in which the Persian monarchs Darius (4.88–89; 5: 11–12) and Xerxes (7.26; 8.10, 85–90) rewarded individuals who performed heroic deeds in battle with generous gifts. It seems likely that this was a known Persian practice. In this particular instance, the reward would have taken the form of a grant that allowed the vassal king to settle Tyrian merchants within the confines of the city walls to conduct trade with local inhabitants in the *bîrâ* proper, with others in the neighboring settlements and, perhaps, with inhabitants throughout the entire province of Yehud (Neh 13:16). Artaxerxes' choice of Jerusalem would have been partly fortuitous in that the city was in the process of being resettled or had recently been resettled.

---

claims that local oils were being produced and sold, which would tend to favor the view that there was a surplus in this commodity and that imports were not necessary. In light of the possibility that commodities like wine, oil, and wheat were being gathered all over the Mediterranean but transported in standardized storage jars (Salles 1994: 196) supplied by the Phoenicians, great caution must be exercised in drawing conclusions about the presence or absence of wares from various countries. It is not good to equate pots with people and then assume that they must have been traded directly by those people. The Phoenicians appear to have served as middlemen in trade, securing goods from all over the Mediterranean and reselling them.

G. E. Markoe has suggested that, in return for their naval services, the Tyrians may have been granted a commercial concession by the Persians in the transit trade that used the canal connecting the Nile with the Red Sea that had been completed during the reign of Darius I (2000: 51). Their involvement in this trade is indicated by the presence of Phoenician inscriptions at Tell el-Kheleifeh at the mouth of the Gulf of Aqabah. While he has not specified the date when this concession might have been enacted, his reasoning is similar to my reasoning here concerning the possible granting of a trade concession in the newly established *bîrâ* of Jerusalem by Artaxerxes I.

The second possible motive may have been a desire to encourage the economic development of Yehud as part of his larger strategy to incorporate the Cisjordanian hill country more fully into the Persian road, military, and economic system. This plan may have involved the granting of trade monopolies to the two main Phoenician cities, Tyre and Sidon, in various *bîrôt* within Samerina and Yehud.[21] These grants would have been designed to exclude Greek merchants from interior markets as punishment for their long history of insubordination, while developing the Phoenicians as duly authorized traders within the realm. The merchants would have engaged in private enterprise, but both the home city-state and the Persian court would have received income from their activities through import, export, road, and head taxes that were assessed on the goods, ships, and caravans as they traversed land and sea.

The inland markets would have supplied Tyre and Sidon with badly needed currency[22] and foodstuffs to help offset the ongoing costs of shipbuilding and the training of crews, as well as food to feed this labor force. In the specific case of Jerusalem, and possibly greater Yehud, Tyre's grant would have supplied marine and other foodstuffs, dyed purple cloth, and novelty items to administrators, soldiers, and civilians newly settled in Jerusalem, in outlying forts, and in more remote

---

21. Such a policy may already have been initiated by a predecessor of Artaxerxes I in Samerina, if this subprovince received earlier attention than Yehud. Further investigation needs to be made to determine whether both areas were incorporated into the imperial system simultaneously or not. Nehemiah's adversary, Sin-u-ballit the Harranite, may have headed a northern "*gôlâ* party" that had been sent into Samerina about the same time that Zerubbabel and his party were sent to Yehud. In both cases, the aim would have been to boost the local population and food production in the rural sectors.

22. This could have taken the form of either coinage or precious metals that were used as a standard of weight. Wallinga (1964: 410–11) has proposed that the Persians needed to pay their crews of oarsmen, just like their soldiers, and that this need accelerated the introduction of coinage in the western Levant.

rural settlements, bringing the material advantages of being a citizen in the Empire to those who could afford them (for various types of commodities, see Elayi 1988: 61–105; Salles 1991; 1994).

Conclusion

A brief review of long-distance trade and the creation of commercial quarters that included resident foreign traders in the ancient Near East has yielded inconclusive results concerning the legal status of foreign merchants in these situations in periods after the Middle Bronze Age. The extant evidence does not provide conclusive proof that self-regulation according to home law continued to be the norm in resident enclaves once empires emerged. Neither does it rule it out. The status of the main Phoenician city-states as vassals or subprovinces within the Persian Empire remains unclear, which in turn precludes our ability to know whether treaties between the Persian kings and the Tyrian kings would have defined the terms under which long-distance Tyrian trade diasporas could be established in various cities within the Empire or whether Tyrian merchants would have been free to set up shop anywhere as Persian citizens.

As a result, a final decision cannot be made regarding the rhetorical function of the Tyrian traders in Neh 13:15–22. A message was sent that all residents in Jerusalem and in Yehud (Neh 7:73; 8:15; 11:1) are bound by the law of Shabbat as expressed in the Torah, whether they are native born, *gērîm*, or possibly residents of a foreign trading enclave with their own laws. This message would have served as an illustration that Shabbat observation applied in all settlements in which the Torah functioned as the legal code. We are unable to determine, however, whether in actuality Tyrian merchants who might have been resident in Jerusalem under Artaxerxes I would have had full rights under Torah as Persian citizens living in a region where Torah was the official Persian law; whether they had the rights extended to *gērîm* under the Torah in spite of possibly being Persian citizens; or whether they were under the law of Tyre while resident in Jerusalem.

Understandings of the historical implications of Neh 13:16 depend on one's view of whether or not the Tyrians portrayed in the narrative world reflect actual traders within Jerusalem during Nehemiah's governorship or during the reign of Artaxerxes I. A decision on this matter is determined in part by the way that one assesses whether Nehemiah 13 is a later addition or an integral part of the original work, when the work was written, and whether the information in 13:16 derives from a postulated "Nehemiah Memoir" that accurately reflects events that transpired during Nehemiah's term of office in Jerusalem. It also depends on the way one understands the economic policies of Artaxerxes I in the southern Levant. Only if historical reliability is assumed can inferences be made concerning the way that the granting of a trade concession to the Tyrians in the *bîrâ* and provincial seat of Jerusalem fit into Artaxerxes' larger policies for the economic development of Yehud. I favor the historical reliability of this detail, and therefore, the historical implications sketched out above in option 1, but I realize that historical reliability cannot be confirmed by current evidence and that, therefore, it is premature and unwise to build too much on such an unstable foundation.

Bibliography

Adams, R. McC.
1974   Anthropological Perspectives on Ancient Trade. *Current Anthropology* 15/3: 239–58.
Ahlström, G. W.
1993   *The History of Ancient Palestine from the Neolithic Period to Alexander's Conquest.* JSOTSup 146. Sheffield.
Blenkinsopp, J.
1988   *Ezra–Nehemiah.* OTL. Westminster.
Boardman, J.
1999   *The Greeks Overseas: Their Early Colonies and Trade.* 4th ed. London.
Borger, R.
1956   *Die Inschriften Asarhaddons, Königs von Assyrien.* AfOB 9. Graz.
Briant, P.
2002   *From Cyrus to Alexander: A History of the Persian Empire,* trans. P. T. Daniels. Winona Lake, Indiana.
Cartledge, P.
1983   "Trade and Politics" Revisited: Archaic Greece. Pp. 1–15 in *Trade in the Ancient Economy,* ed. P. Garnsey, K. Hopkins, and C. R. Whittaker. London.
Çeçen, S., and Hecker, K.
1995   *ina matika eblum:* Zu einem neuen Text zum Wegerecht in der Kültepe-Zeit. Pp. 31–41 in *Von Alten Orient zum Alten Testament: Festschrift für Wolfram Freiherrn von Soden zum 85. Geburtstag am 19 Juni 1993,* ed. M. Dietrich and O. Loretz. AOAT 240. Neukirchen-Vluyn.
Cohen, A.
1971   Cultural Strategies in the Organization of Trading Diasporas. Pp. 266–81 in *The Development of Indigenous Trade and Markets in West Africa,* ed. C. Meillassoux and D. Forde. London.
Cook, J. M.
1983   *The Persian Empire.* London.

Curtin, P. D.
1984   *Cross-Cultural Trade in World History: Studies in Comparative World History.* Cambridge.
Dandamaev, M. A.
1999   Land Use in the Sippar Region during the Neo-Babylonian and Achaemenid Periods. Pp. 363–89 in *Urbanization and Land Ownership in the Ancient Near East, Volume II: A Colloquium Held at New York University, November, 1996, and the Oriental Institute, St. Petersburg, Russia, 1997,* ed. M. Hudson and B. A. Levine. Peabody Museum Bulletin 7. Cambridge, Massachusetts.
Dandamaev, M. A., and Lukonin, V. G.
1989   *The Culture and Social Institutions of Ancient Iran,* trans. P. L. Kohl and D. J. Dadson. Cambridge.
Dercksen, J. G.
2000   Institutional and Private in the Old Assyrian Period. Pp. 135–52 in *Interdependency of Institutions and Private Enterprise (MOS 2): Proceedings of the Second MOS Symposium (Leiden 1998),* ed. A. C. V. M. Bongenaar. Uitgaven van het Nederlands historisch-archaeologisch Instituut te Istanbul 87. Istanbul.
Driel, G. van
2002   *Elusive Silver: In Search of a Role for a Market in an Agrarian Environment. Aspects of Mesopotamia's Society.* Uitgaven van het Nederlands Instituut voor het Nabije Oosten te Leiden 95. Leiden.
Edelman, D.
2005   *The Origins of the 'Second' Temple: Persian Imperial Policy and the Rebuilding of Jerusalem.* London.
Forthcoming   *The Politics of Temple Building.*
Eidem, J.
1991   An Old Assyrian Treaty from Tell Leilan. Pp. 185–207 in *Marchands, diplomates et empereurs: Études sur la civilisation mésopotamienne offertes à Paul Garelli,* ed. D. Charpin and F. Joannès. Paris.
Elat, M.
1978   The Economic Relations of the Neo-Assyrian Empire with Egypt. *JAOS* 98: 20–34.
Elayi, J.
1988   *Pénétration grecque en Phénicie sous l'empire perse.* Travaux et mémoires: études anciennes 2. Nancy.
Eph'al, I.
1982   *The Ancient Arabs: Nomads on the Borders of the Fertile Crescent, 9th–5th Centuries B.C.* Jerusalem.
Frye, R. N.
1984   *The History of Ancient Iran.* Handbuch der Altertumswissenschaft 3/7. Munich.
Fuchs, A.
1994   *Die Inschriften Sargons II. aus Khorsabad.* Göttingen.

Gadd, C. J.
1954   Inscribed Prisms of Sargon II from Nimrud. *Iraq* 16: 173–201.
Grabbe, L. L.
1998   *Ezra–Nehemiah.* Old Testament Readings. London.
Grayson, A. K.
1996   *Assyrian Rulers of the Early First Millenium* BC *II (858–745* BC*).* The Royal Inscriptions of Mesopotamia: Assyrian Periods 3. Toronto.
Gotthard, H.
1958   *Der Text des Buches Nehemia.* Wiesbaden.
Hill, P.
1966   Landlords and Brokers: A West African Trading System. *Cahiers d'é-tudes africaines* 6/23 (3): 349–66.
1971   Two Types of West African House Trade. Pp. 303–18 in *The development of indigenous trade and markets in West Africa,* ed. C. Meillassoux and D. Forde. London.
Hoglund, K.
1992   *Achaemenid Imperial Administration in Syria–Palestine and the Missions of Ezra and Nehemiah.* SBLDS 125. Atlanta.
Holladay, J. S., Jr.
2001   Toward a New Paradigmatic Understanding of Long-Distance Trade in the Ancient Near East: From the Middle Bronze II to Early Iron II—A Sketch. Pp. 136–98 in *Studies in History and Archaeology in Honour of Paul-Eugène Dion,* ed. P. M. M. Daviau, J. W. Wevers, and M. Weigl. JSOTSup 325. Vol. 2 of *The World of the Aramaeans.* Sheffield.
Joannès, F., and Lemaire, A.
1999   Trois tablettes cunéiformes à onomastique ouest-sémitique. *Transeu* 17: 17–34.
Kellermann, U.
1967   *Nehemia: Quellen, Überlieferung und Geschichte.* BZAW 102. Berlin.
Kreissig, H.
1973   *Die sozialökonomische Situation in Juda zur Achämenidenzeit.* Schriften zur Geschichte und Kultur des Alten Orients 7. Berlin.
Lamberg-Karlovsky, C. C.
1975   Third Millenium Modes of Exchange and Modes of Production. Pp. 341–68 in *Ancient Civilization and Trade,* ed. J. A. Sabloff and C. C. Lamberg-Karlovsky. School of American Research Advanced Seminar Series 7. Albuquerque.
Lanfranchi, G. B., and Parpola, S.
1990   *The Correspondence of Sargon II, Part II: Letters from the Northern and Northeastern Provinces.* State Archives of Assyria 5. Helsinki.
Larsen, M. T.
1977   Partnership in the Old Assyrian Trade. *Iraq* 39: 119–49.
1999   The Old Assyrian City State. Pp. 77–87 in *A Comparative Study of Thirty City-State Cultures,* ed. M. H. Hansen. Historisk-filosofiske Skrifter 21. Copenhagen.

2002 *The Assur-nada Archive.* Old Assyrian Archives 1. Uitgaven van het Nederlands Instituut voor het Naboje Oosten te Leiden 94. Leiden.

Lemaire, A., and Lozachmeur, N.
1987 Birah/birta' en araméen. *Syria* 64: 261–66.

Lernau, H., and Lernau, O.
1992 Fish Remains. Pp. 131–48 in *Stratigraphical, Environmental, and Other Reports*, ed. A. De Groot and D. T. Ariel. Qedem 33. Vol. 3 of *Excavations at the City of David 1978–1985, Directed by Yigael Shiloh.* Jerusalem.

Levine, L. D.
1977 Sargon's Eighth Campaign. Pp. 135–51 in *Mountains and Lowlands*, ed. L. D. Levine and T. C. Young. Mesopotamica 7. Malibu, California.

Lewy, J.
1956 On Some Institutions of the Old Assyrian Empire. *HUCA* 27: 1–80.

Luckenbill, D. D.
1927 *Historical Records of Assyria from Sargon to the End.* Vol. 2 of *Ancient Records of Assyria and Babylonia.* Chicago.

Luukko, M., and Buylaere, G. van
2002 *The Political Correspondence of Esarhaddon.* State Archives of Assyria 16. Helsinki.

Malamat, A.
1986 "Doorbells" at Mari: A textual-archaeological correlation. Pp. 160–67 in *Cuneiform Archives and Libraries*, ed. K. R. Veenhof. Leiden.

Markoe, G. E.
2000 *Phoenicians.* Peoples of the Past. London.

Martin, W. J.
1936 *Tribut und Tributleistungen bei den Assyrien.* Studia Orientalia 8/1. Helsinki.

Master, D. M.
2003 Trade and Politics: Ashkelon's Balancing Act in the Seventh Century B.C.E. *BASOR* 330: 47–64.

Myers, J. M.
1965 *Ezra–Nehemiah: A New Translation with Introduction and Commentary.* AB 14. New York.

Na'aman, N.
1979 The Brook of Egypt and Assyrian Policy on the Border of Egypt. *Tel Aviv* 6: 68–90.

Oren, E. D.
1984 Migdol: A New Fortress on the Edge of the Eastern Nile Delta. *BASOR* 256: 7–44.

Parkins, H., and Smith, C.
1998 *Trade, Traders and the Ancient City.* London.

Parpola, S.
1987 *The Correspondence of Sargon II, Part I: Letters from Assyria and the West.* State Archives of Assyria 1. Helsinki.

Parpola, S., and Watanabe, K.
1988   *Neo-Assyrian Treaties and Loyalty Oaths.* State Archives of Assyria 2. Helsinki.

Polanyi, K.
1957   Marketless Trading in Hammurabi's Time. Pp. 12–26 in *Trade and Markets in the Early Empires: Economies in History and Theory,* ed. K. Polanyi, C. M. Arensberg, and H. W. Pearson. Glencoe, Illinois.
1975   Traders and Trade. Pp. 133–54 in *Ancient Civilization and Trade,* ed. J. A. Sabloff and C. C. Lamberg-Karlovsky. School of American Research Advanced Seminar Series 7. Albuquerque.

Postgate, J. N.
1974   *Taxation and Conscription in the Assyrian Empire.* Studia Pohl, Series Maior 3. Rome.

Reich, R.
1984   The Identification of the "Sealed KARU of Egypt." *IEJ* 34: 32–38.

Saggs, H. W. F.
2001   *The Nimrud Letters, 1952.* Cuneiform Texts from Nimrud 5. London.

Salles, J.-F.
1991   Du blé, de l'huile et du vin. . . . Pp. 207–35 in *Asia Minor and Egypt: Old Cultures in a New Empire. Proceedings of the Groningen 1988 Achaemenid History Workshop,* ed. H. Sancisi-Weerdenburg and A. Kuhrt. Achaemenid History 6. Nederlands Instituut voor het Nabije Oosten. Leiden.
1994   Du blé, de l'huile et du vin. . . . Pp. 191–215 in *Continuity and Change: Proceedings of the Last Achaemenid History Workshop, April 6–8, 1990, Ann Arbor, Michigan,* ed. H. Sancisi-Weerdenburg, A. Kuhrt, and M. Root. Achaemenid History 8. Nederlands Instituut voor het Nabije Oosten. Leiden.

Stolper, M. W.
1985   *Entrepreneurs and Empire: The Murāšu Archive, the Murāšu Firm and Persian Rule in Babylonia.* Uitgaven van het Nederlands historisch-archaeologisch Instituut te Istanbul 54. Leiden.

Sullivan, R. D.
1996   Psammetichus I and the Foundation of Naukratis. Pp. 177–95 in *The Survey at Naukratis,* ed. W. D. E. Coulson. Vol. 2/1 of *Ancient Naukratis.* Oxbow Monograph 60. Oxford.

Tadmor, H.
1958   The Campaigns of Sargon II of Assur: A Chronological-Historical Study. *JCS* 12: 22–40.
1966   Philistia under Assyrian Rule. *BA* 29: 86–102.
1994   *The Inscriptions of Tiglath-Pileser III, King of Assyria.* Jerusalem.

Thompson, T. L.
1994   *Early History of the Israelite People: From the Written and Archaeological Sources.* SHANE 4. Leiden.

Veenhof, K. R.
1972   *Aspects of Old Assyrian Trade and Its Terminology.* Studia et documenta ad iura orientis antiqui pertinentia 10. Leiden.

1995   Kanesh: An Assyrian Colony in Anatolia. Pp. 859–71 in vol. 2 of *Civilizations of the Ancient Near East*, ed. J. Sasson. Peabody, Massachusetts.
Wallinga, H. T.
1964   The Ionian Revolt. *Mnemosyne* 37: 401–37.
Williamson, H. G. M.
1985   *Ezra, Nehemiah*. WBC 16. Waco, Texas.
Yardeni, A.
1994   Maritime Trade and Royal Accountancy in an Erased Customs Account from 475 B.C.E. on the Ahiqar Scroll from Elephantine. *BASOR* 293: 67–78.
Yoffee, N.
1994   The Economy of Western Asia. Pp. 1387–1399 in vol. 3 of *Civilizations of the Ancient Near East*, ed. J. Sasson. Peabody, Massachusetts.
Zadok, R.
1976   On the Connection between Iran and Babylon in the Sixth Century BC. *Iran* 14: 67–77.

The Second Temple of Jeb and of Jerusalem

REINHARD G. KRATZ

Göttingen University

The archives of Jedaniah of Jeb (Elephantine) contain an excellent historical analogy to the reconstruction of the Second Temple in Jerusalem and the Aramaic documents of Ezra 4–6: the petition by the Jewish colony (two copies of which exist) to rebuild the temple in Jeb, as well as the reply from the governors of Judah and Samaria.[1] Although the parallels between the two building projects are often alluded to, they are hardly ever employed to critique biblical sources or reconstruct historical events in Jerusalem.[2] This is all the more astonishing given the tendency in contemporary scholarship to prefer the authentic primary sources of a given age over biblical sources, which are separated from events by a longer period of time and are for the most part greatly revised. There are many reasons that the Elephantine documents are treated with kid gloves: in the first place, they do not recount the same event but rather a comparable one that took place about 100 years later; in the second, the Elephantine Papyri portray a

Author's note: During the 2002–3 academic year, I was a fellow at the Berlin Institute for Advanced Study, and I express my heartfelt thanks to the Institute for supporting the writing and translation of this essay. The German version appeared in my *Judentum im Zeitalter des Zweiten Tempels* (FAT 42; Tübingen: Mohr-Siebeck, 2004) 60–78.

1. *TADAE* A4.7–9. If not otherwise noted, the following edition is cited: B. Porten and A. Yardeni (eds.), *Textbook of Aramaic Documents from Ancient Egypt* (4 vols. A–D; Jerusalem: Hebrew University Dept. of the History of the Jewish People, 1986–99). See also B. Porten et al. (eds.), *The Elephantine Papyri in English* (Documenta et monumenta Orientis antiqui 22; Leiden: Brill, 1996) 74–276.

2. An exception is K. Galling, *Studien zur Geschichte Israels im persischen Zeitalter* (Tübingen: Mohr-Siebeck, 1964) 61–77, 78–88, 127–48, and 149–84. Galling attempts to reconcile biblical and extrabiblical material historically. On the other hand, there is not a single reference to Elephantine in the indexes of P. R. Davies (ed.), *Second Temple Studies 1: Persian Period* (JSOTSup 117; Sheffield: Sheffield Academic Press, 1991) or T. C. Eskenazi and K. H. Richards (eds.), *Second Temple Studies 2: Temple and Community in the Persian Period* (JSOTSup 175; Sheffield: Sheffield Academic Press, 1994). Concerning the procedure applied here, see my "Perserreich und Israel," *TRE* 26/1–2 (1996) 211–17.

Jewry that is so different from that of the Old Testament that it is treated as an exception. However, the Egyptian Jews probably had much more in common with the historical Israel of the pre- and post-exilic age in Palestine than do the biblical Jews. The Bible is the exception, not Elephantine. In view of these considerations, I would like to examine biblical accounts of the reconstruction of the Second Temple in Jerusalem in light of later events in Jeb. In my comparison I will focus on three issues: (1) the archaeological evidence, (2) the historical situation, and (3) the religious and political argumentation.

The Archaeological Evidence

The archaeological findings are the most reliable starting point for a historical reconstruction of the two building projects. In the case of Elephantine, the stratigraphic and epigraphic evidence paints a fairly clear picture.[3]

Based on Aramaic papyri and inscriptions, the architecture of the ancient buildings, and the place where the Jedaniah archives were found, scholars have been able to map out what excavator Otto Rubensohn has called the "Aramaic quarter" of Elephantine.[4] This quarter is associated with Stratum 4 of the archaeological site, which lies to the northwest of the Roman temenos wall of the Chnum Temple and dates to the 27th Dynasty (525–404 B.C.E.). The quarter once extended 70 meters to the north, but only the southeastern row of buildings has survived. Topographical and building-ownership information in the papyri have helped fill in the many gaps. Of the diverse attempts to reconstruct the ground plan of the Aramaic quarter, Bezalel Porten's has proved the most persuasive.[5] He interprets the controversial descriptions "above" and "below" as "north" and "south," with his orien-

---

3. For what follows, see C. von Pilgrim, "Textzeugnis und archäologischer Befund: Zur Topographie Elephantines in der 27. Dynastie," in *Stationen: Beiträge zur Kulturgeschichte Ägyptens. Festschrift R. Stadelmann* (ed. H. Guksch and D. Pols; Mainz: von Zabern, 1998) 485–97; idem in *Egypt—Temple of the Whole World: Studies in Honour of Jan Assmann* (ed. S. Meyer; Leiden: Brill, 2003) 303–17; also *MDAIK* 44 (1988) 170–74; 46 (1990) 214–17; 49 (1993) 177–79; 55 (1999) 142–45; and 58 (2002) 192–97.

4. See W. Honroth, O. Rubensohn, and F. Zucker, "Bericht über die Ausgrabungen auf Elephantine in den Jahren 1906–1908," *ZÄS* 46 (1910) 14–61. Also the excavation diaries of O. Rubensohn in W. Müller (ed.), "Die Papyrusgrabung auf Elephantine 1906–1908," *FuB* 20/21 (1980) 75–88; 22 (1982) 7–50; and 24 (1984) 41–44.

5. B. Porten, "The Structure and Orientation of the Jewish Temple at Elephantine: A Revised Plan of the Jewish District," *JAOS* 81 (1961) 38–42; idem, *Archives from Elephantine: The Life of an Ancient Jewish Military Colony* (Berkeley: University of California Press, 1968) 112 and passim; *TADAE* B, 176–82.

tation alternating between the northwest and northeast. His proposal best fits in with the archaeological frame and can be correlated with the intact structures of Stratum 4.

This evidence and more recent excavations at the Chnum Temple have also made it possible to pinpoint the location of the YHW Temple: it stood to the southeast of the Roman temenos wall, underneath the Ptolemaic temple on the southern edge of the Aramaic buildings. It was situated northwest of the "town of Chnum"[6] mentioned in the papyri and confirmed by archaeological excavations. This much-discussed appellation obviously applies to a district of the pre-Ptolemaic Chnum Temple that during the 27th Dynasty was enclosed by a wall. To the west, a northeast–southwest axis (the "street of the king"[7]) and temporarily a second wall separated this area from the Jewish residential quarter and the YHW Temple district bordering on the street.

Unfortunately, not much remains of the YHW Temple, and we have no accurate idea of its floor plan. Including the surrounding streets, the entire property was about 20 meters wide and at least 30 meters long (prior to the Kom destruction). It was thus large enough to hold a shrine the size of Solomon's Temple.[8] The petition to rebuild describes adequate architectural features and furnishings: stone pillars, five stone gates with bronze hinges (obviously the gates of a temenos wall), a roof of cedar wood, wood paneling, as well as gold and silver vessels (A4.7:9–12//4.8:8–10). The few remains of the building and the surrounding walls stem from two phases of construction: the founding of the temple in Stratum 5 (Saite period, 26th Dynasty, 664–525 B.C.E.) and its reconstruction in Stratum 4 (27th Dynasty). The ruins were completely covered by the new building of the Chnum Temple, with construction beginning under Nectanebo II (360–343 B.C.E.)[9] and continuing into the Hellenistic–Roman age.

However, the Egyptian building activities to the south were not the only architectural disruption of the Aramaic quarter. To the northeast

---

6. Original, תמא/תמי זי חנום (B3.4:8; 3.5:10), also translated 'way of Chnum' similar to the expression חמואנתי 'town/way of the god' in B3.10:9. For a discussion, see Porten, *Archives*, 284–85, 309. In both cases the location in question has a wall. This emerges in B3.10:8–9 for the eastern area of the Jewish quarter and is shown by the archaeological evidence for the adjacent Chnum Temple in the south (von Pilgrim, "Textzeugnis," 489–90; idem, *MDAIK* 58, 194–96).

7. Original, שוק מלכא in B3.4:8; 3.5:10f.; the same street is probably meant in 3.12:21.

8. According to 1 Kgs 6:2–3, the measurements are 60 × 20 cubits (including the entrance hall, 70 × 20 cubits), or 30/35 × 10 m.

9. See *MDAIK* 26 (1970) 113ff.

and northwest, the Jewish temple was also enclosed by a "street of the king," that is, a public road owned by the king.[10] The residential neighborhood lay adjacent to this road. Northeast of the temple there was a row of buildings whose ruins have survived and been identified.[11] One of these properties lay between the Jewish temple to the west and a royal storehouse to the east.[12] Ananiah's family archives (B3.1–13) contain information on its fate: between 434 and 420 B.C.E., the Egyptians began erecting, on the southern part of the property, residential buildings for servants of the neighboring Chnum Temple.[13] The documents from 404–402 B.C.E. mention a shrine that was situated to the north of Ananiah's property.[14] East of it, between Ananiah's house and the royal storehouse, was a 'protecting wall' (אגרא זי הנפנא) that "the Egyptians built" and that is identified with the "way/town of God."[15] This "protecting wall," in turn, appears to be identical or, at least, somehow to be connected with the wall (שורא) that was erected near the damaged storehouse in 410 B.C.E., the year that the Jewish temple was destroyed. This wall is mentioned in a petition, which also alludes to the disruption of the Jewish garrison's water supply by the Chnum priests (A4.5). Both mentions of a wall fit with the archaeological evidence of the enclosing walls in the south that separate the Jewish quarter and the "town of Chnum."

Based on the construction measures, which culminated in the destruction of the Jewish temple, we can conclude that the Egyptians began gradually to encircle and isolate the Jewish quarter from the east and the south. However, the invasion was only moderately successful, and the perpetrators were eventually punished and the temple reconstructed in the 27th (Persian) Dynasty. Nevertheless, soon after the change of rulers in Egypt, a new Chnum Temple was erected. During the 30th Dynasty (380–343 B.C.E.) the Egyptians began building over the Jewish quarter from the south, and things did not change during

---

10. Original, שוק מלכא in B3.4:9f.; 3.5:10; 3.11:4–5; 3.12:18–19 as well as ארח מלכא in B2.10:6–7.

11. This included House G, identical with Gaddul's house (B2.7:14), and House H from Stratum 5, which was covered in Stratum 4 by the houses of Shatibar and Ananiah (B3.4:7–10; 3.5:8–11). See the figures in Porten, *Archives*, 215, 218, 246; *TADAE* B, 176; von Pilgrim, "Textzeugnis," 488, 491, and 492–94; idem, *MDAIK* 58, 195.

12. B3.4:9; 3.7:6–7; 3.11:3–4.

13. B3.7:7–8 (3.10:10; 3.11:6) and 3.12:20; see Porten, *Archives*, 284–86.

14. B3.10:8–10; 3.11:3–6; Shatibar's adjacent house had meanwhile changed hands; cf. 3.12:19 with 3.5:11 (3.7:7?).

15. B3.10:8–9. See n. 6 above; regarding the "protection wall" mentioned here, also B3.11:4.

the second Persian Period (31st Dynasty, 343–332 B.C.E.) and continued into the Hellenistic–Roman age.

In Jerusalem there is also a scarcity of archaeological evidence.[16] As blocks in the wall of the Temple Mount suggest, the Second Temple was built over in the Hellenistic–Roman, namely the Herodian age, when the entire complex was enlarged.[17] Whereas third parties constructed their buildings on the ruins of the temple in Elephantine, in Jerusalem the purpose of reconstruction was self-utilization, even if this was not recognized by all. The temple, which had been desecrated under Antiochus IV and then maintained by Hellenistic rulers, was disdained by pious Jews (Chasidim), including those in the Qumran community.

The Herodian enlargement suggests the existence of a predecessor building on the same site. But apart from small traces on the eastern wall, we know of it only from written sources.[18] We are told that the Persian king Cyrus gave the construction order; sources agree that the temple was then built, or completed, under Darius (I). It replaced the preexilic (Solomon) temple that the Babylonians had destroyed upon conquering Jerusalem in 587 B.C.E. Assuming the written sources are reliable, what we have here—as in Elephantine—is the reconstruction of an older, pre-Persian foundation during the Achaemenid era, a structure that had been destroyed by foreign forces (Babylonians or Egyptians).

It thus seems justified to compare the two building projects. While Jeb is not Jerusalem, and the Jewish fortress of Elephantine is not the province of Jehud, I see no reason to distinguish between the two temples in terms of the archaeological evidence. Nor are their differing descriptions of any significance. In Jerusalem the temple is called בית ('house') or היכל ('palace'), and in Jeb it is referred to as אגורא.[19] Though the Aramaic word אגורא is usually derived from the Akkadian *ekurru* (Sumerian é.kur), meaning 'temple, shrine', some scholars have proposed deriving it from the root אגר ('to gather, to assemble') and thus

---

16. See K. Bieberstein and H. Blödhorn, *Jerusalem: Grundzüge der Baugeschichte vom Chalkolithikum bis zur Frühzeit der osmanischen Herrschaft* (BTAVO, series B 100/1–3; Wiesbaden: Harrassowitz, 1994) 1.86ff., 3.370ff.; H. Weippert, *Palästina in vorhellenistischer Zeit* (HdA Vorderasien 2/1; Munich: Beck, 1988) 461–74.

17. See Sir 50:1–4; Josephus *J.W.* 1.21.1 §401; 5.5.1–7 §184–237; *Ant.* 15.11.1–3 §380–402.

18. Haggai; Zechariah 1–8; Ezra 1–6.

19. A4.7//4.8 passim; 4.10:8–9; B2.7:14; 2.10:6; 3.4:9–10; 3.5:10; 3.12:18–19. It is unclear whether the term מסגדא in B7.3, meaning 'place of prostration', refers to the shrine of YHW; the oath is taken to two gods. The name of the first is obliterated; the second is ʿNTYHW.

viewing the building of Elephantine as a walled-in "place of assembly" similar to the *bāmōt* (high places) or to Greek marketplaces (ἀγορά).[20] But even if this is true, it makes no difference to our study. The boundaries between the *bāmōt* (occasionally linked with a building) and the royal temple in the capital are fluid. Disregarding the law of cult centralization expressed in the Bible, even Jerusalem is nothing more than a greatly expanded *bāmā*. In addition, the Egyptian temples are referred to as אגורא in the Elephantine Papyri (A4.7:14//4.8:13). The twice-used[21] expression בית יהו/יהה ('house of YHW/YHH') and the phrase בית מדבחא ('house of the altar'), which is used in the construction permit memorandum (A4.9:3),[22] leave not a shadow of doubt that a temple is meant. Even the phrase "YHW the god, who dwells in Jeb the fortress" (B3.12:2)[23] presupposes a dwelling in the Elephantine settlement of Jeb that is comparable to the Jerusalem temple (see Exod 25:8; Ezra 6:12).

The Historical Situation

The destruction of the Jewish temple of Elephantine and its reconstruction must be seen within the context of the disputes between the leaders and priests of the Jewish colony on the one hand and the priests of the adjacent Chnum Temple on the other. A letter written by Mauziah, son of Natan, dating to the period before 410 B.C.E., alludes to the enmity: ידיע זי חנום הו עלין מן זי חנניה במצרין עד כען 'It is known to you that Chnum is against us since Hananiah has been in Egypt until now' (A4.3:7).

The reason for the hostilities is not entirely clear. Normally the famous Passover Letter that Hananiah wrote to his brothers in Jeb in 419 B.C.E. (A4.1) is cited. Though the interpretation of the badly damaged document is disputed, this much is certain: it refers to a message from King Darius (II) to Arsames, the satrap of Egypt, and afterward details

---

20. D. and M. Kellermann, "YHW-Tempel und Sabbatfeier auf Elephantine?" in *Festgabe für H. R. Singer* Teil 2 (ed. M. Forstner; FAS A.1; Frankfurt a.M., 1991) 433–52. See also H. J. Stoebe, "Überlegungen zum Synkretismus der jüdischen Tempelgemeinde in Elephantine," in *Beiträge zur Kulturgeschichte Vorderasiens: Festschrift R. M. Boehmer* (ed. U. Finkbeiner et al.; Mainz: von Zabern, 1995) 619–26, 620.

21. Used once in the salutation formula שלם בית יהו ביב in A.3.3:1, as in the formula "Greetings to the house of GN" in A2.1–2.4:1; the second time on the Ostrakon D7.18:2–3.

22. The formulation is misleading because the sacrificial altar did not stand inside but in front of the temple building. It merges the temple and altar in A4.7:25–26//4.8:24–25; sacrifices "in" or "at" the temple are also mentioned in A4.7:21–22//4.8:21.

23. See also אהלא שכן ביב ברתא B3.5:2; 3.10:2; 3.11:2.

specific instructions from Hananiah to his brothers. In terms of dates and subject matter, these seem to apply to the Passover festival, even though the name of the festival is never mentioned. Even so, we cannot be sure that the anger of the Chnum priests was indeed provoked by Passover and the planned slaughtering of sheep, or the commemoration of the Exodus and the Jewish victory over the Egyptians, or something entirely different, for which Hananiah went to Egypt.[24] We also do not know exactly who this Hananiah was, except for the fact that he represented Jewish interests in Egypt for a time. It would be rash to identify him with the brother of Nehemiah or the commander of the fortress in Neh 1:2 and 7:2[25] or with the (governor?) ḤN(W)NH[26] whose existence is verified by epigraphic evidence from the fifth century.

What we do know is that Hananiah's mission had to compete for Arsames' favor, as is eloquently recorded in the documents of the Jedaniah archives. Recently Ingo Kottsieper[27] voiced an intriguing theory: Hananiah was able to obtain formal recognition of the Jewish colony, which resulted in its being given the ethnically specific name חילא יהודיא, or 'Jewish garrison' (A4.1:1, 10; C3.15:1). This would explain the diplomatic efforts and hostilities between the opposing parties better than the Passover festival, which had been celebrated earlier.[28]

The usual manner of currying favor with the Egyptian satrap and mastering one's opponent was diplomacy—that is, bribery and intrigue (A4.2; 4.10). A certain Vidranga, who made common cause with the Chnum priests, plays an important role in this context. Vidranga was initially commander of the army in Syene (A4.3:3; B2.10:2–3, 4; 3.9:2) and later advanced to 'governor' (*frataraka*) (A4.5:4; 4.7//4.8:5), whereupon his son Nephaina was made army commander (A4.7:7// 4.8:7; 5.2:7). Vidranga took Mauziah prisoner in Abydos, allegedly for robbery, and perhaps demanded a ransom for his release. The two

---

24. See Porten, *Archives*, 279–82.

25. Ibid., 130; also 279–80.

26. See A. Lemaire, "Das achämenidische Juda und seine Nachbarn im Lichte der Epigraphie," in *Religion und Religionskontakte im Zeitalter der Achämeniden* (ed. R. G. Kratz; Veröffentlichungen der Wissenschaftlichen Gesellschaft für Theologie 22; Gütersloh: Gütersloher, 2002) 210–30, esp. 213ff. Lemaire suggests that this ḤN(W)NH is the son of Zerubbabel in 1 Chr 3:19, 21 ("Juda," 216 n. 35). Hananiah is also a governor of Samaria in the Wadi ed-Daliyeh papyri (WDSP 7:17; cf. with 8:12) and on Samarian coins (Lemaire, "Juda," 221–22).

27. I. Kottsieper, "Die Religionspolitik der Achämeniden und die Juden von Elephantine," in *Religion* (ed. Kratz) 150–78, esp. 157.

28. See D7.6:9–10 (convex); 7.24:5 (concave), and Porten's commentary, *Archives*, 130–33.

aides who secured Mauziah's release "with the help of the God of Heaven" are described as the servants of Anani, who himself was Arsames' scribe and chancellor (A6.2:23). One of them, called Hor, was also, or had previously been, in the service of Hananiah (provided this is the same person). Mauziah sent both servants along with the necessary letter of recommendation to the men and priests of the Jewish colony of Elephantine to curry favor with Anani (A4.3; cf. also A4.2:13–15). It was also Vidranga and his son who destroyed the Jewish temple. In the second, improved version of the petition to rebuild the temple, their actions are put down to a bribe (A4.8:5; cf. A4.5:4). And yet this did not prevent the petitioners from promising the responsible officials a considerable sum to further their interests (A4.10:13–14; uncertain, A4.7:28–29 // 4.8:27).

The leaders and priests of the Jewish colony of Elephantine not only negotiated with the authorities in Egypt but also sought the assistance of Jewish and Persian officials in Judah and Samaria. This is revealed in their extensive correspondence, which has partially survived or is alluded to in intact documents. The surviving documents include a petition to "our lord" (probably Arsames [see A6.1:5] or Anani), which was written just after the destruction of the temple in the 14th year of Darius (410 B.C.E.) and asks for support and a police investigation of the event (A4.5). This letter may be identical with the one to "our lord" that is mentioned in the petition to Bagohi, the governor of Judah, from the 17th year of Darius (A4.7:18 // 4.8:17); but it may also be an earlier letter with the same contents that was written to Bagohi, who is also customarily addressed "our lord" (A4.7 // 4.8:1–2 and passim). After the governors of Judah and Samaria give the go-ahead for the reconstruction project, imposing a few precautionary restrictions on sacrifices (A4.9; cf. A4.10:10–11), an official, who was probably in Egypt and is also addressed as "our lord," is once again asked for orders (A4.10). Two copies of the petition to Bagohi, the governor of Judah, have survived: the first corrected draft and its clean copy. In addition to the earlier letter to "our lord" (mentioned above) are references to letters to the high priest of Jerusalem, Jehohanan,[29] and his colleagues; to Ostanes, Anani's brother; to other members of the Jewish nobility (A4.7:18–19 // 4.8:17–18); and to Delaiah and Shelemiah, the sons of Sanballat,[30] the governor of Samaria (A4.7:29 // 4.8:28).

---

29. See Neh 12:22–23 (Jonathan in 12:10–11). A certain YWḤNN HKHN, or 'Johanan the Priest', is also mentioned on a Judaic coin from the fourth century B.C.E.; see Lemaire, "Juda," 216–17.

30. See Neh 2:10, 19; 3:33; 4:1; 6:1–2, 5, 12, 14; 13:28.

The diplomatic efforts were successful on both fronts. The governors of Judah and Samaria (or their sons) had an envoy inform the satrap of Egypt of their *nihil obstat*, which is recorded in notes of a talk that are stored in Elephantine—the famous memorandum with the message from Bagohi and Delaiah (A4.9). Convinced no doubt by receiving the generosity of leading figures in the Jewish colony (A4.10), the Persian authorities in Egypt apparently gave their consent, thus promoting the interests of the Jewish colony, not those of the Chnum priests. The reconstruction of the temple, which is shown by the archaeological evidence, is proof of this. It is difficult to say why no answer came from Jerusalem. Much depends on how seriously the doctrine of cult centralization was taken there (Deuteronomy 12). Even so, there was no attempt in Jerusalem to stop reconstruction of the temple in Jeb. Perhaps the letter's recipients did not feel responsible or did not want to risk a conflict with the Persian authorities.[31] Perhaps the letter, like the early petition to "our lord," simply got lost in bureaucratic channels. I also think it is possible that there were consultations with the priests and members of nobility in Jerusalem before the governor of Judah and the son of the governor of Samaria issued their *nihil obstat*.

According to the account in Ezra 1–6, the reconstruction of the temple in Jerusalem during the age of Cyrus II and Darius I is also marked by disputes and diplomatic efforts to secure the good will of the Persian authorities. But of course the fault lines run differently here.

As in Egypt, the Jews face local enemies. These enemies are not identical with the destroyers of the temple but are nevertheless defamed as strangers. They are called the "adversaries of Judah and Benjamin" and the "people of the land," and consisted of Israelites who remained in the land and the survivors of the colonies settled under the Assyrians (Ezra 4:1–5; cf. 4:9–10). Opposing them were the (Judaic) Gola, the returnees from Babylon who felt that they alone were entitled to build the temple (Ezra 1–4; 6:16–18, 19–22). In addition to the (high) priest Jeshua, the leaders of the Gola include political officials such as Sheshbazzar, the "prince" and governor of Judah (Ezra 1:8; 5:14), and Zerubbabel, who is probably identical with the governor mentioned in Ezra 6:7 (see Hag 1:1). In Ezra 5–6 the prophets Haggai and Zechariah (5:1–2; 6:14) also put in an appearance, together with the "elders of the Jews" (Ezra 5:5), who are responsible for the construction of the temple and must justify themselves to the Persian authorities.

---

31. See Kottsieper, "Religionspolitik," 164–65 and 171–72 n. 78. Like Galling (*Studien*, 161–65), he alludes to the tensions between Johanan and Bagohi, on which Josephus (*Ant.* 11.7.1 §297–301) reports.

The conflict is essentially an internal one, and one has the impression that it owes more to a theological construct than historical reality. In fact it focuses on a pure anachronism. In terms of content and chronology, the conflict over the start of temple construction anticipates the disputes between Judah and Samaria, which according to the book of Nehemiah took place in the mid-fifth century. There is no mention of these disputes in the Elephantine Papyri from the late fifth century.

In addition, there is a discrepancy between the Gola and the "elders of the Jews" that can only be explained in literary-historical terms.[32] The elders of the Jews are engaged in negotiations with the Persian authorities and are not party to the disputes between the Gola and the "people of the land." Conversely, in factual and literary terms, the tale of the return of the Gola and the start of temple construction in Ezra 1–4 (and 6:16–22) presupposes the account of construction in Ezra 5–6. The story of this earlier period is motivated by the remark in Ezra 5:16 that the temple had been under construction since the first year of Cyrus, and it provides an explanation for the work's interruption, which lasted until the 2nd year of Darius I. It follows that Ezra 1–4 (and 6:16–22) is an addition to Ezra 5–6 and that the conflicts over the beginning of temple construction—in keeping with the diplomatic conventions of the period—are invented.

From this point of view, a judgment is passed on the diplomatic relations that both sides cultivated with the Persian authorities in and outside the country. In this regard, the account also takes the historical situation in the Persian Empire as a model, one it interprets in its own way. For instance, the "adversaries of Judah and Benjamin" in Ezra 4 make use of the instrument of bribery (4:5) and, with the aid of Persian officials, submit various written petitions to foil reconstruction of the city and the temple (4:6ff.). However, in contrast to Elephantine, here bribery and intrigue remain a vice of the Jews' opponents. The Gola (and with them the "elders of the Jews" in Ezra 5–6) do not have to grease any palms to achieve their aims. On the contrary, they receive generous gifts from the Persian kings.

In Ezra 5–6 the "elders of the Jews" are paid a visit by Tattenai, the governor (satrap) of Trans-Euphrates, and his companions, who officially search the temple, though not at the instigation of the Jews' adversaries. Tattenai and his cronies correspond with King Darius on the matter. If we compare their letters with the Elephantine correspon-

---

32. See my *Composition of Narrative Books of the Old Testament* (London: T. & T. Clark, 2005) 52ff.

dence, there are not just time- and place-related differences that catch the eye. Even the form of the letter must raise doubts as to the genuineness of the correspondence. The letters in Ezra 5–6 and Ezra 4 conform with Hellenistic-Roman rather than Imperial Aramaic conventions.[33] Conspicuously, "official channels" were not used. The Elephantine correspondence is conducted within a broad diplomatic web but involves rather lower-level officials. In contrast, the letters in Ezra 5–6 are sent directly to the Persian king. One may argue that in the case of Elephantine it is the petitioners themselves who are writing the letters, while in Ezra 4–6 the writers are high-ranking Persian officials who take up a matter from a lower level of bureaucracy. But then it is all the more significant that the writers have not mastered chancellory style. Furthermore, based on the Passover Letter, one might expect a distinction to be made between the king's order and the details negotiated at the local level. This happens in Ezra 4:21–22 but not in 6:6ff.

Finally, the course of events acquires an entirely new dimension through the involvement of the prophets Haggai and Zechariah (Ezra 5:1–2; 6:14–15), who persuade Jeshua, his fellow priests, and Zerubbabel and his brothers to begin work on the temple. The writers of Ezra 5–6 did not take his information from historical sources but from the books of Haggai and Zechariah. They mention Jeshua/Joshua and Zerubbabel only in editorial additions; and even the appropriation of Zechariah as a prophet of the Second Temple is based on a secondary literary combination in both prophetic books.[34] The appearance of the prophets sheds new light on the diplomatic efforts and points to God as the actual architect of the entire string of events. The political intrigue described in the Elephantine Papyri and practiced in the Persian Empire is thus transported to a theological level. What is at stake is not the fulfillment of particular interests in the Achaemenid multiracial state but the relationship between the Jewish God and the foreign Persian king. This perspective can be noticed in the frame and the body of the narrative and even exercises an effect on the phrasing of the official letters.

Compared with the historical constellation in Jeb, as portrayed in the papyri, the biblical accounts of the reconstruction of the temple in Jerusalem paint an inconsistent picture. On the one hand, they suggest

---

33. See D. Schwiderski, *Handbuch des nordwestsemitischen Briefformulars: Ein Beitrag zur Echtheitsfrage der aramäischen Briefe des Esrabuchs* (BZAW 295; Berlin: de Gruyter, 2000) 343–80.

34. See my *Propheten Israels* (Beck'sche Reihe Wissen; Munich: Beck, 2003) 89–91.

a comparable situation and even include correspondence with Persian authorities. On the other, many of the details that are meant to give the correspondence an official flavor do not sit quite right. It seems reasonable to assume that this is a historical fiction in which the political and diplomatic practices of the Achaemenid Empire and of the later Hellenistic–Roman Period undergo a kind of literary transformation. This interpretation is backed up by the framing story, which shows the political-diplomatic event in a theological light. What is more, not all parts of the narrative come from the same mold; important features that add period flavor, especially in Ezra 1–4 (plus 6:16–18, 19–22), were appended at a later date.

Of course this does not mean that the entire event is made up. In view of the historical analogy in Jeb, one must assume that the temple in Jerusalem could only have been reconstructed after drawn-out negotiations with the various political authorities, ones in which the petitioners availed themselves of all the usual diplomatic instruments to obtain official approval from the responsible officials. But the way that they obtained approval is not necessarily identical with the story told in Ezra 1–6.

It is not easy to say what role Cyrus's decree played in all this because of the dearth of sources, but perhaps the Elephantine correspondence supplies a key. It is striking that the Aramaic version of the decree of Cyrus in Ezra 6:3–5—upon which the Hebrew version in Ezra 1 depends literarily—has survived under the heading of דכרונה, or 'memorandum'. This calls to mind the message from the governors of Judah and Samaria (Bagohi and Delaiah, son of Sanballat), which takes the form of such a memorandum (זכרן, A4.9). I would not rule out the possibility that Ezra 6 presents us with notes of authentic talks from the time of the temple construction, notes that include the information from the Persian authorities and perhaps also the order that King Darius I gave to Governor Tattenai (introduced so abruptly in Ezra 6:6–7).[35] We can no longer establish whether the decree was actually issued by Cyrus. If it is genuine, it included no consequences. However, it is also possible that, just as the heads of the Jewish colony of Elephantine mentioned Cambyses, the conqueror of Egypt,[36] Jewish negotiators

---

35. Compare Ezra 6:3 (שׂם טעם בית אלהא בירושלם ביתא יתבנא אתר די דבחין דבחין) with A4.7:25–26//4.8:24–25; 4.9:8–11; Ezra 6:7 (שׁבקי ל) with A4.7:23//4.8:22–23 (לא שבקן לן למבניה); concerning the expression "Keep away from there," see F. Rundgren, "Über einen juristischen Terminus bei Esr 6,6," *ZAW* 70 (1958) 209–15. The use of official terms, of course, is no proof of authenticity.

36. A4.7:13–14//4.8:12–13; 4.9:5.

celebrated Cyrus as the conqueror of Babylon and perhaps even circulated a rumor about an earlier building permit (recalling the Cyrus Cylinder[37]) in order to obtain the permission from Darius I. Even so, this must remain a matter of conjecture. What we can say is only that the information imparted in Ezra 6:3–7 is the source of the material woven into the construction account in Ezra 5–6 and the frame narrative in Ezra 1–4 (and 6:16–22), both of which were added at a later point in time. Thus the biblical sources (including the books of Haggai and Zechariah) contain little in the way of historically analyzable material.

The Religious-Political Argument

The diverse requests for permission to reconstruct the Jeb temple (A4.5 and 4.7//4.8; also 4.10) use two main arguments: an avowal of unconditional political loyalty to the central Persian powers and an allusion to the earlier conduct of the Persian kings and their officials.

Loyalty is sworn in two ways. First, the petitions make direct reference to the behavior of the Jewish garrison, which did not take part in the Egyptian revolts against Persian rule (A4.5:1).[38] Second, the activities of the Chnum priests and their aides in the Persian administration are linked to disloyal behavior and revolts against the central power. The petitioners accuse their opponents of bribery (A4.5:4; 4.8:5), thus presenting the deployment of troops (under the command of Vidranga and his son Nephaina in Syene) as an abuse of power vis-à-vis the military post loyal to the king. Vidranga's harsh punishment is an additional argument that lends this portrayal credence (A4.7:16–17// 4.8:15–16).

Different details are emphasized depending on the target audience. In the older petition, which is presumably intended for an official in Egypt (A4.5), discussion about the temple is preceded by an extensive description of the destruction of the garrison's infrastructure. It is no coincidence that the writers emphasize the damage done to the royal storehouse and the public well from which the garrison obtains its drinking water. The request for a police investigation underscores the event's relevance for the general public.

In contrast, the letter to Bagohi, the governor of Judah (A4.7//4.8), focuses on the destruction of the temple. The writers describe themselves

---

37. *TUAT* 1/4 (Gütersloh: Gütersloher, 1984) 407–10.

38. For the historical background, see H. Sternberg-el Hotabi, "Die persische Herrschaft in Ägypten," in *Religion und Religionskontakte im Zeitalter der Achämeniden* (ed. R. G. Kratz; Gütersloh: Gütersloher, 2002) 111–49, esp. 124–27.

as "servants" and "friends" of the governor, who is addressed as "our lord" just like the satrap of Egypt (A6.1:5) and the recipients of A4.5 and 4.10. The writers pull off the neat diplomatic trick of appealing to Bagohi as the responsible authority without placing him in the dangerous situation of having to overstep his authority vis-à-vis the governor and the responsible officials in Egypt.[39] To this end, they depict the event as a kind of coup d'état while assuring Bagohi that Arsames, the satrap of Egypt who was absent at the time, knew nothing of it. Furthermore, they do not criticize their "lord," who like the priests and members of nobility in Jerusalem apparently neglected to respond. Finally, they include the governor of Samaria, through his sons, in order to assuage any fears that Bagohi might have of becoming entangled in dangerous intrigue. What the petitioners want of Bagohi is not an official construction permit but a letter of recommendation that will help remove the existing obstacles in Egypt (לא שבקן לן למבניה, A4.7:23//4.8:22–23).

The second argument, the mention of the Persian kings' earlier behavior, is really a reinforcement of the first. It deals with the same loyalty issue around which the report of events and the previously unsuccessful diplomatic efforts have revolved. In a petition to Bagohi, the writers recall the conquest of Egypt by Cambyses. He supposedly came upon the Jewish temple that the "fathers" of the Jewish settlers had built under Egyptian rule and spared it the destruction otherwise wreaked on the temples of the Egyptian gods (A4.7:13–14//4.8:12–13). These historical reminiscences, focusing on a period 100 years earlier, are interesting not only for the information they provide on the founding of the Jewish temple of Elephantine (which they place in the 26th Dynasty, or seventh/sixth century B.C.E., in keeping with the archaeological evidence); they are also remarkable for their gross exaggeration of the destruction of Egyptian temples. They are based on a tradition of Egyptian opposition that generalized individual or specific measures against Egyptian temples in the initial phase of Persian rule and that eventually led to a distorted image of Cambyses in Greek sources.[40] This tradition was appropriated by the Jewish petition writers and used against the Egyptians in order to present the Jews in a better light to the Persians.[41] The risk of defaming the Persian policy was not all

---

39. See Kottsieper, "Religionspolitik," 161ff.

40. See G. Burkard, "Literarische Tradition und historische Realität: Die persische Eroberung Ägyptens am Beispiel Elephantine," *ZÄS* 121 (1994) 93–106; 122 (1995) 31–37.

41. The sources on the Persian conquest of Babylon offer a comparable story in this tradition. See my "From Nabonidus to Cyrus," in *Ideologies as Intercultural Phenomena* (ed.

that great due to the enmity between the loyal Jews and the rebellious Egyptians.

Finally, one must consider the religious dimension of the arguments in the petitions, which are derived from political interests. Even in the salutation, the petitioners commend Bagohi to the God of Heaven, who is to grant him the favor of the royal family and a long life (A4.7// 4.8:1–3). After the destruction of the temple, the inhabitants of the Jewish colony are aggrieved, and they appeal to God with prayers and fasting, which in the past led to the punishment of the conniving Vidranga (A4.7:15–17//4.8:13–16). And yet the fasting cannot end until the temple is rebuilt and the discontinued sacrifices are resumed on the altar of the god YHW (A4.7:19–21//4.8:18–21). The petitioners promise that offerings will be made in the governor's name in return to the diplomatic efforts requested of him (A4.7:25–27//4.8:24–26). His support of temple reconstruction, or so the argument goes, will be a great service that will ensure him a reward (צדקה) "before YHW, the God of Heaven, that is greater than the one bestowed on a person who makes burnt offerings and sacrifices worth 1,000 talents of silver." Thus even the religious practices serve to underscore the avowal of loyalty. No dispute arises over who is the true god or over the purity of worship. Here, as elsewhere, the Jews of Elephantine represent a non-biblical Jewry—an Israelite "heathendom."[42]

These arguments did not fail to achieve the desired effect on the governors of Judah and Samaria. The memorandum that records their answer and recommendations to Arsames (A4.9) uses the very same phrasing and arguments as the petition: the God of Heaven's "house of the altar" that the Jeb garrison constructed before Cambyses' conquests and that was destroyed by the criminal Vidranga in the 14th year of King Darius is to be rebuilt in the very same place where it previously stood, and sacrifices are to be made on the altar, as earlier.

As is well known, there is just one point on which the governors did not comply with the petitioners' wishes. They only allowed food and incense offerings, not the burnt offerings and sacrifices mentioned in the petition. The most-recent intact petition, the bribery letter from the leading men of Elephantine to their "lord" in Egypt (A4.10), shows that this was no coincidence: it expressly excludes the slaughter of

---

A. Panaino and G. Pettinato; Melammu Symposia 3; Milan: Università di Bologna and IsIAO, 2002) 143–56.

42. See E. A. Knauf, "Elephantine und das vor-biblische Judentum," in *Religion und Religionskontakte im Zeitalter der Achämeniden* (ed. R. G. Kratz; Gütersloh: Gütersloher Verlagshaus, 2002) 179–88.

sheep, cattle, and goat—that is, all blood sacrifices (see Lev 1:2). Scholars have discussed three possible reasons for this restriction:[43] (1) a veto by the priests in Jerusalem because of the dictate of cult centralization; (2) a wish to show consideration to the Chnum priests, who worshiped the ram god;[44] and (3) Persian abhorrence of blood sacrifices, which were tolerated only if they had been practiced earlier but were neither sanctioned nor permitted to be initiated. Regarding the veto, one may object that even the son of the governor of Samaria helped frame the resolution and that, while burnt offerings and sacrifices are excluded, none of the other offerings "to YHWH" (mentioned in Deuteronomy 12) are. Regarding showing consideration to ram worshipers, one may raise the objection that cattle and goats were excepted from the practices; and regarding the Persian abhorrence of blood sacrifices, that the sacrifices in question were practiced earlier. Furthermore, the petitioners of Elephantine write about these sacrifices without any self-consciousness in their letter to Bagohi, apparently assuming that the cult practice will continue. The matter remains puzzling.

The two main pillars of the argument in the Elephantine correspondence, the avowal of loyalty and the reference to early decisions of the Persian government, also play a central role in the account of the temple reconstruction in Jerusalem in Ezra 1–6.

In Ezra 4, the "adversaries of Judah and Benjamin" accuse the returnees from the Golah of disloyalty, which they back up with a reference to the revolts against foreign kings in the long history of the city of Jerusalem (4:13, 15–16; cf. vv. 19–20). The letter writers describe themselves as friends of the king, who "eat the salt of the palace" and wish to protect him from harm (4:14; cf. v. 22).

Even so, a search in Ezra 5–6 shows that in fact the "elders of the Jews" who built the temple are loyal servants of the state: they acted on a decree by King Cyrus (Ezra 1; 6:3–5), which is mentioned in a long excursus on the history of the city of Jerusalem (5:12–16) and which eventually secures the Jews the building permit and support of the building project by Darius (6:6ff.). Naturally, Darius benefits too. Here, it is the king himself who, in instructions to his officials, demands that sacrifices and prayers be made for the royal family and at the same time threatens to punish harshly all those who violate his decree and

---

43. See the discussion in Kottsieper, "Religionspolitik," 169–75.
44. See *LÄ*, 1.950–54. Exod 8:21–22 is occasionally referred to in connection with the Egyptian abhorrence of foreign sacrifices.

dare to lay hands on the house of God. The punishment will come not only from the king but from God himself, "who has caused his name to dwell there" (6:10–12; cf. v. 14).

This is all very similar to the Elephantine correspondence, and yet the argumentation in Ezra 4–6 does not correspond exactly to the historical analogy.[45] Apart from time- and place-related differences, which have no bearing on this study, it is particularly the historical survey in Ezra 5 (see vv. 12ff.) that strikes a discordant note. In contrast to the rather sporadic remembrance of the first conquest of Egypt by Cambyses, Ezra has a true historical-religious outline. It provides a succinct chronological view of the pre- and postexilic history of Judah, which, in line with the Cyrus prophecy of the Second Isaiah,[46] experiences a turning point in the first year of Cyrus in Babylon.

The historical outline is narrated for its own sake and not for tactical reasons. The remark in Ezra 5:16 that the temple has been under construction since Sheshbazzar laid the foundation in the first year of Cyrus is not made to demonstrate obedience to a royal order but primarily to show loyalty to God, whose name "dwells" in the temple. As in the historical outline, the loyalty question in Ezra 5–6 becomes a subject of theological reflection. This becomes evident in many other details of the account, particularly in the portrayal of King Darius, who makes the reconstruction of the temple a central concern, furnishes the temple with supplies (cf. Ezra 6:4), demands sacrifices and prayers to the God of Jerusalem, and places the temple under royal protection. The final phrasing in Ezra 6:14 concisely summarizes the theological agenda, placing the orders of the God of Israel and those of the Persian kings on the same level, alongside the prophecies of the prophets Haggai and Zechariah.

Chapters 1–4 in Ezra, which were added to the book at a later date, are written in the same spirit. They explain the background story implied by the remark in Ezra 5:16 (that the temple has been "under construction" since the first year of Cyrus) and ascribe the beginning of the construction to the Babylonian returnees. However, the correspondence in Ezra 4 has a slightly different, more political tone. Apparently this has to do with the subject matter. The reconstruction of the temple by the Jews returning from exile is interpreted here as evidence of the

---

45. See my *Translatio imperii: Untersuchungen zu den aramäischen Danielerzählungen und ihrem theologiegeschichtlichen Umfeld* (WMANT 63; Neukirchen-Vluyn: Neukirchener Verlag, 1991); also T. Willi, *Juda—Jehud—Israel* (FAT 12; Tübingen: Mohr-Siebeck, 1995).
46. See my *Kyros im Deuterojesaja-Buch* (FAT 1; Tübingen: Mohr-Siebeck, 1991).

reconstruction of the city and the city walls and consequently as a politically motivated revolt. However, this correspondence is a secondary interpolation. Modeled on Ezra 5–6 (5:17; 6:1–2), it triggers a search in the royal archives for documents on the city's history (Ezra 4:15, 19–20), which leads to opposite results. In terms of content and chronology, the account anticipates the book of Nehemiah. It is an open question whether the chronology of the correspondence, which extends to Artaxerxes (4:6–7; cf. 6:14), is an anticipation of the age of (Ezra and) Nehemiah or whether the chronology shifts the construction of the temple to the reign of Darius II, with which the reconstruction of the temple of Jeb coincides.

Let me summarize: the archaeological evidence justifies a comparison of the building projects in Jeb and Jerusalem. The Elephantine Papyri give insight into the historical, religious, and political background of such a construction project. The account in Ezra 1–6 must be seen as a theological reflection on and literary appropriation of actual conditions, a sculpting of these conditions into the historical fiction of biblical literature. It is only with great caution that one can tap this source for historical information on the reconstruction of the Temple in Jerusalem; and any information thus obtained must be checked against authentic material. On the other hand, the theological yield is all the greater. YHWH, the God of Israel, is not only the God of his people but of all people, even the foreign kings who rule on his behalf and for the benefit of his people.

Revisiting the Samarian Question
in the Persian Period

GARY N. KNOPPERS
The Pennsylvania State University

The history of the ancient Samaritans has occasionally provoked a keen interest on the part of modern biblical scholars. In the nineteenth and early twentieth centuries, the existence of a Samaritan community was considered to be a key issue for understanding the internal social and religious dynamics of Persian-Period Judah. Employing the writings of Chronicles, Ezra, and Nehemiah as windows into the world of the Second Commonwealth, scholars thought that late biblical authors were anxious to define their own practices and beliefs over against those of the Samaritans. In this common reconstruction, the highly charged relations between Jews and Samaritans dominated the intellectual and religious life of the people. Only such a partisan and acrimonious atmosphere, so it was thought, could explain the complaints about the "peoples of the land" and the interference of Sanballat as portrayed in Ezra–Nehemiah. Ideologically, the Samaritan became the other used to define the Judean self. Wellhausen (1885: 188) states that in the Chronicler's portrayal of the division following Solomon's death, the Chronicler demonstrates his belief that "Israel is the congregation of true worship . . . connected with the temple at Jerusalem, in which of course the Samaritans have no part." Similarly, in von Rad's view (1930: 31), Judah, together with Benjamin, constitute "the true Israel" over against their neighbors to the North.[1]

In an even stronger version of this view, some (e.g., Torrey 1909: 157–73, 188–217; 1954: xviii–xix; Galling 1954: 15; Plöger 1968: 37–38; Rowley 1955–56: 166–98; Mosis 1973: 169–71, 200–201) contended that the Chronicler was engaged in a strident polemic, depicting northern Israel

---

1. The views of Curtis and Madsen (1910: 10, 375–76), Noth (1943: 174–75), and Rudolph (1955: ix, 238) are also relevant. These scholars contend that the Chronicler wrote to delimit Judah from the Northern Kingdom of Israel and hence also Yehud from Samaria. Cf. Welten 1973: 127–29.

as a semiheathen, pagan, or abandoned people. In this view, the Chronicler's portrayal of the Northern Kingdom of Israel is a thinly disguised
attempt to address present problems by rewriting the past: "Behind the
mask of the ancient kingdom of Israel, he [the Chronicler] portrayed
the detested Samaritan community" (Pfeiffer 1948: 811). According to
de Wette (1806–7: 1.126–32), the Chronicler wrote to express his "Vor-
liebe für Juda und Haß gegen Israel." Bewer (1938: 294) wrote that in
the author's estimation, "The [Northern] Israelites were no better than
the heathen. Judah alone was God's people." Pfeiffer (1948: 811) claimed
that the Chronicler's portrayal of the Northern tribes is a guise for a diatribe against the Samaritans, whom the author regarded "ethnically as
alien rabble (Ezra 4:1–3, 7–11; 5:3, 6; 6:6) and religiously as semiheathen
(II [Chr] 13:4–12), Godforsaken (II [Chr] 25:7–10) mobs, over whom the
divine wrath rests because of their abominations (II [Chr] 28:9–15)."

The scholarship of the late twentieth century witnessed a strong reaction against this long-established anti-Samaritan line of interpretation. In the 1960s, Cross (1966: 201–11), Waltke (1965), and Purvis (1968;
1981) pointed out that the anti-Samaritan theory was predicated on the
erroneous assumption that the Samaritan Pentateuch was a relatively
early work. Coggins (1975: 8–100; 1989; 1991) demonstrated that the
view failed to distinguish a variety of voices and multiple stages in the
history of North–South relations. Grabbe (1998; 2000), Hjelm (2000:
273–85), Bedford (2001), Reinmuth (2002), and others have pointed to
the problematic and ideologically-driven nature of the sources for this
period. Scholars, such as Coggins, Crown, Dexinger, Kippenberg, and
Purvis insightfully questioned the theories dating back to Josephus
that a Samaritan schism occurred either early in the postexilic period or
in the aftermath of Alexander's conquest.[2] Scholars had been guilty of
retrojecting the disputes of much later times into the Neo-Babylonian
and Achaemenid eras.[3] Japhet (1968; 1983; 1989; 1993; 1996), William-

---

2. In spite of the rejection of older theories, there is no new consensus on when the
definitive break between Judaism and Samaritanism occurred or whether there ever was
such a "schism." Coggins (1975: 163–74) argues for a gradual separation between the two
communities, but no sudden break. In this context, the comments of Dexinger (1981) and
Hanhart (1982) are also relevant. Kippenberg situates the separation in the early second
century B.C.E. (1971: 60–93). Purvis (1981: 323–50) would date the definitive break a little
later, at the end of the second century B.C.E. But Crown (1991) does not see any clear evidence for a real break until the third or fourth centuries C.E. Helpful reviews of scholarship may be found in Pummer (1976) and Hjelm (2000: 13–75).

3. In Samaritan tradition, the schism is dated to the time of Eli, when Eli established
a rival sanctuary at Shiloh. See the convenient overviews of Pummer (1987: 2–3), Purvis
(1986: 81–98), Hjelm (2000: 76–103, 239–72).

son (1977a; 1982), and more recently Willi (1994; 1995) cast further doubt on the anti-Samaritanism hypothesis by carefully attending to a variety of literary issues. Successfully calling into question the widely-held assumption that the Chronicler wrote both Chronicles and Ezra–Nehemiah, Japhet and Williamson argued that the author of Chronicles was not anti-Samaritan in orientation.[4] Far from it, the Chronicler displays a very open and conciliatory attitude toward residents of the North, whom he unequivocally regards as Israelites. In the view of Williamson (1983; 1989), there is no clear evidence for tensions between Samarians and Jews until the mid- to late fifth century, when the reforms of Ezra and Nehemiah attempt to enforce a demarcation of the members of the Golah community from all others.

In this essay, I have no desire to return to the dominant critical theories of the nineteenth and early twentieth centuries. The work of contemporary scholars has provided a series of healthy correctives to the anachronistic, stereotyped, and reductive views of the past. Nevertheless, I want to argue that recent studies of the material remains from Samaria warrant revisiting Judean–Samarian relations during the Persian Period. The fact that earlier treatments of the issues were so one-sided should not lead us to neglect the issues themselves. The mistakes of the past impel us to gain a better understanding of early Samarian society—its culture, population, and religious practices. In this essay I want to concentrate on some archaeological, epigraphic, and historical matters. Pertinent discoveries warranting discussion include the existence of a significant Samarian population during the Achaemenid era, a time in which the community in Yehud was relatively small, and epigraphic remains indicate significant cultural overlap between the Samarian and Judean communities. At the end of the essay I will return to a few of the complex issues raised by the interpretation of Ezra–Nehemiah.

Samaria during the Late Assyrian, Neo-Babylonian, and Persian Periods

In dealing with the history of Samaria during the seventh through the fourth centuries B.C.E., one has to avoid projecting problems faced

---

4. Following this distinction, references in this essay to the Chronicler designate the author(s) of Chronicles. The work of Ezra–Nehemiah, which evinces variant ideological tendencies, was authored/edited at a different time by other members of the Jerusalem elite. In the editing of the initial chapters of Ezra (especially Ezra 1–3), an attempt has been made to draw the two works (Chronicles and Ezra–Nehemiah) together (Knoppers 2004a).

by Judah onto its neighbor to the North. The province of Samaria seems to have passed from the Neo-Assyrian and Neo-Babylonian Periods to the Persian Period without encountering any of the major destructions that its southern neighbor experienced. From an archaeological perspective, one finds in the territory of Samaria essentially one continuous period (Iron IIC or Iron III) from the late eighth century to the late fourth century.[5] The transitions from the Neo-Assyrian Period to the relatively brief Neo-Babylonian Period and then to the Achaemenid era are very gradual in the North. The decision to speak of a new Persian Period in Samaria, as opposed to an older Neo-Assyrian or Neo-Babylonian Period, is more of a historical judgment than one based on any sudden change in material culture.

The region of Samaria suffered a tremendous demographic decline in the latter part of the eighth century, when the Assyrian armies conquered what was left of the Northern Kingdom and deported a significant part of its population.[6] From this decline, some areas rebounded more quickly than others. The southern region seems to have taken the longest to recover. In the southern Samarian Hills, the Persian Period witnessed slightly less than half the number of sites (90) of the relatively prosperous Iron II period (190; Finkelstein 1993a; 1993b: 1313–14; Finkelstein, Lederman, and Bunimovitz 1997).[7] Most sites in the Achaemenid era were also smaller than their Iron II counterparts. According to Finkelstein, Ledermann, and Bunimovitz, a major recovery in southern Samaria only occurs in the Hellenistic era.[8]

Of the various geographic zones within Samaria, the northern and the western parts seem to have rebounded the most quickly from the

---

5. On the demographics of the Iron II period in Samaria, see Zertal 2001. I am following Zertal's distinction between an Iron II period and an Iron III period (late eighth century B.C.E. onward). Note also the argument of Barkay (1993), for whom the Iron IIC culture in Judah (or Iron III) extends to the late sixth century (530–520 B.C.E.). Barkay sees the late sixth century as the end of "Israelite" material culture, because only at this time does one see the emergence of some features of Achaemenid material culture. Barkay points to the survival of Iron Age culture in the Transjordan, the coastal strip, the northern regions, and the Negev.

6. But hardly the entire people (Knoppers 2004c).

7. I hesitate to attribute this decline to the effects of the destructions of both the Israelite and the Judahite Kingdoms (so Finkelstein), because the latter should not have directly affected this area. If there was a continuing decrease in population in the seventh and sixth centuries, it may have been due to shifts in population within Samaria (toward the west and the north) and economic factors. A distinction between Iron II and III is not observed in the study of Finkelstein. Cf. Zertal 2003: 400–401.

8. O. Lipschits thinks, however, that a recovery began in the seventh century and continued through the fourth century (private communication).

devastations caused by the Assyrian campaigns (Zertal 1990; 1999). The Achaemenid Period witnesses an unprecedented number of sites in the northern region, suggesting that this was a time of considerable demographic expansion. The settlement was particularly heavy in the Dothan Valley and in the areas surrounding the city of Samaria. The Persian Period represents the time in which the hills of Manasseh are the most densely populated (247 sites) of all periods, more than the Iron II period (238 sites) and the Hellenistic Period (140 sites), and considerably more than the Iron III period (95 sites; Zertal 1993). It may be, as Zertal (1988) suggests, that this region was aided by its geography. In northern Samaria numerous springs can be found from north of Jenin to the foot of Mt. Gerizim in the south. Arable soil and broad interior valleys set the Mt. Manasseh region apart from the more rugged hill country to the south.

The recovery may have also been aided by Assyrian investments, an increase in trade, and the absence of major political upheavals. Most sites in northern Samaria show a continuity from the Iron III period (late eighth century) into the Persian Period. Faust (2003a) points to a large number of farmsteads, as well as some hamlets and villages that have been excavated in the Samarian hill country. Almost all of these Iron Age rural sites exhibit continuity into the Persian Period. The internal security and longevity of peace afforded by the Achaemenid era may have contributed to the greater utilization of available land (Zertal 1990: 13). In any event, a decline does not set in until the Hellenistic era. Settlement was roughly cut in half during in the Hellenistic Period, probably as a consequence of the revolt in 332 B.C.E. against the legions of Alexander the Great (Zertal 1997).

The western area of Samaria was intensively settled during the Achaemenid era (Dar 1986; 1993; Applebaum 1986). Already during the latter part of the Iron Age, there was a significant increase of settlements and farmhouses in this territory. In the Persian Period one finds evidence of a dense complex of settlements, although most are small and rarely exceed 2.5 hectares in area (Dar 1992; 1993: 1314–16).[9] Aiding growth during this era was the development of a system of major and minor roads. By means of this network, each village and town was

---

9. One caveat should be offered in this context. Most of the Iron Age rural sites (small farms) that Faust has excavated in the Samarian foothills, that is, the western slopes of Samaria (above the alluvial valley), did not continue to exist during the Persian Period. The date of their destruction/abandonment seems to be earlier than in Judah (Faust personal communication).

connected to near and distant neighbors (Dorsey 1991: 163–80; Dar 1993: 1316).

If recent studies have added much to our knowledge of demographic changes in the various regions of Samaria, much is still unknown about the city of Samaria during the Persian Period. In Samaria, unlike in Jerusalem, one finds a fundamental continuity of settlement from the beginning of the Iron III period to the Achaemenid era. Some of the walls at the site continue in use for a long period of time and the city survives until the end of the Persian Period (Crowfoot 1942: 3–20; 1957a: 1–8; Kenyon 1942: 91–120). According to archaeological surveys, the areas around the town of Samaria were thickly settled during the Achaemenid era. To be sure, much of the material evidence from the city itself stems from the Iron Age and the Hellenistic Period. There are few building remains dating to the Neo-Babylonian and Persian Periods (Stratum VIII). Small finds from this era include Persian-Period pottery (Kenyon 1957: 98), a clay cup that the excavator deemed to be a direct Achaemenid import (Crowfoot 1957b: 216), several fragmentary ostraca in palaeo-Hebrew script (Birnbaum 1957: 11–25), several Aramaic ostraca,[10] a large amount of Attic ware (Crowfoot 1957b: 213–16), a number of local coins, three Sidonian coins from the reign of Straton I (ca. 370–358 B.C.E.; Kirkman 1957: 43–70), a late Achaemenid coin that may stem from the reign of Darius III (Stern 2001: 425–26), and bronze parts of a throne probably belonging to one of Samaria's governors (Tadmor 1988).

Three major factors are at work limiting our knowledge of the city in this period: the shortcomings of older excavations and archaeological methods, the severity of the destruction wrought by the forces of Alexander the Great in the latter part of the fourth century (Josephus, *Ant.* 11.302, 331; Curtius Rufus 4.8, 9–11) and the extensive rebuilding that went on during the Hellenistic era.[11] Further reconstruction occurred during Herodian and Roman times. Estimates of the city's stature during the Achaemenid age are therefore inevitably speculative, being based on the city's size during the Iron III and Hellenistic Periods, existing material remains from the Persian Period, epigraphic finds, and the large cluster of towns and villages surrounding the site during the Persian Period. Over half of the Persian Period-sites that

---

10. But the ostraca are unstratified (Birnbaum 1957: 25–33). Birnbaum dates them to the fourth century B.C.E.

11. The devastation may have been coupled with the displacement of the native Samarians by the Macedonians, resulting in a massive transformation of the city (Stern 2001: 424–27).

have been found in the region of Samaria have been found within a 10-km radius of the capital (Zertal 1990: 14). This evidence would suggest that the city of Samaria prospered and grew during much of the Persian era. Employing the central place theory, Stern (2001: 424) thinks, in fact, that Samaria was one of the most important urban areas in all of Palestine during the Achaemenid era. Zertal (2003: 380) goes a step further in claiming that Samaria became the largest and most important city of Palestine.

Summary

There is still much that is unknown about the history of Samaria from the fifth through the fourth centuries, but archaeological studies suggest that the transition to the Persian Period was not nearly as traumatic for the region of Samaria as it was for certain cities along the Mediterranean coast and for parts of Judah. After suffering a tremendous demographic decline at the beginning of the Iron III period, most of the region recovered and grew. In this context, some contrasts may be drawn between Samaria and postmonarchic Judah. Within the past few generations, population estimates for Yehud in the early Persian Period have varied wildly. Albright (1963: 87) surmised that the population of early postexilic Judah was scarcely more than 20,000 people, but others such as Kreissig (1973: 38) thought that the true number was five times that, around 100,000.[12] Weinberg (1996: 37–38) thought that this figure was still too small and put the tally much higher, at well over 200,000 people.

The work of recent archaeologists has cast serious doubt on the high figures presented by Kreissig and Weinberg. Studies of the material remains have indicated that the Babylonian campaigns caused substantial destruction and depopulation in certain areas of the southern Levant. Some sites along the coast, such as Ashqelon, and sites inland, such as Jerusalem, Lachish, Tell Beit Mirsim, and Tel Batash, suffered major damage during the Neo-Babylonian era with fateful consequences for their regional economies (Miller and Hayes 1986: 377–436; Finkelstein 1993a; Ahlström 1993: 733–803).[13] The destruction affected not only urban areas but also rural areas (Faust 2003b). To be sure, there is also evidence for continuity of occupation at some sites such as Gibeon,

---

12. Note also the comments of Janssen 1956: 39–54.

13. Although Jerusalem suffered tremendous damage, the destruction was not total. Barkay's excavations (1986) in the Hinnom Valley have yielded some burial artifacts from the sixth century, perhaps as late as 500 B.C.E.

Mizpah, and Bethel (Lipschits 1998; 2001; Blenkinsopp 2002). Areas north of Jerusalem in Benjamin were largely spared destruction (Mazar 1990: 548–49; Lipschits 1999; Carter 2003). In any event, the most recent population estimates for early Achaemenid Judah have hovered far closer to the original estimate of Albright than they have to the much higher estimates of Kreissig and Weinberg. The estimate given by Carter (1999: 201) to his Persian I Period (538–450 B.C.E.)—13,350—is, in fact, about one-third smaller than that of Albright.[14] The appraisal of Lipschits (2003; 2005) is more generous, about 30,000 in the Achaemenid era.[15] Whatever the case, scholars are confronted with modest demographic assessments of the postmonarchic period in Judah.

By comparison, the region of Samaria seems to have escaped any large-scale damage from the Babylonian campaigns. Because the residents of Samaria evidently did not participate in the rebellions against the Babylonians, they did not suffer any major deportations.[16] There are gradual changes in the material record from the late eighth century to the late fourth century, but no sudden breaks or sharp deviations. Site surveys indicate that the populations of northern and western Samaria actually grew substantially during the Persian Period. The Achaemenid era witnesses a larger number of inhabited sites in northern Samaria than at any time during the Iron Age. Very few population estimates have been offered for Samaria during this time. In one of his early studies, Zertal (1990: 11–12) put the number of residents on Persian-Period Mt. Manasseh at about 42,000. Based both on Zertal's more recent archaeological work, in which new sites have been found, and the fact that his estimate only addressed one section, albeit the most populous section, of Samaria, we would have to estimate the figure for the province as a whole higher than this partial figure.

The Jerusalem of the Achaemenid era has been described as a village with an administrative center.[17] In contrast, the Samaria of the

---

14. The number goes up to 20,650 in his Persian II Period (450–332 B.C.E.).

15. Lipschits's estimate (2003) deals with the Persian Period as a whole. He does not think that it is possible to distinguish between Persian I and Persian II sub-periods on the basis of the material remains.

16. The point may be implicitly conceded by Nehemiah in his imprecations against Sanballat and his allies, "Hear our God, for we have become (the subject of) contempt. Return their taunts upon their heads! Deliver them up as plunder in a land of captivity!" (Neh 3:36).

17. King and Stager (2001: 389) conclude that "postexilic Jerusalem was limited to the confines of the City of David (4.4 hectares excluding the Temple Mount) and was probably only half that size, with a few hundred inhabitants." See further de Groot 2001: 77–81; Faust 2001, 2003b; Kloner 2001: 91–95; Eshel 2001. For a somewhat higher estimation

Achaemenid era has been described as one of ancient Palestine's larger urban areas. If so, we are dealing not with a situation of comparability but with a situation of disparity. One regional center was substantially larger and wealthier than the other. The difference between the two provinces and their two capitals cannot but have affected the intelligentsia of Jerusalem. During the Achaemenid era, members of the Judean elite were not dealing with a depopulated outback to the north. Quite the contrary, they were dealing with a province that was larger, better-established, and considerably more populous than was Yehud.

Cultural Continuities

Recognition of Samaria's important status vis-à-vis Yehud compels us to inquire further into the character of its culture(s) during the Persian Period. Up to a few decades ago, this subject was completely foreboding due to the paucity of evidence. Recent discoveries have begun to change this picture. The topic may be approached by several different angles. It may be useful to begin by briefly discussing language and scripts.[18] The long-awaited publication of the fourth-century Samaria papyri is helpful, in this respect. Also helpful is the discovery over the past few decades of hundreds of Samarian coins and inscriptions dating to the late Persian and Hellenistic ages. Some of these inscriptions and coins, especially those dating to the Persian Period from Mt. Gerizim, have yet to be formally published.[19] But those that have been published provide important clues about linguistic usage and the employment of scripts in different historical contexts.

In his study of the language of the Samaria papyri, Gropp (1990: 170) shows that the language of the papyri is a conservative version of Official Aramaic. The language used is virtually identical to the language employed in the fifth-century Elephantine papyri and the Arsames correspondence. There is, in fact, little typological development from the

---

of the town's size (but not necessarily population) during the Achaemenid era, see Ussishkin, in this volume, pp. 147–166.

18. The following treatment is necessarily selective. One could add other criteria. One such prominent standard appearing in some previous discussions is the relative absence of so-called pagan cults and cultic figurines during the Second Commonwealth. In Stern's view (1989; 2001: 479, 488), there is a complete absence of such artifacts both in the material remains relating to Persian-Period Judah and in the material remains relating to Persian-Period Samaria. This is a very important issue, but note the reservations raised by Schmitt (2003) in his recent treatment of the archaeological evidence stemming from a variety of sites.

19. A sample may be found in Magen, Tsfania, and Misgav 2000.

fifth-century Elephantine texts to the fourth-century Samaria papyri. Despite their late provenience, the Samaria papyri show little or no Persian influence in either vocabulary or syntax (Gropp 1990: 170–71; 1997). The fifth-century Elephantine papyri and the Arsames correspondence exhibit more-extensive Achaemenid influence than the Samaria papyri do. Comparative study demonstrates, however, many differences in the composition of legal formulas, suggesting important divergences in legal traditions between the Samaria papyri and the Elephantine papyri (Gropp 1986: 130–39; 1990: 186–87; 1993; 1997). The Samaria papyri show a greater proportion of specifically late Neo-Babylonian loans than do the Elephantine papyri. Gropp (2001: 32) thinks that the former may have been affected by a Babylonian-Aramean symbiosis, whereas the latter may have been affected by an Assyro-Aramean symbiosis. It is surely interesting, in the context of this discussion, that the Samaria papyri share a large number of isoglosses with the later Murabbaʿat and Naḥal Ḥever deeds (Gropp 2001: 5). Given the shared scribal conventions, these documents evidently belong to the same legal tradition. The fragmentary Samaria papyri thus provide useful evidence for reconstructing the history of early Jewish law.

The information gleaned from the Samaria papyri may be supplemented by other types of epigraphic evidence, as well as by numismatics. The hundreds of short inscriptions found in Samaria dating to the late Persian and Hellenistic Periods suggest that the Samarians wrote and spoke the same language as the Judeans did during this time. Aramaic evidently was employed, as it was in other provinces in western Asia, as the language of governance and international diplomacy. Hebrew was employed, but not restricted to, certain official or sacred purposes.[20] The scribes of both communities employed a similar system of scripts, an Aramaic script for diplomatic and commercial activities and a Hebrew script (the so-called palaeo-Hebrew) for certain religious purposes (Ephʿal 1998; cf. Lipiński 1990). Both the Judeans and the Samarians used the two scripts as late as the Hellenistic era. Naveh (1998: 91) has gone so far as to declare: "No differentiation whatsoever is discernible in the scripts used in Judah and Samaria in the Persian Period." One caveat should be offered, however, in this context. From the fifth through the third centuries, the Hebrew script was used on both official seals and on coins in Yehud. Only a few coins

---

20. Lemaire (1995) discusses the complications in distinguishing between spoken Hebrew and written Hebrew in Yehud and in pinpointing the features of regional dialects during this time.

with Aramaic legends are known from Yehud so far (Machinist 1994; Mildenberg 1996; Naveh 1998: 91–93). In the third century and on-ward, the so-called early Jewish script developed in Yehud.[21] But in Persian-Period Samaria, many coins were issued with Aramaic leg-ends (e.g., Jeroboam, Ḥananiah, Abdiel, Yeho'anah). Coin legends with a Hebrew script, comparable to the Yehud types, are rare if not un-attested. There are, however, Persian-Period seals from Samaria en-graved in a Hebrew script. For example, the seal of one of Sanballat's sons discovered among the Samaria papyri reads, "[Belonging to Ye-sha]yahû son of Sanballat, governor of Samaria" (Avigad and Sass 1997: 176 [#419]).[22] This Hebrew inscription was impressed upon a bulla sealing an Aramaic legal document written in an Aramaic script. Hence, the more general point about the use of Aramaic and Hebrew scripts stands.

We have been discussing questions of language and script in the an-cient province of Samaria with special reference to possible contempo-rary Judean practices. One type of comparison that is useful in this context is the composition of proper names. The linguistic and reli-gious features of onomastica can be used to provide some indication of their bearers' religious identities. One may begin by observing the large number of proper names shared with Judah. It is also relevant to point out that of the many personal names found within the fourth-century Samaria papyri, the vast majority are Yahwistic (Zsengeller 1996; Eshel 1997; Eph'al 1998: 110–11). It has sometimes been claimed that the Yahwistic theophorics found within these documents are largely restricted to the names of the sellers and buyers, but Gropp's recent study (2001: 6–7) indicates that most of the personal names of the slaves mentioned in these documents are also Yahwistic in charac-ter. In sum, proper names also attested in Judean literature predomi-nate in the Samaria papyri, and most of these apellatives—whether they be of owners, buyers, or slaves—are Yahwistic in character.

It has been suggested that the papyri indicate some diversity in the ethnic composition of Samaria in the fourth century (e.g., Cross 1974: 20–22). This may be true, as there is an instance of a proper name with

---

21. Referring to the archaic or proto-Jewish script that appears in 250–150 B.C.E. (Cross 1961: 136–53; Naveh 1971). Given recent epigraphic discoveries in Samaria, it may be debated whether "Jewish script" is the best nomenclature for what was previously thought to be simply one local development from the standard Aramaic cursive of the late Persian Empire.

22. The Sanballaṭ referred to is probably Sanballaṭ II, the grandson of Sanballaṭ I, the contemporary of Nehemiah.

the theophoric 'Qaws' (*qwsnhr*; Lemaire 2001: 105). There are also a few instances of Babylonian and Persian names. Yet, one hesitates to read too much into the appearance of an Akkadian name such as *Sin-ʾuballaṭ* ('Sanballat').[23] To begin with, the names attested for Sanballat's sons—"Delaiah," "Shemaiah," and "[Yeshaʿ]yahu" (or "[Yadaʿ]yahu") —are all Yahwistic in nature. Second, there are also a variety of Akkadian names attested in the literature from Yehud, such as 'Shenazzar' (*šenʾaṣṣar*), 'Sheshbazzar' (*šēšbaṣṣar*), and 'Zerubbabel' (*zĕrubbābel*). But rarely, if ever, is the argument made that these names show that Shenazzar, Sheshbazzar, and Zerubbabel adhered to Babylonian cultic practices. It is usually assumed that these individuals were Judeans who had Akkadian names. Similarly, in the very few instances of Persian names found among the Samaria papyri, the evidence does not necessarily point to some sort of Persian religious identity. One of the two Persian names attested, *yhwbgh*, features the Yahwistic name element with the Persian element *baga* 'god', hence 'Yahu is god'. The other Persian personal name is more ambiguous, *bgbrt* 'by god lifted up, esteemed'.

In addition to the Yahwistic nomenclature found within the Samaria papyri, Yahwistic names have also been found on the legends of fourth-century Samarian coins (Meshorer and Qedar 1999: 20–28). These include 'Hananyah' (*ḥnnyh*),[24] 'Jehoʿanah' (*yhwʿnh*), 'Bodyah' (*bdyh*), a name appearing on four different coin types (cf. Ezra 10:35 *bēdyāh*), *dl* probably short for *dlyh* 'Delaiah', *šl*, probably short for *šlmyh* 'Shelemiah' (*šlmyh*), and *wny*, perhaps short for *wnyh*.[25] In dealing with the numismatic evidence, one would be remiss if one did not mention those coins with the legend *yrbʿm* 'Jeroboam'. Obviously, this appellative is not specifically Yahwistic, but it possibly does bear larger national connotations. Five different fourth-century coin types are attested with the name of this Samarian governor (or governors), the most for any personal name (Meshorer and Qedar 1999: 24–25). The

---

23. Extrabiblical references to Sanballat(s) may be found in TAD 1 A4.7:29 (cf. TAD 1 A4.8:28); WDSP 11 recto 13; WD 22 attached to WDSP 16; Josephus, *Ant.* 11.302–3, 310–11, 315, 321–24, 342; Gropp 2000.

24. Probably the same Hananiah who evidently appears as a governor in the Samaria papyri—Ḥ[*nnyh*] (WDSP 7.17); [Ḥ]*nnyh pḥt šmryn* (WDSP 9.14; Gropp 2001: 80–85, 93–96).

25. See MT Ezra 10:36: וַנְיָה (Vulg. *Vania*); cf. a few Heb. MSS זניה; LXX *Ouiechōa*; LXX α *kai Anōs*. Among the Elephantine papyri, one finds ונו 'Vanah' (AP 22.40). But the evidence is inconclusive. See, for example, the inscription engraved in the Jewish script of the Herodian era, found at ʿIllar, which reads דמנשה בן ונו '(The tomb) belonging to Manasseh son of Wannay' (cited in Naveh 1998: 94).

reuse of the name of two of the most prominent kings in (Northern) Israelite history suggests that at least some residents of Samaria felt an attachment to the traditions of the former Northern Kingdom.[26]

In contrast with the Samarian coins bearing Yahwistic appellatives, there are a few Samarian coins featuring non-Yahwistic theophorics.[27] One Samarian coin type with the divine name 'Zeus' (IEYΣ) is attested, along with an image of this deity (Meshorer and Qedar 1999: 29, 90–91). On the reverse of this coin is the name 'Jehoʿanah' (*yhwʿnh*). On yet another coin one finds the face and short form of the name of the god '[Hera]cles' (KΛEYΣ; Meshorer and Qedar 1999: 29, 104). The appearance of these Greek deities may indicate a stronger western cultural influence in Samaria than in contemporary Yehud (Lemaire 2001: 107–9). The date of these coins is, however, disputed. The decision by Meshorer and Qedar to situate these coins in the fourth century is predicated on the assumption that Samarian coinage ended with the Macedonian conquest. But as Oren Tal points out (personal communication), the presence of Greek letters formulating the names of Greek deities would be highly unusual in a Persian-Period context. Hence, the coins may date to the early Hellenistic era. In any case, it must be acknowledged that Yehud was not immune to external influences either. During the Persian Period, imports from the west (and local imitations thereof) increased and spread inland in both Samaria and Yehud. The fifth and fourth centuries were a time of rapid Hellenization in the Levant (Elayi 1987; 1988; 1994; Stern 2001: 217–27, 518–34, 552–54, 558–59; Knoppers 2003). Such western influences are evident by developments in pottery, numismatics, weights, weaponry, fortifications, and glyptic art (Stern 1995: 432–35; Leith 1997).

If proper names found on bullas, coins, and papyri are any reliable indication of religious affiliation, the extant evidence from Samaria suggests that the majority of people in this province in the fourth century, or at least the majority of the elite, were Yahwistic.[28] The question arises how best to explain the strong cultural overlap between Samaria and Yehud. It does not seem possible to explain the lines of continuity between the two administrative units simply by recourse to historical explanations focusing on the common roots of these two communities.

---

26. But not necessarily to the Former Prophets or to many of the books that were to constitute the Writings (Ben Zvi 1995: 143).

27. There is also a coin type with a personal name with the divine element El, 'Abdiel' (*ʿbdʾl*).

28. Legitimate questions may be raised about how representative some of the merchants' names may have been of the populace as a whole (Eshel 1997).

The projected time of origins would be far too distant in the past (the tenth century and before) to account for the cultural parallels in the Achaemenid and Hellenistic eras. Rather, one must assume contacts between these two neighboring areas during the Achaemenid and Hellenistic Periods, if not before. Moreover, the links must have been substantial and persistent, rather than superficial and sporadic. These associations undoubtedly took different forms: trade, travel, migrations, including migrations in time of war, and scribal communications.

Some tantalizing pieces of evidence pertaining to the character of Samaria's relations to Yehud are found among the Elephantine papyri. When the Jews at Elephantine wished to rebuild their temple in the late fifth century, they appealed to the authorities in both Jerusalem and Samaria for assistance (TAD 4.5–4.10; Vincent 1937: 253–55; Porten 1968: 278–98). Certainly, the colonists at Elephantine must have felt some affinity with the community of Samaria, or they would not have written them to ask for their help. Moreover, the fact that Jedaniah and his priestly colleagues saw fit to mention their appeal to the Samaria authorities—Delaiah and Shelemiah, the sons of Sanballat, the governor of Samaria—in their correspondence with Bagavahya (Bagohi), the governor of Judah, suggests ongoing ties between the leaders of Yehud and Samaria (TAD 4.7:29; 4.8:28).

That the Jerusalem leadership shared normal diplomatic relations with the Samarian leadership is evidently confirmed by the joint communiqué written by Bagavahya, the governor of Judah, and Delaiah the son of Sanballat, the governor of Samaria, supporting the Elephantine community's bid to gain permission from Arsames, the satrap of Egypt, to rebuild the Elephantine Temple (literally, 'the altar house' בית מדבחא; TAD 4.9:3).[29] One could argue the contrary point and maintain that this joint communiqué represented a unique or highly unusual instance of cooperation between the Jerusalem and Samaria authorities. But there is no hint of this within the draft of the missive itself. All the indications from the letters point to regular relations between the leadership in Jerusalem and Samaria. Indeed, even the authors of Ezra–Nehemiah concede some close relations between the elites of Jerusalem and Samaria (e.g., Neh 6:10–14; 13:28; cf. Josephus, Ant. 11.306–12). The same writers acknowledge intermarriage between

---

29. With the proviso that it only present cereal offerings (מנחה), drink offerings (נסך), and incense (לבונה; TAD 4.9:9; 4.10:11; Grelot 1972: 417–19). Sheep, oxen, and goats were not to be offered there as burnt sacrifice (מקלו; TAD 4.10:11).

members of the leading families of Jerusalem and Samaria during the latter part of the fifth century B.C.E. (Neh 13:28).[30]

Conclusion

At the end of this essay, I wish to return to the issues of self-definition and opposition raised at the beginning of this work. Two points are relevant. On the one hand, the available material evidence grants some credence to the claims made in Ezra–Nehemiah that Samaria and its leadership were a force to be reckoned with. Because of Samaria's size, status, and population, it may have posed special challenges for certain members of the elite in Jerusalem. In the Persian Period, as we have seen, the leaders of Yehud were faced with a bigger, more well-to-do, and more populous neighbor to the north.

On the other hand, the material evidence for cultural continuity between the two regions contrasts with the tensions and opposition found in Ezra–Nehemiah. Culturally speaking, Samaria and Yehud shared much in common. Indeed, in speaking of two separate provinces of Samaria and Yehud, one has to recognize that such a distinction is inherently an administrative and political one and not so much a cultural one. Attempts at self-definition may have been necessary for some of the elite in Jerusalem precisely because of the similarities between the Yahwists living in the two territories. If, as recent excavations suggest, some sort of sanctuary or temple existed on Mt. Gerizim already during the Persian Period, this would only have added further impetus for Jerusalem Temple scribes to authenticate the distinctive positions of their city and shrine (Magen 1993: 104–8; 2000; Stern and Magen 2000; 2002).[31]

As the ideological differences among Zechariah, Chronicles, and Ezra–Nehemiah attest, there was no unanimity among writers in Yehud about how to define Israelite identity, the community's institutions, and the people's relations to their neighbors (Japhet 1983; 1996; Williamson 1977a; 1987; Meyers and Meyers 1988; Albertz 1994; Willi 1995; Knoppers 2000; 2001; 2004b). One of the major mistakes made by major nineteenth- and early-twentieth-century interpreters was to take the negative and defensive sentiments expressed toward Sanballat

---

30. If the reconstruction of Cross is well founded, this pattern of intermarriage continued well into the fourth century (1974: 20–22; 1998: 173–202). For cautions about the confused state of the testimony provided by Josephus (*Ant.* 11.297–312, 321–25), see Williamson 1977b: 49–66 and Grabbe 1987: 231–46; 1992: 1.112–14.

31. This is a subject in itself. I plan to devote a future study to this topic.

by Nehemiah as representative of North–South relations during the entire Achaemenid era. Historically speaking, it might be better to view Nehemiah's measures as rear-guard actions against what he deemed to be improper Samarian interference in the internal affairs of his province. But such actions, undertaken in the tenure of one particular governor, cannot be allowed to obfuscate the common traits shared by the Yahwistic residents residing in the two regions. Even the authors of Ezra–Nehemiah acknowledge that Nehemiah's position was not recognized by many leadership elements within Jerusalem. One of the advantages to the study of the material evidence is to provide a much-needed corrective to the literary evidence or, at least, to place the literary remains in a better perspective. The archaeological and epigraphic remains suggest that major contacts between Yehud and Samaria preceded the time of Nehemiah and continued after his term(s) of office ended. The Persian Period was an era of cultures in contact. For many residents of Yehud and Samaria, close relations between their two communities were a fact, not an issue.

Bibliography

Ahlström, G. W.
1993   *The History of Ancient Palestine from the Palaeolithic Period to Alexander's Conquest.* JSOTSup 146. Sheffield: JSOT Press.

Albertz, Rainer
1994   *From the Exile to the Maccabees.* Vol. 2 of *A History of Religion in the Old Testament Period.* OTL. Louisville: Westminster John Knox.

Albright, W. F.
1963   *The Biblical Period from Abraham to Ezra.* New York: Harper.

Applebaum, A.
1986   Historical Commentary. Pp. 257–70 in *Landscape and Pattern: An Archaeological Survey of Samaria 800 B.C.E.–636 C.E.* BAR International Series 308/1. Oxford: BAR.

Avigad, N., and Sass, B.
1997   *Corpus of West Semitic Stamp Seals.* Jerusalem: Israel Academy of Sciences and Humanities.

Barkay, G.
1986   Ketef Hinnom: A Treasure Facing Jerusalem's Walls. Jerusalem: The Israel Museum.
1993   The Redefining of Archaeological Periods: Does the Date 588/586 B.C.E. Indeed Mark the End of Iron Age Culture? Pp. 106–12 in *Biblical Archaeology Today, 1990: Proceedings of the Second International Congress on Biblical Archaeology,* ed. A. Biran and J. Aviram. Jerusalem: Israel Exploration Society.

Bedford, P. R.
2001   *Temple Restoration in Early Achaemenid Judah.* JSJSup 65. Leiden: Brill.
Ben Zvi, E.
1995   Inclusion and Exclusion from Israel as Conveyed by the Use of the Term *Israel* in Post-monarchic Biblical Texts. Pp. 95–149 in *The Pitcher Is Broken: Memorial Essays for Gösta W. Ahlström*, ed. S. W. Holloway and L. K. Handy. JSOTSup 190. Sheffield: Sheffield Academic Press.
Bewer, J. A.
1938   *The Literature of the Old Testament.* Rev. ed. Records of Civilization: Sources and Studies 5. New York: Columbia University Press.
Birnbaum, S. A.
1957   Inscriptions: Ostraca. Pp. 9–32 in *The Objects from Samaria*, ed. J. W. Crowfoot, G. M. Crowfoot, and K. M. Kenyon. Samaria–Sebaste: Reports of the Work of the Joint Expedition in 1931–1933 and of the British Expedition in 1935, no. 3. London: Palestine Exploration Fund.
Blenkinsopp, J.
2002   The Bible, Archaeology and Politics or The Empty Land Revisited. *JSOT* 27: 169–87.
Carter, C. E.
1999   *The Emergence of Yehud in the Persian Period.* JSOTSup 294. Sheffield: Sheffield Academic Press.
2003   Ideology and Archaeology in the Neo-Babylonian Period: Excavating Text and Tell. Pp. 301–22 in *Judah and the Judeans in the Neo-Babylonian Period*, ed. O. Lipschits and J. Blenkinsopp. Winona Lake, Indiana: Eisenbrauns.
Coggins, R. J.
1975   *Samaritans and Jews: The Origins of Samaritanism Reconsidered.* Atlanta: John Knox.
1989   After the Exile. Pp. 229–49 in *Creating the Old Testament: The Emergence of the Hebrew Bible*, ed. S. Bigger. Oxford: Blackwell.
1991   The Samaritans and Northern Israelite Tradition. Pp. 99–108 in *Proceedings of the First International Congress of the Société d'études samaritaines.* Tel Aviv: Chaim Rosenberg School for Jewish Studies.
Cross, F. M.
1961   The Development of the Jewish Scripts. Pp. 133–202 in *The Bible and the Ancient Near East: Essays in Honor of William Foxwell Albright*, ed. G. E. Wright. Garden City, New York: Doubleday.
1966   Aspects of Samaritan and Jewish History in Late Persian and Hellenistic Times. *HTR* 59: 201–11.
1974   The Papyri and Their Historical Implications. Pp. 17–29 in *Discoveries in the Wâdī ed-Dâliyeh*, ed. Paul W. Lapp and Nancy L. Lapp. AASOR 41. Cambridge, Massachusetts: ASOR.
1998   *From Epic to Canon: History and Literature in Ancient Israel.* Baltimore: The Johns Hopkins University Press.

Crowfoot, J. W.
  1942   Buildings round and below the Summit. Pp. 5–20 in *The Buildings at Samaria*, ed. J. W. Crowfoot, K. M. Kenyon, and E. L. Sukenik. London: Palestine Exploration Fund.
  1957a   Introduction. Pp. 1–8 in *The Objects from Samaria*, ed. J. W. Crowfoot, G. M. Crowfoot, and K. M. Kenyon. Samaria–Sebaste: Reports of the Work of the Joint Expedition in 1931–1933 and of the British Expedition in 1935, no. 3. London: Palestine Exploration Fund.
  1957b   Pottery: Imported Wares. Pp. 210–16 in *The Objects from Samaria*, ed. J. W. Crowfoot, G. M. Crowfoot, and K. M. Kenyon. Samaria–Sebaste: Reports of the Work of the Joint Expedition in 1931–1933 and of the British Expedition in 1935, no. 3. London: Palestine Exploration Fund.
Crown, A. D.
  1991   Redating the Schism between the Judaeans and the Samaritans. *JQR* 82: 17–50.
Curtis, E. L., and Madsen, A. A.
  1910   *The Books of Chronicles.* ICC. Edinburgh: T. & T. Clark.
Dar, S.
  1986   *Landscape and Pattern: An Archaeological Survey of Samaria 800 B.C.E.–636 C.E.* BAR International Series 308/1. Oxford: BAR.
  1992   Samaria (Archaeology of the Region). Pp. 926–31 in vol. 5 of *ABD*.
  1993   Survey of Western Samaria. Pp. 1314–16 in vol. 4 of *NEAEHL*.
Dexinger, F.
  1981   Limits of Tolerance in Judaism: The Samaritan Example. Pp. 88–114 in vol. 2 of *Jewish and Christian Self-Definition*, ed. E. P. Sanders, A. I. Baumgarten, and A. Mendelson. 2 vols. Philadelphia: Fortress.
Dorsey, D. A.
  1991   *The Roads and Highways of Ancient Israel.* Baltimore: Johns Hopkins University Press.
Elayi, J.
  1987   *Recherches sur les cités phéniciennes à l'époque perse.* Supplemento 51 agli *Annali* 47/2. Naples: Instituto Universitario Orientale.
  1988   *Pénétration grecque en Phénicie sous l'empire Perse.* Nancy: Presses universitaires de Nancy.
  1994   Présence grecque sur la côte palestinienne. Pp. 245–60 in *La Palestine à l'époque perse*, ed. E.-M. Laperrousaz and A. Lemaire. Études annexes de la Bible de Jérusalem. Paris: Cerf.
Eph'al, I.
  1998   Changes in Palestine during the Persian Period in Light of Epigraphic Sources. *IEJ* 48: 106–19.
Eshel, H.
  1997   Israelite Names from Samaria in the Persian Period. Pp. 181–89 in *These Are the Names: Studies in Jewish Onomastics*, ed. A. Demsky, J. Tabory, Y. A. Raif, and E. D. Lawson. Ramat Gan: Bar Ilan University Press. [Hebrew]

2001   Nehemiah's Walls of Jerusalem. Pp. 97–110 in *New Studies on Jerusalem*, ed. A. Faust and E. Baruch. Jerusalem: Ingeborg Rennert Center for Jewish Studies. [Hebrew]

Faust, A.
2001   Jerusalem's Countryside during the Iron Age II–Persian Period Transition. Pp. 83–89 in *New Studies on Jerusalem*, ed. A. Faust and E. Baruch. Jerusalem: Ingeborg Rennert Center for Jewish Studies. [Hebrew]
2003a   The Farmstead in the Highlands of Iron III Israel. Pp. 91–104 in *The Rural Landscape of Ancient Israel*, ed. A. M. Maeir, S. Dar, and Z. Safrai. BAR Int. Series 1121. Oxford: Archaeopress.
2003b   Judah in the Sixth Century B.C.E.: A Rural Perspective. *PEQ* 135: 37–53.

Finkelstein, I.
1993a   Environmental Archaeology and Social History: Demographic and Economic Aspects of the Monarchic Period. Pp. 56–66 in *Biblical Archaeology Today, 1990: Proceedings of the Second International Congress of Biblical Archaeology*. Jerusalem: Israel Exploration Society.
1993b   Southern Samarian Hills Survey. Pp. 1313–14 in vol. 4 of *NEAEHL*.

Finkelstein, I.; Lederman, Z.; and Bunimovitz, S. (eds.)
1997   *Highlands of Many Cultures: The Southern Samaria Survey.* 2 vols. Tel Aviv: Institute of Archaeology of Tel Aviv Publications Section.

Galling, K.
1954   *Die Bücher der Chronik, Esra, Nehemia.* ATD 12. Göttingen: Vandenhoeck & Ruprecht.

Grabbe, L. L.
1987   Josephus and the Reconstruction of the Judean Restoration. *JBL* 106: 231–46.
1992   *Judaism from Cyrus to Hadrian.* 2 vols. Philadelphia: Fortress.
1998   *Ezra–Nehemiah.* Old Testament Readings. London: Routledge.
2000   *Judaic Religion in the Second Temple Period: Belief and Practice from the Exile to Yavneh.* London: Routledge.

Grelot, P.
1972   *Documents araméens d'Égypt.* Paris: Cerf.

Groot, A. de
2001   Jerusalem during the Persian Period. Pp. 77–81 in *New Studies on Jerusalem*, ed. A. Faust and E. Baruch. Jerusalem: Ingeborg Rennert Center for Jewish Studies. [Hebrew]

Gropp, D. M.
1986   *The Samaria Papyri from Wâdī ed-Dâliyeh: The Slave Sales.* Ph.D. dissertation. Harvard University.
1990   The Language of the Samaria Papyri: A Preliminary Study. *Maarav* 5–6: 169–85.
1993   The Origin and Development of the *šallīṭ* Clause. *JNES* 52: 31–36.
1997   Imperial Aramaic. Pp. 144–46 in vol. 3 of *OEANE*.
2000   Sanballat. Pp. 823–25 in *Encyclopaedia of the Dead Sea Scrolls*, ed. L. S. Schiffman and J. C. VanderKam. Oxford: Oxford University Press.

2001   *Wadi Daliyeh II: The Samaria Papyri from Wadi Daliyeh.* DJD 28. Oxford: Oxford University Press.

Hanhart, R.
1982   Zu den ältesten Traditionen über das Samaritanische Schisma. *ErIsr* 16 (Orlinsky volume): 106–15.

Hjelm, I.
2000   *The Samaritans and Early Judaism.* JSOTSup 303. Copenhagen International Seminar 7. Sheffield: Sheffield Academic Press.

Janssen, J.
1956   *Juda in der Exilszeit.* FRLANT 69. Göttingen: Vandenhoeck & Ruprecht.

Japhet, S.
1968   The Supposed Common Authorship of Chronicles and Ezra–Nehemiah Investigated Anew. *VT* 18: 330–71.
1983   People and Land in the Restoration Period. Pp. 103–25 in *Das Land Israel in biblischer Zeit,* ed. G. Strecker. GTA 25. Göttingen: Vandenhoeck & Ruprecht.
1989   *The Ideology of the Book of Chronicles and Its Place in Biblical Thought.* BEATAJ 9. Frankfurt am Main: Peter Lang.
1993   *I and II Chronicles.* OTL. Louisville: Westminster John Knox.
1996   L'Historiographie post-exilique: Comment at pourquoi? Pp. 123–52 in *Israël construit son histoire: L'historiographie deutéronomiste à la lumière des recherches récentes,* ed. A. de Pury, T. Römer, and J.-D. Macchi. *MdB* 34. Geneva: Labor & Fides.

Kenyon, K. M.
1942   The Summit Buildings and Constructions. Pp. 91–120 in *The Buildings at Samaria,* ed. J. W. Crowfoot, K. M. Kenyon, and E. L. Sukenik. London: Palestine Exploration Fund.
1957   Pottery: Early Bronze and Israelite. Pp. 91–209 in *The Objects from Samaria,* ed. J. W. Crowfoot, G. M. Crowfoot, and K. M. Kenyon. Samaria–Sebaste: Reports of the Work of the Joint Expedition in 1931–1933 and of the British Expedition in 1935, no. 3. London: Palestine Exploration Fund.

King, P. J., and Stager, L. E.
2001   *Life in Biblical Israel.* Library of Ancient Israel. Louisville: Westminster John Knox.

Kippenberg, H. G.
1971   *Garizim und Synagoge: Traditionsgeschichtliche Untersuchungen zur samaritanischen Religion der aramäischen Periode.* Religionsgeschichtliche Versuche und Vorarbeiten 30. Berlin: de Gruyter.

Kirkman, J. S.
1957   The Evidence of the Coins. Pp. 43–70 in *The Objects from Samaria,* ed. J. W. Crowfoot, G. M. Crowfoot, and K. M. Kenyon. Samaria–Sebaste: Reports of the Work of the Joint Expedition in 1931–1933 and of the British Expedition in 1935, no. 3. London: Palestine Exploration Fund.

Kloner, A.
2001 Jerusalem's Environs in the Persian Period. Pp. 91–95 in *New Studies on Jerusalem*, ed. A. Faust and E. Baruch. Jerusalem: Ingeborg Rennert Center for Jewish Studies. [Hebrew]

Knoppers, G. N.
2000 "Great among His Brothers," but Who Is He? Heterogeneity in the Composition of Judah. *Journal of Hebrew Scriptures*. http://www.purl.org/jhs.
2001 Intermarriage, Social Complexity, and Ethnic Diversity in the Genealogy of Judah. *JBL* 120: 15–30.
2003 Greek Historiography and the Chronicler's History: A Reexamination. *JBL* 122: 627–50.
2004a *I Chronicles 1–9.* AB 12A. New York: Doubleday.
2004b *I Chronicles 10–29.* AB 12B. New York: Doubleday.
2004c In Search of Postexilic Israel: Samaria after the Fall of the Northern Kingdom. Pp. 150–80 in *In Search of Preexilic Israel*, ed. J. Day. JSOTSup 406. Edinburgh: T. & T. Clark/Continuum.

Kreissig, H.
1973 *Die sozialökonomische Situation in Juda zur Achëmenidzeit.* Schriften zur Geschichte und Kultur des Alten Orients 7. Berlin: Akademie.

Leith, Mary Joan Winn
1997 *Wadi Daliyeh I: The Seal Impressions.* Oxford: Oxford University Press.

Lemaire, A.
1995 Ashdodien et judéen à l'époque Perse: Ne 13:24. Pp. 153–63 in *Immigration and Emigration within the Ancient Near East: Festschrift E. Lipiński*, ed. K. van Lerberghe and A. Schoors. OLA 65. Leuven: Peeters.
2001 Épigraphie et religion en Palestine à l'époque achéménide. *Transeu* 22: 97–113.

Lipiński, E.
1990 Géographique linguistique de la Transeuphratène à l'époque achéménide. *Transeu* 3: 95–107.

Lipschits, O.
1998 Nebuchadrezzar's Policy in 'Ḫattu-Land' and the Fate of the Kingdom of Judah. *UF* 30: 467–87.
1999 The History of the Benjamin Region under Babylonian Rule. *TA* 26: 155–90.
2001 Judah, Jerusalem, and the Temple 586–539 B.C. *Transeu* 22: 129–42.
2003 Demographic Changes in Judah between the Seventh and Fifth Centuries B.C.E. Pp. 323–76 in *Judah and the Judeans in the Neo-Babylonian Period*, ed. O. Lipschits and J. Blenkinsopp. Winona Lake, Indiana: Eisenbrauns.
2005 *The Fall and Rise of Jerusalem: The History of Judah under Babylonian Rule.* Winona Lake, Indiana: Eisenbrauns.

Machinist, P. B.
1994 The First Coins of Judah and Samaria: Numismatics and History in the Achaemenid and Early Hellenistic Periods. Pp. 365–80 in vol. 8 of

Achaemenid History, ed. H. Sancisi-Weerdenburg, J. W. Dijvers, and M. Cool Root. Leiden: Brill.

Magen, Y.
1993 Mount Gerizim and the Samaritans. Pp. 89–148 in *Early Christianity in Context*, ed. F. Manns and E. Alliata. Studium Biblicum Franciscanum Collectio Maior 38. Jerusalem: Franciscan Printing Press.
2000 Mt. Gerizim: A Temple City. *Qadmoniot* 33/2: 74–118. [Hebrew]

Magen, Y.; Tsfania, L.; and Misgav, H.
2000 The Hebrew and Aramaic Inscriptions from Mt. Gerizim. *Qadmoniot* 33/2: 125–32. [Hebrew]

Mazar, A.
1990 *Archaeology of the Land of the Bible 10,000–586 B.C.E.* ABRL. Garden City, New York: Doubleday.

Meshorer Y., and Qedar, S.
1999 *Samarian Coinage.* Numismatics Studies and Researches 9. Jerusalem: Israel Numismatics Society.

Meyers, C., and Meyers, E.
1988 *Haggai, Zechariah 1–8.* AB 25b. Garden City, New York: Doubleday.

Mildenberg, L.
1996 *Yěhūd und šmryn*: Über das Geld der persischen Provinzen Juda und Samaria im 4. Jahrhundert. Pp. 119–46 in *Geschichte-Tradition-Reflexion: Festschrift für Martin Hengel zum 70. Geburtstag*, ed. H. Cancik, H. Lichtenberger, and P. Schäfer. Tübingen: Mohr.

Miller, J. M., and Hayes, J. H.
1986 *A History of Ancient Israel and Judah.* Philadelphia: Westminster.

Mosis, R.
1973 *Untersuchungen zur Theologie des chronistischen Geschichtswerkes.* Freiburg: Herder.

Naveh, J.
1971 Hebrew Texts in Aramaic Script in the Persian Period? *BASOR* 203: 27–32.
1998 Scripts and Inscriptions in Ancient Samaria. *IEJ* 48: 91–100.

Noth, M.
1943 *Überlieferungsgeschichtliche Studien: Die sammelnden und bearbeitenden Geschichtswerke im Alten Testament.* Tübingen: Max Niemeyer.

Pfeiffer, R. H.
1948 *Introduction to the Old Testament.* 2nd ed. New York: Harper.

Plöger, O.
1968 *Theocracy and Eschatology.* Oxford: Blackwell.

Porten, B.
1968 *Archives From Elephantine.* Berkeley: University of California Press.

Pummer, R.
1976 The Present State of Samaritan Studies: I. *JSS* 21: 48–55.
1987 *The Samaritans.* Iconography of Religions 23/5. Leiden: Brill.

Purvis, J. D.
1968   *The Samaritan Pentateuch and the Origins of the Samaritan Sect.* HSM 2.
         Cambridge: Harvard University Press.
1981   The Samaritan Problem: A Case Study in Jewish Sectarianism in the
         Roman Era. Pp. 323–50 in *Traditions in Transformation: Turning Points in
         Biblical Faith. Essays Presented to Frank Moore Cross, Jr.,* ed. B. Halpern
         and J. D. Levenson. Winona Lake, Indiana: Eisenbrauns.
1986   The Samaritans and Judaism. Pp. 81–98 in *Early Judaism and Its Modern
         Interpreters,* ed. R. A. Kraft and G. W. E. Nickelsburg. Atlanta: Scholars
         Press.

Rad, G. von
1930   *Das Geschichtsbild des chronistischen Werkes.* Stuttgart: Kohlhammer.

Reinmuth, T.
2002   *Der Bericht Nehemias: Zur literarischen Eigenart, traditionsgeshichtlichen
         Prägung und innerbiblischen Rezeption des Ich-Berichts Nehemias.* OBO
         183. Freiburg: Universitätsverlag.

Rowley, H. H.
1955–56 Sanballat and the Samaritan Temple. *BJRL* 38: 166–98.

Rudolph, W.
1955   *Chronikbücher.* HAT 21. Tübingen: Mohr.

Schmitt, R.
2003   Gab es einen Bildersturm nach dem Exil? Einige Bemerkungen zur
         Verwendung von Terrakottafiguringen im nachexilischen Israel.
         Pp. 186–98 in *Yahwism after the Exile: Perspectives on Israelite Religion
         in the Persian Era,* ed. R. Albertz and B. Becking. Studies in Theology
         and Religion 5. Assen: Van Gorcum.

Stern, E.
1989   What Happened to the Cult Figurines? *BARev* 15/4: 22–29, 53–54.
1995   Between Persia and Greece: Trade, Administration and Warfare in the
         Persian and Hellenistic Periods. Pp. 432–45 in *The Archaeology of Society
         in the Holy Land,* ed. T. E. Levy. London: Leicester University Press /
         New York: Facts on File.
2001   *The Assyrian, Babylonian, and Persian Periods 732–332* BCE. Vol. 2 of *Ar-
         chaeology of the Land of the Bible.* ABRL. New York: Doubleday.

Stern E., and Magen, Y.
2000   The First Phase of the Samaritan Temple on Mt. Gerizim: New Ar-
         chaeological Evidence. *Qadmoniot* 33/2: 119–24. [Hebrew]
2002   Archaeological Evidence for the First Stage of the Samaritan Temple
         on Mount Gerizim. *IEJ* 52: 49–57.

Tadmor, M.
1979   Fragments of an Achaemenid Throne from Samaria. *IEJ* 24: 37–43.

Tappy, R. E.
2001   *The Archaeology of Israelite Samaria, Volume II: The Eighth Century* BCE.
         HSS 50. Winona Lake, Indiana: Eisenbrauns.

Torrey, C. C.
1909 The Chronicler as Editor and as Independent Narrator. *AJSL* 25: 157–73, 188–217.
1954 *The Chronicler's History of Israel.* New Haven: Yale University Press.
Vincent, A.
1937 *La Religion des Judéo-Araméens d'Éléphantine.* Paris: Geuthner.
Waltke, B. K.
1965 *Prolegomena to the Samaritan Pentateuch.* Ph.D. dissertation. Harvard University.
Weinberg, J. P.
1996 *Der Chronist in seiner Mitwelt.* BZAW 239. Berlin: de Gruyter.
Wellhausen, J.
1885 *Prolegomena to the History of Ancient Israel.* Edinburgh: Black.
Welten, P.
1973 *Geschichte und Geschichtsdarstellung in den Chronikbüchern.* Neukirchen-Vluyn: Neukirchener Verlag.
Wette, W. M. L. de
1806–7 *Beiträge zur Einleitung in das Alten Testament.* 2 vols. Halle: Schimmelpfennig.
Willi, T.
1994 Late Persian Period Judaism and Its Conception of an Integral Israel according to Chronicles. Pp. 146–62 in *Second Temple Studies 2: Temple and Community in the Persian Period,* ed. T. C. Eskenazi and K. H. Richards. JSOTSup 175. Sheffield: JSOT Press.
1995 *Juda–Jehud–Israel: Studien zum Selbstverständnis des Judentums in persischer Zeit.* FAT 12. Tübingen: Mohr.
Williamson, H. G. M.
1977a *Israel in the Books of Chronicles.* Cambridge: Cambridge University Press.
1977b The Historical Value of Josephus' *Jewish Antiquities* XI.297–301. *JTS* 28: 49–66.
1982 *1 and 2 Chronicles.* NCB. Grand Rapids: Eerdmans.
1983 The Composition of Ezra i–vi. *JTS* 34: 1–30.
1987 Postexilic Historiography. Pp. 189–207 in *The Future of Biblical Studies: The Hebrew Scriptures,* ed. R. E. Friedman and H. G. M. Williamson. Atlanta: Scholars Press.
1989 The Concept of Israel in Transition. Pp. 141–60 in *The World of Ancient Israel,* ed. R. E. Clements. Cambridge: Cambridge University Press.
Zertal, A.
1988 The Water Factor during the Israelite Settlement Process in Canaan. Pp. 341–52 in *Society and Economy in the Eastern Mediterranean c. 1500–1000 B.C.,* ed. M. Heltzer and E. Lipiński. OLA 23. Leuven: Peeters.
1990 The Pahwah of Samaria (Northern Israel) during the Persian Period: Types of Settlement, Economy, History and New Discoveries. *Transeu* 3: 9–30.

1993   The Mount Manasseh (Northern Samarian Hills) Survey. Pp. 1311–12 in vol. 3 of *NEAEHL*.

1997   Survey of Northern Samaria. Pp. 164–66 in vol. 4 of *OEANE*.

1999   The Province of Samaria during the Persian and Hellenistic Periods. Pp. 75*–98* in *Michael: Historical, Epigraphical and Biblical Studies in Honor of Professor Michael Heltzer*, ed. Y. Avishur and R. Deutsch. Tel Aviv: Archaeological Centre Publications. [Hebrew]

2001   The Heart of the Monarchy: Patterns of Settlement and Historical Considerations of the Israelite Kingdom of Samaria. Pp. 38–64 in *Studies in the Archaeology of the Iron Age in Israel and Jordan*, ed. A. Mazar. JSOTSup 331. Sheffield: Sheffield Academic Press.

2003   The Province of Samaria (Assyrian *Samerina*) in the Late Iron Age (Iron Age III). Pp. 377–412 in *Judah and the Judeans in the Neo-Babylonian and Persian Periods*, ed. J. Blenkinsopp and O. Lipschits. Winona Lake, Indiana: Eisenbrauns.

Zsengeller, J.

1996   Personal Names in the *Wadi ed-Daliyeh* Papyri. *ZAH* 9: 181–89.

Bethel:
The Israelite Impact on
Judean Language and Literature

ERNST AXEL KNAUF

University of Berne, Switzerland

Bethel is, after Jerusalem, the place most frequently mentioned in the Bible.[1] This essay seeks to explain why.

Introduction

There was no Torah before the Torah.[2] Canaan/Israel was not only linguistically cantonized[3]—and remains so to this very day, at least on the level of the spoken language[4]—but Israel and Judah were also cantonized with regard to local traditions. The legends involving Father Abraham emerged at Mamre, in northern Judah, during the Iron I period.[5] It is conceivable that the name of Abraham was unheard of in Jerusalem prior to 597 B.C.E.,[6] if even by that time, and that the tradition

---

Author's note: This essay was researched and written at the Institute for Advanced Studies, The Hebrew University of Jerusalem, and would never have been completed without the bibliographical resources of the Jewish National and University Library. All dates are B.C.E. unless specified otherwise.

1. Bethel has 71 references (with Jer 48:13 not counted and "Beth Aven" disregarded) vis-à-vis 669 references to Jerusalem (synonyms such as "Zion," "City/Citadel of David," "Shalem," etc. disregarded).

2. Cf. Knauf 2002b: 165–74; nor was there "biblical" literature (in the sense of canonical literature) prior to the Torah, that is, 398 B.C.E.—the existence of Judean literature since at least the seventh century B.C.E. notwithstanding; the latter was used as source material in the redactions of the various biblical books; see Knauf 2002a: 193–98.

3. "Canaan was linguistically cantonized": Halpern 1987: 139.

4. This goes without saying for colloquial Arabic but also holds true for Modern Hebrew, in which the untrained ear of the present writer distinguishes at least the dialects of Tel Aviv and Jerusalem.

5. See for the archaeology of Abraham, Knauf 2002c: 280–82.

6. See Ezekiel 10–11 in the interpretation of Dietrich 1997: 350–76. The same movement from Judah into Jerusalem after 597 may have brought Amos and Micah into Jerusalem—if these traditions did not bypass Jerusalem and move directly to Bethel after

was only committed into writing at Bethel in the first half of the sixth century.[7] Most contemporary scholars would agree that the prophet Isaiah of the late eighth century, whoever he was,[8] knew nothing of an Exodus out of Egypt. The local traditions that one might discern with some degree of confidence comprise Dan (Amos 8:14; Psalm 42f.?[9]), Shechem (Jacob), Bethel (Jacob, Moses, Hosea[10]), Jericho (Genesis 2;[11] Elisha, and also Elijah?), Jerusalem (David, Zion), and Hebron (David; Amos?[12]). Local traditions—or some sanitized version of them—become national traditions only with the establishment of a national educational network. According to the Bible, such a notion was introduced by Ezra and not before (Ezra 7:25–26; Neh 8:7–8).[13]

---

586 (or, in the case of Amos, had never had another place of tradition). The question is linked to the problem of the historicity of Jeremiah 7 and 26:1–19: did Jeremiah actually pronounce these words against the temple prior to 586, and did his audience then check their book of Micah (3:12 = Jer 26:18), or is the condemnation of the temple a piece of Bethel-theology dating after 586, and the reference to Micah due to the fact that the editors of Jeremiah had this book in their library too? See further below n. 169.

7. Below, with n. 166.

8. For the near impossibility of discerning the prophetic personality around which the Isaianic tradition crystallized, see Knauf 2000a.

9. Probably not Judges 17–18; cf. Niemann 1999: 25–48.

10. Linked together, and to the place, by Hosea 12, on which see de Pury 2001a: 105–14; 2001b: 213–41; 1994a: 95–131; 1994b: 413–39; 1992: 175–207.

11. As Müller (1980: 99–142) already pointed out, Genesis 2 presupposes an oasis environment.

12. The way of the Amos tradition from Tekoa to Bethel—via Jerusalem or not?—remains largely enigmatic. The discussion of the book's various strata, their number, nature, and dating, is far from anything resembling a consensus; compare recently the positions of Becker 2001: 141–65; Levin 1995: 307–17; Blum 1994: 23–47; Loretz 1992: 179–215; Fritz 1989: 29–43; Fritz leaves Amos 3:12abα*; 5:3; 7:1–6 to the (?) eighth-century prophet. How the prophetic traditions looked before they were edited into full-blown books might be illustrated by comparison with the Assyrian records. At first, individual prophecies of public interest were recorded by the administration and reported to the king, if deemed necessary; at a second stage, various prophecies concerning the same event (as, e.g., Esarhaddon's [illegitimate] ascension to the throne) were collected, if judged to be of interest to further generations (and the stability of the ruling dynasty). See for seminal empirical research into the phenomenon of prophecy and prophetic books M. Nissinen 2002: 4–9; 1998: 157–70; 1996: 172–95; 1993: 217–58. According to recent (Germanic) research, it was the book of Amos that came to Bethel in the course of the sixth century. Or, should a sheep magnate from Tekoa indeed have come to Bethel in the times of Jeroboam II and said something unflattering about the status and the future prospects of the sanctuary, which led to a bureaucratic notice (Amos 9:1–2?) that two years later was endorsed by the facts, enriched with a further remark (Amos 1:1*?), and returned to the archive? In this case, the real Amos might long have gone home when his prophetic gifts were finally recovered— and the book, in its early stages, may have been compiled at Bethel in the first place.

13. Even if this educational effort was not immediately set in motion in 398, it must have been in place when the book of Ezra–Nehemiah was written (end of the fourth century). A similar educational effort is conspicuously absent in 2 Kings 22–23, where the king

When and how did Northern traditions, such as the Exodus and the stories of the saviors/judges[14] arrive in Judah? The conclusion that these were brought by Northern fugitives after 720, which is also used to explain the growth of Jerusalem at the end of the eighth century, rests on a number of wrong assumptions:

(a) The growth of Jerusalem and the refortification of the city—the first refortification since the Middle Bronze Age[15]—date to the time of Hezekiah. But it is more likely that both should be attributed to Manasseh.[16]

(b) Israelites left Israel for religious reasons—but they had no reason to do so. Within the ugly anti-Samarian polemic in 2 Kings 17, the information that a Yahwistic Temple and cultural center was established (or emerged) at Bethel is trustworthy and squares well with the archaeological and documentary record for Samaria, Shechem, and Bethel,[17] and equally well with the development of the Jacob tradition, notably

---

is the only targeted reader of the book, and the people are only called upon to swear allegiance to him as the designated executor of its ordinances (23:1–3); just as conspicuous is the absence of further public readings of the book, as ordained by Deut 31:9–17. Josiah's reform might have consisted of promoting Yhwh to the position of supreme god in the official pantheon of Jerusalem, a position Yhwh was striving for unofficially beginning in the time of Manasseh, and this became politically feasible with Ashur's demise; a reform that would have been meaningless to the fifth-century Deuteronomists who projected the final result of this reform, monotheism, into Israel's very beginnings. Cf. Knauf 2000a; Levin 1984: 351–71; Niehr 1995: 33–55; Uehlinger 1995: 57–89; Handy 1995: 252–75.

14. See for the Northern origin of Judges, denied by redactional critics (such as, e.g., Becker 1990, against the better judgment of Richter 1966; and now, notably, P. Guillaume forthcoming). The Becker-Richter controversy elucidates the limits of redaction criticism and the need for "content criticism" (for the term, see Knauf 2002c: 275f.).

15. Cf. most recently D. Ussishkin, in this volume, pp. 147–166.

16. Cf. 2 Chr 33:14 and Halpern 1991; Reich and Shuqrun 2000: 338.

17. *Samaria*: it was in the provincial capital (Nimrud Prism IV 37; Becking 1992: 28f.) that the deportees of Sargon's Arabian campaign of 716 were settled (Cyl. 20; Becking 1992: 32 n. 53). Of two cuneiform documents from the province of Samaria, one from 698/97 contains Akkadian names only, whereas the other one from 664/63 has only one Akkadian name together with five indigenous ones. The bearer of one of those is called "Egyptian" in the text; another one (Padi) could be Philisto-Canaanite; cf. Naʾaman and Zadok 2000: 159–88. One gets the impression that it is not so much population change that is attested by these documents but the acculturation of the local elite to cuneiform law and documents. Two cuneiform contracts from Gezer, dated 651 and 649, contain nine Akkadian names, five Aramaic names (Ṭebetay, *Saggiʾ, Adad-tadin, Bur-Rapi, Ṭurilay), one Egyptian, and two Canaanite names, Sinʾi and Natanyahu, the latter an Israelite and owner of a field that is sold; cf. Galling 1935: 81–85; Becking 1981/82: 76–89; Reich and Brandl 1985: 41f. In Renz and Röllig (vol. 1) there are 12 Hebrew inscriptions from the Assyrian provinces of Samaria and Megiddo (BSea [8]:2; [7/8]:1; Kh [8]:1; Or [8]:2, 4, 5; Qas [8]:1; [8]:2; Gez [7]:6f.; Meg [7]:2; Qad [7]:2). Seventh-century *Shechem* was a poor shadow of its pre-Assyrian urban predecessor; contrast Stratum VI (seventh–sixth centuries; Campbell 2002: 295–99) with Strata IX through VII (ninth and eighth centuries; Campbell 2002: 247–95). See for the archaeology of *Bethel* below, nn. 80–92.

Jacob's "migration" from Shechem to Bethel, Gen 35:1. The (partial!) depopulation of the Israelite countryside that can be observed during the seventh century is not due to the Assyrian deportations of 733–720, which did not affect more than 10–20% of the population,[18] but to the Assyrian policy of sidelining Phoenicia (the natural agrarian hinterland of which Israel had been a part) and to Assyria's promoting of the Philistine trade hub instead (which contributed to the economic prosperity of Judah under Manasseh). Many Israelites may have left for economic reasons, but in this case, they would not have moved to Jerusalem, which had its own problems, being filled to the brim with refugees from the Shephelah; rather, they would have moved to Philistia and, farther down the road, to Egypt.[19]

(c) The Israelite traditions were known to every Israelite. Most likely, this was not the case—there was no Bible prior to the first Bible (the Torah, issued in 398), and prior to 720 Israel did not even have a standard administrative language, so there is even less reason to assume that this kingdom developed anything like a national tradition (as opposed to dynastic ideologies, which can be supposed to have existed and then were exterminated after the next coup). The Israelites who left Samaria in the eighth and seventh centuries for economic reasons were not exactly Huguenots.

Contrary to the assumption of a significant influx of Israelite people and traditions into Judah after 720, Israelite linguistic influence on Judean Hebrew cannot be traced prior to the sixth century (see below, §2). In the fifth and fourth centuries, the Israelite form of the theophoric element in personal names, *-yw* instead of Judean *-yhw*, is attested among Judeans in Yehud, in the Shephelah, and in Babylonia.[20]

A model of how a national identity—and the cultural expression of such an identity—might emerge in a country as geographically, ethnically, and economically fragmented as Israel/Palestine can be studied by means of Palestinian ethnogenesis during the course of the twentieth century C.E. The *keffiyah* became the male accoutrement expressing "being Palestinian" in the course of what can now be called the "first intifada," 1936–39 C.E.[21] Prior to that date, no upper-class Jerusalemite or Nabulsi would have donned such a rustic piece of headgear. In the case

---

18. Sargon deported 27,280 or 27,290 persons (Nimrud Prism IV 31–33; Becking 1992: 28f.; Display-inscription 24; Becking 1992: 26) and Tiglath-pileser III had previously deported 13,520 people (Naʾaman 1993: 105) out of a population of ca. 350,000; cf. Finkelstein and Silberman 2000.

19. Hos 7:16; 9:3, 6; Oren 1984: 7–44.

20. Cf. Ephʿal and Naveh 1996: 92.

21. For a balanced history of the Palestinians in the twentieth century C.E., see Krämer 2002.

of female garb, the traditional "Palestinian" dress celebrated local identity and regional diversity with a passion. If the basic color of the Bethlehem dresses was black, then in neighboring Beth Jala it could hardly
have been anything but white. . . . A pan-Palestinian pattern of embroidery emerged after 1949 in the camps.[22] The "nation," as it emerged in
nineteenth-century C.E. Europe and became firmly established there by
the beginning of the twentieth century, can by no means be projected
into earlier Europe or other countries. Pre-nineteenth-century political
reality is well described by the Spanish General Don Alvaro Navia Oso-
rio, Marqués de Santa Cruz y Marcenado (1684–1732):

> It is rare to find a country where the people are not at daggers drawn
> with the aristocracy, or the nobles are not divided among themselves. . . .
> The inhabitants of two neighboring localities will usually be on bad
> terms. Their hostility derives from the endless disputes over right to
> water, woodland or pasture along their borders; each village wishes to
> extend its borders at the expense of the other.[23]

Prima facie, the assumption that the Bible as "Jewish national literature" emerged from the Exile and during the Persian Restoration is
highly attractive. To forge a new identity out of the ruins of the failed
states, Israel and Judah required not only collecting but also organizing
and editing the traditions hailing from the First Temple Period.[24] It
would, however, be overly simplistic to assume that the Bible—or what
was to become the Tanakh between 398 and ca. 100 C.E.—emerged in
the Exile. The thesis now to be presented is that Bethel played a part
of equal importance with Babylon in the literary history of the Neo-
Babylonian Period and was only superseded by Jerusalem in the Persian Period; and notably, that it was the Northern traditions that came
to Judah via Bethel, a process that started when Judah incorporated
Bethel and its local temple, school, and library.

1. Demography and Archeology [25]

There can be no doubt that the territory of Benjamin with Bethel
was attached to Judah in the course of the seventh century. The northern border of Yehud as fairly well attested for the fifth and fourth

---

22. Völger, Welck, and Hackstein 1987; cf. further El-Khalidi 1999; Azzazi 1992; Weir
and Shahid 1988.
23. Quoted from Duffy 1998: 9.
24. Auerbach 1953; Kratz 2000a: 2157.
25. *Archeology* is a branch of social and political anthropology, aiming at the reconstruction of past societies and their social and economic behavioral patterns on the basis

centuries[26] could not have been established in the eighth century, when Bethel still functioned as an Israelite sanctuary. The act of Gedaliah, the last Judean king,[27] of taking up residence in Mizpah is a strong argument for the incorporation of Bethel into Judah prior to 586 (Gedaliah would not have chosen a town on the extreme northern border of his territory for his central place).

The story of Bethel's profanation in 2 Kgs 23:15–20 is usually interpreted as an indication of Judah's extension to the north under Josiah, whereas older assumptions, based on the same text, that Josiah "restored" more or less the whole Davidic kingdom from Dan to Beer-sheba have been given up lately.[28] Based on the excavations, no destruction at Bethel is attested between 733 and 586.[29] One might argue that the exact site of the sanctuary has not been excavated (yet) and that Josiah's action need not be visible in the archeological record such as it now stands. But the text reads more like a mischievous fantasy concocted in Jerusalem at a time when there was actual competition between Bethel and Jerusalem,[30] of the same ilk as 2 Kgs 17:7–41 (we will discuss this further below, §3, pp. 318–330). The textual basis having been found insufficient for historical conclusions, we must again look at the facts on the ground other than artifacts. After the loss of the Shephelah, colonization in neither the Negev nor the immediate Judean vi-

---

of material culture remains, which include not just artifacts but also ecofacts (such as floral and faunal remains) and geofacts (such as earthquakes and landslides). Archeology is an empirical social science. *Archaeology*, on the other hand, is the study of artifacts and is instead rooted in the humanities. Archaeology has something to offer to archeology (and history), but sometimes, not very much.

26. Carter 1999: 75–100.

27. A strong argument for Gedaliah's claim to the royal title is the seal found at Mizpah and belonging to one of Gedaliah's officials; cf. Becking 1997: 65–83. That Gedaliah is not given his title in the Bible is of small importance—he was not a descendant of David and, therefore, was illegitimate for the Deuteronomistic editors of Kings (and, to a lesser degree, Jeremiah). What is indicative in this context is that he is not called a governor either; in the Bible, he is simply Gedaliah. Since it is clear that he did not act as a private citizen, it stands to reason that his title has been suppressed, and that, in this case, it would not have been a designation of office which with the Deuteronomists could easily have lived.

28. Na'aman 1991: 3–71.

29. See below, with nn. 80–92.

30. These among many other features (most notably the destruction of sanctuaries in 2 Kgs 23:8–20, which either were not destroyed at the end of the seventh century [Bethel] or had ceased to exist previously [Beer-sheba], or were out of Josiah's reach anyway [Samaria]) strongly suggest that 1 Kings 22f. in its present form is fifth-century B.C.E. programmatic writing; see Spieckermann 1982: 112f. n. 179 (*Wunschvorstellung*).

cinity of Jerusalem could have easily fed the ca. 15,000 inhabitants of
Jerusalem in the seventh century, whereas the primary agricultural
area of Benjamin[31] would have found a market for its products in its
immediate vicinity. In other words, the shift of Benjamin from the
sphere of Samaria into that of Jerusalem in the course of the seventh
century was dictated by demographic and economic factors. When this
shift was acknowledged, by changing the border between Judah and
Samaria accordingly, is subject to speculation: it may have happened as
early as 662, when Esarhaddon/Ashurbanipal held court on the borders of Samaria[32] and may have found it advisable to honor his loyal
vassal Manasseh, whose troops (and logistic support) he needed for his
Egyptian campaign; or as late as 640/630, when Assyria virtually gave
up its possessions in southern Syria (or handed them over to its Egyptian vassal, now ally, Psammetichus).[33] It may be noteworthy in this
connection that Isa 9:1–6, now usually understood as a celebration of
the child-king Josiah's accession to the throne,[34] seems to be the first
Judean text betraying knowledge of the Northern tradition of (Gideon
and) the Midianites (9:2).[35]

---

31. Carter's precise delimitation and evaluation of the ecological niches within Yehud (Carter 1999: 100–113) elucidates Benjamin's economic precedence over Judah quite
sufficiently.

32. It is only "Aphek of the Land of Šame[ri]na" that Esarhaddon, Frt. F verso 16
(Borger 1956: 112), mentions between Tyre and Raphia, indicating that this was probably
the place where his southern Syrian vassals, such as Manasseh, were to join his army
bound for Egypt.

33. A tax-stamp of the type usually attributed to the reign of Josiah from the Benjamin region (MP #100) bears the date "Year 10," which would mean that Bethel and its environs came to Judah well before 630 (and would disprove any theory of a campaign of
Northern conquest in 622; cf. Renz 2000: 113; unfortunately, the item comes from the antiquities market, which means that doubts concerning its authenticity cannot be ruled
out). Kottsieper (2000: 368–92) dates an anti-Babylonian Assyrian edict (in Aramaic) from
southern Syria/northern Lebanon to 626–610; a date during the Shamash-shumukin revolt of 653–648 seems more likely.

34. Barth 1977: 141–52; 166–77 = idem 1989: 199–229; against postexilic datings, such
as Werner 1982: 20–46, 77f. (followed by Becker 1997: 216f.). Werner's arguments are
wrong or inconclusive; there is no justification whatever for translating the x-*qatal*s, *qatal*-
x's, and *wayyiqtol*s (!) of the text as "present" (Werner 1982: 20f.) and referring them to the
future. The text arrives at the author's present in v. 6 with a nominal sentence and may
look into the future with its very last clause (x-*yiqtol* l), which either means "The zeal
of the Lord will provide that things remain as they are now" or is a gloss in the extra-
temporal mode: "The zeal of the Lord always acts in such a way."

35. Alternatively, one would first have to postulate an independent Judean Midian
tradition, which must, in addition, have equally been a story of suppression and rescue.
The first proposition is possible (cf. Gen 36:35; but this note may represent an educated
guess at synchronizing "Israelite" and "Midianite" history, not a tradition independent

The importance of Bethel and Benjamin in the Neo-Babylonian and Persian Period is best seen on the basis of demographics.[36] Prior to 597, Judah had ca. 110,000 inhabitants. The loss of southern Judah and the Negev in 597 would have subtracted 12–13,000 from this number.[37] The deportations of 597, 586, and 582 led 4,600 men—that is, ca. 20,000 people—to Babylon.[38] Lipschits estimated the population of Judah in the sixth century at 40,000 altogether, of which 20,000 must have lived in the Benjamin region and the rest "in ruins, caves, and tents" (Ezek 33:27). The 35,000 people not accounted for must have fallen victim to "the sword, hunger, and pestilence" (Jer 14:12; 21:7, 9; 24:10; 27:8, 13; 29:17f.; 32:24, 36; 34:17; 38:2; 42:7, 22; 44:13; Ezek 5:12, 17; 6:11f.; 7:15; 12:16; 14:21),[39] and, more decisively, because populations under favorable circumstances recover quickly, must have left the country for better pastures such as, for example, Egypt[40] or even Arabia.[41]

---

of Judges 6–8; cf. Knauf 1985: 252); the second is rather unlikely, because it was only in the context of the (Northern) "Book of Saviors" that a vague memory of Gideon and the Midianites was transformed into a story of occupation and liberation (for a version of the Gideon story in which Gideon is the successful aggressor, bound by the noble tribal motive of blood revenge, see Judg 8:4–17*; for a tradition originally independent of Judges 7, see Becker 1990: 174).

36. I am using the figures and estimates in Lipschits 2003: 323–76, which improve upon earlier calculations. The relative devastation of Judah—in contrast to Benjamin (Faust 2003: 46)—is further elucidated by the material presented by Faust 2003: 37–53. There remains, however, the problem that it is nearly impossible to distinguish sixth-century pottery from seventh-century ceramics. In addition, there is the growing number of sites without Persian pottery but with Persian-Period inscriptions, coins, and "Iron IIC" pottery; see below, nn. 85–91.

37. Descendants of these Judeans under Edomite (and, from ca. 550 until ca. 375, Qedarite) rule can still be traced in Neh 11:25–30 and the Idumean ostraca (Porten, in this volume, pp. 457–488; for the kingdom of Qedar, cf. Knauf 1989a: 102–4; and Lemaire, in this volume, pp. 413–456; for 597 as more likely than 586 for the transfer of the old Judean South from Hebron to Edom, following a Judean war of aggression against Edom, 601 = 598, see Knauf 2000b: 56–61, 60 n. 27.

38. The exact figures in Jer 52:28–30 seem to derive from the Babylonian administration at Mizpah; the parallel account in Kings, presumably written in Babylonia, gives round numbers; probably because its authors did not have access to official documents.

39. The distribution of the rhetorical triad of "sword, hunger, and pestilence" suggests strongly that it reflects a reality of the sixth century (in addition to the above, the triad is only attested in 1 Chr 21:12 and 2 Chr 20:9, two pieces of innerbiblical exegesis depending on the finalized prophetic canon). In Ezek 5:17 and 14:21, "wild beasts" join the triad; in Ezek 33:27, they replace "hunger."

40. See Jer 41:11–43:7; the Jews of Elephantine claimed to have established themselves before 525, but their religion, as has been observed long since, points to Bethel and Benjamin as their place of departure; cf. Weippert 1990: 156 n. 54 = 1997: 15; and the archaeology of Elephantine suggests that they did not arrive before the sixth century; cf. Pilgrim 1999: 142–45.

41. Cf. Ben-Zvi 1961: 145–49; 1963: 141–75.

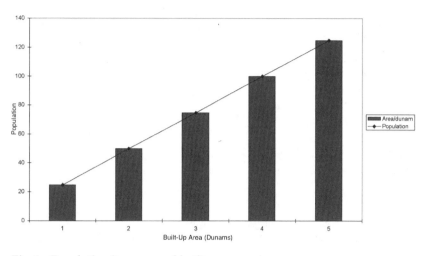

Fig. 1. Population increase and built-up area.

These demographic calculations are sound within a margin of error that remains to be determined (see fig. 1). For the time being, a simple model, enhanced by some ethnoarcheological information, may suffice. The current estimate is 25 people per built-up dunam (0.1 ha). If the population declined dramatically, by an epidemic or a subsistence crisis, it still took 50 years or longer until the unoccupied buildings fell down.[42] If a population increase occurred, at first the rooms were more crowded; traditionally people did not add another bedroom to their house for every newborn child. Once the rooms became overcrowded, more rooms were created within the family complex (note that the courtyard area is included in the built-up area of surveyed sites) or on the roofs.[43] These building activities do not go into the standard demographic calculation. Only when there were no more space reserves within the boundaries of the settlement, then either the boundaries were enlarged or satellite settlements were founded in outlying agricultural areas. These areas may have been previously colonized by our model village, at first without permanent structures at these sites, and perhaps only on a seasonal basis.[44] While population

42. Cf. Ziadeh-Seely 1999: 127–50.
43. Mershen 1992: 409–15.
44. For such settlement processes in the Ottoman Period, see Mershen and Knauf 1988: 128–45.

growth was continuous, settlement expansion was discontinuous. If we assume that settlement expansion did not set in below an increase of 50% of the population, 37 people would still occupy one dunam, whereas 38 people would need two dunams, bringing the population per dunam down to 19 people. This is merely a model calculation that needs to be refined by ethnoarcheological data. But it is already quite likely that the 49,897 or 49,942 inhabitants of Yehud (as documented by Ezra 2:64–65, Neh 7:66–67) lay well within the margin of error that goes with an estimate of 30,000 inhabitants, whereas the assumption that the list(s) only comprise(s) heads of households (leading to a population estimate of more than 200,000 inhabitants) does not.

In the Persian Period, the region of Benjamin seems to have declined demographically (did some Benjaminites resent the reestablishment of Jerusalem and go off to join their brothers in Egypt?). Benjamin still represented 40% of Yehud's overall population of 30,000 people; of even more importance is the fact that more than 90% of luxury items and agricultural installations from the Persian Period were found within Benjamin.[45] Whoever resettled Jerusalem and designed its official traditions in the fifth century could not completely ignore the Benjaminites. At the end of the Persian Period, ca. 45,000 Jews seem to have lived in Judah,[46] ca. 75,000 in Babylonia,[47] and ca. 20,000 in Egypt.[48] Whoever finalized the Torah could not ignore the point of view of the Babylonian Golah (the exiles) either: they had the money to finance the restoration of Jerusalem, and finance it they did.[49] Jerusalem and its immediate

45. Cf. Carter 1999: 249–68 with figs. 19–24.

46. Based on the statistics of Ezra 2 / Nehemiah 7, previously interpreted as giving the number of heads of households only, thus leading to a widely erroneous estimate of Yehud's population, see Lipschits 2003: 358 n. 127.

47. Based on the number of 20,000 deportees and the assumption of an annual population growth of 0.7% (calculated on the assumption that the 30,000 Judeans from 500 had grown into ca. half a million under Herod the Great). This figure means that every woman had three surviving and reproducing children, an assumption that is by no means out of bounds.

48. Based on ca. 3,500 Jews at Elephantine (Knauf 2002b: the Jewish ḥaylā [brigade] had 4, later 3 daglīn [battalions], each of which had at least 2 but probably more centuria or "hundreds" [companies]; the brigade could hardly have comprised less than 600 fit men; most likely more Jews lived on Elephantine than in Jerusalem in the fifth century, for which Neh 11:1–19 gives 3,036 inhabitants) and the number of Jewish towns in Egypt in Isa 19:18f. Jer 44:1 lists 4 Jewish settlements in Egypt, among which Jeb (Elephantine) is not mentioned.

49. Cf. Ezra 1:4, 6, 9–11; 2:69 = Neh 7:70; Ezra 7:16; 8:25–30, 33f.; Zech 6:9–15. The investments of the Babylonians were largely unproductive—temple, cult, the restorations of largely symbolic and completely oversized walls of Jerusalem (see Ussishkin, in this

environs had 2,500–3,000 inhabitants—less than Elephantine, which makes the Egyptian colony much less marginal than it appears from its representation—or rather, its neglect—in previous historical studies of the period.

The demography of Achaemenid Judah, as established by the archaeological record, calls for a reevaluation of the "Judean census list" in Ezra 2 and Nehemiah 7. The list claims to be a list of the returnees, but this is hardly the case.[50] The variants between the two versions[51] indicate that a basic document was slightly revised and partially updated at a later period. Some features are suspicious, for example, the double occurrence of (the) *Benê Elam* with exactly the same number. Remarkably, however, the sum of all persons listed is 29,818 in Ezra and 31,089 in Nehemiah, matching the demographic estimate for the fifth century exactly. Three classes of Judeans can be distinguished: (a) the priests and other temple personnel: 5,022 (16.84%) in Ezra and 5,041 (16.21%) in Nehemiah; (b) the *'ănāšîm* (people) of particular places;[52]

---

volume, pp. 147–166); thus not diminishing but increasing the economic weight of the Benjamin region. Not everybody needs to study Torah day and night, but everybody, including those who study Torah, needs to eat at least once a day. The walls of Jerusalem were already symbolic during the reign of Manasseh, when they were built for the first time (see above, p. 293)—with 10 city gates for a city of 50 ha, there were too many gates for the city wall to be really defensive, at least against an Assyrian army (the same can be concluded from the course of the wall in the Kidron Valley). For this inflation of city gates, Sennacherib's Nineveh with its 15 gates (Stronach and Codella 1997) may have provided the model (but then, Sennacherib's Nineveh covered 664 ha [Röllig 1995: 931f.] in comparison with Jerusalem's 50–60 ha). To build a little Nineveh—this was Manasseh's intention. In comparison, Suleiman the Magnificent's wall of Jerusalem (including 100 ha) was broken up by only 6 gates, and this wall was more symbolic than military in nature: it looked good, especially to fellahin and bedouin, but it would not have withstood Suleiman's own artillery. That the Babylonians needed one and a half years to conquer the place sheds a not-too-favorable light on their military capabilities. Evidently, they had neither a corps of engineers nor the high-quality archers of the Assyrian army. They may not have been able to put into the field more than a tribal rabble, enforced with Greek mercenaries (who were not exactly archers either, nor very useful in siege warfare—just think of Troy).

50. Myers 1965: 15f.; Gunneweg 1985: 65f.

51. Neh 7:15 has Binnui for Bani, Ezra 2:10; Magbish, Ezra 2:30, is missing after Neh 7:33; for Jorah, Ezra 2:18; Neh 7:24 has Hariph with an equal number of descendants; the sequence is Bezai–Jorah–Hashum in Ezra 2:17–19, and Hashum–Bezai–Hariph in Neh 7:22–24; Lod–Jericho in Ezra 2:33f., and Jericho–Lod in Neh 7:36f.; Bethlehem and Netophah have two entries in Ezra 2:21f. and one in Neh 7:26. Sixteen out of 41 numbers differ between the two versions (numbers of animals disregarded).

52. The place-names are better preserved in Nehemiah 7 (Gibeon, Neh 7:25 for Gibbar, Ezra 2:20; Beth-azmaveth, Neh 7:28 for Azmawet, Ezra 2:24; Kiriath-jearim, Neh 7:29 for Kiriatharim, Ezra 2:25; Addon, Neh 7:61 for Addan, Ezra 2:59; one expects *'ănāšîm*,

4,083 (13.69%) in Ezra and 3,822 (12.29%) in Nehemiah; and (c), the "descendants of PN/CN," which make up the rest. It is tempting to see in the distribution of "people" versus "descendants" a stage of the tradition that precedes the attribution of the Golah to all of them—that is, to regard the "descendants" as returnees and the "people" as descendants of the left-behinds. This, at least, seems to be the intention of the different designations. It is obvious that the percentage of returnees is far too high. This observation, together with the decline of the absolute and relative numbers of those who stayed behind, in the Nehemiah version, suggests that in fifth century Yehud it became fashionable to register as a "returnee" rather than as an "indigenous of the land," a process well in accordance with what is known about ancient Near Eastern clientelism and patronage. The returnees had the money (only the Babylonian Jews could support such a high number of unproductive temple personnel), and they made sure that their view of the world and its history dominated public life. The numbers given for Bethel, 223 in Ezra and 123 in Nehemiah, consequently do not reflect the actual number of the place's inhabitants (but do indicate that the town still existed) but only those among them who stubbornly kept up a "Bethelian" identity, ranking it 6th out of 13 towns or regions in Ezra and 8th out of 12 in Nehemiah, indicating a severe loss of prominence in between.

It is equally remarkable that the sums of people actually listed do not square at all with the sums given at the end of the lists: 29,818 to 49,897 in Ezra, and 31,089 to 49,942 in Nehemiah (the rejected priests, for whom no census figure is given, cannot have amounted to 18–20,000 people). From the demographical point of view, the actual sums fit the fifth century, whereas the sums quoted look like an update from the end of the fourth century, when the book of Ezra(–Nehemiah) was composed.[53]

---

when inhabitants of towns and villages are counted, and *bānîm*, if we are dealing with members of a family or clan, and this is generally the case in Nehemiah 7 (while Ezra 2 has *bānîm* for *'ănāšîm* in vv. 21, 24, 25, and 29), but even in Nehemiah 7 there are "descendants" of Gibeon, Jericho, and Lod.

53. The dating is based on the observation that the intentional distortion of Persian imperial history and chronology (see Japhet, this volume, pp. 491–508) was eased by the Persian Empire's demise in 332 (for Israel/Palestine) and that, on the other hand, the composition of Ezra(–Nehemiah) precedes Chronicles, which shows traits of Ptolemaic Hellenism; cf. Mathys 2000: 41–155.

Excursus:
Mass Return or Privately Sponsored aliyah and
the Degree of Persian Involvement in the Restoration of Yehud

One of the questions that was openly declared unresolved at the end of the Heidelberg conference was the question of how much concern was paid to Judean affairs by the imperial administration. It is clear that the leading circles of Achaemenid Yehud, whose voice we hear in Ezra(–Nehemiah) present themselves as loyal servants of the Persian Crown who did not undertake anything without the orders, or at least the consent, of the Great King. It is also clear from the biblical record itself that there was no mass return in 538 (thus 2 Chr 36:20–23[54]) but a trickle of relatively small groups between 528(–520) and 398.[55] This trickle accords well with comparable groups of returnees that are visible in the archeological record, among Arameans[56] as well as among Edomites.[57] The general picture supports the assumption of return as a private enterprise for the time before Nehemiah. Even the Aramaic edict of Cyrus in Ezra 6:3–5 might easily have been fabricated by the Golah. From the Cyrus Cylinder we know[58] that Cyrus favored the restoration of sanctuaries despoiled by Nabonidus in Babylonia.[59] So, when the construction of the Jerusalem Temple ruffled some feathers in the Persian administration at Mizpah (where people had been quite content with the nearby sanctuary of Bethel, presumably), it was a good decision to produce the edict that Cyrus would probably have issued had he had time to think about the Temple of Jerusalem.[60] Things must

---

54. The source of this passage, Ezra 1:1–11, still indicates between the lines that it was a minority which returned, dependent on the financial support of the majority that stayed where they were.

55. Ezra 1:4, 6, 9–11; 2:69 = Neh 7:70; Ezra 8:25–30, 33–34; and cf. Galling 1964.

56. Timm 1995: 276–88.

57. The cuneiform document concerning the delivery of sheep to Harran, found in Edomite Ṭawīlān, must also (like the Neirab tablets) have been brought back by returning Edomites from the vicinity of Harran, for the delivery of a flock of sheep at a distance of more than 500 km (from Ṭawīlān near Petra to Harran) does not make the slightest sense; see for the tablet Weippert 1987: 97–105, 102. Bienkowski (2001: 206), dating the cuneiform contract from Ṭawīlān as late as 423 misses the pertinence of this piece of evidence.

58. As the Aramaic version of Darius's Bisitun inscription found at Elephantine demonstrates, the Achaemenids (as the Assyrians before them) made sure that their wonderful propaganda was not confined to rocks or archives in scripts that hardly anybody could read but were distributed in Aramaic copies for the moral fortification of their scribes— and to the remotest spots of Achaemenid Egypt. For the Assyrians' adoption of the same practice, there is, for the time being, only iconographic evidence: the Great King dictating the record of his deeds to two scribes, the one writing on clay (ergo, in cuneiform) and the other on leather or papyrus (ergo, in Aramaic).

59. NB: only in Babylonia, and only to counteract the "misdeeds" of vilified Nabonidus; for the texts, see now Schaudig 2001.

60. For the view that the Aramaic correspondence in Ezra 4–6 was heavily edited (to reflect Nehemiah's favorite enemies), see Grabbe, in this volume, pp. 531–570.

have changed, however, with the arrival of Nehemiah in 445. From 445 onward, but not before, one might call Yehud together with the *bîrtā* of Jerusalem "a Persian colony."[61] Both the relocation of the seat of administration from Mizpah to Jerusalem[62] and the rebuilding of the walls of Jerusalem were acts that only the central administration could command. In addition, Jerusalem was rebuilt as a royal *bîrtā* (Heb. *bîrâ*) 'fortress', very much like Elephantine.[63] It is not inconceivable that the Persians thought of re-deporting some of the Babylonian deportees back to Jerusalem. Evidently, this did not meet with much enthusiasm, so Nehemiah was restricted to local ends and means, and the walls of Jerusalem, rebuilt by him as close to their Manassean splendor as he could manage, remained largely empty for 200 more years. A lack of returnees from Babylonia, however, might have partially been compensated for by emigrants from Moab (Ezra 2:6; Neh 7:11[64])—or Transjordan in general— and Idumea (Ezra 2:59; Neh 7:61[65]).

Persian military interest in the redevelopment of Jerusalem ca. 450 after unrest in the coastal regions is highly conceivable because of the strategic position of Jerusalem, which is often overlooked. Jerusalem not only controls one of the main east–west connections between the two sides of the Jordan,[66] it also provides a flanking position from which the southern coastal plain can be controlled, or, at least, be harassed by light troops until (imperial) military arrives. This thought must have been predominant in Sennacherib's mind in 701, when

---

61. Berquist 1995: 10 with n. 45.

62. Neh 3:7; cf. Blenkinsopp 1998 and translate: "Mizpah of the seat of the official (Gunneweg 1987: 65) of Transeuphratene." Cf. Williamson 1985: 197; Klein 1999: 768. The genitival dependence on Mizpah is expressed by *l-*, for Mizpah, as a proper name, is considered definite.

63. Neh 2:8; 7:2; and cf. Edelman, in this volume, pp. 207–246. According to Neh 11:6, 8f., and 14, the garrison of Jerusalem had 596 or 1,524 members—that is, soldiers with their wives, children, and slaves, indicating, that a *degel* (battalion) or, less likely, only a *centuria* (company) was stationed at Jerusalem, as opposed to two brigades, one Jewish and one Aramean, at Elephantine.

64. Could the reference to the "governor of Moab" as "father" of this group of returnees imply that he was asked by his Persian superiors to send Jews (or settlers) to Jerusalem? Under the impact of the "Babylonian" origin of all the clans listed in Ezra 2 / Nehemiah 7, Pahath-moab came to be treated as a personal name, which the term obviously is not; cf. Ezra 8:4; 10:30; Neh 10:14. Bidirectional migration across the Rift Valley is attested during the Persian Period by the book of Ruth.

65. Compare for the localities Tel-melah, Tel-harsha, Cherub, Addan (Addon, Neh 7:61) and Immer, which are usually supposed to have been the abode of Babylonian exiles (but there is nothing specifically Babylonian in theses names), with the following toponyms from the Negev: Tell el-Milḥ / Tel Malḥata, Jebel el-Ḥirthe (Musil 1907: 249; 1908: 177); Jebel el-Khrāshe (Musil 1907: 176); and for Cherub either al-Krèm (Musil 1908: 192) or Umm al-Kharrūba (with ⟨k⟩ for Arabic /ḫ/ ≠ Hebrew/Aramaic /ḥ/). *Immer* is Aramaic for 'sheep' and fits any steppe environment. See for Tel-melah also the toponym *mlḥt* in the Idumean ostracon 108:3 (Ephʿal and Naveh 1996: 58), which is not necessarily to be sought in the immediate vicinity of Maqqedah.

66. Cf. Keel 2000: 7–14.

he mustered the cooperation of the beaten enemy, as Napoleon did with the Prussian and Austrian armies for his Russian campaign.[67] The same thought forced Allenby in 1917 first to fight off the Turkish VIII Army at Jerusalem after the third battle of Gaza before he could take up the VII Army again at Megiddo. The mountains of Judea form a natural fortress that can only be attacked from the plain with great difficulty, as Allenby experienced when he had to fight the first battle for Jerusalem without his heavy or field artillery and without armored cars.[68]

Evidence for the functioning of the Bethel Temple throughout the sixth century is amply provided by the Bible.[69] The pilgrims of Jer 41:4f. could not have been on their way to the Jerusalem Temple,[70] because it was destroyed and nobody seems to have lived in the city's ruins[71] prior to the first returnees.[72] Jer 48:13 refers to Israel's god by use of the name "Bethel" (a polemic against Gen 35:7,[73] insofar as Bethel is here relegated to Israel's past). As the theonyms Ishim-Bethel and ʿAnat-Bethel show, as well as anthroponyms such as Bethel-natan/Ḥerem-natan, Bethel-shezib/Ḥeremshezib, Bethel-nuri, Bethel-raʿi from Elephantine show, "Bethel" was another designation for Yhwh for sixth–fifth-century Judeans (ʿAnat-Bethel TAD C3.15:128 = Anat-Yaho TAD B7. 3:3[74]) or, more specifically, the deified sanctuary[75] itself. Ezek 33:25

67. Cf. Knauf 2003a: 141–49.

68. Cf. Bruce 2003: 154–64. The conquest of Jerusalem was not just a matter of prestige, and Wavell's evaluation, "the occupation of Jerusalem itself had no special strategical importance" (Bruce 2003: 165), is belied by the facts on the ground as they presented themselves in December 1917 (2003: 165f.).

69. I have no qualms about using data retrieved from the Bible as long as they are not under suspicion of being construed according to the agenda of the various biblical authors.

70. Blenkinsopp 1998: 25–43.

71. Lipschits 2003: 332f.

72. Addressed by Haggai as *haʿam hazzeh*, 2:1 (which is not identical with the ʿam ha-ʾaretz, Hag 2:4, as shown by L. S. Fried, in this volume, pp. 123–145 and differentiated from those who had stayed, notably in the Benjamin region). The application of that expression to the Samaritans as by, for example, Rudolph (1976: 49f.) is baseless; cf. Meyers and Meyers 1987: 57 (but the identification of this ʿam/goy with the temple-building community [thus Ackroyd 1975: 167f.; Smith 1984: 161] does not hold water either). So is the assumption of an exilic Jerusalem cult of lamentations based on an ahistorical reading of Lamentations? See for the date of these texts: Kaiser 1992. Only Lamentations 5* (minus the Zion- and Golah-theology) might be exilic and could easily have been composed at Bethel.

73. See §3.1 and n. 156 below.

74. For references, see Porten and Yardeni 1986–99. The vocalization of the divine name as Yaho is evidenced by the orthographic variants יהו (19 attestations) and יהה (11 attestations) at Elephantine.

75. A deity "Bethel" did not exist, nor was it either Phoenician or Aramaic: the elements -*natan* and -*nuri* in personal names with the theophoric element "Bethel" are, in a

criticizes those left behind for their polytheistic and iconic cult. The cult of Elephantine, deriving from sixth-century Bethel as already argued, was both.[76] In Zech 7:2–3, Bethel asks Jerusalem for a priestly ruling, dated to 4 IX Darius 4 = Dec. 12, 518, while the Second Temple (of Jerusalem) is under construction.[77]

The question of the Bethel Temple's destruction or abandonment cannot be answered, for the time being, with any precision; it might have happened sooner, or later after the inauguration of the Second Jerusalem Temple in Adar 515, violently,[78] or by consent. The archeology

---

fifth-century context, more Canaanite than Aramaic, and the persons who swear by Ḥerem-Bethel in TAD B7.2:7, and by Ḥerem and Anat-Yaho in TAD B7.3:3 are indisputably Jewish. As the interchange of Yaho/Bethel, Bethel/Ḥerem/Ishim (Ishim-Bethel = 'the Name of/at Bethel') demonstrates, the locale of the divine presence, be it the temple, the altar, or the *maṣṣebâ* (Greco-Phoenician *bethylos*) was deified in turn. "Bethel" thus served as a theophoric *passe-partout* and represented different deities for different people, unless they had (as the Jews of Elephantine probably did) a specific sanctuary in mind. The Babylonian sanctuary of Esangila was still revered as a deity by the people of Taima in the fifth–fourth century (*sngl*' KAI 228.16). American families who want to stress their Bavarian or Polish descent might call a daughter Maria Altotting or Maria Czenstochowa in a similar vein.

76. The most likely purpose of the 126 shekels collected for Yaho, the 120 shekels for ʿAnat-Bethel, and the 70 shekels for Ishim-Bethel (TAD C3.15) was the reproduction of the divine statues of a male head of the pantheon, his slightly smaller wife, and their considerably smaller son, lost in the pogrom and mentioned in the correspondence with Jerusalem (TAD A4.7 and 8) under "other things" pillaged, the Jews of Elephantine being well aware that Jerusalem was aniconic.

77. Cf. Pfeiffer 1999: 81; it is syntactically and semantically impossible to see in "Bethel" anything but the subject of the sentence (Rudolph 1976: 137) or to construe "Bethel-shar-ezer" as a personal name (1976: 138). Cf. also Hoffman 2003: 200–202 pace Blenkinsopp 2003: 100f. The little story, composed after 515 (because of the "seventy years," v. 5; cf. n. 91), shows Bethel trying to come to terms with Jerusalem and being rebuked.

78. It is by no means impossible that a fanatic mob enacted the fantasy of 2 Kgs 23:15–20 sometime between 515 and 445, and it is easily conceivable that at the core of the Aramaic correspondence in Ezra 4–6, in its present state heavily edited if not outright fictitious (see Grabbe, in this volume, pp. 531–570), lay a conflict between Mizpah/Bethel and Jerusalem, brought before the higher echelons of the Persian administration. It is equally possible that the rebuilders of the walls of Jerusalem in 445/44 had to have "one hand at work and one hand at the sword" to defend themselves, not against the Samarians, Ashdodites, and Qedarites, but against disaffected Benjaminites, who resented the relocation of the province's capital from Mizpah to Bethel. This, then, was a reenacting, by the shift of neighbors to enemies, the externalization of internal conflicts that was prefigured by the Deuteronomist's denunciation of Israel's and Judah's preexilic religious practices as "Canaanite"; on this aspect of Israel's religious history and biblical theology, see Keel 2001: 245–61; 1995: 95–113; Uehlinger 1999: 546–78; 2000: 173–98; Knauf 2001a: 41–44; Levenson 1985: 242–60.

of Bethel is nonexistent; its archaeology a mess.[79] There was a destruction, usually dated to the end of the sixth century,[80] but nobody can say whether or not it was humanly induced. Although the excavator claims, "Somewhere between 553 and 521 B.C. Bethel was completely destroyed,"[81] there are no top-plans, locus-lists, locus-descriptions, or sections to allow the reader to check whether this destruction was indeed encountered in all excavated areas. The excavator's evaluation has to be taken with more than one pinch of salt; he postulates the destruction or abandonment of Bethel in the beginning of the Assyrian Period on the basis of a "pottery gap" that is absent from the published pottery.[82] The pottery from the "sixth-century destruction layer," which is clearly sub-Iron IIC in nature, is dated according to the observation that "the lack of characteristic Persian Period forms means that we cannot date the destruction of Bethel beyond the end of the sixth century B.C."[83] Unfortunately (for the pertinence of this conclusion), Iron IIC pottery has turned out to cover the Persian Period as well (with few, if any, new "Persian" forms) in the Jordan Valley (Tell el-Mazar),[84] Eilat

---

79. The archaeology of Bethel/Beitin is thoroughly misrepresented by Albright and Kelso; cf. Dever 1992: 651–52; there may have been a (partial) destruction in the second half of the sixth century (or 50–100 years later), but there is also evidence for continuity of occupation through the Persian and into the Hellenistic Period (with a possible gap in the fourth century); cf. Lipschits 1999: 171f. with nn. 30 and 31 (the interpretation of the evidence is mine). A settlement at Bethel is presupposed by Ezra 2:28; Neh 7:31; 11:31 (ca. 450/400 B.C.E., based on the demography [cf. n. 46]). The discrepancy between the two lists (223 or 113 inhabitants?) may just indicate when the town and sanctuary of Bethel was visited by a catastrophe, without being completely annihilated.

80. Lipschits 1999; 2003.

81. Kelso 1993: 192–94; 1968: 37 §150. For the cavalier manner in which old style "biblical" archaeology jumped to conclusions whenever the finds seemed to fit the biblical narrative, see, for example, A. Biran's interpretation of a thin ash layer preceding the Iron I resettlement of Tel Dan (resulting from burning the macchia that had grown all over the place during a century or so of abandonment) as a "massive conflagration" testifying to the Danites' conquest of Canaanite Laish.

82. Plate 79.4 shows a clear case of an Assyrian bottle, which may have come to the place or been produced there between the late eighth through the fifth centuries. Sequences of local household ware cannot (and could not in the times of Albright either) be dated with a precision that would make a gap of ca. 50 years visible.

83. L. A. Sinclair in Kelso 1968: 75.

84. Mazar I, dated by Yassine to the fourth century (too early), already has Hellenistic pottery (Yassine 1983: pl. 110:1–5); Mazar II, fifth (and early fourth) century has largely pottery that survey-archeologists would regard as representative for Iron IIC, with the exception of a lamp (pl. 110:9). Cf. Yassine 1983: 495–513, and for the epigraphic evidence, Knauf 1999a: 31–34.

(Tell el-Kheleifeh),[85] Buṣeyra and Ṭawīlān,[86] the Feinan region[87] (Edom), Rujm el-Malfuf North, Khirbet el-Ḥajjār[88] (Amon), and Akh-ziv[89] (Phoenicia). Even more unfortunately for Kelso et al. Persian pot-tery does show up on the plates of the Bethel excavation report but is unrecognized and classified as "Iron II";[90] stratigraphically, it would then predate the "sixth-century destruction," if there were any stratig-raphy in the Bethel excavations. The report is largely useless; as far as the published evidence goes (mostly in the form of pottery drawings), no gap or man-made destruction is discernible at Bethel between the eighth and the third centuries. A partial (?) destruction, if it happened at all, might have occurred between the second half of the sixth century and the first half of the fifth century without interrupting the continu-ity of occupation.

The history of Bethel (and Jerusalem) in the sixth and fifth centuries may be summarized as follows:

586–515   Jerusalem is destroyed; Mizpah is the seat of the administration, and Bethel the cultic and cultural center of Yehud.

515–445   The Temple of Jerusalem is reinaugurated;[91] the administration remains at Mizpah. The Temple at Bethel is attested for the last time in 518/7 (Zech 7:2).

445/4   Yehud's seat of administration relocates to Jerusalem. It stands to reason that the Temple of Bethel has no more

---

85. Cf. Bienkowski 2001: 210 and, for the epigraphic evidence from Eilat reaching down as far as the fourth/third centuries, Knauf 1990a: 201–17.

86. Bienkowski 2001: 206; for the date of the cuneiform contract from Tawīlān, how-ever, see n. 57.

87. In the Feinan area, at Khirbet el-Ghuweibeh, a smelting site was dated to the fourth/third centuries without any pottery postdating the Edomite Iron IIC ware; for the C14 dates, see Hauptmann 2000.

88. Cf. Sauer 1986: 18; 1982: 82.

89. At Akhziv, pottery dated no later than the sixth century is associated with terra-cotta figurines from the fifth century: Akhziv Cemeteries figs. 7.13 (certainly), 7.5, 7.12, and 7.23 (probably) and inscriptions (fig. app. 1.6; possibly fifth century) in Dayagi-Mendels 2002.

90. Kelso 1968: pl. 63.25 is a mortarium (the jug and bowl pl. 79.3 and 5 are possibly Persian; cf. also above, n. 82). In the north (and in coastal Palestine), this type has a lifespan of ca. 650–440; cf. Lehmann 1996; note, however, that the Assyrian carinated bowl dies out there after 580, which is attested, in the southern Palestinian periphery, well into the fourth century (cf. n. 84). The "sixth-century" assemblage from Bethel would date in the north to ca. 650–580 and may easily belong to 540–440 in the south and the peripheral mountains.

91. Following the traditional (biblical) chronology; it may or may not be significant that from Ab 9, 586 to Adar 3, 515, 70 years passed (Fried 2003: 52).

official backing and ceases to function, if this did not already happen sometime before.

2. Language:
From Judean Hebrew to Biblical and Mishnaic Hebrew

Recent research has refined the perception of the Hebrew language's history and dialectology to a degree that surpasses my earlier attempts.[92] Biblical Hebrew (BH) is broken down into Archaic Hebrew (AH), Classical Hebrew (CH), and Late Biblical Hebrew (LBH).[93] Judean Hebrew (JH, of the late eighth through sixth centuries), which has a clear orthographical, morphological, and syntactical profile, contrasts with Israelite Hebrew (IH), which remains more diffuse; and recently, Transitional Classic Hebrew (TCH) together with informal, versus elaborate/cultured, Spoken Hebrew have entered the scene.[94] There is, furthermore, sufficient reason to assume that Mishnaic Hebrew (MH) was the spoken language of Yehud as early as the fifth or even the sixth century.[95] The scholars and scribes at Bethel and Jerusalem in the Neo-Babylonian and Persian Periods must have been trilingual: in addition to Aramaic, the language of the imperial administration, and their own spoken, early MH, they mastered BH. It was with BH that they edited the Torah and large parts of the Prophets and with which they creatively wrote, in the form of LBH.

It is not possible, however, simply to postulate "the Exile" as the watershed between BH and LBH.[96] Apart from the "Exile's," or better, the sixth century's rather complex nature in regard to Hebrew language(s) and literature (as is argued in this essay), BH as evidenced by the Torah in its present orthographic state was in itself a creation of Jerusalem

---

92. The following section reformulates some points in Knauf 1990b: 11–23, and modifies others.

93. For the tripartite division of BH, *in nuce*, see Blau 1998a: 12–14.

94. Cf. Polak 1998: 59–105; 2001: 53–95; and Polak, in this volume, pp. 589–628.

95. The best argument for this conclusion is the influence of contemporary spoken Hebrew on LBH, especially in cases where the deviation from BH cannot be explained by way of the Aramaic adstrate, as, for example, in the case of *še-* for *ʾăšer*; cf. Kutscher 1982: 116, 118. The same adstrate is operative in Qumran Hebrew; cf. Bar Asher 2000: 12–19; Blau 2000: 20–25; Hurvitz 2000b: 110–14; pace Qimron 2000: 232–44. The differences between the language of the Mishnah and the Copper Scroll, listed by Qimron (pp. 233–35), or dialectical traits in MH (perhaps better be called "Middle Hebrew" to prevent an overly literal application of the term) as, perhaps, deviations in the MH of Lod and Jerusalem (pp. 235–36) do not make QH a language of its own. Prior to the Bar Kochba letters, MH is attested epigraphically at the tomb of the Benei Ḥezir in Jerusalem, probably for the first century (B.C.E.) and certainly no later than 70 C.E.; cf. Barag 2003: 92–94.

96. Thus Hurvitz 2000a: 143–60; 1997: 301–15; and Polak 1998.

after 520. At Bethel in the sixth century, the scribes still wrote JH, as will be shown. The basic difference between JH and BH is orthographic:

	JH	BH
ms noun with 3 ms suffix	אהלה	אהלו
mp noun with 3 ms suffix	אהלו	אהליו

This orthography is not attested in Judea or anywhere else prior to the fifth century[97] and is in this writer's opinion sufficient reason to date the creation of this literary dialect (or at least, the fixation of its orthography) to the Persian Period. On the other hand, there can be no doubt that BH is, in terms of syntax and semantics, a prolongation or rather, a preservation,[98] of preexilic JH. In addition, the editors of the Torah and the Prophets in Acheamenid Judah had a rather large collection of literature from eighth- through sixth-century Judah at their disposal that was written, as can be discerned by some *kethiv*s and *qere*s and other bonuses of textual transmission,[99] in JH.

A chronological reevaluation of the detailed statistics provided by Polak leads to ca. 400, rather than the "Exile," as being the separator between BH and LBH. Polak's sample for LBH is based on texts deriving from the fourth through second centuries, with only one exception.[100] His "transitional class," dated by Polak to the seventh/sixth centuries, contains a text, Joshua 22, that could hardly have been written before the end of the fifth century.[101] TH should then be dated be-

---

97. Pace Cross 2003: 18*–24*, whose "Type 2" orthography (p. 18*) is simply not attested except for first and second person.

98. For differences between the language of the texts that the redactors received and the literary language that they mastered, see also Schüle 2000: 14–25; 1997: 115–25 (note, however, that in Schüle's idiosyncratic terminology, inherited from his teacher, Beyer, the following equations operate: *althebräisch* = IH, JH, CH and TCH; *mittelhebräisch* = LBH; and *neuhebräisch* = MH. Proclaiming the absence of *Althebräisch*, as Schüle does, on the basis of the epigraphic evidence, misses the categorical distinction between narrative and discursive texts or, in the categories of F. Polak, between CH and TCH.

99. That pre-Persian Judean literature was written in Judean Hebrew, not Biblical Hebrew, is evidenced by a number of scribal mistakes or deviations: אהלה Gen 9:21; 12:8; 13:3; 35:21 for אהלו (inconsistently marked *kethiv* in L, and with deviations in this respect, between L and A), הגוי לא / לו, Isa 9:2 < הגילה.

100. Polak 1998: 69; in Polak's judgment, only Job 1:1–3:1; 42:7–17 belongs to the fifth century, whereas the samples from Ezra and Nehemiah date to the late fourth century (see above, n. 13, and below, n. 201), Chronicles and Esther probably to the third century, and the Hebrew Daniel definitely from the second century.

101. Not only style and language but also the theological program of Joshua 22 show the confluence of the P and the D traditions, which place the text at the very end of the

tween the seventh and fifth centuries and most likely overlaps with both BH and LBH. That the Mesha stele is more "written" than the older strata of the Abrahamic cycle[102] is without chronological bearings: this observation indicates that the Abrahamic texts were oral literature indeed, until put into writing in Bethel during the course of the sixth century.[103] The demise of the Judean royal chancellery in 586 (the scribes of which used JH) should not be overestimated:[104] a temple and its schools continued to function, initially in Bethel and later in Jerusalem, and the Babylonian general neglect of southern Syria suggests that the impact of the new language of administration,[105] Aramaic, was rather light during the sixth century. It is only in the course of the late sixth and fifth centuries that Aramaic bureaucracy must have intensified, and its impact on the tradition of scribal Hebrew was, for sure, initially neither sweeping nor prominent. Again, 400 becomes a more likely date for the BH/LBH divide than 586.

Diachronically, one can be sure that a text written in LBH does not antedate the fifth century; on the other hand, one cannot be sure that a text in BH predates it. How "Classical" or Torah-like or, on the other side, how "vernacular" or MH-like an author wanted to write was a matter of choice, not ability. Job (fifth century B.C.E.)[106] to some extent and Qohelet and Canticles (third century B.C.E.) to a very large extent indicate their difference from (not: denial of) traditional thought by the degree of their deviation from the classical language. These authors did not want to write the Torah but commentaries about some aspects of, or theological problems in, the Torah. An early-fourth-century text such as Joshua (final redaction), on the other hand, intentionally presenting itself as a supplement to the Torah (or the sixth book of the Pentateuch), uses the Classical language.[107]

Torah/Pentateuch redaction; in addition, Joshua 22 may form the biblical, or Jerusalemite, version of the rescript to the petition of the Jews in Elephantine concerning the rebuilding of their temple (cf. Knauf 2002b).

102. Polak 1998: 105. I can agree with Polak's concluding remarks with slight modifications: "Classical biblical narrative was transmitted by the redactors of the seventh *through fifth* (P: and sixth) centuries, but it was *coined* (P: formulated) much earlier."

103. See §3.2 and n. 163 below.

104. As does Polak 1998: 62f.

105. Which was, on the other hand, not so new for the scribes, having been the language of diplomacy and international relations since the seventh century, if not the end of the eighth centuries.

106. For Job (with the exception of chaps. 32–37) as a fifth-century text, see Knauf 1988: 65–83.

107. See for Joshua preliminarily Knauf 2000c: 395f.

BH developed into LBH under the influence of both Aramaic and MH; the construction *beto shel hammelek* parallels Aramaic *bayteh di malka*, but *shel < she l-* has an unquestionable Canaanite pedigree.[108] It is equally evident that spoken JH became MH under the impact of Aramaic and IH; MH, in other words, has strong Northern roots in addition to Southern ones.

The main problem of Israelite Hebrew is its bad attestation and, secondarily, that more than one language was spoken in the Kingdom of Israel. Especially the north (Galilee) and the east (Gilead) seem to have come under Aramaic influence at a very early point in time.[109] The linguistic differences between the Gezer calendar (late tenth/early ninth century) and the Samaria ostraca (eighth century)[110] could be due to their locale as well as temporal distance. The use of q to express etymological /ź/ (conventionally transcribed ḍ) is restricted to Gilead in the eighth century[111] but seems to have been *en courant* in ninth-century Samaria as well.[112] The situation would improve if an Israelite royal inscription were found that contained more than the relative particle אשר,[113] or if one could confidently reassert Segert's proposal that the

---

108. Kutscher 1982: 125 notes the parallel development from *ʾaš* to *še-* in Phoenician-Punic.

109. Pre-hellenistic inscriptions from Galilee (Dan, Hazor, Kabul, et-Tell, Kinneret, seventh/sixth-century Megiddo and Yoqneam) are predominantly Phoenician or Aramaic. Only from the eighth century B.C.E. are there Hebrew (Israelite) inscriptions and seals, documenting the (re-)conquest of Galilee by Jeroboam II. Because conquerors in premodern times did not, as a rule, impose their languages on the conquered, it is hardly thinkable that Hazael set up an elaborate display inscription at Dan in Damascene Aramaic without a significant part of the local elite's being able to read it. The Galilean language mix is well attested in the tribal saying about Naphtali in Gen 49:21, which is at least half Aramaic: the free-roaming hind is supposed to produce "kids of beauty," not "good words" (cf. Speiser 1964: 367).

110. Gezer: 3ms suff. -∅; mp -*m*; etymological /ź/ and relative particle not attested; — Samaria: 3ms suff. not attested, mp -*m* (Aḥituv 1992: 202 = Renz and Röllig 1995: 136–39), צ for /ź/ (*rāḥūṣ*), relative particle *ʾšr*. The Israelite texts from Kuntillet ʿAjrud seem to reflect the dialect of eighth-century Samaria, as is to be expected by people who invoke Yhwh of Shomron: suff. 3ms -*h*; mp -*m* (read *yāmīm* for *yōmām*, Aḥituv 1992: 159; the text on p. 160 is probably Phoenician); /ź/ not attested; relative particle *ʾšr* (Aḥituv 1992: 156).

111. Tell Deir ʿAlla (TDA) *qrn* = * źōrrīn* 'foes'; *qqn* = *qōźīn* 'judges'.

112. Cf. קלעים for צלעים, 1 Kgs 6:34; and for the Israelite impact on the architecture of Jerusalem in the ninth century, I. Finkelstein 2001: 105–15; on ninth-century Judean literature, Knauf 2002d. This "Israelitism" was already noted by C. Rabin (1979: 73 with n. 11, 294 with n. 12). In the archaic Israelite Song of Deborah, which might well have been committed to writing in the course of the ninth century, there are, of course, the cases of מצקה (explained as מחצה) and the pseudocorrection מחקקים (for מחצצים).

113. Renz and Röllig 1995: 1.135 (Sam [8]:14) with the curious translation ʿ. . . der . . .ʾ (according to the common and most sensible restoration of the text, [*mṣbt*] *ʾšr* [*nṣb* PN *bn* PN *mlk yśrʾl*], one would expect ʿ. . . die . . .ʾ).

language of the Mesha stele is indeed Israelite.[114] Some corollary evidence that this might indeed be the case, or, at least, that Mesha's Moabite was at least deeply influenced by IH, has recently come forth in the form of more Moabite inscriptions: the Heshbon ostraca[115] and the incense burner of Mudayyineh[116] This distribution might help to establish the two Mesha-features, the masculine plural in -*īn* and the relative particle *'šr* as elements of ninth-century Israelite Hebrew.[117] Both are attested in Israelite inscriptions or in biblical texts of presumably Northern origin.[118]

	Mesha	Mudayyineh	Heshbon
mp noun ending	*īn*	not attested	*îm*
relative particle	*'šr*	*'š*	*'š*

The complexity of IH is further elucidated by the fact that, in addition to *'šr* (attested prior to 720), IH also had the relative exponent *š-*, first attested in the seventh century[119] but presumably much earlier in the spoken IH of at least some regions. The relative particle is the most

---

114. Segert 1961: 255–57. The export of Israel's standard language to a vassal of Omride Israel, however, could well have happened without the vehicle of Israelite prisoners of war, who theoretically taught the Moabites how to write.

115. That Heshbon was a Moabite not an Ammonite town and that its local language should, therefore, be classified as Moabite has been pointed out by Hübner 1988: 68–73 (whose point was weakened by his not discussing the linguistic problems involved in that reclassification, notably vis-à-vis the Mesha inscription; on Heshbon's territorial affiliation, see also Knauf 1992: 124–28). One cannot, as Aḥituv (1992: 228) does, argue against Hübner on paleographical grounds, for paleography is quite irrelevant for the linguistic classification.

116. Dion and Daviau 2000: 1–13. Their reading and translation is not without problems. I propose *mqṭr 'š 'š 'lšm' lnsk bt 'wt* 'Incense stand that Elshamaʿ made for the prince/idol of Bet Awit'.

117. For the evidence on eighth-century Israelite, see above, n. 110. In this case it seems that Omrides and Nimsides preferred different dialects as the bases for their written languages.

118. This constellation renders Young's conclusion, that the Israelites wrote "Standard Hebrew," on the sole basis of *'šr*, premature; cf. Young 1995: 67.

119. Cf. Weippert 1999: 195 with n. 33 (Paris BN N3316), another piece of evidence that Young still misclassifies (1995: 67 with n. 22). In the case of שקמתי, Judg 5:7, I maintain the view that we are dealing with *šapʿel* (and not the only ones in this text, cf. שריד = **šōrīd* Judg 5:13). There is no reason to postulate a perfective in this context ('Until you would have stood up, Deborah'—how very undramatic!), because the simple past is expressed, after *ʿd 'šr* in narrative contexts, by *yiqṭol l* in BH (cf. Ruth 1:13), whereas the *qaṭal* in this position expresses the accomplished future (Gen 28:15; Num 32:17; Isa 6:11) or a lasting state resulting from the action (Exod 32:20 = Deut 9:21; Josh 3:17; 8:26; Judg 4:24; 2 Sam 17:13; 1 Kgs 10:7 = 2 Chr 9:6, "until I have entered—and now am—here"; 1 Kgs 17:7; 2 Kgs 17:20, 23; 21:16; Ezek 34:21).

striking IH trait in MH; however, it is joined by quite a few more such traits,[120] even though their identification is somewhat more difficult and less indisputable than sometimes thought.[121] As already discussed, various Israelite dialects (for example, Gileadite) feature isoglosses with Aramaic,[122] and parallel developments such as the one leading to *qaṭal* for past, *qoṭel* for present/future, and *yiqṭol* for subjunctive (roughly the syntax of Qoheleth) must also be envisioned.[123] Whereas the loss or very restricted use[124] of the *Qal* passive and the *Pual* in MH are either influenced by Aramaic or constitute a parallel development, the MH *Nitpael* customizes the very Aramaic t-passive/reflexive with the very un-Aramaic prefix of the old *Nipal*.[125]

There can be little doubt about the fact that MH developed under the impact of IH, and recalling the demography of sixth- and fifth-century Judah, there can be less doubt about how IH came to change JH into (early) MH: by the incorporation of Benjamin into Judah, which accounted for 40% of the Judean population in the late seventh and fifth centuries and for more than 50% in the sixth century.

Yehud's demography thus ends an amusing history of errors regarding the origin(s) of MH. It is outright impossible that MH emerged from

---

120. Gordon 1955: 85–88; Rabin 1979: 73 with n. 12 (p. 294); Gevirtz 1986: 25–29; Rendsburg (1991a: 241–51) lists 12 features linking northern Canaanite with MH, though not all are wholly convincing, and adds another one in Rendsburg 2000: 83–88. The relevant features are, in my view: (1) relative *š-* (Judg 6:17; 7:12; and 8:26 are, however, late); (2) *zōh* for *zō't*: Hos 7:16; 2 Kg 6:19; (3) *'ellū* for *'ellēh*; cf. Plautus. *Poen.: ily*; (4) nomen actionis *qĕṭilāh*: Judg 5:16; 14:12, 19; 1 Sam 13:21; 1 Kgs 19:8; (5) double plural of the type *rā'šê šānîm*, Gen 49:23; Judg 5:6, 10; (6) *pō'ēl* for *'ōśēh*: Hos 7:10; (7) *hyh* + ptc. for "past continuous," 2 Sam 3:6, 17; 1 Kgs 22:35; 2 Kgs 6:8; (8) pl. ימות, Deut 32:7; (9) *zh h'm* for *h'm hzh*.

121. Rendsburg seems to be overconfident that a text with a Northern subject was also written by (Northern) Israelites. If LBH is BH under the influence of MH, and if MH emerged under the impact of IH, then an IH feature in a biblical text implies no more (at least not without further arguments) than that it is Northern, or late, or both. See also the criticism of Young 1995: 63–70, who aptly notes that *š-* is put into the mouth of an Aramean king in 2 Kgs 6:11, probably in order to make his speech more "foreign."

122. Like the mp in *-în*; cf. מדין, Judg 5:10; עין, Mic 3:12 (and see below, §3.2, pp. 322–326); and TDA (above, n. 111). *Ṣîdōnîn*, 1 Kgs 11:33 may be trying to imitate Northern language in a Southern text (for "dialect" used as a literary device, see Young 1995). Aramaic and/or Israelite influence on MH (and TCH and LBH) is a partially mute question; see, for example, *qāṭōl* for nomen agentis in Jeremiah and MH, cf. Rendsburg 1991b: 355 n. 30.

123. It would not have hurt his argument if Rendsburg (1991c: 1265–77) had also considered these. For a balanced view of Hebrew heritage and Aramaic influence in MH, see Kutscher 1982: 118–20; and also Rendsburg 1991a: 234.

124. Kutscher 1982: 127.

125. The passive *Hitpael*s in Mic 6:16, Prov 31:30, and Eccl 8:10 are not "Northern" (pace Rendsburg 1991a: 233) but late and presuppose *Nitpael*s in the spoken language of the authors.

Southern Judah (thus Blau[126]) or received its Northern features as early as in the period of the supposed "United Kingdom" (thus Rabin[127]) or emerged from the merging of Judeans and Israelites during the Exile (thus Gordon[128]). The hypothesis that it came from Galilee (Rendsburg[129]) is most unlikely. Prehellenistic inscriptions from Galilee are predominantly Phoenician or Aramaic. Only from the eighth century B.C.E. are there some Israelite inscriptions and seals, documenting the (re-)conquest of Galilee by Jeroboam II.[130] Because conquerors in premodern times did not, as a rule, impose their languages on the conquered,[131] it is hardly thinkable that Hazael set up an elaborate display inscription at Dan in Damascene Aramaic without a significant part of the local elite's being able to read it. The Galilean language mix is well attested in the tribal saying on Naphtali in Gen 49:21.[132] There are no signs of a massive Jewish presence in Galilee prior to Aristobul's conquest of the area: 1 Macc 5:14–23 attests to scattered Jewish settlements

---

126. J. Blau 1998a: 13: ". . . the dialect spoken by the authors and scribes was the precursor of RH, . . . perhaps spoken in southern Judaea."

127. Rabin 1979: 73 with n. 11 (p. 294). The assumption of a considerable impact of the "United Kingdom" on the emergence of "Classical Hebrew" is irreconcilable with the epigraphic evidence (cf. nn. 109 and 110, above); it is also irreconcilable with the actual extent and cultural power of this shortlived political entity; cf. Knauf 2001b; 2002d.

128. Gordon 1955: 85–88; for the fate of the Israelite deportees, who did no go into "exile" because they lost all connections with their homeland, and possibly happily so, see Dalley 1985: 31–48; Oded 2000: 91–103; Becking 2002: 153–66. Soldiers, officials, scribes, and other experts were deported; no "tribes" were "exiled," and those who still look for tribal descendants all over Asia may as well hunt goblins or leprechauns.

129. Rendsburg (1991a), whose reference to "the Galilean origin of the Mishnah itself" (p. 234) invalidates the wholly justified assumption that MH was the language spoken in Judah prior to 135 C.E., and why not in the region of Lod (which, like the environs of Bethel, had an Israelite past), as postulated by Qimron 2000? Kutscher (1982: 116) quite correctly states: "Other parts of the country, e.g., the Galilee . . . were probably monolingual, speaking only Aramaic"—and from the second century B.C.E. on perhaps also a little Greek, at least some of them.

130. Finkelstein 1999: 61; of the three names attested at et-Tell ("Bethsaida"), two are more Aramaic than anything else (*ʿqbʾ* and *mky*), one is Israelite (*zkryw*; pace Naʾaman 2002: 206)—the texts are no more precisely stratified than dating to pre-733 B.C.E.; cf. Finkelstein 2002: 126f. For the Persian Period, which is not covered by Renz and Röllig 1995, see Lemaire 1990: 63f.; Weippert 1999: 191–200. The epigraphic evidence is well corroborated by archaeology; cf. Faust 2000: 2–27.

131. The success of Latin in Spain, France, and Romania was due to the fact that these areas evidently were extremely fragmented linguistically. $n(n-1)/2 > n$ for $n > 3$; in a linguistic situation in which one needs three languages or more in order to communicate with one's neighbors, it is feasible to adopt a common language, even if this common language is not one in this particular environment (reducing the languages one has to master from ≥ 3 to 2). A hundred years from now, all Europe will be an English-speaking area.

132. Cf. above, n. 109 (and Speiser 1964: 367).

only.[133] It seems that Judaism was adopted by the inhabitants of Galilee with fervor, because it gave them an identity that allowed them to be different from their Arabic, Aramaic, and Phoenician neighbors.

After 597, or 586 at the latest, the old Judean south with Hebron was lost to the Edomites.[134] Between 630 and 620, the Israelite south, Benjamin, was joined to Judah and remained Judean throughout the Babylonian and Persian Periods. In the sixth century, more than 50% of the inhabitants of Yehud were descendants of speakers of (southern) Israelite Hebrew. BH/MH diglossia started at Bethel in the sixth century, when the scribes edited and wrote literature in JH,[135] whereas the local population spoke early MH.

*   *   *

That Bethel and not just Jerusalem played a decisive role in the early transmission of biblical literature may be reflected by some IH loanwords in BH. It is fairly certain that IH did not have the phoneme /ś/ but used /š/ instead. This feature is attested (a) by Shoshenq's transcription *šwkw* for Sokho; (b) by Shalmaneser's transcription *sirʾilayya* for "Israel(i)";[136] and (c) the pronunciation of Samaritan Hebrew.[137] By this phonological feature—/š/ in BH where /ś/ is expected—three Israelite loanwords can be identified.

(a) תשוקה 'desire'. This is a clear case, both on the basis of the cognates, which prove that the root is /śwq/,[138] and on the basis of the literary attestations: Gen 3:16; 4:7; Cant 7:10. The environment presupposed in Genesis 2–3 is an oasis.[139] The only major oasis that ever was

---

133. Pace Rendsburg (1991a: 235), who follows a later, problematic source, Josephus. Nor is his distinction of "Israelites" (who would have resented being called "Jewish") and Samaritans warranted. There was emigration from Persian-Period Yehud in all directions, for obvious economic reasons.

134. At least some Judeans persisted, as evidenced by the Beer-sheba, Arad, and Idumean ostraca (and by Neh 11:25–30 as well), necessitating the use of Aramaic as (one of) the spoken language(s) in this province, as attested by the Aramaization (besides Arabization) of the inherited stock of Edomite personal names.

135. As evidenced by the orthography in Gen 12:8;13:3; 35:21; and see above, n. 99 and below, §3.2 with n. 165.

136. Shoshenq's (Shishak's) Karnak List, #38; *sir-ʾi-la-a-a*: Shalmanesar's Monolith Inscription II 91f. It is unlikely that both did not transcribe the name as heard but transliterated its alphabetic form. For Assyrian ⟨s⟩ representing West Semitic /š/, see Fales 1978: 91–98; Knauf 1989b: 13–19.

137. Cf. Ben-Ḥayyim and Tal 2000: 36f.

138. Safaitic *taśawaqqa ʾilā* 'he longed for' (frequent), Mehri *śátwĕq*; cf. also Blau 1998b: 92 = 1977: 75.

139. See above, n. 11.

part of Israel is Jericho—a place that came, together with Bethel, from Israel/Samaria to Judah in the course of the seventh century. More or less like Joshua, the garden story migrated from Jericho, not to Jerusalem at first, but to Bethel, where it was continued by a Southern tradition, the origin myth of the Kenites, inscribing the Northern word *tĕšûqâ* into this Southern text.[140] In spite of desperate attempts to make Canticles a Northern rather than a LBH text[141] or a naïve reading of the book as a haphazard collection of love lyrics from different times and places, Canticles has turned out to be a sophisticated lyrical treatise on the nature, possibilities, and impossibilities of love[142] that deals with no less a question than "Paradise regained."[143]

(b) The word רעש 'to shake, tremble' (of heaven/sky and earth) and noun 'earthquake'. This case is less clear, for there is also *rˁš* in the sense of 'rumbling, rattling' attested in at least two preexilic texts, Isa 9:4; Nah 3:2; and, in Arabic, it has not only the corresponding root *rˁš* (leading to Semitic *rˁś*) but also *rˁs* (root *rˁš*).[144] Both problems can be addressed by means of the Syriac, which has *rˁas* 'to immerse a garment' (in water or dye) and *rˁaš* 'to smash, shatter'. I suggest linking 'rumbling, rattling' with this Aramaic cognate (root *rˁš*) and 'to shake,

---

140. It is not inconceivable, of course, that the garden was already linked to the Kenites in the traditions of Jericho. The merging of Northern and Southern traditions is, on the other hand, typical of the "story of the patriarchs" (Genesis 12–35*), which was composed, with a high degree of probability, at Bethel in the sixth century; see below, §3.2. A movement of traditions, rather than real persons, between Jericho and Bethel is also implied by Josh 2–8; 2 Kgs 2:1–4 (where Bethel is represented in a neutral, or even positive, manner); and 2 Kgs 2:23f. (which presents some inhabitants of Bethel rather negatively). N.B.: Bears are much more likely to have haunted the vicinity of Bethel in the Assyrian, Neo-Babylonian, and Persian Periods (when there was considerable reforestation in northern and central Israel) than under the Omrides; see for the reforestation, Knauf 2003b: 166f.

141. Notably Young 1993: 5. If LBH < MH < IH, as presented above and, it seems, widely agreed upon, the question "Northern or late?" needs extralinguistic evidence to be settled.

142. Keel 1986; Müller, Kaiser, and Loader 1992; 1976: 23–41; Heinevetter 1988; Sadgrove 1979: 245–48.

143. Landy 1987: 318: "More centrally, the Song is a reflection on the story of the Garden of Eden, using the same images of garden and tree, substituting for the traumatic dissociation of man and animals their metaphoric integration. Through it we glimpse, by the grace of poetry, the possibility of paradise." See also Baildam 1999: 178, 211; Tromp 1982.

144. J. Blau 1998b: 96 [79]: "Hebrew *rˁš* is matched not only by Arabic *rˁš*, but also by Arabic *rˁs* (which is, admittedly, less frequent)" (and not attested in Wehr and Cowan, wheras *rˁš* is): either dialect mixture in Arabic or contamination of two roots; cf. Syriac *raˁsā* 'submersion of a garment in the process of washing or dying' (root *rˁś*) and *rˁaš* 'to break' (root *rˁš*). I could not find the root in a Semitic language that has phonetically preserved /ś/.

tremble' with r‘as[145] (root r‘š). In Arabic, the two roots seem to have coalesced semantically (if ra‘asa is not simply a dialectal form). The older attestations are all Northern, as is probably the "theophany" tradition in itself: Judg 5:5; Ps 46:3; 68:8; 1 Kgs 19:11f. It does, however, show up in late preexilic Judean texts (Ps 60:2; 72:19)[146] and is found in the course of the sixth century both in Judah (i.e., at Bethel): Jer 4:24; 8:16; 10:10; 49:21; 50:46; 51:29; Ps 77:18; and in Babylonia: Ezek 26:10; 26:15; 27:28; 31:16; 37:7; 38:19–20. In the late preexilic Moses–Joshua narrative,[147] for which Bethel must have provided both the Moses and the Joshua traditions, צרד is used instead of רעש (Exod 19:18).[148] Amos 9:1 (and hence, the use of the "earthquake" in the superscription, Amos 1:1) is not a problem if the preexilic tradition of Amos was never transmitted to a temple, school, or library/archive other than Bethel.[149]

(c) אל שדי 'El Shaddai'. A clear example, again, if one accepts the most plausible etymology, 'The/a god (who protects us) from (the beasts) of the wild', in JH *’ēl śādēh.[150] All preexilic attestations are Northern: Gen 49:25; Ps 68:14. In P, the term became the name of God for Abraham's non-Judean descendants, possibly intentionally maintaining its non-Judean phonology. All other biblical references to El Shaddai, in my opinion, are dependent on, or at least later than, P.

The discussion of the three Israelite loanwords in BH suggest that Northern traditions entered the South—via Bethel—by the end of the seventh century. The impact of Bethel on Judean literature must by necessity have increased when its sanctuary, school, and library/archive were the only ones remaining and operating in Judah for most of the sixth century and possibly extending into the fifth century.

3. Literature:
Or, Bethel and Jerusalem—A Tale of Two Towns

The dualism of Bethel and Jerusalem as Judah's cultic and cultural centers can be traced in the Torah as well as in the Prophets. According

---

145. For the semantic development, see the use of *hpk* in Gen 19:25.
146. See Knauf 2000b for the date (600–598) of Ps 60:2. For the date of Ps 72:19, see Arneth 2000.
147. Schmid 1999; Knauf 2002c: 290–92.
148. Other terms for earthquake in JH: *mdd* (Hab 3:6); *nwṭ* (Ps 99:1); *rgz* (Josh 2:10, Job 6:9).
149. Cf. above, n. 12. The above stratification of the references implies that 2 Sam 22:8 = Ps 18:7; Isa 13:13; 14:16; 24:18; 29:6; Josh 2:10; 3:16; Nah 1:5; Hag 2:6–7, 21; Zech 14:5 are regarded as postexilic (together with some of the Jeremiah and Ezekiel references, which need not be discussed further in the present context).
150. Knauf 1999b: 749–53.

to §1 ("Demography and Archeology"), the drama can be expected to have evolved in 3 + 1 acts:[151]

a. ca. 650–586: Bethel (and its tradition) are incorporated into Judah. Bethel traditions (Jacob, Exodus) soon take precedence over Jerusalem traditions (David).

b. 586–ca. 520: Jerusalem is temporarily knocked out; the Jerusalem traditions either go to Babylonia—or to Bethel. Bethel is the only place within Judah where preexilic traditions are collected, preserved, and elaborated upon.

c. ca. 520–445: Jerusalem is reestablished as a cultural but not yet political center. The traditions that had been taken to Babylonia come back, revised and enlarged. The conflict between Bethel and Babylonia becomes a conflict between Jerusalem and Bethel. Finally, the sanctuary and school of Bethel is annihilated.

d. ca. 450–ca. 300: Reconciliation. The Bethel traditions are integrated into the "constitution of Yehud," the Torah, but can still be identified as a voice of its own in ca. 300 (Nehemiah 9).

How many and which traces did the rivalry between Jerusalem and Bethel leave in the text? This should now be elucidated in some detail.

3.1. Bethel's Ascendancy, 650–586

The Exodus tradition was already institutionalized at Bethel in the eighth century by Jeroboam II (rather than I).[152] In the late eighth or early seventh century, the Jacob cycle, the (first) book of Hosea, and the "Book of Saviors" (= Judges*), all of which deal with the problem of Israel under foreign rule, were added to the Exodus tradition.

In the Jacob tradition, as is universally acknowledged, an older stratum of the tradition has Jacob moving between Gilead (the home of the "easterners," *běnê qedem*), and Shechem (Gen 29:1; 31:25–33:20*). Geographically, this stage of the tradition presupposes an Israel as it was defined between Eshbaal and Jeroboam I. In the present story, the "easterners" are relocated to Harran, a feature that becomes credible in

---

151. The last act cannot be derived from the known history of the two towns; it is based on a historical reading of a number of biblical texts, for which see below, §3.4 (pp. 329–330).

152. For the historical presuppositions for this conclusion, see Knauf 2002d with n. 98. Bovid religious imagery has a firm place in the ninth through seventh centuries; cf. Keel and Uehlinger 1988: 144–46 (§89, figs. 167a–169b, Syrian imports); 291 (§170); Bernett and Keel 1998. It is mostly absent during the twelfth through tenth centuries (especially now that the bull from the "bull-site" has turned out to be a MB/LB leftover; cf. Finkelstein 1998: 94–98). For Jeroboam (II) and the Exodus, see also Blanco Wißmann 2001: 42–54.

the light of our knowledge of the fact that Sin of Harran was regarded by the Assyrians as the "lord of the west" and by Assyria's western population as the god whom they adopted to show that they were good subjects of the Assyrian king.[153] By sending Jacob right into the lion's den and having him prosper and succeed there, the author insinuates that Israel could well marry and trade, wheel and deal with the Assyrians and their other subjects, profit from it (by a kind of cunning collaboration), and still enjoy Yhwh's blessings on the road and, especially, in the land given to its tribal ancestor (but not necessarily in the form of a state).

Bethel appears prominently in this version of the Jacob story. It is at Bethel, at the height of the narrative crisis, that Yhwh reveals himself to Jacob as his tutelary deity. According to the older tradition, Jacob returns first to Shechem and pays his respects to El, the older head of the divine council[154] (Gen 33:18, 20). But here, Jacob is commanded to go to Bethel "and settle there" as his final destination. The "foreign gods," not just Laban's teraphim, but presumably also the pantheon of Shechem and other sanctuaries of the ex-state of Israel, have to be left behind, interred at Shechem (Gen 35:1–4). El of Shechem no longer counts;[155] the God of Jacob is the Yhwh of Genesis 28, now identified with the El of Bethel (35:7).[156] Finally, it is Jacob (not the Jeroboams or the Assyrian king) who founds Bethel's sanctuary (Gen 35:7).

There can be little doubt that the core of Hosea, chaps. 4–11, was composed at Bethel after 720. Later redactions notwithstanding, these eight chapters are a unified composition, using prophetic utterances from the period immediately preceding the fall of Israel but recording them for other purposes than antiquarian interests. The traditions are instead integrated into a single speech by Yhwh as a state's attorney, proving Israel's guilt and the justice of his own judgment, ending, however, on a positive note: there will be a future for Israel as Yhwh's people but not necessarily for a state of Israel (Hosea 11).

---

153. Keel 1994: 135–202; Knauf 1994: 160–63; Perlitt 1977 = 1994: 32–49; Staubli 2003: 65–89.

154. Indirectly presupposed in Genesis 28 insofar as Yhwh, as one of El's subordinates, *stands* at the top of the ladder, whereas El is enthroned, invisible to Jacob and most of the story's readers so far, at the back of his audience hall. The relevance of Yhwh's corporal position is well emphasized by Zenger (1999: 287), who misses the point, however, that at the end of Psalm 82 Yhwh has usurped the position of El.

155. Cf. Hos 12:1, which is, as rarely understood, critical of Judah.

156. This is the background for the polemic in Jer 48:13, which, therefore, belongs to one of the postexilic, Jerusalemite strata of the book.

Pre-Assyrian Bethel is addressed as "Beth-aven" (Hos 4:15;[157] 5:8; 10:5); the transition to post-state Bethel begins in 10:15 (and continues to 12:5; see below), where the town is addressed by its real name. The polemic against the golden bulls (and horses?) serves the quite utilitarian purpose that, if Yhwh himself has always been against this cult paraphernalia, there is no reason to replace them (the Assyrians probably took them away, as was their custom), nor is it necessary to postulate that Yhwh himself has decided to travel to Assyria.[158] In addition, the book of Hosea presupposes the Exodus tradition. It is unclear how many Israelites in the eighth and seventh centuries knew some or all of this tradition, but it is clear that the people in Bethel did.

The "Book of Saviors" (Judges*) is ideologically close to Hosea: there had been an "Israel" before the state,[159] and this "primordial Israel" had already been subject to periods of foreign occupation, none of which lasted forever. The message is: there will again be an Israel of free peasants on their own land but not necessarily again a state of Israel.[160]

Bethel appears in the Book of Saviors/Judges by relocating Deborah to a palm tree between Ramah and Bethel (Judg 4:5). She must have had a strong voice indeed if she managed to shout from there to Kedesh-Naphtali—and have Barak understand her message (Judg 4:6).

After 650, Judah was included among the addressees of the book of Hosea by the addition of the appendix, Hosea 12–14 (repeating/emulating the structure of chaps. 4–11: from indictment and judgment to pardon): Hosea 12 presupposes both the Jacob cycle (in more or less its present form, as far as contents are concerned) and the Exodus tradition. The chapter proves itself to be an early form of academic writing in pointing out some basic differences between the ideologies implied by these traditions.[161]

After 640, Bethel even furnished the tradition for the etiology of Josianic (or post-Josianic) Judah, which was formulated in the Exodus–Joshua narrative, to the detriment of the Jerusalemite Beit-David story, which may still have been unacceptable for Judah's Northerners (the

---

157. Probably part of a postexilic Hosea–Amos redaction; see the close parallel in Amos 5:5; see also below, nn. 169 and 170.

158. For both possibilities, see Berlejung 2002: 196–230. According to Esarhaddon, it was Marduk who handed himself and his city over to Sennacherib, and according to Ezek 1:10, Yhwh had left Jerusalem for Babylonia even before the first deportees did.

159. Which is, of course, an ideological construct of seventh-century, post-state Israel; cf. Kratz 2000b: 1–17; Levin 2000a: 385–403.

160. Cf. Guillaume 2002: 12–17.

161. Cf. de Pury 2001a: 105–14; 2000b: 213–41; 1994a: 95–131.

Benjaminites) and may have been tarnished, in the eyes of the revolutionaries of 640, by its successful implementation (adding royal central control to royal ideology) by Manasseh.

3.2. The Years 586–520

The Jacob and Exodus traditions had become so much a part of Judah's intellectual heritage that Ezekiel, in 597, took them with him to Babylonia. There he was joined, not necessarily to his liking, by a second wave of deportees in 586, who brought Samuel/Kings with them, indicating that between 597 and 586 Jerusalem may have experienced a "Davidic revival," which would better explain Benjamin's spiritual secession from Judah after 586.[162]

This spiritual secession is well expressed by means of the Abraham-cycle (Genesis 12–19*), which never existed (in written form) independent of the Jacob story, to which it was added in the course of the sixth century—an innovation that Ezekiel 33 greeted with contempt and revulsion. By the addition of Abraham, the ideology of the Jacob-cycle (Israel living on the land given to its ancestor by Yhwh) is extended to Judah. It is true that the tradition originated in the South, but it entered the sphere of (biblical) literature at Bethel. Jerusalem does not figure in the older strata of the Abraham tradition (unless it was under the code name "Sodom"[163]), but Bethel appeared prominently in the text: it is near Bethel (Gen 13:3 with 12:8) that Yhwh shows Abraham the exact extent of the land (from Bethel to Mamre!) promised to him and his descendants (Gen 13:14–18), which equates with the borders of Judah/Yehud after 597.[164] The spelling אהלה in Gen 12:8; 13:3 indicates that in sixth-century Bethel, the orthography was still that of JH.

The same spelling reveals that Gen 35:21f. is an addition to the older Jacob story by the authors of the Abraham–Jacob story, whereas, other than in the P version (which has to bring Jacob back to Isaac at Mamre/Hebron), the Abraham–Jacob story could have lived well with a Jacob permanently settled at Bethel (Gen 35:1). However, it ends with Jacob's foray into the territory of Abraham.[165] Gen 35:21f. is written in the style of the classical narrative, but it is a fragment, needed to introduce the

---

162. Guillaume 2001: 31–32.

163. For Sodom = Jerusalem, see Deut 29:18–28; 32:16–36; Isa 1:7–10; 3:1–9; Jer 23:14; Lam 4:6; Ezek 16:43–58; Amos 4:11. None of these references to Sodom is preexilic.

164. For a detailed discussion of the geography of this textual stratum, see Knauf 2000d: 152–55.

165. Mic 4:8 identifies the place with Jerusalem. Regardless of whether this is the point of view of the sixth century or not, the term refers to the Judean south with its "tent-dwellers" (cf. above, p. 298, with n. 39).

curse on Reuben in Gen 49:3f. It stands to reason that the Abraham–Jacob story at that time concluded with a core of Jacob's blessings now contained in Genesis 49, probably contrasting Reuben, as representative of the old (and deceased) Israel and Judah, with Joseph (Gen 49:22–26), as representative of the New Bethel community of survivors.[166] Joseph has survived the onslaught of the archers (Gen 49:23) to live in the kind of agricultural bliss envisaged by Jeremiah 31* and the core of the Asaph psalms.[167] The militance of the blessings of Judah (Gen 49:8–12) and Benjamin (49:27) does not square well with the post-state ideology of the Jacob and Abraham–Jacob stories, nor does the geographical scope of the Twelve Tribes (represented by the Galilean tribes in Gen 49:13–21) fit the Yehud-orientation of the Abraham–Jacob story.[168] Literary archeology is able to reveal, identify, and date strata of the tradition prior to its final form but cannot restore them in their entirety.

Hosea was developed into a book of "Four Minor Prophets":[169] Hosea, Amos, Micah, and Zephaniah. Of these, Hosea had always been at Bethel and possibly also Amos.[170] Micah, who was violently anti-Jerusalem, probably made it directly from the Shephelah, throroughly devastated once again in 588–586, to Bethel. Northern influence in the writing of Micah is exhibited by the plural -*în* (עיין 3:12), part of the oldest textual stratum. These three books (or booklets) were joined by Zephaniah, even more violently anti-Jerusalem than Micah, stating that Josiah's Jerusalem was not any better than Azariah's or Hezekiah's Jerusalem. It is wholly unlikely that such a text could have been uttered, preserved, and transmitted while Josiah was actually ruling.[171]

---

166. One has the impression that Joseph, the paradigmatic descendant of Abraham and Jacob and heir to the promise of the land, here comprises Judah and Benjamin as well.

167. The end of Gen 49:25 renounces Hos 9:14.

168. That these blessings are secondary in their present literary context does not mean that all of them are postexilic (the sayings about Dan and Naphtali clearly are not). On the other hand, the Simeon-and-Levy episode in Gen 49:5–7 presupposes the insertion of Genesis 34 into the story of Genesis.

169. Albertz (2003a: 232–51), who, however, cannot make up his mind whether this book was edited in Bethel or in Babylonia, due to the fact that he attributes far too much text to the sixth-century stratum of "The Book of Four" and misdates some of the co-texts (Ezek 22:25–31 may well be dependent on Zeph 3:3–8, and 2 Kings 23 is an early postexilic text, as I will show).

170. If Amos took a stayover in Jerusalem between 701/597 and 586, he was now "renaturalized" in Bethel by the insertion of the biographical piece in Amos 7:10–17, the secondary character of which has been elucidated by Utzschneider 1988: 76–101 and Levin 1995: 307–17 (whose distinction between Jeroboam I and II, in this context, has been neutralized; cf. above, with n. 152).

171. There was a "voice of the opposition" under the monarchy, but it expressed itself with much more subtlety, and with good reason; cf. Knauf 2000a; 2001c: 200–204.

As it stands, the book condemns Jerusalem's recent past from the point of view of Bethel's present.

That Jeremiah went to Mizpah in 586 is explicitly stated. A first edition of the book may have served as Gedaliah's inauguration address or address to the nation, especially the idea of a Northern restitution or a restitution of both Judah and Israel as two nations under the same god but not necessarily the same king (cf. Jer 30:18–22; 31:15?; 31:18–20?; 31:31–34?). It seems that Bethel's role of cultic/cultural center of Samaria had never been forgotten, and now that the border between Judah and the Babylonian province had fallen, it again lived up to this task. When Jeremiah disappeared in 582, Egypt-bound, it is possible but not very likely that some of the deportees of 582 took the Jeremiah tradition to Babylonia. From Jeremiah 45, as the final chapter of one of the book's major editions, we are instead led to the conclusion that Baruch stayed behind in Mizpah/Bethel and edited another, bleaker version of the book.

Gedaliah's care for the Samarian North and the Northerners' continued interest in the cult of Bethel (Jer 41:4f.) may also be reflected in the psalms of Asaph.[172] The original, sixth-century, collection cannot, however, comprise more than Psalms 75*, 77*, 80–82*, and [85][173] and was subsequently subject to several redactions, prominent among them a pro-Jerusalem-Zion redaction.

The transmission of the book of Isaiah in the sixth century poses a problem in that Deutero-Isaiah supposedly was added in Babylonia, but Isaiah 3* attests to such an augmentative redaction as having taken

---

172. For the thematic unity and geographical background of the Asaph psalms, see Goulder 1995: 71–81; 1996; it goes without saying that I do not share Goulder's presupposition that Israelite literature must have gone to Judah immediately after 722 in order to survive.

173. Psalm 85 is attributed to the sons of Korah, but seems to be of "Northern" origin. There is a Zion-redaction in the Asaph collection (Psalms 76, 78f., 84, and 87, and the latest additions derive from the second century B.C.E.: Psalms 73f., 78?, 79, 83); cf. Zenger 1999: p. 278 with n. 22. Psalm 89 reacts, in my opinion, not to 586, but to the disappearance of Zerubbabel between 520 and 515, on whom hopes for a Davidic restitution had rested. The shorter and older version of this psalm is preserved in 11QPs; the longer, MT version seems to have been produced after the transmission of Psalms separated, that is, after 150; Glessmer 1992: 55–73; against the assumption of exilic "rituals of lamentation" (Veijola 1982), see now Volgger 1995: 231–35. With Volgger (1995: 237), Psalm 89 MT can be regarded as an exegetical construct, responding to Psalm 2 in framing an edition of the Psalter that comprised Psalms 2–89. But with Glessmer, there is an earlier core in Psalm 89 that was (with Steymans 1998: 143f.) already postexilic, whereas the final redaction of Psalm 89 is Hellenistic. According to Heim (1998: 306–14) Isa 55:1–5 responds to Psalm 89 and therefore cannot predate the fourth/third centuries, presupposing, as it does, a rather advanced stage of the monetarization of the Judean economy.

The Growth of the Biblical Tradition: Its Chronology and Geography

Date	Bethel	Jerusalem	Babylon

early seventh century	Hosea 4–11*
	Genesis 26–35* (Jacob)
	Exodus 1–
	  Deuteronomy 34*
	  (Moses)
	Judges 3–9* (Saviors)
		1 Samuel 8–2 Kings 10*
		Isaiah 6–8*	

late seventh century	Hosea 12–14*	→Exodus 1ff.* + Joshua 1–11* →Jacob Isaiah 5–9*	
598		Isaiah 5–32*	→Exodus 1–Joshua 11* →Jacob
586	Jeremiah 1–31* Isaiah 5–32*← Amos*← Micah*← Exodus 1–Joshua 11*←		→1 Samuel 8–2 Kings 10* →??Isaiah 5–32*
582–525	Jeremiah 1–45* Zephania* Genesis 12–35* (Abraham and Jacob) Isaiah 3–32* Psalms 75–82*		Ezekiel 1–39* 1 Samuel–2 Kings* ??Isaiah 40–48*
520		→Genesis 12–Joshua 11* Genesis 1–Joshua 18* (P) →Isaiah 4–32* ?? Isaiah 40–48* ← Ezekiel 1–39* ← →Jeremiah 1–45* →Hosea–Zephania* 1 Samuel–2 Kings* ← → Judges 2–18*	
450		Judges 1–21* →Psalms 75–82* Ezekiel 1–48*	
398		Genesis–Deuteronomy; Joshua	
ca. 150		Genesis–Malachi	

place in the land of Israel.[174] There are several possible solutions: (a) After 586, one copy of Isaiah* went to Babylonia and another to Bethel, to be happily reunited after 520 in Jerusalem. (b) Deutero-Isaiah is not Babylonian at all but a sixth-to-fourth century augmentation of Isaiah

---

174. Becker 1997: 162–68.

from Jerusalem.[175] (c) A minimal textual core of Deutero-Isaiah (Isaiah 40–48*) did originate in Babylonia but was not intended to take up and continue First Isaiah.[176]

The polemics between Ezekiel and the "Sons of Abraham," between Ezekiel and Jeremiah, or between the Samuel–Kings Deuteronomists (who denied Gedaliah the title of king) and the Jeremiah Deuteronomists (who showed Gedaliah acting as if he were a king) are basically polemics between Bethel and Babylonia, between the Judeans in Palestine and the Judeans in exile, during the sixth century. They became polemics between Bethel and Jerusalem when the Babylonian Golah started the restoration of Jerusalem and pushed it through.

3.3. The Years 520–450: Conflict

The conflict between Jerusalem and Bethel during the initial Restoration Period is marked by the Jerusalemite takeover of Bethel traditions and texts, augmented by polemics against their place of origin.

In the beginning, there was denial. P (the *hieros logos* of the Second Temple when it was finished) contains a variant of the Jacob-Bethel tradition (Gen 35:9–13), but he relocates it to Shechem. Shechem (Gen 33:18) is the only place-name in addition to Mamre–Hebron mentioned by P at all in his version of the patriarch's story. That El Shaddai spoke to Jacob there and not at Bethel is, in his opinion, underlined by the repeated reference to בבאו מפדן ארם (Gen 33:18; 35:9).[177] P is sympathetic to Samaria, the other nation under Yhwh, indicated by the repetition of the promise of kings springing forth from the patriarch (Gen 17:6; 35:11), most likely referring to the kings of Israel in addition to the kings of Judah. By the time P was writing, it was only during the past two generations, and possibly not for everyone, that Jacob had become Abraham's grandson. The Samarians may have their own cultural (not cultic) center, placed outside the pale of Yehud. In a like manner, the goddess was divorced from Yhwh in these years and sent

---

175. Davies 1995: 207–25.

176. Thus Steck 1992. For some basic criticism of such a view, see Albertz (1990), who, however, seems to have abandoned this (one of his best) idea; cf. now Albertz 2003b: 371–83. Kratz (1994: 243–61) does not really help, for Jeremiah was not in Babylonia either. For a concise overview of the "Second Isaiah" problem, see Schmid 1999: 266f. and n. 552.

177. The references to Bethel/Luz in Gen 35:6 and 35:15 are in mixed redactional contexts and, if claimed for P, would leave the note on Shechem without a function—not at all the style of P, who tries to be precise and does not waste words.

packing to Babylonia.[178] P prefigures, on one hand, the cooperation between Yehud and Samaria as evidenced by the Elephantine correspondence and, on the other hand, proposes a degree of independence for
the Samarians that they were not to take up before the fourth century.[179] In accordance with his Golah orientation, P insists that all 12
sons of Jacob were born in Mesopotamia (Gen 35:22–26).[180] This polemic
against (Judah's and) Benjamin's autochthonos status does not necessarily presuppose Gen 35:16–20;[181] it may simply address the claim
quoted in Ezek 33:24. The intention of P's shift of Bethel to Shechem is
squarely summarized by P[s] in Gen 35:15, where Shechem is finally
called "Bethel."[182]

The Jerusalemite takeover of the book of Saviors/Judges unwinds
P's yarn some inches farther.[183] Judg 1:21, in blatant contradiction to
Josh 15:63,[184] presents the Benjaminite view, probably still formulated
at Bethel: Jerusalem should be a town of Benjamin, but unfortunately,
Benjamin has to share the place with "Jebusites"[185] to this very day.
The notion is borrowed from the Golah's evaluation of preexilic Jerusalem (Ezekiel 16) and turns it against the returnees. Jerusalem retaliates
with Judg 1:22–26: Bethel was not inaugurated by Jacob, nor is it part
of the patrimony of Benjamin, but it was conquered by "the house of Joseph"—not an old tribal designation either.[186] A Canaanite collaborator

---

178. Cf. Uehlinger 1994: 93–103.

179. For the archeology of this temple and its settlement, see Magen 2000: 74–118;
Stern and Magen 2000: 119–24; Magen, Tsfania, and Misgav 2000: 125–32.

180. P or P[s]? The list of the sons of Jacob is original in Exodus 1 (Knauf 2001d: 291–
300) but has a clear function here: to deny the autochthony of Benjamin.

181. The literary stratigraphy in this case depends on whether one dates the addition
of the Joseph novella to the "story of the patriarchs" to pre-P (thus Schmid 2002) or post-
P (thus Knauf 2001d).

182. The verse could not possibly have flowed out of P's pen, for there are no place-
name etymologies in P[g]. On the other hand, it could not have been produced by the final
redaction either, because Bethel had already been mentioned a couple of times, the last
time in 35:8.

183. Judges 19–21 reflects the same attitude toward the Judean north by the elites of
restoration Jerusalem but will not be discussed here; cf. Guillaume forthcoming; Amit,
in this volume, pp. 647–661; Blenkinsopp, in this volume, pp. 629–645.

184. For Judges 1 as a late compilation, see Smend 1983; and Auld (1975: 265, 276),
who recognizes the postdeuteronomistic character of the chapter as opposed to R. Boling
1975: 29–38; see also, against Boling, Brettler 1989: 399–402.

185. For the Jebusites as an ideological construct, see Hübner 2002; for a possible etymology of the term, see Knauf 2002c: 288.

186. Nearly all references to "Beth Joseph" are exilic or postexilic (Josh 17:17; 18:5;
Amos 5:6 [cf. above, nn. 157 and 163]; Obad 18 (‖ Jacob); Zech 10:6. The same holds
true for Joseph as an ethnonym: Ezek 37:15–19; Amos 5:15; 6:6); Ps 77:15 (‖ Jacob); 78:67

was spared and went off to establish "New Luz" in the "Land of the Hittites," for which one should not look too far north. *Louza* was the name of the settlement on Mt. Gerizim from Hellenistic times onward.[187] Judg 1:22–26 contains P's idea of a Samaritan Bethel, but without P's philo-Samari(ta)n attitude.

It is in Kings that the anti-Bethel polemic reaches it apogee. Establishing the sanctuary was the "sin of Jeroboam" (II; cf. also the reoccurrence of Bethel in 2 Kgs 10:29, under Jehu), which finally led to the downfall of Samaria. It is the Samari(t)ans who, under Assyrian control, continue the "sin" even after the downfall of the state (2 Kgs 17:28).[188] From a historical point of view, this construction is utter nonsense; the redactors of Kings could have found better reasons for Israel's demise, if not in (the Assyrian royal inscriptions and) the Babylonian chronicles series, then in the books of Hosea and Amos—but then, these books were kept at Bethel and were not at the disposal of the Babylonian Golah or of the first returnees, apparently. The intensity of the anti-Bethel propaganda is most conceivable under a constellation in which the existing sanctuary at Bethel provided an obstacle to the restoration of Jerusalem,[189] and a fierce competition ensued during the first decades of the Restoration.

Under the impact of the anti-Bethel propaganda of the returnees, Bethel finally was destroyed or abandoned, and Amos finally came to Jerusalem as well. Whereas the Bethel addition in Amos 7:10–17 served to differentiate between Old Bethel and New Bethel (as did the Beth-

---

(‖ Ephraim); 80:1 (‖ Israel); 81:5 (= Israel), and see above, nn. 172 and 173. In 2 Sam 19:21, a Benjaminite identifies with the "Beth Joseph"; the Shimei episode is difficult to stratify but paints a picture that has nothing to do with Israel's situation after the Absalom revolt, when the country was under Judean occupation; cf. Halpern 2001. 1 Kgs 11:28 is equally difficult to date; 1 Kgs 11:40 is better prepared by 3 Kgdms 12:24a–z; cf. Talshir 1993; cf. also Edelman 1995: 166–91; Bosshard-Nepustil 2000: 95–109.

187. Eusebius, *Onom.* 120.11; Horvat Luza / Khirbet Lauze 175178, a settlement on Mt. Gerizim south of the summit (and Samaritan Temple); cf. Hüttenmeister and Reeg 1977: 2.615–17. In the Samaritan tradition, Mt. Gerizim is identified with the 'House of God' (הר גריזים בית אל), whereas Luz is sometimes identified with Samaria, supposedly built by King Joshua (Adler and Séligsohn 1902–3: 207). Nodet (1997) goes so far as to regard the Samaritan sanctuary as the original referent of Bethel as mentioned in the Torah, an assumption that seems somehow linked to his astounding claim that Beitin "stopped being occupied from the beginning of the Iron Age" (1997: 173).

188. The only historical information to be retrieved from this theological trash is the notion that Bethel served as the cultic and cultural center of Samaria after 720—probably not because it was established as such by the Assyrians but because it was not destroyed between 733 and 720, whereas Samaria and Shechem were.

189. Pakkala (2002: 86–94) dates the Deuteronomistic Bethel polemic to the Exile.

aven / Bethel references in Hosea), the Bethel polemics in Amos 3:14; 4:4; and 5:5f. are aimed at New Bethel. It has long been observed that they form a redactional bracket around chaps. 3–5 and are rather late.[190] What "Amos" is meant to say is not so much "Don't go to church, but instead adopt a responsible life-style"; the intention is, rather, "Don't go to Bethel (or Jericho), but spend your temple money on Jerusalem."

A similar redaction, only slightly more subtle, transformed the anti-Jerusalem book of Jeremiah into pro-Zion prophecy. Whereas Jer 29:1–7 advises the Golah to stay where they are, and Jeremiah 45 declares that every believer is immediate to Yhwh regardless of where she or he is geographically, Jer 29:10–14 terminates the "Exile" and buys into the myth of the "empty land."[191] We learn even more about Gedaliah from Jeremiah than from Kings, but even in Jeremiah his title is deleted, and the "great oracle" for (Gedaliah and) Bethel-centered Israel (Jeremiah 30–31) is heavily revised in favor of the Golah, Zion, and a *David redivivus* (30:9–11, 17f.; 31:6, 8, 12, 16f., 23, 38–40).[192]

3.4. Reconciliation, 450–300

After Bethel ceased to be a threat, Jerusalem made peace with the Bethel tradition, by now only a literary memoir. The post-P material in Genesis 35 is partially redactional and epexegetical, tying up loose ends. Gen 33:19 and 35:5 are needed to anchor Genesis 34[193] in that context. Gen 35:8 tries to find a solution for the problem of Judg 4:5–6 by finding another Deborah who might have sat under that tree.[194] Gen 35:16–20 prepares the ground for the story of Joseph. Now it has become possible to admit the version, at last, that Benjamin was born in the land and not in Babylonia. But by the same token, his original name, Ben-Oni, recalls Beth-aven, and Rachel's tomb is relocated from Benjaminite Ephrah[195] to Judean Bethlehem (35:19). In 35:7, the calling

---

190. Cf. Spieckermann 1982: 112f. n. 130: "So sehr die Verbindung der betreffenden Stellen des Amos-Buches ... mit der einschlägigen Passage des R[eform-]B[erichts] 2 Kön 23,15–20 zutreffen mag, sowenig kann diese Verbindung aufgrund der Reformtat Josias in Bethel zustandegekommen sein" which can only be regarded as factual by someone who "verwechselt Historiographie mit schriftgelehrter Arbeit" (p. 112); for the postexilic editions of Hosea and Amos, the appropriate paragraphs in Levin 2001 are quite pertinent.

191. A happy formulation by Barstad 1997; 1996.

192. For the similar fate of the psalms of Asaph, see above, with n. 170.

193. On the development of this very late extension of the Jacob tradition, see Levin 2000b.

194. See above, after n. 160.

195. Cf. 1 Sam 10:1; Jer 31:15.

of the name (unnecessary as it is; we just read it in the preceding verse) anticipates 35:15 and robs this verse of its anti-Bethel impact. More importantly, 35:14 clarifies that Jacob did not—heaven forbid—build an altar at Bethel but just a memorial and equally devaluates Gen 28:17f. of its cultic implications. Overachieving the intentions of Joshua 22, these late verses contribute to the lasting memory of Bethel and of what it once was, which is contained in the columns of the text (for the literary stratigraphy of Genesis 35, see the appendix below).

The Bethel tradition of the stay-at-homes who never went into exile resurfaces once again, in Nehemiah 9. The controversy between Rendsburg, who hears in the text the voice of Israelites, and H. G. M. Williamson, who identifies the prayers with non-exiled Judeans, misses the point:[196] Bethel and the people of the Judean north were both. Due to the phrasing of the prayer, it presupposes the canonical Torah and the Former Prophets in a form already very close to the present form. Nevertheless, it does not feel bound to reproduce the story of Israel as it became standardized with the canonization of the Prophets.[197] It was the promise to the fathers (9:8)[198] as well as the Exodus that immediately led the people into the land. History ended with Judges; with Judges the story arrived in the author's present, as was the intention of the "Book of the Saviors" in the seventh century. Kings are known to have existed[199] and disappeared, but there is no Exile.[200] It is advisable to date that prayer to the very last stage of the formation of Ezra(–Nehemiah), that is, to the last third of the fourth century.[201] The stability of the Persian Period is gone, the local elites who had relied on Persian backing, in their self-perception perhaps more than in political reality, are in danger of losing their grip. The situation of the stay-at-homes of the seventh and sixth century is now their situation too: late justice to Bethel and its non-Jerusalemite, non-Golah traditions, but justice nevertheless.

---

196. Rendsburg 1991b: 365; Williamson 1988: 117–31.

197. Mathys 1994: 4–21. Prior to M. Noth, the "Deuteronomistic History" had never enjoyed canonical standing.

198. Schmid 1999: 303f.

199. Mentioned in passing in Judg 9:32, 34, and among many other officials.

200. Inasmuch as I do not understand the qualification of 9:30f. and 9:36f. as "exile" by Schmid 1999: 302–6, 305. In 9:36f., the perspective is from the land to the outside world, not vice versa. In 9:30f. it is, accordingly, in their own land that the people are handed over to foreigners—as in Judges.

201. For another view, see Oeming, in this volume, pp. 571–588.

Appendix:
The Stratigraphy of Genesis 35

Post-P Pss	P [possibly Ps]	Pre-P: Gilead-Shechem story Harran-Bethel story Jacob-Abraham story
ויחן את פני עיר 33:19 ויקן את צלקת השדה אשר נטה שם אהלו מיד בני חמור אבי שכם במאה קשיטה	ויבא יעקב עיר שכם אשר בארץ כנען בבאו מפדן ארם	33:18 ויבא יעקב שלם עיר שכם 33:20 ויצב שם מזבח ויקרא לו אל אלהי ישראל
		35:1 ותאמר אלהים אל יעקב קום עלה בית אל ושב שם ועשה שם מזבח לאל הנר ארה אליך בברחך מפני עשו אחיך 35:2 ויאמר יעקב אל ביתו ואל כל אשר עמו הסרו את אלהי הנכר אשר בתכם והטהרו והצליפו שמלתיכם 35:3 ונקומה ונעלה בית אל ואענה שם מזבח לאל הענה אתי ביום צרתי ויהי עמדי בדרך אשר הלכתי 35:4 ויתנו אל יאקב את כל אלהי הנכר אשר בידם ואת הנזמים אשר באזניהם ויטמן אתם יעקב תחת האלה אשר עם שכם
ויסאו ויהי חתת אלהים על הערים אשר סביבותיהם ולא רדפו אחרי בני יעקב לוזה אשר בארץ כנען היא הוא וכל העם אשר עמו 35:8 ותמת דברה מינקת רבקה ותקבר מתחת לבית אל תחת האלון ויקרא שמו אלון בכות עוד	35:9 וירא אהלים אל יעקב	35:6 ויבא יעקב בית אל 35:7 ויבן אם מזבח ויקרא למקום אל בית אל כי שם נגלו אליו האלהים בברחו מפני אחיו

Post-P Pss	P [possibly Ps]	Pre-P: Gilead-Shechem story Harran-Bethel story Jacob-Abraham story
	בבאו מפדן ארם ויברך אתו 35:10 ויאמר לו אלהימשמך יעקב לא יקרא שמך עוד יעקב כי אם ישראל יהיה שמך ויקרא את שמו ישראל 35:11 ויאמר לו אלהים אני אל שדי פרה ורבה גוי וקהל גוים יהיה ממך ומלכים מצלציך יצאו 35:12 ואת הארץ אשר נתתי לאברהם וליצחק לך אתננה ולזרעך אחריך אתן את הארץ 35:13 ויעל מעליו אלהים במקום אשר דבר אתו	
35:14 ויצב יקב מ<u>שבה</u> במקום אשר דבר אתו מצבת אבן ויסך עליה נסך ויצק עליה שמן 35:16 ויסעו מבית אל ויהי עוד כברת הארץ לבוא אפרתה ותלד רחל ותקש בלדתה 35:17 ויהי בהקשתה בלדתה ותאמר לה המילדת אל תיראי כי גם זה לך בן 35:18 ויהי בצאת נפשה כי מתה אתקר שמו בן אוני ואביו קרא לו בנימן 35:19 ותמת רחל ותקבר בדרך אפרתה היא בית לחם 35:20 ויצב יקעב מצבהעל קברתה היא מצבת קברת רחלעד היום	35:15 ויקרא <u>יעקב</u> את שם המקום אשר דבר אתושם אלהים בית אל	
		35:21 ויסע ישראל ויט אהלה מהלאה למגדל עדר 35:22 ויהי בשכן ישראל בארץ ההיא וילך ראובן וישכב את בלחה פילגשאביו וישמע ישראל
	ויהיו בני יעקב שנים עשר 35:23 בני <u>לאה</u> בכור יעקב ראובן ושמעון ולוי ויהודה	

Post-P P^{ss}	P [possibly P^s]	Pre-P: Gilead-Shechem story Harran-Bethel story Jacob-Abraham story
	וישׁשׂכר וזבלון 35:24 <u>בני רחל</u> יוסף ובנימן 35:25 <u>ובני בלהה</u> שׁפחת רחל דן ונפתלי 35:26 <u>ובני זלפה שׁפחת לאה</u> גד ואשׁר אלה בני יעקב אשׁר ילד לו בפדן ארם 35:27 ויבא יעקב אל יצחק אביו ממרא קרית הארבע היא חברון אשׁר גר שׁם אברהם ויחצק 35:28 ויהיו ימי יצחק מעה שׁנה ושׁמנים שׁנה 35:29 ויגוע יצחק וימת ויאסף אל עמיו זקן ושׂבע ימים ויקברו אתו עשׂו ויעקב בניו	

Bibliography

Ackroyd, P. R.
　1975　*Exile and Restoration: A Study of Hebrew Thought of the Sixth Century* B.C. Old Testament Library. Philadelphia.

Adler, E. N., and Séligsohn, M.
　1902–3　Une nouvelle chronique samaritaine. *Revue des études juives* 44: 188–222; 45: 70–98; 46: 123–46.

Aḥituv, S.
　1992　*Asurat ketuvot ʿivriyot.* Jerusalem.

Albertz, R.
　1990　Das Deuterojesaja-Buch als Fortschreibung der Jesaja-Prophetie. Pp. 241–56 in *Die hebräische Bibel und ihre zweifache Nachgeschichte: Festschrift für Rolf Rendtorff zum 65. Geburtstag,* ed. E. Blum et al. Neukirchen-Vluyn.

　2003a　Exile as Purification: Reconstructing the "Book of the Four." Pp. 232–51 in *Thematic Threads in the Book of the Twelve,* ed. P. E. Redditt and A. Schart. Beihefte zur Zeitschrift für die alttestamentliche Wissenschaft 325. Berlin and New York.

　2003b　Darius in Place of Cyrus: The First Edition of Deutero-Isaiah (Isaiah 40.1–52.12) in 521 BCE. *Journal for the Study of the Old Testament* 27: 371–83.

Arneth, M.
2000 *"Sonne der Gerechtigkeit": Studien zur Solarisierung der Jahwe-Religion im Lichte von Psalm 72.* Beihefte zur Zeitschrift für altorientalische und biblische Rechtsgeschichte 1. Wiesbaden.

Auerbach, E.
1953 Die große Überarbeitung der biblischen Bücher. Pp. 1–10 in *Congress Volume: Copenhagen, 1953.* Vetus Testamentum Supplement 1. Leiden.

Auld, A. G.
1975 Judges I and History: A Reconsideration. *Vetus Testamentum* 25: 261–76.

Azzazi, S. al-Sayyed
1992 *Photographs of the Palestinian Village's Tradition.* Amman.

Baildam, J. D.
1999 *Paradisal Love: Johann Gottfried Herder and the Song of Songs.* Journal for the Study of the Old Testament Supplement 298. Sheffield.

Barag, D.
2003 The 2000–2001 Exploration of the Tombs of Benei Ḥezir and Zechariah. *Israel Exploration Journal* 53: 78–110.

Bar Asher, M.
2000 A Few Remarks on Mishnaic Hebrew and Aramaic in Qumran Hebrew. Pp. 12–19 in *Diggers at the Well: Proceedings of a Third International Symposium on the Hebrew of the Dead Sea Scrolls and Ben Sira,* ed. T. Muraoka and J. F. Elwolde. Studies on the Texts of the Desert of Judah 36. Leiden.

Barstad, H. M.
1996 *The Myth of the Empty Land: A Study in the History and Archaeology of Judah during the 'Exilic' Period.* Symbolae Osloenses: Supplementum 28. Oslo.
1997 *The Babylonian Captivity of the Book of Isaiah, 'Exilic' Judah and the Provenance of Isaiah 40–55.* Instituttet for Sammenlignende Kulturforskning: Skrifter Serie B 102. Oslo.

Barth, H.
1977 *Die Jesaja-Worte in der Josia-Zeit.* Wissenschaftliche Monographien zum Alten und Neuen Testament 48. Neukirchen-Vluyn.
1989 Jes 8,23b–9,6. Pp. 199–229 in *Studien zum Messiasbild im Alten Testament,* ed. U. Struppe. Stuttgarter biblische Aufsatzbände 6. Stuttgart.

Becker, U.
1990 *Richterzeit und Königtum. Redaktionsgeschichtliche Studien zum Richterbuch.* Beihefte zur Zeitschrift für die alttestamentliche Wissenschaft 192. Berlin and New York.
1997 *Jesaja: Von der Botschaft zum Buch.* Forschungen zur Religion und Literatur des Alten und Neuen Testaments 178. Göttingen.
2001 Der Prophet als Fürbitter: Zum literarhistorischen Ort der Amos-Visionen. *Vetus Testamentum* 51: 141–65.

Becking, B.
1981–82   The Two Neo-Assyrian Documents from Gezer in Their Historical Context. *Jaarboek Ex Oriente Lux* 27: 76–89.
1992   *The Fall of Samaria: An Historical and Archaeological Study.* Studies in the History of the Ancient Near East 2. Leiden.
1997   Inscribed Seals as Evidence for Biblical Israel? Jeremiah 40.7–41.15 par Exemple. Pp. 65–83 in *Can a "History of Israel" Be Written?* ed. L. L. Grabbe. Journal for the Study of the Old Testament Supplement 245. Sheffield.
2002   West Semites at Tell Šeḫ Ḥamad: Evidence for the Israelite Exile? Pp. 153–66 in *Kein Land für sich allein: Studien zum Kulturkontakt in Kanaan, Israel/Palästina und Ebirnari für Manfred Weippert zum 65. Geburtstag,* ed. U. Hübner and E. A. Knauf. Orbis Biblicus et Orientalis 186. Freiburg, Switzerland.
Ben-Ḥayyim, Z., and Tal, A.
2000   *A Grammar of Samaritan Hebrew.* Jerusalem.
Ben-Zvi, I.
1961   Les origins de l'établissement des tribus d'Israël en Arabie. *Le Muséon* 74: 143–90.
1963   *The Exiled and the Redeemed.* 2nd ed. Philadelphia.
Berlejung, A.
2002   Notlösungen: Altorientalische Nachrichten über den Tempelkult in Nachkriegszeiten. Pp. 196–230 in *Kein Land für sich allein: Studien zum Kulturkontakt in Kanaan, Israel/Palästina und Ebirnari für Manfred Weippert zum 65. Geburtstag,* ed. U. Hübner and E. A. Knauf. Orbis Biblicus et Orientalis 186. Freiburg, Switzerland.
Bernett, M., and Keel, O.
1998   *Mond, Stier und Kult am Stadttor: Die Stele von Betsaida (et-Tell).* Orbis Biblicus et Orientalis 161. Freiburg, Switzerland.
Berquist, J. L.
1995   *Judaism in Persia's Shadow.* Minneapolis.
Bienkowski, P.
2001   New Evidence on Edom in the Neo-Babylonian and Persian Periods. Pp. 198–213 in *The Land That I Will Show You: Essays on the History and Archaeology of the Ancient Near East in Honor of J. Maxwell Miller,* ed. J. A. Dearman. Journal for the Study of the Old Testament Supplement 343. Sheffield.
Blanco Wißmann, F.
2001   Sargon, Mose und die Gegner Salomos: Zur Frage vor-neuassyrischer Ursprünge der Mose-Erzählung. *Biblische Notizen* 110: 42–54.
Blau, J. [Y.]
1977   "Weak" Phonetic Change and the Hebrew śîn. *Hebrew Annual Review* 1: 67–119.
1998a   Introduction: On the History and Structure of Hebrew. Pp. 11–19 in Blau 1998b.
1998b   *Topics in Hebrew and Semitic Linguistics.* Jerusalem.

2000 A Conservative View on the Language of the Dead Sea Scrolls. Pp. 20–25 in *Diggers at the Well: Proceedings of a Third International Symposium on the Hebrew of the Dead Sea Scrolls and Ben Sira*, ed. T. Muraoka and J. F. Elwolde. Studies on the Texts of the Desert of Judah 36. Leiden.

Blenkinsopp, J.
1998 The Judean Priesthood during the Neo-Babylonian and Achaemenid Periods: A Hypothetical Reconstruction. *Catholic Biblical Quarterly* 60: 25–43.
2003 Bethel in the Neo-Babylonian Period. Pp. 93–107 in *Judah and the Judeans in the Neo-Babylonian Period*, ed. O. Lipschits and J. Blenkinsopp. Winona Lake, Indiana.

Blum, E.
1994 "Amos" in Jerusalem: Beobachtungen zu Am 6,1–7. *Henoch* 16: 23–47.

Boling, R. G.
1975 *Judges*. Anchor Bible 6A. Garden City, New York.

Borger, R.
1956 *Die Inschriften Asarhaddons, Königs von Assyrien*. Archiv für Orientforschung Beiheft 9. Graz.

Bosshard-Nepustil, E.
2000 Hadad, der Edomiter: 1 Kön 11,14–22 zwischen literarischem Kontext und Verfassergegenwart. Pp. 95–109 in *Schriftauslegung in der Schrift: Festschrift für Odil Hannes Steck zu seinem 65. Geburtstag*, ed. R. G. Kratz, T. Krüger, and K. Schmid. Beihefte zur Zeitschrift für die alttestamentliche Wissenschaft 300. Berlin and New York.

Brettler, M.
1989 The Book of Judges: Literature as Politics. *Journal of Biblical Literature* 108: 395–418.

Bruce, A.
2002 *The Last Crusade: The Palestine Campaign in the First World War*. London. [Paperback edition, 2003]

Campbell, E. F.
2002 *Text*. Vol. 1 of *Shechem III: The Stratigraphy and Architecture of Shechem / Tell Balâṭah*. American Schools of Oriental Research Archaeological Reports 6. Boston.

Carter, C. E.
1999 *The Emergence of Yehud in the Persian Period: A Social and Demographic Study*. Journal for the Study of the Old Testament Supplement 294. Sheffield.

Cross, F. M.
2003 Some Problems in Old Hebrew Orthography with Special Attention to the Third Person Masculine Singular Suffix on Plural Nouns [-âw]. *Eretz-Israel* 27: 18*–24*.

Dalley, S.
1985 Foreign Chariotry and Cavalry in the Armies of Tiglath-Pileser III and Sargon II. *Iraq* 47: 31–48.

Davies, P. R.
1995   God of Cyrus, God of Israel: Some Religio-Historical Reflections on Isaiah 40–55. Pp. 207–25 in *Words Remembered, Texts Renewed: Essays in Honour of John F. A. Sawyers*, ed. J. Davies et al. Journal for the Study of the Old Testament Supplement 195. Sheffield.

Dayagi-Mendels, M.
2002   *The Akhziv Cemeteries: The Ben-Dor Excavations, 1941–1944*. Israel Antiquities Authority Reports 15. Jerusalem.

Dever, W.
1992   Beitin, Tell. Pp. 651–52 in vol. 1 of *Anchor Bible Dictionary*, ed. D. N. Freedman. New York.

Dietrich, W.
1997   Wem das Land gehört: Ein Beitrag zur Sozialgeschichte Israels im 6. Jahrhundert v.Chr. Pp. 350–76 in *Ihr Völker alle, klatscht in die Hände!* ed. R. Kessler, K. Ulrich, and M. Schwantes. Exegese in unserer Zeit 3. Münster.

Dion, P. E., and Daviau, P. M. M.
2000   An Inscribed Incense Altar of Iron Age II at Ḥirbet el-Mudēyine (Jordan). *Zeitschrift des Deutschen Palästina-Vereins* 116: 1–13.

Duffy, C.
1998   *The Military Experience in the Age of Reason*. 2nd ed. Ware, Hertfordshire.

Edelman, D. V.
1995   Solomon's Adversaries Hadad, Rezon and Jeroboam: A Trio of "Bad Guy" Characters Illustrating the Theology of Immediate Retribution. Pp. 166–91 in *The Pitcher Is Broken: Memorial Essays for Gösta W. Ahlström*, ed. S. W. Holloway and L. K. Handy. Journal for the Study of the Old Testament Supplement 190. Sheffield.

Eph'al, I., and Naveh, J.
1996   *Aramaic Ostraca of the Fourth Century BC from Idumaea*. Jerusalem.

Fales, F. M.
1978   A Cuneiform Correspondence to Alphabetic in West Semitic Names of the I Millennium B.C. *Orientalia* 47: 91–98.

Faust, A.
2000   Ethnic Complexity in Northern Israel during Iron Age II. *Palestine Exploration Quarterly* 132: 2–27.
2003   Judah in the Sixth Century BCE: A Rural Perspective. *Palestine Exploration Quarterly* 135: 37–53.

Finkelstein, I.
1998   Two Notes on Northern Samaria: The "Einun Pottery" and the Date of the "Bull Site." *Palestine Exploration Quarterly* 130: 94–98.
1999   Hazor and the North in the Iron Age: A Low Chronology Perspective. *Bulletin of the American Schools for Oriental Research* 314: 55–70.
2001   The Rise of Jerusalem and Judah: The Missing Link. *Levant* 32: 105–15.
2002   Chronology Rejoinders: *Palestine Exploration Quarterly* 134: 118–29.

Finkelstein, I., and Silberman, N. A.
2000   *The Bible Unearthed: Archaeology's New Vision of Ancient Israel and the Origin of Its Sacred Text.* New York.

Fried, Lisbeth S.
2003   The Land Lay Desolate: Conquest and Restoration in the Ancient Near East. Pp. 21–54 in *Judah and the Judeans in the Neo-Babylonian Period*, ed. O. Lipschits and J. Blenkinsopp. Winona Lake, Indiana.

Fritz, V.
1989   Amosbuch, Amosschule und historischer Amos. Pp. 29–43 in *Prophet und Prophetenbuch: Festschrift für Otto Kaiser zum 65. Geburtstag*, ed. V. Fritz. Beihefte zur Zeitschrift für die alttestamentliche Wissenschaft 185. Berlin and New York.

Galling, K.
1935   Assyrische und persische Präfekten in Geser. *Palästina-jahrbuch* 31: 75–93.
1964   *Studien zur Geschichte Israels im persischen Zeitalter.* Tübingen.

Gevirtz, S.
1986   Of Syntax and Style in the "Late Biblical Hebrew"–"Old Canaanite" Connection. *Journal of the Ancient Near Eastern Society of Columbia University* 18: 25–29.

Glessmer, U.
1992   Das Textwachstum von Ps 89 und ein Qumranfragment. *Biblische Notizen* 65: 55–73.

Gordon, C. H.
1955   North Israelite Influence on Postexilic Hebrew. *Israel Exploration Journal* 5: 85–88.

Goulder, M.
1995   Asaph's History of Israel (Elohist Press, Bethel, 725 BCE). *Journal for the Study of the Old Testament* 65: 71–81.
1996   *The Psalms of Asaph and the Pentateuch.* Vol. 3 of *Studies in the Psalter.* Journal for the Study of the Old Testament Supplement 233. Sheffield.

Guillaume, P.
2001   Jerusalem 586 BC: Katastrophal? *Biblische Notizen* 110: 31–32.
2002   From a Post-monarchical to the Pre-monarchical Period of the Judges. *Biblische Notizen* 113: 12–17.
2004   *Waiting for Josiah: The Judges.* Journal for the Study of the Old Testament Supplement 385. London.

Gunneweg, A. H. J.
1985   *Esra.* Kommentar zum Alten Testament 19/1. Gütersloh.
1987   *Nehemia.* Kommentar zum Alten Testament 19/2. Gütersloh.

Halpern, B.
1987   Dialect Distribution in Canaan and the Deir Alla Inscriptions. Pp. 119–39 in *Working with No Data* (Festschrift for T. O. Lambdin), ed. D. M. Golomb. Winona Lake, Indiana.
1991   Jerusalem and the Lineages in the Seventh Century BCE: Kinship and the Rise of Individual Moral Liability. Pp. 11–107 in *Law and Ideology in*

Monarchic Israel, ed. B. Halpern and D. W. Hobson. Journal for the Study of the Old Testament Supplement 124. Sheffield.

2001   *David's Secret Demons: Messiah, Murderer, Traitor, King.* Grand Rapids.

Handy, L. K.

1995   Historical Probability and the Narrative of Josiah's Reform in 2 Kings. Pp. 252–75 in *The Pitcher Is Broken: Memorial Essays for Gösta W. Ahlström*, ed. S. W. Holloway and L. K. Handy. Journal for the Study of the Old Testament Supplement 190. Sheffield.

Hauptmann, A.

2000   *Zur frühen Metallurgie des Kupfers in Fenan/Jordanien.* Der Anschnitt Beiheft 11. Bochum, Germany.

Heim, K. M.

1998   The (God-)Forsaken King of Psalm 89: A Historical and Intertextual Enquiry. Pp. 296–322 in *King and Messiah in Israel and the Ancient Near East: Proceedings of the Oxford Old Testament Seminar*, ed. J. Day. Journal for the Study of the Old Testament Supplement 270. Sheffield.

Heinevetter, H.-J.

1988   "Komm nun, mein Liebster, dein Garten ruft dich!" Das Hohelied als programmatische Komposition. Athenäums Monografien: Theologie 69. Frankfurt am Main.

Hoffman, Y.

2003   The Fasts in the Book of Zechariah and the Fashioning of National Rememberance. Pp. 169–218 in *Judah and the Judeans in the Neo-Babylonian Period*, ed. O. Lipschits and J. Blenkinsopp. Winona Lake, Indiana.

Hübner, U.

1988   Die ersten moabitischen Ostraka. *Zeitschrift des Deutschen Palästina-Vereins* 104: 68–73.

2002   Jerusalem und die Jebusiter. Pp. 31–42 in *Kein Land für sich allein: Studien zum Kulturkontakt in Kanaan, Israel/Palästina und Ebirnari für Manfred Weippert zum 65. Geburtstag*, ed. U. Hübner and E. A. Knauf. Orbis Biblicus et Orientalis 186. Freiburg, Switzerland.

Hüttenmeister, F., and Reeg, G.

1977   *Die antiken Synagogen in Israel.* Vols. 1–2. Beihefte zum Tübinger Atlas des Vorderen Orients B 12. Wiesbaden.

Hurvitz, A.

1997   The Historical Quest for "Ancient Israel" and the Linguistic Evidence of the Hebrew Bible: Some Methodological Observations. *Vetus Testamentum* 47: 301–15.

2000a   Can Biblical Texts Be Dated Linguistically? Chronological Perspectives in the Historical Study of Biblical Hebrew. Pp. 143–60 in *Congress Volume: Oslo, 1998*, ed. A. Lemaire and M. Sæbø. Vetus Testamentum Supplements 80. Leiden.

2000b   Was QH a "Spoken" Language? On Some Recent Views and Positions. Pp. 110–14 in *Diggers at the Well: Proceedings of a Third International Symposium on the Hebrew of the Dead Sea Scrolls and Ben Sira*, ed. T. Muraoka and J. F. Elwolde. Studies on the Texts of the Desert of Judah 36. Leiden.

Kaiser, O.

1992   Die Klagelieder. Pp. 91–198 in *Das Hohelied, Klagelieder, Das Buch Ester*, ed. H. P. Müller, O. Kaiser, and J. A. Loader. Das Alte Testament Deutsch 16/2. Göttingen.

Keel, O.

1986   *Das Hohelied*. Zürcher Bibelkommentar AT 18. Zurich.

1994   *Studien zu den Stempelsiegeln aus Palaestina, Israel, Vol. IV: Mit Registern zu den Bänden I–IV*. Orbis Biblicus et Orientalis 135. Freiburg, Switzerland.

1995   Der zu hohe Preis der Identität oder von den schmerzlichen Beziehungen zwischen Christentum, Judentum und kanaanäischer Religion. Pp. 95–113 in *Ugarit und seine altorientalische Umwelt*, Vol. 1 of *Ugarit: Ein ostmediterranes Kulturzentrum im Alten Orient. Ergebnisse und Perspektiven der Forschung*, ed. M. Dietrich and O. Loretz. Abhandlungen zur Literatur Alt-Syrien-Palästinas 7. Münster.

2000   Das kanaanäische Jerusalem und sein Nachwirken: Versuch, ein dominierendes Bild zu dekonstruieren und ein neues zu umreißen. *Welt und Umwelt der Bibel* 16: 7–14.

2001   Das Land der Kanaanäer mit der Seele suchend. *Theologische Zeitschrift* 57: 245–61.

Keel, O., and Uehlinger, C.

1988   *Gods, Goddesses and Images of God in Ancient Israel*. Edinburgh.

Kelso, J. L.

1968   *The Excavations of Bethel (1934–1960)*. Annual of the American Schools of Oriental Research 39. Cambridge, Massachusetts.

1993   Bethel. Pp. 192–94 in vol. 1 of *New Encyclopedia of Archaeological Excavations in the Holy Land*, ed. E. Stern. Jerusalem.

Khalidi, L. El-

1999   *The Art of Palestinian Embroidery*. London.

Klein, R. W.

1999   The Books of Ezra and Nehemiah: Introduction, Commentary, and Reflections. Pp. 661–851 in *The New Interpreter's Bible*, ed. L. E. Keck et al. Nashville.

Knauf, E. A.

1985   Alter und Herkunft der edomitischen Königsliste. Gen 36,31–39. *Zeitschrift für die alttestamentliche Wissenschaft* 97: 245–53.

1988   Hiobs Heimat. *Die Welt des Orients* 19: 65–83.

1989a   *Ismael Untersuchungen zur Geschichte Palästinas und Nordarabiens im 1. Jahrtausend v. Chr Abhandlungen des Deutschen Palästina-Vereins* 2, expanded ed. Wiesbaden.

1989b   Assur, Šuaḥ und der stimmlose Sibilant des Assyrischen. *Biblische Notizen* 49: 13–19.

1990a   The Persian Administration in Arabia. *Transeuphratène* 2: 201–17.

1990b   War Biblisch-Hebräisch eine Sprache? Empirische Gesichtspunkte zur Annäherung an die Sprache der althebräischen Literatur. *Zeitschrift für Althebraistik* 3: 11–23.

1992 Jeremia xlix 1–6: Ein zweites Moab-Orakel im Jeremia-Buch. *Vetus Testamentum* 42: 124–28.

1994 *Die Umwelt des Alten Testaments.* Neuer Stuttgarter Kommentar AT 29. Stuttgart.

1999a Supplementa Ismaelitica 19: Zur Ethnolinguistik des Tell el-Mazar. *Biblische Notizen* 97: 31–34.

1999b Shadday. Pp. 749–53 in *Dictionary of Deities and Demons in the Bible,* ed. K. van der Torn, B. Becking, and P. W. van der Karst. 2nd ed. Leiden.

2000a Vom Prophetinnenwort zum Prophetenbuch: Jesaja 8,3f im Kontext von Jesaja 6,1–8,16. *Lectio difficilior: European Electronic Journal for Feminist Exegesis* 2000/2 (www.lectio.unibe.ch).

2000b Psalm LX und Psalm CVIII. *Vetus Testamentum* 50: 55–65.

2000c Does 'Deuteronomistic Historiography' (DtrH) Exist? Pp. 388–98 in *Israel Constructs Its History,* ed. A. de Pury et al. Journal for the Study of the Old Testament Supplement 306. Sheffield.

2000d Der Umfang des verheißenen Landes nach dem Ersten Testament. *Bibel und Kirche* 55: 152–55.

2001a Mythos Kanaan. Oder: Sex, Lügen und Propheten-Schriften. *Welt und Umwelt der Bibel* 21: 41–44.

2001b Saul, David and the Philistines: From Geography to History. *Biblische Notizen* 109: 15–18.

2001c Prophetie und Dissidenz. *Zeitschrift/Reformatio* 50: 200–204.

2001d Genesis 36,1–43. Pp. 291–300 in *Jacob. Commentaire à plusieurs voix de Gn. 25–36: Mélanges offerts à Albert de Pury,* ed. T. Römer and J.-D. Macchi. Le Monde de la Bible 44. Geneva.

2002a Der Kanon und die Bibeln: Die Geschichte vom Sammeln heiliger Schriften. *Bibel und Kirche* 57: 193–98.

2002b Elephantine und das vor-biblische Judentum. Pp. 165–74 in *Religion und Religionskontakte im Zeitalter der Achämeniden: Sechs Jahre "Arbeitsgemeinschaft zur Erforschung der altorientalisch-hellenistischen Religionsgeschichte des 1. Jahrtausends" in Göttingen,* ed. R. G. Kratz. Veröffentlichungen der Wissenschaftlichen Gesellschaft für Theologie 22. Munich.

2002c Towards an Archaeology of the Hexateuch. Pp. 275–94 in *Abschied vom Jahwisten: Die Komposition des Hexateuch in der jüngsten Diskussion,* ed. J. C. Gertz, K. Schmid, and M. Witte. Beihefte zur Zeitschrift für die alttestamentliche Wissenschaft 315. Berlin and New York.

2002d The Queens' Story: Bathshebah, Maacah and Athaliah and the 'Historia' of Early Kings. *Lectio difficilior. European Electronic Journal for Feminist Exegesis* 2002/2 (www.lectio.unibe.ch).

2003a 701: Sennacherib at the Berezina. Pp. 141–49 in *'Like a Bird in a Cage': The Invasion of Sennacherib in 701 BCE,* ed. L. L. Grabbe. Journal for the Study of the Old Testament Supplement 363 = European Seminar for Historical Methodology 4. Sheffield.

2003b "Kinneret I" Revisited. Pp. 159–69 in *Saxa Loquentur* (Festschrift for Volkmar Fritz), ed. C. G. den Hertog et al. Alter Orient und Altes Testament 302. Münster.

Kottsieper, I.

2000 Der Mann aus Babylonien: Steuerhinterzieher, Flüchtling, Immigrant oder Agent? Zu einem aramäischen Dekret aus neuassyrischer Zeit. *Orientalia* 69: 368–92.

Krämer, G.

2002 *Geschichte Palästinas: Von der osmanischen Eroberung bis zur Gründung des Staates Israel*. Munich.

Kratz, R. G.

1994 Der Anfang des Zweiten Jesaja in Jes 40,1 f. und das Jeremiabuch. *Zeitschrift für die alttestamentliche Wissenschaft* 106: 243–61.

2000a *Die Komposition der erzählenden Bücher des Alten Testaments: Grundwissen der Bibelkritik*. Uni-Taschenbücher 2157. Göttingen.

2000b Israel als Staat und als Volk. *Zeitschrift für Theologie und Kirche* 97: 1–17.

Kutscher, E. Y.

1982 *A History of the Hebrew Language*. Jerusalem.

Landy, F.

1987 The Song of Songs. Pp. 305–19 in *The Literary Guide to the Bible*, ed. R. Alter and F. Kermode. Cambridge.

Lehmann, G.

1996 *Untersuchungen zur späten Eisenzeit in Syrien und Libanon: Stratigraphie und Keramikformen ca. 720 bis 300 v. Chr.* Archäologie des Vorderen Orients 5. Münster.

Lemaire, A.

1990 Population et territoires de Palestine à l'époque perse. *Transeuphratène* 3: 31–74.

Levenson, J. D.

1985 Is There a Counterpart in the Hebrew Bible to New Testament Antisemitism? *Journal of Ecumenical Studies* 22: 242–60.

Levin, C.

1984 Joschija im deuteronomistischen Geschichtswerk. *Zeitschrift für die alttestamentliche Wissenschaft* 96: 351–71.

1995 Amos und Jerobeam I. *Vetus Testamentum* 45: 307–17.

2000a Das vorstaatliche Israel. *Zeitschrift für Theologie und Kirche* 97: 385–403.

2000b Dina: Wenn die Schrift wider sich selbst lautet. Pp. 61–72 in *Schriftauslegung in der Schrift: Festschrift für Odil Hannes Steck zu seinem 65. Geburtstag*, ed. R. G. Kratz, T. Krüger, and K. Schmid. Beihefte zur Zeitschrift für die alttestamentliche Wissenschaft 300. Berlin and New York.

2001 *Das Alte Testament*. Beck Wissen 2160. Munich.

Lipschits, O.

1999 The History of the Benjaminite Region under Babylonian Rule. *Tel Aviv* 26: 155–90.

2003   Demographic Changes in Judah between the Seventh and Fifth Centuries B.C.E. Pp. 323–76 in *Judah and the Judeans in the Neo-Babylonian Period*, ed. O. Lipschits and J. Blenkinsopp. Winona Lake, Indiana.

Loretz, O.
1992   Die Entstehung des Amos-Buches im Licht der Prophetien aus Mari, Assur, Ishchali und der Ugarit-Texte: Paradigmenwechsel in der Prophetenbuchforschung. *Ugarit-Forschungen* 24: 179–215.

Magen, Y.
2000   Har Gerizim: ʿIr miqdash. *Qadmoniot* 33 (120): 74–118.

Magen, Y.; Tsfania, L; and Misgav, H.
2000   *Ha-ketuvot ha-ʾaramiyot we-ha-ʿivriyot me-Har Gerizim.* *Qadmoniot* 33 (120): 125–32.

Mathys, H.-P.
1994   *Dichter und Beter: Theologen aus spätalttestamentlicher Zeit.* Orbis Biblicus et Orientalis 132. Freiburg, Switzerland.
2000   Chronikbücher und hellenistischer Zeitgeist. Pp. 41–155 in *Vom Anfang und vom Ende: Fünf alttestamentliche Studien.* Beiträge zur Erforschung des Alten Testaments und des antiken Judentums 47. Frankfurt am Main.

Mershen, B.
1992   Settlement History and Village Space in Late Ottoman Northern Jordan. Pp. 409–16 in vol. 4 of *Studies in the History and Archaeology of Jordan.* Amman.

Mershen, B., and Knauf, E. A.
1988   From Ǧadar to Umm Qais. *Zeitschrift des Deutschen Palästina-Vereins* 104: 128–45.

Meyers, C. L., and Meyers, E. M.
1987   *Haggai, Zechariah 1–8.* Anchor Bible 25B. Garden City, New York.

Müller, H.-P.
1976   Die lyrische Reproduktion des Mythischen im Hohenlied. *Zeitschrift für Theologie und Kirche* 73: 23–41.
1980   Gott und die Götter in den Anfängen der biblischen Religion: Zur Vorgeschichte des Monotheismus. Pp. 99–142 in *Monotheismus im Alten Israel und seiner Umwelt*, ed. O. Keel. Biblische Beiträge 14. Fribourg.
1992   Das Hohelied. Pp. 1–90 in H.-P. Müller, O. Kaiser, and J. A. Loader, *Das Hohelied, Klagelieder, Das Buch Ester.* Das Alte Testament Deutsch 16/2. Göttingen.

Musil, A.
1907   *Arabia Petraea.* Vol. 2/1. Vienna.
1908   *Arabia Petraea.* Vol. 2/2. Vienna.

Myers, J. M.
1965   *Ezrah–Nehemiah.* Anchor Bible 14. Garden City, New York.

Naʾaman, N.
1991   The Kingdom of Judah under Josiah. *Tel Aviv* 18: 3–71.
1993   Population Changes in Palestine Following Assyrian Deportations. *Tel Aviv* 20: 104–24.

2002 In Search of Reality behind the Account of David's Wars with Israel's Neighbours. *Israel Exploration Journal* 52: 200–224.

Na'aman, N., and Zadok, R.

2000 Assyrian Deportations to the Province of Samerina in the Light of Two Cuneiform Tablets from Tel Hadid. *Tel Aviv* 27/2: 159–88.

Niehr, H.

1995 Die Reform des Joschija: Methodische, historische und religionsgeschichtliche Aspekte. Pp. 33–55 in *Jeremia und die "deuteronomistische Bewegung,"* ed. W. Groß. Athenäums Monografien. Theologie: Bonner biblische Beiträge 98. Weinheim.

Niemann, H. M.

1999 Zorah, Eshtaol, Beth-Shemesh and Dan's Migration to the South: A Region and its Traditions in the Late Bronze and Iron Ages. *Journal for the Study of the Old Testament* 86: 25–48.

Nissinen, M.

1993 Die Relevanz der neuassyrischen Prophetie für die alttestamentliche Forschung. Pp. 217–58 in *Mesopotamica–Ugaritica–Biblica: Festschrift für Kurt Bergerhof zur Vollendung seines 70. Lebensjahres am 7. Mai 1992,* ed. M. Dietrich and O. Loretz. Alter Orient und Altes Testament 232. Kevelaer.

1996 Falsche Prophetie in neuassyrischer und deuteronomistischer Darstellung. Pp. 172–95 in *Das Deuteronomium und seine Querbeziehungen,* ed. T. Veijola. Schriften der Finnischen Exegetischen Gesellschaft 62. Göttingen.

1998 Prophecy against the King in Neo-Assyrian Sources. Pp. 157–70 in *"Lasset uns Brücken bauen . . .": Collected Communications to the XVth Congress of the International Organization for the Study of the Old Testament, Cambridge 1995,* ed. K.-D. Schunck and M. Augustin. Beiträge zur Erforschung des Alten Testaments und des antiken Judentums 42. Frankfurt am Main.

2002 Prophets and the Divine Council. Pp. 4–19 in *Kein Land für sich allein: Studien zum Kulturkontakt in Kanaan, Israel/Palästina und Ebirnari für Manfred Weippert zum 65. Geburtstag,* ed. U. Hübner and E. A. Knauf. Orbis Biblicus et Orientalis 186. Freiburg, Switzerland.

Nodet, É.

1997 *A Search for the Origins of Judaism: From Joshua to the Mishnah.* Journal for the Study of the Old Testament Supplement 248. Sheffield.

Oded, B.

2000 The Settlements of the Israelite and Judean Exiles in Mesopotamia in the 8th–6th Centuries BCE. Pp. 91–103 in *Studies in Historical Geography and Biblical Historiography Presented to Zecharia Kallai,* ed. G. Galil and M. Weinfeld. Vetus Testamentum Supplements 81. Leiden.

Oren, E. D.

1984 Migdol: A New Fortress on the Edge of the Eastern Nile Delta. *Bulletin of the American Schools of Oriental Research* 256: 7–44.

Pakkala, J.
2002   Jereboam's Sin and Bethel in 1 Kgs 12:25–33. *Biblische Notizen* 112: 86–94.

Perlitt, L.
1977   Sinai und Horeb. Pp. 302–22 in *Beiträge zur alttestamentlichen Theologie: Festschrift für Walther Zimmerli zum 70. Geburtstag*, ed. H. Donner, R. Hanhart, and R. Smend. Göttingen.
1994   *Deuteronomium-Studien.* Forschungen zum Alten Testament 8. Tübingen.

Pfeiffer, H.
1999   *Das Heiligtum von Bethel im Spiegel des Hoseabuches.* Forschungen zur Religion und Literatur des Alten und Neuen Testaments 183. Göttingen.

Pilgrim, C.
1999   Der Tempel des Jahwe. *Mitteilungen des Deutschen Archäologischen Instituts Kairo* 55: 142–45.

Polak, F. H.
1998   The Oral and the Written: Syntax, Stylistics and the Development of Biblical Prose-Narrative. *Journal of the Ancient Near Eastern Society of Columbia University* 26: 59–105.
2001   The Style of the Dialogue in Biblical Prose Narrative. *Journal of the Ancient Near Eastern Society of Columbia University* 28: 53–95.

Porten, B., and Yardeni, A.
1986–99   *Textbook of Aramaic Documents from Ancient Egypt.* Vols. 1–4. Jerusalem.

Pury, A. de
1992   Osée 12 et ses implications pour le débat actuel sur le Pentateuque. Pp. 175–207 in *Le Pentateuque: Débats et Recherches*, ed. P. Haudebert. Lectio divina 151. Paris.
1994a   Las dos leyendas sobre el origen de Israel (Jacob y Moisés) y la elaboración del Pentateuco. *Estudios bíblicos* 52: 95–131.
1994b   Erwägungen zu einem vorexilischen Stämmejahwismus: Hos 12 und die Auseinandersetzung um die Identität Israels und seines Gottes. Pp. 413–39 in *Ein Gott allein?* Jahweverehrung und biblischer Monotheismus im Kontext der *israelitischen und altorientalischen Religionsgeschichte*, ed. W. Dietrich and M. A. Klopfenstein. Orbis Biblicus et Orientalis 139. Freiburg.
2001a   Le choix de l'ancêtre. *Theologische Zeitschrift* 57: 105–14.
2001b   Situer le cycle de Jacob: Quelques réflexions, vingt-cinq ans plus tard. Pp. 213–41 in *Studies in the Book of Genesis: Literature, Redaction and History*, ed. A. Wénin. Bibliotheca Ephemeridum Theologicarum Lovaniensium 155. Leuven.

Qimron, E.
2000   The Nature of DSS Hebrew and Its Relation to BH and MH. Pp. 232–44 in *Diggers at the Well: Proceedings of a Third International Symposium on the Hebrew of the Dead Sea Scrolls and Ben Sira*, ed. T. Muraoka and J. F. Elwolde. Studies on the Texts of the Desert of Judah 36. Leiden.

Rabin, C.

1979   The Emergence of Classical Hebrew. Pp. 71–78, 293–95 in *The Age of the Monarchies: Culture and Society*, ed. A. Malamat. Vols. 1 and 4/2 of *The World History of the Jewish People*. Jerusalem.

Reich, R., and Brandl, B.

1985   Gezer under Assyrian Rule. *Palestine Exploration Quarterly* 117: 41–54.

Reich, R., and Shuqrun, E.

2000   The Excavations at the Gihon Spring and Warren's Shaft System in the City of David. Pp. 327–39 in *Ancient Jerusalem Revealed*, ed. H. Geva. Reprinted and expanded ed. Jerusalem.

Rendsburg, G. A.

1991a   The Galilean Background of Mishnaic Hebrew. Pp. 241–51 in *The Galilee in Late Antiquity*, ed. L. I. Levine. New York and Jerusalem.

1991b   The Northern Origin of Nehemiah 9. *Biblica* 72: 348–66.

1991c   Parallel Developments in Mishnaic Hebrew, Colloquial Arabic, and other Varieties of Spoken Semitic. Pp. 1265–77 in vol. 2 of *Semitic Studies in Honor of Wolf Leslau on the Occasion of His Eighty-Fifth Birthday, November 14th, 1991*, ed. A. S. Kaye. Wiesbaden.

2000   An Irregular Usage of the Demonstrative Pronoun in Biblical Hebrew: Additional Device for Northern Hebrew in the Biblical Period. *Shnaton* 12: 83–88. [Hebrew]

Renz, J.

2000   Dokumentation neuer Texte. *Zeitschrift für Althebraistik* 13: 106–20.

Renz, J., and Röllig, W.

1995   *Handbuch der althebräischen Epigraphik*. 3 vols. Darmstadt.

Richter, W.

1966   *Traditionsgeschichtiche Untersuchungen zum Richterbuch*. Bonner biblische Beiträge 18. 2nd ed. Bonn.

Röllig, W.

1995   Ninive. Pp. 931–92 in vol. 2 of *Neues Bibel-Lexikon*, ed. M. Görg and B. Lang. Düsseldorf.

Rudolph, W.

1976   *Haggai—Sacharja 1–8—Sacharja 9–14—Maleachi*. Kommentar zum Alten Testament 13/4. Gütersloh.

Sadgrove, M.

1979   The Song of Songs as Wisdom Literature. Pp. 245–48 in *Studia biblica 1978: Sixth International Congress on Biblical Studies*, ed. E. A. Livingstone. Journal for the Study of the Old Testament Supplement 11. Sheffield.

Sauer, J. A.

1982   Prospects for Archeology in Jordan and Syria. *Biblical Archaeologist* 45: 73–84.

1986   Transjordan in the Bronze and Iron Ages: A Critique of Glueck's Synthesis. *Bulletin of the American Schools of Oriental Research* 263: 1–26.

Schaudig, H.

2001   *Die Inschriften Nabonids von Babylon und Kyros' des Grossen samt den in ihrem Umfeld entstandenen Tendenzschriften: Textausgabe und Grammatik.* Alter Orient und Altes Testament 256. Münster.

Schmid, K.

1999   *Erzväter und Exodus: Untersuchungen zur doppelten Begründung der Ursprünge Israels innerhalb der Geschichtsbücher des Alten Testaments.* Wissenschaftliche Monographien zum Alten und Neuen Testament 81. Neukirchen-Vluyn.

2002   Die Josephsgeschichte im Pentateuch. Pp. 83–118 in *Abschied vom Jahwisten: Die Komposition des Hexateuch in der jüngsten Diskussion,* ed. J. C. Gertz, K. Schmid, and M. Witte. Beihefte zur Zeitschrift für die alttestamentliche Wissenschaft 315. Berlin and New York.

Schüle, A.

1997   Zur Bedeutung der Formel *wajjehi* im Übergang zum mittelhebräischen Tempussystem. Pp. 115–25 in *Studien zur hebräischen Grammatik,* ed. A. Wagner. Orbis Biblicus et Orientalis 156. Freiburg, Switzerland.

2000   Deutung und Neugestaltung. Althebräische Grammatik in alttestamentlichen Texten. *Zeitschrift des Deutschen Palästina-Vereins* 116/1: 14–25.

Segert, S.

1961   Die Sprache der moabitischen Königsinschrift. *Archiv Orientální* 29: 197–267.

Smend, R.

1983   Das uneroberte Land. Pp. 91–102 in *Das Land Israel in biblischer Zeit: Jerusalem-Symposium 1981 der Hebräischen Universität und der Georg-August-Universität,* ed. G. Strecker. Göttinger theologische Arbeiten 25. Göttingen.

Smith, R. L.

1984   *Micah–Malachi.* Word Bible Commentary 32. Waco, Texas.

Speiser, E. A.

1964   *Genesis.* Anchor Bible 1. Garden City, New York.

Spieckermann, H.

1982   *Juda unter Assur in der Sargonidenzeit.* Forschungen zur Religion und Literatur des Alten und Neuen Testaments 129. Göttingen.

Staubli, T.

2003   Sin von Harran und seine Verbreitung im Westen. Pp. 65–89 in *Werbung für die Götter: Heilsbringer aus 4000 Jahre,* ed. Th. Staubli. Freiburg.

Steck, O. H.

1992   *Gottesknecht und Zion: Gesammelte Aufsätze zu Deuterojesaja.* Forschungen zum Alten Testament 4. Tübingen.

Stern, E., and Magen, Y.

2000   *Ha-shalav ha-rishon shel ha-miqdash ha-shomroni be-Har Gerizim: ʿEduyot arkeʾologiyot ḥadashot.* Qadmoniot 33 (120): 119–24.

Steymans, H. U.
1998   Der (un-)glaubwürdige Bund von Psalm 89. *Zeitschrift für Altorientalische und Biblische Rechtsgeschichte* 4: 126–44.

Stronach, D., and Codella, K.
1997   Nineveh. Pp. 144–48 in vol. 4 of *The Oxford Encyclopedia of the Ancient Near East*, ed. E. M. Meyers. Oxford.

TAD   See Porten and Yardeni 1986–99

Talshir, Z.
1993   *The Alternative Story of the Division of the Kingdom: 3 Kingdoms 12:24a–z.* Jerusalem Biblical Studies 6. Jerusalem.

Timm, S.
1995   Die Bedeutung der spätbabylonischen Texte aus Nerab für die Rückkehr der Judäer aus dem Exil. Pp. 276–88 in *Meilenstein: Festgabe für Herbert Donner zum 16. Februar 1995*, ed. M. Weippert and S. Timm. Ägypten und Altes Testament 30. Wiesbaden.

Tromp, N.
1982   *Mens is meervout: Het hooglied, vertaald en ingeleid.* Cahiers voor levensverdieping 38. Averbode.

Uehlinger, C.
1994   Die Frau im Epha (Sach 5,5–11): Eine Programmvision von der Abschiebung der Göttin. *Bibel und Kirche* 49: 93–103.

1995   Gab es eine joschijanische Kultreform? Plädoyer für ein begründetes Minimum. Pp. 57–89 in *Jeremia und die "deuteronomistische Bewegung,"* ed. W. Groß. Athenäums Monografien. Theologie: Bonner biblische Beiträge 98. Weinheim.

1999   The "Canaanites" and Other "Pre-Israelite" Peoples in Story and History (Part I). *Freiburger Zeitschrift für Philosophie und Theologie* 46: 546–78.

2000   The "Canaanites" and Other "Pre-Israelite" Peoples in Story and History (Part II). *Freiburger Zeitschrift für Philosophie und Theologie* 47: 173–98.

Utzschneider, H.
1988   Die Amazjaerzählung (Am 7,10–17) zwischen Literatur und Historie. *Biblische Notizen* 41: 76–101.

Veijola, T.
1982   *Verheissung in der Krise: Studien zur Literatur der Exilszeit anhand des 89. Psalms.* Annales Academiae Scientiarum Fennicae B 220. Helsinki.

Völger, G.; Welck, K. V.; and Hackstein, K. (eds.)
1987   *Pracht und Geheimnis: Kleidung und Schmuck aus Palästina und Jordanien: Katalog der Sammlung Widad Kawar zu einer Ausstellung des Rautenstrauch-Joest-Museums der Stadt Köln in Zusammenarbeit mit dem Institute of Archaeology and Anthropology der Yarmuk Universitaet in Irbid.* Ethnologica n.s. 13. Cologne.

Volgger, D.
1995   *Notizen zur Textanalyse von Ps 89.* Arbeiten zu Text und Sprache im Alten Testament 45. St. Ottilien.

Weippert, M.
1987   The Relations of the States East of the Jordan with the Mesopotamian Powers during the First Millennium B.C. Pp. 97–105 in vol. 3 of *Studies in the History and Archaeology of Jordan*, ed. A. Hadidi. Amman.
1990   Synkretismus und Monotheismus: Religionsinterne Konfliktbewältigung im alten Israel. Pp. 143–79 in *Kultur und Konflikt*, ed. J. Assmann and D. Harth. Frankfurt.
1997   *Jahwe und die anderen Götter: Studien zur Religionsgeschichte des antiken Israel in ihrem syrisch-palästinischen Kontext.* Forschungen zum Alten Testament 18. Tübingen.
1999   Eine phönizische Inschrift aus Galiläa. *Zeitschrift des Deutschen Palästina-Vereins* 115: 191–200.

Weir, S., and Shahid, S.
1988   *Palestinian Embroidery: Cross-Stitch Patterns from the Traditional Costumes of the Village Women of Palestine.* London.

Werner, W.
1982   *Eschatologische Texte in Jesaja 1–39: Messias, Heiliger Rest, Völker.* Forschung zur Bibel 46. Würzburg.

Williamson, H. G. M.
1985   Ezra, Nehemiah. Word Biblical Commentary 16. Waco, Texas.
1988   Structure and Historiography in Nehemiah 9. Pp. 117–31 in *Proceedings of the Ninth World Congress of Jewish Studies—Panel Sessions: Bible Studies and Ancient Near East.* Jerusalem.

Yassine, K.
1983   Tell El Mazar, Field I. Preliminary Report of Area G, H, L and M: The Summit. *Annual of the Department of Antiquities of Jordan* 27: 495–513.

Young, I. M.
1993   *Diversity in Pre-exilic Hebrew.* Forschungen zum Alten Testament 5. Tübingen.
1995   The "Northernisms" of the Israelite Narratives in Kings. *Zeitschrift für Althebraistik* 8: 63–70.

Zenger, E.
1999   Psalm 82 im Kontext der Asaf-Sammlung: Religionsgeschichtliche Implikationen. Pp. 272–92 in *Religionsgeschichte Israels: Formale und materiale Aspekte*, ed. B. Janowski and M. Köckert. Veröffentlichungen der Wissenschaftlichen Gesellschaft für Theologie 15. Gütersloh.

Ziadeh-Seely, G.
1999   Abandonment and Site Formation Processes: An Ethnographic and Archaeological Study. Pp. 127–50 in *Archaeology, History and Culture in Palestine and the Near East: Essays in Memory of Albert E. Glock*, ed. T. Kaplan. American Schools of Oriental Research Books 3. Atlanta.

Cyrus II, Liberator or Conqueror? Ancient Historiography concerning Cyrus in Babylon

DAVID VANDERHOOFT

Boston College

Cuneiform and archaeological evidence has led scholars to conclude that the transfer of power from Nabonidus to Cyrus the Great did not effect massive or immediate disruptions within the society or economy of Babylonia (Oppenheim 1985; Kuhrt 1988; Dandamayev 1989: 55; Bongenaar 1997; Briant 2002: 70–71). Nevertheless, from a historiographic perspective it is noteworthy how much attention was paid in the ancient world to analysis of this power transfer, its causes, and its signficance. Ancient writers expended considerable effort discussing Cyrus's accession to the throne of Babylon and the reasons for Babylon's fall, not only in the Babylonian cuneiform tradition, but also in biblical and Greek sources. Moreover, a near consensus of opinion characterizes those sources: in them, Cyrus is understood as a liberator, as an exemplar of the highest aspirations for kingship in each of the traditions that reflects on his rise to power in Babylon. The Hebrew Bible is no exception, and traditions within it invariably reckon Cyrus's rise and Babylon's fall as elements in God's overall plan for the restoration of his people.

This essay offers a comparative evaluation of a particular problem: the mechanics and historiography of the Persian takeover of Babylon in the autumn of 539. Its purpose is to investigate the historiographic logic that informs the cuneiform, Greek, and select biblical traditions concerning Cyrus's accession to the throne of Babylon and to explain

---

Author's note: Assyriological abbreviations follow those in CAD R. This essay expands on an analysis of the question presented in Vanderhooft 1999: 193–202. I am grateful to numerous scholars who have discussed the issues presented here with me, including Paul-Alain Beaulieu, Baruch Halpern, Reinhard Kratz, Oded Lipschits, Peter Machinist, Daniel Master, Mark Munn, David Schloen, and Larry Stager. None of these individuals bears responsibility for the views expressed.

351

his portrait as a liberator (for another recent attempt in this mode, see Kratz 2003).

Documentary evidence proves that in 539 B.C. Babylon passed rapidly from the control of Nabonidus to Cyrus. The Babylonian Chronicle reports that Ugbaru, governor of Gutium, together with the army of Cyrus, entered Babylon without a battle. This occurred on the 16th day of *Tašrītu*, in the 17th year of Nabonidus (Grayson 1975: 109–10 iii 15–16; the Julian date is Oct. 12, 539, on which see Parker and Dubberstein 1956: 29; Beaulieu 1989: 230). The Chronicle reports that 17 days later, on the 3rd of Araḫsamnu (Oct. 29, 539), Cyrus entered Babylon. In the interval between these two events, the Chronicle notes that armed Gutians surrounded the gates of Esagil but that cult practices were not interrupted.

Meanwhile, administrative tablets dated by regnal years of the king of Babylon confirm that rule was transferred. The first known cuneiform text dated to the accession year of Cyrus, "king of Babylon, king of lands," comes from Sippar and dates to the 19th day of *Tašrītu* (Oct. 15, 539; CT 57, 717). This was 5 days after the Persians captured Sippar, 3 days after Ugbaru entered Babylon, and 16 days before Cyrus's reported arrival in the capital on Oct. 29.[1] On the other hand, scribes elsewhere did not immediately recognize the change of ruler. On the day after Ugbaru entered Babylon, a tablet from Uruk dates to the reign of Nabonidus (GCCI 1.390; Parker and Dubberstein 1956: 13). Strassmeier assigned another contract to an even later date, the 10th of Araḫsamnu in Nabonidus's 17th year (Nov. 5, 539; Nbn. 1054: 8–9).[2] Even allowing for a slight delay in diffusion of the news about the transfer of power from Nabonidus to Cyrus, that transfer is a fact, the chronology relatively straightforward, and there is no room for skepticism.

---

1. For a survey of the administrative texts associated with the change of rulers, see Parker and Dubberstein 1956: 13–14; Petschow 1987. The mechanisms in place for legitimating Cyrus's status as king are not known. Note that the preferred titulary for Persian kings in Babylon, LUGAL TIN.TIR.KI *u* KUR.KUR 'king of Babylon and the lands' comes into use almost immediately (Petschow 1987: 45), even though LUGAL KUR.KUR was largely in abeyance during the Neo-Babylonian era, even for Nabonidus (Vanderhooft 1999: 16–23; on Cyrus's titulary, see Schaudig 2001: 26–27).

2. The month name is shaded in Strassmeier's copy, and Parker and Dubberstein therefore concluded that "this date cannot be accepted" (1956: 13). But the beginning of the sign is not shaded (Nbn. 1054: 8), and the two horizontals strongly argue in favor of the APIN sign. Strassmeier even dated another tablet (Nbn. 1055) to Kislev, the 9th month of Nabonidus's 17th year. However, the text refers only to disbursements from the *maššartum* (staples for assignment to craftsmen) allotted for Kislev, which may well have been laid up earlier and cannot serve as a reliable indicator of the terminal date of Nabonidus's reign (CAD M/1 389 s.v. *maššartu*, c 2'; Parker and Dubberstein 1956: 14).

We can be certain about the outlines of the power transfer because of the cuneiform sources. Discussion of the same event in different sources—including Greek and biblical texts—muddies the waters of historical reconstruction, and questions remain. Did Babylon capitulate, or was the city captured or conquered? Was power simply transferred from Nabonidus to Cyrus? Why and how did it happen? A second set of questions is also relevant. What significance did various ancient writers assign to the event and why? Why did ancient writers choose to emphasize one or another element in their reconstructions? These historiographical questions should be just as much a part of the modern historian's goals in analyzing the different accounts as are the problems of what happened.

The Babylonian Chronicle and the Cyrus Cylinder relate that Persian forces entered Babylon without a battle. The Babylonian Chronicle reads: UD 16 $^{m\lceil}Ug^\rceil$-ba-ru ^{lú}NAM ^{kur}Gu-ti-um u ERÍN.MEŠ ^{m}Ku-$raš$ ba-la $ṣal$-tum ana E^{ki} KU$_4$ 'On the sixteenth day (of *Tašrītu*), Ugbaru,[3] governor of Gutium, and the army of Cyrus entered[4] Babylon without battle' (Grayson 1975: 109–10 iii 15–16).[5] The Cyrus Cylinder reads: ba-lu qab-li $ù$ ta-$ḫa$-zi $ú$-$še$-ri-ba-$áš$ $qé$-reb ŠU.AN.NA^{ki} URU-$šu$ KÁ.DINGIR.MEŠ^{ki} i-$ṭe$-er i-na $šap$-$ša$-$qí$ 'Without a battle or attack, he (Marduk) made him (Cyrus) enter Šuanna, his city; he saved Babylon from hardship' (Schaudig 2001: 552, 17). The so-called Persian Verse Account of Nabonidus preserves no specific description of the entry into Babylon, although both the Verse Account and the cylinder claim that Cyrus was welcomed as a liberator (Schaudig 2001: 563–78). Scholars long ago recognized the anti-Nabonidus sentiment in all of these texts (see, e.g., Oppenheim 1985: 540–41; Machinist and Tadmor 1993; Beaulieu 1989; 1995; Sack 1997; now Schaudig 2001: 25–26; 563 with literature). The existence of such an animus, however, hardly seemed reason enough for modern historians to propose that there was a military encounter, even if the texts do not clarify why or how Cyrus's forces were able to enter the city without a battle. As Pierre Briant has recently stated,

---

3. The identity of Ugbaru and his relationship to Gubaru, the *pīḫāt bābili* (Grayson 1975: 110 iii 20) remains uncertain. The effort to link him to the Greek Gobryas has been disproved (Grayson 1975: 109 note).

4. The semantic range of *erēbu* 'to enter' includes the notion of the 'penetration' or 'invasion' into a city, foreign country, and so forth in military contexts (CAD E s.v. *erēbu* 1 f 1′).

5. Note the slightly different wording for Sippar, which 'was captured without a battle' (*ba-la ṣal-tum ṣa-bit*, Grayson 1975: 109 iii 14). Did the scribe's choice of different verbs reflect different processes for taking the cities?

however, it is reasonable to wonder if Babylon would have fallen entirely without resistance (2002: 41–43).

The historian may consider the following evidence. The Babylonian Chronicle relates that the Persians conquered Upê (Opis) on the east bank of the Tigris several days before Ugbaru entered Babylon. The battle at Upê involved a defeat of Babylonian field forces and plunder and slaughter of the people (Grayson 1975: 109 iii 12–14). The battle at Upê was followed by the capture (*ṣabātu*) of Sippar without a battle two days before Ugbaru's entry into Babylon. The Chronicle also reports that after the Persian capture of Sippar, Nabonidus fled (*iḫliq*), which implies that the author of the chronicle assumed that Nabonidus participated in the encounter at Sippar. Nabonidus was later seized (*ṣabit*) in Babylon, apparently after Ugbaru's entry (Briant 2002: 51). We know too that Nabonidus had already prepared Babylon for attack. The Chronicle reports that Nabonidus began transferring the gods of Babylonia into the capital late in his 16th year, or early in his 17th, and continued right up through Elul (Aug.–Sept. 539; Grayson 1975: 109 iii 10). Beaulieu has illuminated the scope of this program by an analysis of administrative documents showing the movement of numbers of people, boats, and materiel into Babylon; the goal, evidently, was to keep the cult statues safe in the fortified capital (Beaulieu 1993). All of this information points to the expectation and the reality of military engagement, as Briant has likewise remarked (2002: 43).

The laconic Chronicle text, not to mention the Cyrus Cylinder or Verse Account, says little in detail about how the city of Babylon came under Ugbaru's and then Cyrus's control. Did the population or at least the elite in Babylon hate Nabonidus so much that they would have welcomed Cyrus as a liberator, as the cylinder states (Schaudig 2001: 556, 36) and the Verse Account implies? Why were Nabonidus's preparations for the Persian assault so spectacularly ineffective and Babylon's prodigious defences overcome so swiftly? I will return to the cuneiform accounts with these questions in mind after review of the Greek traditions, especially Herodotus.

Greek traditions preserved by Herodotus and others suggest that the Greek writers knew or invented traditions about Babylon's fall that were different from the cuneiform traditions.[6] Herodotus (*Hist.* 1.188–

---

6. For discussions of the relationship between the cuneiform and Greek texts concerning the event, see Smith 1924: 102–6; Dougherty 1929: 167–85; Barnett 1963: 12–13; Wohl 1969: 28–38; MacGinnis 1986: 79; Black 1987: 15–25; Kuhrt 1987: 20–55; Beaulieu 1989: 225–26; Cole 1994: 95; Rollinger 1993: passim; Dalley 1996: 525–32; and Kratz 2003: 143–56.

91) and, later, Xenophon (*Cyr.* 7.5.7–15) relate an elaborate stratagem of Cyrus: he captured Babylon by diverting the flow of the Euphrates and infiltrating the city by its channel. The Greek accounts rest on several assumptions. First, both Herodotus (*Hist.* 1.178–81, 190) and Xenophon (*Cyr.* 7.5.7) assume that Babylon's defenses were impregnable.[7] Second, they agree that the city had been provisioned to hold out in a siege. Third, the plan to divert the river's flow and infiltrate the city through its empty or lowered channel is credited to Cyrus's brilliance. Finally, the diversion of the river's flow coincided with a festival in Babylon that diminished its defenders' vigilance (*Hist.* 1.191; *Cyr.* 7.5.15).

Particular evidence appears to undergird these assumptions. As Sack and others have shown, one of the Neo-Babylonian kings' principal claims to fame in Greek historiography was their monumental building achievements, including their defensive works around Babylon (Sack 1991: 115 n. 1; more generally Ravn 1942; and MacGinnis 1986). This affinity for grandeur notwithstanding, the Greek writers were aware of the massive fortification of Babylon conducted by Nebuchadrezzar and his successors, and possessed numerous details about the nature and scope of these defenses.[8] Their assumption that a conventional assault or siege would fail at Babylon followed from evidence that they possessed concerning Babylon's immense fortifications; in this sense, their reconstruction is at least well founded.

Second, the assumption that Babylon had been provisioned to withstand a Persian siege depends on a sound assessment of the evidence: Nabonidus's preparation for a Persian assault began considerably earlier. Transport of Babylonian gods and their retinues to Babylon began many months before the Persian campaign in October. Such activity in and around Babylon, recorded by the Chronicle in terms of the transport of the gods, could certainly support the later reconstruction of the Greeks. Herodotus, in any case, concluded that the Babylonians must already have been well aware of Cyrus's "expansionist ambitions," and they thus provisioned the city for siege (1.190).

Third, Herodotus and Xenophon agree that Cyrus conceived and executed a plan to manipulate the Euphrates to conquer Babylon, although they diverge in their descriptions. Herodotus's narrative has

---

7. A ground plan of the city can be had in George 1992: 24, fig. 4; and for a plan including the defenses and moats, p. 141, fig. 7.

8. For a survey of the debate concerning whether or not Herodotus in particular ever visited Babylon, see Ravn 1942; MacGinnis 1986; George 1992; Rollinger 1993 (negative); Dalley 1996 (possible). On the fortifications at Babylon, see Wetzel 1930; Koldewey 1990; and the synthetic work of George 1992.

long attracted interest in terms of its reliability. No doubt elements of folklore infuse the narrative, and the modern historian should retain a healthy skepticism about its details. On the other hand, Herodotus shows a frequent interest in military tactics designed to exploit or overcome river and water barriers and can dismiss those that seem improbable to him (e.g., 1.75). In fact, Herodotus states that Darius I attempted Cyrus's strategy of lowering the Euphrates to capture Babylon, but Babylonian vigilance prevented the success of such an assault on the city (3.152). In any case, the historian should ask whether Herodotus's reconstruction represents merely a colorful tale. He was fairly well informed about defenses and building techniques at Babylon and connects them plausibly to Cyrus's strategy. He offers a detailed description of the construction of the quay walls along the river in his description of the reign of Queen Nitocris. His description rests on precise knowledge about Babylonian building techniques (e.g., 1.186). We know from the inscriptions of Nabopolassar, Nebuchadrezzar, and Nabonidus that the Neo-Babylonian kings exerted massive energies in constructing quay walls of baked bricks set in bitumen, particularly along the east bank of the Euphrates (Cole 1994: 93–95).[9] The main reason for these construction projects was the high water table at Babylon and the danger that the Euphrates, which bisected the city, would shift out of its channel or erode the fortifications (Bergamini 1977: 111–52; Koldewey 1990; Cole 1994). Herodotus also accurately notes the existence of a bridge over the Euphrates, which the German excavations at the city uncovered (Koldewey 1990: 155–57). Herodotus knew that the builders in Babylon had the ability to reduce the water level of the river to construct the quay walls. This too is confirmed by excavations, which reveal that Nabonidus's quay wall "was built almost entirely in the river bed" (Bergamini 1977: 128).

Herodotus then explicitly states that Cyrus adopted the procedure of lowering the river as a prelude to investing Babylon:

> he posted his army at the place where the river enters the city, and another part of it where the stream issues from the city, and bade his men enter the city by the channel of the Euphrates when they should see it to be fordable. . . . He himself marched away . . . and when he came to the

---

9. Herodotus had exact knowledge of the Neo-Babylonians' use of bitumen and reed meshing in the baked brick walls: "using hot bitumen for cement and interposing layers of wattled reeds at every thirtieth course of bricks, they built first the border of the fosse and then the wall itself in the same fashion" (1.179). MacGinnis notes that the reeds generally were interposed at smaller intervals (1986: 75).

lake, Cyrus dealt with it and with the river just as had the Babylonian queen: drawing off the river by a canal into the lake, which was till now a marsh, he made the stream to sink till its former channel could be forded. When this happened, the Persians who were posted with this intent made their way into Babylon by the channel of the Euphrates, which had now sunk about to the height of the middle of a man's thigh (1.191).

It should be added that the Persian tactic, as described by Herodotus, would have been undertaken, if we adopt the Chronicle's date, in October (*Tašrītu*), when the Euphrates is at its lowest level (Charles 1988: 38, table 5). Barnett already argued some decades ago that the Greek historians probably did not conclude that Cyrus flooded the area north of the cross-country wall near the Aqar-Quf depression but, rather, that he "sent a detachment on to Falluja to switch the Euphrates into the course of the Pallakattu channel" (1963: 13). Cole has shown that the marsh area around Borsippa, fed by the Pallakattu, was referred to in the sixth century simply as *tamtu* 'sea'; he tentatively suggests that this may have been the outlet that accomodated increased water and reduced the flow through Babylon (1994: 95). Herodotus also narrates that Cyrus personally supervised the diversion of the river after installing his troops near Babylon (1.191).[10]

Other Greek writers knew that Babylon was vulnerable to penetration via the Euphrates. Berossus, in his *Babyloniaca*, says of Nebuchadrezzar's fortification of Babylon: "in order to prevent the possibility in any future siege of access being gained to the city by a diversion of the course of the river, he enclosed both the inner and the outer city with three lines of ramparts, those of the inner city being of baked brick and bitumen, those of the outer city of rough brick" (in Josephus, *Ag. Ap.* 1.139).[11] Berossus here seems to explain the purpose of Nebuchadrezzar's defensive installations under the influence of the Greek traditions about invaders having diverted the Euphrates. It is thus unclear whether Berossus provides independent evidence for a military threat from the Euphrates or whether the Cyrus tradition informs his comments. Still, he is cognizant of the military mechanism of diverting the river.

---

10. Xenophon's reconstruction is derivative of Herodotus's and apparently rests on less intimate knowledge of the city's defenses (*Cyr.* 7.5.10, 15–16).

11. The passage is also quoted in *Ant.* 10.220–26, where the defensive purpose of fortifying the river walls is described slightly differently: "in order that besiegers might no longer be able to divert the course of the river and direct it against the city, he surrounded the inner city with three walls and the outer one with three." On the *Babyloniaca*, see Burstein 1978.

In practical terms, it is not clear how lowering the river would have facilitated infiltration into the city. In Herodotus's view, if the Babylonians had been aware of the ruse, then "they would have shut all the gates that open on the river and themselves mounted up on to the walls that ran along the river banks, and so caught their enemies as in a trap" (1.191). Herodotus concluded that the Persian forces gained access to the city by the gates that opened on the river. But why did the river need to be lowered for this strategy to work? The gates gave access to the river even in high water periods (Bergamini 1977). Whatever the answer, Wetzel noted that gates were built into the defensive towers that lined Nabonidus's quay wall along the east bank; he speculated that they might have been the *pylidas* that Herodotus linked to the Persian infiltration (1930: 53 and pl. 49).

The Greek reconstruction of Cyrus's infiltration may also have been influenced by native Babylonian concerns about penetrating the city from the Euphrates. One of Nebuchadrezzar's royal inscriptions mentions the possibility of infiltration through canals that flowed eastward through the river quay wall into Babylon's eastern quadrant. The text describes Nebuchadrezzar's fortification of a canal outlet. The text is not without difficulties, but it reads as follows:

> *aš-šum in* ^{id}*mu-ṣe-e me-e-ša ḫa-ab-ba-a-tim mu-ut-ta-ḫa-li-lum la e-ri-bi in pa-ar-zi-il-lum e-lu-tim àṣ-ba-at mu-ṣa-a-ša in ḫu-qu gu-ul-la-tim pa-ar-zi-il-lum ú-uš-ši-im-ma ú-uš-ši-iṭ ri-ki-is-sa*

> so that robbers and thieves do not enter the canal's water outlet, I secured its outlet with pure iron. In crossbars I installed iron discs??, and I reinforced its (the outlet's) joint(s).[12]

Archaeological evidence for reinforcement of canal outlets appears near what is designated "Turm 1" in Wetzel's reconstruction (1938: pl. 49). Bergamini also described grates in the canal mouths in his analysis of the water levels of the Neo-Babylonian city and noticed their possible relationship to Nebuchadrezzar's inscription, although Bergamini preferred to interpret the grate as a filter for river water (1977: 122 n. 41 and fig. 72). These grates served no architectural purpose: they were designed for defense or for water regulation, or both. Might such native Babylonian concerns and defenses or, at least, the knowledge of the existence of such defenses have contributed to a reconstruction of the Persian infiltration such as the one presented in Herodotus?

---

12. VAB 4 84 (Nbk. 5 = Zyl II, 5) ii 1–10; H. Winckler, *ZA* 2 (1887) 126.

Another, quite different theory linking water diversion to the Persian infiltration has been suggested by Dalley (1996). We know that the so-called "Median Wall," built by Nebuchadrezzar, ran between Opis and Sippar and permitted defensive flooding of regions to the north (the 'Aqar Quf depression). Some have suggested that Cyrus's actions against Upê and Sippar, mentioned in the chronicle, may have permitted the switching of the Euphrates out of its channel and penetration into the area south of the Median Wall. Information about actions at the "Median Wall" may have been conflated by the classical writers with action at the inner walls of Babylon. On this view, the Persian entry into the vicinity of Babylon from Opis and Sippar was instead construed by Herodotus as entry directly into the city (e.g., Burn 1984: 54–56). He naturally concluded that the wall in question was the Imgur-Enlil. Rollinger has vociferously criticized such views, arguing that they represent a desparate attempt to salvage something from Herodotus (1993). On the other hand, Rollinger never really engages the question of why Herodotus offers the reconstruction he does, and thus he fails to respond to the historiographical question.

The tradition that the people of Babylon were celebrating a festival at the time of the Persian assault—the fourth assumption of the Greeks (*Hist.* 1.191; *Cyr.* 7.5.15)—has been widely dismissed as another folkloristic element. Certainly the motif "Nero plays while Rome burns" should not be accepted uncritically. In fact, however, Babylon did celebrate a "mid-year" Akitu-festival in the seventh month, *tašrītu*.[13] While this hardly means that the Greek narratives are strictly accurate, it once again shows that Herodotus in particular may have based his reconstruction on better information than scholars formerly suspected.[14]

---

13. Cohen writes:

> As at Uruk, Babyon celebrated an *akītu*-festival in the seventh month as well. Although the tablets do not mention the festival by name, the ritual information contained clearly refers to an *akītu*-celebration. This kinship with the *akītu* in *Nisannu* is noted in a letter to the Assyrian king: '[The king, my lo]rd, knows that the god Bēl is dressed (for the festival) [on the 3]rd day of Tašritu; on the 6th day the gate (of the temple) is kept open, (and the procession of Bēl sets out like in the month Nisa[nnu]. [The cere]monies of the city of Der are conducted in the same way.' (Cohen 1993: 451; the text is ABL 956, the translation by S. Parpola)

14. Such a tradition may also be reflected indirectly in Jer 51:39: "When they are heated, I will put out their drink, and I will make them drunk, that they may become hilarious. They will sleep the eternal sleep, and will not waken, says Yhwh." See also Jer 51:7; Isa 21:5; and, in the later tradition connected to Belshazzar, Dan 5:1–4 (Collins 1993: 243–46). None of these texts preserves specific information about the nature or timing of the festival, and certainly they are not primary witnesses. There is no direct connection

Even if celebration of the Akitu in the month *Tašritu* was not the cause of the Persian success, it would be reasonable for a writer, if he possessed such information, to conclude that the contemporaneity of the two events was not mere happenstance.

The Greek narratives about Cyrus's ruse for penetrating Babylon should not simply be read as a description of the Persian entry. The assumptions that inform the reconstruction, however, are at least explicable in view of the physical geography, seasonal timing, defensive architecture and installations around Babylon, and even the timing of the liturgical calendar. It turns out that defensive flooding around Babylon was widely used during the Neo-Babylonian Period and that this depended on the ability to divert or lower the Euphrates. Such diversion took place upstream, probably near Falluja, and the Babylonian Chronicle reports that the Persians captured Sippar, in that vicinity, days before they entered Babylon. Defensive flooding of the approach to cities in Babylonia was a longstanding military procedure, especially designed to prevent assault by chariotry (Powell 1982; Scurlock 1997). According to Herodotus, Cyrus pursued exactly the opposite strategy (lowering the river rather than flooding the city's approaches), but it was dependence on hydrological engineering in Babylonia that made it possible to switch the main flow of the Euphrates out of its channel.

On the whole, the Greek accounts provide a different historiographical perspective on Babylon's submission to Cyrus than the cuneiform accounts. Herodotus's narrative is largely shorn of theological considerations and avoids commentary on the competing religious claims for royal legitimacy that animate the cuneiform tradition. Herodotus focuses on Babylon's grandeur and Cyrus's genius. In this respect, he provides what might cautiously be called a rationalization for the more religiopolitical perspectives in the cuneiform tradition.[15]

The cuneiform accounts, meanwhile, comprise a series of indictments against Nabonidus. The Cyrus Cylinder and the Verse Account argue that Nabonidus was impious and, through his devotion to the moon god, Sîn, destructive of Babylonian mores. Very likely Cyrus's Babylonian apologists were drawing attention away from his role in capturing the city to portray him as a peaceful liberator. In any event,

---

between these traditions and the notice in the Babylonian Chronicle of "a libation of wine" in Nabonidus's 17th year (Grayson 1975: 109 iii 7).

15. I am grateful to Mark Munn of the Pennsylvania State University for discussion of this point.

as Kuhrt noted, these texts provide a ceremonial and, I would add, theological perspective that emphasizes that the coronation of Cyrus, a foreigner, need not be an impediment to legitimate rule, "on condition that the new king pledged himself to and showed himself active in maintaining traditional order" (Kuhrt 1987: 48). The texts are, in that respect, not merely propagandistic; they conform to a particular piety characteristic of the Babylonian viewpoint. Harmonization of the details of the cuneiform and Greek traditions is not required. As Kratz has also suggested, to discern the logic in the reconstructions is to enter into analysis of the history of ideas in the ancient world (Kratz 2003: 145). To dismiss Herodotus as inaccurate or as a liar does not further historiographical research.

This leads to a last set of observations about historiography in the Babylonian Chronicle. It is possible to reinterpret the report of Ugbaru's peaceful entry into Babylon, followed by Cyrus over two weeks later. The implication of the Chronicle, of course, is that Cyrus was absent at the initial entry into Babylon, even though he is said to have led his forces in the battle at Opis days earlier (see also Oppenheim 1985: 542–43). Rather, Ugbaru led the troops to enter the city, and he is designated "governor of Gutium." As Stephanie Dalley has noted, by the Neo-Babylonian Period, "Gutium is an archaic designation" that "refers to the barbarian from the eastern mountains who leaves nothing undamaged." In the Babylonian literary tradition, "Gutians are the archetypal sackers of cities" (Dalley 1996: 528; so also, earlier, Oppenheim 1985: 547 n. 2).[16] Although Ugbaru is not described as having sacked Babylon, the Chronicle does carefully report that armed Gutians "surrounded the gates of Esagil" but without interfering with temple rites. The purpose of this statement may well have been to rule out the conclusion that a learned, ancient audience would naturally have drawn: Cyrus let loose the brutal and uncivilized Gutians on the holy city, a religiopolitical act unworthy of the liberator (Oppenheim 1985: 542–43).

On the other hand, the Chronicle also reports that Ugbaru died eight days after Cyrus entered the city (Grayson 1975: 110 iii 22). The death of the Gutian may well have been interpreted as divine punishment for actions in or against Babylon (Dalley 1996: 528). To pose the

---

16. Beaulieu notes that there are other references to Gutians in Neo-Babylonian documents, including two in the Cyrus Cylinder and one in VAB 4, Nbn. 8. The last is a clear case in which Gutians are described as "archetypical barbarians and enemies of Babylonia"; the other two may be as well, even if the cylinder implies that Gutium is an actual region in the east (Beaulieu 1989: 228–29).

historiographical question: why should Cyrus's Gutian governor, who was active according to the Chronicle for a total of only a few weeks, have merited mention at all? Why should the entry into Babylon have been credited to Ugbaru rather than to Cyrus? After all, Cyrus is reported in the Chronicle and other cuneiform accounts to have been solicitous of the cults of Marduk and the other Babylonian deities when he did finally arrive. Would the statement that he presided over the peaceful liberation of the city not be a feather in his cap? A plausible case can be made that the Chronicle sought to emphasize that Cyrus was not involved with the initial entry into the city. Instead, as Dalley supposes, the author of the Chronicle identifies Ugbaru as the one immediately responsible for entering Babylon under Persian arms. (Note that the Chronicle takes no such pains with respect to the capture of Sippar.) Now one could argue that this is simply because the Chronicle gives just the facts: Ugbaru did it. But such an argument fits ill with the overwhelming tendency to identify the accomplishments of the king's deputies with those of the king himself. What is more, Zawadski has noted that proper names of nonroyal individuals appear very infrequently in the Babylonian Chronicles series (1988: 118–19). Ugbaru, in short, sticks out like a sore thumb in this notice.

Perhaps he appears prominently for the simple reason that he died immediately after the seizure of Babylon, and such a portentous circumstance both required comment and contributed to an agenda.[17] The strategy of the chronicler seems to be to encourage the reader to conclude that Ugbaru was a scapegoat, noting his death almost immediately after Cyrus the liberator arrives in Babylon. The implication is that Ugbaru absorbed the divine judgment that otherwise might have been meted out to Cyrus (Dalley 1996: 528). The careful presentation of the Chronicle permits the author fully to insulate Cyrus from activities associated with conquest. Cyrus is not Sennacherib.

We have compared the cuneiform accounts of Cyrus's takeover of Babylon with a Western, Greek perspective. Biblical traditions offer still another perspective. Where they touch directly on Cyrus (such as in the Second Isaiah and Ezra–Nehemiah), they are thoroughly positive. Cyrus normally appears as the liberator of the Judeans. On the other hand, biblical texts rarely bring Cyrus's rise and Babylon's fall together in an explicit way.[18] Several groups of prophetic oracles, however, do dwell

---

17. No indication is given for the cause of death, and the text certainly does not state that it was a result of a wound received in conflict.

18. An exception may be Isa 48:14–15, where God designates an unnamed individual who will יעשה חפצו בבבל וזרעו כשדים אני אני דברתי אף־קראתיו הביאתיו והצליח דרכו 'carry out

extensively on the issue of Babylon's demise, whether hoped for or already accomplished. The most extensive group of oracles dealing with the topic appears in Jeremiah 50–51, and these chapters deserve investigation in the present context. The oracles in Jeremiah express the conviction that Babylon will fall (or has fallen) in a military calamity and that the fortunes of the Judean exiles to Babylonia, the Golah, will be reversed (e.g., Jer 50:4–5, 8). Cyrus is personally absent from these oracles,[19] but it will be worthwhile to investigate what they say about Babylon's fall.

Jeremiah 50–51 frequently states that God will arrange a military assault against Babylon. In many texts, this is something that is impending, while others describe it as a fait accompli. Numerous examples of the latter could be cited. The opening lines state: נלכדה בבל הביש בל חת מרדך 'Babylon is captured, Bel is shamed, Merodach is dismayed' (Jer 50:2). In 50:23 we read: איך נגדע וישבר פטיש כל־הארץ איך היתה לשמה בבל בגוים 'How the Hammer of the whole earth has been hewn down and shattered; how Babylon has become a desolation among the nations'. At the end of chap. 50, the text has, מקול נתפשה בבל נרעשה הארץ 'at the sound of Babylon's capture, the earth quakes' (50:46). Or this: פתאם נפלה בבל ותשבר 'suddenly Babylon fell and was shattered' (51:8). Again, כי־נגע אל־השמים משפטה ונשא עד־שחקים 'For her judgment has reached the heavens, has been raised as high as the skies' (51:9). Or again: איך נלכדה ששך ותתפש תהלת כל־הארץ 'How has Sheshach[20] been captured, the praise of the whole earth been seized?' (51:41). Jer 51:44 reads, גם חומת בבל נפלה 'moreover, the wall of Babylon has fallen'. These statements all include verbs that are morphologically in the past tense (although the problem of verbal tense in prophetic oracles remains a vexing one). Given the clearly heterogenous nature of the oracles in

---

his [God's] intent in Babylon, and his might against Chaldea. I, I myself spoke, even called him; I have brought him and his way will prosper'. The prophet refers here to the individual whom God raises to carry out his intent in Babylon. The passage is consistent with the more explicit references to Cyrus as God's agent of restoration for his people in the Second Isaiah and justifies the identification, but it does not definitively name the Persian. Baltzer wonders whether the verb הביאתיו 'I have brought him (in)' might "indicate that the fall of Babylon is already presupposed" (Baltzer 1999: 291 n. 164). This is an intriguing possibility, but the reference in this context need not mean more than that God has "brought him" to the verge of success.

19. Numerous references to the enemy from the north who will attack Babylon (just as Babylon attacked Judah as the enemy from the north) may have the Persians in view (e.g., Jer 50:2); this is possible too for the reference to "the king[s] of the Medes" (Jer 51:11, 28). Even so, Cyrus remains unnamed.

20. Sheshach is an atbash cipher: *b* = *š* (second = second last); *k* = *l* (eleventh from beginning = eleventh from the end; i.e., adjacent middle letters).

Jeremiah 50–51, we may ask whether any of them reconstructs or comments on Babylon's fall to the Persians as a past event or whether they represent wishful thinking from before the period of Persian ascendancy. There is no decisive evidence, after all, demanding the conclusion that the oracles derive from before 539 (Reimer 1993; Albertz 2003: 194–96; Kessler 2003; differently, Holladay 1989: 391–431).

If the author or compiler of these oracles possessed concrete information about Babylon, then that might inspire confidence that the comments about Babylon's demise rest upon an informed reconstruction. Where Babylon's topography and defensive architecture are concerned, the writer does know some details. One example of this appears in Jer 50:15: הריעו עליה סביב נתנה ידה נפלו אשויתיה נהרסו חומותיה 'Raise a shout over her all around, she has surrendered; her turrets have fallen, her walls are thrown down'. The term אשיותיה[21] 'its (Babylon's) turrets', a hapax legomenon, is a loan of the Akkadian cognate *asītu*, a defensive turret or tower attached to a city wall.[22] The use of such a term evidently reflects more than a casual familiarity with Babylon. Elsewhere, the writer mentions that military officers, cavalry, and archers were to be arrayed against Babylon, and in one instance he uses an Akkadian loanword for the military officer, טפסר, Akk. *ṭupšarru* (Jer 51:27).[23] Jer 51:57 lists a series of terms encompassing Babylon's officialdom. Among them are פחות וסגנים 'governors and prefects'. The terms accurately reflect the Babylonian official titles *pīḫātu* and *šaknu*. It remains unclear how much precise knowledge of Babylonian administration such usage reflects, because the terms came into usage in Hebrew during the sixth century and are also assigned to Babylon's Median foes in the present oracles (51:23, 28; for a survey of the Hebrew usage of the terms, see Petit 1988). Still, the words are not misused and seem to underscore the effort in these oracles to achieve verisimilitude.

The writer of these oracles also puns on geographical terms associated with names for Babylon and its edifices, refers to ethnic groups

---

21. Thus the *Qere*; *Kethiv* אַשְׁוִיתֶיהָ is a simple transposition of letters.

22. The Akkadian parallel was recognized already by Zimmern (1917: 14); see also AHw 74 and CAD A/2 332–33, s.v. *asītu*; also Kaufman 1974: 37; Cohen 1978: 46–47; and Mankowski 2000: 52–53, who notes that the term may have been loaned into Akkadian from Northwest Semitic. It was earlier thought to be an exclusively Assyrian term, but in fact it describes architectural elements of Babylon's defenses known from Nebuchadrezzar's royal inscriptions (see Vanderhooft 1999: 190–91 n. 256).

23. The Hebrew word appears also in Nah 3:17; see the discussion of Machinist 1983: 732 n. 79; and Mankowski 2000: 60–61. The realization of *š* with *s* suggests it was a Neo-Assyrian loan into Hebrew.

within Babylonia, and mentions its contempoary foes. Twice the oracles use cryptograms: Sheshach for Babylon (51:44; see above, n. 20) and לב קמי 'Leb-qamai', an atbash cipher for כשדים (51:1). These are possibly intended to communicate a kind of insider knowledge, an ironic reversal of Babylon's own pretensions to learning, which will be discredited (cf. Isaiah 47). The reference to הר שרפה 'a burned mountain' or 'mountain of fired (bricks)' has also been understood by some scholars as a kind of pejorative reference to the ziggurat of Marduk—Etemenanki. The tale of the מגדול built in Babylon in Genesis 11 includes a reference to the builders' construction techniques: נלבנה לבנים ונשרפה לשרפה 'let us form bricks and fire them into burnt [bricks]' (Gen 11:3).

As for Babylon's foes, the oracles twice state that מלכי מדי 'the king[s] of the Medes' will attack Babylon (Jer 51:11, 28).[24] Also, the kingdoms of אררט מני ואשכנז 'Ararat, Minni, and Ashkenaz' are summoned by God to attack Babylon (Jer 51:27). The first of these three should be identified with Urartu, the second with the Manneans of northwestern Iran (southeast of Lake Urmia), and the third with the Scythians of central Asia. Hebrew אשכנז, therefore, is to be identified with the *Aškuzāya*, Scythians, mentioned in Neo-Assyrian cuneiform sources. In the so-called Table of Nations in Genesis, אשכנז is the offspring of Gomer, identified with the Cimmerians, also of central Asia (Gen 10:3). The three kingdoms named in the Jeremiah oracle had been subsumed into the territory of the Medes by the end of the seventh or beginning of the sixth century. The Medes, in turn, were conquered by Cyrus the Great before his campaign into Babylonia. What significance might the prophetic reference to these kingdoms have for our discussion? In the first place, their mention brings to mind the designation of Cyrus's general Ugbaru, who was "governor of the Gutians" and who was the first to enter Babylon, according to the Chronicle. The archaic ethnicon Guti shares several important characteristics in common with the biblical references to Manneans, Urartu, and the Scythians: these were all located in or adjacent to the Zagros Mountains to the east and north of Mesopotamia and were all subsumed within Median territory by the early sixth century (Diakonoff 1985: 124–25; Young 1988: 20–22). Is there a similar interpretive intention in the Jeremiah oracle to that

---

24. The LXX and Syriac both read, possibly correctly, a singular for the MT plural construct. On the other hand, the notion that a centralized Median empire developed in the mid-seventh century and was then ruled by a singular "king of the Medes" remains an unproved model in any case (Young 1988: 6–23; Briant 2002: 24–27). The author of these oracles may have understood the "Medes" to be a loose coalition of distinct peoples with more than one king.

found in the Babylonian Chronicle? The typological barbarians are summoned to the gates of Babylon. For the Chronicle, the issue is to show that this did not precipitate calamity and that Cyrus was indeed a liberator and Marduk's chosen. For the biblical oracle, the issue is the sovereignty of the God of Israel, not the efficacy of the conquering king or the power of Marduk. In this view, wicked Babylon will receive its comeuppance from traditional enemies from the north, directed now by the deity of a small, exiled population.

Do particular references to Babylon's fall from after the fact appear in Jeremiah? I have argued that one particular text describing Babylon's capture, Jer 51:30–32, resembles some elements in the Classical accounts. It reads as follows:

30 חדלו גבורי בבל להלחם ישבו במצדות
נשתה גבורתם היו לנשים הציתו משכנתיה נשברו בריחיה:
31 רץ לקראת־רץ ירוץ ומגיד לקראת מגיד
להגיד למלך בבל כי־נלכדה עירו מקצה:
32 והמעברות נתפשו ואת־האגמים שרפו באש
ואנשי המלחמה נבהלו:

30. The warriors of Babylon have ceased fighting, they remain in the strongholds. Their strength has dried up, they have become women! Its dwellings are burned; its bars are smashed.[25]
31. Runner runs to meet runner, messenger to meet messenger, to report to the king of Babylon that his city is taken from the outskirts:
32. "the fords are seized and they have burned the reed marshes, the soldiers are terrified."

This passage may well reflect *ex eventu* Judean traditions about Babylon's fall. The two Hebrew terms המעברות and האגמים evidently refer to topographical elements around Babylon. The Akkadian cognate of the first is *nēberu* 'crossings, fords'; these appear commonly in Akkadian texts that describe the capture of such fords as a military strategy.[26] The Hebrew term אגנים can mean 'pools' but here probably refers to the reed marshes around Babylon.[27] The Akkadian cognate *agammu* 'swamp,

---

25. Compare Isa 43:14 and 45:1–2 on the destruction of the doors and bars of Babylon. It would be incautious, however, to suggest a direct link between these references and the Greek tradition of infiltration into Babylon as it appears in Herodotus, not least because the smashing of bars is a common metonymic device in the Hebrew Bible for military destruction of a fortified city (e.g., Judg 16:3; Amos 1:5; Lam 2:9).

26. See CAD N/2 s.v. 1 a. On the physical characteristics of such fords, see Cole 1994: 93 and n. 62.

27. This was noted by Holladay (1989: 427); see also Isa 14:23, where an editorial addition brings the older poem in vv. 4b–21 into connection with the fall of Babylon and likewise mentions that the city will be turned into "marshes."

marsh' refers to a topographical item well known in the vicinity of Babylon. The term is in fact an Akkadian loan into Hebrew.[28] Akkadian texts, much like the report in Jeremiah, also refer to the burning of such marshes, usually in connection with curse formulas or as a military tactic for flushing out fugitives (Vanderhooft 1999: 201).

What prompted the use of such language in this oracle? Is it possible that the military tactics alluded to by the Babylonian messengers in Jer 51:31–32, seizing of fords and burning of reed marshes, were influenced by the Persian penetration into Babylonia in the autumn of 539? Perhaps the fords referred to in Jer 51:32 were crossing points or key points along the Euphrates where the river's flow could be diverted out of the main channel. Whether or not the author has in mind the manipulation of the river's water level through such diversion, as does Herodotus, remains unclear. The tactics described, however, are clearly at home in the Mesopotamian heartland. Seizure of fords and burning of marshes are practices well known in Mesopotamian military tactics, much less so in the Levant. The notice in Jer 51:31 that the messengers report to the king that the city was captured *miqqāṣeh*, from the outskirts, finds a parallel earlier in the anti-Babylon oracles, when the injunction is given to Babylon's enemies: באו־לה מקץ 'enter her (Babylon) from the extremity' (50:26). These may be general statements about invading the city, of course, but are rare, and one wonders about their topographical referents. Rare too is the comment that Babylon's attackers should חרבו כל־פריה 'destroy all her bulls' (50:27). The verb in the MT (from חרב III [BDB] or II [HALAT]), is rare, and the noun פר 'bull-calf' is not used elsewhere in Jeremiah. Human leaders could certainly be in view. One might even speculate that this is a reference to the famed Processional Street of Babylon, the Ay-Ibur-šabu, lined as it was with images of bulls, lions, and composite beasts in glazed tile. Such a hypothesis is clearly speculative, but these oracles provide numerous indications of an effort to achieve verisimilitude, even if, as Beaulieu suggests, these indications are not overwhelming.[29] Given the traditions preserved by the Greek historians and the reticence of the Babylonian accounts, however, it is worth investigating whether these oracles simply express a proleptic hope for the destruction of Babylon or whether they reflect traditions about its fall that had reached the Judean

---

28. The date of the loan cannot be precisely established, given its distribution in Hebrew (e.g., Exod 7:19; 8:1; Isa 41:18; 42:15; Ps 107:35; 114:8). See the discussion of Mankowski (2000: 25–26).

29. In private communication.

community in the mid-sixth century. If so, they may augment the native cuneiform sources, which, as argued above, were not intended as straightforward military accounts of the events of Autumn 539.

In the aggregate, the Greek and Biblical traditions caution the historian that cuneiform sources can be flawed sources for historical reconstruction notwithstanding their proximity or formulation in Akkadian.

Each of the historiographical perspectives discussed so far is basically transparent. There were reasons why Cyrus's Babylonian apologists might have hesitated to describe his military capture of the city: he was a liberator, not a conqueror. The Chronicle and the Cyrus Cylinder also assert that Cyrus showed proper respect for the Babylonian cultic establishment. Could such a king—designated by Marduk—have orchestrated a ruse to penetrate the holy city? The cuneiform sources continually emphasize that the transfer of power from Nabonidus to Cyrus deserved comment precisely because the theological stakes in interpreting its significance were so high. The Greek accounts—and that of Herodotus in particular—on the other hand, emphasize the glory and impressive might of Babylon, a typical motif in Greek historiography, and couple this with an account of the brilliance of Cyrus, whom they honor to show his extraordinary gifts. Here the theological component recedes altogether. The prophetic oracles in Jeremiah, meanwhile, likely date to the end of the Babylonian imperial era or early Persian Period and assume that Babylon is no longer a force with which to reckon. Now it stands under Yahweh's judgment and will finally be destroyed because of crimes against his people. The descriptions of the city's fall are not specific enough in every detail to allow for a reconstruction of that event, but there are some intriguing indications, most notably Jer 51:32, that the writer had already witnessed the fall of Babylon to the Persians. If this is correct, then these oracles and the more explicit Classical accounts (their historiographical assumptions notwithstanding) provide an interesting alternative tradition to the cuneiform accounts about the fall of the great imperial city, and indeed of the Babylonian imperial state. Utlimately, however, it was the Persian-inspired propaganda about Cyrus that carried the day and decisively influenced the Western historiography of Cyrus as liberator.

Bibliography

Albertz, R.
    2003   *Israel in Exile: The History and Literature of the Sixth Century* B.C.E., trans. D. Green. Studies in Biblical Literature 3. Atlanta.

Baltzer, K.
1999 *Deutero-Isaiah.* Hermeneia. Philadelphia.
Barnett, R. D.
1963 Xenophon and the Wall of Media. *Journal of Hellenic Studies* 83: 1–26.
Beaulieu, P.-A.
1989 *The Reign of Nabonidus King of Babylon, 556–539 B.C.* Yale Near Eastern Researches 10. New Haven, Connecticut.
1993 An Episode in the Fall of Babylon to the Persians. *Journal of Near Eastern Studies* 52: 241–61.
1995 King Nabonidus and the Neo-Babylonian Empire. Pp. 969–79 in vol. 2 of *Civilizations of the Ancient Near East*, ed. J. M. Sasson et al. New York.
Bergamini, G.
1977 Levels of Babylon Reconsidered. *Mesopotamia* 12: 111–52.
Berger, P.-R.
1974 Der Kyros-Zylinder mit dem Zusatzfragment BIN II Nr. 32 und die akkadischen Personennamen im Danielbuch. *Zeitschrift für Assyriologie* 64: 192–234.
1989 *Die neubabylonischen Königsinschriften: Königsinschriften des ausgehenden babylonischen Reiches (625–539 a. Chr).* Alter Orient und Altes Testament 4/1. Kevelaer and Neukirchen-Vluyn.
Black, J. A.
1987 Babylonian Textual Evidence. Pp. 15–25 in vol. 1 *Ḫabl aṣ-Ṣaḫr 1983–85: Nebuchadnezzar II's Cross-Country Wall North of Sippar*, ed. J. A. Black, H. Gasche et al. Ghent.
Bongenaar, A. C. V. M.
1997 *The Neo-Babylonian Ebabbar Temple at Sippar: Its Administration and Its Prosopography.* Nederlands Historisch-Archaeologisch Instituut te Istanbul. Istanbul.
Borger, R.
1956 *Die Inschriften Asarhaddons Königs von Assyrien. Archiv für Orientforschung* 9. Graz.
1996 *Beiträge zum Inschriftenwerk Assurbanipals.* Wiesbaden.
Briant, P.
2002 *From Cyrus to Alexander: A History of the Persian Empire*, trans. P. T. Daniels. Winona Lake, Indiana.
Burn, A. R.
1984 *Persia and the Greeks.* 2nd ed. London.
Burstein, S.
1978 *The Babyloniaca of Berossus.* Source for the Ancient Near East 1/5. Malibu, California.
Charles, M. P.
1988 Irrigation in Lowland Mesopotamia. *Bulletin on Sumerian Agriculture* 4: 1–39.
Cohen, C.
1978 *Biblical Hapax Legomena in the Light of Akkadian and Ugaritic.* Society of Biblical Literature Dissertation Series 37. Misoula, Montana.

Cohen, M.
1993   The Cultic Calendars of the Ancient Near East. Bethesda, Maryland.
Cole, S. W.
1994   Marsh Formation in the Borsippa Region and the Course of the Lower Euphrates. Journal of Near Eastern Studies 53: 81–109.
Collins, J. J.
1993   Daniel. Hermeneia. Philadelphia.
Dalley, S.
1996   Herodotus and Babylon. Orientalistische Literaturzeitung 91: 525–32.
Dandamayev, M.
1989   A Political History of the Achaemenid Empire, trans. W. J. Vogelsang. Leiden.
1997   Assyrian Traditions in Achaemenid Times. Pp. 41–48 in Assyria 1995, ed. S. Parpola and R. Whiting. Helsinki.
Diakonoff, I.
1985   Media. Pp. 36–148 in The Median and Achaemenian Periods, ed. I. Gershevitch. Vol. 2 of The Cambridge History of Iran. Cambridge.
Dougherty, R. P.
1929   Nabonidus and Belshazzar: A Study of the Closing Events of the Neo-Babylonian Empire. Yale Oriental Researches 15. New Haven, Connecticut.
Gadd, C. J.
1958   The Harran Inscriptions of Nabonidus. Anatolian Studies 8: 35–92.
George, A. R.
1992   Babylonian Topographical Texts. Leuven.
Grayson, A. K.
1975   Assyrian and Babylonian Chronicles. Locust Valley, New Jersey. [Repr. Winona Lake, Indiana, 2000.]
Holladay, W. L.
1986   Jeremiah 1. Hermeneia. Philadelphia.
1989   Jeremiah 2. Hermeneia. Philadelphia.
Kaufman, S. A.
1974   Akkadian Influences on Aramaic. Assyriological Studies 19. Chicago.
Kessler, M.
2003   Battle of the Gods: The God of Israel versus Marduk of Babylon: A Literary/Theological Interpretation of Jeremiah 50–51. Studia Semitica Neerlandica. Assen.
Koldewey, R.
1990   Das wieder erstehende Babylon, ed. B. Hrouda. 5th ed. Munich.
Kratz, R.
2003   From Nabonidus to Cyrus. Pp. 143–56 in Melammu Symposia III (Milano 2002), ed. A. Panaino and G. Pettinato. Helsinki.
Kuhrt, A.
1988   Babylonia from Cyrus to Xerxes. Pp. 112–38 in Persia, Greece and the Western Mediterranean c. 525–479 B.C., ed. J. Boardman et al. Vol. 4 of The Cambridge Ancient History. Cambridge.
1997   Usurpation, Conquest and Ceremonial: From Babylon to Persia. Pp. 20–55 in Rituals of Royalty: Power and Ceremonial in Traditional Societies, ed. David Cannadine and Simon Price. Cambridge.

Langdon, S.
1912 *Die neubabylonische Königsinschriften.* Vorderasiatische Bibliothek 4. Leipzig.

MacGinnis, J.
1986 Herodotus' Description of Babylon. *Bulletin of the Institute of Classical Studies* 33: 67–86.

Machinist, P.
1983 Assyria and Its Image in the First Isaiah. *Journal of the American Oriental Society* 103: 719–37.
1997 The Fall of Assyria in Comparative Ancient Perspective. Pp. 179–95 in *Assyria 1995,* ed. S. Parpola and R. Whiting. Helsinki.

Machinist, P., and Tadmor, H.
1993 Heavenly Wisdom. Pp. 146–51 in *The Tablet and the Scroll: Near Eastern Studies in Honor of William W. Hallo,* ed. M. Cohen, D. Snell, and D. Weisberg. Bethesda, Maryland.

Mankowski, P. V.
2000 *Akkadian Loanwords in Biblical Hebrew.* Harvard Semitic Studies 47. Winona Lake, Indiana.

Oppenheim, A. L.
1985 The Babylonian Evidence of Achaemenian Rule in Mesopotamia. Pp. 529–87 in *The Median and Achaemenian Periods,* ed. I. Gershevitch. Vol. 2 of *The Cambridge History of Iran.* Cambridge.

Parker, R. A., and Dubberstein, W. H.
1956 *Babylonian Chronology, 626 B.C.–A.D. 75.* Providence, Rhode Island.

Petit, T.
1988 L'évolution sémantique des termes hébreux et araméens *phh* et *sgn* et accadiens *pāḫatu* et *šaknu. Journal of Biblical Literature* 107: 53–67.

Petschow, H.
1987 Zur Eroberung Babyloniens durch Cyrus: Die letzten vorepersischen und ersten persischen Datierungen aus den Tagen um die persische Eroberung Babyloniens. *Nouvelles assyriologiques brèves et utilitaires* 3: 44–45.

Powell, M.
1982 Merodach-Baladan at Dur-Jakin: A Note on the Defense of Babylonian Cities. *Journal of Cuneiform Studies* 34: 59–61.

Ravn, O. E.
1942 *Herodotus' Description of Babylon.* Copenhagen.

Reimer, D. J.
1993 *The Oracles against Babylon in Jeremiah 50–51.* San Francisco.

Rollinger, R.
1993 *Herodots Babylonischer Logos.* Innsbruck.

Sack, R.
1991 *Images of Nebuchadnezzar: The Emergence of a Legend.* Selinsgrove, Pennsylvania and London.
1997 Nabonidus of Babylon. Pp. 455–73 in *Crossing Boundaries and Linking Horizons: Studies in Honor of Michael C. Astour,* ed. G. D. Young, M. W. Chavalas, and R. E. Averbeck. Bethesda, Maryland.

Schaudig, H. P.
2001   Die Inschriften Nabonids von Babylon und Kyros' des Großen, samt den in ihrem Umfeld entstandenen Tendenzinschriften. AOAT 256. Münster.
Scurlock, J. A.
1997   Neo-Assyrian Battle Tacitics. Pp. 491–517 in Crossing Boundaries and Linking Horizons: Studies in Honor of Michael C. Astour, ed. G. D. Young, M. W. Chavalas, and R. E. Averbeck. Bethesda, Maryland.
Smith, S.
1924   Babylonian Historical Texts relating to the Capture and Downfall of Babylon. London.
Unger, E. A.
1970   Babylon: Die Heilige Stadt nach der Beschreibung der Babylonier. 2nd ed., ed. R. Borger. Berlin.
Vanderhooft, D. S.
1999   The Neo-Babylonian Empire and Babylon in the Latter Prophets. Harvard Semitic Monographs 59. Atlanta.
2003   New Evidence Pertaining to the Transition from Neo-Babylonian to Achaemenid Administration in Palestine. Pp. 219–35 in Yahwism after the Exile: Perspectives on Israelite Religion in the Persian Period, ed. Rainer Albertz and Bob Becking. Studies in Theology and Religion 5. Assen-Maastricht.
Wetzel, F.
1930   Die Stadtmauern von Babylon. Wissenschaftliche Veröffentlichungen der Deutschen Orientgesellschaft 48. Leipzig.
Wetzel, F., and Weissbach, F. H.
1938   Das Hauptheiligtum des Marduk in Babylon, Esagila und Etemenanki. Wissenschaftliche Veröffentlichungen der Deutschen Orientgesellschaft 59. Leipzig.
Wiseman, D. K.
1956   The Chronicles of the Chaldean Kings (625–556 B.C.). London.
1985   Nebuchadrezzar and Babylon. The Schweich Lectures, 1983. Oxford.
1991   Babylonia 605–539 B.C. Pp. 229–51 in The Assyrian and Babylonian Empires and Other States of the Near East, from the Eighth to the Sixth Centuries B.C., ed. J. A. Boardman et al. Vol. 3/2 of Cambridge Ancient History. Cambridge.
Wohl, H.
1969   A Note on the Fall of Babylon. Journal of Ancient Near Eastern Studies 2: 28–38.
Young, T. C.
1988   The Early History of the Medes and the Persians and the Achaemenid Empire to the Death of Cambyses. Pp. 1–52 in Persia, Greece and the Western Mediterranean c. 525–479 B.C., ed. J. Boardman et al. Vol. 2 of The Cambridge Ancient History. Cambridge.
Zawadski, S.
1988   The Fall of Assyria and Median-Babylonian Relations in Light of the Nabopolassar Chronicle. Poznan.
Zimmern, H.
1917   Akkadische Fremdwörter als Beweis für babylonischen Kultureinfluss. 2nd ed. Leipzig.

Neo-Babylonian and Achaemenid State Administration in Mesopotamia

M. A. DANDAMAYEV
Oriental Institute, St. Petersburg

Our information on the Babylonian administrative system during the Chaldean and Achaemenid Periods is very limited. This can easily be explained by the fact that Babylonian cuneiform documents of the first millennium B.C.[1] come mostly from temple and private archives. State archives, which naturally contained primary information on governmental administration, with a few exceptions have not come down to us. Apparently, the state chancellery as early as Chaldean times and then during the Achaemenid Period was maintaining records mainly in Aramaic on leather and papyrus, and such texts easily deteriorated in the climatic conditions of Mesopotamia. The aim of this essay is to study documentary evidence on state administration, while the temple, military, financial, and judicial administrative systems cannot be considered here. As seen from documents discussed below, terminology of the Babylonian administration, as well as functions of various officials were essentially the same during Chaldean and Persian times (i.e., the seventh through fourth centuries).

The palace administration itself was controlled by the 'head of the palace' (*rab ekalli*) and included a large number of court employees and a net of messengers. During Neo-Babylonian times, one of the high administrative positions was held by *Zazakku*, who was a close counselor of the king in the relations between palace and temples. This office, however, was given up under the Achaemenids (cf., MacGinnis 1996: 19–20, with previous lit.). There were also overseers of royal canals and

---

1. All dates in this essay are B.C. Abbreviations are those of the *Assyrian Dictionary of the Oriental Institute of the University of Chicago* and of the *Reallexikon der Assyriologie und Vorderasiatischen Archäologie*. My estimates of Babylonian capacity measures are based on the assumption that one *qa* was about one liter. Several unpublished cuneiform documents from the State Hermitage Museum in St. Petersburg are designated by the abbreviation *Erm*. These texts are being prepared for publication by N. Czechowicz.

moorings, officials in charge of customs stations, and other lesser functionaries. A number of royal officials were stationed in temples of various cities. The most important among them were *ša-rēš šarri*, who were the royal controllers introduced into the temple administrative staff (cf. Bongenaar 1997: 105–6; MacGinnis 1994: 207–11). They supervised the exact and prompt payments of barley, dates, sheep, and so on to the crown, as well as performance of state duties by the temples.

Along with the autochthonous population of Babylonia, there were in the country about 30 ethnic groups, some of which had their own area under the jurisdiction of their prefects, who were overseers of landholders of these groups. For instance, an "assembly of Egyptian elders" functioned in Babylon that made decisions concerning lands belonging to individuals of Egyptian extraction (Camb. 85). Also known are "the elders of Judah" (Ezek 8:1), that is, chiefs of Judahite settlements in Babylonia who decided problems related to the internal administration of these communities (a prototype of the Hellenistic *politeumata*).

The chief state officials bore a variety of titles. The highest administrative title was *šakin māti* (spelled GAR.KUR), that is, 'governor of the country' (see San Nicolò 1941: 61). However, "the sign sequence GAR. KUR, which originally stood for *šakin māti*, could be (and in fact, usually was) used for writing simple *šaknu* as well" (CAD Š/1 191; cf. also Ebeling 1953: 221–22). Da Riva assumes that during early Neo-Babylonian times (640–580), all the provinces were under direct royal control (Da Riva 2002: 385). There is, however, some evidence that in the period under consideration the provinces were under direct jurisdiction of the governor of the country. No explicit evidence on the term of the governors' office exists. In this connection, some interest has been shown in a Neo-Assyrian letter, according to which a governor of Nippur was in office for 10 years, while during the year that the letter was composed three holders of the office left it (CT 54 no. 22: rev. 9–10; see SAA 10 no. 112). It is also known from a little earlier time that a governor of Dilbat retained his office for at least 17 years (see Brinkman 1968: 108).

The first governor of the country known to us was Terikšarrussu, before whom in 555, on the orders of the last Chaldean king, Nabonidus, a contract was drawn up, according to which the Eanna Temple rented out some lands located near Uruk (YOS 6 no. 11). The next governor of Babylonia was Nabû-aḫḫe-bulliṭ who came to this office during Nabonidus's reign and retained his post, after the Persian conquest of Mesopotamia in 539, for four years. In 548 he ordered a settlement of some accounts in the Eanna Temple (YOS 6 no. 145). A document from 536 states that a debtor must be delivered to Eanna officials by his guarantors or else they would have to pay ten minas of silver to this governor (YOS 7 no. 33). In 535 three cousins appealed to him to make a decision about a transaction made by their dead grandfather. The governor sent them to Imbija, the governor of Uruk, and judges there for a verdict (BIN 2 no. 134).

The same title is mentioned in a number of letters from temple archives in Uruk, with no reference to any names. For instance, a governor orders Eanna officials not to be negligent in guarding the temple (YOS 3 no. 154). Another message says: "immediately purchase bows and other weapons" (YOS 3 no. 170; see CAD Š/1 189). To judge from a letter, some royal soldiers were under one governor's command (BIN 1 no. 41; cf. CAD Š/1 189). Another letter contains a governor's order to compile a list of the members of the Eanna collegium (YOS 3 no. 57; cf. also ibid. no. 161). One governor, together with another person, presented some iron and bronze to the Eanna Temple (BIN 1 no. 41). The sender of one letter asks his addressee to deliver him some oxen in order to present them to a governor (YOS 3 no. 179).

A number of documents from the Ebabbar Temple archives in Sippar mention "the house of the governor," some individuals of which were issued 237 talents of bitumen (CT 55 no. 335), a sheep (CT 44 no. 72), etc. The son of another governor handed over a sheep as an offering to the Ebabbar (VS 6 no. 213). One governor's architects were paid money and beer for their work (CT 56 no. 600). Some Nippureans were collecting taxes under the jurisdiction of their governor (TMH 2/3 no. 238). One merchant of a governor is listed among several officials (VS 6 no. 215:15). The sender of one letter asks his addressee to let him know the governor's verdict regarding a slave woman who was being held as security for a debt (UET 4 no. 174). Finally, one text refers to the manager of a governor's household (PBS 2/1 no. 198:23–24).

The title "governor of the country" (or simply "governor") is attested also in one document drafted in Ur in 496 (UET 4 no. 101:4). This man apparently was a district governor (*šaknu*). In a number of Murašû documents composed in Nippur in the second half of the fifth century, several individuals with Babylonian names bear the title *šaknu* (BE 9 no. 23; PBS 1/1, 35, 70, 170, etc.). Usually they are listed among witnesses in records concerning various obligations, and frequently their seals are affixed to the tablets (PBS 2/1 nos. 22, 27, 29, etc.). In Nippur this title usually designated the overseers of various groups of landholders. Stolper has shown that there were five different *šaknus* of Nippur over a period of 25 years but "no two of them appear in the same year" (Stolper 1988: 130). He assumes that they did not have much status (1988: 131). But it seems to me that these officials appear in Nippur with approximately the same responsibilities as governors of other cities. Therefore the distinction should be made between a *šaknu* of Nippur, which was an administrative title on the city level, and simple *šaknus* who were the overseers of various professional groups dependent on the state administration. As *The Assyrian Dictionary* states, "in all periods, *šaknu* could refer to officials on two distinct levels of the administrative hierarchy: provincial governors (appointed by the king), and officials subordinate to provincial governors and other high officials" (CAD Š/1 191). At Nippur, beginning in the ninth century, the governor bore the title *šandabakku* (Brinkman 1968: 298). According to Oppenheim, governors of Nippur had this title until Xerxes' reign, and after that time they were called *paqdu* (Oppenheim 1985: 569 n. 2). Zadok assumes that at the beginning of the Achaemenid period the activity of the *šandabakku* was restricted to religious and economic spheres, the carrying out of the functions of the head of the Enlil Temple (Zadok 1978: 274). As Stolper indicates, a certain Širiktu-Ninurta was a *šandabakku* from the last year of Nabonidus until the accession year of Darius I, that is, from 539 to 522 (Stolper 1988: 129; cf. CAD Š/1 373). However, the exact functions of these officials during the period under consideration remain elusive.

In 535 the Persian King Cyrus made Mesopotamia and the regions to the west of the Euphrates (Across-the-River, i.e., Syria and Palestine) into a single province and appointed an Iranian, Gubaru by name, its governor. His official title was *bēl pīḫāti or pīḫātu* (LÚ EN.NAM or LÚ NAM), that is, 'lord of a province'. It was a synonym for "governor of the country" as well as a designation for the office of provincial and city administrator.

Gubaru held his post for at least ten years, until 525, and is referred to in many documents from Babylonian temple archives, which give abundant information about his administrative functions. His residence was in Babylon. At his orders, the Eanna Temple frequently sent its slaves from Uruk to Babylon to perform state duties and perhaps to work in the palace household. He also ordered Eanna officials to supply a royal palace located near Uruk with sheep, beer, and dates. He was regularly informed about the number of dead and runaway temple slaves. The persons who had stolen temple property were sent from Uruk to Babylon for his interrogation and punishment. He had at his disposal several scribes and a number of messengers. His administration ordered the assignment of a canal in the Nippur region to some military settlers (BE 8 no. 80; on similar functions of Neo-Assyrian governors, see ABL 327 rev. 11). Thus, his control was extensive. In particular, he exercised authority over the Babylonian temples (for references to sources and previous literature, see: Dandamayev 1992: 73–78; Zadok 2002: 883 no. 2; Jursa 1996: 198–200; see also Erm. 15562, according to which this official was informed in 527 about an Eanna slave who had left his job of feeding temple oxen and had run away; the governor ordered him put in shackles).

In 520 a certain Uštanu (an Iranian name) became the governor of Babylonia and Across-the-River (Dar. 27:3: LÚ NAM; BRM 1 no. 101:4 LÚ *pe-ḫat-tum*). He apparently was an Iranian. The tablets referring to him as governor belong to the period between 521 and 516 (Eph'al 1988: 154). They come from Babylon, Sippar, and some other cities. According to BRM 1 no. 101, three scribes and one Aramaic scribe (*sepīru*) of the Ebabbar Temple in Sippar recorded orders by Uštanu and the priest of Sippar about regulations for the lease of temple fields. In 520 he authorized several persons to issue 35,986 liters of barley to make beer (see Dar. 27, which probably comes from the Borsippa region).

During his service, a certain Tattannu was appointed governor of Transpotamia. His name is Semitic. As is well known, he is mentioned also in the book of Ezra (5:3, 6; 6:6, 13). A promissory note drafted in Babylon in 502 mentions one of his slaves (VS 4 no. 152). He was subordinate to Uštanu (for references, see Stolper 1989: 292).

One of the governors of Across-the-River was Belšunu. He was governor of Babylon between 421 and 414 (but possibly as early as 429). Later (between 407 and 401) he was given the governorship of Across-the-River (see Stolper 1989: 392–400).

A number of Murašû documents from Nippur mention a certain Gubaru, who in 420–419 was "governor of the Land of Akkad," or "governor of the Akkadians" (for references, see Stolper 1989: 290). According to Oppenheim, he was an important satrap (Oppenheim 1985: 564). Thus, *bēl pīḫāti* or *pīḫātu* was a synonym for the office of *šakin māti* or *šaknu* (cf. Frame 1992: 226) and "sometimes served as the Babylonian equivalent of satrap" (see Brinkman 1968: 304).

However, it was not just the title of the chief official of Babylonia or Across-the-River. For instance, in some Murašû texts it designates officials in charge of canals (see Stolper 1985: 39). Furthermore, in one text from Sippar this title is applied to an official who was "perhaps in charge of a settlement of Egyptians" (MacGinnis 1994: 210 n. 66 with reference to Camb. 344). One Murašû text mentions a field that belonged to 'the governor' (LÚ NAM) of the Aramaic ethnic group Hindanu in the Nippur region in the second half of the fifth century (BE 10 no. 54:5). Finally, in a document from Sippar a "governor," together with one other individual, asked Ebabbara officials to lease them water from a canal for five minas of silver per year (Jursa 1995: 145 no. 53). Apparently, they both were tenants of temple fields situated in the Sippar region, and this *pīḫātu* was only a village head (cf. 1995: 111 n. 218).

Several texts mention the title governor without personal names. For instance, in 529 in Borsippa a governor and another person acted as guarantors for a certain man who owed 25,740 liters of dates to the manager of the palace (*rab ekalli*) (VA 3 no. 71). One governor detained some individuals (BIN 1 no. 86; also YOS 3 no. 65). Frequently scribes, messengers, and other officials subordinate to the governors are mentioned (BIN 1 no. 54; CT 55 no. 256; VS 6 no. 303, etc.).

Finally, the title under consideration was also used to designate city governors, although most commonly their office (especially in big cities) was called *šakin ṭēmi* (LÚ GAR.KU 'lord of appointment'). Documentary evidence on city governors will now be discussed in an alphabetized list of the cities. Their titles are indicated where they are stated (*bēl pīḫāti*), otherwise they were called *šakin ṭēmi*.

Arpad. One of its governors (his name is not indicated) is mentioned in two documents from Sippar composed in 586 that state that he delivered two oxen as an offering to the god Šamaš (CT 56 no. 439; Nbk. 74; see Joannès 1994: 22).

Babylon. In 560 Mušezib-Bel, son of Eli-ilani-rabi-Marduk together with several judges sealed a document on a sale of land (5 R 67, no. 1 rev. 12; cf. Frame 1984: 749 n. 17). The next year he (again together with some judges) judged a lawsuit, and the tablet contains his seal impression (Dalley 1979: no. 69).

Nabu-iddin is known from several Sippar documents (cf. Bongenaar 1997: 9; for the list of governors in economic texts from Sippar, see Frame 1984: 749). In 552 he paid a certain amount of silver to the Ebabbara for a house (Nbn. 170:12–14). The dates of other texts are broken off, or they are undated. According to one of them, he was issued a quantity of wool from the same temple that provided his income (*pappasu*) (CT 56 no. 310:4). Together with Nabu-mukin-apli, governor of Borsippa, he ordered some "prisoners" fettered who were making a royal statue in the royal storehouse in the Ebabbara (MacGinnis 1995: 181–82). A legal document records a statement made by a certain man before Nabu-iddin concerning some property (Wunsch 1997: 159–64 no. 12). Finally, he is listed among the witnesses in a contract in which King Nabonidus rented out a palm grove that belonged to the Ebabbara (Jursa 1995: 88 no. 24).

Gubaru was the first Persian governor (LÚ NAM) of Babylon (on governors of this city during Persian times, see Stolper 1989: 290). According to the Babylonian Chronicle, in 539 he "appointed the district officials in Babylon" (Grayson 1975: 110, col. III 15, 20). But he died soon after the conquest of Mesopotamia by the Persians.

Marduk-zakir-šumi is attested in two documents from 531 and 525. According to the first of them, a certain man contracted to marry a girl without the knowledge of his father. The father appealed to a court of law, which decided that the contract was illegal. This court consisted of the governor himself and three royal judges (Cyr. 312). As seen from Camb. 276, a certain Hašdaja was to go into military service, but he hired another person to perform the duty instead and paid him one mina of silver for two years of expenses there. This sum was entrusted to the governor to hand over to a royal official. The document itself was drafted in a town, the location of which is unknown. It can also be noted that a certain Bit-irani-šar-uṣur is mentioned as *pīḫātu* in Babylon in 528 (Camb. 127). Perhaps he was an official over only part of the city.

Bel-apla-iddin in 517 sent his "men of the chariot" to Elam (Dar. 154). As we know from a document composed in 516, a slave smith was hired for a term of two years, but the man who hired him failed to pay the slave's master any money until the governor ordered him to (Dar. 206).

Bagapanu was an Iranian governor (LÚ *pa-ḫa-⟨tum⟩*) of Babylon. In 503 one of his slaves bought a female slave (Stigers 1976: 36 no. 22; here his name is spelled Bagapa'; see Stolper 1987: 396). A legal decision concerning the lease of several fields and palm groves belonging to the royal treasury was made before Bagapanu and several judges (Zadok 2002: 884). The name of the man who held the office in 499 is only partly preserved (Dar. 577).

In 496–494 Guzanu is attested as governor. He ordered Širku, a member of the Egibi business house, to pay 56,880 liters of dates to a palace official (BRM 1 no. 81:2–5). In the same year he entrusted Širku to collect toll from boats "at the bridge or at the harbor, going downstream or upstream" (TCL 13 no. 196; see CAD 1 197–98). He also ordered an official to issue 324 liters of barley from the Ebabbara storehouse in Sippar (CT 56 no. 411; cf. Frame 1984: 749 with n. 18). The letter CT 22 no. 74 was sent from Guzanu to his "brother" Širku. Van Driel assumes that they were governor and Širku from the Egibi family. Guzanu writes: "The soldiers belonging to the *gardu* about whom I gave you an order, you must allow to go, realize that the guards at the gate and the charioteers are all at your disposal and that the troops from Bit-Dakuru who stay in Babylon are (also) at your disposal. Do not complain about the men of my chariot fief" (the translation is from van Driel 1989: 207).

Marduk-eriba, son of Belšunu, was governor (*pa-ḫa-ti*) in 429 (Wunsch 1997: 185 no. 36). He was the same man who is attested in other texts as Eriba, "Governor of Babylon." Probably, he was the son of and successor to Belšunu, governor of Babylon, who was promoted later to the governorship of Across-the-River (see Stolper 1995: 224).

The term *pīḫātu* continued to be used in Babylon during the Hellenistic Period as well (see Oppert-Ménant Doc. jur.: 285–90). The latest known reference to the title "governor (LÚ *pa-ḫat)* of Babylon" comes from 94 (CT 49 no. 156:12).

But in some cases it is difficult to determine the exact position of the officials who bore this title. For instance, a certain Šamaš-aḫ-iddin (his patronymic is not given) is referred to by this title in two documents that come from two different cities and were drafted in 551 and 547. According to the first of them, three shekels of gold from his income (*irbu*) were delivered to the Eanna Temple goldsmiths in Uruk for work (GCCI 1 no. 386:4). The second document states that 795 liters of sesame belonging to him were paid as tithe to the Ebabbara Temple in Sippar. The payment was made through his secretary (Nbn. 362). In all probability, this was one and the same person. The question arises: Was he governor of Babylonia or of one of its provinces? It would be logical to assume that he was the chief administrator of the whole country. However, as we have seen above, in 548 the post of Babylonian governor belonged to Nabû-aḫḫe-bulliṭ who bore the title *šakin māti*. Thus, we still do not know where this Šamaš-ah-iddin was governor.

Another difficult case is the governorship of Nergal-epuš, who was a *bēl pīḫāti* and in 550 delivered five oxen to the Eanna Temple in Uruk as an "offering of the king" (TCL 13 no. 123). He could have been governor of Babylonia after Terikšarrussu, who held the office in 555. However, the problem is that Erm. 15539 (lines 19–20), drafted in Uruk in 533, mentions a "message" of the high-ranking Persian official Parnaka concerning an investigation into some gold that had been stolen from the Eanna Temple, and in connection with this matter refers to a Nergal-epuš, who is called the *bēl pīḫāti* (the text is damaged). His patronymic is not given, and it is difficult to decide whether these two names referred to one and the same person.

The following texts also give some information about governors of Babylon, although their names are not indicated. In 544 a certain man undertook to make a repair on a harbor in Babylon and, "according to the decision of the governor of Babylon," was issued a quantity of asphalt and lime, as well as beams (VS 6 no. 84). A letter states that 120 talents of asphalt and 10 talents of lime were issued from the Ebabbara Temple storehouse in Sippar to a "messenger of the governor of Babylon" (CT 55 no. 334). In 540 an agent of the governor of Babylon received five shekels of silver as half payment for the equivalent for military service (*ilku*) of a certain Arad-Gula, who paid for it himself (Nbn. 962). It can also be noted that the sender of another letter informs his addressee that he is going to visit the governor and therefore asks him to send him (in Babylon) 4 "excellent" sheep and 18 liters of milk to give to the governor (CT 22 no. 142).

Finally, a document drafted in Babylon records that Bel-iddin, "governor (LÚ EN.NAM) of Esagil" (i.e., the Temple of Marduk in Babylon) was issued $42\frac{1}{2}$ minas of silver as the rental payment incumbent on the temple lands for the years 512–511. The actual recipient apparently was the Esagil Temple, and the tenant of the field was the Egibi business firm (Dar. 315).

Borsippa. All of the documents for this entry come from Borsippa, except the fragmentary CT 56 no. 396, which probably was drafted in Sippar.

Mardukaja in 614 attended a lawsuit regarding a field (VS 6 no. 9). The next governor was Ukin-Marduk, a descendant of Carpenter, in whose presence in 594 Nebuchadnezzar II killed a conspirator right at the people's (or army's) assembly (Weidner 1954–56: 1ff.).

Nabu-eṭir-napšati (I), son of Balassu, descendant of Ilu-bani, was governor in 592, and before him a land-sale contract was made (VS 5 no. 6). In 567 he sold five cubits of land for four shekels of silver. The text does not mention his title, and apparently by that time he had become a private citizen (TCL 12 no. 55; on him, see also Zadok 1997/1998: 298).

Nabu-mukin-apli was governor during the reign of Nabonidus (the date is broken off; MacGinnis 1995: 181, BM 62602). On him, see above in the entry on governors of Babylon, s.v. Nabu-iddin.

Nabu-eṭir-napšati (II) was authorized to collect money from those who entered the gate of Borsippa, and in 532 he passed on this right to another man (OECT 12 no. A 110). The document stipulates that his secretary should receive a share of the income. The long gap between this document and VS 5 no. 6, in which an individual with the same name is mentioned as governor in 567, excludes the possibility that they were one and the same person.

Mušezib-Bel's seal is affixed to a document composed in 510 (VS 6 no. 128). It records the obligation of a certain man for the monthly delivery of a quantity of barley and flour to some people. This obligation was announced in the presence of two judges and some other individuals, including the governor's scribe.

Finally, a fragmentary text seems to record the delivery of 1 talent, 45 minas of (wool?) to a "governor of Borsippa" (CT 56 no. 396:15).

Byblos. A certain Rikis-kalamu-Bel is attested as governor (LÚ. NAM) of the city Gubbal (i.e., Byblos; CT 55 no. 435:10). The document comes from the Ebabbara archive in Sippar and was composed during the reign of Darius I (the year is destroyed). It records that he paid a tithe to the Ebabbara Temple. This tax consisted of silver, blue purple, wine, and a trunk of a cedar tree. It is unknown whether Byblos in Phoenicia or its possible namesake in the Sippar region is meant here. I cannot accept the assumption of Zadok (1985: 120) and Stolper (1987: 396 n. 35) that the toponym under discussion should be read *Dubal* (see Dandamayev 1995: 30).

Cutha. The earliest-known governor of this city was Nergal-tabni-uṣur, who settled a suit in the second year of Cyrus (537) regarding a piece of land that had been sold (Joannès 1996: 63–64).

Nergal-šar-uṣur is mentioned in a land-sale contract from the reign of Cambyses (the year is destroyed), to which his seal is affixed (Camb. 432:20).

A certain Nabu-kešir declared before the governor Nergal-zer-ibni and the assembly of the Cuteans that the paternal grandmother and aunt gave him nothing from his father's property. The governor and members of the assembly of Cutha examined witnesses, studied related documents, and made their decision (BM 77425; see Joannès 1996: 62–63).

OECT 10 no. 247 is an undated text that records that "the governor of Cutha" (his name is not given) was issued 30 liters of barley. Other recipients of the same quantity of barley were a judicial scribe, a judge, an official in charge of fodder, and so on. In all probability, the distribution was made from the local temple.

A governor (EN.NAM) of *Der* is mentioned in a letter, according to which he visited Uruk and discussed with Eanna officials there the status of a man who presumably was from that city (YOS 3 no. 59).

Kiš.   Lawsuits concerning property were conducted before Governor Zababa-napišti-(iddin) in 596 (OECT 10 nos. 48:11 and 50:6–7).

Marduk-eriba, son of Banija, is mentioned as governor in 579 and a recipient of 3 minas of silver (OECT 10 no. 315:65).

In 557 Bel-kaṣir set a deadline for a certain man to settle an account with his contracting party (Watelin Kish III, p. 145:6).

Zababa-iddin, son of Etellu, descendant of Ahutu, appears in 505 as a recipient of 23 minas of silver. The debtor was the well-known Marduk-naṣir-apli of the Egibi firm (Abraham 1997: 79, BM 33936:8; see also the duplicate text, Liv. 25).

Finally, a document from 517 mentions a palm grove belonging to the governor (line 4: LÚ *pi-ḫa-tum*) of Kiš (his name is broken off; Dar. 194).

In *Nippur* governors were called *šaknu* (see above in the entry on the governors of the country).

Qadeš.   Milki-ṭiri, "governor (LÚ EN.NAM) of the city of Qadeš" was responsible to deliver three cows with their calves at a specified time to a certain Aplaja or else to pay him 5 minas of silver. The document was composed in 565 in the city of Ṣurru (Tyre; Pinches 1917: 129). It is unknown whether these were the Phoenician cities or their possible Babylonian namesakes.

Šahrinu was a town in the region of Babylon. Its governor (LÚ *pi-ḫa-tum*) Liblut, son of Mušezib-Marduk, bought dates in 510 for 5 minas of silver from a member of the Egibi firm (Dar. 338).

From *Uruk* we have much more information on the office of the governor (on the lists of governors from there, see: Kümmel 1979: 139–40; Frame 1991: 80; Sack 1994: 30–32). Anu-ah-iddin was governor in 626–625. His seal is affixed to a contract on the sale of a temple prebend (von Weiher, AUWE 12 no. 221:27). AnOr 9 no. 4 is a land sale contract dated to his administration (cols. I 35, II 32, and IV 31). He is also mentioned in BagM 5:342 no. 30:3.

Marduk-šum-uṣur, son of Nabu-šum-iškun of the Ḫunzû family, was governor in 612–611. A land-sale contract is dated to his tenure (BIN 1 no. 130:26), and his seal is affixed to another such contract (von Weiher Uruk 2 no. 55:33).

In 603 a land-sale contract was made in the presence of Šamaš-zer-iqiša of the Gimil-Nanaja family (AnOr 8 no. 2:30). In Gehlken AUWE 11 no. 179:9, Governor Iqišaja received part of an offering to Eanna of mutton. Jursa assumes that these were both probably the same individual (Jursa 1997/1998: 424).

Bel-šum-iškun, son of Bel-iddin of the Kuri family, is listed without any title among witnesses to a promissory note drafted in 601 (Kessler AUWE 8:41 no. 90:14). Apparently at that time he was still a private citizen. In OECT 10 no. 51 he appears as a 'deputy' (LÚ *šanû*) of the governor of Uruk and a debtor owing 5 minas, 10 shekels of silver (in this text, his ancestral name is omitted). The document was drafted sometime after 594. Finally, in YOS 17 no. 357 he is referred to as governor (line 6). The document comes from the Eanna Temple archives but was composed in Borsippa in 592. It records a payment to him of an amount of silver by somebody else. The money was destined for another individual, whose slave had been held as security for the debt.

Marduk-eriba, son of Zerutu, was governor in 588–586. Nbk. 109, drafted in Babylon, records a lawsuit over a house between two parties. One of the partners was a resident of the Sealand, located on the south of Mesopotamia. The court was attended by several people, including the governor (*qīpu*) of the Sealand and his deputy (*šanû*), as well as by the governor of Uruk, Marduk-eriba, and governor (*šangû*) of Ur, Imbi-ili. In TCL 12 no. 36, a certain man presented to his wife a slave woman together with her sons with the stipulation that they serve her until the end of her life and then become temple slaves. The document was composed "at the time when Marduk-eriba was governor of Uruk" (lines 22–24). In another text, 34 shekels of silver belonging to the Eanna Temple constituted the price of barley that a certain man was to pay. The document adds that the barley was given to this governor (Walker AfO 24:126 no. 14). In all probability, the text was composed in 588 (see Kümmel 1979: 139). Finally, Pinches ET 25 (1913/14) 420 no. 18, drafted in Babylon in 586 records that the above-mentioned governor of the Sealand, his deputy, and a scribe were to pay 1 mina, $22\frac{1}{2}$ shekels of gold to the Eanna Temple. Governor Marduk-eriba and Imbi-ili, governor of Ur (mentioned also above in Nbk. 109), are listed among the witnesses.

Anu-šar-uṣur was governor of Uruk in 561 (TCL 12 no. 62:4). This document was drafted in Babylon and records that he owed 3 minas of silver to an administrator of the Esagil Temple, while an Eanna official stood as guarantor (see also a reference to an unpublished text in Sack 1977: 47 n. 17).

Marduk-šum-iddin, son of Nabu-balassu-iqbi of the Gimil-Nanaja family was issued a quantity of barley from the Eanna Temple in 572 (GCCI I no. 230:4). Van Driel has noted that in 564 this person addressed an official of Eanna with these words:

Give me the king's cash in Eanna, the cash of the office of *šatammu*, all the prebendary income held by the king of the functions of brewer, cook, slaughterer, oil presser, measurer and . . . all prebends held by the king and the *šatammu*, as many as exist in Eanna and the prebends of the king which individuals illegally pocket in Eanna . . . , and I will give you the three minas of gold which the king imposed upon you. I will also give a horse of good quality to the king. (TCL 12 no. 57; the translation is from van Driel 1989: 213)

In 561 the administrator of the Enlil Temple in Nippur delivered 90,000 liters of barley to the Eanna in exchange for wool from the Sealand. This transaction was completed through Marduk-šum-iddin (YOS 40 38, unpublished; see Sack 1977: 43–44). In none of these texts does he bear the title of governor. As Sack notes, he "was involved with the hierarchy of Eanna before he ever held the office of *šakin ṭēmi*" (1977: 46). He appears as Uruk's governor first in a document from 559 (see 1977: 46 n. 9 with reference to an unpublished text). The next year he is mentioned as governor in connection with the payment of an amount of barley to the Eanna (UCP 9 no. 34:4). The following documents were drafted in 555: YOS 6 no. 11 records that an enormous area of land belonging to the Eanna temple was rented out at King Nabonidus's orders. The contract was concluded before this governor as well as others. In PTS 2097 (see Frame 1991: 39), the royal commissioner in the Eanna informed the governor, the temple collegium, and scribes about a royal edict. Another text contains a list of sacred vessels taken from the Eanna for religious ceremonies. To judge from the tablet, which is in bad condition, these vessels were delivered through this governor (YOS 19 no. 266). The latter is mentioned also in YOS 19 no. 266, which is a receipt for alum given to the Eanna by Crown Prince Belshazzar through the governor. In 554 a messenger of this governor received from the Eanna 19 minas, 15 shekels of silver and 13 spades of iron for some purpose (GCCI 1 no. 410). Finally, in the same year, before the governor and temple officials, the royal commissioner in the Eanna made a statement about the status of a temple slave's daughter (YOS 19 no. 91). As Frame has noted, he is attested as governor from the first year of Neriglissar to the second year of Nabonidus—that is, 559–554 (Frame 1991: 80).

Ṭabija, son of Nabu-nadin-šumi of the Ḫunzu family, was governor in 551–543. San Nicolò (1941: 13) and Kümmel (1979: 140) give 551–545 as the years of his governorship. Frame (1991: 80) considers the 13th year of Nabonidus (543) to be the last year that reference is made to him as governor. The last time he is mentioned by name is in the 14th year of Nabonidus (542) in YOS 19 no. 1, which records the sale of a house located in the city of Uruk. It bordered specifically on the house of Ṭabija, who apparently was a private citizen by that time. The first time his name occurs is in the fourth year of Nabonidus (552), when he is mentioned as a witness for an estimation of the yield of an Eanna date grove (YOS 19 no. 83). But in this text he is referred to as a private individual. TCL 12 no. 123 contains a list of royal offerings to Eanna, including 3 oxen and 10 sheep from this governor. He also delivered there a quantity of gold (Erm. 15487), as well as some bronze and iron (YOS 19 no. 295 from 543). According to YOS 6 no. 95, he owed the same temple 50 shekels of silver, "the remainder of the price for wool." YOS 6 no. 92 is a record of the proceedings of a court of law regarding a house that had been sold in 583 and about which litigation arose in 550. The case was considered in 549 at the assembly of the Babylonians and Urukeans, including this governor, judges, and temple officials. His seal is also affixed to the tablet. An Eanna financial claim against an individual was registered in the presence of *zazakku* (a high royal official), a temple administrator, and the governor (YOS 6 no. 228). *Zazakku* and the governor were also among those before whom the Eanna officials and scribes filed for payment from a certain man 1 mina, 29 shekels of silver to be paid to the temple (AnOr 8 no. 25). A widow dedicated her two small sons to the Eanna Temple in order to save them from starvation. Her statement was made before a number of individuals, including the governor (YOS 6 no. 154). As Kümmel noted, he was the father of Šulaja, who also served as governor of Uruk (Kümmel 1979: 140 n. 232).

We used to assume that Nadinu, son of Balaṭu, descendant of Ekurzakir, was governor in 541–538 (see San Nicolò 1941: 13; Kümmel 1979: 140; Frame 1991: 80). Now a document from 543 has been found in which he is already mentioned as governor (YOS 19 no. 92). It describes a session of the assembly of Uruk in the 13th year of Nabonidus, with the participation of Nadinu and the chief administrator of the Eanna. This session determined the date of the composition of a document regarding a field located in the Nippur neighborhood. ROMCT 2 no. 6 contains a financial claim against an individual from the Sealand made by some Eanna officials in front of some citizens, including this governor and a deputy of the governor of the district of Tuplijaš. According to another document, Eanna officials arrested a certain individual, hoping to turn him into a slave, because his grandmother was a temple slave. The investigation was conducted in Nadinu's presence (YOS 6 no. 224). He is also listed among individuals before whom a certain man declared that nobody had touched the vegetable oil while he was bringing it by boat from the Esagil Temple in Babylon to Eanna (TCL 13 no. 124). YOS 7 no. 7 is a court protocol concerning a temple slave charged with 12 counts of stealing Eanna property. The body of citizens that decided this matter included Nidintu. Finally, in 524 he was among some citizens who considered a litigation regarding a house (YOS 7 no. 198). But in this case he acted as a private citizen and therefore is referred to without any title. Furthermore, we know that at this time the office of governor was occupied by a man named Imbija.

Šulaja, son of Ṭabija of the Hunzu family, was governor in 537. As we have seen, his father also held the same office. In 538 he is listed in a list of witnesses as a private citizen (TCL 13 no. 124). The following year he became governor. A rent collector from the Eanna estate complained to him that in 539 he gave 16,200 liters of dates to Imbija, son of Nanja-ereš, descendant of Kidin-Marduk (a future governor) "in an exchange" but that he received nothing from him (YOS 7 no. 23; see also its duplicate BIN 2 no. 115). In the same year, the assembly of Uruk, including this governor, judged a case in which a cow from the temple herd was appropriated by an individual (AnOr 8 no. 38).

Nabu-šar-uṣur, son of Bunana (536) together with a judge and other individuals was informed that 5 oxen belonging to Eanna had been stolen (YOS 7 no. 30).

Imbija, son of Nanaja-ereš, descendant of Kidin-Marduk, was governor from 535? to 524 (see San Nicolò 1941: 13; Kümmel 1979: 140). As we have seen from the entry on Šulaja, a rent collector complained that this Imbija had not paid for dates received from the Eanna (YOS 7 no. 23). The document was composed in 537 when he had not yet been appointed governor. In BIN 2 no. 134, three cousins appealed to the governor of Babylonia, requesting that he make a decision regarding the house that had been mortgaged by their grandfather. In his turn, he sent them to the governor and judges of Uruk for a verdict. The date is lost. It probably was the fourth year of Cyrus (535/34; see San Nicolò 1941: 24 n. 21). In YNER 1 no. 1, Eanna officials informed artisans who were working for this temple about their status. This statement was made before Imbija and some other individuals. According to a document from 531, lamentation-priests set up the kettledrum after sunset and declared: "There is an eclipse of the moon!" (see CAD K 93). This announcement was made at the assembly of Uruk, a member of which was Imbija (Boissier 1926: 13–17; see also YOS 7 no. 71 with similar contents). TCL 13 no. 233 is a receipt for various expenditures of the

Eanna Temple, including 9 minas of silver for the purchase of 190 sheep that Imbija delivered to the Eanna stables. In TCL 13 no. 147 he is listed among the members of the assembly who decreed that a stolen sheep was to be compensated 30-fold to Eanna. In BIN 1 no. 128 he acts as a witness regarding rent payment to Eanna. YOS 7 no. 198 from 524 is the latest document that mentions him. In it he, together with some other officials and citizens, considered a case about livestock and fowl missing from Eanna. The tablet also contains his seal impression. Finally, in a document from 552 his father is listed among citizens of Uruk (AnOr 8 no. 21:9).

A number of letters from the Eanna archives mention a certain Imbija, who probably was the same person. Among them, YOS 3 no. 129 is of a special interest: its sender urges the addressee to return everything taken from the house of a certain Guzanu, because Guzanu was going to convince Imbija to complain (?) to the king about this matter.

The title *šakin ṭēmi* is also mentioned in some letters from the Eanna archives without personal name. For instance, a governor arrested the slave of a smith, telling him: "You are to deliver 12 swords a year" (YOS 3 no. 107:28–29). A man was imprisoned at the orders of a governor (BIN 1 no. 19:24–25). A letter from the royal commissioner in the Eanna to "the governor, my father," informs him about a message from the crown prince regarding work to be done in the temple (TCL 9 no. 132). Another letter commands: "Do not be negligent about the document which the governor has given to you" (YOS 3 no. 57). In one letter "the boats of the governor" are mentioned (YOS 3 no. 173:21).

Yabatamru (?). In 536 Yabatamru's governor (EN.NAM) Marduk-šar-uṣur, together with his boatman rented out a boat for 5 shekels of silver per month (Frame 1986: 39 no. 6). This city probably was located in the area of Uruk (1986: 40).

In addition to the titles discussed above, there are several other words used to designate governors. One of them is *qīpu*, which was borne by the "administrator of a region, a city, or a temple" (CAD Q 266). During Neo-Babylonian and Achaemenid times, it mainly referred to a temple official but in a few texts is also used for governors. In particular, two governors who bore this title are referred to in a text that probably belongs to Nebuchadnezzar II's time (Unger Babylon: 286 no. 26 IV 17–18 and 21–22). Other references to this title are given below. In 544, the governor of the city of Akkad and a scribe delivered 100 sheep to the Ebabbara Temple in Sippar (CT 55 no. 151:5–6). CT 55 no. 746 states that the administrator of Akkad paid the same temple some money. One text mentions a slave of the governor of the town of

Birati (VS 6 no. 248:21, 28). In BIN 1 no. 169 a "governor of Larsa" appears among citizens of Uruk, before whom a statement was made about guarding the Eanna Temple in 530. Finally, Nbk. 109 from 588 records a lawsuit regarding a house in Babylon. One of the litigants (or possibly both of them) was an individual from the Sealand. One of the people who attended was the governor of the Sealand and his deputy.

The word *šangû*, usually denoting "chief administrator of a temple" (CAD Š/1 377), in some cases was also used as a title for governors of small towns. For instance, a *šangû* of the town of Baṣ is mentioned together with five judges and an administrator of the Temple Esagil in Babylon among witnesses in a document about Egibi slaves used as pledges (TCL 13 no. 193; cf. Stolper 1996: 517). In Nbk. 109, the governor of Ur is also designated *šangû*.

An opinion has been expressed that city governors of Sippar and Larsa were called *šangûs* (Beaulieu 1989: 116; 1991: 74–76). However, Bongenaar (1997: 21–22, 40, etc.) and Jursa (1996: 202) assume that the functions of the governor of these cities were carried out by *ḫazannu* or *pīḫātu*, while *šangûs* were the chief temple administrators. According to Bongenaar, the *šangû* of Sippar was involved in cultic functions. But the texts to which he refers actually deal with the administrative aspects of some religious rituals.

While the chief administrators of the main temples were called *šatammu*, the Ebabbar of Sippar was headed by the *šangû* of Sippar. It is important to note that, although about 5,000 documents from first-millennium Sippar have already been published, they contain no clear reference to any governor of this city, although they do mention the governors (*šakin ṭēmi*) of Babylon, Dilbat, and some other cities. It is true that one letter mentions the NAM of Sippar, who gave instructions about some barley (CT 22 no. 76:30). But it does not contain sufficient evidence regarding his authority and functions. It is also worth noting that the chief official of Ebabbar was called the *šangû* of Sippar but not of its temple. Moreover, this official presided over the king's tribunal and judged various private litigations. For instance, Cyr. 332 is the protocol of a court inquiry concerning the case of a slave who had been sold, but later a suit was brought against the buyer in an attempt to get the slave back. The decision on this case was made by the *šangû* of Sippar, the elders of the city, and the temple collegium. Two documents drawn up in Sippar in 531 contain a complaint brought by a creditor to the *šangû* of Sippar against the relatives of a boy who had been held as debt security; they had freed him and had taken one mina of silver with them from his house. The case was turned over to the assembly of

Sippar elders for a verdict (Cyr. 328, 329). Together with "the elders of the city," the *šangû* of Sippar also settled a case concerning 2 minas of silver that constituted the business capital of two persons (Camb. 412). These are the functions that were normally carried out by the governors of various cities, and apparently the *šangû* of Sippar was the chief magistrate of the city and at the same time the chief administrator of the Ebabbara.

As stated above, the chief administrative temple official was usually called the *šatammu*. But in some cases, this word was also used as a title for governors (see San Nicolò 1941: 26 n. 40; Landsberger 1965: 62). For instance, a deputy of the governor of the Sealand turned over a slave to the estate manager of Eanna to be confined to the temple workhouse. This action was taken in the presence of the governor (*šatammu*) of the town of Udannu and some other individuals. The document was drafted in Uruk in 529 (YOS 7 no. 106).

A *šatammu* of the city of Kiš is mentioned in the fragmentary Nbn. 306 from 548 (the provenance is unknown). It states that a certain man was appointed "feeder" of the ducks, which probably belonged to the *šatammu*. Before the governor of the same city (his name is lost) and a scribe, 30 shekels of silver were paid to another man (Nbn. 1024; provenance is unknown).

The same title is also used to designate a district governor in two documents from Nabonidus's reign (Nbn. nos. 233:15; 417:16). The name of the province (*mātu*) is broken off, but it appears to have been the same in both of them. The first text records the income and expenditures of a temple (possibly Ebabbara in Sippar) and was composed in 549 in the presence of "Šamaš-uballiṭ, governor (*šatammu*) of the province of Qa(. . .)." The second text was drafted in Babylon in 546 and records the handing over of some cattle to the care of two shepherds, which was done in front of several persons, including the governor of the same province. Perhaps the name of the same governor should be restored here.

Governors of provinces and big cities had deputies or assistants called *šanû* (CAD Š/1 397; for text references, see above in the entry on Uruk governors; see also Erm. 15496:3).

One important administrative title was *ḫazannu*, the "chief magistrate of a town, of a quarter of a larger city, a village or large estate— mayor, burgomaster, headman" (CAD H 163; see also Brinkman 1968: 298).

A document drafted in 539 states that the remainder of the price for a field was determined before a *ḫazannu* of Borsippa, three judges, and two scribes (VS 4 no. 32). A boat belonging to a *ḫazannu* was put at the disposal of two individuals, who sublet it for $1\frac{1}{2}$ shekels of silver per day. The document was composed in 540 in a town located in the region of Babylon (Nbn. 1019; see Frame 1986: 39–40). In 527 the palace steward (*rab ekalli*) in Borsippa was issued one sheep, which had been exacted by the *ḫazannu* from a certain Ardi-Gula and was destined for the king (TCL 13 no. 153). BRM 1 no. 101 records that two tenants of the temple land were to deliver a sheep to *ḫazannu* in addition to their rental payment to the Ebabbara Temple. The document was drafted in Sippar during the reign of Darius I. Another document from the same city states that 6 minas of silver, "tithe of the king, along with the silver of the *ḫazannu*," have been deposited in the temple storehouse (see MacGinnis 1994: 218 no. 5).

The following documents also come from Sippar and its region. In 553, 30 containers of sesame oil and one container of pitch were put at the disposal of a *ḫazannu*, and then he delivered them to an Ebabbara storehouse (Nbn. 108). Six thousand three hundred liters of roasted barley flour were issued from the same storehouse to a *ḫazannu* (Nbk. 131:21). CT 55 no. 702 is a receipt for the delivery of "fat" oxen to the Ebabbar Temple, in addition to oxen from a man who is referred to as the 'associate' (*aḫu*, literally 'brother') of the *ḫazannu* (line 7). The date is lost. Nbn. 920 from 541 states that the commander of a division of 1,000 soldiers (*rab lim*) owed 11,880 liters of dates to a man who is designated as an "associate of the *ḫazannu*" (on this term in Sippar texts, see also CT 55 702; and Nbn. 920). It can also be noted, in passing, that in Erm. 154514 a tenant's personal name is *Ḫa-za-an-nu*.

As was said above, Bongenaar and Jursa assume that, during the reign of Nebuchadnezzar II and later, the functions of the governor of Sippar were carried out by its mayor, who bore the title *ḫazannu*. However, this word is not attested at all in combination with Sippar (i.e., *ḫazannu* of Sippar). The opposite opinion of Da Riva, that a document from Kandalanu's time mentions a *ḫazannu* of Sippar (Da Riva 2002: 50) seems to be misleading, because this text mentions an official who bore such a title but does not describe him as the *ḫazannu* of Sippar. Moreover, the documents from there do not contain any information to support the view that a *ḫazannu* was the mayor of Sippar. It is more likely that the functions of Sippar's governor were carried out by *šangû*, and as to the *ḫazannu*, he was an administrative official subordinate to him.

The latter term also appears in two texts from Uruk. In 526, an Eanna Temple slave took his daughter from Uruk to Babylon and sold her there. When authorities learned about this deal, the case was heard in Babylon, and the chairman of the court and the *ḫazannu* (probably the administrator of a city district) considered the contract illegal, because the girl belonged to the same temple as her father (AnOr 8 no. 74). A letter from the same archives records that a *ḫazannu* arrested an individual for some violation but then let him go (TCL 9 no. 123).

The title *bēl āli* (ruler of a city) in Babylonia is attested only in letters from the Kouyunjik Collection (see CAD A/1 388). In Late Babylonian and Achaemenid times, *ša muḫḫi āli* may have designated a "village headman." We know that one of the bearers of this title was a gardener (CT 2 no. 10b:2; see Jursa 1995: 42, s.v. Balassu), and other persons of the same designation are attested as witnesses (Jursa 1995: 127–28 no. 36:22; Nbk. 70:9; VS 6 no. 12:11; Zadok 1995: 447 no. 2:11). In two texts from 549–548, the words *bēl piqitti* mean the administrators of a locality situated near Babylon and of the harbor there (Nbn. 268, 280). The most inferior post was perhaps *ša muḫḫi sūqi* 'the street inspector', which is mentioned in a broken context drafted in 542 (VS 6 no. 94:5; CAD S 406 and other references given there). Camb. 394 mentions a *šinamû* of a town. It was perhaps a low-ranking administrative position (see also Nbn. 640; cf. CAD Š/3 38). Finally, *ša rēš āli* ('head of a city'), attested in Late Achaemenid and Seleucid texts, does not refer to any kind of regional administration but means an administrator in the temple (see CAD K 290; Beaulieu 1995: 90, with previous literature).

The Babylonian texts also contain several Iranian administrative vocabulary words. One of them is *aḫšadrapanu*, which is a Babylonian transcription of the Old Persian title *xšaçapāvan-* 'satrap'. First of all, in ROMCT 2 no. 48 a certain Belšunu is referred to as 'satrap'. The document was composed in the 35th year of Artaxerxes, but the place where it was written is not indicated in the text. As Stolper has noted, he could have been Belesys, satrap of Syria, mentioned by Xenophon (*Anabasis* 1.4.10). He previously was district governor (*pīḫātu*) of Babylon (or perhaps of all the country). The above-mentioned text was in all probability composed in Nippur. It states that a temple official was ordered to issue 5 shekels of silver to a subordinate of satrap Belšunu as the equivalent of 30 shekels of wool. Probably the text belongs to the reign of Artaxerxes I, and in this case Belšunu was the satrap at Babylon as early as 429, and around 407 was promoted to the governorship of Across-the-River (see Stolper 1987: 398–400).

The title *aḫšadrapannu* is also attested in several Murašû documents from the last quarter of the fifth century (for text references, see CAD A/1 195; also PIHANS 54 no. 109; PIHANS 79 no. 105). As seen from

PBS 2/1 no. 2, a rental payment incumbent on some land belonging to royal workmen (*gardu*) was collected by written order of a Babylonian, who was called the "satrap" and was also the foreman (*šaknu*) of the same workmen, and of one more person without a title. This satrap could hardly have been governor of Babylonia or of any of its city and at the same time hold the post of foreman of the workmen. Apparently the title "satrap" was held not only by governors of administrative districts but also by royal officials of inferior rank (see Stolper 1987: 399). In BRM 2 no. 56, which belongs to the Hellenistic Period, the title "satrap" seems to have designated governor of Uruk.

Umarzanapāta is a transcription of the Old Persian *vardana-pāti*, 'chief of the city' (AHW 1447). It is attested only in a letter with instructions to deliver a certain quantity of barley to an individual and then to inform the temple manager and "the governor of the city," who bore a typical Babylonian name, Iddin-Nergal (CT 22 no. 73).

Another Iranian term for a city governor was *uppadētu* which is used in a document probably drafted in 523 (Pinches 1891/92: 134). It records the sale of two slaves in the presence of a certain Umar'mira' (an Iranian name), who was "*uppadētu* of the country of Humadešu," which was located in the region of Persepolis. The principals of the document were Babylonians, who went there for some business. In all other texts in which this place is mentioned, it is called "city."

Summarizing the information contained in the documents examined above, the following conclusions can be made. Mesopotamia was divided into administrative districts headed by officials who bore a variety of titles. The highest administrative designation was 'governor of the country' (*šakin māti*). This title, however, was a synonym for the office of *bēl pīḫāti* (or simply *pīḫātu*), a title commonly used for provincial administrators. In the majority of cases, the district governors were called *šaknu*. All of these titles were partly equivalent to the word *satrap*, which usually designated chief officials of the provinces. *Šaknu*, however, also designated officials in charge of canals, foremen of foreign ethnic groups, and other minor supervisors. City governors were usually called *šakin ṭēmi*. They had deputies or assistants whose title was *šanû* 'second'. There are also some cases in which these deputies later occupied the governor's office.

Several other words are also used to designate governors. For instance, chief administrators of the cities of Akkad and Larsa were *qīpu*. In some cases the word *šangû* was also used as a title for city governors. For instance, the *šangû* of Sippar was the chief magistrate of the city. In Udannu and Kiš the title *šatammu* denoted governors of these cities.

One of the important administrative titles was *ḫazannu* 'mayor' in a number of towns (e.g., Borsippa) and headmen of quarters in big cities. There were also minor civil servants down to village administrators and street inspectors.

Although Mesopotamia was conquered by the Persians in 539, local administrative traditions were not disrupted, and indigenous officials retained their posts. However, gradually, significant changes occurred in the structure of the administrative system. Some of these changes occurred as early as Cyrus's reign. For instance, under the last Chaldean king, Nabonidus, the governor of the country was a Babylonian. At first, Cyrus left him in his office, but four years later he made Mesopotamia and Across-the-River into a single province and appointed an Iranian as its governor. In this satrapy, civilian and military functions were in the hands of one and the same governor. Later, under Darius I's time, the governor's functions were mainly limited to civilian ones. During Achaemenid times, several Iranian administrative titles are attested in Babylonian documents (such as *aḫšadrapanu* 'satrap', *vardana-pāti* 'chief of the city', etc.).

The governors of all levels were at the head of the administration of their own regions and had at their disposal various officials, as well as scribes, messengers, and sometimes even merchants. They were obliged to keep order and carry out justice, as well as supervising the economics of their districts and their local civil servants, and overseeing the receipt of state taxes and tolls and the fulfillment of duties. For instance, at the orders of the governor of Babylonia and Across-the-River, temple officials of various cities sent workmen to Babylon to perform state duties. The governor was regularly informed about the number of dead and runaway temple slaves and about livestock and fowl missing from temple estates. He also gave orders about regulations for the lease of temple fields.

City governors' functions included the supervision of construction projects, control of state-funded land worked by tenants, and collection of payment due to the crown. Frequently land-sale contracts and many other documents from private archives as well as temple transactions were drawn up in their presence and sealed by the city governors. Together with royal judges, they exercised judicial authority, presided over the king's tribunal, and judged various private litigations. For instance, when several men appealed to the governor of Babylonia, requesting him to make a decision concerning a house, he sent them to the governor and judges of Uruk, where the house was located. The governor had a great deal of influence in the management of the Eanna Temple and sometimes acted as the chairman of the local popular assembly. Some documents indicate that governors paid tithe to temples and brought offerings of oxen, sheep, and other animals. Finally, city governors acted as witnesses in both temple and private documents.

We do not know whether there was a fixed term of office for governors on the various levels. In any case, Nabu-aḫḫe-bulliṭ was governor of Babylonia for at least twelve years; Gubaru served as governor of Babylonia and Transpotamia for ten years, and some governors of Uruk held their posts about five years or more. There were two instances in which a father and son were governors of Babylon and Uruk, although this office was not handed directly from one to another. In all probability, there was no limitation on the governor's term of office.

Almost nothing is known about the remuneration of state officials, including governors. When temple lands were rented out, standard payments were made to district governors out of the harvest. Governors also received allowances of barley and wool from the temples, part of the mutton destined for sacrifices, and so on.

With the exception of a few cases in which governors of Babylonia or its capital were Iranians (such as Bagapanu, Gubaru, and Uštanu), high-ranking officials of the state administration, including district and city governors, were usually Babylonians. Even the governor of Across-the-River, Belšunu, was a Babylonian. We also know that several prominent families of Uruk provided its governors.

Bibliography

Abraham, Kathleen
  1997   Šušan in the Egibi Texts from the Time of Marduk-nāṣir-apli. *OLA* 28: 55–85.
Beaulieu, P.-A.
  1989   *The Reign of Nabonidus 556–539 B.C.* New Haven: Yale University Press.
  1991   Neo-Babylonian Larsa: A Preliminary Study. *Or* 60: 58–81.
  1995   The Brewers of Nippur. *JCS* 47: 85–96.
Boissier, A.
  1926   Extrait de la chronique locale d'Uruk. *RA* 23: 13–17.
Bongenaar, A. C. V. M.
  1997   *The Neo-Babylonian Ebabbar Temple at Sippar: Its Administration and Its Prosopography.* PIHANS 80. Leiden: Nederlands Historisch-Archeologisch Instituut te Istanbul.

Brinkman, J. A.
1968   *A Political History of Post-Kassite Babylonia.* AnOr 43. Rome: Pontifical Biblical Institute.

Dalley, S.
1979   *A Catalogue of the Akkadian Cuneiform Tablets in the Collection of the Royal Scottish Museum, Edinburgh.* Information Series. Art and Archaeology 2. Edinburgh: Royal Scottish Museum.

Dandamayev, M. A.
1992   *Iranians in Achaemenid Babylonia,* ed. Ehsan Yarshater. Columbia Lectures on Iranian Studies 6. New York: Mazda.
1995   A Governor of Byblos in Sippar. *OLA* 65: 29–31.

Da Riva, Rocío
2002   *Der Ebabbar-Tempel von Sippar in frühneubabylonischer Zeit (640–58 v. Chr.).* AOAT 291. Münster: Ugarit-Verlag.

Driel, G. van
1989   The Murašûs in Context. *JESHO* 32: 203–29.

Ebeling, E.
1953   *Glossar zu den neubabylonischen Briefen.* Munich: Bayerischen Akademie der Wissenschaften.

Eph'al, I.
1988   Syria–Palestine under Achaemenid Rule. Pp. 139–64 in *Persia, Greece and the Western Mediterranean c. 525 to 479 B.C.* Vol. 4 of *CAH.* Cambridge: Cambridge University Press.

Frame, G.
1984   Neo-Babylonian and Achaemenid Economic Texts from the Sippar Collection of the British Museum. *JAOS* 104: 745–52.
1986   Some Neo-Babylonian and Persian Documents Involving Boats. *OrAnt* 25: 29–50.
1991   Nabonidus, Nabû-šarra-uṣur, and the Eanna Temple. *ZA* 81: 37–86.
1992   *Babylonia 689–627 BC: A Political History.* PIHANS 69. Leiden: Nederlands Historisch-Archeologisch Instituut te Istanbul.

Grayson, A. K.
1975   *Assyrian and Babylonian Chronicles.* TCL 5. Locust Valley, N.Y.: Augustin. Repr. Winona Lake, Indiana: Eisenbrauns, 2000.

Joannès, F.
1994   Une visite du gouverneur d'Arpad. *NABU:* 21–22.
1996   Textes judiciaires néo-babyloniens. *NABU:* 62–64.

Jursa, M.
1995   *Die Landwirtschaft in Sippar in neubabylonischer Zeit. AfO* 25. Horn: Berger.
1996   Akkad, das Eulmaš and Gubāru. *WZKM* 86: 196–211.
1997–98   Review of E. Gehlken, *Uruk: Spätbabylonische Wirtschaftstexte aus dem Eanna-Archiv* (AUWE 11. Mainz am Rhein: von Zabern, 1990). *AfO* 44–45: 424.

Kümmel, H. M.
   1979   *Familie, Beruf und Amt im spätbabylonischen Uruk.* Abhandlungen der Deutschen Orient Gesellschaft 20. Berlin: Mann.
Landsberger, B.
   1965   *Brief des Bischofs von Esagila an König Asarhaddon.* Mededelingen der Koninklijke Nederlandse Akademie van Wetenschappen, Afd. Letterkunde n.s. 28/6. Amsterdam: Neord-Hollandsche.
MacGinnis, J.
   1994   The Royal Establishment at Sippar in the 6th Century BC. *ZA* 84: 198–219.
   1995   Statue Manufacture in Sippar. *WZKM* 85: 181–85.
   1996   A Further Note on the *zazakku*. *NABU*: 19–20.
Oppenheim, A. L.
   1985   The Babylonian Evidence of Achaemenian Rule in Mesopotamia. Pp. 529–67 in *The Median and Achaemenian Periods*, ed. I. Gershevitch. Vol. 2 of *Cambridge History of Iran*. Cambridge: Cambridge University Press.
Pinches, T. G.
   1891–92   Old Persian Names in Babylonian Contracts. *Hebraica* 8: 134–35.
   1917   From World-Dominion to Subjection. *JTVI* 49: 107–31.
Sack, R. H.
   1977   The Scribe Nabû-bāni-aḫi, Son of Ibnâ, and the Hierarchy of Eanna as Seen in the Erech Contracts. *ZA* 67: 42–52.
   1994   *Cuneiform Documents from the Chaldean and Persian Periods.* Selinsgrove: Susquehanna University Press.
San Nicolò, M.
   1941   *Beiträge zu einer Prosopographie neubabylonischer Beamten der Zivil-und Tempelverwaltung.* SBAW 2/2. Munich: Bayerischen Akademie der Wissenschaft.
Stigers, H. G.
   1976   Neo-and Late Babylonian Business Documents from the John Frederick Lewis Collection. *JCS* 18: 3–59.
Stolper, M. W.
   1985   *Entrepreneurs and Empire: The Murašû Archive, the Murašû Firm, and Persian Rule in Babylonia.* PIHANS 54. Leiden: Nederlands Historisch-Archeologisch Instituut te Istanbul.
   1987   Bēlšunu the Satrap. Pp. 387–402 in *Language, Literature, and History: Philological and Historical Studies Presented to Erica Reiner*, ed. F. Rochberg-Halton. New Haven: American Oriental Society.
   1988   The *šaknu* of Nippur. *JCS* 40: 127–55.
   1989   The Governor of Babylon and Across-the-River in 486 B.C. *JNES* 48: 283–305.
   1995   The Babylonian Enterprise of Belesys. *Pallas* 43: 217–38.
   1996   A Paper Chase after the Aramaic on TCL 13 193. *JAOS* 116: 517–21.

Weidner, E. F.
1954–56   Hochverrat gegen Nebuchadnezar II. *AfO* 17: 1–5.
Wunsch, C.
1997   Neu- und spätbabylonische Urkunden aus dem Museum von Mont-
        serrat. *AuOr* 15: 139–94.
Zadok, R.
1978   The Nippur Region during the Late Assyrian, Chaldean and Achae-
        menian Periods Chiefly according to Written Sources. *IOS* 8: 266–332.
1985   *Geographical Names according to New- and Late-Babylonian Texts*. RGTC
        8. Wiesbaden: Reichert.
1995   Foreigners and Foreign Linguistic Material in Mesopotamia and
        Egypt. *OLA* 65: 431–47.
1997–98 Review of M. Sigrist, H. H. Figulla, and C. B. F. Walker, *Catalogue of
        the Babylonian Tablets in the British Museum*, vol. 2 (London: British Mu-
        seum, 1996). *AfO* 44–45: 293–306.
2002   Contributions to Babylonian Geography, Prosopography and Docu-
        mentation. Pp. 871–97 in *Ex Mesopotamia et Syria Lux: Festschrift für
        Manfred Deitrich*, ed. O. Loretz, K. A. Metzler, and H. Schaudig. AOAT
        281. Münster: Ugarit-Verlag.

New Evidence for Judeans in Babylonia

LAURIE E. PEARCE

San Francisco, California

Even in the early days of Assyriology, recovery of cuneiform documentation attesting to the presence of Judeans in late-first-millennium Babylonia was hardly surprising. Biblical reports of Assyrian and Babylonian deportations of conquered peoples and their repopulation of vanquished lands in the wake of military activities were corroborated by the appearance of Israelite and Judean names in cuneiform documents composed after those events took place. Of course, there is a great variety of textual and archaeological evidence that confirms the biblical record on a number of important events, including Nebuchadnezzar's attack on Jerusalem (Stern 2001: 323–24; Lipschits 2001; 2003: 328, with literature cited there). The most direct cuneiform evidence of that event remains the Weidner tablets, which record not only the name of the deported Judean king but also the generous grain rations given to him and his sons while in captivity (Weidner 1939). Nonetheless, this text contains only scraps of information and fails to provide significant evidence to help elucidate the picture of events related to the Babylonian destruction of Jerusalem and Judah and its aftermath.

Evidence of the economic activities of individuals who may be presumed to be descendants of Judeans exiled to Babylonia comes from the Murašû "archive,"[1] a group of approximately 730 cuneiform texts from Nippur that furnish a wealth of information for Assyriologists,

Author's note: It is a great pleasure to thank Professors Oded Lipschits and Manfred Oeming for their invitation to participate in the conference Judah and the Judeans in the Persian Period. I also thank many of the participants for their responses and input, both at the time of and subsequent to the conference. In particular, I benefited from the insights and comments of B. Becking, A. Lemaire, N. Naʾaman, B. Porten, C. Uehlinger, and D. Vanderhooft. They are, of course, in no way responsible for any limitations or errors in this work.

1. In chronological order of appearance, the major publications of the texts belonging to the Murašû archive are: Hilprecht and Clay 1898; 1908; 1912; Augapfel 1917; Cardascia 1951; Stolper 1985; Donbaz and Stolper 1997.

historians of the ancient Near East, and biblical scholars alike.[2] Of particular interest to the latter is the evidence from the onomastic corpus of a significant number of West Semitic names, including many compounded with the theophoric element YHWH. Analyses of the Murašû-corpus Yahwistic names began to appear soon after the texts were excavated, beginning with S. Daiches's (1910) work, *The Jews in Babylonia in the Time of Ezra and Nehemiah according to Babylonian Inscriptions*, and continued into the mid- to late-twentieth century.[3]

Notwithstanding the evidence from the Weidner and Murašû tablets, the published cuneiform documentation reveals very little about the Judeans in Babylonia in the last half of the first millennium B.C.E. The lacunas result from limitations inherent in the evidence itself. Chronologically, little or no cuneiform documentation related to the Judean exiles and their descendants has heretofore been recovered for the approximately 150 years between the 597 deportation and the earliest Murašû text, which dates to 454 B.C.E. (Stolper 1985: 17). Because they were excavated in Nippur, the Murašû texts document activity in that city and its immediate environs (Stolper 1985: 11). Although demonstrable onomastic links prove that economic transactions took place between the Murašûs and individuals in Babylon, they do not connect the Judean populations in Nippur and Babylon (Stolper 1990), the city or area to which the earliest deportees were presumably brought.

Recently, texts have been published that incrementally expand the documentation for the presence and activities of Judeans in Neo-Babylonian and Achaemenid Babylonia. Francis Joannès and André Lemaire (1999) published three cuneiform texts that not only include additional West Semitic and Yahwistic names but also mention locations that were home to many individuals who were undoubtedly of Judean origin. For the study of Judeans in postexilic Babylonia, the most significant pieces of information that these texts provide are the names of the places in which texts 1 and 2 were composed. Text 2 was written in ālu ša Našar, a place known from previously published texts (TuM 2/3 91; VS 4 177; Waerzeggers 1999–2000). Text 1 was written in āl-Yāhūdu, a previously unattested place-name. Its name, to be translated 'the city of Judah', reflects the geographic origin of a major component of its popu-

---

2. Stolper (1985) notes that the total number of texts and fragments is 879. Once joins are accounted for, the number is reduced to an approximate count of 730 items.

3. Among the significant studies of the Yahwistic names in Babylonian documents are: Sidersky 1929; Coogan 1973; 1976; Stolper 1976; Zadok 1979; 1980.

lation.[4] Joannès and Lemaire (1999: 26) referred to this town as "Jérusalem de Babylonie," in view of the fact that much of the deported population of Judah came from Jerusalem and its immediate environs. In the present essay, I am offering a preliminary report on the contents of a text corpus, provisionally designated TAYN,[5] that contributes significant numbers of additional texts from āl-Yāhūdu, Našar, as well as other places that offer a great deal of new evidence for the presence of Judean deportees and their descendants in Mesopotamia.

The corpus consists of nearly 100 texts, approximately one-third of which were composed in āl-Yāhūdu, a second third in Našar; the remainder were composed in a variety of locales, both known and previously unattested.[6] While the largest representation of texts comes from Našar, the intriguing place-name is that of āl-Yāhūdu, only recently recovered as a toponym with Joannès's and Lemaire's publication of the tablet written there. Previously published cuneiform references to the geographic region of Judah are few. Some are attested in the Weidner tablets (Weidner 1939: 925–26, Text B ii 38, 39; Text C rev. ii 17, 18; Text D, Z 20, 21), and one appears in a Nebuchadnezzar chronicle (Grayson 2000), where it certainly refers to the Judean capital, not to a Babylonian town.

The new texts preserve a number of orthographies for the toponym āl-Yāhūdu,[7] almost all of which appear in the notation at the end of the tablet that records the name of the scribe, the date on which the transaction took place and the place in which the document was composed. One of these orthographies, URU *šá* LÚ *ia-a-ḫu-du-a-a*, adds the standard Akkadian gentilic ending (*-a-a*) to the geographical term[8]

---

4. The practice of naming a town (often a newly established settlement) for the place from which most of its occupants originally came is well attested in Babylonia. See, for example, Eph'al 1978: 80–83.

5. The acronym TAYN stands for Texts from āl-Yāhūdu and Našar. The texts are in a private collection that is being prepared for publication.

6. Among the other locations in which these texts were composed are Babylon, a town (named for an individual) known as ᵐAmurru-šar-uṣur, and a town called 'royal town', *āl šarri*, sometimes further designated 'royal town of the new bow fief' *āl šarri ša qašti eššēti*.

7. ᵁᴿᵁ*ia-a-ḫa-du*; ᵁᴿᵁ*ía-ḫu-du*; ᵁᴿᵁ*ia-a-ḫu-du*; ᵁᴿᵁ*ia-a-ḫu-di*; ᵁᴿᵁ*ia-a-ḫu-du*; ᵁᴿᵁ*ia-ḫu-du*; ᵁᴿᵁ*ia-ú-du*; ᵁᴿᵁ*i-ḫu-du*; ᵁᴿᵁ*ú-ḫa-du*; URU *šá* LÚ *ia-a-ḫu-du-a-a*.

8. At the time of writing his important work, *The Jews in Babylonia during the Chaldean and Achaemenian Periods*, Zadok (1979) stated: "The ethnic designation 'Judean' (ᴸᵁ*Ia-a-ḫu/ú-da-a-a*) is not found in Babylonian records from the periods in question except for those referring to King Jehoiachin." The presence of this orthography in the TAYN corpus

and positively demonstrates that the town was named for individuals who came from Judah. In addition to firmly establishing the place of origin of the former residents, it is noteworthy that the orthography *ālu šá* ^LÚ*Yāḫūdāia* appears in the earliest text of the corpus, which dates to Nebuchadnezzar 33 (572 B.C.E.), 15 years after the 587 B.C.E. deportation. The next-oldest tablet dates to Amēl-Marduk 1 (= 561 B.C.E.) and already preserves the orthography ^URU*ia-a-ḫu-du* for the toponym. All subsequent attestations of the toponym āl-Yāhūdu also lack the gentilic ending, suggesting that the Judean deportees and their descendants were sufficiently established in the social and economic life of Babylonia that their town could simply be called "Judah-ville" or the like. The integration of Judeans into Babylonian economic life is evidenced by their participation in very ordinary economic transactions in which they are recorded as the creditors and debtors in a variety of loan documents and receipts. Of course, this process of acculturation may well have begun earlier than the destruction of Jerusalem. The happenstance of recovery is such that, at the present, no texts that document the existence of āl-Yāhūdu also antedate the destruction of Jerusalem. While the transformation of the toponym from one that identifies it on the basis of its residents' being from somewhere else to a place-name that merely recalls their origins might appear to point to a rapid acculturation of Judeans into Babylonian life, this assumption would ignore the likelihood that the process of acculturation may have begun earlier than the destruction of Jerusalem. In light of the fact that thousands of people were alleged to have accompanied Jehoiachin to Babylonia,[9] it is conceivable that, by the third decade of the sixth century B.C.E., a town named for its residents' Judean origin was already well established and no longer had to be identified by the name of the former "newcomers."

On the basis of geographical and onomastic information both within and from outside the TAYN corpus, it is believed that āl-Yāhūdu lay in the Babylon-Borsippa region.[10] This conclusion in part depends on

---

expands the evidence for this orthography to a short period beyond the destruction of Jerusalem and the deportation of its residents.

9. The biblical record provides varying estimates of the numbers of people deported in the first wave of the Exile. 2 Kgs 24:12–16 reports that 10,000 captives went along with Jehoiachin, his mother, and palace retinue. Jer 52:28–30 reports that 3,023 persons were deported at that time.

10. Contra Joannès and Lemaire (1999: 26), who theorized that āl-Yāhūdu might have been located in the Sippar region, based on the fact that it is in this region that later Talmudic academies of Sura and Pumbedita were established, and therefore may have been

establishing the proximity of āl-Yāhūdu and Našar, for which there is compelling evidence. A promissory note for repayment of dates notes that the payment is to take place in āl-Yāhūdu, although the tablet was written in Našar. It is unlikely that repayment would take place at a great distance from the place in which the document was composed. Even more convincing is the evidence from a text written in Cambyses 1 in Bīt Našar that mentions the *dēkû*, the 'summoner (for taxes or corvée)',[11] of āl-Yāhūdu. The text records payment by Šalam-Yāma, acting as an agent (*ina našparti*) of Yāmu-[i]zri, the *dēkû*, to Ahiqar, son of Rimut, whom Joannès and Lemaire had already identified as the "governor" (Joannès and Lemaire 1999), certainly a chief fiscal administrator, of Bīt Našar. It is improbable that the *dēkû*-official for one town would be mentioned in a text composed in another unless the two towns were in close proximity.

In *Repértoire Géographique*, Zadok (1985: 98) suggested that Našar ought to be located in the Borsippa region. The recent publication of a small family archive from the Borsippa region (Waerzeggers 1999–2000) confirms this suggestion. The activities of Inṣabtu, daughter of Iddin-Nabû, descendant of Naggāru, are preserved in a group of twelve documents written in Babylon, Borsippa, and its environs, including at least three from Bīt Našar. Combining this concrete evidence for locating Našar in the Babylon-Borsippa region with the suggestions that āl-Yāhūdu and Našar were neighboring towns implies that āl-Yāhūdu lay in the Babylon-Borsippa area as well.

Onomastic evidence from within this group further substantiates these claims. The name Naggāru 'carpenter' is a well-attested Borsippean family name (Waerzeggers 1999–2000: 192). It appears in three āl-Yāhūdu tablets, always as the family name of the tablet scribe: ᵐIddin-ᵈNabû, son of ᵐᵈMarduk-ēṭir, descendant of ᵐNaggāru. Evidence from the theophoric names in the TAYN onomasticon, specifically the presence of a nearly 100 names compounded with the name

---

the center of the initial repopulation of the deportees. However, from the establishment of those academies in 219 and 259 C.E., respectively, there is sufficient time for the population to have grown and expanded geographically to places beyond their original places of settlement. Joannès and Lemaire also tentatively suggested that the presence of a name (ᵈBunene-ibni) that contains a theophoric element reflective of a Šamaš cult might further point to the Sippar region for the text's place of origin. However, the expansion of the onomastic evidence from āl-Yāhūdu and Našar has yielded only a total of 25 names that could suggest strong association with the Sippar cult. Despite the admitted limitations of onomastic evidence for locating individuals' origins, the paucity of evidence hardly strengthens the suggestion of āl-Yāhādu and Sippar's proximity.

11. For the office of *dēkû*, see Stolper 1985: 83 n. 59.

of the deity Nabû, city-god of Borsippa, corroborates the suggestion that āl-Yāhūdu lies in the Borsippa region.[12]

The onomasticon of the TAYN corpus provides striking new evidence for the study of Judeans in Babylonia. At this early stage in the study of the corpus, any attempt at a "statistical analysis" of the data must be provisional. Nonetheless, some patterns and rough approximations can be observed. By a conservative count, the tablets preserve nearly 500 different names.[13] Of these, approximately one-half are Akkadian and one-quarter West Semitic.[14] Unfortunately, the language of almost one-fifth of the names cannot be determined, either because they are too badly damaged or because they present unusual orthographic and/or linguistic problems. The remaining names (roughly 5%) contain a mixture of West Semitic and Akkadian elements; only 2 Persian names belong to individuals other than kings. Approximately 80 names contain some form of the Yahwistic theophoric element, a figure that represents slightly more than two-thirds of the preserved West Semitic names and about 15% of the total number of names in the corpus. When individuals are counted, the preliminary statistics suggest that approximately 600 individuals can be identified in the corpus and that, of these, approximately 120 bear Yahwistic names.[15] This proportion stands in sharp contrast to the 2.8% of people in Nippur that Zadok (1979: 78) claims can be identified as Judeans or Jews. The greatest number the individuals bearing Yahwistic names appear in texts written at āl-Yāhūdu; fewer than a dozen appear in texts written in āl Našar; roughly 30 individuals with Yahwistic names appear in texts written in other towns or in tablets in which the toponym is not preserved. These approximations point to a concentra-

---

12. While an argument ex silencio is hardly conclusive, the fact that a cursory examination of the onomastica of Sippar and Murašû Nippur texts does not reveal the name Naggāru adds to the weight of this argument. For the Sippar onomasticon, see Jursa 1995; Bongenaar 1997; for the Murašû onomasticon, see Stolper 1985; Hilprecht and Clay 1898; Clay 1912.

13. Not included in this number are partially preserved names that cannot be identified as belonging to unique or duplicate individuals, as well as the names of the kings by whose reigns the tablets are dated. All numerical data presented in this discussion must be regarded as preliminary.

14. Until the etymologies of all names are identified, even names that can be securely labeled Hebrew, Aramaic, or Arabic are subsumed under the general rubric "West Semitic."

15. Because of damage to the texts, an additional 20 or so Yahwistic names cannot be securely identified as belonging to unique individuals. They have been omitted from these calculations.

tion of individuals of Judean descent in āl-Yāhūdu, although their presence is attested in other settlements (assumed to be) in the vicinity.

In the writing of the Yahwistic element in TAYN names, the divine determinative is not always included, a convention typical in the cuneiform scribes' treatment of non-Mesopotamian gods, particularly the deities with which they were not as familiar (Zadok 1979: 9). Most of the orthographies of this theophoric element are attested in publications of the Murašû texts and those published by Joannès and Lemaire. However, the TAYN corpus adds at least one new writing (^{d}e-ḫu-ú) to the repertoire of writings with the Yahwistic element. A complete analysis of the orthographies in this corpus and a consideration of their relationship to those previously known will be forthcoming.

The prosopographic record provides valuable information on the naming practices among the Judeans in Babylonia. Within a family, names are given largely along linguistic lines. In one-half of the approximately 300 name pairs in which the linguistic origin of both names can be securely identified, both father and son bore Akkadian names. The next largest group is that in which sons and fathers both bore West Semitic names, with 65–75 such pairings.[16] There are approximately 35 pairings of fathers with West Semitic names and sons with Akkadian names, and about 20 pairings of fathers with Akkadian names and sons with West Semitic names.

The TAYN corpus records economic and administrative activities of the community of Judeans in Babylonia in well-attested text types: receipts for payments, debt notes for commodities owed, sales of livestock, and leases of houses and people. Prices for commodities and property lie well within the ranges typical for this time period. In addition to the small amount of information about officials connected with the Judean community, as already noted in the discussion of the *dēkû*, the corpus proves the existence of an administrative fiscal district populated in large measure by Judeans. In Nippur and its environs, these districts were known as *ḫaṭru*. While this term seems to be used almost exclusively in the Mursašû archives, the institution it denotes is a characteristic means of fiscal control and production in the Achaemenid Empire (Stolper 1985: 71–72). Because the geographical distribution of the term indicates that the instititution did not exist exclusively in Nippur (Stolper 1985: 71), it is plausible that such an organization, whether termed *ḫaṭru* or not, operated in the Babylon-Borsippa region

---

16. The upper end of this range accounts for fathers with West Semitic names whose sons have hybrid Akkadian–West Semitic names.

as well. Thus, for ease of reference, we can reasonably speak of the existence of a Judean *ḫaṭru*.

Although a *ḫaṭru* is often identified by a population or professional designation, the existence of a *ḫaṭru* can be detected on the basis of several criteria, notably its presence in a text of officials associated with the *ḫaṭru* organization (Stolper 1985: 71–72). Among these officials are *šušānû*, members of a semi-free class bound to their holdings of Crown lands by restrictions on alienation and by tax and service encumberances (Stolper 1985: 79–82; Dandamaev 1984: 626). Documents from the Murašû archive show that *šušānû* could be assigned to groups based on professional, institutional, and ethnic affiliation (Dandamaev 1984: 629; Stolper 1985: 72–79). In the TAYN corpus, three tablets refer to *šušānû* of the Judeans, providing the first evidence for the existence of a Judean *ḫaṭru*.[17]

In addition to contributing to the identification of the Judean *ḫaṭru*, three tablets mention a certain *Uštanu ša ēbir nāri*. The Akkadian term *piḫātu* (LÚNAM) 'governor', which often identifies Uštanu (Dar. 27:3; 82:2), does not appear in these texts. It remains to be determined whether these attestations can be assumed to represent an abbreviation of his title to include reference only to the geographical region and whether they thus provide unique and early attestations of Uštanu's being associated with the province Across-the-River as a geographical region distinct from the province of Babylon,[18] or whether this title defines Uštanu's position in some other way.

The TAYN texts offer a few insights into the early stages of the administration of royal landholdings and the organization of various lands and populations as economic supportors of the Empire. One point that is illustrative comes from four texts written in *āl-šarri* 'the royal city' and two in *āl šarri ša qašti eššēti* 'the royal city of the new bow-fief'. The two texts written in *āl šarri ša qašti eššēti* date to the accession and second years of Cambyses, the first quarter of his eightyear reign. This geographical term, in either its long or short form, is not the name of a particular site. Rather, it seems to refer to lands be-

---

17. Zadok (1979: 74) postulated that such a *ḫaṭru* could well have existed, and he attributed its lack of apparence in the textual record to the incomplete nature of the Murašû archive documentation of *ḫaṭru* organizations.

18. Stolper (1989a) tabulates the evidence for titles borne by specific governors of the united province of Babylon and Across-the-River and of the divided provinces, Babylon and Across-the-River. There, Uštānu bears only the title Governor of Babylon and Across-the-River; the earliest attestation of the title Governor of Across the River was borne by Tattannu, evidenced in a document dated to 502.

longing to the Crown that have yet to be given a proper name. Amélie Kuhrt suggests that the text Cambyses 85, which belongs to the time of the Cyrus–Cambyses co-regency, points to the existence of bowlands in the early years of the Achaemenid Period and reflects the "reorganization or development of elements that were already in place at the time of the conquest."[19] This assertion, combined with textual evidence for the existence of bowlands already near the end of the reign of Nebuchadnezzar (Jursa 1998) remove any doubt that the development of such organizations was part of an exclusive innovation implemented in Darius's reign and reforms.

We should also point out that, while the TAYN corpus provides much new information, it is frustratingly silent about many areas of inquiry. Some may have hoped that the texts would furnish information about the social status of Judean deportees in Babylonia. From the biblical records, we know that, along with Jehoiachin, "his mother, his courtiers and commanders and officers . . . and all the men of property, ten thousand . . . and all the artisans and smiths" were deported (2 Kgs 24:12–15). Unfortunately, the TAYN texts do not provide evidence for the professional status of deportees or their descendants, nor do they provide any indication of the participation of those deportees in cultic activities, Babylonian or otherwise. The exceptional reference to two individuals as *dēkû* reflects the Babylonian concern with insuring the smooth functioning of its administrative and economic order, a process for which the identification of individuals' professions was unimportant or irrelevant.[20] The previously published materials that deal directly with the deportees, the Weidner tablets and the Murašû texts, only provide evidence for the two extremes of the exiled population—namely, royalty and the lower echelons of society—whose reduced economic condition is evident in the Murašû texts (Eph'al 1981: 109–10). Eph'al notes that the people who came with Jehoiachin "were the socio-economically advantaged, who absorbed later waves of deportees from Judah and established the character of the Jewish exile in Babylonia for the coming generations. They could hardly have been the ancestors of those poor farmers mentioned in the Bīt Murašû documents, who were settled in the Nippur region." To the extent that the

---

19. Stolper (1989b) cites the argument presented by Kuhrt (1988).

20. TuM 2/3 238 (dated to Nebuchadnezzar 43) demonstrates the administration's lack of interest in an indiviudal's profession. In this text, which lists the names and patronyms of 55 individuals who are paying tithes, few are identified by profession. See Dandamaev 2000: 148.

TAYN texts record promissory notes and other forms of indebtedness, they demonstrate that at least a portion of the Judean deportees and their descendants provided a ready supply of labor for the official administration.[21]

The TAYN corpus also corroborates another conclusion drawn from previous studies of deported populations. Unlike deportees in the Neo-Assyrian Period, conquered populations in the Neo-Babylonian and Achaemenid Periods were resettled in communities defined by the large majority of the population composition. These communities functioned largely intact within the administrative structures of the Neo-Babylonian and Achaemenid Empires. A notable example of such a community is that of the Mesopotamian town of Neirab, a town named for its population's original home in Syria. The Neirabeans appear to have returned to their homeland shortly after (and in much the same manner as did) Judean deportees and their descendants returned to Judah (Eph'al 1981: 108). The populations of these two communities (and we may extrapolate this experience for other exile communities as well) returned to their places of origin with a portion of the community intact. This, of course, is the broad implication of the Cyrus Edict, which according to Tadmor and Bickerman, "implies a tendency to restore various groups of exiles, and not only the Jews" (Eph'al 1981: 108).

Thus, the TAYN corpus adds to our knowledge of Judeans in Babylonia in the late Neo-Babylonian and Achaemenid Periods in the following ways: (1) it documents the presence of Judeans participating with Babylonian natives and other Judeans in common agricultural and economic activities at a point in time earlier than previously known; (2) it enlarges the corpus of Yahwistic personal names and provides evidence for additional naming patterns among the Judeans; and (3) it adds a number of new place-names to the Babylonian landscape, some of which are particularly identified with the Judean deportees. In spite of these features, it is important to bear in mind that the picture that emerges of the experiences of the populations in āl-Yāhūdu and ālu ša Našar is remarkably similar to the experiences known for other foreign populations resettled in late (Neo-)Babylonia and Achaemenid Babylonia.

---

21. Given the concerns of the Babylonian and Achaemenid administrations, it is not surprising that the information recorded deals with workers associated in some connection with providing capital or produce for the state. The presence of the professional classes (scribes, judges, etc.) are usually noted in cuneiform docuementation only when their services are the subject of the matter at hand.

Bibliography

Augapfel, J.
1917 *Babylonische Rechtsurkunden aus der Regierungszeit Artaxerxes I und Darius II.* Kaiserliche Akademie der Wissenschaften in Wien: Philosophisch-historische Klasse, Denkschriften 59/3. Vienna.

Bongenaar, A. C. V. M.
1997 *The Neo-Babylonian Ebabbar Temple at Sippar: Its Administration and Its Prosopography.* Leiden: Nederlands Historisch-Archaeologisch Instituut te Istanbul.

Cardascia, G.
1951 *Les archives des Murašu.* Paris: Imprimérie nationale.

Clay, A. T.
1908 *Legal and Commercial Transactions Dated in the Assyrian, Neo-Babylonian and Persian Periods, Chiefly from Nippur.* Babylonian Expedition of the University of Pennsylvania, Series A: Cuneiform Texts 8/1. Philadelphia: Department of Archaeology, University of Pennsylvania.
1912 *Business Documents of Murashû Sons of Nippur Dated in the Reign of Darius II.* Philadelphia: University Museum Press.

Coogan, M. D.
1973 Patterns in Jewish Personal Names in the Babylonian Diaspora. *Journal for the Study of Judaism in the Persian, Hellenistic and Roman Period* 4: 183–91.
1976 *West Semitic Personal Names in the Murašû Documents.* Missoula, Montana: Scholars Press.

Daiches, S.
1910 *The Jews in Babylonia in the Time of Ezra and Nehemiah according to Babylonian Inscriptions.* London: Jews College.

Dandamaev, M.
1984 *Slavery in Babylonia.* DeKalb, Illinois: Northern Illinois University Press.
2000 State Taxes in Neo-Babylonian and Achaemenid Mesopotamia. Pp. 147–62 in *Studi sul Vicino Oriente Antico dedicati alla memoria di Luigi Cagni,* ed. S. Gaziani. Naples: Istituto Universitario Orientale.

Donbaz, V., and Stolper, M. W.
1997 *Istanbul Murašû Texts.* Istanbul: Nederlands Historisch-Archaeologisch Instituut te Istanbul.

Eph῾al, I.
1978 The Western Minorities in Babylonia in the 6th–5th Centuries B.C.: Maintenance and Cohesion. *Orientalia* n.s. 47: 74–90.
1981 On the Political and Social Organization of the Jews in Babylonian Exile. Pp. 106–12 in *XXI. Deutscher Orientalistentag. Vorträge,* ed. Fritz Steppat. Wiesbaden: Franz Steiner.

Grayson, A. K.
2000 *Assyrian and Babylonian Chronicles.* Repr., Winona Lake, Indiana: Eisenbrauns.

Hilprecht, H., and Clay, A. T.
1898   *Business Documents of Murashû Sons of Nippur Dated in the Reign of Artaxerxes I (464–424 B.C.).* Philadelphia: Department of Archaeology and Palaeontology of the University of Pennsylvania.

Joannès, F., and Lemaire, A.
1999   Trois tablettes cunéiformes à l'onomastique ouest-sémitique. *Transeuphratène* 17: 17–33.

Jursa, M.
1995   *Die Landwirtschaft in Sippar in neubabylonischer Zeit.* Vienna: Instituts für Orientalistik der Universität Wien.

Kuhrt, A.
1988   Babylonia from Cyrus to Xerxes. Pp. 112–38 in *Persia, Greece and the Western Mediterranean.* Vol. 4 of *Cambridge Ancient History.* Cambridge: Cambridge University Press.

Lipschits, O.
2001   Judah, Jerusalem and the Temple. *Transeuphratène* 22: 129–42.
2003   Demographic Changes in Judah between the Seventh and the Fifth Centuries B.C.E. Pp. 323–76 in *Judah and the Judeans in the Neo-Babylonian Period,* ed. O. Lipschits and J. Blenkinsopp. Winona Lake, Indiana: Eisenbrauns.

Sidersky, D.
1929   L'onomastique hébraïque des tablettes de Nippur. *Revue d'études juives* 87: 177–99.

Stern, E.
2001   *The Assyrian, Babylonian and Persian Periods 732–332 B.C.E.* Vol. 2 of *Archaeology of the Land of the Bible.* New York: Doubleday.

Stolper, M. W.
1976   A Note on Yahwistic Personal Names in the Murašû Texts. *BASOR* 222: 25–28.
1985   *Entrepreneurs and Empire: The Murašû Archive, the Murašû Firm, and Persian Rule in Babylonia.* Leiden: Nederlands Historisch-Archaeologisch Instituut te Istanbul.
1989a   The Governor of Babylon and Across-the-River in 486 B.C. *Journal of Near Eastern Studies* 48: 283–305.
1989b   On Interpreting Tributary Relationships in Achaemenid Babylonia. Pp. 147–156 in *Le tribut dans l'empire perse,* ed. P. Briant. Travaux de l'Institut d'études iraniennes de l'Université de la Sorbonne nouvelle 13. Paris: Peeters.
1990   The Kaṣr Archive. Pp. 195–205 in *Centre and Periphery: Proceedings of the Groningen 1986 Achaemenid History Workshop,* ed. H. Sancisi-Weerdenburg and A. Kuhrt. Achaemenid History 4. Leiden: Nederlands Instituut voor het Nabije Oosten.

Waerzeggers, C.
1999–2000   The Records of Inṣabtu from the Naggāru Family*. *Archiv für Orientforschung* 46–47: 183–200.

Wallis, G.
1980   Jüdische Bürger in Babylonien während der Achämeniden-Zeit. *Persica* 9: 129–88.

Weidner, E.
1939   Jojachin, König von Juda, in babylonischen Keilschrifttexten. Pp. 923–35 in *Mélanges Syriens offerts à monsieur René Dussaud.* Bibliothèque archéologique et historique 30. Paris: Geuthner.

Zadok, R.
1979   *The Jews in Babylonia during the Chaldean and Achaemenian Periods according to the Babylonian Sources.* Haifa: University of Haifa Press.
1985   *Geographical Names according to New- and Late-Babylonian Texts.* RGTC 8. Wiesbaden: Reichert.

New Aramaic Ostraca from Idumea and Their Historical Interpretation

ANDRÉ LEMAIRE

The Sorbonne

Clearly, since 1985 (Naveh 1985: no. 7; Lemaire 2002: no. 22), and very likely, since 1971 (Holladay 1971a; 1971b; Geraty 1972: 28, no. 8; Lemaire 1996: no. 101; Yardeni 2000: 198)—that is, as far back as salvage excavations by John S. Holladay—several hundred Aramaic ostraca have appeared on the antiquities market. They are now dispersed in several private and public collections. At the end of 1996, I published about 200 of them (L), which were a gift from Mr. and Mrs. Robert Feuer (New York) to the Israel Museum. Two months later, I. Eph'al and J. Naveh published another 201 Aramaic ostraca (EN) available to them in the form of good photographs. A few months later, with Mrs. H. Lozachmeur, I published 9 others from the Moussaieff collection in London (LL) and, later on, Y. Avishur published one ostracon in the *Heltzer Volume*, while I published 4 ostraca from the Schoyen collection (S) in *Transeuphratène*. At the end of 2002, I published a second volume, *Nouvelles inscriptions araméennes d'Idumée*, with some 400 ostraca from various collections, mainly from the Moussaieff, Jeselsohn, and Welch collections (AL), and B. Porten and A. Yardeni are preparing the publication of several hundred more ostraca. So, at least 1,600 (ca. 1,400 legible) Aramaic ostraca came from this find, which is probably to be located at Khirbet el-Kôm/Makkedah, about halfway between Hebron and Lachish, because *Makkedah* appears at least 25 times in these ostraca,[1] and the identification of Khirbet el-Kôm with Makkedah is generally accepted today (Dorsey 1980; de Vos 2003: 402–3, 406, 411–14).

I should like, first, to illustrate how the *new ostraca* are of interest to the various fields of dating, administration, way of life, religion, history, and the redactional history of the Bible.

---

1. EN read, first, MQRH or MNQRH, but I. Eph'al now accepts the reading MQDH or MNQDH (*IEJ* 47, 1997, p. 291).

413

Status Quaestionis

Dating

Eph'al, Naveh, and I have disagreed about interpreting the dating according to the years of "Alexander." I proposed a local calculation system according to the years of Alexander III (the Great), and Eph'al and Naveh have connected these dates with his son, Alexander IV.

In addition to EN no. 56, 3 new ostraca are now dated to the third year of Antigonus:

- AL no. 92 to "Tammuz, Year 3 of A(n)tigonus"
- AL no. 93 to "6th of Ab, Year 3 of Antigonus"
- AL no. 94 to "[Ye]ar 3 of Antigonus"

These ostraca, especially no. 93, clearly confirm the reading "Antigonus," which was not recognized by Eph'al and Naveh. Furthermore, "Year 3 of Antigonus" corresponds to the year 315/314, and this makes the interpretation of "Alexander" as Alexander IV, as proposed by Eph'al and Naveh, very unlikely because Year 2 of Alexander IV, with references to the same month, Tammuz, would appear in AL no. 88[2] and would be from the same year 315/314 as the ostracon from Year 3 of Antigonus, while there would not be any ostracon from the 10 years (332–323) of Alexander the Great's reign. These new ostraca confirm my interpretation of the dating by Alexander as referring to a local calculation system of Alexander the Great, as well as the general dating of the ostraca between 362 and 312. Because a similar calculation is also attested in a bilingual Greek/Phoenician inscription from Piraeus (Baslez and Briquel-Chatonnet 1991: 235–39), this local calculation, beginning in the spring of 332, also was probably in use in the neighboring province of Judea.

Administration, Taxes

The great number of Aramaic ostraca and their dating scheme make clearer and clearer that they are somehow connected with Achaemenid administration. Most of the ostraca probably record taxes in kind (barley, wheat, oil, and so on), and it is no surprise that quantities of barley, wheat, and oil were, at the time of the harvesting of each crop, entering the storerooms of Makkedah. Some of the ostraca may be drafts of a land-registry indicating the quantity of barley to be given for each field. A few ostraca mention quantities of silver, perhaps connected

---

2. In my view, this ostracon contradicts Porten and Yardeni's interpretation of the chronology (below, pp. 484–485).

with taxes to be paid in silver. However, because I intend to deal in more detail with the problem of taxes elsewhere (Lemaire 2000a; 2002: 230; Janzen 2002: 152–54; Lemaire 2004), I shall not address this problem here.

There are also several references to taxes in Judea during the Persian Period in the books of Ezra and Nehemiah, and the Judean taxes were probably similar to the Idumean taxes. So, indirectly, these ostraca could help us understand Judean taxes during the Persian and beginning of the Hellenistic Periods.

Way of Life

Ostracon AL 365 was broken and, although it is still incomplete, most of it is readable. It was probably a scribal exercise, as shown by the beginning of one abecedary at the top and two abecedaries at the bottom. However, the main part is a presentation of two lists of personal names of people from the village of Idnah, probably the Arabic village of Idnah today, about three kilometers from Khirbet el-Kôm:

1. ʾBGDHWZḤṬY
2. ŠMHT ZY ʿRBW
3. KSPʾ BʾDNH
4. ZKWR BR YHWKL
5. GNY QWSYTB BR
6. ḤNNYH ʿZRYQM
7. ZY ŠṬYW ḤMRʾ
8. BʾDNH QWSḤNN
9. QWSḤNN QWSY
10. ʿZ[RY? B?]R SMWK—[
11. [QWSY?]TB B[R?
12. GNY ʿK[BR?
13. YHŠMʿ [?
14. ʾBGDH[?
15. ʾBGDHWZḤṬ[?

2. Names: (those) who guaranteed
3. silver in *Idnah*:
4. Zakkour, son of Yehôkal,
5. Ganî, Qôsyatab, son
6. of Hananyah, ʿAzrîqam.
7. (Those) who drank wine
8. in Idnah: Qôshanan,
9. Qôshanan, Qôsî,

10. ʿAz[rî? so]n *of* Sammouk . . . [?
11. [Qôsya]tab, s[on of . . .
12. Ganî, ʿAk[bar?
13. Yahshamaʿ?

So, we have two lists of names: 'those who garanteed silver' and 'those who drank wine'. This last feature is not completely surprising since the onomastics reveal many North Arabic names, very similar to the onomastics of Nabatea, and Diodorus 19.94.3 tells us that the Nabateans did not drink wine. Actually, in the list of people drinking wine, no name is North Arabic: the names are Edomite, general Northwest Semitic, or Judean. The same is true regarding the names of those who guaranteed silver, which was probably characteristic of the "Canaanite" people but not of the North Arabic people. So we have, among the local population, various cultures and various ways of life.

We can compare the coexistence of various cultures in Idumea with what we know about the situation in Judea. From the literary tradition of the books of Ezra and Nehemiah, Haggai, and Zechariah, we know that there was apparently a trend toward a more unified culture. Even if there was some tension between local Judeans and new settlers from Babylonia, the majority of the Judeans trace their roots to the Hebrew culture. Especially after Ezra's mission and his probable proclamation of the Torah, the Jewish Law seems to have been enforced among the whole Judean population.

Religion

The onomastica found in these ostraca include several theophoric elements characteristic of the various ethnicities (Lemaire 2001b): besides the North Arabic names (with the theonyms El, El-Baalî, and Manat/Manawat), we have many Edomite names with "Qôs," the national deity of Edom, and various Aramaic names (with Shamash, Nabu, and Sin), as well as a few Phoenician/Canaanite names with Baal, Sidq, Shalem, Isis, Apis, or Osiris,[3] and a minority group of names with "Yaho." This diversity not only appears in the onomastica: ostracon AL 283, probably a list of fields that were not cultivated, also reveals names of the various sanctuaries with theophoric elements:

1. TL ᶻʸ ṬḤT MN BYT ʿZ
2. WḤYBL ZY BYT YHW

---

3. Isis, Apis, and Osiris are Egyptian deities. However, they are also attested in Phoenician onomastica.

3. *ZBR ZBY* RPYD^ɔ ZY BṬN^ɔ
4. BZ^ɔ S^cD/RW KPR GLGWL
5. RQQ ZY BYT K/NBD/R/W
6. KPR YNQM

1. The *hill/ruin* that is below the house of ʿUzzâ
2. and the *strip/rope* of the house of Yahô,
3. the *marshland* of Zabî, the terrace of the terebinth tree,
4. *the wasted (field) of Saʿad/ru, the tomb of Gilgoul,*
5. (the) pool of the house of Nabu,
6. *the tomb of Yinqom.*

Although the reading 'the house/temple of Nabu' is very uncertain at the end of line 5, we clearly have BYT ʿZ^ɔ and BYT YHW at the end of lines 1 and 2. The similarity of the syntagms reveals that both are referring to temples: the Temple of the Arabic deity ʿUzza, well known in Lihyanite, Thamudic, and Nabatean inscriptions, and the Temple of Yaho, also known during this period at Elephantine, Jerusalem, and Mount Gerizim. The coexistence of these temples in the same place, probably Khirbet el-Kôm/Makkedah, is also evidence of the mixed ethnicities and religions characteristic of the Idumean province during the fourth century B.C.E.

The existence of a Yahwistic minority group in Idumea may explain the enigma of the list of towns with a Judean population in Neh 11:25–30 (Lemaire 1990: 40).

Furthermore the existence of a Temple of "Yaho" in Idumea can be compared with the existence of a Temple of Yaho at Elephantine and on Mount Gerizim. Unfortunately we have no information about the kind of cult that was practiced in the Idumean temple. What we can underline is the fact that it is no longer possible to speak about the Yahwistic cult during the Persian Period by taking into account only the Temple of Jerusalem.

It is probably in this context that the absence of a reference to Jerusalem in the Torah makes sense. From the Samaritan tradition, we can infer that the Ezra Torah was accepted in Samaria. One may propose that it was also accepted by the minority Yahwistic population in Idumea. This would probably have been impossible if people were obliged to celebrate their cult in Jerusalem. However, this was not the case, as is shown by the Samaritans who could accept the Torah and keep their temple on Mount Gerizim. The absence of an explicit reference to Jerusalem and its temple explains that the Ezra Torah was acceptable to the Yahwistic population outside Judea.

History of Southern Palestine

These Aramaic ostraca, directly or indirectly, illuminate five centuries of the history of southern Palestine with many political changes, very often in relation to the Judean situation. One may distinguish nine steps:

(1) About 600, southern Palestine was part of the Kingdom of Judea, which probably controlled the Negeb as far as far as Aroer.

(2) In approximately 599, King Jehoiakim revolted against Nebuchadnezzar and, according to the corrected text of 2 Kgs 24:2 (Lemaire 1997: 89), the king of Babylon sent "raiding parties of Chaldeans, *Edomites*, Moabites, and Ammonites, letting them range through Judah and ravage it." The activity of Edomite raiding parties seem to be confirmed by the Arad ostraca, especially Arad ostracon 24:20. More generally, most of the Elyashib ostraca are probably to be interpreted as the bookkeeping of the last month of the fortress: Tebet 597 (Lemaire 1977: 231–32). So, from February 597 on, the Edomites controlled the Judean Negeb, as has already been well argued by A. Alt (1925: 108; 1953: 280–81) and M. Noth (1953: 256), interpreting Jer 13:19: "Your cities in the Negeb are closed and nobody opens them."

(3) During the second Judean revolt, the Edomites apparently chose to help Nebuchadnezzar and, in 587 and/or 582, invaded the southern Judean Shephelah and the southern Judean Hills as far as Lachish, Hebron, and Ein-Gedi.

(4) The famous campaign of Nabonidus in Arabia in 553/552 began with the invasion of Edom. In early 552, Edom was defeated and the Edomite Kingdom became part of the (Neo-)Babylonian Empire, more precisely part of the great province of Arabia, with its capital at Teima, where Nabonidus stayed for ten years (Lemaire 2003).

(5) In 539, Cyrus took over Babylon. The great province of Arabia became the allied Kingdom of Kedar, controlling as far as the Mediterranean coast between Palestine and Egypt. One of the incense altars from Lachish probably mentions the name of one of these kings of Kedar (Lemaire 1974). Another one was "Geshem/Gashmu, the Arab" mentioned in the Bible as an adversary of Nehemiah (2:19; 6:1, 2, 6). A third one, his son "Qaynu," is mentioned on a silver bowl found at Tell el-Maskhuta near Ismaelia (Gibson 1975: 122–23).

(6) At the beginning of the fourth century, after 387/6 and before 362 B.C.E., this great Kingdom of Kedar disappeared, probably because it, with Egypt and Evagoras, revolted against Persia (see Diodorus 15.2.4). At this time, southern Palestine was reorganized under firmer

control of the Great King. Gaza became a Persian garrison town and the rest of southern Palestine became the Achaemenid province of Idumea, as shown clearly by the Aramaic ostraca dating to 362–312 B.C.E. (Lemaire 2002: 147–50).

(7) These ostraca also show clearly that the province of Idumea became, from 332 on, apparently without any problem, the Hellenistic province of Idumea under Alexander, his successors (the Diadochi), and later on the Ptolemaic kings.

(8) After the battle of Paneion in 200, this Lagid province was controlled by the Seleucid kings, as confirmed by an Aramaic ostracon from Maresha (Eshel and Kloner 1996). The province was an important base for the Seleucid armies against the Maccabean revolt.

(9) Finally, in 112/111, the province was invaded by John Hyrcanus and became part of the Hasmonean kingdom of Judea (Barag 1992–93).

Thus, for nearly five centuries, this entire portion of the country was not a dependency of Jerusalem.

Redactional History of the Bible

Without delving any further into the general historical interest of the ostraca (which is to be done when all of them are published), I should like to share with the reader some thoughts about the relevance of these ostraca for our interpretation of the biblical tradition.

This relevance does not seem obvious because no biblical figure has been mentioned so far. Of course, it is possible to research the significance of the few Jewish names mentioned, as well as information on the location of biblical Makkedah. However, I think that the main interest of the ostraca lies elsewhere.

Because these ostraca confirm that most of southern Palestine was outside the direct influence of Jerusalem for nearly five centuries, most, if not all, of the biblical traditions concerning this part of the country are probably to be dated earlier, that is, during the period of the Kingdom of Judah. This seems obvious from the detailed geographical description contained in Joshua 15 (de Vos 2003; cf. also "Simeon": Josh 19:1–9), but it is also true of the conquest legend regarding this territory and especially of Makkedah in Josh 10:6–40. And it is also true of the David stories connected with the territory of Judah: Keila, Zif, Maon, Carmel, Ziklag, Hebron . . . in most of 1 Samuel 23–2 Samuel 5.

Let us go one step farther: it is a well-known fact that the patriarchal traditions about Abraham are centered around Hebron and Mamre, and those about Isaac, around Beer-sheba. What we have to realize now is that, after 587 and for nearly five centuries, all of these places were outside Judea and were inhabitated mainly by Edomites or North Arabian population. Because a literary composition of these traditions after 112 B.C.E. is obviously impossible, the bulk of them were probably written down during the First Temple Period (Lemaire 2000b).

So, indirectly, in revealing the extent of the political and cultural break in the history of southern Palestine from the beginning of the sixth century to the end of the second century B.C.E., this new documentation tends to push back most of the biblical traditions about this part of the territory to the First Temple Period.

New, Unpublished Aramaic Ostraca

As already stated, there are still many Aramaic ostraca from this discovery to be published, and the collection of this material from the market and from private collectors appears to be without end. I would like to present here 30 new items as well as discuss a few problems of interpretation.

Memorandum Ostracon

1. (= P8) This ostracon is written on a quadrangular sherd (118 × 70 × 8 mm) from the wall of a jar; it is light brown on the outside and a little darker inside. The inscription is written at about −10° in relation to the potter's wheel traces. In the lower part of the ostracon, the left part of lines 5 and 6 is missing, and it seems impossible to determine the number of lines that may be missing in the lower part.

Transcription

1. LDKRWN Š⁀RN ZY WHBY ⁀L QWSNHᴿ
2. Š S X III II ⁀L QWSḤNN Š X III II
3. ⁀L ⁀DRNY Š X III II ⁀L QWSDKR
4. WB⁀L⁀YR Š X III II ⁀L NṬYR⁀
5. Š S III III II ⁀L ⁀ḤYW[?] Q?[?
6. ⁀L ⁀B/D/RB/D/R⁀[?

Translation

1. As a memorandum: barley of Wahabî upon Qôsnahar,
2. b(arley) s(eah) 15; upon Qôshanan, b(arley) 15;
3. upon ⁀Adarnî, b(arley) 15; upon Qôsdakar,
4. and Baal⁀îr, b(arley) 15; upon Netyrâ
5. b(arley) s(eah) 8; upon Ahyô, [?] q(ab?) ?[?]
6. upon ⁀Adrâ[?

Ostracon 1 (P8).

Paleography

The Aramaic script of this ostracon looks formal or semiformal, close to the monument script attested on the contemporary Trilingual Xanthus Stele and especially close to the classical script of the Baga-want manuscripts, to be published by Shaked. Even though there is still ambiguity concerning the D/R, reading is easy enough because the ink is generally well preserved.

Commentary

At the beginning of line 1, LDKRWN seems to be a kind of title. The Aramaic word *dikrôn*(/*dikkārôn*?) is well attested in Nabatean, Palmyrenian, and Hatrean funerary inscriptions, especially in the syntagm DKRN ṬB 'good memory' (Hoftijzer and Jongeling 1995: 331). However, here the context is not funerary and is closer to the use of the graphic variant ZKRN in Imperial Aramaic, especially in the documents from Egypt. One can especially quote Cowley 32:1, 2, where ZKRN is also a title, 'memorandum', that presents the main points of Bagohî and Delayah's answer. This last meaning seems close to the reference to *dikronāh* in Ezra 6:2 (Fitzmyer 1974: 210), where it appears to be an archivial summary of an official decision. However, the context of Cowley 61–63 (Porten and Yardeni 1993: C3, 13; cf. C3:8IIIB.16), a "fragmentary record of memoranda" concerning cups of bronze, vessels, barley, rods, seems closer to our ostracon because it is an account, more precisely, a barley account.

The syntagm ŠʿRN ZY + PN + ʿL + PN seems similar to formulas attested on Aramaic tablets recording loans of barley (Fales 1986: nos. 46–48; Lemaire 2001a: no. 15).[4] WHBY '(the deity) gave' is already well attested on several ostraca and inscriptions on jars from Idumea (L 72:3; EN 56:2; 181:6; AL 336–38). QWSNHR, probably 'Qôs is light', is already attested on a Beer-sheba Aramaic ostracon (Naveh 1979: 183).

In lines 2, 3, and 4, one notes that the scribe did not repeat the abbreviation S (for *seah*) before the same quantity of barley. The name QWSḤNN is very well attested in these ostraca (about 18 times).

In line 3, the reading ʿDRNY is practically certain when one looks carefully at the original. This new name, which means '(the deity) helped me', is probably a graphic variant of ʿDRN known from two ostraca (AL 13:3; 246:1?). QWSDKR 'Qôs remembered' is probably already attested on three ostraca from the same find (L 145:2[!]; EN 125:1; AL 233:3).

At the beginning of line 4, BʿLʿYR is probably an associate of QWSDKR. It is a well-known name in these ostraca. The last letter is a D/R. EN chose to read D (EN 1:2; 3:2; 4:2, 5:2; 9:2 . . .) but R seems preferable, because it gives the meaning 'Baal protected'.[5]

At the end of line 4, NṬYRʾ, probably 'protected (by the deity)', is a new personal name in these ostraca, but it is already attested in the contemporary Samaria papyri from Wadi Daliyeh (Gropp et al., eds. 2001: nos. 5:3, 12; 8:9, 10; 9:5) and in the Saqqarah papyri (Segal 1983: 86–87).

At the end of line 5, the fragmentary reading ʾḤYW is uncertain. This name is already well attested in Nabatean (Negev 1991: 11, no. 60). After this name, one might complete with Š + number + Q II (above the line). However, this would be very conjectural.

General Interpretation

The general interpretation of this ostracon is not clear because the formulas are very short and the ostracon incomplete. However, the formula LDKRN at the beginning of the ostracon probably indicates the "literary genre" of an accounting memorandum about barley, which

---

4. See also the similar formula with ŠʿRN L + PN + ʿL + PN (Fales 1986: nos. 53, 54, 56; Lemaire 2001: nos. 7–12, 19).

5. L 13:1; 98:1; AL 41:2; 46:3. . . . Cf. also W. Röllig, *Die Welt des Orients* 28 (1997) 221 n. 3.

apparently belongs to Wahabî and is connected in various quantities to various people. One can imagine four different interpretations:

1. Because the formula is similar to one of the Aramaic tablets recording loans of barley, Wahabî could be the owner/creditor and the various names, the names of the debtors. In this case, the lack of an interest rate is a bit strange but interest may not have been absolutely necessary if Wahabî was consistently lending barley at the same rate (often 50%).
2. Wahabî could be the owner of fields and the various names, the names of his farm tenants. In this case, the list would indicate the amount of the rent in kind.
3. Wahabî could be a perceptor/tax-farmer, and the list would indicate the amount of barley to be given as taxes in kind.
4. Since the Aramaic preposition ʿL is ambiguous and could also mean 'to/towards', the ostracon could refer to a distribution of rations to people working for Wahabî.

Perhaps it will be possible to choose from among these four interpretations when all of the ostraca from the same find are published.

Ostraca Mentioning BNY/BYT + PN

2. (= P2) Quadrangular sherd from the wall of a jar, pink on both sides, measuring 54 × 50 × 9 mm; it is inscribed at about −10° in relation to the potter's wheel traces. The ostracon is incomplete: the lower left part is missing.

Transcription

1. B XXI LTMWZ ŠNT III Iᴵ
2. ʿTRN ZBDʾRH
3. LBNY YHWKL[?
4. Š S II[?

Translation

1. On the 21st of Tammuz, Year 5,
2. ʿAtaran (son of) Zebadurah
3. (belonging) to the sons of Yehukal[?
4. b(arley), s(eahs) 2[?

Commentary

At the end of line 1, a fifth unit has been added above the first four. The dating can be compared with AL 44 ("On the 27th of Tammuz,

Ostracon 2 (P2).

Year 5"). The precise reign is not given: it could be that of Artaxerxes III, Alexander, Philip, or Antigonus, so that the earliest possible date (in the 5th year of Artaxerxes III) is "July 15, 354."

At the beginning of line 2, the first letter seems to be either ʾ*alep* or ʿ*ayin*, but a detailed exam reveals that ʿ*ayin* is preferable. ʿTRN may be compared with ʿTR[? (L 58:3) and probably ʿTRY? (L 46:2). Before the ending -N, one can identify the theophoric ʿTR, known from the Aramaic onomastics (Maraqten 1988: 58, 201–2). At the end of line 2, there is the ambiguous reading D/R. Ephʿal and Naveh prefer to read this name with a *dalet* EN 87:1; 97:2) but a *reš* is also possible (L 121:1; EN 46:1; 50:2; 55:2; 56:2; 58:2; 59:2; 102:2; 126:1; 179:2; 184 (right, vertically); AL 42:2; 210:1; 255:7).

At the end of line 3, the syntagm BNY YHWKL 'the sons of Yehukal' is already attested in EN 78:1; 96:2; AL 35:2–3; 90:2–3. It is to be compared with BYT YHWKL 'house of Yehukal', attested in EN 76:1; 106:2; AL 83:2. The Yahwistic name YHWKL 'Yahô is able, has power' (Fowler 1988: 82, 347) is already mentioned in the book of Jeremiah (37:3; cf. 38:1) and in Hebrew epigraphy (Davies 1991: 368).

3. (= P3) Quadrangular sherd from the wall of a jar of whitish/clear gray color. It measures 78 × 56 × 11–13 mm. The ostracon is probably

Ostracon 3 (P3).

complete and the inscription written at about −50° in relation to the potter's wheel traces. Ink is partly faded and the inscription difficult to decipher.

Transcription

1. B X L*NYSN* ŠNT III II*I* II
2. ZW/YM/S'W/Y ḤNWN 'L YD
3. 'TNY *LBNY* QS*Y*
4. MN '(R)BT ḤW/ZRW

Translation

1. On the 10th of Nisân, Year 8,
2. . . . . (*son of*) Hanun by (*the intermediary of*)
3. 'Otnî (*belonging*) *to the sons of* Qosî,
4. from the ste⟨p⟩pe of Ḥazziru.

Commentary

The reading of line 1 is almost certain, even though the name of the month is partly blurred. Year 8 can be related either to Artaxerxes III (= April 4, 351) or to Alexander the Great (= April 16, 325).

Ostracon 4 (P7).

At the beginning of line 2, the reading of the name is uncertain; it is probably followed by ḤNWN 'Hanun', not yet attested in these ostraca but already known in Aramaic (Maraqten 1988: 81).

At the beginning of line 3, the uncertain name ʿTNY ''Otnî' would be already attested in L 83:1; EN 174:4; 188:6; AL 41:2; 296:1. At the end of line 3, the syntagm BNY QSY is probably a graphic variant of BNY QWSY, already attested in EN 95:1; AL 109:2(?).

In line 4, ʿBT would be a new word and its meaning uncertain. However, one can compare the syntagm MN ʿBT ḤZRW to MN ʿRBT ḤNZRW, already attested in L 39:2–3(!); EN 100:3; AL 87:2–3. So, one can propose reading line 4: MN ʿ(R)BT ḤZRW, 'Hazziru' being a graphic variant of 'Hanziru'. However, the reading ḤWRW is also possible.

4. (= P7) Sherd from the wall of a jar, brown on both sides, measuring 63 × 48 × 6 mm. The ostracon seems complete; the inscription is written at about +80° in relation to the potter's wheel traces.

Transcription

1. ḤLPN LBNY QWṢY
2. MRYŠ ḤD
3. B XX III III III LʾB

Ostracon 5 (W4').

Translation

1. Halipan (*belonging*) to the sons of Qôṣî:
2. one timber.
3. On the 29th of Ab.

Commentary

The formula of this ostracon is similar to the one on EN 86, written 'on the 28th of Ab' and mentioning 'one beam (ŠRY ḤDH)'. Without the date, the formula is also similar to EN 67, '1 beam (ŠRY 1)'. Judeo-Aramaic MRYŠ 'timber, beam' translates *kĕrutot* (*'ărāzīm*) in 1 Kgs 6:36.

In line 1, ḤLPN LBNY QWṢY can be compared with 'BYDW LBNY GYR (EN 67:1) and ZBYD LBNY B'RWM (EN 87:1). The syntagm BNY QWṢY is already attested in EN 92:2; 93:1; 119:2(!); AL 82:2; 150:1–2; 184:1; 185:2 (cf. BNY QṢY: EN 94:1) and can be compared to BYT QWṢY (AL 94:2; 130:1–2).

5. (= W4') Sherd from the wall of a jar, brown on both sides, measuring 88 × 52 × 7 mm. The ostracon seems complete; the inscription is written at about –60° in relation to the potter's wheel traces.

Transcription

1. 'DRB'L MN BNY 'LB'L
2. MRYŠN QRY*N*

Translation

1. ʿAdarbaal from the sons of ʿAlbaal,
2. *two* timbers *covering*.

Commentary

The formula of this ostracon is in some ways similar to EN 67 and to the ostracon just above.

The name ʿDRBʿL is already attested in EN 47:4. At the end of line 1, BʿL is partly blurred but still legible. The syntagm BNY ʿLBʿL is already well attested in EN 41:2; 42:1; 55:2–3; 72:2; 73:1; 74:1–2; 77:1; LL 1:4; AL 99:2?; 104:1; 245:3–4 and can be compared with BYT ʿLBʿL (EN 76:1).

In line 2, MRYŠN is probably dual since it is not followed by a number. QRYN is difficult to interpret; it could be used to specify the meaning of MRYŠ, that is, the kind of timber.

6. (= W5′) Fairly large sherd from the wall of a jar, cream outside, and clear brown inside. It measures 114 × 95 × 6 mm and is written at about +15° in relation to the potter's wheel traces. The ink is sometimes blurred and the reading uncertain.

Transcription

1. *B—W/D/R* YHB ʿL YD?
2. [ŠM]ʿYH [*MN*] B*Y*T Q[??
3. PSY Š S III II*I B*???
4. BB ʾ*H*YW *MN GBRW* Š *S* III [?
5. *Y*HBLH *H*LPH BŠWQ *H* S X III [III]
6. MN BYT *QWS*[*Y*?] S X II

Translation

1. . . . . gave by (*the intermediary of*)
2. [*Shema*]ʿyah [*from the*] *house of* Q[?
3. Pasî: b(arley), s(eah) 6???
4. Bab (*son of*?) Ahyô *from* Gabbaru: b(arley), s(eah) 3 [?
5. *Yehablah* (*son of*?) Halipah *in the market*: w(heat), s(eah) 16
6. from the house of *Qôs*(*î*?): s(eah) 12.

Commentary

The first name at the beginning of line 1 is practically illegible, and there may be another name at the end of the line.

At the beginning of line 2, the uncertain name ŠMʿYH is already attested in EN 201:3, 4 (cf. also YHŠMʿ in AL 365:13). At the end of the

Ostracon 6 (W5').

line, the name of the 'house' is practically illegible, although the first letter may be Q.

At the beginning of line 3, PSY is a name already attested in EN 133:2; AL 69a:3; 80:2; 156:1; 174:1. The last letters of the line are blurred and illegible.

At the beginning of line 4, BB is already attested in EN 58:4(!); AL 13:3; 115:2, while GBRW is already known from AL 324:2. For 'Aḥyô', see above, no. 1:5.

At the beginning of line 5, YHBLH 'God has given' is new and probably is a graphic variant of YHBꞋLH (cf. ꞋWŠꞋLH/ꞋWŠLH in Nabatean: Negev 1991: 10–11). However, it would not be impossible to understand it as '(Halipah) gave him'. ḤLPH seems new in these ostraca but can be compared with ḤLPN and ḤLPT. In the middle of the line, BŠWQ is somewhat uncertain. ŠWQ 'street, market' would be a synonym of MḤWZ, probably 'market' in EN 90:3(!); AL 52:3; 53:3.

At the beginning of line 6, the uncertain syntagm BYT QWS[Y?] 'the house of Qôs[î?]' is comparable to BNY Q(W)SY (see above, no. 3:3).

These six ostraca contain the syntagm BNY/BYT + personal name. It seems clear enough that in these syntagms BNY and BYT are practically synonymous and designate a 'house', either with an economic meaning (all the people living and working on a farm) or with a social meaning (all the members of a [large] family or of a clan). People are connected with this group, either with the preposition L '(belonging) to', or with the preposition MN 'from/part of'. Two other references to these groups may be signified when the personal name is followed directly by L + another PN or when the personal name is followed by BR + another PN. This interpretation is not quite certain and will need to be rechecked when all of the ostraca are published. The expression PN + L + PN may be a shortened form of PN + L (+ BYT/BNY) + PN, directly referring to the head of the farm or of the clan. So these expressions probably indicate some kind of social or economic organization in Idumea and will need to be studied in detail when all of the ostraca are published.

Ostracon on Stone

7. (= P6) Chip off a flat, whitish/gray, calcareous stone, more or less triangular, measuring 83 × 77 × 4/18 mm. It is apparently the first ostracon on stone among these ostraca. However, we may compare it with the stone ostraca found at Deir el-Medineh (Egypt).[6] Another so-called Hebrew ostracon on stone, found on the surface at Lachish, was published by B. Rocco (1966; Rinaldi 1967); however, the existence of an ink inscription on this small stone is doubtful (Lemaire 1977: 89; Renz 1995: 437 n. 3). Here, on this stone ostracon, there is clearly an Aramaic inscription, although it is sometimes difficult to read it because it is cursive and partly worn away.

Transcription

1. B XX L'B ḤZ/BYR/BW Š S XX *III*
2. *III II* 'L YD ZBD'L
3. Ḥ S XX *II* Q *II*

Translation

1. On the 28th of Ab, *Huzayru/Hubaybu*: b(arley), s(eah) 2*8*
2. *by (the intermediary of) Zebadel*
3. w(heat), s(eah) 22, q(ab) 2.

---

6. See, for instance: www.uni-muenchen.de/dem-online or www.lmu.de/dem-online: ostraca Berlin 14 233, 14 246, 14 253ff.

Ostracon 7 (P6).

Commentary

At the beginning of line 1, the date, with no mention of the year (cf. a similar dating in no. 4:3), seems clear enough. The somewhat uncertain name ḤZYRW is already attested in L 103:1(?); EN 182:4; AL 139:1. The reading ḤBYBW is also possible.

At the end of line 2, the somewhat uncertain name ZBDʾL is already well attested in L 6:3(!); EN 7:4; 10:3; 71:4; 109:4; 160:3; AL 112b:3; 162:2; 193:3; 215:1(?); 282:3.

Other Ostraca

8. (= P1) Rectangular clear brown sherd from the thin wall of a jar. It measures 63 × 59 × 5 mm. The inscription follows the potter's wheel traces; it is easier to read the inscription on the ostracon itself than in the photo.

Transcription

1. B XX III I *LSYWN* ŠNT II
2. ?Q . . . [Š]ʿRN S X III III II

Ostracon 8 (P1).

Translation

1. On the 24th of Siwân, Year 2,
2. . . . .[*b*]*arley:* s(eah) 18.

Commentary

'Year 2' does not allow us to determine a precise date, but one may compare it with EN 9 ('On the 4th of Siwân, Year 2'); 12 ('On the 22nd of Siwân, Year 2'); and AL 23 ('On the 19th of Siwân, Year 2').

On line 2, the reading Š'RN is conjectural.

9. (= P15) Thick trapezoidal sherd from the wall of a jar, brown outside and a little clearer inside. It measures 77 × 62 × 22 mm. The two-line inscription is difficult to read because it is partly covered by calcareous deposit.

Transcription

1. *B XX IIIII L'DR ŠNT* ??
2. *'TNY Š'RN* K III I *S* ???

Ostracon 9 (P15).

Translation

1. *On the 25th of Adar, Year* ??
2. *ʿOtnî, b(arley):* k(or) 4, s(eah) ???

Commentary

The reading of this ostracon is generally very uncertain.

In line 2, the (very uncertain) reading ʿTNY is already attested in L 83:1; EN 174:4; 188:6; AL 41:2; 296:1 and above, no. 3:3. After this word, the reading ŠʿRN is conjectural.

10. (= Mo2) Clear brown sherd from the wall of a jar. The inscription follows the potter's wheel traces.

Transcription

1. ZBWD Š K I
2. *S X III* III I Q III

Translation

1. Zabbud: b(arley), k(or) 1,
2. s(eahs) *17*, q(abs) 3.

Ostracon 10 (Mo2).

Commentary
ZBWD is already attested in AL 211:3 and 285:1.

11. (= P13) Thin sherd from the wall of a jar, clear brown outside and a little darker inside. It measures 77 × 82 × 8 mm. The inscription is written at about +10° in relation to the potter's wheel traces.

Transcription

1. *SMWK* BYT [?]
2. *R'Š* III III [?]

Translation

1. *Sammuk* house [?]
2. *barley groats* 6 [?]

Commentary
This ostracon is enigmatic. It seems to be palimpsest: under the actual inscription, there are probably traces of an older inscription that may be read, in the second part of line 1, LŠMTW LQWS?. Furthermore, there are traces of two other previous lines, with several Ls.

The actual inscription is difficult to read and to understand. The (uncertain) name SMWK is already known in these ostraca (EN 11:2;

Ostracon 11 (P13).

79:2; 150:1; 186:1; LL 8:1; AL 365:10). BYT is clear but, strangely enough, apparently not followed by a name.

At the beginning of line 2, the reading RʾŠ is highly uncertain; one could also propose the reading ḤŠ. RʾŠ is all the more uncertain because it is not followed by the abbreviation S for s(eah), as usual.

12. (= Mo3) Whitish/gray sherd from the wall of a jar, measuring 78 × 75 × 8 mm. The inscription is written at about −5–10° in relation to the potter's wheel traces.

Transcription

1. LYTᶜ MŠTL I
2. LŠMYRW

Translation

1. (*Belonging*) to Yataᶜ, *bundle* 1,
2. (*Belonging*) to Shumayru

Commentary

YTᶜ is probably attested in AL 116:2; 164:1.
For a discussion of the precise meaning of MŠTL, see AL, p. 46.

Ostracon 12 (Mo3).

The North Arabic name ŠMYRW seems to be new in these ostraca; it is to be compared with the Aramaic hypocoristic ŠMWR (AL 255:1).

13. (= P11) Gray sherd from the wall of a jar measuring 120 × 45 × 7–8 mm. The ostracon seems to be complete. The inscription is written at about +20° in relation to the potter's wheel traces.

Transcription

1. ḤYRW WḤYRW
2. GRGRN III I

Translation

1. Hayru and Hayru
2. *shriveled olives* 4

Commentary

The writing is very cursive: for instance, *reš* seems to be a simple vertical stroke and can be confused with *zayin*.

In line 1, ḤYRW is new in these ostraca. However, it is already known from Nabatean (Negev 1991: 29).

In line 2, the precise meaning of GRGR is still uncertain (Lemaire 2002: 77).

Ostracon 13 (P11).

Ostracon 14 (W1').

14. (= W1') Large dark brown sherd from the wall of a jar, measuring 102 × 94 × 8 mm. The inscription is perpendicular to the potter's wheel traces.

Transcription

1. QWSKHL GRGRN X III III I

Translation

1. Qôskahel: *shriveled olives* 17.

Ostracon 15 (P12).

Commentary

The name Qôskahel is well known in these ostraca (15 times).

15. (= P12) Whitish sherd from the wall of a jar measuring 89 × 69 × 8 mm. The ostracon contains a single line perpendicular to the potter's wheel traces.

Transcription

1. 1. ZBYDW LʿLYʾL G X III

Translation

1. 1. Zubaydou (*belonging*) to ʿAliél, *sh*(*riveled olives?*) 13.

Commentary

In these ostraca, ZBYDW is already attested 12 times and ʿLYʾL 4 times (EN 69:1; 189:1; LL 9:1; AL 110:2). The abbreviation G is already attested in AL 231:1, 2; it is probably an abbreviation for GRGR(N) (above, nos. 13–14).

16. (= P4) Large roughly triangular sherd from the wall of a jar, brown on both sides. It measures 118 × 117 × 6–7 mm. The inscription

Ostracon 16 (P4).

is written at about –70° in relation to the potter's wheel traces. The ostracon seems complete, but the ends of the lines are worn away.

Transcription

1. B III II LTŠRY ŠNT *XX*[?
2. QWSLYTᶜ LYD QWSML[K
3. *M[Š?]Ḥ* S III II Q III II

Translation

1. On the 5th of Tishri, Year *20*[+?
2. Qôsluyataᶜ *under the authority of* Qôsmala[k
3. *o*[*i*]*l*, s(eah) 5, q(ab) 5.

Commentary

The precise date of this ostracon may be interesting but is very uncertain. After ŠNT, the number XX is probable, and it may be followed
by a diagonal stroke for '1'; however, a second XX is not excluded, and
there is still room for two strokes. Because of the general date of these
ostraca, I hesitate between three solutions:

1. With the minimal reading 'XX', it would be dated during Artaxerxes III's reign, that is, on the 11th of October 339 B.C.E.
2. With the possible reading 'XX I', it would also be dated during
   Artaxerxes III's reign, that is, on the 30th of September 338 B.C.E.

Ostracon 17 (Mo6).

Actually, it may be the only document dated during the 21st year of Artaxerxes III, that is, the last year of his reign, since "no contemporary cuneiform documents help to establish his 21 years of rule" (Parker and Dubberstein 1956: 19). If this were the correct reading, this ostracon could help to determine the date of Artaxerxes III's death, which had not yet been announced in Idumea 'on the 5th of Tishri'.

3. With the very conjectural reading 'XX XX II', this would be a date during Artaxerxes II's reign and might be the earliest ostracon of the find, because the dating of EN 48 ('on the 26th of Siwân, Year 42') is paleographically uncertain.

In line 2, QWSLYT‘ 'May Qôs save' is already attested several times in these ostraca (L 27:2; 76A:7?; AL 195:1; 261:4; 289:2?), and QWSMLK occurs frequently (21 times).

At the beginning of line 3, MŠḤ is conjectural.

17. (= Mo6) Whitish sherd from the wall of a jar, measuring 80 × 480 × 8 mm. The inscription is perpendicular to the potter's wheel traces.

Transcription

1. B III III LNYSN *QWSY*
2. *MŠḤ* S X I Q *II*

Translation

1. On the 6th of Nisan, *Qôsî*,
2. *oil:* s(eahs) 11, *q(ab)* 2.

Commentary

QWSY is already attested 11 times in these ostraca.

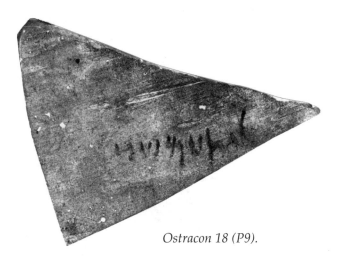

Ostracon 18 (P9).

18. (= P9) Small triangular sherd from the wall of a jar, measuring 61 × 46 × 7 mm. The inscription contains only one line, which approximately follows the potter's wheel traces.

Transcription

1. LYTᶜ MŠḤ

Translation

1. (Belonging) to Yataᶜ, oil.

Commentary
Although the letters are the same size as on the ostraca, this could well be an inscription on a jar citing the name of the owner and the contents of the jar. YTᶜ is already attested above, no. 12:1.

19. (= W3′) Small dark brown sherd measuring 43 × 39 × 7 mm. The inscription approximately follows the potter's wheel traces.

Transcription

1. ḤZY *MN*[?
2. MRYŠN III[?

Translation

1. Hazî *from* [?
2. timbers 3[?

Ostracon 19 (W3').

Commentary

The original ostracon may have contained only two lines.

ḤZY is already attested in AL 214:3 and in a Beer-sheba ostracon (Naveh 1979: 186, no. 34B:8).

For MRYŠ 'timber', see above, nos. 4 and 5.

20. (= W2') Small clear brown sherd measuring 45 × 52 × 8 mm. The inscription is perpendicular to the potter's wheel traces. The ostracon is incomplete: we have only the ends of three lines.

Transcription

1. ?*TMW*]Z ŠNT II
2. ?*N*]ŠRW ŠʿRN
3. ?*MR*]YŠN III I

Translation

1. . . . ?*Tammu*]z, Year 2
2. . . . . . ? *Na*]shru orge
3. . . . ?*tim*]bers 4.

Commentary

In this ostracon, only 'Year 2' seems certain. The other readings are very conjectural.

Ostracon 20 (W2′).

21. (= P5) Quadrangular thin sherd from the wall of a jar, dark brown outside and brick pink inside. It measures 46 × 57 × 5/7 mm. The ostracon seems complete, and the inscription is almost perpendicular to the potter's wheel traces.

Transcription

1. ʿYDW PʿLN III II
2. B XX III III LTMWZ

Translation

1. ʿAydou: laborers 5.
2. On the 26th of Tammuz.

Commentary

ʿYDW is already attested in L 63:2; 72:6; 73:3; 90:1; 166:1; EN 156:1; S 4:2; AL 318:1?.

The formula of this ostracon is quite similar to EN 69; 87; 95 and AL 114. The role played by these (1 to 8) laborers is difficult to determine, but they seem to be connected to (directed by? sent by?) one person. Is this a reference to some kind of forced labor?

Ostracon 21 (P5).

22. (= P10) Small sherd from the wall of a jar, gray on both sides and measuring 65 × 40 × 6–7 mm. The ostracon could be complete: it has been written following the potter's wheel traces.

Transcription

1. QWSYD/R LQWS
2. ʿ/YKBD/RN XXX

Translation

1. Qôsîd/r (*belonging*) to Qôs
2. *mice* 30

Commentary

The last letter of the first name is uncertain. QWSYD is probably attested in EN 85:1(!) and AL 211:2. The second name may be complete because the hypocoristic QWS is already known from these ostraca.

In line 2, the probable reading ʿKBRN is difficult to explain here. Are these 'mice' animals, or is this an appellation for another product?

23. (= Mo5) Brown sherd, probably from the wall of a jar, measuring 87 × 47 × 7 mm. The inscription follows the potter's wheel traces. Re-

Ostracon 22 (P10).

Ostracon 23 (Mo5).

stored from two pieces, the ostracon seems complete, but part of the inscription is worn away.

Transcription

1. *KRM* YT'W *S XX* II Q III II
2. *KRM B*{'*]L*{*Y*] S X II
3. '/*YLL—ZY LW/D/RT KPR*' S III II

Ostracon 24 (Mo4).

4. —?*LWY S* III I
5. -Ḥ————————?*S I*

Translation

1. *Vineyard of Yetaʿu: s(eahs)* 22, q(abs) 5.
2. *Vineyard of Ba(a)l(y): s(eahs)* 12.
3. . . . . . ? . . . . . . *who/which (is) near the tomb: s(eahs)* 5.
4. . . . . . ? . . . . . . s(eahs) 4
5. . . . . . . ? . . . . s(eah) 1.

Commentary

This ostracon probably belongs to the category of drafts for a land-registry (Lemaire 2002: 133–56, 230).

In line 1, YTʿW is already attested in L 31:1; 74B:2; AL 65:2; 73:2 and 252:1.

In line 2, the name BʿLY (L 114:2?; 154:4; EN 190:5; LL 8:7?) is very conjectural.

In line 3, KPRʾ[7] could be a personal name or a common name. In the latter case, it probably means 'the tomb' as in AL 283:4, 6 and in Nabatean (Lemaire 2001b: 1154–55; Lemaire 2002: 151).

24. (= Mo4). Clear brown sherd from the wall of a jar. The inscription is written inside, at about –5° in relation to the potter's wheel traces.

---

7. This form already appears in EN 118:2 in a fragmentary context.

One part of the ostracon is missing in the upper right angle. The beginnings of the lines are lacking.

Transcription

1. ?]*B III LZBWL ZY*
2. ?]*I/L WPLG ʾŠL ʿLT*^Y
3. ?*P*]*LG ʿṢL*

Translation

1. ?]? *3 to Zebul of/who*[?
2. ?]? *and* half of the cord of *ʿAlaty,*
3. ?*h*]*alf of ʿAzil.*

Commentary

The reading of this ostracon is often uncertain. It may also be a draft for a land-registry.

In line 1, ZBWL could be either a proper name (cf. Judg 9:28–38) or a common name. In the latter case, it could mean either 'prince' or a 'residence/princely dwelling place', as in Biblical Hebrew. The meaning of this word is very uncertain.

In line 2, the syntagm PLG ʾŠL is already attested in AL 258:2. ʿLTY, with the last letter written above the line, is probably a new personal name in these ostraca. It may be compared with Nabatean ʿLT (Negev 1991: 52).

In line 3, the reading PLG is conjectural. ʿṢL could be a personal name comparable to ʿṢLʾ (AL 258:8).

25. (= Mo1) Large brown sherd from the wall of a jar, broken in three pieces. It measures 137 × 157 × 8–10 mm. On the left side, it contains the remains of seven lines, partly covered by a calcareous deposit.

Transcription

1. —*Y QWSN*R
2. ʾ*WBL SM*Y*R*
3. *Y*??? *SM*Y*R*
4. ? *NŠ*Y*R*
5. *DRD/Wʿ NŠ*Y*R*
6. *T/QY/W/RSʿ/BYN SM*Y*R*
7. *Ṭ/LP/BD/RʿL SM*Y*R*

Translation

1. . . . . Qôsn*er*

Ostracon 25 (Mo1).

2. Obil Sumair
3. . . . . . . *Sumair*
4. . . . . . . Nashîr
5. *Dardaᶜ* Nashîr
6. ????? Sumair
7. ????? Sumair

Commentary

This ostracon apparently presents a list of names in which the second name in each line is probably the patronym. If this is correct, the names in lines 2, 3, 6, and 7 on the one hand, and lines 4 and 5 on the other hand, would be the names of brothers. Although the left part of the ostracon may have been broken, it is also possible that we have here a complete ostracon with a list of seven names with patronyms. Unfortunately, the reading of these names is sometimes effaced and often uncertain. Their interpretation is tentative.

Ostracon 26 (P14).

In line 1, QWSNR is already attested in EN 175:8; 201:2; AL 35:2; 47:1.

At the beginning of line 2, 'WBL may be comparable to *'ôbîl*, the man in charge of the camels in 1 Chr 27:30.

At the end of lines 2, 3, 6, and 7, SMYR is almost clear. It is a new name among these ostraca and it could be a North Arabic name (Harding 1971: 328; Winnett and Harding 1978: 583).

At the end of lines 4 and 5, NŠYR could also be compared with North Arabic *an-Nusair* (Harding 1971: 615, 621) and with the later Greek transcription Νοσαειρ (Wuthnow 1930: 84, 153).

At the beginning of line 5, the (uncertain) name DRDᶜ is already mentioned in the Bible as a famous wise man among the *Benê-Qedem*, that is, the North Arabians.

26. (= P14) Quadrangular sherd from the wall of a jar, pink outside and gray inside. The incomplete ostracon measures 81 × 59 × 9 mm. The inscription follows approximately the potter's wheel traces.

Transcription

1'. ᶜQB[?
2'. PŠW/T[?
3'. NQM[?

Ostracon 27 (P16).

Translation

   1′. ʿAqa*b*[?
   2′. Pash*u*?
   3′. Neqa*m*[?

Commentary

This fragmentary ostracon probably contained a list of names written in a kind of formal script.

In line 1, ʿQB is already attested in AL 49:3 and perhaps in L 187:1.

In line 2, the name PŠW may be Egyptian and comparable to PŠWBSTY, attested in the Aramaic documents from Egypt (Kornfeld 1978: 92).

In line 3, NQM[? may be comparable to NQMW, attested in LL 7:8 and to NQWM, attested in AL 312:2.

Ostracon 28 (P17).

27. (= P16) Sherd from the wall of a jar, clear brown outside and pink/bricky red inside. It measures 104 × 78 × 8 mm. There may be a few traces of illegible letters.

28. (= P17) Pentagonal thin sherd from the wall of a jar, whitish outside and clear brown inside. It measures 59 × 45 × 5/7 mm and contains many irregular half circles, probably from experiments with a calamus or beginning attempts at learning to write.

29. (= P18) Triangular sherd from the wall of an orange jar (restored from two fragments). It measures 81 × 81 × 8/10 mm. The inscription follows the potter's wheel traces, and it is very likely an inscription on a jar.

    1. ?]RMBʿL
    2. ?]Rambaal.

The inscription is written in the Phoenician cursive writing of the fourth century B.C.E. The color and type of sherd are similar to other Phoenician inscriptions on jars from this find (L 203; AL 394).

RMBʿL is already attested in Phoenician (Benz 1972: 179).

Ostracon 29 (P18).

30. (= W6′) Clear brown sherd measuring 40 x 58 x 6 mm. It is written on the outside, perpendicularly to the potter's wheel traces.

Transcription

1′. ?[?
2′. B[?
3′. ʾDNY[?
4′. MHRH T[?
5′. WʿT M-H[?

Translation

1′. ?[?
2′. came[?
3′. my master [?

Ostracon 30 (W6').

4'. quickly . . . [?
5'. *and now* . . . . .[?

Commentary

The reading of line 5' is conjectural.

Paleographically this *Paleo-Hebrew* ostracon dates to about 600, or the seventh century B.C.E. It is very fragmentary, but the few legible words indicate that it was a message. It probably comes from the same place as the Aramaic ostraca (Lemaire 2002: 166, 385–89).

Bibliography

A = Avishur 1999
AL = Lemaire 2002
Alt, A.
    1925   Judas Gaue unter Josia. *Palästina Jahrbuch* 21: 100–117.
    1953   Vol. 2 of *Kleine Schriften zur Geschichte des Volkes Israel*. Munich.
Avishur, Y.
    1999   An Edomite Ostracon. Pp. 33–37 in *Michael: Historical, Epigraphical and Biblical Studies in Honor of Prof. M. Heltzer*, ed. Y. Avishur and R. Deutsch. Tel Aviv. [abbreviated as A]

Barag, D.
1992–93 New Evidence on the Foreign Policy of John Hyrcanus I. *Israel Numismatic Journal* 12: 1–12.

Baslez, M. F., and Briquel-Chatonnet, F.
1991 Un exemple d'intégration phénicienne au monde grec: Les Sidoniens au Pirée à la fin du IVe siècle. Pp. 229–40 in vol. 1 of *Atti del II congresso internazionale di studi fenici e punici, Roma, 9–14 novembre 1987*. Rome.

Benz, F. L.
1972 *Personal Names in the Phoenician and Punic Inscriptions*. Studia Pohl 8. Rome.

Davies, G. I.
1991 *Ancient Hebrew Inscriptions: Corpus and Concordance*. Cambridge.

Dorsey, D. A.
1980 The Location of the Biblical Makkedah. *Tel Aviv* 7: 185–93.

EN = Eph'al, and Naveh 1996

Eph'al, I., and Naveh, J.
1966 *Aramaic Ostraca of the Fourth Century BC from Idumaea*. Jerusalem. [abbreviated as EN]

Eshel, E., and Kloner, A.
1996 An Aramaic Ostracon of an Edomite Marriage Contract from Maresha, Dated 176 B.C.E. *Israel Exploration Journal* 46: 1–22.

Fales, F. M.
1986 *Aramaic Epigraphs on Clay Tablets of the Neo-Assyrian Period*. Studi semitici n.s. 2. Rome.

Fitzmyer, J. A.
1974 Some Notes on Aramaic Epistolography. *Journal of Biblical Literature* 93: 201–25.

Fowler, J. D.
1988 *Theophoric Personal Names in Ancient Hebrew*. Journal for the Study of the Old Testament Supplement 49. Sheffield.

Geraty, L. T.
1972 *Third Century B.C. Ostraca from Khirbet el-Kom*. Ph.D. dissertation. Harvard University.

Gibson, J. C. L.
1975 *Aramaic Inscriptions*. Vol. 2 of *Textbook of Syrian Semitic Inscriptions*. Oxford.

Gropp, D. M., et al. (eds.)
2001 *Wadi Daliyeh II: The Samaria Papyri from Wadi Daliyeh and Qumran Cave 4: Miscellanea, Part 2*. Discoveries in the Judaean Desert 28. Oxford.

Harding, G. L.
1971 *An Index and Concordance of Preislamic Arabian Names and Inscriptions*. Toronto.

Hoftijzer, J., and Jongeling, K.
1995 *Dictionary of the North-west Semitic Incriptions*. Leiden.

Holladay, J. S.
1971a Khirbet el-Qôm. *Israel Exploration Journal* 21: 177.

1971b Khirbet el-Kôm. *Revue biblique* 78: 593–95.

Janzen, D.
2002 *Witch-Hunts, Purity and Social Boundaries*: The Expulsion of the Foreign Women in Ezra 9–10. Journal for the Study of the Old Testament Supplement 350. Sheffield.

Kornfeld, W.
1978 *Onomastica Aramaica aus Ägypten.* Vienna.

L = Lemaire 1996

Lemaire, A.
1974 Un nouveau roi arabe de Qédar dans l'inscription de l'autel à encens de Lakish. *Revue Biblique* 81: 63–72.

1977 *Les ostraca.* Vol. 1 of *Inscriptions hébraïques.* Littératures anciennes du Proche-Orient 9. Paris.

1990 Populations et territoires de la Palestine à l'époque perse. *Transeuphratène* 3: 31–74.

1996 *Nouvelles inscriptions araméennes d'Idumée au musée d'Israël. Supplément à Transeuphratène* 3. Paris. [abbreviated as L]

1997 D'Édom à l'Idumée et à Rome. Pp. 81–103 in *Des Sumériens aux Romains d'Orient: La perception géographique du monde,* ed. A. Sérandour. Antiquités sémitiques 2. Paris.

1999 Quatre nouveaux ostraca araméens d'Idumée. *Transeuphratène* 18: 71–74. [abbreviated as S]

2000a L'économie de l'Idumée d'après les nouveaux *ostraca* araméens. *Transeuphratène* 19: 131–43.

2000b Vues nouvelles sur la tradition biblique d'Abraham. Pp. 21–31 in *Les routes du Proche-Orient: Des séjours d'Abraham aux caravanes de l'encens,* ed. A. Lemaire. Paris: Desclée.

2001a *Nouvelles tablettes araméennes.* Hautes Études Orientales 34. Geneva: Droz.

2001b Les religions du sud de la Palestine au IVe siècle av. J.-C. d'après les ostraca araméens d'Idumée. *Comptes rendus de l'Académie des Inscriptions et Belles-Lettres*: 1141–58.

2002 *Collections Moussaïeff, Jeselsohn, Welch et divers.* Vol. 2 of *Nouvelles inscriptions araméennes d'Idumée.* Supplément à *Transeuphratène.* Paris. [abbreviated as AL]

2003 Nabonidus in Arabia and Judah in the Neo-Babylonian Period. Pp. 285–98 in *Judah and the Judeans in the Neo-Babylonian Period,* ed. O. Lipschits and J. Blenkinsopp. Winona Lake, Indiana.

2004 Taxes et impôts dans le sud de la Palestine (IVe s. av. J.-C.). *Transeuphratène* 28: 133–42.

LL = Lozachmeur and Lemaire 1996

Lozachmeur, H., and Lemaire, A.
1996 Nouveaux ostraca araméens d'Idumée (Collection Sh. Moussaieff). *Semitica* 46: 123–42. [abbreviated as LL]

Maraqten, M.
1988 *Die semitischen Personennamen in den alt- und reichsaramäischen Inschriften aus Vorderasien.* Texte und Studien zur Orientalistik 5. Hildesheim.

Naveh, J.
1979 The Aramaic Ostraca from Tel Beer-Sheba (Seasons 1971–1976). *Tel Aviv* 6: 182–98.
1985 Published and Unpublished Aramaic Ostraca. *ʿAtiqot* 17: 114–21.
Negev, A.
1991 *Personal Names in the Nabatean Realm.* Qedem 32. Jerusalem.
Noth, M.
1953 *Geschichte Israels.* Berlin.
Parker, R. A., and Dubberstein, W. H.
1956 *Babylonian Chronology 626 B.C.–A.D. 75.* Providence, Rhode Island.
Porten, B., and Yardeni, A.
1993 *Literature, Accounts, Lists.* Vol. 3 of *Textbook of Aramaic Documents from Ancient Egypt.* Jerusalem.
Renz, J.
1995 Vol. 1 of *Die althebräischen Inschriften.* Handbuch der althebräischen Epigraphik 1. Darmstadt.
Rinaldi, P. G.
1967 Ostraco Canfora. *Bibbia e Oriente* 9: 117 and pl. 6.
Rocco, B.
1966 L'ostrakon Canfora. *Rivista biblica italiana* 14: 201–8.
S = Lemaire 1999
Segal, J.-B.
1983 *Aramaic Texts from North Saqqarah.* London.
Vos, J. C. de
2003 *Das Los Judas: Über Entstehung und Ziele der Landesbeschreibung in Josua 15.* Vetus Testamentum Supplements 95. Leiden.
Winnett, F. W., and Harding, G. L.
1978 *Inscriptions from Fifty Safaitic Cairns.* Toronto.
Wuthnow, H.
1930 *Die semitischen Menschennamen in griechischen Inschriften und Papyri des vorderen Orients.* Leipzig.
Yardeni, A.
2000 *The Documents.* Vol. A of *Textbook of Aramaic, Hebrew and Nabataean Documentary Texts from the Judaean Desert.* Jerusalem.

Social, Economic, and Onomastic Issues in the Aramaic Ostraca of the Fourth Century B.C.E.

BEZALEL PORTEN AND ADA YARDENI
The Hebrew University

In the beginning there was Lenny Wolfe. Porten writes the following memoir:

> A decade or so ago, when I was deeply immersed in the final preparations of volume 3 of our *Textbook of Aramaic Documents from Ancient Egypt*, I went to visit Lenny, who showed me photographs of Aramaic ostraca from an unknown source. As I recall, the batch was going for some $25,000. The pieces were not from Egypt, and I knew of no sugar daddy prepared to shell out such dough for some broken potsherds, so I thanked Lenny for his time and left. As a scholarly gesture, Lenny passed the photos on to Joseph Naveh, who, together with Israel Eph'al, published some 200 out of 275 of them in 1996. But what of the ostraca themselves? One batch of 50 or so were acquired by the late Elie Borowski, who soon turned them over to the Bible Lands Museum in Jerusalem (= BLM). Another 91 were acquired by Dr. David Jeselsohn, who divides his time between Zurich and Jerusalem. Another 32 pieces were divided between Robert and Liane Feuer of Woodmere, New York (11), and Shlomo Moussaieff (21), who moves back and forth between London and Jerusalem. Moussaieff turned his pieces over to André Lemaire (Paris) for publication. So, while the whereabouts of 170 of Lenny's photographs are known, another 100 or so are at this point still lost to the scholarly world.

> While the site of the ostraca remains obscure, new pieces keep cropping up all the time and ownership changes hands. Pride of place goes to Dr. David Jeselsohn, who holds ca. 560 pieces; 91 appeared in the publication of Eph'al–Naveh and 54 in Lemaire 2000 (= AL). The remaining 440 or so are unpublished. Of these, ca. 150 have recently been acquired from a previous collector. Next to him comes the Feuer family, Robert and Liane of Woodmere, New York, their daughter Marilyn of New York City, and their brother Robert Forbes of Baltimore, Maryland. Marilyn had already acquired and donated 23 pieces to the Jewish Theological Seminary of New York, and the Feuers, 218 pieces to the Israel Museum of Jerusalem (= IM), which entrusted them to André Lemaire for publication (Lemaire

1996 = L). I first met Feuer in a synagogue, as a friend of my classmate Rabbi Burton Cohen. He told me of his donations to the Israel Museum and of the existence of more ostraca for sale. Already possessed of such a large number, the Israel Museum was indifferent to receiving more. "I'll take them," I said. "You can donate them to my tax-exempt Institute, incorporated in the State of Pennsylvania." And so he did. Over a period of seven years, from 1995 to 2002, the Feuers and Forbes have acquired 468 pieces, donated them through the auspices of the American Friends of the Hebrew University to the Institute for the Study of Aramaic Papyri (= ISAP), whence they have been deposited in the Institute of Archeology of the Hebrew University (= IA).

Next to the Feuers and Forbes is Shlomo Moussaieff, who has acquired 354 pieces, 340 of which have been published by André Lemaire (Lemaire 2002 = AL), including 9 with Hélène Lozachmeur (Lozachmeur and Lemaire 1996 = LL). Lemaire scrounged around and picked up 4 pieces from Martin S. Schøyen in Norway (Lemaire 1999), 7 from Mike Welch in Florida, 6 more from Moussaieff, 18 and 6 from two anonymous collectors, respectively, and 8 from someone known only as "B." Thirty of these (18 + 6 + 6) are published in this volume (pp. 413–456). Gil Chaya of Jerusalem has made available to us 88 pieces, while James Charlesworth of Princeton acquired 10 pieces and had access to another 14. Smaller holdings include 3 pieces acquired by the Jerusalem collector Arnold Spaer and 2 pieces by Reuben Hecht, now in the Reuben and Edith Hecht Museum affiliated with the University of Haifa, all 5 included in Eph'al and Naveh 1996. Other unpublished pieces are held by owners who prefer to remain anonymous: one, made known to us through Shmuel Aḥituv, has 58; another possesses, or had access to, 43; a third had access to 26; and a fourth acquired a single piece. As we go to press, a fifth piece has turned up.

Out of these 1,900 tabulated pieces, less than 1,700 are legible. With the exception of the 100 or so unknown pieces photographed for Lenny Wolfe, the 11 pieces of Schøyen and Welch, and 5 of the 30 pieces published by Lemaire (in this volume), we have had access to, photographed, and hand-copied all the remaining pieces. Our projected corpus will extend beyond the Idumean pieces from an unknown source to include the Aramaic pieces from Arad, Beer-sheba, el Kom, Tell Jemma, and elsewhere, since these come from the same period—the fourth century B.C.E.

Lacking site location that accompanies excavated material such as the Lachish, Arad, and Beer-sheba ostraca, the scholar must fall back on the dealer's collection, in the hope that pieces that lay together in situ also came together in the collector's hands, allowing, of course, for the migration of a piece here and a piece there. We may isolate at least three dossiers—that is, documents that center around a dominant person or subject and derive primarily from a single collection or from one or more related collections. Many of the ostraca we deal with are dated and record the payment of a quantified commodity by a named person, often to another named person and/or to some destination. In studying them, we pay attention to the interplay between onomastics, subject matter, chronology, and script. Because of their formulaic nature, the ostraca lend themselves to tabular recording that greatly facilitates the process of understanding and interpretation. Composing such tables, we wish to let the reader into the workshop of the editors who seek to bring order out of chaos, discover natural links, and see if the whole is greater than the sum of its parts. Bear in mind all the time that ours is a work in progress.

The first natural collection comprised nos. 1–36 in the publication of Eph'al and Naveh 1996 (= EN) because the photographs of these "were received together" (1996: 10). They called it the "archive of Ḥalfat" because he was "the person who provides the goods," while the dominant recipient was Baalghayr. Further study shows that 4 of the 8 texts seen on the antiquities market by Lemaire ("B"), photographed and published by him, belong to this "Ḥalfat dossier" (AL 46, 108–9, 202). Nine more documents from elsewhere, including 3 from Eph'al and Naveh's own publication, may also be added, bringing the total to just under 50 (EN 37, 38, 57; L 1!, 13; AL 191; ISAP 271, 804, 823). The thrust of the transactions is made explicit by the use of synonymous verbs in 8 documents, all of which share a nuance of payment or delivery: "brought" (היתי [EN 1:2, 13:2, 27:1, 31:1, 35:1]) has the meaning of bringing a gift to a family member (*TAD* A2.1:10) and of bringing tribute to the satrap (*TAD* A6.13:5); 'brought in' (הנעל [EN 34:1]) refers to bringing leaven into one's storage chamber (*TAD* A4.1:8) and bringing the bride's dowry into the groom's house (*TAD* B3.8:22); 'delivered' (המטא [EN 26:1]) never appears elsewhere in the *Hafel*, but in the *Peal* it refers to the coming to someone of an heir's portion (*TAD* B2.11:1–12); and 'gave' (יהב [EN 16:2]), of course, is the all-purpose word for conveyance and occurs only here in all our ostraca. The verbs הנעל and היתי, usually together, are the standard ones used in the Nisa ostraca for the delivery of wine to the royal treasury (Diakonoff and Livshits 1976: texts 1:1–2; plates 1:1–2). The most proximate parallels to our texts are the numerous demotic tax receipts from Ptolemaic Egypt. These invariably begin with the word *ỉn* 'bring', and their study informs us that the term 'dossier' is more apt than the designation 'archive' (Mattha 1945;

Devauchelle 1983; Vleeming 1994; el Aguizy 1994). In earlier Egyptian we find the noun *ỉnw* 'that which is brought', namely tribute, or in the more banal sense, 'delivery', a meaning that would suit our context perfectly (Erman and Grapow 1926: 1.90–91; Spalinger 1996: 361–62).

Less than half of the documents, 22 in all, are fully dated, that is, day, month, and year (EN 1–15, 28, 57; L 1, 13; AL 41, 46; ISAP 271). Another 13 are dated only by day and month (EN 16, 19, 22, 24, 31, 33, 35, 37–38; AL 108–9; ISAP 804, 823) and an equal number have no date at all (EN 18, 20–21, 23, 25–27, 29–30, 32, 34; AL 191, 202?). One or two have only a day as date (EN 24; AL 202?). The documents begin on 27 Ab, Year 43 (August 19, 362 B.C.E. [L 1!]) and move through 19 Tammuz, Year 46 (August 8, 359). Clearly, this must be Artaxerxes II, for he alone ruled so many years. Parker and Dubberstein (1956: 19) tell us that he "died and was succeeded by Artaxerxes III between late November, 359 and April, 358." Our next dated document comes in seamlessly on 4 Elul, Year 1 (September 10, 358 [EN 6]). Not until we go through two more documents for Year 1 (EN 7–8), four for Year 2 (EN 9–12), and one for Year 4 (EN 15), do we come upon one whose date is composed in full, like those regularly employed in the Elephantine contracts. It reads "On the 16th of Tammuz, Year 4 of Artaxerxes the king" (July 21, 355 [EN 13]) and continues with the verb "brought" (היתי), not regularly employed in these texts. Fortunately, this is one of the pieces that was acquired by the Bible Lands Museum (BLM 3168) and we were able to copy it (ISAP 1813). Whereas the date in the Aramaic documents was usually written at the beginning, the date in the demotic documents invariably came at the end. Being tax receipts, the demotic documents are fully dated by day, month, and year, but like the Aramaic documents, they, too, rarely give the name of the king (Mattha 1945: 8).

There are three more documents in our collection for Year 4 (EN 14, 17; AL 41), one or two for Year 6 (L 13; AL 46?), and we reach the end of the dated documents with 25 Tammuz, Year 9 (August 5, 350). Halfat in this document is not the payer but the agent ("by the hand of Halfat"), and if we did not include it in the archive, then the latest document would be dated to 9 Ab, Year 6 (August 20, 353 B.C.E.). Similarly, the earliest dated document wherein Halfat is a payer is dated to 2 Iyyar, Year 45 (May 4, 360). We would thus have a minimalist period of less than 7 years (360–353 B.C.E.) and a maximalist period of some 12 years (362–350 B.C.E.). A document such as a papyrus contract, which was meant to be long-lived, would naturally contain the date in full. An isolated document dated to Year 1 would be enigmatic for the modern scholar. The ancient scribes of our dossier knew that Year 1 followed hard upon Year 46 and, since the shelf life of the document itself was brief, there was no need to add the name of the king—how brief is seen by the fact that so many lacked year date, and an equal number were not dated at all. While the dated pieces may have been entered into a papyrus ledger every month, it is hard to see how the undated pieces would have been classified (Diakonoff and Livshits 1976: texts 1:1–2; plates 1:1–2).

Almost all the ostraca were written on the convex side, as were the Egyptian demotic pieces. Scholars of those ostraca attribute this to the fact that the outside was "smoother and therefore better adapted for writing than the concave or inner side, the furrowed surface of which is mostly useless for the purpose" (Mattha 1945: 7; Vleeming 1994: 150). Yet, it should be noticed that almost all of the Elephantine Aramaic ostraca were written on the concave (*TAD* D7).

The first dossier falls into six groups (table 1, pp. 462–463).

(1) Fourteen documents (nos. 1–14) wherein Ḥalfat (no. 7 [EN 9]) provides goods from Makkedah for Baalghayr, who is four times designated by his patronym, the Egyptian name Ḥori (EN 1, 3–4, 25). Ten of the documents are dated, though two lack the year (AL 108–9). At least six documents conclude with a sign resembling an archaic *’alep* (EN 1, 3, 5; AL 46, 108–9; bottom missing in EN 4) and two of these are followed by a signatory, Yazidu (EN 3, 5). As noted already by Ephʿal and Naveh (1996: 10), this features regularly in the Arad ostraca (Naveh 1981: nos. 1–2, 4–9, 12–13, 15, 17, 20, 22, 26, 28, 36, 52, 57–58, 61–63, 65–66, 68, 70–71, 82), indicating a common dating. Three and perhaps four of our six documents were written by a single scribe (EN 1, 3?, 4, 5), while the other two were written by a second scribe, who wrote the date at the bottom but omitted the year (AL 108–9). Taken together, the six documents demonstrate a payment pattern. They cover three months in a period of a year and three months from May 4, 360 to August 7, 359. In each of these three months a small payment of the same product is made at the beginning (on days 2, 7, and 6) and at the end of the month (on days 30, 22, and 19), with that at the end tending to be larger. Barley groats are paid in Iyyar (EN 1; AL 108); semolina and flour in Sivan (AL 109; EN 3) and pretty much the same in the following month of Tammuz but designated as "from the later grind" (EN 4–5). As will become clear below, Yazidu is not the scribe of the document but an official validating the payment. Other dated documents, not being bunched together, reveal no pattern but do indicate that Ḥalfat made large payments to Baalghayr as well as small ones: between

Table 1. The Dossier of Ḥalfat and Baalghayr

No.	EN/L/ AL/ ISAP	Babylonian Date	Julian Date	Scribe	Payer	Payee	Commodity
1.	1	2 Iyyar, 45	May 4, 360	1	Ḥalfat brought (היתי)	Baalghayr son of Ḥori	barley groats: 2 seahs, 3 qabs; ʾalep; signatory
2.	AL 108	30 Iyyar, (45)	June 1, 360	2	Ḥalfat	Baalghayr	barley groats: 4 seahs, 1 qab; ʾalep
3.	AL 109	7 Sivan, (46)	June 27, 360	2	Ḥalfat	Baalghayr	semolina: 4 qabs; flour: 1 seah, 5 qabs; ʾalep
4.	3	22 Sivan, 46	July 12, 359	1	Ḥalfat	Baalghayr son of Ḥori	semolina: 2 seahs; flour: 2 seahs, 1 qab; ʾalep; Yazidu
5.	4	6 Tammuz, 46	July 25, 359	1	Ḥalfat	Baalghayr son of Ḥori	from later grind: flour: 3 seahs, 3 qabs; ʾalep missing?
6.	5	19 Tammuz, 46	August 7, 359	1	Ḥalfat	Baalghayr	from later grind: semolina: 1 seah, 2 qabs; flour: 1 seah, 2 qabs; ʾalep; Yazidu
7.	9	4 Sivan, 2	June 1, 357		Ḥalfat from Makkedah	Baalghayr	barley: 1 kor, 26 seahs, 5 qabs
8.	14	22 Tammuz, 4	July 27, 355		Ḥalfat	Baalghayr	barley: 15 seahs; [. . .]
9.	L 13	9 Ab, 6			Ḥalfat	Baalghayr	crushed grain: 2 seahs
10.	AL 191	[. . .]			Ḥalfat	Baalghayr	wheat: 16 seahs, 4 qabs, a half
11.	AL 46	[-.-.], 6[+?]			Ḥalfat	Baalghayr	2 jars; ʾalep
12.	18	—			Ḥalfat	Baalghayr	2 bales
13.	25	—			Ḥalfat	Baalghayr son of Ḥori	1 load of wood
14.	21	—			Ḥalfat	Baalghayr	[. . .]
15.	6	4 Elul, 1	September 10, 358		Ḥalfat	—	semolina: 5 qabs, 3 quarters; flour: 2 seahs, 2 qabs; Saadel
16.	7	11 Elul, 1	September 17, 358	3	Ḥalfat	—	semolina: 5 qabs; flour: 1 seah, 2 qabs; Zabdiel
17.	8	23 Elul, 1	September 29, 358		Ḥalfat	—	wheat: 4 seahs, 3 qabs
18.	12	22 Sivan, 2	June 19, 357		Ḥalfat	—	wheat: 2 seahs, 2 qabs
19.	10	24 Ab, 2	August 19, 357	3	Ḥalfat	—	wheat: 6 seahs, half qab; Zabdiel
20.	15	4 Shebat, 4	February 1, 354		Ḥalfat from Makkedah	—	wheat: 12 seahs, 1 qab; Qosyatha wrote
21.	35	3 Tammuz			Ḥalfat brought	—	wheat: 3 kors, 2 seahs, 1 qab
22.	13	16 Tammuz, 4 Artaxerxes	July 21, 355		Ḥalfat brought	—	wheat: 1 kor, 5 seahs, 4 qabs; barley: 1 kor, 12 seahs, 4 qabs
23.	31	4 Ab			Ḥalfat		wheat: 20 seahs; barley: 29 seahs, 5 qabs
24.	33	15 Sivan			Ḥalfat brought	—	barley: 2 kors, 4 seahs; mark; Zaydu

Table 1. The Dossier of Ḥalfat and Baalghayr (cont.)

No.	EN/L/ AL/ ISAP	Babylonian Date	Julian Date	Scribe	Payer	Payee	Commodity
25.	28	14 Adar II	(April 3, 356)		Ḥalfat	—	50 pegs; mark; Saadel
26.	11	25 Adar II, 2	April 14, 356		Ḥalfat son of Sammuk	—	oil: 2 qabs, 2 quarters, 1 eighth
27.	17	25 Shebat, 4			Ḥalfat	—	oil: 1 eighth
28.	32	—			Ḥalfat		oil: 1 seah, 1 qab, half qab
29.	29	—			Ḥalfat		wheat: 2 seahs; barley: 3 kors, 2 seahs; Qosyatha ⸢wrote⸣
30.	26	—			Ḥalfat delivered (המטא) from Makkedah	—	semolina: 1[+?] seah, [?]; flour: [. . .]
31.	30	—			Ḥalfat	—	semolina: 1 qab, a half; flour: 2 qabs
32.	16	28 Kislev			Ḥalfat gave (יהב)	Yehoanah	8 maahs = price of wine
33.	34	—			Ḥalfat brought in (הנעל) from Makkedah	Ab(i)yatha	wheat: 2 kors, x seahs, 3 qabs; by the hand of PN; barley: 6 kors
34.	AL 202	20			Ḥalfat	Palaqos	barley: 16 seahs, 4 qabs, a half
35.	57	29 Ab, 4	September 2, 355		Nuhayru	Baalghayr	5 jars; Abdmilk
36	AL 41	6 Tishri, 4	October 8, 355		Othni	Baalghayr	3 bales (פחלצן) of chaff; by hand of PN
37.	38	13 Sivan			Zabdi	Baalghayr from Makkedah	1 bale
38.	19	10 Elul			Zabdi	Baalghayr	1 bale
39.	22	30 Marcheshvan		4	Zabdi	Baalghayr	14 DRIED FIGS (גרגרן)
40.	20	—		4	Zabdi	Baalghayr	1 bale
41.	23	—		4	Zabdi	Baalghayr	2 bales
42.	37	20 Ab			Abdi	Baalghayr	1½ bundles (משתלן); by hand of Amittai
43.	L 1	27 Ab, 43	August 19, 362		Baalghayr	Qoskahel	barley groats: 1 kor, 4 qabs
44.	ISAP 823	22 Sivan		5	Baalghayr	Qoskahel	grindings of Iyyar and Sivan: barley groats: 1 seah, 3 qabs
45.	ISAP 804	22 Sivan		5	Baalghayr	Samitu	(grindings) of Iyyar and Sivan: barley groats: 1 seah
46.	24	25 26			Ḥaniel Baalghayr	— —	12 bundles 8 bundles
47.	ISAP 271	25 Tammuz, 9	August 5, 350		Qo[s . . .]	PN	barley: 23 seahs, 3 qabs; by the hand of Ḥalfat

close to 2 kors and $\frac{1}{2}$ kor of barley in Tammuz and Sivan (EN 9, 14), $\frac{1}{2}$ kor of wheat (AL 191), and 2 seahs of crushed grain on Tisha b'Av of Year 6 (L 13). Moreover, Ḥalfat supplied Baalghayr with other products besides grain: 2 jars (AL 46), 2 bales (probably of chaff [EN 18]), 1 load of wood (EN 25) and an unknown product (EN 21). Though the document for the two jars bore a date (damaged) and an archaic *'alep*, the other two payments were considered more ephemeral and were undated.

(2) Seventeen documents (nos. 15–31) wherein Ḥalfat, once designated by his patronym, Sammuk (EN 11), provides goods to an unnamed recipient, whose identity was taken for granted, presumably Baalghayr. Thirteen are dated (EN 6–8, 10–13, 15, 17), four lacking the year (EN 35, 31, 33, 28). With the exception of barley groats, the goods provided are essentially the same, with the addition of small quantities of oil (EN 11, 17, 32) and pegs (EN 28). Semolina and flour, provided in Sivan and Tammuz, Year 46 to Baalghayr and validated by Yazidu are provided just over one year later, again twice in the month, with Saadel validating the payment on 4 Elul, Year 1 (EN 6) and Zabdiel on 11 Elul (EN 7). While the scribe who wrote this latter document also wrote one for a small payment of wheat (EN 10), his signature in two other documents (EN 71, 109 [not listed here]) is in quite a different hand, demonstrating that he was not the scribe. Likewise, the two documents signed off by Saadel, the second one being for 50 pegs (EN 28), do not appear to be in the same hand. Assuming the unidentified recipient is Baalghayr, we again have sets of twice-monthly payments of grain in June, 357—almost 2 kors of barley on 4 Sivan, Year 2 (EN 9) and just over 2 seahs of wheat on 22 Sivan, Year 2 (EN 12); and July, 355—over one kor each of wheat and barley on 16 Tammuz, Year 4 (EN 13) and at least 15 seahs of barley on 22 Tammuz, Year 4 (EN 14). The signatories warrant payments small and large, and three other names appear—Zabdu for 3 kors of wheat (EN 35) and Zaydu for 2 kors of barley (EN 33). Once we find an expanded notation—"from Makkedah" and "Qosyatha wrote" (EN 15)—and in a second document— "Qosyatha ⌈wrote⌉" (EN 29). The addition of "wrote" may have meant that the responsible official was also the scribe. Though warranted, this latter document for wheat was the only such to be undated (contrast EN 8, 10, 12–13, 15, 31, 35). Usually dated and warranted, semolina and flour were also delivered in undated and unwarranted documents (EN 26, 30). Two of the three documents for minuscule quantities of oil are dated (EN 11, 17; contrast EN 32), one being the only document to give Ḥalfat's patronym, Sammuk (EN 11).

· (3) Three documents (nos. 32–34) in which Ḥalfat makes payment to a party other than Baalghayr. One undated ostracon that appears to be in the same hand as the partially dated, marked, and warranted one by Zaydu for over 2 kors of barley (EN 33) states that Ḥalfat "brought in from Makkedah to Ab(i)yatha by the hand of PN" the large amounts of over 2 kors of wheat and 6 kors of barley (EN 34). A strange document for over 16 seahs of barley reads "on the 20th to Palaqos" (AL 202). Most unique among all the documents is a record of 8 maahs of wine given to Yehoanah "for the price of wine" (EN 16). Ephʿal and Naveh reasonably conjectured that he was a nonresident Jewish wine merchant. If so, then these documents would truly constitute Ḥalfat's own record of expenses. But . . .

(4) Eight documents (nos. 35–42) record payments made by four different individuals to Baalghayr. None is for grain. Five are for bales of chaff; one is for bundles; one is for jars (EN 57); and one is for "dried figs" (גרגרן; cf. *m. Nazir* 2:1 [גרגרות]; Yadin and Naveh 1989: 47, pl. 42). One by Nuhayru is delivered by Abdmilk (EN 57); one by Othni is delivered by Abdelbaali (AL 41); and one by Abdi is delivered by Amittai (EN 37). Three of the payments by Zabdi are dated (EN 19, 22, 38), and 3 are written by the same scribe (EN 20, 23), only 1 dated (EN 22). Payments were made almost monthly, from spring through late fall: Sivan, Ab (twice), Elul, Tishri, Marcheshvan, with only the year date for Year 4 added (EN 57; AL 41). Only 2 of the 31 payments by Ḥalfat, one undated at that, were for jars (AL 46) and bales (EN 18), respectively. Clearly, for these items he had suppliers other than Ḥalfat. But what are these suppliers doing in the dossier of Ḥalfat?

(5) Four documents (nos. 43–46) record payments by Baalghayr to other parties. These bring us around full cycle. The earliest Ḥalfat documents were for a couple seahs of barley groats in Iyyar, Year 45, to Baalghayr. Here we have two ostraca by the same scribe for 22 Sivan, a month later but in an undated year, where Baalghayr turns around and presents Qoskahel in one document and Samitu in another with a seah or so of "grindings of Iyyar and Sivan: barley groats" (ISAP 804, 823). More striking is a document of two years earlier (27 Ab, Year 43), in which Baalghayr gave the same Qoskahel no less than 1 kor, 4 qabs of barley groats (L 1). Similarly, in one document with only a day date, a certain Ḥaniel gives 12 bundles on the 25th, while Baalghayr, who on a certain 20 Ab, received $1\frac{1}{2}$ bundles, paid out on the 26th 8 bundles (EN 24). Whether or not these dates are sequential in the same year, they show both a receipt of one quantity and a payment of a larger quantity by Baalghayr of barley groats and bundles. So this is not just a dossier of Ḥalfat but essentially a record of his payments to Baalghayr, some explicit but most not, and also of payments made to Baalghayr by others and of a few by Baalghayr *to* others.

(6) A single document (no. 47) wherein Ḥalfat is agent. This is the latest document in the group, dated to 25 Tammuz, Year 9 (August 5, 350). It is a payment of over 23 seahs of barley, and the names of both parties are unclear. What is clear is that the payment was made through the agency of Ḥalfat (ISAP 271). So here, and here alone, this fellow who is so often making payments is delivering a payment for someone else.

If the first dossier was dominated by the party of the first part, whom we designate the payer, the second one was dominated by the party of the second part, whom we shall designate the payee. Fifty-four texts put at our disposal by the collector Gil Chaya were said to have been found together at the bottom of a well (ISAP 883–936). Thirty-seven of these come together, either because of common date or common person. That person is Saadel, and we call this his dossier. A smaller collection of 19 texts belonging to Chaya (ISAP 864–82) contains 7 ostraca from this dossier. A third collection, of 14 documents, seen by James Charlesworth (ISAP 538–51), contains 4 documents of this same person. Isolated pieces drawn from other collections bring the total Saadel documents up to 62. At least 36 are dated, from 24 Elul, Year 2 through 20 Elul, Year 6 of an unnamed monarch. One isolated document is dated to 27 Ab, Year 17, which can only be September 7, 342. Can we fit this date in with the others?

The documents fall into nine groups (table 2, pp. 468ff.).

(1) A group of four documents (nos. 1–4), in which three documents name Saadel of/from Baalrim as payer (ISAP 1742, 903, 899) and three list the storehouse of Makkedah as the recipient of the payment (ISAP 909, 903, 899). Two payments were made on the same day (24 Sivan, Year 3), but the scribal hand of the documents is different (ISAP 909, 903). Two written six months apart are by the same scribe and record large payments of barley, over $7\frac{1}{2}$ kors on 24 Sivan and 8 kors on 26 Kislev (903, 899). An isolated jar inscription (no. 5) reads "(Belonging) to Saadel" (AL 346), and we may imagine the jar as containing the barley or other grain that Saadel gave to the storehouse. On the same day that he brought his very large payment, Abdidah brought just over 21 seahs of barley (ISAP 909). These are the only texts in which Saadel is the payer; but their real common denominator is the storehouse.

(2) Twelve dated ostraca by different persons (nos. 6–17), almost all for unstated recipients, mostly recording small amounts of semolina and flour. Five were written on 2 Kislev Year 3, and 5 on 5 Kislev. Four of the first 5 (ISAP 898, 902; 887 and 896 [fig. 1a and 1b]) and all of the second 5 (ISAP 545, 894, 925; 886 and 888 [fig. 1c and 1d]) were possibly

Fig. 1. Plena (a and b) and defective (c and d) spellings of נשׁ(י)ף written by the same scribe.

written by the same hand. Despite the *plena* spelling of נשׁיף 'semolina' for 4 of the 5 ostraca of 2 Kislev (fig. 1a and b) and the defective spelling of נשׁף for the 5 ostraca of 5 Kislev (fig. 1c and d), we note the spacing between the lines and between the letters in the respective groups, the relative size of the letters one to another and their slant, and the common appearance of specific words, such as כסלו and קמח. Yet when the scribe came to write each ostracon, he displayed not insignificant variation in the shape of individual letters, which, of course, might also be due to a change of reed pen. Two ostraca in this group are deviant. Both are from Saadel and differently dated (22 Elul and 20[+?], without year date). One is for a huge amount, a full kor, and concludes with the notation בגת, perhaps 'in Gath', and the other presents several times the normal amount of semolina to one *Danq[os]* (ISAP 897, 920). Wherever the other 10 payments went, there were specific scribes for each day, and 2 for one of the days, to record the payments.

Table 2. The Dossier of Saadel

No.	ISAP/ AL	Babylonian Date	Julian Date	Scribe	Payer	Payee	Commodity
1.	1742	—			Saadel of Baalrim	[. . .]	flour: 8 seahs
2.	909	24 Sivan, 3		1	Abdidah	storehouse of Makkedah	barley: 21 seahs, 2 qabs
3.	903	24 Sivan, 3		1	Saadel of Baalrim	storehouse of Makkedah	barley: 7 kors, 18 seahs, 2 qabs
4.	899	26 Kislev, 3		1	Saadel from Baalrim brought	storehouse of Makkedah	barley: 8 kors
5.	AL 346					(Belonging) to Saadel	jar inscription
6.	898	2 Kislev, 3		2	Malku	—	semolina (נשׁיף): 3 seahs, 3 qabs; flour: 7 seahs
7.	887	2 Kislev, 3		2	Bayyun	—	semolina (נשׁיף): 3 seahs, 3 qabs; flour: 6 seahs, 3 qabs
8.	896	2 Kislev, 3		2	Zabdiel	—	semolina (נשׁיף): 2 seahs; flour: 3 seahs, 5 qabs; 1 rooster
9.	902	2 Kislev, 3		2	Qosmilk/ malak	—	semolina (נשׁיף): 1 seah, 2 qabs; flour: 2 seahs, 2 qabs
10.	702	2 Kislev, 3		2	Qoslanṣur	—	semolina (נשׁף): 2 seahs, 3 qabs, a half; flour: 7 seahs
11.	894	5 Kislev, 3		2	Zabdi	—	semolina (נשׁף): 1 seah,1 qab, 1 quarter; flour: 2 seahs, 4 qabs
12.	925	5 Kislev, 3		2	Ḥanziru	—	semolina (נשׁף): 5 qabs; flour: 1 seah, 5 qabs
13.	886	5 Kislev, 3		2	Zaydi	—	semolina (נשׁף): 1 seah, 2 qabs; flour: 2 seahs, 4 qabs
14.	888	5 Kislev, 3		2	Ḥayyan	—	semolina (נשׁף): 4 qabs; flour: 1 seah, 3 qabs
15.	545	5 Kislev, 3		2	ˀᵒb s. Annui	—	semolina (נשׁף): 4 qabs; flour: 1 seah, 1 qab
16.	897	22 Elul			Saadel	—	semolina (נשׁיף): 1 kor; in Gath(?)
17.	920	20[+? of x]			Saadel	Danq[os]	semolina (נשׁיף): 8 seahs
18.	904	18 Tammuz, 4		3	Qosghayr of Baalrim	to the hand of Saadel; storehouse	wheat: 5 seahs
19.	893	29 Sivan, 5			Qosyinqom of Baalrim	storehouse	wheat: 8 seahs, 4 qabs
20.	908	29 Sivan, 5			Adarbaal and Zabdiel of Baalrim	storehouse	wheat: 1 kor, 3 seahs, 4 qabs, a half
21.	890	29 Sivan, 5		3	Qoskhair	to Saadel; storehouse	barley: 2 seahs, 4 qabs, a half

Table 2. The Dossier of Saadel (cont.)

No.	ISAP/ AL	Babylonian Date	Julian Date	Scribe	Payer	Payee	Commodity
22.	889	1 Tammuz, 5		3	Ammiqos of Baalrim	storehouse	wheat: 17 seahs, 4 qabs
23.	924	1 Tammuz, 5		3	Qosyinqom of Baalrim	storehouse	wheat: 17 seahs, 1 qab
24.	932	5 Tammuz, 5		3	Zaydi [of Baalrim]	storehouse	wheat: 17 seahs, half qab
25.	928	5 Tammuz, 5		3	Ani of Baalrim	storehouse	wheat: 17 seahs, half qab
26.	927	6 Tammuz, 5		3	Ammiel of Baalrim	storehouse	wheat: 4 seahs
27.	13	9 Tammuz, 5		3	Zubaydu	storehouse	wheat: 16 seahs; Palaqos
28.	543	19 Tammuz, 5		3	Qosyinqom of Baalrim	storehouse	wheat: 13 seahs, 4 qabs, a half
29.	917	19 Tammuz, 5		3	Qosyinqom	storehouse of Makkedah	barley: 5 seahs, 3 quarters
30.	914	18 Tammuz, [4]		3	Dikru of Baalrim	to the hand of Saadel (supra–linearly); storehouse	wheat: 6 seahs, 1 qab; wheat: 1 seah, 1 qab, a half (in exchange) for (ב) barley: 2 seahs, 3 qabs
31.	900	16 Tammuz			Abenašu	Saadel; by the hand of Żabdi	wheat: 3 kors, 2 seahs, 3 qabs
32.	901	26 Elul			Ḥazira	Saadel; by the hand of Żabdi	wheat: 1 kor, 24 seahs, 3 qabs
33.	544	27 Tammuz			Qosyaqim/ yaqum	——; by the hand of Zabdi	wine: 24 seahs, 1 qab, a half
34.	1532	27 Tammuz, 5		3	Qosrim of Gur	storehouse	wheat: 5 seahs (in exchange) for (ב) barley: 10 seahs
35.	873	—			*Amru*	Saadel	wheat: 8 seahs; *x* qabs
36.	865	24 Elul, 2			PN	Saadel	wheat: 3 seahs, 2 qabs, a half
37.	891	1 Mar-cheshvan, 2			Ḥori	Saadel	crushed grain: 3 seahs, 5 qabs, a half
38.	926	—			Ḥori	Saadel	'plaster' (גיר gypsum])/ (or: גיד [coriander]): 7 seahs
39.	911	—			Malku	Saadel	'plaster' (גיר gypsum]): 14 seahs, 3 [qabs]
40.	868	—			Aḥiqam/ yaqim	Saadel	'plaster' (גיר gypsum]): 1 kor
41.	923	—			Aḥiqam/ yaqim	Saadel	'plaster' (גיר gypsum]): 7 seahs
42.	548	—			Abdidah	Saadel	'plaster' (גיר gypsum}): 25 seahs
43.	913	---			Qosmilk/ malak	Saadel	'plaster' (גיר gypsum]): 22 seahs
44.	1762	—			Zubaydu & Baa[l . . .]	Saadel	'plaster' (גיר gypsum]): 10 seahs

Table 2. The Dossier of Saadel (cont.)

No.	ISAP/ AL	Babylonian Date	Julian Date	Scribe	Payer	Payee	Commodity
45.	912	—			Qamṣa Ṭabio	Saadel	'plaster' (גיר gypsum]): 1 seah, 3 qabs; 'plaster' (גיר gypsum]): 4 seahs, 2[+?] qabs
46.	874	—			Ab(i)yatha	Saadel	'plaster' (גיר gypsum]): 1 seah
47.	885	5 Adar, 2			Saadi	—	oil: 4 seahs, 3 qabs
48.	870	—			Nahri	Saadel	oil: 1 seah, 1 qab, 1[+?] quarters; Qosqam
49.	866	—			$_{\circ\circ}\frac{d}{r}t$	Saadel	oil: 3 qabs; Qosqam
50.	546	—			Qosyad	Saadel	oil: 2 seahs, 3 qabs, 3 quarters
51.	929	—			$\frac{dd}{rr}y\frac{d}{r}w$	Saadel	oil: 4 qabs, 3 quarters
52.	AL 182	—			Qosab	*Saadel*	*a half log*
53.	921	—			Bayyun	Saadel; by the hand of Ešmiel	2 roosters
54.	551	—			Qosgʿ	Saadel	6 *m* (= maah?)
55.	883	20 Elul, 6			Ḥaṭamu	Saadel	4 jars
56.	879	—			Dikru	Saadel	[. . .]
57.	859	18[+?] Tebeth			Uzayzu from ʾmoʾ	—	[. . .], 8 seahs, 5 qabs; by the hand of Saadel
58.	860	—				(Belonging) to Uzayzu	jar inscription
59.[a]	AL 82	27 Ab, Year 17	*September 7, 342*		Natanṣidq from Qoṣi	—	. . . : 14 *x*, 3 qabs; Saadel calculated

a. Numbers 60–64 constitute payment orders drawn up by or for Saadel.

(3) Thirteen documents (nos. 18–30) are for payments mostly of wheat, with 2 for barley. Ten are for persons belonging to Baalrim and are destined for the storehouse (ISAP 893, 908, 889, 924, 932, 928, 927, 543), to (the hand of) Saadel and the storehouse (ISAP 904, 890, 914), or to the storehouse of Makkedah (ISAP 917). Eleven of these 13 documents were written by the same scribe (ISAP 904, 890, 889, 924, 932, 928, 927, 13, 543, 917, 914, 1532). Qosyinqom of Baalrim brings in three payments: 8+ seahs on 29 Sivan (ISAP 893); 17+ on the next day, the 1st of Tammuz (ISAP 924); and 13+ seahs less than 3 weeks later, on 19 Tammuz (ISAP 543). We note that on 1 and 5 Tammuz, 4 persons of Baalrim bring in virtually the identical amount: 17 seahs and a qab or so of wheat (ISAP 889, 924, 932, 928). A similar amount (16 seahs) was brought in by Zubaydu on 9 Tammuz. When 2 persons join together on

the same ostracon, the amount they bring in is double that—a little over 1 kor (ISAP 908). In that 18 Tammuz document, Dikru brought in to Saadel to the storehouse just over 6 seahs of wheat and exchanged a small amount of wheat for barley at the rate of 1:2 (ISAP 914; cf. 2 Kgs 7:1). Similarly, on 27 Tammuz, Qosrim of Gur exchanges 5 seahs of wheat for 10 of barley (ISAP 1532). These exchanges reveal the store-house to be also something of a store. It was located in Maqqedah and was probably under the jurisdiction of Saadel.

(4) Seven documents (nos. 31–37; 5 dated), each by a different scribe for a different person, are grouped together because 5 specify Saadel as the recipient (ISAP 873, 900–901, 865, 891) and 3, Zabdi as the agent (ISAP 900–901, 544). They deliver 3 different kinds of foodstuff. Two deliveries by Zabdi are for large amounts of wheat: over 3 kors (16 Tammuz) and close to 2 kors (ISAP 900, 901). The third names no recip-ient (27 Tammuz) and is the first payment of wine that we encounter (ISAP 544). Two payments for Saadel are fully dated: some 3 seahs of wheat on 24 Elul, Year 2 (ISAP 865), and almost 4 seahs of crushed grain just over one month later, on 1 Marcheshvan (ISAP 891). An un-dated document is for just over 8 seahs of wheat (ISAP 873).

(5) Nine undated documents (nos. 38–46) present Saadel with a com-modity found nowhere else in the whole corpus: גיר 'gypsum, plaster'; or, less likely, גיד 'coriander'. The amounts vary from very small to large, from one seah (ISAP 874) to one kor (ISAP 868), with intermediate quantities of 4, 7, 10, 14, 22, and 25 seahs (ISAP 912, 926, 1762, 911, 913, 548). There are a couple of repeat payers: Hori had presented Saadel with crushed grain in a dated document (ISAP 891), and Ahiqam/ya-qim made two payments to Saadel, one of 1 kor and another of 7 seahs (ISAP 868, 923). Clearly, the day of payment was unimportant.

(6) Five documents (nos. 47–51) record small quantities of oil pay-ments, ranging from 3 qabs to $4\frac{1}{2}$ seahs. These payments, too, must have been considered ephemeral, because only one is dated—5 Adar, Year 2, by Saadi to an unnamed recipient (ISAP 885). It would be tempting to take this name as hypocoristic for Saadel and assume the payment is to the storehouse. Though undated, two bore a signatory, Qosqam (ISAP 870, 866). Unfortunately, the names of two payers are unintelligible or illegible (ISAP 866, 929).

(7) Five documents (nos. 52–56) record miscellaneous or illegible objects: *a half log* (AL 182); 2 roosters brought in by the agent Ešmiel/ Ešmuel (ISAP 921 [NB: a rooster was sent by Zabdiel along with the semolina and flour on 2 Kislev, Year 3]); 6 *m* (= maah? ISAP 551); and 4 jars on 20 Elul, Year 6, the latest of the group of 54 Gil Chaya texts (ISAP 883).

(8) Two documents (nos. 57–58) showing Saadel as agent. On 28 Tebeth, Uzayzu from ʾmoʾ delivered 8 seahs, 5 qabs of an unspecified grain "by the hand of Saadel" (ISAP 859). Alongside this ostracon in the same collection was a jar inscription in lapidary script, reading "(Belonging) to Uzayzu" (ISAP 860). Whatever purpose the other ostraca served, this one may have been a label that accompanied the delivery, similar to the Samaria ostraca that recorded the delivery of wine and oil (Aḥituv 1992: 162–63) and the Nisa ostraca that recorded the delivery of wine and vinegar (Diakonoff and Livshits 1976: texts 1:1–2; plates 1:1–2).

(9) A final document (no. 59) made out on 27 *Ab*, Year 17 (September 7, 342) for Natanṣidq from Qoṣi for a certain amount of grain. It concludes with the statement, "Saadel calculated."

We conclude: at least 3 times Saadel of Baalrim appears as payer; twice an anonymous Saadel is payer; and once Saadi is payer. At 6-month intervals (24 Sivan and 26 Kislev, Year 3), Saadel of Baalrim turned over to the storehouse of Makkedah between $7\frac{1}{2}$ and 8 kors of barley (ISAP 903, 899; cf. 1742); on 22 Elul and 20[+?] *x*, respectively, the anonymous Saadel paid one kor and 8 seahs of semolina, the former "in Gath" and the latter to *Danq*[*os*] (ISAP 897, 920); and on 5 Adar, Year 2, Saadi paid 4+ seahs of oil (ISAP 885). But most of the documents concern Saadel as payee and four times his name as recipient is coupled with the storehouse (ISAP 890, 904, 914) of Makkedah (ISAP 917). Surely, he was the storehouse administrator, and the documents derive from his dossier. There is no certainty, however, that either anonymous Saadel was identical with Saadel from Baalrim. In line with the large biannual multiple kor payments made *by* the latter, there are bimonthly large payments *to* the anonymous Saadel "by the hand of Zabdi" (ISAP 900–901). Otherwise, almost all the payments received by Saadel the administrator, or by the storehouse, measured only in the seahs. These included some 10 dated ostraca of Year 5 and one of Year 4, where the payee almost always stems from Baalrim (ISAP 543, 889, 890, 893, 904, 908, 914, 924, 932, 927–28); 9 undated documents for relatively small amounts of "plaster" (ISAP 548, 868, 874, 911–13, 923, 926, 1762); and various other documents for small amounts of oil and the like.

Not only did an anonymous Saadel make deposits in the storehouse and receive deposits in the storehouse, but he also issued payment orders, presumably to be made from the storehouse. There are 5 such orders (nos. 58–62), uniquely found in these two collections, 3 mentioning Saadel and all posing difficulties of reading. They are reminiscent of the Hebrew payment orders from Arad that read "Give to the Kittiyim such-and-such a commodity"(Aharoni 1981: nos. 1:2, 2:1–2, 4:1, 7:2, 8:2, 10:2, 11:2, [14:2]). There are 2 such orders in Aramaic, and one presents a formula found in our ostraca: "Give (הב) to Pedael one s(eah) of b(arley). Yaddua. On the 5th" (Naveh 1981: no. 5; cf. no. 9). Ours reads, "Give (הב) to Ḥayyan son of Qosi 2 loads of wood. . . . On the 7th. From Saadel" (ISAP 895). Were Saadel the source of the payment and not the authorizing party, we should have expected the text to read, "Give to Ḥayyan from Saadel," along the lines of Arsames' payment order on behalf of Nakhthor to the officials en route to Egypt, "You, give (הבו) [him ra]tions from my estate which is in your province(s), day by day" (*TAD* A6.9:2). Nonetheless, another text, also drawn up "On the 7th," which allots to Shobai the scribe 3 bales of chaff and possibly 1 seah of wheat, signs off with what appears to be "from Makkedah," instead of a personal name (ISAP 864). We have seen above how Saadel appears together with the storehouse (ISAP 890) and is interchangeable with "storehouse of Makkedah" (ISAP 917). Another authorization is likewise for 3 bales of chaff; the name of the recipient is obscure, but we seem to read "from ˹the hand of˺ (מן ˹יד˺) Saadel" at the end (ISAP 907). A fourth authorization is for 3 qabs of semolina and 6 seahs of wheat, but the name of the recipient is obscure and the name Saadel itself is very faint (ISAP 933). The fifth payment order is to give to the Akrabatians "flour, kors [*x*], white (חור)" (cf. *TAD* A6.9:3). It signs off "on the 15th" (ISAP 910), with no other name. Akrabattene, a border town (see Num 34:4; Josh 15:1–3; cf. Judg 1:36), apparently at that time in Edom, was the place where Judas Maccabee dealt the "sons of Esau" a heavy blow (1 Macc 5:3; Görg 1992). The fact that these 3 dates do not even mention the month indicates that payment was to be expected within the month of issuance. It was authorized by Saadel and came from Saadel—alternately, perhaps from Makkedah—that is, from the storehouse there.

The third dossier is not of a person but of a group. Within each of 2 of the collections that Feuer and Forbes presented to the Institute for the Study of Aramaic Papyri for deposit in the Institute of Archeology was a group of texts sparsely represented in the publication of Eph'al and Naveh (EN 69, 87, 95, 118) and unrecognized by Lemaire in his publication (L 44, 81, 114). These texts deal not with the transfer of a commodity but with the supply of a worker, Aramaic פעל. The first collection has 157 texts, of which 106 are legible (ISAP 201–357). Among these are 12 worker texts (ISAP 201, 209–10, 216, 221, 225, 236, 243, 259–60, 264, 269). The second collection contains 126 texts (ISAP 401–527), 82 being legible, while 27 are worker texts (ISAP 404, 406, 408, 417, 423–

25, 428–29, 431–32, 443, 446–49, 451–52, 457, 460, 465–67, 470, 479, 495, 522). Two worker texts emerged from the first Feuer collection of 66 texts (ISAP 101–66), 42 being legible. Altogether, then, these three collections have supplied 41 worker texts. Careful study revealed that 28 of these ostraca were written by a single scribe, all but one within a period of less than a month. Three from another collection were written by a second scribe, 3 days apart. Additions from other collections bring the total up to 57 texts (tables 3a [pp. 476f.] and 3b [pp. 478f.]).

Scribe 1 wrote a single document on 4 Elul (ISAP 443) and then a whole string of ostraca from 25 Marcheshvan down through 20 Kislev. He was a registrar of workers sent by the four/five major clans and wrote out an ostracon for each person showing up for work. With one exception (ISAP 446), he wrote a day and month date at the beginning, followed by "PN_1 of the house of [less frequently, 'sons of'] $PN_{2:}$ worker(s), 1 [or more]." For each of the three clans, respectively, a person regularly affiliated by "house of" appeared once by "sons of" (Zabdimilk [ISAP 406, 264], Dikri [ISAP 425, 465]), and Ramel [ISAP 443, 417]. Each ostracon is usually for one worker; 5 ostraca have 2 workers each (ISAP 443, 424, 209, 417, 460) and 3 have 3 workers each (ISAP 210, 470, 452). His busiest days were 25 Marcheshvan, 1 and 2 Kislev, when he wrote 6, 7, and 6 ostraca, respectively. On 5 Kislev he wrote 3 ostraca, and one each on 11, 14, and 20 Kislev (ISAP 465, 429, 225). Three of the 5 major clans appeared some dozen times each, Gur (also written Gir, Guru) with 13 ostraca (nos. 29–41; nos. 40–41 not Scribe 1), Qoṣi (nos. 18–28) and Baalrim (nos. 7–17) with 11 each (nos. 14–18, 25–26, 28 not Scribe 1); Yokal, with only 3 or 4 (nos. 3–6; no. 3 not Scribe 1), Albaal with 1 or 2 (nos. 2–3 not Scribe 1), and Qosi (no. 1 not Scribe 1) with 1. Each of the 3 large clans appeared on 25 Marcheshvan, 1 and 2 Kislev and each of the 3 clans had persons that came to work more than once. Gur sent 3 such persons—Ramel 4 times, on 1 Kislev, and with his brother on 4 Elul and 2 and 5 Kislev; Qosyahab twice, on 25 Marcheshvan and 1 Kislev; and Ḥanina twice, on 25 Marcheshvan and 20 Kislev. Qoṣi sent 2 persons—Qosdalani 3 times, on 25 Marcheshvan, with Qosata on 5 Kislev, and with 2 other persons on [. . . +?]1 Kislev; and Dikri twice, on 1 and 11 Kislev. Baalrim sent one person 3 times—Zabdimilk on 25 Marcheshvan, 1 and 2 Kislev. It is clear that the clan was the primary dispatcher because in one case the name listing is "sons of Qoṣi, Dikri" (ISAP 465 [no. 23]), and not the other way around, and in another we have "sons of Baalrim, [PN]" (ISAP 1639).

These workers were day laborers, as seen from the fact that both Zabdimilk of Baalrim and Ramel of Qoṣi show up on two successive days, Kislev 1 and 2, and on the second day Ramel brings his brother along. Moreover, even though each clan sent more than one person on a given day, they were generally not recorded together on a single ostracon, but each one separately. Thus, 3 persons from Gur were recorded individually on 25 Marcheshvan (nos. 33, 35, 38); 3 from Gur (nos. 30, 34, 37) and 2 from Qoṣi (nos. 22, 24) appear separately on 1 Kislev; and 2 for Qoṣi on 5 Kislev (nos. 20, 27). There are 4 exceptions, 2 of which are probably instructive for the other 2. As noted, Ramel of Gur is recorded once alone and three times with his unnamed brother, while Zubaydu of Gur is recorded with his sons = "3 workers" (ISAP 452 [no. 39]). Qosdalani of Qoṣi is recorded once alone (no. 19), once with an unidentified Qosata (no. 20), and once with 2 other, illegible names (no. 21). Qosladin and Zubaydu of Yokal appear together on a single ostracon (no. 5). Like Ramel and his brother and Zubaydu and his sons, these latter pairs probably lived together in the same household, unlike the others mentioned above, who were members of the clan but not residents in the same household.

Scribe 1 was the major registrar but not the only one for the clans. For each, there are documents, dated and undated, written by different hands (Baalrim: EN 87, 118; ISAP 201, 1639, 1647; Gur: EN 69, 118; Qoṣi: AL 130; ISAP 495, 522, 861). Though clan designation regularly displaced patronymic, there is one possible exception. One ostracon that starts out in the regular fashion, comes up surprising at the end. "On the 5th of Kislev, Qosnatan of the sons of Qoṣi, 1 worker," with the addition of a name, "Ḥazir son of Abdilahi" (ISAP 423 [no. 29]). It was taken for granted that the person whose name appeared following the date was the worker himself. Is Qosnatan here sending a substitute, a fellow named Ḥazir son of Abdilahi? Or did he belong to the clan of Qoṣi? Who was he if he was not the actual worker?

There are four undated texts from Baalrim (EN 118; ISAP 201, 1639 [Scribe 1] 1647) and two for Gur (EN 69, 118) but only three dated examples of workers sent by the clans on dates other than Kislev/Marcheshvan and registered by other scribes: Qoṣi on 7 Tishri (AL 130), Baalrim on 21 Shebat (EN 87), and [Albaa]l/[Yehoka]l on 26 Ab, Year 7 (ISAP 259). There is one undated document for Albaal (ISAP 109), who is otherwise dated to August 8 and 17, 359 (AL 41; LL 1; cf. ISAP 1723). The other worker documents are all written by different scribes, for isolated individuals and not clans, and cover 6 months: 5 Nisan (ISAP 449); 15 and 22 Sivan (L 44; ISAP 431); 20 Tammuz (ISAP 816; AL 114); 26 Ab, Year 7 (ISAP 259); 13 Elul (ISAP 243); 13 Shebat, Year 6 (ISAP 221); and 24 Adar, Year 2 (L 114). Perhaps a single scribe (Scribe 2)

Table 3a. Workers Listed according to Families;
28 Ostraca Written by Scribe 1

No.	ISAP/Lemaire Number/EN	Babylonian Date	Julian Date	Workers	Scribe	Persons/Clan: Qosi 1; Albaal 1/2; Yokal 3/4; Baalrim 11; Qoṣi 11; Gur 13
1.	210 = EN 95 (IA 11821)	—	—	3	1	sons of Qosi
2.	109 = IA 11892	—	—	5		. . . the Sons of Al(i)baal
3.	259 = IA 11749	26 Ab, Year 7	—	1		Barik [of the Sons of Al(i)baa]l/[Yehoka]l
3.	259 = IA 11749	26 Ab, Year 7	—	1		Barik [of the Sons of Al(i)baa]l/[Yehoka]l
4.	408 = IA 11386	25 Marcheshvan	—	1	1	Ḥabibu of the House of Yokal
5.	424 = IA 11387	1 Kislev	—	2	1	Qosladin and *Zubaydu* of the House of Yokal
6.	429 = IA 11402	14 Kislev	—	1	1	Dikri of the House of Yokal
7.	264 = IA 11752	25 Marcheshvan	—	1	1	Zabdimilk of the Sons of Baalrim
8.	406 = IA 11306	1 Kislev	—	1	1	Zabdimilk of the House of Baalrim
9.	467 = IA 11363	2 Kislev	—	1	1	Zabdimilk of the House of Baalrim
10.	428 = IA 11326	2 Kislev	—	1	1	Samku of the House of Baalrim
11.	447 = IA 11358	2 Kislev	—	1	1	Qos [. . .] of the House of Baalrim
12.	466 = IA 11419	2 Kislev	—	1	1	Yabneel of the House of Baalrim
13.	1639	—	—	1	1	The Sons of Baalrim, PN
14.[b]	1909 = EN 118	—	—	1		The Sons of Baalrim
15.	201 = IA 11804	—	—	19		PN of the Sons of Baalrim
16.	1647	—	—	2		Qoswahab to PN [from] the House of Baalrim
17.	1881 = EN 87	21 Shebat	—	2		Zabdidah s. Naqru/Naqdu of House of Baalrim
18.	1243 = AL 130	7 Tishri	—	3		Qosyadli, Wah(a)bu, Dalael: House of Qoṣi
19.	446 = IA 11341	25 Marcheshvan		1	1	Qosdalani of the House of Qoṣi
20.	460 = IA 11323	[4+]1(=5) Kislev	—	2	1	Qosdalani and Qosata of the House of Qoṣi
21.	470 = IA 11397	[. . . +]1 Kislev	—	3	1	Qosdalani (erased—and Qosata [?]) of the House of Qo[ṣi]
22.	425 = IA 11383	1 Kislev	—	1	1	Dikri of the House of Qoṣi
23.	465 = IA 11300	11 Kislev	—	1	1	The Sons of Qoṣi, Dikri
24.	269 = IA 11751	1 Kislev	—	[1]	1	*Kalel* of the Sons of Qoṣi
25.	495 = IA 11384	2 Kislev; date end	—	2		Zubaydu and PN of the House of Qoṣi
26.	522 = IA 12126 (Feuer 1)	2 Kislev; date end	—	1		Qosaiti son of Palatiah of the House of Qoṣi
27.	423 = IA 11322	5 Kislev	—	1[a]	1	Qosnatan of the Sons of Qoṣi
28.	861 = IA 12453	23 Kislev	—	⟨1⟩		Natanṣidq from the Sons Of Qoṣi
29.	443 = IA 11319	4 Elul	—	2	1	Ramel and his brother of the House of Gur
30.	457 = IA 11407	1 Kislev	—	1	1	Ramel of the House of Gur
31.	209 = IA 11771	2 Kislev	—	2	1	Ramel and his brother of the House of Gur

Table 3a. Workers Listed according to Families;
28 Ostraca Written by Scribe 1 *(cont.)*

No.	ISAP/Lemaire Number/EN	Babylonian Date	Julian Date	Workers	Scribe	Persons/Clan: Qosi 1; Albaal 1/2; Yokal 3/4; Baalrim 11; Qoṣi 11; Gur 13
32.	417 = IA 11342	5 Kislev	—	2	1	Ramel and his brother of the Sons of Gur
33.	260 = IA 11766	25 Marcheshvan	—	1	1	Qosyahab of the House of Gur
34.	448 = IA 11311	1 Kislev	—	1	1	Qosyahab of the House of Gur
35.	216 = IA 11421	25 Marcheshvan	—	1	1	Ḥanina of the House of Gur
36.	225 = IA 11808	20 Kislev	—	1	1	Ḥanina of the House of Gir
37.	479 = IA 11361	1 Kislev	—	1	1	PN of the Sons/House of *Gir*
38.	432 = IA 11340	25 Marcheshvan	—	1	1	Qoshanan of the House of Gur
39.	452 = IA 11396	2 Kislev	—	3	1	Zubaydu and his sons of the House of Gur
40.	236 = EN 69 = IA 11780	—	—	1		Aliel of the Sons of Gur
41.[b]	1909 = EN 118	—	—	3		The Sons of [Gur]u
42.	449 = IA 11362	5 Nisan	—	6		Maanu to Nutaynu
43.	431 = IA 11343	15 Sivan	—	1		Qosbarak of the House of [PN]
44.	1044 = L 44 = IM 91.16.23	22 Sivan date end	—	1		Zabdidah
45.	1600 = AL 114 = M402	20 Tammuz	—	8		Qosaz
46.	816 = IA I2199	20 Tammuz date end	—	1		Qoskahel
47.	1641	23 Tammuz date end	—	2	2	Aydu/Iyadu
48.	1640	25 Tammuz date end	—	3	2	Aydu/Iyadu
49.	1659	26 Tammuz date end	—	4	2	Aydu/Iyadu
50.	243 = IA 11811	13 Elul date end	—	7		[PN]
51.	221 = IA 11773	13 Shebat, Yr 6	—	2		Zabdiel
52.	1114 = L 114 = IM 91.16.45	24 *Tammuz*, Yr 2 date end	—	1		Suaydu and Malku . . .
53.	110 = IA 11869	—	—	5+		Workers of the Gate: Ḥaggagu, Qosyatha, Dikru, Mannukišamaš, Wah(a)bu
54.	404 = IA 11312	—	—	1		*Qosiwah*
55.	818 = IA 12201	—	—	1		*Qoslanṣur*
56.	1081 = L 81 = IM 91.16.3	—	—	1		Wahabil to Qosyatha
57.	451 = IA 11313	—		for 15:2 [sh(ekels)]		Naamel son of Nattun

a. *Ḥazir* son of Abdilahi
b. Numbers 14 and 41 are same text.

Table 3b. Workers Listed according to Dates

No.	ISAP/Lemaire Number/AL/ EN	Babylonian Date	Julian Date	Workers	Scribe	Dates for Clans: 4 Elul 1; 7 Tishri 1; 25 Marheshvan 6; 1 Kislev 8; 2 Kislev 8; 5 Kislev 2; 11 Kislev 1; 14 Kislev 1; 20 Kislev 1; 23 Kislev 1; 21 Shebat 1
1.	1114 = L 114 = IM 91.16.45	24 *Tammuz*, Year 2		1		Suaydu and Malku . . .
2.	221 = IA 11773	13 Shebat, Year 6		2		Zabdiel
3.	259 = IA 11749	26 Ab, Year 7		1		Barik [of the Sons of Al(i)baa]l/[Yehoka]l
4.	449 = IA 11362	5 Nisan	—	6		Maanu to Nutaynu
5.	431 = IA 11343	15 Sivan		1		Qosbarak of the House of [PN]
6.	1044 = L 44 = IM 91.16.23	22 Sivan	—	1		Zabdidah
7.	816 = IA 12199	20 Tammuz		1		Qoskahel
8.	1600 = AL 114 = M402	20 Tammuz		8		Qosaz
9.	1641	23 Tammuz	—	3	2	Aydu/Iyadu
10.	1640	25 Tammuz	—	2	2	Aydu/Iyadu
11.	1659	26 Tammuz	—	4	2	Aydu/Iyadu
12.	443 = IA 11319	4 Elul	—	2	1	Ramel and his brother of the House of Gur
13.	243 = IA 11811	13 Elul	—	7		[PN]
14.	1243 = AL 130	7 Tishri		3		Qosyidli, Wah(a)bu, Dalael: House of Qoṣi
15.	216 = IA 11421	25 Marcheshvan	—	1	1	Ḥanina of the House of Gur
16.	260 = IA 11766	25 Marcheshvan	—	1	1	Qosyahab of the House of Gur
17.	432 = IA 11340	25 Marcheshvan	—	1	1	Qoshanan of the House of Gur
18.	264 = IA 11752	25 Marcheshvan	—	1	1	Zabdimilk of the Sons of Baalram
19.	446 = IA 11341	25 Marcheshvan	—	1	1	Qosdalani of the House of Qoṣi
20.	408 = IA 11386	25 Marcheshvan	—	1	1	Ḥabibu of the House of Yokal
21.	448 = IA 11311	1 Kislev	—	1	1	Qosyahab of the House of Gur
22.	457 = IA 11407	1 Kislev	—	1	1	Ramel of the House of Gur
23.	479 = IA 11361	1 Kislev	—	1	1	PN of the Sons/House of *Gir*
24.	406 = IA 11306	1 Kislev	—	1	1	Zabdimilk of the House of Baalrim
25.	269 = IA 11751	1 Kislev	—	[1]	1	*Kalel* of the Sons of Qoṣi
26.	425 = IA 11383	1 Kislev	—	1	1	Dikri of the House of Qoṣi
27.	423 = IA 11322	1 Kislev	—	1ª	1	Qosnatan of the Sons of Qoṣi
28.	424 = IA 11387	1 Kislev	—	2	1	Qosladin and *Zubaydu* of the House of Yokal
29.	209 = IA 11809	2 Kislev	—	2	1	Ramel and his brother of the House of Gur
30	452 = IA 11396	2 Kislev	—	3	1	Zubaydu and his sons of the House of Gur
31.	428 = IA 11326	2 Kislev	—	1	1	Samku of the House of Baalrim

Table 3b. Workers Listed according to Dates (cont.)

No.	ISAP/Lemaire Number/AL/ EN	Babylonian Date	Julian Date	Workers	Scribe	Dates for Clans: 4 Elul 1; 7 Tishri 1; 25 Marḥeshvan 6; 1 Kislev 8; 2 Kislev 8; 5 Kislev 2; 11 Kislev 1; 14 Kislev 1; 20 Kislev 1; 23 Kislev 1; 21 Shebat 1
32.	447 = IA 11358	2 Kislev	—	1	1	Qos[. . .] of the House of Baalrim
33.	466 = IA 11419	2 Kislev	—	1	1	Yabneel of the House of Baalrim
34.	467 = IA 11363	2 Kislev	—	1	1	Zabdimilk of the House of Baalrim
35.	495 = IA 11384	2 Kislev	—	2		Zubaydu and PN of the House of Qoṣi
36.	522 = IA 12126 (Feuer 1)	2 Kislev	—	1		Qosaiti son of Palatiah of the House of Qoṣi
37.	417 = IA 11342	5 Kislev	—	2	1	Ramel and his brother of the Sons of Gur
38.	460 = IA 11323	[4+]1 (= 5) Kislev	—	2	1	Qosdalani and Qosata of the House of Qoṣi
39.	470 = IA 11397	[. . . +]1 Kislev	—	3	1	Qosdalani (erased—and Qosata [?]) of the House of Qo[ṣi]
40.	465 = IA 11300	11 Kislev	—	1	1	The Sons of Qoṣi, Dikri
41.	429 = IA 11402	14 Kislev	—	1	1	Dikri of the House of Yokal
42.	225 = IA 11808	20 Kislev	—	1	1	Ḥanina of the House of Gir
43.	861 = IA 12453	23 Kislev	—	⟨1⟩		Natanṣidq from the sons of Qoṣi
44.	1881 = EN 87	21 Shebat	—	2		Zabdidah son of Naqru/Naqdu of the House of Baalrim

a. Ḥazir son of Abdilahi.

wrote three ostraca for Aydu/Iyadu on 20, 23, and 25 Tammuz (ISAP 1640–41, 1659 [nos. 47–49]). [The *yod* in 1640 עידו is drawn in an unusual loop.] The only two months in the year that lack worker texts are Iyyar and Tebeth. In contrast to the ostraca written by Scribe 1 for the clans, usually one worker per piece, those for the non-clan persons record 6 (ISAP 449), 7 (ISAP 243), and 8 (AL 114) workers. The three pieces on successive days for Aydu/Iyadu record 2, 3, and 4 workers. Did individuals other than Aydu/Iyadu have to supply workers on successive days, and is it mere chance that we do not have this documentation? Finally, an undated ostracon for the sons of Baalrim records 19 unnamed persons (ISAP 201 [no. 15]). This is something of a work detail.

For whom or for what were these workers meant? For the workers from the clans, we note that Kislev is the month of December, and we may cite the standard study of Lucian Turkowski, "Peasant Agriculture in the Judean Hills": "The first plowing [the shallow ploughing] takes place in the mountainous country in December. . . . The farmers know how to take advantage of the short breaks between the rains for the completion of the first and second plowing. The interval between these two lasts from three to four weeks" (Turkowski 1969: 27–28). In the Gezer Calendar this period would correspond to the first of the two months designated there as זרע 'sowing' (Aḥituv 1992: 149–51). These day laborers would be the counterpart to the harvesters appearing in the book of Ruth (2:3–7, 14), though the latter may have slept in the field during the harvest period rather than coming and going daily. In whose fields our Idumean workers may have worked is not indicated. How did the tasks of these individual day laborers differ from, say, the un-dated 19 workers of the sons of Baalrim? Were they, too, day laborers? Sumerian documents (called to our attention by Tania Notarius) pro-vide some analogy. One reports, "16 male workers for 1 day at the weir of Dubla-Utu and the *barla*-basin of the orchard of A'abba, (and also) at the inlet of the Eduna canal filled up the earth . . . 28 male workers for 1 day carried reed from the Endudu (field) to the Ganunkara (field) . . . 16 male workers for 1 day weeded out rush at the reed bank of Urabba (canal). 15 male workers were sick" (Kang 1973: 61–62). More recent documents from Erech from the time of Nebuchadnezzar (called to our attention by Paul-Alain Beaulieu) list groups of 4, 5, and 11 workers belonging to so-and-so (Dougherty 1923: vol. 1, no. 168 [December 26, 573]) and at the disposal of someone else (Dougherty 1923: vol. 2, no. 271).

One document from the Feuer and Forbes collection is entitled "Workers of the Gate" and lists 5 names before breaking off (ISAP 110). So perhaps not all workers did fieldwork. Seven ostraca conclude with the term לתרען 'for (the) gatekeepers'. Five of them appear to have been drawn up by the same scribe, three weeks apart, and a fragmentary 5th on an unknown date. Though the handwriting sports a certain variation, they are distinguished by the plena spelling of the measure and quantity and were doubtless drawn up by the same scribe, though his documents became scattered among three collections. As the clans supplied workers, so here they brought barley and flour for one class of workers, the gatekeepers: 5[+?] seahs and x qabs of x by Natanṣidq [of PN] on 6 Nisan (AL 102); 19 seahs and 2 qabs of barley on 7 Nisan by Qosmilk/malak of Baalrim (ISAP 12); 5 seahs, 3 qabs of flour on 18 Nisan by Badan of Albaal (AL 104); 1 kor, 4 qabs on 1 Iyyar by Qos-milk/malak and Aydan of Baalrim (AL 197); 3 seahs, 4 qabs on the same date by Alqos of Qoṣi (EN 93!); and x seahs, [1] qab by Ammiqos (EN 144 = BLM 660!). If the wealth of the clan be judged by the amount brought, we would have to judge Baalrim as the most affluent. Accord-ingly we find that on 20 Shebat, Year 3[+?] someone from Baalrim brought 1 kor, 25 seahs of barley (Lozachmeur and Lemaire 1996: no. 2 = ISAP 1223). Not only flour and grain were delivered to the gatekeep-ers but also heavy stuff. On June 12, 340 / February 4, 339 Baalmilk/

malak transferred 6 loads (L 24). An Aramaic ostracon from Tel el Farʿah (south) opens with "Give (הב) to Qosdakar" and may conclude with the word תרעיא 'the gatekeepers' (Naveh 1985: no. 3 and pl. 19.3). Gatekeepers abound in the biblical sources, both the sacred ones of the sanctuary and temple and the profane ones of the city. The Chronicler reports that 4 chief gatekeepers, who were accounted Levites, were in charge of the temple chambers and treasuries, slept by the temple, where they did guard duty, opened up the temple gates every morning, and were joined by their kinsmen on regular seven-day shifts (1 Chr 9:22–27). Nehemiah appointed officials to take charge of the stores of produce gathered in "from the fields of the towns" for the priests, Levites, singers, and gatekeepers. Further, "in the time of Zerubbabel and in the time of Nehemiah, all Israel contributed daily portions of the singers and the gatekeepers . . ." (Neh 12:44–47). Whether sacred or profane, the Idumean gatekeepers were receiving allotments from the major clans. And of course the gate, as again illustrated by the book of Ruth (4:1–12) as well as other sources (Gen 23:10, 18; Prov 31:23; Job 29:7), was a center of public life. But were the workers at the gate the same as the gatekeepers? Our guess is that they were not but, rather, were comparable in status to the day laborers in the field.

The Bible does not know the term פעל with the meaning 'worker'. Instead it has שכיר 'hired (worker)', and פעל is used to designate the wages he receives (Job 7:2). He is often paired with תושב "resident (alien)" (Exod 12:45; Lev 25:6, 10, 40). The standard service contract ran for three years (Deut 15:18; Isa 16:14), though one-year (Isa 21:16) or annually renewable (Lev 25:50, 53) contracts were also known. Equally well known was the day laborer (Job 14:6), who might be either an Israelite or a resident alien. He was poor, and considerable solicitude is shown to him (Deut 24:14–15). He was to be paid at the end of each day, and it was expressly forbidden to hold over his wages even until the next morning (Lev 19:13). Hours of work, how early the worker had to come, how late he had to stay, and provision of meals varied from place to place, and mutual obligations in these matters are discussed in the Mishnah. It is clear from these discussions that the workers labored in fields of grain and vegetables, in vineyards, and among fruit trees. Not only are they envisioned as having wives and children, but slaves and handmaidens as well (*m. B. Meṣiʿa* 7:1–7). According to a New Testament parable, workers were hired daily in the market at about 6 a.m. to work in a householder's vineyard for a denarius, which was paid to them in the evening (Matt 20:1–16). Were the day laborers supplied by the Idumean clans in the same category as these indigent workers? One text from the Feuer and Forbes collection reads, "Naamel son of Nattun: 2 silver for 15 workers" (ISAP 451). A puzzling piece. Is Naamel paying 2 shekels instead of supplying 15 workers, or is he paying wages for 15 workers? If we assume 2 shekels = 24 maahs, then each worker would be worth .133 shekels. If the denarius equals a half-shekel (= 0.50; cf. Yadin et al. 2002: *P. Yadin* 46:11–12), then the Idumean day laborer of the fourth century B.C.E. received just $\frac{2}{5}$ times less than his Judean successor in the first century C.E. In an unpublished Aramaic ostracon of the first century B.C.E. from the vicinity of Jerusalem, two lines record payments to workers (פעליא): 1 denarius, 2 maahs to an unspecified number; and 4 denarii, 3 maahs to 10 workers, that is .225 shekels (or less that $\frac{1}{2}$ a denarius) per worker. In two separate passages, the Laws of Hammurabi stipulate the wages of a hired worker: the equivalent of 240 seahs of grain a year (= 4 qabs/day) for an agricultural laborer (*ikkaram* = Heb./Aram. אכר; LH 257), or .033 shekels a day for a hireling (*agram*; cf. Aram. אגיר) for the first five months of the agricultural year and .027 shekels for the next seven months (LH 273; Driver and Miles 1960: 1.470–71). A Neo-Babylonian text from Erech dated January 24, 565 (Dougherty 1923: vol. 1, no. 207) records 5 kors of barley for 10 workers. Averaged out, that would come to 15 seahs (= $\frac{1}{2}$ kor) per worker, presumably per month, paid at the beginning of the month (3 Shebat), amounting to only 180 seahs per year.

Can we supply these documents with absolute dates? As noted, three of them have year dates, Years 2, 6, and 7. But of what ruler? The same problem applies to the dossier of Saadel. There we have ostraca dated to Years 2, 3, 4, and 5. Cross-references come to our aid. Both dossiers make several references to Baalrim. The workers' dossier shows Baalrim to be a contemporary of Yehokal. A document mentioning him is dated to 2 Adar, Year 3 of Philip the king (EN 96), which is March 14, 320 B.C.E. As we were working on these texts, we noticed that the following number in the Eph'al and Naveh collection (no. 97) was written by our Scribe 1. This piece is held by the Reuben and Edith Hecht Museum of the University of Haifa (H-2579) and was copied by Yardeni (fig. 2d). We select two workers texts from Baalrim (ISAP 428, 466 [fig. 2a and b]) and one from Gur (ISAP 260 [fig. 2c]) and note in all four texts such common paleographic features as the broad left leg of the *'alep*, the tail of the *'ayin*, and the curving in of the *lamed*. Moreover, EN 97 (fig. 2d) was explicitly dated to 12 Kislev, Year 7 which is December 12, 317 B.C.E. Years 2 through 7 of Philip III would be 322 to 317. It would not be impossible for a young Saadel who "calculated" at the end of the document dated to 27 *Ab*, Year 17 = September 7, 342 (AL 82) to be active as

Fig. 2. Applying paleography to date undated workers' texts (a, b, and c) according to a dated payment record (d).

a mature or senior official in the Years 322 to 319. Were he the same Saadel who warranted the transactions in the Ḥalfat dossier in 4 Elul, Year 1 = September 10, 358 (EN 6), he would have been young then (in his 20s), mature in 342 (ca. 40), and advanced in years in 320 (ca. 60). Is he identical with the Saadel of the clan of Baalrim? To be sure, homonymy or even papponymy should not be excluded. Two contemporaneous fellows bore the name Dikri among our workers. One belonged to the house/sons of Qoṣi (ISAP 425, 465) and the other to the house of Yokal (ISAP 429). On the other hand, Qosyinqom of Baalrim (ISAP 543, 893, 924) is identical with the unaffiliated Qosyinqom (ISAP 917).

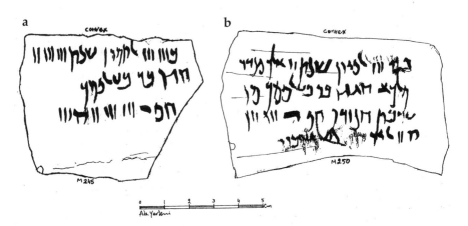

Fig. 3a–b. Determining the identity of Alexander on the basis of paleography.

There are 6 ostraca dated according to the reign of Alexander. Three are bunched together in Year 2—23 Sivan (AL 87), 26 Sivan (L 38), and 8 Tammuz (AL 88), and one in that year has the day and month missing (L 39). A fifth is dated to 20 Shebat, Year 5 (EN 111 = AL 89) and the sixth is dated 5 Kislev, but the year is missing (EN 112). Scholars are divided over the identity of Alexander. Eph'al and Naveh (1996: 16–17) maintained that it was Alexander IV, whose years ran from 316 to 312. Lemaire (1996: 41–46; above, p. 414) preferred Alexander III the Great. Taking his cue from the computing of his reign in Egypt, which began in the autumn of 332 and ran till his death in June, 323 (Year 9), he assumes a similar calculation for Idumea, beginning in the spring of 332. Only three demotic texts are dated to his reign (Pestman 1967: 10; Hughes and Jasnow 1997: no. 2), while at least fourteen texts are dated to the reign of Alexander, son of Alexander (Pestman 1967: 13). If Lemaire's attribution is correct, it would be a chronological windfall. But is it? The 23 Sivan text was written for Ḥaggagu son of Baalsamak (AL 87 [fig. 3b]). On 6 Tammuz, Year 8 a text was written for Ḥaggu son of Baalsamak (AL 57 [fig. 3a]). Noting the near-identity of names, Lemaire assigned this "Year 8" to Alexander III, yielding July 9, 325. The earlier text he assigned to July 3, 331, a gap of six years. Yet we will get a gap of but one year between these two documents (AL 57 and 87) if we note that both were written by the same scribe, as evidenced by his signatory *nun*, starkly curved to the right in the word שנת and in חנזרו

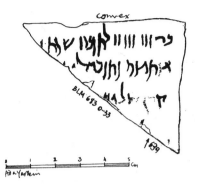

Fig. 4. Restoring a fragmentary date in a text of Antigonus.

in AL 87:3 (fig. 3a and b). "Year 8" may be assigned to Philip III, yielding June 30, 316, while the Alexander date (23 Sivan, Year 2) would apply to son not father and yield July 7, 315. The 26 Sivan document (L 38) would bring Alexander's date down to July 10, 315. Quite strikingly, a document for an anonymous Ḥaggagu (AL 50!) is dated 7 Tammuz, 3 Arti*gonus* (= Antigonus), which would be July 20, 315. This date is "touch and go" with one for Alexander: 8 Tammuz, Year 2 = July 21, 315. Dates in August are firmly Antigonus: August 7 (25 Tammuz, 3 Antigonus [EN 56]) and August 19 (7 Ab, 3 Antigonus [אנתגס] {AL 93!}). A third ostracon may push this date up by about a week. The piece was among the photos supplied to Ephʿal and Naveh by Lenny Wolfe, not published by them, acquired by the Bible Lands Museum (BLM 683), and copied by Yardeni. The first 1½ lines read, "On the 18th of Tammuz, Year 1[+?] of *ʾntgns*, Natanbaal. . . ." This is the first time we find the ruler's name spelled with initial *nun*, just as in Greek—Antigonus. As clear from the drawing (fig. 4), the ostracon breaks off in the middle of the numeral "1" with no numeral visible to its left. Paleographically, a second numeral would have been suitable, because it would have slanted left from top to bottom. Chronologically, this is unsuitable because it would yield Year 316, a year before Antigonus's arrival. A third stroke tilting left in the same fashion would yield a date of July 31, 315. We find a paleographical parallel to this method of writing three numeral strokes in line 3 of the ostracon just above (fig. 3a). Diodorus (19.58–59) tells us that in the early summer of 315 Antigonus wrested Coele-Syria from Ptolemy. Accepting our chronology allows us to date the transition to the end of July/beginning of August.

Fig. 5. Proposing a reading of a unique name, Saadaniqos.

In conclusion, let us say a few words about the names. The corpus contains some 220 theophorous names, with the dominant deities being Qos, El, and Baal. Most of the non-theophorous elements are well known from Biblical Hebrew and epigraphic Ammonite and Moabite names, often in variant forms. Thus Elephantine יהועלי is Edomite עליאל (EN 69). We can follow the spectrum in Qos names—Edomite Qos-ḥanan, Aramaic Qosyahab, and Arabic Qoswahab—as well as in Baal names—Edomite Baalḥanan, Aramaic Yahabbaal, and Arabic Baal-ghayr. The onomastic, and perhaps ethnic mix, is further evident in patronyms. The Baalghayr in our first dossier was son of Ḥori, an Egyptian name. Such mixed names were prevalent at Elephantine (Porten 2002: 298). Other compound Egyptian names include Abdisi and Abdosiri. Ḥalfat seems to be a profane name and his father bore a familiar *qāttul* type hypocoristicon, Sammuk. On the face of it, Saadel, with a *śin*, seems to be Arabic, to be pronounced Saadil. We have such hypocoristica as Saadi, Saadu, and Suaydu. Yet up popped a strange name that we originally read as שקניקוס. When it became apparent that this must be a ghost name, Yardeni decided that we could squeeze out שעדניקוס, the alleged *qop* in fact being *ʿayin* and *dalet* written without spacing (cf. the form of the *ʿayin* in קוסעני [line 4]). Furthermore, we take the *śin* for *samek* and interpret 'Qos has assisted me' on the model of Qosdalani, 'Qos has rescued me' (fig. 5). This spelling, with *samek*, is now warranted by the appearance of this name in a recently acquired ostracon in the Jeselsohn collection (ISAP 2544). Meanwhile, we propose an improved reading in an ostracon from the Moussaieff collection (ISAP 1461): סעדניקוס instead of the editor's סיוני ח ס ר (*sywny ḥ s* 10). The investigation is ongoing.

Bibliography

Aguizy, O. el
1994   Some Demotic Ostraca in the Cairo Museum. *Egitto: Vicino Oriente* 17: 125–44.
Aharoni, Y.
1981   *Arad Inscriptions.* Jerusalem.
Ahituv, S.
1992   *Handbook of Ancient Hebrew Inscriptions.* Jerusalem. [Hebrew]
Devauchelle, D.
1983   *Ostraca démotiques du Musée du Louvre.* Bibliotheque d'Étude 92/1. Paris.
Diakonoff, I. M., and Livshits, V. A.
1976   *Parthian Economic Documents from Nisa.* Corpus Inscriptionum Iranicarum. London.
Dougherty, R. P.
1923   *The Goucher College Cuneiform Inscriptions: Archives from Erech, Time of Nebuchadrezzar and Nabonidus.* 2 vols. New Haven, Connecticut.
Driver, G. R., and Miles, J. C.
1960   *The Babylonian Laws.* 2 vols. Oxford.
Eph'al, I., and Naveh, J.
1996   *Aramaic Ostraca of the Fourth Century from Idumea.* Jerusalem.
Erman, A., and Grapow, H.
1926   *Wörterbuch der ägyptischen Sprache.* Berlin.
Görg, M.
1992   Akrabattene; Akkrabim. Pp. 140–41 in vol. 1 of *Anchor Bible Dictionary*, ed. D. N. Freedman. New York.
Hughes, G. R., and Jasnow, R.
1997   *Oriental Institute Hawara Papyri.* Chicago.
Kang, S. T.
1973   *Sumerian Economic Texts from the Umma Archive.* Urbana, Illinois.
Lemaire, A.
1996   *Nouvelles inscriptions araméennes d'Idumée au Musée d'Israel.* Vol. 1. Paris.
1999   Quatre nouveaux *ostraca* araméens d'Idumée. *Transeuphratène* 18: 71–74.
2002   *Nouvelles inscriptions araméennes d'Idumée au Musée d'Israel.* Vol. 2. Paris.
Lozachmeur, H., and Lemaire, A.
1996   Nouveaux ostraca araméens d'Idumée (Collection Sh. Moussaieff). *Semitica* 46: 123–52.

Mattha, G.
    1945   *Demotic Ostraka from the Collections at Oxford, Paris, Berlin, Vienna and Cairo*. Cairo.
Naveh, J.
    1981   The Aramaic Ostraca from Tel Arad. Pp. 153–76 in Y. Aharoni, *Arad Inscriptions*. Jerusalem.
    1985   Published and Unpublished Aramaic Ostraca. ʿ*Atiqot* 17: 114–21 + pls. 19–20.
Parker, R. A., and Dubberstein, W. H.
    1956   *Babylonian Chronology 626 B.C.–A.D. 75*. Providence, Rhode Island.
Pestman, P. W.
    1967   *Chronologie égyptienne d'après les textes démotiques*. Leiden.
Porten, B.
    2002   Egyptian Names in Aramaic Texts. Pp. 287–327 in *Acts of the Seventh International Conference of Demotic Studies: Copenhagen, 23–27 August 1999*, ed. K. Ryholt. Copenhagen.
Spalinger, A.
    1996   From Local to Global: The Extension of an Egyptian Bureaucratic Term to the Empire. *Studien zur Altägyptischen Kultur* 23: 352–76.
Turkowski, L.
    1969   Peasant Agriculture in the Judean Hills. *Palestine Exploration Quarterly* 101: 21–33, 101–12.
Vleeming, S. P.
    1994   *Ostraka Varia: Tax Receipts and Legal Documents on Demotic, Greek, and Greek-Demotic Ostraka, Chiefly of the Early Ptolemaic Period, from Various Collections (P. L. Bat 26)*. Leiden.
Yadin, Y., and Naveh, J.
    1989   *Masada I: The Yigael Yadin Excavations 1963–1965 Final Reports. The Aramaic and Hebrew Ostraca and Jar Inscriptions*. Jerusalem.
Yadin, Y., et al.
    2002   *The Documents from the Bar Kokhba Period in the Cave of Letters*. Jerusalem.

PART 2

Biblical Perspectives

Periodization between History and Ideology II: Chronology and Ideology in Ezra–Nehemiah

SARA JAPHET

The Hebrew University

The present essay is a follow-up to two earlier works that related to the two components of its title: "Chronology and Composition in Ezra–Nehemiah,"[1] and "Periodization between History and Ideology: the Neo-Babylonian Period in Biblical Historiography."[2] This review of Ezra–Nehemiah (= EN) from the perspective of these three aspects—chronology, composition and periodization—and in their conjunction, will bring to light the work's particular nature and its historical and ideological goals. It will expose the figure of the historian who undertook to write the history of the Restoration Period and determined for generations the historical picture of the period. It will also elucidate the phenomenon and concept of periodization—a backbone of the historical genre and an indispensable aspect of the historian's work[3]—by its illustration in EN. It will also demonstrate how the most basic aspects of the historical genre are informed by ideology, which in turn is a product of the historian's cultural context and his overall ideological goals.

Among the many problems that face the student of EN are the two major issues of the book's unclear chronology and its apparent erratic composition. Although I presented and discussed these problems in some detail in "Composition and Chronology in the Book of Ezra–Nehemiah" (Japhet 1994), some measure of repetition seems unavoidable, but I will restrict the presentation in this context to the essential points.

Chronology

Unlike all other historical books in the Bible, EN does not seem to have a consistent chronological skeleton or a systematic chronological

---

1. Japhet 1994: 189–216.
2. Japhet 2003: 75–89.
3. See Ritter 1985: 313–18; Japhet 2003: 75–76.

framework from which the individual dates receive their meaning.[4]
Although EN describes events in consecutive order and occasionally
provides chronological data, no overall chronological system seems to
be discerned in the work. As a result, studies of the biblical chronological systems tend to ignore the evidence of EN altogether.[5]

What is the cause for this apparent lack? Does it mean that EN has
no clear concept of time and thus defies the book's genre-definition as
history? We begin with the most basic question: Can a specific concept
of time be discerned in EN ? If there is such a concept, what is it?

The fact that immediately strikes the eye is the abundance of indications of time and references to dates in EN—full-fledged dates, partial
or general dates, and various other indications of time. Predominantly
in EN, references to time include precise dates based on the reigns of
the Persian emperors: Ezra 1:1; 4:24; 5:13; 6:3, 15; 7:7–9; Neh 1:1; 2:1;
5:14; 13:6.[6] Next to this group, and also in reference to the reigns of the
Persian emperors, are general statements of time, such as: "All the
years of King Cyrus of Persia, and until the reign of King Darius of Persia" (Ezra 4:5; also Ezra 4:6, 7; 7:1; 8:1; Neh 12:22).[7]

Another group of dates uses different time referents, such as: "the
second year after their arrival . . . in the second month" (Ezra 3:8) or,
"in the days of Yoiakim" (Neh 12:12), and so on.[8] There are also references to the months of the year without any indication of which year is
intended.[9] And finally, there are rather vague statements: "after these

---

4. This fact has been noticed by many scholars. See, for example, Tadmor 1962: 303.

5. See, for example, Tadmor 1962. Even Hughes, who views biblical chronology almost entirely from the perspective of "myth," refers only to isolated dates in EN but not
to its overall chronology (Hughes 1990: 51–54).

6. "In the first year of King Cyrus" (Ezra 1:1; 5:13; 6:3); "the second year of the reign
of King Darius of Persia" (4:24); "the third of the month of Adar, in the sixth year of the
reign of King Darius" (6:15); "the seventh year of King Artaxerxes . . . in the fifth month
in the seventh year of the king" (7:7–9); "in the month of Kislev of the twentieth year"
(Neh 1:1); "in the month of Nisan, in the twentieth year of King Artaxerxes" (2:1); "from
the twentieth year of King Artaxerxes until his thirty-second year, twelve years in all"
(5:14); "in the thirty-second year of King Artaxerxes" (13:6). The English renderings
generally follow the NJPSV, with a few deviations, as required.

7. "In the reign of Ahasuerus, at the start of his reign" (Ezra 4:6); "in the time of
Artaxerxes" (4:7); "during the reign of King Artaxerxes" (7:1); "in the reign of King Artaxerxes" (8:1); "the reign of Darius the Persian" (Neh 12:22); six in all.

8. "In the days of Eliashib, Yoiada, Yohanan and Yaddua" (Neh 12:22); "to the time of
Yohanan son of Eliashib" (12:23); "in the time of Yoiakim son of Jeshua . . . and in the time
of Nehemiah the governor and of Ezra the priest, the scribe" (12:26); "in the time of
Zerubbabel and in the time of Nehemiah" (12:47).

9. Such as "the seventh month" (Ezra 3:1; Neh 7:72 [8:1]; 8:14); "the first day of the seventh month" (Ezra 3:6); "the fourteenth day of the first month" (Ezra 6:19); "the twelfth

events" (Ezra 7:1); "at that time" (Ezra 8:34); "on that day" (Neh 12:44; 13:1); "before that" (13:4); "in these days" (13:15, 23); and more.

The most instructive of these time indications is the first group, in which the dates synchronize the recorded events with the reigns of the Persian emperors.[10] Although EN does not provide a systematic list of these kings or a register of the length of their reigns, a comparison of the data with the chronology established by modern scholarship on the basis of Babylonian, Persian, and Greek sources allows a precise dating for the events marked by these dates.[11] We are also able to calculate, among other things, the length of the period covered by EN as it stands, that is, from the first chapter to the last. The book begins with the first year of Cyrus (Ezra 1:1), and the last date mentioned is the 33rd year of Artaxerxes (Neh 13:6). Assuming that the "first year of Cyrus" refers to his first year as king of Babylon, the beginning of the period should be placed at 538 B.C.E.; keeping in mind that the date of the 33rd year of Artaxerxes is taken from "The Words of Nehemiah" and that according to the prevailing scholarly view the king in whose time Nehemiah was active was Artaxerxes I (465–424), this year can be determined with certainty as 432 B.C.E. Thus, the span of time covered by EN as it stands would be 107 years in all.[12]

However, notwithstanding the abundance of dates referring to Persian chronology and the great significance of the Persian emperors in the historical philosophy of EN,[13] the reigns of the Persian kings do not constitute the chronological skeleton of the book. This statement appears untrue on a superficial reading because there seems to be correspondence between the order of the Persian kings in EN and their actual historical sequence.[14] However, it is sustained by a careful historical consideration of the problem. The inevitable conclusion

---

day of the first month" (Ezra 8:31); "the ninth month, the twentieth of the month" (10:9); "the first day of the tenth month . . . the first day of the first month" (10:16–17); "the twenty-fifth of Elul" (Neh 6:15); "the twenty-fourth day of this month" (Neh 9:1). In some cases the intended year may be inferred from the present context, whether or not it was the original setting.

10. As was indeed the common procedure in the Achaemenid Period. See Briant 2002.

11. For the reconstruction of these dates, see the classic work by Parker and Dubberstein 1971: 11–16. See also Briant 2002.

12. On the tension between this chronological picture and the actual historical span of time represented in EN, based on historical-critical considerations, see below, pp. 501–2.

13. For which, see Japhet 2000: 153–55.

14. This is indeed the picture proposed by Dequeker (1993: 75–76) and adopted by D. Edelman (personal communication). See also Liver 1974.

remains that the Persian chronology does not constitute the chronological framework of EN.[15]

Is it possible to discern in EN another chronological system that could be considered the work's framework? The existence of two chronological systems may be inferred from the quoted dates of EN: the sequence of the governors of Judah with the length of their office, and the sequence of the high priests. However, the first system is illustrated in EN only for the governorship of Nehemiah (Neh 5:14; 13:6) and even this one is incomplete, because the end of Nehemiah's second term of office is not recorded.[16] The system based on the sequence of high priests, as listed in Neh 12:10–11 and 12:22, lacks precise chronological data.[17]

The inevitable conclusion seems to be that there is no obvious or "objective" chronological system upon which the historical description of EN is based. This impression, however, is immediately reversed when the matter is reviewed from a different perspective. A more careful study of EN shows that, not only does EN have a clear concept of time, but this concept forms the basis for both its chronological setting and its literary composition. A brief presentation of the problem of composition is therefore indicated at this point.

Composition

Although problems relating to EN 's composition are found in each of its parts,[18] the most difficult appear in Nehemiah 1–13. Formally, these chapters bear the stamp of a literary unit, with its own opening (Neh 1:1) and conclusion (Neh 13:31).[19] However, it seems to show no literary integrity and to include a great variety of styles and literary

---

15. For a detailed discussion of this matter, see Japhet 1994: 201–6.

16. This is characteristic of EN, which never mentions the end of the historical figures. At undefined points Sheshbazzar, Zerubbabel, Jehoshua, Ezra, and Nehemiah simply disappear from the historical scene.

17. Following the reconstruction of Cross, who repeated this view in several articles, the list is regarded by some scholars as incomplete. See Cross 1975: 9–18 and a critique of this view by Widengren 1977: 506–9; VanderKam 1991: 67–91.

18. For a presentation of these difficulties and different proposals for their solution, see the commentaries, e.g., Rudolph 1949: xxiii–xxiv; Williamson 1985: xxiii–xxxv; Blenkinsopp 1988: 41–47. See also Japhet 1991: 203–5.

19. Consequently, some scholars regard Nehemiah as a distinct literary work, independent of the book of Ezra. See Segal 1943: 93–96, 103; VanderKam 1992; Kraemer 1993; Becking 1999. For the unity of EN, which is supported also by the present essay, see, e.g., Williamson 1985: xxi–xxii; Gunneweg 1985: 28–31.

genres that point to a variety of literary sources and a complex composition. Without going into controversial issues (and allowing for differences in details), Nehemiah 1–13 comprise the following literary components:

a. "The Words of Nehemiah," with its own linguistic and stylistic stamp, in Neh 1:1–7:5 and 13:4–31.[20] The first part is appended in Neh 7:6–72 by a list of "the people of the province," which is also found, with slight textual variations, in Ezra 2.

b. A narrative describing the events of the seventh month of Ezra (Neh 8:1–18). This passage most likely belongs to "The Story of Ezra," the main part of which is found in Ezra 7–10.

c. An account of the events of the "twenty-fourth of this month," which include, after the introduction (9:1–5): a long prayer of the Levites (9:6–37) and "the covenant" (Neh 10:1–40). Although the events are placed in the time of Nehemiah (10:2), the account does not seem to stem from "The Words of Nehemiah"; it refers to Nehemiah in the third person, and its style is different.

d. Some short passages may have been extracted from "The Words of Nehemiah" and inserted into the story outside their original sequence or in a reworked form (Neh 11:1–2; 27–43).

e. Some narrative sections seem to owe their origin to either the author of EN or some later hand (Neh 12:44–47; 13:1–3).

f. Miscellaneous lists of various functions and origin in Neh 11:3–12:26.

The most important feature of this literary conglomerate—and the one that indeed has attracted the greatest scholarly attention—is the way it deals with the two major sources of EN, "The Words of Nehemiah" and "The Story of Ezra." The greater part of "The Words of Nehemiah" is placed at the beginning of this section (Nehemiah 1–6), and a smaller part of it at the end (Neh 13:4–31), while the greater part of the Ezra story is placed in Ezra 7–10 and another part of it in Nehemiah 8. These breaks in literary continuity, the apparent displacement of the materials derived from the sources, and the strong mixture of styles and genres are evidence of what seems to be an insurmountable tension between the final structure of EN and the continuity, uniformity, and unity of its component parts.[21] As I already hinted above, the solution

---

20. For a possible two-stage process of composition of "The Words of Nehemiah," see Williamson 1985: xxvii–xxviii, and recently Reinmuth 2002.

21. These problems presented a challenge to all of EN's students; for a discussion of some proposed solutions, see Japhet 1994: 197–201.

to this problem should be sought in EN's specific time structure—our next step.

Periodization

A review of EN from a different vantage point soon reveals that the "chaos" of both chronology and composition in EN is only apparent. There does exist a "miraculous key" to EN that offers a solution to the problems presented above and opens the door to a better understanding of many aspects of the work. The tag of this key is *periodization*, the system of time-structuring that constitutes the foundation of the entire work. When this aspect of EN is elucidated, many aspects of the work come into focus, opening the way to a new set of questions and evaluations.

Analyzed from the perspective of historical periodization, EN is very clearly seen to comprise two parts:

(a) Ezra 1–6, the story of the rebuilding of the temple, which begins with Cyrus's decree in the first year of his reign (Ezra 1:1) and ends with the dedication of the temple and the celebration of the Passover in the sixth year of Darius's reign (Ezra 6:15). These two ends by themselves do not supply the precise length of the period but, according to the chronology of the Persian Empire as established by modern scholarship, it was a period of 22 years: 538–516 B.C.E.

(b) Ezra 7–Nehemiah 13, the combined acts of Ezra and Nehemiah. This action begins with Ezra's arrival in Jerusalem in the seventh year of the reign of Artaxerxes (Ezra 7:7), continues with Nehemiah, in the 20th year of Artaxerxes (Neh 1:1; 2:1), and ends with Nehemiah's second term of office, in the 33rd year of Artaxerxes (Neh 13:6–7). This is a period of 26 years, from the 7th to the 33rd year of Artaxerxes and, according to Persian chronology, 458–432 B.C.E.

It should be emphasized again that, while the chronology of the Persian kings provides the numerical data on which the calculation of the periods is based, it does not constitute the chronological framework by which the historical periods are determined. The first period includes the full reign of two kings, one of whom is not even mentioned, and part of the reign of a third king (Cyrus, 538–530 B.C.E.; Cambyses, 530–522 B.C.E.; Darius, 522–516). The second period comprises part of the reign of one king (Artaxerxes); it does not begin with his ascent to the throne and does not end with the termination of his reign. The historical periodization defines the periods by internal criteria, according to topics and events related exclusively to the Restoration of Judah and Jerusalem: the building of the temple for the first period, the consolidation of the Judean community under the leadership of Ezra and Nehemiah for the second.

The two periods are structured along the same lines, each of them covering a time span of one generation. The actual length of the generations, however, is established in each case by the historical data, as their lengths are neither standard nor typological.

Another characteristic feature of the two periods is the view of the particular political system prevailing in Judah during each of them. In each period the people of Judah are presented as headed by two leaders: Zerubbabel, son of Shealtiel, and Jehoshua, son of Jehozadak, in the first period; Ezra and Nehemiah in the second.[22] One of the leaders is a layman, responsible for the political administration; the other is a priest, responsible for the religious or spiritual sphere. The actual portrayal of these leaders, however, is not standardized, and the peculiar features are determined for each period by the historical data.

During the first period, both leaders are presented as heads of the respective establishments: Zerubbabel is the political leader while Jehoshua, the high priest, heads the religious establishment (Ezra 3:2, 8; 4:2, 3; 5:2). In both cases, however, their titles are absent from EN and have to be learned from other sources.[23] For the second period, both leaders derive their authority from their appointment by the Persian emperor: Nehemiah is the head of the political establishment as the appointed governor of Judah (Neh 5:14, 18; 12:26), while the position of Ezra is described as "the priest, the scribe" (Ezra 7:11, 12; Neh 8:9; 12:26), commissioned by Artaxerxes.[24] Notwithstanding the differences between the figures of the leaders, the sociopolitical concept of a society headed by two leaders is retained for the two periods.

Another common feature of both periods is the internal periodization of each, with all the events clustered at definite focal points. In the first period there is a concentration of events at the beginning of the period and then at its end. Cyrus's decree, the return from Babylon, and the laying of the foundations of the temple, are all placed in the first years of the period,[25] while all the events connected with the

---

22. This system was greatly emphasized by Talmon, in all his works on Ezra–Nehemiah, most recently 2001: 137, 145. See also Japhet 1982: 94.

23. For the meaning of this omission, see Japhet 1982: 80–89.

24. The double title gave rise to many conjectures regarding Ezra's status, authority, and mission. See, among others, Grabbe 1994; Steiner 2001 (and the bibliography cited by both).

25. Although only the beginning of the historical process is marked by a date, "the first year of King Cyrus" (Ezra 1:1), the return from Babylon is described as having followed

completion of the building are clustered at the end, from the second to the sixth year of Darius (Ezra 4:24, 6:15). Concerning the period between these two ends which, chronologically speaking, is its longest part, the author has nothing to say. This is the time when the building of the temple was stopped, "all the years of King Cyrus of Persia and until the reign of King Darius of Persia" (Ezra 4:5), and the author passes over it in a single sentence (4:24).

The second period is structured according to the same historiographical principle: all the events are clustered at three, very short points in time—two beginnings and one conclusion. The first focus is Ezra's return to Jerusalem, around which are concentrated the events described in Ezra 7–10: the return from Babylon, from the first to the fifth month of the year (Ezra 7:7–9; 8:31), and the struggle over the mixed marriages, from the ninth month of the year to the first month of the next (10:9, 17). The second point in time is Nehemiah's arrival in Jerusalem, 12 years later, in the 20th year of Artaxerxes. Everything recounted in Nehemiah 1–12, taken from a variety of sources, is presented as having occurred in a single year: Nehemiah's departure for Jerusalem in the first month (Neh 2:1), the completion of the wall of Jerusalem in the sixth month of Elul (Neh 6:15), and the ingathering of the people in "the seventh month" (7:72; 9:1), followed by the dedication of the wall (12:27–43). The third point in time, which is again about 12 years later is the final one: the description in a single sequence of all of Nehemiah's acts in his second term of office (Neh 13:6–31).

The periods between these points in time are treated similarly on all occasions: these are times when "history stands still"; nothing happens, and the role of the historian is just to pass over them briefly (Ezra 4:24; Neh 5:14).

Another aspect of the periodization of EN is the sequence of the two periods, presented as consecutive, with the transition between them marked by the vague phrase "after these events" (Ezra 7:1). This literary strategy creates an impression of direct sequence in time, although, as is now well known, there is an interval of at least 58 years between the 6th year of Darius (516 B.C.E.; Ezra 6:15) and the 7th year of Artaxerxes (458 B.C.E.; Ezra 7:7)—if these kings were Darius I and Artaxerxes I—or much longer—if the second is Artaxerxes II. The impression of immediate continuity created by this strategy was so compelling that it determined the traditional view of the Persian Period for

---

immediately afterward (Ezra 1:5), and the laying of the foundations is explicitly dated "in the second year after their arrival" (Ezra 3:8).

a long time, as expressed in the famous chronological work *Seder Olam Rabbah*, and following it, by traditional exegesis.[26]

The specific concept of periodization underlying EN 's chronological and literary structure is also expressed in an editorial note in Neh 12:47. In summing up the arrangements for the portions and tasks of the priests and Levites, as implemented by David, the conclusion is: "And in the time of Zerubbabel, and in the time of Nehemiah, all Israel contributed the daily portions of the singers and the gatekeepers" (Neh 12:47). In the presentation of the writer of this passage—whether the author of EN or a later hand—the whole Persian period is composed of two terms, the same principle on which the whole book of EN is structured.

When EN is studied from the perspective of its periodization, not only the chronology but also the composition becomes abundantly clear. It is indeed the author's time concept—expressed by his method of periodization—that forms the basis for the literary composition. Thus, it turns out (quite unexpectedly), that EN 's historical methodology is similar in principle to that of the Deuteronomist on the one hand, and the editorial framework of the Pentateuch, on the other. While the actual chronological systems are very different,[27] in all these works it is the time-concept as expressed in the method of periodization that determines their literary structure.

As I showed elsewhere, EN introduced into biblical historiography a specific literary methodology, in which existing documents were integrated as they stood into a narrative framework.[28] The combination of this literary method with the specific system of periodization resulted for the author of EN in the following procedures. For the "first period" (Ezra 1–6) the author of EN did not possess complete literary sources but miscellaneous documents and some biblical material (such as the prophecies of Haggai and Zechariah), and therefore he undertook to write the unit himself, integrating the available documents into

---

26. *Seder Olam Rabbah* 30:11–15 (with the remarks of the editor) and 30:49. The exegetical means by which the textual problems emanating from this chronology were overcome was the view that "Artaxerxes" was a royal title rather than a proper name (similar to Pharaoh for the kings of Egypt), and therefore the king referred to in chap. 7 as Artaxerxes was actually Darius (30:12: "The kingship is called Artaxerxes"). In this view, the duration of the Persian Period was calculated as having lasted 52 years. See First 1997.

27. The best-known systems are the synchronistic chronology of the book of Kings and the cyclical periodization determined by typological generations in the book of Judges.

28. Japhet 1983: 181–82; Williamson 1983.

the historical narrative.[29] For the "second period" (Ezra 7–Nehemiah 13), the author had at his disposal two rather long, quite uniform literary works with decided literary stamp—"The Words of Nehemiah" and "The Story of Ezra"[30]—as well as some shorter passages of various kinds and miscellaneous lists. Following his concept of periodization—one generation under the leadership of Ezra and Nehemiah—the author forwent the literary integrity of each of the two major sources, bisected each of them into two parts, and combined them with each other. Thus, he began his account with the story of Ezra, to which he prefaced his own introduction (Ezra 7:1–10), and recounted several of Ezra's actions (Ezra 7:11–10:44). He then interrupted the story and began with "The Words of Nehemiah" (Neh 1:1). Here again, he did not present this work in a single sequel but severed the last part from the main body and placed it, or part of it, at the end of his work (Neh 13:4–31). After using "The Words of Nehemiah" up to Nehemiah 7, he interrupted the continuity of the story and assembled its continuation from various components: an additional passage from "The Ezra Story" about the reading of the Torah (Nehemiah 8); various paragraphs taken from other sources (Nehemiah 9, 10); a cluster of lists, with information about the inhabitants of Judah and Jerusalem and the clerical orders (11:3–12:26); and passages from "The Words of Nehemiah" in reworked form (11:1–2; 12:27–43). To this conglomerate of source material (in either its original or reworked form) the author of EN added some passages of his own. The final result of this "cut and paste" method was a full synchronization of Ezra and Nehemiah and a comprehensive picture of settlement and administration during this one generation and under their combined leadership.

---

29. This method is followed in both the Hebrew and Aramaic parts of this section. The Hebrew documents are Ezra 1:2–4, 9–11a; and 2:3–67; and the Aramaic documents are Ezra 4:8–16, 17–22; 5:6–17; and 6:3–12. The Hebrew narrative passages are Ezra 1:1, 5–6, 7–8, 11b; 2:1–2, 68–70; chap. 3; 4:1–5, 6–7; and 6:19–22; and the Aramaic narrative passages are 4:23–24; 5:1–5; and 6:1–2, 13–18. The uniqueness of the literary method, on the one hand, and its uniformity throughout Ezra 1–6, on the other, speak loudly against the preexistence of an "Aramaic source" (as claimed, e.g., by Kaufmann 1960: 514–15, or Gunneweg 1982: 299–302, 1985: 36, following earlier works). See also Williamson 1985: xxiii–xxiv; Blenkinsopp 1988: 42, 112.

30. For "The Words of Nehemiah," see above, p. 495. For the definition of "The Ezra story" and the research concerning its authenticity, authorship, and purpose, see the concise presentation in Williamson 1985: xxviii–xxxii. While "certainty is unattainable" (Blenkinsopp 1988: 46), it seems that the existence of an original "Ezra source" is accepted today by most scholars. For a different view of Ezra 9–10, with consequences for its composition, see Dor 2003.

The artificial nature of EN's periodization and its literary consequences are quite obvious. EN's conscious attempt to impose on the sources alien chronological and historical principles interferes with and impairs the original unity and integrity of these sources. In their original form (as much as it can be reconstructed from the material included in EN), "The Words of Nehemiah" covered a period of over 13 years[31] and did not mention Ezra; "The Story of Ezra" did not include Nehemiah, and the material now included in EN related to his deeds in about one year.[32] Two editorial notes—intended to support the synchronization between Ezra and Nehemiah by adding Nehemiah to the reading of the Torah (Neh 8:9) and Ezra to the dedication of the wall (Neh 12:36), as well as their joint appearance in the subscription of Neh 12:26—are not sufficient to blur the original separateness of these persons and the different styles of the works that tell their deeds.

The impact of EN's method of periodization on its historical account raises a series of chronological and historical questions. Were Ezra and Nehemiah indeed contemporaries? Were they active during the reign of the same "Artaxerxes"? Did Ezra's office indeed precede that of Nehemiah?[33] Does the material included in Nehemiah 9–12 indeed belong to the period of Nehemiah's governorship, or does it relate to later periods, as may be learned from the list of the high priests and the reference

---

31. The period covered by "The Words of Nehemiah" includes the 12 years of his first term of office (Neh 5:14), his absence from Jerusalem, probably for one year (Neh 13:6), and an undefined second term (described in Neh 13:4–31), the conclusion of which is not given. The most we can do is accept the estimate of 13+ years.

32. Taken from this source is the account of three events: the return from Babylon, between the first and the fifth month of Artaxerxes' 7th year (Ezra 7:7–9; 8); the account of the mixed marriages (Ezra 9–10), in which the dates span from the ninth month to the first (Ezra 10:9, 16, 17), and the reading of the Torah in the seventh month (Neh 8:1). If this order is original, the time span is about a year and a half (from the first month of the seventh year to the 7th month of the next year). If, however, the reading of the Torah preceded the affair of the mixed marriages, as suggested by most scholars (see, e.g., Rudolph 1949: xxiv; Williamson 1985: xxx; Blenkinsopp 1988: 45), the time span would be just over one year, from the first month of the 7th year to the same month of the next.

33. Williamson's introductory statement that "no critical issue raised by the books of Ezra and Nehemiah has evoked more discussion than this question" (1985: xxxix) is an adequate description of the situation. The most common alternative to the view of EN is that Ezra's mission took place at the time of Artaxerxes II, his return to Jerusalem to be dated about 30 years after the end of Nehemiah's office, at 398 B.C.E. For a concise discussion of this issue, see Widengren 1977: 503–9; Williamson 1985: xxxix–xliv; and Blenkinsopp 1988: 139–44. Although certainty seems unattainable here as well, the arguments for placing Ezra at the time of Artaxerxes II seem to me more convincing than otherwise.

to Darius the Persian (Neh 12:22)?[34] I have already mentioned the untenable view of the immediate sequence of the two periods.[35] All these questions create a feeling of discomfort regarding the credibility of EN. If the most basic aspects of chronology and periodization are a construct, how can the work's claim to history be taken seriously? Only a very concise statement on this topic is possible in this context, but before attending to it, we must look at another major issue: the big question "Why?" What was the motivation for structuring time and history in this way? What are the meaning and purpose of this construct?

History and Ideology

Once the question is put forward, the answer seems rather obvious. The picture of the Restoration as a time span of two consecutive generations, with a political system characterized by the leadership of two leaders, a laymen and a priest, follows a venerable historical and literary model: the Exodus from Egypt, followed by conquest and settlement in the land of Israel.

The analogy between the return from the Babylonian Exile and the Exodus from Egypt is a well-known biblical concept and is explicitly proclaimed by Jeremiah and Second Isaiah.[36] The impact of this idea on EN, as reflected in various details of the story, has been observed and pointed out by several scholars.[37] So far, however, no one has observed that through its specific time concept and mode of periodization this analogy constitutes the foundational infrastructure for the entire historical account of EN. The first generation of the Restoration is conceived as parallel to the departure from Egypt. The people of Israel left the Babylonian Exile to go back to Jerusalem, with the pronounced purpose of building the temple, similar to the Exodus from

---

34. Most scholars regard "Darius the Persian" to be a reference to either Darius II (Notus, 424–404 B.C.E.) or Darius III (Codomanus, 336–331 B.C.E.)—in any case, after Nehemiah's time. Williamson explains it as a reference to Darius I but regards the note as a gloss of Hellenistic origin (1985: 364–65).

35. Above, pp. 498–499.

36. See, in particular, Isa 48:20; 51:9–11; 52:4; Jer 16:14–15 (= 23:7–8); and Anderson 1962.

37. See, among others, Rudolph 1949: 6 (following earlier scholars); Koch 1974: 184–89; Williamson 1985: 16, 93, 296; Blenkinsopp 1988: 75–76 ("the first of many allusions to the early traditions which form a kind of deep structure to the history of this new beginning"); 136, 175, 290, 292; Hughes 1990: 39–40.

Egypt to worship the Lord (Exod 5:1–3) and build the tabernacle.[38] The second generation is parallel to that of settlement, when Israel consolidated its hold on the land, withstood the temptations represented by the local population, and strove to create a pure and holy community.

The periods of Exodus and settlement are also the only times in the history of Israel characterized by a two-leader political system, a layman and a priest. Moses and Aaron were the leaders during the first period; Joshua, the son of Nun, and Eleazar, the son of Aaron, were the leaders in the second (Josh 14:1; 17:4; 19:51; 21:1; 24:29–30, 33).[39]

This analogy with the Exodus provides an adequate explanation for many other features of EN,[40] among which is the point in time at which the author of EN began his story.[41] Choosing from several possible alternatives, the author began his story with the proclamation of Cyrus, who was presented as the antithesis of the Egyptian Pharaoh. Rather than letting the people go after having been bitten by ten plagues, Cyrus let the people go of his own free will. "The Lord hardened the heart of Pharaoh" (Exod 9:12; also: 7:3, 13, 22; 8:11, 15; 10:1 and more), but he "roused the spirit of King Cyrus of Persia" (Ezra 1:1)

---

38. The temple of the Restoration Period has points of contact with both the wilderness tabernacle and Solomon's Temple. The description of the first steps taken by the returnees toward the building of the temple have points of contact with the building of Solomon's Temple (in particular, Ezra 3:7–8). However, the most basic premise—that the place of worship was to be built before the achievement of political independence (or without reference to it), that is, without "rest round about" (2 Sam 7:1–3; 1 Chr 22:9–10, 18; following Deut 12:9–11)—is shared by the temple of the Restoration and the tabernacle. For this aspect of the Restoration temple, see Japhet 1991: 228–33, 240–42.

39. Talmon has repeatedly posited that the picture of the Qumran community, of Israel headed by two leaders, was influenced by the model of the Restoration. See recently Talmon 2001: 145. I suggest, however, that both views—the historical picture of the Restoration and the eschatological picture of the Qumran community—derive their inspiration from the model of the Exodus.

40. I venture to suggest that even the internal periodization of EN, that is, the clustering of events in the focal points of beginning and end, is based on the same analogy. According to pentateuchal chronology all the events described from Exodus 3 to Numbers 14 are presented as having taken place in a very brief period, of less than two years. The mission of the spies (Numbers 13–14), which resulted in 40 years of wandering in the wilderness, is placed just over a year after the departure from Egypt, and the same chronology is expressed in another way by the biography of Moses, who was 80 years old when "he spoke to Pharaoh" (Exod 7:7), and 120 at his death (Deut 34:7). At the other end, at least according to Numbers 20, where the story of Aaron's death in the 40th year of the wandering is recorded (Num 20:22–29; 33:38), all the events belong to the last phase of the people's wanderings, before the entrance to the land of Canaan. The 40 years of wandering in the wilderness are passed over by just one chapter (Numbers 33).

41. See Japhet 2003: 79–81.

and charged him "with building him a house in Jerusalem, which is in Judah" (1:2).

Another common feature of the two eras in the history of Israel is the presentation of the overarching historical cycle, of enslavement and deliverance, as a fulfillment of the word of God. The Exodus is the fulfillment of God's vision to Abraham: "Know well that your off-spring shall be strangers in a land not theirs, and they shall be enslaved and oppressed four hundred years, but I will execute judgement on the nation they shall serve, and in the end they shall go free with great wealth" (Gen 15:13–14). Cyrus's decree is the fulfillment of Jeremiah's word (Ezra 1:1), which proclaimed the dominance of the Babylonian Empire over the world, its eventual fall, and the return of the Judeans to Zion (Jer 25:9–14; 27:6–8; 29:10–14). According to this view, the entire history of the Restoration was a realization of Jeremiah's words, that "assuredly, a time is coming—declares the Lord—when it shall no more be said, 'As the Lord lives who brought the Israelites out of the land of Egypt,' but rather, 'As the Lord lives who brought the Israelites out of the northland, and out of all the lands to which he had banished them'" (Jer 16:14–15; and, with slight changes, 23:7–8).

The conclusion seems inevitable: the motive behind the specific periodization and the literary structure of EN is straightforwardly ideological: the analogy between the period of the Restoration and the Exodus from Egypt. With this realization, however, the question of historicity comes forcefully to the fore: how much of the historical picture is determined by historical "fact" and how much is "constructed," directed by historical concepts and ideological goals?

As I mentioned before, the answer to this question can be given only in its broadest contours. It seems that two features of EN should provide the balance in answering this question. The first is the fact that there is a limit to the imposition of ideology on the historical account of EN. As we saw several times in the discussion, and as one may illustrate further, the author of EN creates an analogy with the Exodus and settlement, but not a typology. The contents of the events and the presentation of the figures is determined in the first place by the actual historical data at the author's disposal. The second feature of EN, and perhaps of greater significance in this regard, is the particular historiographical method of EN, mentioned above. The author of EN derived his material from available sources and in most cases left them untouched. Rather than writing his account in his own words, he preferred to leave the sources as they were, expressing his own views mainly through the restructuring and reworking of the borrowed material, the creation of a chronological and historical framework, and the writing of some passages of his own. Thus, the data of EN's sources bear their own witness, and they should be examined and scrutinized for their own historical value.[42]

As our discussion has demonstrated, no aspect of the historical work, including what might be regarded as "objective" data, that is, chronology and periodization, is free from the impact of ideology. Periodization has been adequately defined as "a tool for the reconstruction of the past,"[43] and as such it is a conveyer of the historian's message, from his own perspective and toward his own goals. It seems that a balanced conclusion is that no historical work is totally "fact" or totally "fiction"—in the same way that historical events themselves are not free from ideological components. The modern historian who wishes to write his own history would do well not to found his work on any one historical source. Only the accumulation of as many sources as possible and their constant critical scrutiny would help him in his search for the "historical truth." In writing his history, however, the modern historian should be aware not only of the facts but also of the ideologies that his ancient predecessor may have shared with his contemporaries and by which he was motivated and guided. These ideologies too are "historical facts."

---

42. See, for example, in this volume Grabbe, pp. 531–570.
43. Golden and Toohey 1997: 93. See Japhet 2003: 75.

Bibliography

Anderson, B. W.
   1962   Exodus Typology in Second Isaiah. Pp. 177–95 in *Israel's Prophetic Heritage*, ed. B. W. Anderson and W. Harrelson. London.
Becking, B.
   1999   Continuity and Community: The Belief System of the Book of Ezra. Pp. 256–75 in *The Crisis of Israelite Religion: Transformation of Religious Tradition in Exilic and Post-exilic Times*, ed. B. Becking and M. C. A. Korpel. Leiden.
Blenkinsopp, J.
   1988   *Ezra–Nehemiah: A Commentary.* OTL. London.
Briant, P.
   2002   *From Cyrus to Alexander: A History of the Persian Empire.* Winona Lake, Indiana.
Cross, F. M.
   1975   A Reconstruction of the Judean Restoration. *JBL* 94: 9–18.

Dequeker, L.
1993 Darius the Persian and the Reconstruction of the Jewish Temple in Jerusalem (Ezra 4:24). *OLA* 55: 67–92.

Dor, Y.
2003 The Composition of the Episode of the Foreign Women in Ezra IX–X. *VT* 53: 26–47.

First, Mitchell
1997 *Jewish History in Conflict: A Study of the Major Discrepancy between Rabbinic and Conventional Chronology.* Northvale, New Jersey.

Golden, M., and Toohey, P.
1997 *Inventing Ancient Culture: Historicism, Periodization and the Ancient World.* London.

Grabbe, L. L.
1994 What was Ezra's Mission? Pp. 286–99 in *Second Temple Studies 2*, ed. T. C. Eskenazi and K. H. Richards. JSOTSup 175. Sheffield.
2006 The "Persian Documents" in the Book of Ezra: Are They Authentic? Pp. 531–570 in *Judah and the Judeans in the Persian Period*, ed. O. Lipschits and M. Oeming. Winona Lake, Indiana.

Gunneweg, A. H. J.
1982 Die aramäische und die hebräische Erzählung über die nachexilische Restauration: Ein Vergleich. *ZAW* 94: 299–302.
1985 *Esra: Mit einer Zeittafel von Alfred Jepsen.* KAT. Gütersloh.
1987 *Nehemia: Mit einer Zeittafel von Alfred Jepsen und einem Exkurs zur Topographie und Archäologie Jerusalems von Manfred Oeming.* KAT. Gütersloh.

Hughes, J.
1990 *Secrets of the Times: Myth and History in Biblical Chronology.* JSOTSup 66. Sheffield.

Japhet, S.
1982–83 Sheshbazzar and Zerubbabel against the Background of the Historical and Religious Tendencies of Ezra–Nehemiah. *ZAW* 94: 66–98; 95: 218–29.
1983 Biblical Historiography in the Persian Period. Pp. 176–202; 295–303 in vol. 6 of *World History of the Jewish People*, ed. H. Tadmor and I. Ephʿal. Jerusalem. [Hebrew]
1991 The Temple in the Restoration Period: Reality and Ideology. *Union Seminary Quarterly Review* 44: 195–251.
1994 Composition and Chronology in the Book of Ezra–Nehemiah. Pp. 189–216 in *Second Temple Studies 2*, ed. T. C. Eskenazi and K. H. Richards. JSOTSup 175. Sheffield.
2000 Postexilic Historiography: How and Why? Pp. 144–73 in *Israel Constructs Its History: Deuteronomistic Historiography in Recent Research*, ed. A. de Pury, T. Römer, and J. D. Macchi. JSOTSup 306. Sheffield. [original French version, 1996]
2003 Periodization: Between History and Ideology—The Neo-Babylonian Period in Biblical Historiography. Pp. 75–89 in *Judah and Judeans in the Neo-Babylonian Period*, ed. O. Lipschits and J. Blenkinsopp. Winona Lake, Indiana.

Kaufmann, Y.
1960   *From the Babylonian Captivity to the End of Prophecy.* Vol. 6 of *History of the Religion of Israel.* Tel Aviv. [Hebrew]
Kellermann, U.
1967   *Nehemia: Quellen, Überlieferung und Geschichte.* BZAW 102. Berlin.
Kraemer, D.
1993   On the Relationship of the Books of Ezra and Nehemiah. *JSOT* 56: 73–92.
Koch, K.
1974   Ezra and the Origins of Judaism. *JSS* 19: 193–97.
Liver, J.
1974   Regarding the Problem of the Order of the Kings of Persia in the Books of Ezra and Nehemiah. Pp. 127–38 in *Studies in Bible and Judean Desert Scrolls.* Jerusalem. [Hebrew]
Parker, R. A.
1942   *Babylonian Chronology 626 B.C.–A.D. 45.* Chicago. [Rev. ed. with W. H. Dubberstein, *Babylonian Chronology 626 B.C.–A.D. 45.* Providence, 1956, 1971.]
Ratner, B.
1897   *Seder Olam Rabbah.* Vilnius.
Reinmuth, T.
2002   *Der Bericht Nehemias: Zur literarischen Eigenart, traditionsgeschichtlichen Prägung und innerbiblischen Rezeption des Ich-Berichts Nehemias.* OBO 183. Göttingen.
Ritter, H.
1985   Periodization. Pp. 313–19 in *Dictionary of Concepts in History.* New York.
Rudolph, W.
1949   *Esra und Nehemia samt 3. Esra.* HAT. Tübingen.
Segal, M. Z.
1943   The Books of Ezra and Nehemiah. *Tarbiz* 14: 81–103.
Steiner, R. C.
2001   The MBQR at Qumran, the EPISOKOPOS in the Athenian Empire, and the Meaning of LBQR in Ezra 7:14: On the Relation of Ezra's Mission to the Persian Legal Project. *JBL* 120: 623–46.
Tadmor, H.
1962   Chronology. Pp. 245–310 in vol. 4 of *Encyclopedia Biblica,* ed. B. Mazar et al. Jerusalem. [Hebrew]
Talmon, S.
2001   "Exile" and "Restoration" in the Conceptual World of Ancient Judaism. Pp. 107–46 in *Restoration: Old Testament, Jewish and Christian Perspectives,* ed. J. M. Scott. Leiden.
VanderKam, J. C.
1991   Jewish High Priests in the Persian Period: Is the List Complete? Pp. 67–91 in *Priesthood and Cult in Ancient Israel,* ed. G. A. Anderson and S. M. Olyan. JSOTSup 125. Sheffield.

1992 Ezra–Nehemiah or Ezra and Nehemiah? Pp. 55–75 in *Priests, Prophets and Scribes: Essays on the Formation and Heritage of Second Temple Judaism in Honour of Joseph Blenkinsopp*, ed. E. Ulrich et al. JSOTSup 149. Sheffield.

Widengren, G.
1977 The Persian Period. Pp. 489–538 in *Israelite and Judean History*, ed. J. H. Hayes and J. M. Miller. London.

Williamson, H. G. M.
1983 The Composition of Ezra i–vi. *JTS* 34: 1–30.
1985 *Ezra, Nehemiah*. WBC. Waco, Texas.

The Missions of Ezra and Nehemiah

TAMARA COHN ESKENAZI

Hebrew Union College—Jewish Institute of Religion, Los Angeles

Newer interpretations of Ezra–Nehemiah increasingly supplement, and in some cases supplant, earlier interpretations of the missions of Ezra and Nehemiah. This is especially true regarding the assessment of priestly and Persian vested interests. My essay explores this subject by building on the contributions made by a number of new studies of Ezra–Nehemiah (= EN). Reviewing EN's own presentation of events (including its vocabulary) and examining material from Classical Athens, this essay (among other things) challenges views of Persian and priestly interests as *the* driving force behind the missions of Ezra and Nehemiah.

My thesis in a nutshell is this: Ezra–Nehemiah, like some writers in Periclean Athens, is concerned with a form of citizenship rights. The preoccupation with so-called mixed marriage in both communities is a product of new social structures that emerge in both societies, with Deuteronomy as the newly defining framework, even polity,[1] for EN and Judah. The issues expressed through these marriage laws are unique to Periclean Athens and EN in the fifth century. The wealth of evidence from this era shows no parallels in other groups under Persian control. Therefore, it is not useful to look for the impetus for these reforms in the Persian royal court. Class conflicts play a role, but not as J. L. Berquist (1995) and others envision it, with Ezra and Nehemiah supporting the priestly and aristocratic elite. Instead, Ezra's and Nehemiah's efforts suggest a challenge to these elite groups.

Aspects of these claims are by no means original. Some elements in my essay can be construed as a return to earlier scholarly positions. But a reiteration of these possibilities is necessary in the wake of Peter Frei's seminal articles on Persian authorization of the Torah (Frei 1984; 2nd ed., 1996: 8–131).[2] Moreover, I trust that I bring to bear certain

---

1. On Deuteronomy as polity, see McBride 1987: 229–44. See also Steiner 2001.
2. See also Frei's later reformulation (2001: 5–40).

arguments and evidence that have not been used previously in quite this manner.

A number of studies propose or presume (on the basis of Frei's articles) that Ezra and Nehemiah, and even the Torah itself, functioned primarily as instruments of Persian control (Frei 2001).[3] Some also suggest that these reformers represent the collaboration of priests and other elites for the benefit of the Empire. J. Berquist, for example, writes regarding Ezra and Nehemiah (both of whom, he claims, were governors) that: "Whatever their differences, they were both politicians with responsibility for governing the province to keep it in line with Persian interests. . . . Artaxerxes I sent Ezra *to enforce the law of the Persian Empire and also to provide helpful service to the temple.*"[4]

The recent reevaluation of Frei's original thesis resulted in a compelling critique of Frei's premises and conclusions, drastically weakening his position. Thus Watts summarizes the book that contains responses to Frei's thesis as follows:

> Taken together, these articles suggest that the available evidence will not support Frei's comparison of Persian policy with modern federal arrangements governing the relationships between local and national governments. The examples of Persian influence on local laws seem too diverse and sporadic to be the product of a systematic "federal" policy. Nevertheless, the extant evidence does show some Persian involvement in local legal affairs.[5]

Taking the form of an alternate construction of certain events in Judah, the present essay is another, indirect critique of views of Frei and others, such as Berquist.

Describing Judaism in the first century, Seth Schwartz writes in his *Imperialism and Jewish Society* that the "ideological complex . . . God-Temple-Torah, was symbolically central in the Palestinian Judaism of the first century" (Schwartz 2001: 49). He rightly insists, however, that "the centrality of Temple and Torah in ancient Jewish self-definition requires argumentation because it is not a priori an eternal truth of Jewish identity, uncontingent on changing social and political conditions. Rather, it was the result of a long and obscure series of historical processes" (pp. 50–51).

---

3. For some evidence of influential discussions, see, for example, works cited in Watts 2001: 1 n. 2.

4. Berquist 1995: 10; emphasis added.

5. Watts 2001: 3.

EN presents Ezra and Nehemiah as pivotal figures in this "series of historical processes" and attributes some specific achievements to them. An analysis of historical conditions suggests that this representation in general is supportable, given what we do know about the era. Ezra's achievements according to EN can be described as the establishment of such a community around the axis of God-Temple-Torah, one that defines itself according to the Torah. The earlier returnees had built the temple and recreated a context as well as a focus for renewed identity and worship for the people of Israel. In building the temple, Israel joined other nations who had their distinct shrines and traditions under the umbrella of the Persian overlords. But under Ezra's guidance, Judahites and exiles become Jews, to use S. J. D. Cohen's terminology (Cohen 1999).[6] According to Cohen, the word *Judahites* defines people's identity on the basis of biology and geography; the word *Jews* defines Israelites on the basis of deliberate dedication to Israel's God and the Torah.[7] A key to this newly revised identity for EN is separation from other groups. This position contrasts with the requirement that the "other" be eradicated (the model propagated by the book of Joshua) as well as with advocacy of socioreligious affiliation or intermingling with "the other" (the view held apparently by Ezra's opponents in fifth-century Judah).[8]

---

6. Cohen devotes a full chapter in *The Beginnings of Jewishness: Boundaries, Varieties, Uncertainties* (1999) to distinguishing among various terms. His major claim is that *Judean* (the term used in the Hellensitic Period, analogous to *Judahite* in the Persian Period) is an "ethnic geographic term" (p. 104). It refers to "those who hailed originally from the ethnic homeland" (p. 104). "In contrast, 'Jew' (at least in English) is a religious term: a Jew is someone who venerates the God of the Judaeans, the God whose temple is in Jerusalem. . . . 'Jew' then, denotes culture, way of life, or 'religion,' not ethnic or geographic origin" (p. 105).

7. As Cohen observes, "Greek *Ioudaios*, Latin *Iudaeus*, and Hebrew *Yehudi* are almost always translated as 'Jews,' but in all occurrences of the term before the end of the second century B.C.E. this translation is wrong, because before this point these words always and everywhere mean 'Judaean' not Jew" (Cohen 1999: 104). In EN the term יהודי still has the geographical and/or biological connotations when applied to persons (e.g., Neh 5:1). It is therefore best to translate these occurrences as 'Judahite' or 'Judean'.

8. It is safe to conclude that returning exiles arrived with mixed motives, as is true of immigrants throughout history. Although Ezra 1 describes religious enthusiasm as motive, Haggai and Zechariah show a different preoccupation. Personal gain, economic opportunities, and instability in Babylonia most likely contributed to persons' readiness to traverse the hundreds of miles between Babylonia and Judah. That returnees also had diverse visions of what was to be accomplished is apparent in Isaiah 56–66. Ezra (as depicted in EN) seeks to instill in them a sense of communal obligation and a specific understanding, one in which the Torah plays a specific role.

Nehemiah moves the agenda further, turning a city *with* Jews into a Jewish city, changing a place with Jews into a Jewish place. The book of Deuteronomy serves as the authoritative source for the reforms. In the process that leads to the normativity of Judaism as a God-Temple-Torah axis and to the very categories that eventually persist, key moments belong, then, to the time of Ezra and Nehemiah as they are portrayed in EN. This claim is hardly new, of course, but it does require reiteration in light of recent scholarly tendencies. What I hope is useful and instructive in my presentation are some of the details I bring into view in support of this position.

It is my contention that Ezra's reforms are the beginning of the process of reducing the monopoly of the priests as well as of creating a more egalitarian community. The concern with "mixed" marriages, like the empowering of the Levites, serves to broaden religious and political authority at the expense of priests and other elites. The public role of the Torah serves the same purpose. While acknowledging the priests' sphere of influence, the Torah demystifies their role and authority. Priests cease to be the source of "Torah." Instead, authority becomes vested in a book, and priestly authority becomes derivative. The textualization of the Torah removes authority from the priests and reverses the hierarchy of obedience to God's teachings: with cult legislation now "an open book," priests can be scrutinized by the wider community.[9]

In this version of the essay I concentrate on making three points, developed through attention to Periclean Athens:

1. that the reforms of Ezra and Nehemiah have a specific group in mind as the target;
2. that the opposition to the so-called "mixed marriages" is part and parcel of the formation of more-egalitarian structures;[10]

---

9. Like the majority of scholars working on EN today, I date Ezra's mission to 458. For a balanced discussion of the theories concerning the dates of Ezra and Nehemiah, see Suiter 1992.

10. Whatever the reasons, the opposition to foreign women is not to be confused with simple misogyny. Although certain women are unquestionably victimized by these measures, other women are expected to have benefited from them: the rejection of one category of women as eligible partners protects the position of other women in the community (see, e.g., the plea for remaining faithful to the wife of one's youth in Mal 2:14–16 and its close association with foreign marriages in 2:11). The pressures on new immigrants to marry up and out is well documented in ancient and modern situations. Sympathetic readings of Ezra 9–10 recognize the need to secure partners and families for the women of the new Judahite community in the face of competing possibilities. Such readings consider the opposition to foreign women not simply a misogynistic restriction

3. that the similarities with Classical Athens drastically reduce the likelihood that we must look to the Persian court as an impetus for the reforms.

The Reforms of Ezra and Nehemiah Targeted a Specific Group

It is necessary to consider the attack on marriages as a subterfuge for or a symptom of another issue, namely, a struggle against some specific (male) leaders or a class/group of leaders. Both evidence internal to EN and comparative information from Athens support such a view.

R. Albertz (1994) suggests that the social and economic dynamics in postexilic Judah were more complex than bifurcated models such as those construed by Berquist or P. Hanson. According to Albertz, the priesthood itself was not a monolithic group with unified interests (1994: 464–510). J. Schaper (2000: 226–65) and N.-J. Min (2002), who focus on priests and Levites, offer a somewhat different perspective, although largely compatible with Albertz's. Both Schaper and Min concur that tension between priests and Levites is apparent in the sources. According to Min, EN itself is a Levitical document, at odds on occasion with priestly vested interests. Min documents the progression that moves power from priests to Levites in EN and attributes this representation to Levitical authorship. Schaper suggests that priests' vested interests in Nehemiah's time indeed corresponded with those of the aristocracy but that Nehemiah supported the Levites against the priests. Given these studies and explicit attacks on the priesthood by Nehemiah, such as Neh 13:28–30, the case for Nehemiah's challenge to the priesthood is more readily apparent and available to scholars. The case of Ezra is different and requires further elucidation because Ezra the priest has been more persistently identified as a spokesperson for priestly vested interests.

Several elements support the view that Ezra's reforms, like Nehemiah's, aim at priests and their cohorts and do not, as Berquist argues, primarily support priestly interests. Ezra's recruiting of Levites is a case in point. He not only insures that Levites accompany him in his journey to Jerusalem (Ezra 8:15–19), but he also empowers them and delegates sacred responsibility to them. The Levites thereby serve alongside the priests and in equal measure to them (Ezra 8:24–30). The events in Ezra 9–10 further support this view.

---

but, rather, a defense of the rights of women in the community against outside competition and as a means for maintaining communal cohesiveness and continuity.

The notion of class is introduced in Ezra 9:1–10. Ezra's informants (9:1) include leaders who bring charges, especially against other leaders (9:2). The concern with the priests and the high proportion of cultic personnel among the offenders in Ezra 10 (17 out of 110 or 111) undermine the assumption that the priestly elite are driving Ezra's reforms. To the contrary, the entire process can be seen as a challenge to the elite on the basis of the Torah, with Deuteronomy as the overarching model.

Ezra 9–10 charges only men with exogamy. A number of explanations have been proposed to account for the opposition (see below). In what follows I add to those who emphasize socioeconomic factors by using Periclean Athens to help shed some light on the possibilities.

A specific opposition to priests can be derived from the conclusion of Ezra 10. Trailing a long list of offenders comes the problematic concluding statement:

10:44: כָּל־אֵלֶּה נָשְׂאוּ נָשִׁים נָכְרִיּוֹת וְיֵשׁ מֵהֶם נָשִׁים וַיָּשִׂימוּ בָּנִים׃

All these had married foreign women, and there are from them women who had placed children.[11]

1 Esdras reads instead, "All these had married (συνῴκισαν) foreign women, and they *put them away* with their children (τέκνοις)" (9:36; NRSV; emphasis added). Most English translations replace Ezra 10:44 with the conclusion from 1 Esdras. The NRSV 1994 edition, for example, has this translation for Ezra 10:44: "All these had married foreign women, and they sent them away with their children." The note cross-references 1 Esd 9:36, adding: "Meaning of Heb uncertain."[12] Thus most readers conclude that the women were in fact expelled, even though EN (in both the MT and the LXX) does not quite say this.[13]

---

11. Williamson translates the latter part of the verse as "and some of the women had even borne children." This rendition is among the better ones, and Williamson's note is especially helpful because he adjudicates among alternatives (Williamson 1985: 144–45 n. 44a-a). The JPSV renders it similarly: "among whom were some women who had borne children," adding in a note that the Hebrew is uncertain. However, the verb שׂים or שׂום in the *Hiphil* does not mean 'to bear children' elsewhere. Rather, it means 'to place' or 'put', often in a very concrete sense of placing an object (see, e.g., Gen 9:23), or more abstractly, meaning 'to establish' (Exod 1:11). BDB defines the verb in general as meaning 'put, place, set' (962b). The significance of this translation will become clearer when we discuss the verbs used to indicate matrimony in EN.

12. The Hebrew itself is basically clear. The uncertainty results from an ambiguity regarding the significance of the phrase, not from textual or translation problems.

13. Ezra 9–10 is silent about the fate and circumstances of the women. Marriage agreements, especially among the upper class, entailed the transfer of wealth between families. Marriage agreements from Persian-Period Babylonia and Egypt show that women were

But did all the men in fact divorce their wives? EN surprisingly does not say so, at least not explicitly. *Only the priests of Jeshua's family (i.e., a high priest family) explicitly promise to divorce their wives and bring a guilt-offering* (Ezra 10:18–19)![14] EN may expect readers to infer the same for all others listed. However, in its present form, the MT leaves open the possibility that, while all the relevant cases had been identified, some husbands took no action.[15] The point of the process, then, was to establish communal norms and future practice, with less interest in their immediate implementation, except in the case of these priests.[16]

The emphasis on the cooperation of the priests may reflect priestly concern with establishing and reiterating cultic purity. However, the entire episode may be told in detail in order to show how to exert communal pressure on the priests. In other words, reform of the priesthood may be a central goal of Ezra's reforms in Ezra 9–10 (note also that it marks the climax of Nehemiah's reforms as well according to Nehemiah in Neh 13:29). The concern, then, is not merely about pollution but also about communal power over cultic leaders. EN addresses questions such as the following: How does a community bring about change when those entrusted with teaching the Torah appear to act in violation of it? How does a community compel the leaders to act in accordance with the interests of the community as a whole and in line with the teachings of Deuteronomy? Ezra's behavior in Ezra 9–10 models a successful response to these problems.

Too little attention has been paid to the ways that Ezra's response to the report in Ezra 9:1–2 demonstrates a procedure for redistributing power within the community. However, this emphasis is integral to EN's central concern and the focus of my subsequent remarks in this section.

---

protected against arbitrary dismissal by certain financial arrangements already built into the marriage contract (see Kraeling 1953: #2). It seems probable that, if the women were divorced, economic restitution of some sort was required. Of course it is not likely that these could adequately compensate for the pain inflicted on the women or the men.

14. Note that according to Lev 5:17–18 guilt-offerings were used for inadvertent transgressions. On this point, see also Japhet 1988: 112.

15. For an interesting hypothesis concerning the ritualistic significance of removing "foreign wives" from the community, see Dor 2001. Using a cultural-conceptual interpretation and anthropological studies, Dor suggests that EN is concerned with a ritual separation, at the conclusion of which families nonetheless remained intact.

16. S. Japhet makes an analogous point in her discussion of the Torah in EN: "The focus of the matter is the establishment of a dogmatic stance toward intermarriages, its definition as a sin" (Japhet 1988: 110).

In describing Ezra's actions, the narrative emphasizes communal participation and process. Ezra does not use authority vested in him by biblical tradition (his priestly credentials) or by Persian law (Artaxerxes' letter in Ezra 7:11–26). Instead, he expresses persuasively the nature of the problem and its consequences—as much by behavior as by word—and then awaits the people's reaction. Only when others concur and invite him to take charge (10:1–3) does he assume a leadership role. A full assembly is convened, and procedures for action are devised by this broader constituency (10:4–17).[17]

This process is extremely important to EN's theological and political agenda and has long-lasting consequences. It represents a major step in developing participatory government. In line with Deuteronomy's democratizing tendencies, these measures create communal infrastructures for social and religious life, shifting the balance of power. They also set in motion a new process for communal decision-making and action.

H. Zlotnick-Sivan interprets the conflict in EN as analogous to the tension in Rome between *patria* and *familia*. She speaks of the spectacle in Rome as a revealing analogue to Ezra 9–10.[18] She also highlights the function of spectacles as test cases for assessing a leader and describes the tactics a leader uses to demonstrate his power in such events. Ezra 9–10, in her view, functions similarly, with Ezra manipulating public events.[19] But I suggest that, although both settings illustrate a new role for the public, the goals and results differ sharply. Ezra's reforms aim at consolidating certain strata within the postexilic community, while his goals include consensus-building and a model of citizenship based on deliberate affiliation. He also helps create a community that takes the initiative and does not merely wait for leaders to offer solutions (hence a key difference from Roman spectacles). Attention to what EN lingers upon—the process itself—brings this emphasis into view. The concluding celebration in Nehemiah 8–12, especially 8–10, demonstrates the success of such procedures. In these chapters, the people themselves come to assume responsibility for the religious life and struc-

---

17. For fuller details, see my book on this subject (Eskenazi 1988), especially pp. 136–44.

18. H. Zlotnick-Sivan 2000. One can look back to classical Greece and its conflict between *oikos* and *polis*, expressed, for example, in Sophocles' *Antigone*.

19. Zlotnick-Sivan draws upon Livy, who writes: "For not only the performance of duty draws but also their enthusiasm for the spectacle (*studium spectaculi*), so that they might see the leader to whose power and planning they have entrusted the protection of the state itself" (Livy 42.49.1–6, cited by Zlotnick-Sivan 2000: 7 n. 13).

tures of postexilic Judah; the Torah serves as their authoritative source for praxis.

Parallels with Periclean Athens are instructive in highlighting another aspect of the reforms. As is well known, Aristotle mentions that Pericles' law of 451 requires that a citizen be an offspring of two Athenians (the date itself, some seven years after a probable date for Ezra's arrival in Jerusalem in 458, is intriguing). According to Aristotle, during Pericles' rule, "on account of the large number of citizens it was decided on the proposal of Pericles that a man should not be a member of the citizen body unless both his parents were Athenians."[20]

Eherenberg writes:

> It seems certain that the law was not generally retrospective nor was it immediately put into effect. It seems even more certain that it was directed only against sons of marriages between Athenian men and foreign women (*metroxenoi*); the opposite would hardly occur. It is a curious coincidence that Cimon, who was the son of a foreign mother, had recently returned from exile. Was there a connexion between his return and the new law? Modern views differ. Perhaps it is more important to see how the law fitted into Pericles' democracy. (Eherenberg 1968: 225–26)[21]

Eherenberg further observes that, "In fact, intermarriage with non-Athenian women had been fairly frequent only in the upper classes" (1968: 226). He concludes that the law most likely was "a weapon, or perhaps only the threat of a weapon, *in the internal struggle against the oligarchs*" (p. 226; emphasis added). "In those years, when Pericles was pursuing the most determined policy both at home and abroad, he met with the *strong opposition of the aristocracy; the law on citizenship was most likely directed against them*" (p. 226; emphasis added). I suggest that EN reflects a similar concern, with certain priestly families as an implicit target.

"Mixed Marriages" and More-Egalitarian Structures

Ezra himself directs our attention to land rights as contingent upon endogamy. According to him, marriage with peoples of the land is

---

20. Aristotle, *The Athenian Constitution* (*Athenaion Politeia*, 26.3). For the report about grain distribution and the law of citizenship, see also Philochorus (*FGH* 328 F 119). He reports that grain distribution six years later led to accusations regarding citizenship, and Pericles' law was invoked in the controversies.

21. Although aspects of Eherenberg's analysis have been challenged, and in some cases superseded by newer studies, this point remains standing. I cite him rather than newer publications because he expresses this point succinctly.

dangerous if one seeks to possess and retain the land (Ezra 9:12). Although he presents the problem in theological and cultic terms, one cannot avoid considering the pragmatic, economic, and political aspects of the conflict over land rights. The redistribution of land during the Babylonian era was bound to create conflict between the Judahites who had remained in Judah and the exiles who had returned. If the accounts in Jeremiah are reliable (Jer 39:9–10 and 52:15–16)—and there are good reasons to suppose that they are on this point—class issues played a role: surviving Judahites in the land belonged to the lower classes while the deportees included the elite. Tension between the exiles and those who remained in the land would have been inevitable. Both the biblical texts (Jeremiah, Isaiah, EN) and analyses of patterns of dislocation and repopulation point in this direction. Despite the implicit ideology of an "empty land" lying fallow in its expiating Sabbath rest (so 2 Chr 36:21), archaeological, biblical, and extrabiblical evidence indicates that Judah continued to be inhabited, even if sparsely. Immigrants claiming to repatriate would have encountered their former Judahite neighbors who in the meantime had settled more of the land, as well as persons from other nations that had made incursions into the area (see, for example, Lemaire 1990).

EN does not perpetuate the myth of an empty land (Blenkinsopp 2002 notwithstanding).[22] On the contrary; it makes the problem of populated land a central challenge to be addressed. The question of land rights, expressed in theological, ideological, and political terms, is one of the chief concerns of the book.

A number of scholars offer compelling interpretations of the way that political and economic considerations about land rights account for EN's perspective on marriage. Weinberg (1992), Hoglund (1992), and Smith-Christopher (1994), among others, explain some ways in which communal and national ownership of land was at stake. I also develop this point elsewhere (Eskenazi 1992). The precise nature of land rights is envisioned differently by these scholars; but the underlying consensus is that, from a historical perspective, land is of para-

---

22. There is a lively debate about the population density in Judah and Benjamin in the sixth and fifth centuries B.C.E. For a good review of the various positions, see A. Faust 2003, esp. his "endnote" (pp. 46–47). Faust's archaeological analysis challenges the view advanced, for example, by Berquist (1995: 15–18), that the majority of Judahites in what used to be the kingdom of Judah remained in the land after Jerusalem fell in 586 B.C.E. According to Faust, the data show discontinuity between the Babylonian- and Persian-Period settlements in rural Judah and hence support the view that the population in the rural areas was also drastically reduced in the aftermath of the destruction of the temple.

mount importance in this dispute, even when the rhetoric masks this issue in a theological garb.

Weinberg (1992: 127–38) suggests that more is at stake than conflict over personal property. He infers from the text a particular configuration of national, communal security. According to Weinberg, the defining structure of the newly organized Jewish community was *Bürger-Tempel-Gemeinde* ('Citizens-Temple-Community'), a structure that Dandamaev identifies for temple organizations in Babylonia and for other ANE communities. These socioeconomic units in Babylonia comprised temple personnel and landowners, and functioned as a relatively autonomous economic system accountable to the imperial government.

K. G. Hoglund emphasizes group control of land, with landrights granted only secondarily to individuals who were members in good standing of that group. He uses the model of "dependent populations" to explain the status of the returnees. According to him, the king granted land in Judah to the group as a group. Hoglund finds a clue to such a group structure in the threat of *ḥrm* imposed by the community (Ezra 10:8). Like Weinberg, he argues that ethnicity and religious identity have thus become politically and economically significant for retaining land (see, for example, Hoglund 1992: 234–38). What was at stake was not only religious cohesiveness but actual communal and national ownership of land. These models largely connect the reforms to external patterns and Persian control.

In an earlier article I emphasized women's inheritance rights as a factor in EN's marriage controversies (Eskenazi 1992; 1994). I suggested that a potential loss of land would have played a role if women in Judah could inherit, as did Jewish women in Egypt. If so, then marriages with women not fully integrated into the community would threaten the transfer of land to other groups or communities. The story of Zelophehad's daughters exemplifies the concern over losing communal (tribal) land (see Numbers 36, esp. 36:2–4). A similar concern may be involved here, once men married "foreign" women.

These economic considerations proposed, for example, by Weinberg, Hoglund, and my earlier work, help explain the severity of the opposition to intimacy with the peoples of the land. Yet the case for the connection between landrights and Ezra's reforms in these prior discussions largely depend on indirect or circumstantial evidence, with parallels elsewhere (Babylonia or Egypt) applied to Judah. What has been overlooked is important evidence *in the text*, supporting the position that landrights are preeminently in view in this conflict. As far as

I can tell, scholars have overlooked the way that concern with land in
EN is consistently embedded in the very language of the text.[23] In
other words, the significance of the very terminology used to refer to
marriage has been ignored.

The Hebrew expression that is most telling is obscured in virtually
all English translations. Ezra 10:2, Shecaniah's exhortation of Ezra to
take up leadership, is a case in point. The Hebrew has:

אֲנַחְנוּ מָעַלְנוּ בֵאלֹהֵינוּ וַנֹּשֶׁב נָשִׁים נָכְרִיּוֹת מֵעַמֵּי הָאָרֶץ

Thus Shecaniah says, 'We have trespassed against our God וַנֹּשֶׁב foreign women from the peoples of the land' (10:2). The important word
is וַנֹּשֶׁב. As one can see below, this verb is translated consistently as
forms of 'marry':

> We have broken faith ... and have *married* foreign women (NRSV and
> NEB)

> We have acted faithlessly ... and have *married* foreign women (Blenkin-
> sopp 1988: 186)

> We have been unfaithful ... in *marrying* foreign women (Williamson
> 1985: 139. Williamson adds an explanatory note)

Better but still not sufficiently accurate are the following two translations:

> We have trespassed ... by *bringing into our homes* foreign women (JPSV)

> We ... have *taken* (Koren)

What most English translations render 'married' or 'taken' (here
and in Ezra 10:10, 14, 17, 18, as well as Neh 13:23, 27) is the Hebrew
root ישב in the *Hiphil* form. As is well known, this verb ישב in the *Qal*
refers consistently in the Bible to 'sitting' or 'settling'. The *Hiphil* להושיב
consistently means 'to cause to settle' or 'to set', usually upon the land
(see, e.g., Gen 47:11).

Only *EN persistently uses the verb* ישב *in the Hiphil when referring to
what translators render as 'marriage' (Ezra 10:2, 10, 14, 17, 18; Neh 13:27)!*
Such references are unique to EN, distributed throughout both the Nehemiah Memoir (NM) and Ezra 10. Moreover, only the context in EN
implies that this act, להושיב, might concern taking wives in marriage.
Indeed, the term הושיב is the most common one used in connection with
the foreign women.

---

23. I allude to this evidence in my entry on "Daughters of Judah and Foreign Daugh-
ters/Wives" (Eskenazi 2000). The present essay is the fuller development of that point.

The other examples include Ezra 10:10, where Ezra reiterates the nature of the transgression in 10:10:

(1)　　　וַיָּקָם עֶזְרָא הַכֹּהֵן וַיֹּאמֶר אֲלֵהֶם אַתֶּם מְעַלְתֶּם וַתֹּשִׁיבוּ נָשִׁים נָכְרִיּוֹת לְהוֹסִיף
עַל־אַשְׁמַת יִשְׂרָאֵל:

And Ezra the priest arose and said to them: "You have trespassed וַתֹּשִׁיבוּ foreign women, to add to the guilt of Israel."

Again, in 10:14, the people propose:

(2)　　　יַעֲמְדוּ־נָא שָׂרֵינוּ לְכָל־הַקָּהָל וְכֹל אֲשֶׁר בְּעָרֵינוּ הַהֹשִׁיב נָשִׁים נָכְרִיּוֹת יָבֹא
לְעִתִּים מְזֻמָּנִים

Let our leaders stand for the entire congregation, and everyone in our towns who הַהֹשִׁיב foreign women will come at the appointed time.

In 10:17 and 18 the narrator reports:

(3)　　　וַיְכַלּוּ בַכֹּל אֲנָשִׁים הַהֹשִׁיבוּ נָשִׁים נָכְרִיּוֹת עַד יוֹם אֶחָד לַחֹדֶשׁ

And they concluded with all the men who הַהֹשִׁיבוּ foreign women until the first day of the month.

(4)　　　וַיִּמָּצֵא מִבְּנֵי הַכֹּהֲנִים אֲשֶׁר הֹשִׁיבוּ נָשִׁים נָכְרִיּוֹת

And it was found from among the descendants of the priests who הֹשִׁיבוּ foreign women.

It is very interesting and consequential for a source analysis of EN, especially for the relationship between the NM and the Ezra material, that the same unusual vocabulary is repeated twice in Nehemiah 13, as part of NM (Neh 13:23 and 26–27).

(5)　　　גַּם בַּיָּמִים הָהֵם רָאִיתִי אֶת־הַיְּהוּדִים הֹשִׁיבוּ נָשִׁים אַשְׁדּוֹדִיּוֹת [אַשְׁדָּדִיּוֹת] עַמֳּנִיּוֹת
מוֹאֲבִיּוֹת

Also in those days I saw the Judahites הֹשִׁיבוּ Ashdodite, Ammonite, Moabite women.

(6)　　　וְלָכֶם הֲנִשְׁמַע לַעֲשֹׂת אֵת כָּל־הָרָעָה הַגְּדוֹלָה הַזֹּאת לִמְעֹל בֵּאלֹהֵינוּ לְהֹשִׁיב
נָשִׁים נָכְרִיּוֹת:

And as for you, is it heard of to do all of this great evil, to trespass against our God לְהֹשִׁיב foreign women?

It is not sufficient merely to say, as several interpreters do, that this is postexilic usage, unique to this era. We need to examine what this unique use of a common verb communicates in this particular book, and this book alone.

Since the literal meaning suggests settlement or establishment of persons on the land, this issue is the one apparently foremost in the writer's mind. It is not clear whether the use of the verb in EN is intended literally or metaphorically. If literal, it could refer to specific technical or legal processes involving settling (or settlement). It may mean that marriage already implied ownership of the land by women. Or it could mean that some people, the ones EN opposes, allotted property to such women, perhaps as a part of a marriage contract. In either case, such unions may also entailed legal membership in the social structure of Judah. If metaphorical, then the verb is used to equate marriage itself with the de facto settling of "Canaanites" on the land instead of dispossessing them. Either way, the use of this verb explicitly specifies that an important reason for the opposition to foreign women is concern with settling foreigners on what God intended as land for Israel. The use of the verb וַיָּשִׂימוּ (from שׂוֹם or שִׂים 'to place' or 'to put') in Ezra 10:44 further underscores this point (see n. 16 above). It expresses a preoccupation with establishing foreigners on the land. Doing so is reversing God's plans and promises. Changed demographic conditions make such a concern especially significant in a world transformed by the expansion of the Persian Empire, a time of extensive mobility and of land and people ceasing to be tied together as they had been earlier.[24]

---

24. I do not discuss the notion of *race* in this connection because I do not consider it central to EN's agenda. The notion of familial kinship (Herodotus's "community of blood"; see his *Histories*, 8.144.2) is very much a component of identity in EN, as in most societies in antiquity (Christianity being the exception). It cannot be reduced, however, to a racial designation. Although the reference to the intermingling of the "holy seed" (Ezra 9:2) has been on occasion interpreted as designating racial superiority, it is important to see that in Ezra 7–10 holiness is not an inherent category; "holiness" is not something that can be transmitted biologically or genetically. The only other occurrence of the term "holy seed," namely, in MT Isa 6:13, is also devoid of what might be called "racial" connotations. The central notion is of a remnant in the face of widespread destruction, with an emphasis on smallness and vulnerability, as well as potential for growth. Holiness is an acquired trait, determined by dedication, not origin. Thus the personnel and vessels in Ezra 8:28 *become* holy when they are dedicated to the service of God. Ezra's informants allege loss of devotion, not loss of genetic purity. The same idea with a different vocabulary recurs in Nehemiah's objection to foreign wives (Neh 13:25–27). As for "intermingling" in Ezra 9:2, the term refers to association with other nations at the risk of imitating their religious practices in Ps 106:34. The same idea appears unmistakably also in 2 Kgs 18:23, where it means "to make a deal." Both these senses account for its meaning in Ezra 9:2: the informants are concerned with improper association and dealings with "the peoples of the lands," not with biological criteria. Indeed, some of the opponents of Ezra's reforms have strong genealogical credentials. One of EN's points is that such credentials are not sufficient. For others who also reject racial interpretation, see Hoglund 1992: 232; Williamson 1885: 132; Smith-Christopher 1994: 247–55.

In drawing attention to the unique way that EN employs the verb יָשַׁב that elsewhere means 'to settle' or 'establish', I am not importing something new into the text of EN. Rather, I advise caution about construing this verb as 'marry' without examining the reasons why EN does not use other common words for marriage. Terms such as "give" and "take" and the verb נָשָׂא that eventually becomes the familiar term for marriage appear in Ezra 7–10 (see, e.g., Ezra 9:12). Indeed, the verb נָשָׂא, which can be read as 'lifted' or 'supported' (see Ezra 1:4), appears both at the beginning (Ezra 9:2) and the end (Ezra 10:44) of the episode about problem marriages.[25] The availability of this and other terms throws into even sharper relief the polemical insistence on the unusual term 'to settle'.[26]

In her monograph on Pericles' law of citizenship, Cynthia Patterson observes that Pericles promoted large-scale participation of Athenians in the city's institutions (1981: 94–95). While many interpreters assume that Pericles' law is about marriage, Patterson argues that it is, rather, about citizenship. "The Athenians were now a closed 'familial' group; 'adoption' was possible only on the decision of the group as a whole. . . . It does not say that only those born of two Athenian parents are legitimate or can inherit property, but that only they will 'have a share in the *city.*' It is a public, 'state,' criterion for public status" (Patterson 1981: 130; Patterson's emphasis).

"The law is only one piece of a larger development, the emergence of a public status of being an Athenian" (Patterson 1981: 115). Midcentury was a time of intense development of the Athenian *polis*, both in the physical and institutional sense (Patterson 1981: 114). Development of an urban civic center and of civic institutions entailed the broadening of the base of participation in the drive for a cohesive city.

---

25. The shift in vocabulary in Ezra 9:12 between "giving" daughters to foreigners' sons and 'lifting up' (וּנְשָׂאתֶם) foreigners' daughters may imply an understanding of marriage with a member of the community as a step up. I am suggesting that the general use of נָשָׂא for marriage embodies an interpretation of this union as an elevation of the woman. In EN it may stand for improperly elevating "people of the land."

26. Although all dictionaries and concordances, to my knowledge, consider the reference to הוֹשִׁיב in these instances in EN to be the *Hiphil* of יָשַׁב, nevertheless the characteristic *waw* of the *Hiphil* does not appear in any of these references. David Noel Freedman suggested (in private correspondence) that the root may not be יָשַׁב but שׁוּב. A relevant example is the case in Ps 23:6 (on Ps 23:6, see his article "The Twenty-Third Psalm," Freedman 1980: 298–300). Freedman does not contest the meaning 'to settle' or 'to sit' (in either place). One may note that the *Hiphil* of יָשַׁב in a defective form (as is EN's also) appears in 2 Kgs 17:16, 24 and Jer 32:37. More often, however, the *plene* spelling is used in late texts (see Isa 64:3 and Zech 10:6). The verb יָשַׁב in the *Hiphil* appears twice in Chronicles (2 Chr 8:2 and 23:20), where it definitely pertains to settling or establishing.

The language in the Greek records is interesting, especially Aristotle's and others' expression "to have a share in the city" (Patterson 1981: 135)—a parallel to the expression used in Hebrew by Nehemiah against Sanballat and Tobiah (Neh 2:20). Also interesting is the fact that while the law fell into disuse, its reinstatement in 403 corresponded with the restoration of democracy. Alongside these developments one should observe the codification of the laws of Solon in 410 and the new stature for written codes. The law quoted by Andocides (1.85.87) has it "that magistrates should not use an unwritten law" as the only authoritative legal tradition at that time (Patterson 1981: 145).

I trust that the discussion of Athenian reforms sufficiently hints at how developments in Judah can be construed.[27] Deuteronomy redistributes power and decentralizes authority. It is probably an overstatement to suggest, as Dean McBride does, that Deuteronomy is a model for democracy, since officials were not elected.[28] Nevertheless, the redistribution of power and responsibility is at work in EN, with Deuteronomy as the overarching "constitution."[29]

Similarities with Athens versus
Similarities with the Persian Court

To what extent did the episode concerning marriage with foreign wives reflect Achaemenid policies? Blenkinsopp concludes that it did not. Indeed, the uproar generated by Ezra's activities led, according to Blenkinsopp, to his recall (Blenkinsopp 1988: 200–201). On the other

---

27. Let me make clear that my point is made in full awareness of the fundamental differences between Athens and Jerusalem at this juncture. The similarities I pursue are striking precisely because of these basic differences. For other examinations of the relation between fifth-century Athens and Jerusalem, see R. J. Littman (1995) and the earlier essay by F. M. Heichlheim (1951). A great deal of attention has been bestowed on the relationship between these two communities during the Hellenistic Period. The light that the two communities shed on each in the fifth century B.C.E. deserves more exploration. An important work in this area is D. B. Small 1995.

28. See Schwartz's chapter on "Hellenization and Democratization" (Schwartz 2001: 12–14), in which he questions the appropriateness of the term to Jewish communities in antiquity.

29. Schwartz writes concerning pre-70 Jewish society that "it would not be an exaggeration to say that the Torah was the constitution of the Jews of Palestine" (Schwartz 2001: 56). As Japhet points out, the "democratizing" elements appeared in EN earlier: "We have seen that the narrative in Ezra 1–6 is formed along the line of 'democraziation,' attempting to moderate the role of individual leaders and to describe the whole people, with its representatives, as the historical protagonist" (Japhet 1983: 218–29).

hand, both Smith-Christopher and Hoglund see the issue as intimately related to the Persian government, but they each interpret the situation along sharply differing lines. According to Smith-Christopher, mixed marriages were supported and encouraged by Persian rulers as part of colonizing other regions. He therefore interprets the resistance to foreign marriages in Ezra 9–10 as one of several gestures of Judean resistance to foreign control (Smith-Christopher 1994: 243–65). Hoglund, on the other hand, sees Ezra's mission from the start as establishing community boundaries for the sake of Achaemenid administrative policies. He uses the example of "dependent population" to argue that the Persian administration needed community boundaries in order to determine which group was to be governed by which indigenous traditions. The ban against mixed marriages that Ezra endorsed was, according to this interpretation, primarily enforcing Persian imperial agenda (Hoglund 1992: 241–47).

The parallels to fifth-century Athens imply that we need not explain Ezra's reforms in terms of the vested interests of the Persian imperial court, as Hoglund, Berquist, and others suggest. Athens, after all, was not subject to Persian control. Indeed, its rise to power was due largely to resistance to Persian control. It is therefore necessary to examine other factors operating in Judah and its environs. I have suggested a number of these factors above.

Conflict over "mixed" marriages is part and parcel of "identity crisis," although such terminology should not be construed in a modern, individual, existential, or psychological sense. It concerns citizenship and the political, economic, and social privileges that accompanied citizenship in the fifth century B.C.E. Shared concerns about "mixed" marriages in Athens and Judah, as well as the absence of such concerns in Mesopotamia and Egypt, may reflect shared concern with new political structures for community.

Monarchic structures made such questions less significant. But the rise of democracy in Athens caused questions of citizenship to become a much-contested subject (see Davies 1977: 105–21). I suggest that one reason for the conflict over marriages and membership in the community emerging in Judah is that a more-participatory social structure, à la Deuteronomy, is being implemented by Ezra, Nehemiah, and their supporters. John K. Davies describes decades of fierce battles in Athenian legal and political circles precisely over this issue (Davies 1977). One important factor in this battle, then, was the need to establish boundaries for internal governance.

Ezra 10 illustrates such a role when describing the formal assembly that is convened and that then legislates, or at least ratifies, decisions under Ezra's leadership and influence. Nehemiah 10 depicts an even greater formality and assigns greater authority to this communally representative body.

EN claims that the missions of Ezra and Nehemiah originated with these two individuals who then successfully solicited royal support (Ezra 7:6 states that the king gave Ezra whatever he asked for; Nehemiah 2 describes how Nehemiah received his commission). The probability of initiative from such individuals is supported by other cases in EN, which show that imperial attention to Judah/Yehud was typically reactive, not proactive. I reiterate that these descriptions seem consistent with the fact that Judah, though important to biblical writers, was, from an imperial perspective, statistically insignificant. That Judah would have been largely off the imperial "radar screen" is evident from historians such as Herodotus, who ignores it. The silence in non-Jewish accounts of Alexander's conquest also suggests that this backwater province was not of great importance.[30]

There can be no doubt that Persian authorization was required for any of these events to transpire and that value to the Empire would have been an important feature of any authorized reforms. Anyone receiving imperial authorization would have had to make a case in terms of Persian vested interests. Stability and loyalty would have been part of Ezra's value to the Empire, especially in 458 B.C.E.; greater economic prosperity (hence more taxes) would have been Nehemiah's.[31] But recognizing these advantages to the Persian court does not mitigate against the prior concern that EN articulates: reconstructing life in Judah on a new, hitherto untested, basis of actual adherence to Deuteronomy.

---

30. On Alexander's conquest, see Schwartz 2001: 25–26.

31. There has been a scholarly tendency to attribute military goals to Nehemiah's mission (see, e.g., Hoglund, who interprets the fifth-century fortresses in the region as an aspect of such military strategy in his *Achaemenid Imperial Administration*). The Peace of Callias in 450–449, which formally ended the Persian Wars, most likely changed Persian strategies for the region. It seems to me more likely that the fortresses that Hoglund describes (structures too small to be serious military defenses) were outposts to protect commercial routes and the transfer of taxes rather than to protect the borders from enemies. Nehemiah asks to build Jerusalem. His efforts aim at socioeconomic renewal and revitalization of the city. Urban prosperity serves imperial interests in that it produces taxes. For an economic perspective on Nehemiah's tactics, see J. A. Friedman, "Theology and Economics: Nehemiah's Reform and the Reconstruction of Judah in the Post-Exilic Period" (1999). Friedman uses economic theories to show the fiscal benefits of Nehemiah's reforms.

Bibliography

Albertz, R.
1994   *From the Exile to the Maccabees.* Vol. 2 of *A History of Israelite Religion in the Old Testament Period.* OTL. Louisville: Westminster John Knox.

Berquist, J. L.
1995   *Judaism in Persia's Shadow: A Social and Historical Approach.* Minneapolis: Fortress.

Blenkinsopp, J.
1988   *Ezra–Nehemiah.* OTL. Philadelphia: Westminster.
2002   The Bible, Archaeology and Politics; or The Empty Land Revisited. *JSOT* 27/2: 169–87.

Cohen, S. J. D.
1999   *The Beginnings of Jewishness: Boundaries, Varieties, Uncertainties.* Berkeley: University of California Press.

Davies, J. K.
1977   Athenian Citizenship: The Descent Group and the Alternatives. *Classical Journal* 73: 105–21.

Davies, P.
1992   *In Search of "Ancient Israel."* JSOTSup 148. Sheffield: Sheffield Academic Press.

Dor, Y.
2001   *The Theme of the Foreign Women in Ezra–Nehemiah.* Ph.D. dissertation. Hebrew University of Jerusalem.

Ehrenberg, V.
1968   *From Solon to Socrates: Greek History and Civilization during the 6th and 5th centuries* BC. London: Methuen.

Eskenazi, T. C.
1988   *In an Age of Prose: A Literary Approach to Ezra–Nehemiah.* SBLMS 36. Atlanta: Scholars Press.
1992   Out from the Shadows: Biblical Women in the Post-Exilic Era. *JSOT* 54: 25–43. Reprinted pp. 252–71 in *A Feminist Companion to Samuel and Kings,* ed. A. Brenner. The Feminist Companion to the Bible 5. Sheffield: Sheffield Academic Press.
2000   Daughters of Judah and Foreign Daughters/Wives. Pp. 285–86 in *Women in Scripture,* ed. Carol Meyers. Boston: Houghton Mifflin.

Eskenazi, T. C., and Richards, K. H. (eds.)
1994   *Second Temple Studies 2: Temple and Community in the Persian Period.* JSOTSup 175. Sheffield: Sheffield Academic Press.

Faust, A.
2003   Judah in the Sixth Century B.C.E.: A Rural Perspective. *PEQ* 135: 37–53.

Freedman, D. N.
1980   The Twenty-Third Psalm. Pp. 275–302 in *Pottery, Poetry, and Prophecy: Studies in Early Hebrew Poetry.* Winona Lake, Indiana: Eisenbrauns.

Frei, P.
1996 Zentralgewalt und Lokalautonomie im Achämenidenreich. Pp. 8–131 in *Reichsidee und Reichsorganisation im Perserreich*, ed. P. Frei and K. Koch. OBO 55. 2nd ed. Freiburg: Universitätsverlag. [1st ed., 1984]
2001 Persian Imperial Authorization: A Summary. Pp. 5–40 in *Persia and Torah: The Theory of Imperial Authorization of the Pentateuch*, ed. J. W. Watts. SBLSymS 17. Atlanta: Society of Biblical Literature.

Friedman, J. A.
1999 Theology and Economics: Nehemiah's Reform and the Reconstruction of Judah in the Post-Exilic Period. Unpublished paper presented at the SBL Annual Meeting, Boston.

Hanson, P. D.
1987 Israelite Religion in the Early Postexilic Period. Pp. 485–508 in *Essays in Honor of Frank Moore Cross: Ancient Israelite Religion*, ed. P. D. Miller, P. D. Hanson, and S. D. McBride. Philadelphia: Fortress.

Heichlheim, F. M.
1951 Ezra's Palestine and Periclean Athens. *Zeitschrift für Religions und Geistesgeschichte* 3: 251–53.

Hoglund, K. G.
1992 *Achaemenid Imperial Administration in Syria–Palestine and the Missions of Ezra and Nehemiah*. SBLDS 125. Atlanta: Scholars Press.

Janzen, D.
2000 The "Mission" of Ezra and the Persian-Period Temple Community. *JBL* 119: 619–43.

Japhet, S.
1983 Sheshbazzar and Zerubbabel Against the Background of the Historical and Religious Tendencies of Ezra–Nehemiah. *ZAW* 95: 218–29.
1988 Law and "The Law" in Ezra–Nehemiah. Pp. 99–115 in *Proceedings of the Ninth World Congress of Jewish Studies, Panel Session: Bible Studies and Ancient Near East*. Jerusalem: Magnes.

Kraeling, E. G. H. (ed.)
1953 *The Brooklyn Museum Aramaic Papyri: New Documents of the Fifth Century B.C. from the Jewish Colony at Elephantine*. New Haven: Yale University Press.

Lemaire, A.
2003 Populations et territoires de la Palestine à l'époque perse. *Transeuphratène* 3: 31–74.

Lipschits, O.
2003 Demographic Changes in Judah between the Seventh and the Fifth Century B.C.E. Pp. 323–76 in *Judah and the Judeans in the Neo-Babylonian Period*, ed. O. Lipschits and J. Blenkinsopp. Winona Lake, Indiana: Eisenbrauns.

Lipschits, O., and Blenkinsopp, J. (eds.)
2003 *Judah and the Judeans in the Neo-Babylonian Period*. Winona Lake, Indiana: Eisenbrauns.

Littman, R. J.
1995 Athens, Persia and the Book of Ezra. *TAPA* 125: 251–59.

McBride, S. D., Jr.
   1987   Polity of the Covenant People: The Book of Deuteronomy. *Int* 41/3:
          229–44. [Reprinted: Pp. 17–33 in *Constituting the Community: Studies on
          the Polity of Ancient Israel in Honor of S. Dean McBride Jr.* (ed. John T.
          Strong and Steven S. Tuell; Winona Lake, Indiana: Eisenbrauns,
          2005).]
Min, N.-J.
   2002   *The Levitical Authorship of Ezra–Nehemiah.* Ph.D. dissertation. Univer-
          sity of Durham.
Patterson, C.
   1981   *Pericles Citizenship Law of 451–50 b.c.* Monographs in Classical Studies.
          New York: Arno.
Schaper, J.
   2000   *Priester und Leviten im achämenidischen Juda.* Forschungen zum Alten
          Testament 31. Tübingen: Mohr Siebeck.
Schwartz, S.
   2001   *Imperialism and Jewish Society: 200 b.c.e. to 640 c.e.* Princeton: Princeton
          University Press.
Small, D. S. (ed.)
   1994   *Methods in the Mediterranean: Historical and Archaeological Views on Texts
          and Archaeology.* Leiden: Brill.
Smith-Christopher, D.
   1994   The Mixed Marriage Crisis in Ezra 9–10 and Nehemiah 13: A Study of
          the Sociology of Post-Exilic Judaean Community. Pp. 243–65 in *Second
          Temple Studies 2: Temple Community in the Persian Period*, ed. T. C. Es-
          kenazi and K. H. Richards. JSOTSup 175. Sheffield: Sheffield Aca-
          demic Press.
Steiner, R. C.
   2001   The *mbqr* at Qumran, the *episkopos* in the Athenian Empire, and the
          Meaning of *lbqr'* in Ezra 7:14: On the relation of Ezra's Mission to the
          Persian Legal Project. *JBL* 120: 623–46.
Suiter, D.
   1992   *The Contribution of Chronological Studies for Understanding Ezra–Nehe-
          miah.* Ph.D. dissertation. Iliff School of Theology and the University of
          Denver.
Watts, J. W. (ed.)
   2001   *Persia and Torah: The Theory of Imperial Authorization of the Pentateuch.*
          SBLSymS 17. Atlanta: Society of Biblical Literature.
Weinberg, J.
   1992   The Postexilic Citizen-Temple Community: Theory and Reality. Pp.
          127–38 in *The Citizen-Temple Community.* JSOTSup 151. Sheffield: Shef-
          field Academic Press.
Williamson, H. G. M.
   1985   *Ezra, Nehemiah.* WBC 16. Waco, Texas: Word.
Zlotnick-Sivan, H.
   2000   The Silent Women of Yehud: Notes on Ezra 9–10. *JJS* 51/1: 3–18.

The "Persian Documents" in the Book of Ezra: Are They Authentic?

LESTER L. GRABBE

University of Hull, England

If the "Persian documents" of Ezra were to appear as previously un-known texts on the antiquities market today, they would be promptly labeled Hellenistic forgeries. No text from the Achaemenid Period looks like them in language, orthography, or epistolary style. Yet the texts have been widely accepted as authentic in recent English-language scholarship.[1] This has not necessarily been the case in German-language scholarship, where the authenticity has often been doubted.[2] I called for the question to be reopened almost fifteen years ago and prepared a preliminary study that has been summarized in several publications but not published in full.[3]

In the present essay, I aim to put my argument in a fuller form. The documents to be examined are:

Author's note: I wish to thank Dr. Oded Lipschits, who kindly invited me to give a paper at this conference and to participants for their comments on it. Professor Bezalel Porten graciously provided a copy of his essay from the Baruch Levine Festschrift. Professors Stephan Kaufman, Jan Willem van Henten, and Mark Geller commented on an earlier draft of my paper, for which I am grateful. Professor Philip Davies kindly invited me to present an early draft to a seminar in the Department of Biblical Studies at Sheffield. This does not imply the agreement of these individuals with the conclusions of this essay or any particular point in it.

1. For a sampling of opinion, see Batten 1913; Myers 1965; Widengren 1977: 496–97; Clines 1984; Williamson 1985; Porten 1978–79; 1983; 2002; 2003; cf. also Blenkinsopp 1989, though his opinion is much more nuanced. An exception was, of course, Torrey (1896; 1970), who denounced them as late "pseudepigraphs."

2. See, for example, Gunneweg 1985; Lebram 1987. An exception to this is Rudolph (1949), who accepts them as genuine and, most important, Meyer (1896: 8–71), who was possibly the first to make a case for their authenticity (cf. Schaeder 1930a, 1930b).

3. I raised the issue in a paper read in the summer of 1990 (published as Grabbe 1991). A call for the question to be thoroughly investigated, with a summary of some of the main issues, was made in my *Judaism from Cyrus to Hadrian* (Grabbe 1992: 32–36). The preliminary study was presented orally to the Aramaic Section at the Society of Biblical Literature annual meeting in San Francisco, November 1992.

- the (Hebrew) decree of Cyrus (Ezra 1:2–4)
- the letter to Artaxerxes (Ezra 4:8–16)
- the reply of Artaxerxes (Ezra 4:17–22)
- the letter of Tattenai and Shethar-bozenai to Darius (Ezra 5:7–17)
- the (Aramaic) decree of Cyrus (Ezra 6:2–5)
- the reply of Darius (Ezra 6:6–12)
- the decree of Artaxerxes to Ezra (Ezra 7:12–26)

Although a monograph could easily be devoted to the question, I hope that this study will encompass most of the main issues of relevance to the question.

General Issues Relevant to Judging Authenticity

Four points will be considered preliminary to looking at the specific texts. They constitute general issues important for evaluating the documents themselves that need to be kept in mind throughout the detailed study.

Parallel Documents for Purposes of Comparison

We are fortunate in possessing a great many Persian documents in readily accessible editions at the present time. Nevertheless, the problem is greater than it might appear at first sight. For parallel documents we have some letters by Persian officials: in Aramaic is the Arsames correspondence;[4] we also have some material in Egyptian.[5] Five of the seven alleged official Persian documents of Ezra are royal decrees, four of them in Aramaic. When it comes to Persian royal decrees, we have the Cyrus Cylinder in Akkadian;[6] the Behistun inscription in Persian and Elamite, as well as translations;[7] and a letter of Xerxes in Greek in Thucydides, which is of doubtful authenticity.[8] Other alleged royal decrees in Greek are inauthentic, such as some documents in Herodotus[9] and the Gadatas inscription.[10] It is very im-

---

4. Driver 1957 = *TAD* A6.1–16.
5. Hughes 1984: 75–86; Spiegelberg 1928: 604–22.
6. See especially Berger 1975; Schaudig 2001: 550–56.
7. It is debatable whether the original was the Persian or the Elamite version. For the Persian text, see Kent 1953. The Elamite text is given in transliteration in Weissbach 1911. The Babylonian text is given by von Voigtlander 1978. Fragments of an Aramaic version are edited by Greenfield and Porten 1982.
8. Thucydides 1.128–29. Olmstead (1933) accepted it as authentic, but Briant (2003: 120 n. 55) questions it.
9. This includes the letters in Herodotus 1.123; 3.40, 128; 5.14, 35; 6.4; 7.239; 8.22, 128. See further van den Hout 1949: 19–41, 138–53.
10. For a discussion, see below (p. 539).

portant to recognize that *we have not a single document in Aramaic to compare with the four alleged Aramaic royal decrees in Ezra.* Thus, to demonstrate the genuine or nongenuine nature of these alleged Persian documents is made much more difficult.

Language of the Ezra Documents

If the Aramaic passages in Ezra are taken as they stand, from a linguistic point of view they are almost certainly not from the Achaemenid Period, just based on the orthography alone. For example, the documents of Ezra all use די as the relative pronoun and sign of the genitive. There are only a few sporadic uses of די in any documents from the Achaemenid Period,[11] and no known document from the Persian administration has anything but זי.[12] The inescapable conclusion is that if these are Persian-Period documents, copyists have systematically "updated" the orthography so that no examples of זי and other pronouns with ז remain. If so, the question then is whether other scribal interventions were made or, alternatively, whether the documents were not written in Achaemenid times in the first place but at a later time when the orthography had changed. Yet when the Aramaic of the Greek Period (that is, Standard Literary Aramaic,[13] such as we find in Daniel) is examined, the language of the Ezra documents definitely looks earlier.

What we must keep in mind is a basic principle: *early forms can occur in late texts, but late forms cannot occur in early texts.* We can find many parallels to the language of the Ezra documents in Achaemenid texts, but many of these continued into Standard Literary Aramic. Therefore, my examination, while far from exhaustive, will focus on some obvious features that distinguish Imperial Aramaic from what is now frequently referred to as Middle Aramaic:[14]

---

11. E.g., *TAD* B2.7:7, 11, 16 = Cowley 1913: 13.7, 11, 16; *TAD* B3.4:12; B3.12:30, 31 = Kraeling 1953: 3.12; 12.30, 31. These few occurrences are in documents that normally and overwhelming use the זי orthography.

12. We are of course dealing with the orthography, not necessarily the pronunciation. The Proto-Semitic *ḏ* was probably pronounced [d] in some dialects by this time, though not necessarily all (cf. Folmer 1995: 62–63). In any case, professional scribes seem to have changed the orthography only gradually.

13. This term was coined by J. C. Greenfield (1974: 280–89). It is the successor to Imperial Aramaic and tends to have many of the latter's characteristics.

14. This term comes from the scheme of Fitzmyer (1979), who divides the phases of Aramaic into Old Aramaic, Official (Imperial) Aramaic, Middle Aramaic, and Later Aramaic. He begins Middle Aramaic only about 200 B.C.E., whereas I would argue that the language of the Ezra framework and Daniel is already Middle Aramaic, or at least has many of the features of Middle Aramaic.

- the 2nd-person plural pronominal suffixes
- the 3rd-person plural pronominal suffixes
- some other grammatical features and characteristic vocabulary
- the Persian loanwords[15]

In all official Achaemenid documents known so far, the 2nd- and 3rd-person plural pronouns are consistently כם- and הם-. In Middle Aramaic (such as Daniel), however, we find consistently כון- and הון-. The latter forms (though with defective spelling) are also found sporadically in material from Persian Egypt,[16] but they mostly occur in texts that represent a Syrian form of the language.[17]

Epistolary Formulas

Several studies by B. Porten (1978–79; 1983) have mentioned the epistolary formulas of the Ezra letters, but until recently no thorough study had been done. Now a detailed investigation of the epistolary formulas has been made by Dirk Schwiderski (2000). He surveyed the Hebrew and Canaanite letters from the ninth century on, letters in Early and Official (Imperial) Aramaic, and Hebrew and Aramaic letters from the Hellenistic Period (along with Greek parallels). He then used the results of this study to compare with the letters in Ezra to see where they fitted in the diachronic development of the epistolary formulas. It should be noted that he does not deal with the Hebrew Cyrus decree of Ezra 1:2–4 or the "memorandum" of Ezra 6:2–5. In the investigation of the individual documents below, the details of Schwiderski's study will be given.

The Persian Policy toward Temples and Cults

It has often been asserted that the Persian government promoted local cults.[18] While the Persians were generally tolerant of local cults, this was also the case with the Assyrians and Babylonians. The Persian attitude was not generally different from their predecessors, and sup-

---

15. The study of loanwords in this paper depends primarily on the data and references found in Koehler and Baumgartner 2001.

16. Especially in the Hermopolis Papyri, e.g., 1.3; 2.10; 5.9 = *TAD* A2.2:10; A2.3:3; A2.5:9; also Cowley 1923: 16.4; 34.6–7; 37.4, 14 = *TAD* A4.2:4, 14; A4.4:6–7; A5.2:4; Kraeling 1953: 12.19, 21 = *TAD* B3.12:19, 21. It should be noted that these are usually spelled כן- and הן- (i.e., without the vowel letter *waw* that is normal in Standard Literary Aramaic). The plene forms are not documented before the third century B.C.E. (Muraoka and Porten 1998: 53–54).

17. See E. Y. Kutscher 1971: 109.

18. De Vaux 1971: 77–78. Cf. Blenkinsopp 1987: 413.

posed differences are usually the result of Persian propaganda (cf. Kuhrt 1983). While the Persians tolerated the local shrines and temples, they also taxed them.[19] Any supposed deviation from this general practice needs to be looked at carefully to see whether it represents a genuine exception to policy or is only an example of Jewish propaganda. Here is a brief survey of some of the main Persian-Period sources bearing on the question.[20]

Some of the most direct evidence about how subject peoples appealed to the Persian administration and how the latter responded in turn is found among the correspondence of the Jewish community at Elephantine.[21] The original request was to restore the temple as it has been, including holocausts on the altar as well as cereal and incense offerings.[22] A later document, however, promises payment if the temple is allowed to be rebuilt and includes the names of those who pledged silver.[23] This offer includes the statement that, if permission is granted, animals will no longer be offered on the altar. Finally, a document from Bagohi (or Bagavahya?), the governor of Judah, and Delaiah (presumably the son of Sanballat, governor of Samaria) authorizes the rebuilding of the Jewish temple that had been destroyed, though only cereal and incense offerings were allowed and not animal sacrifice.[24]

What these letters make clear is that the original request asked to renew the animal sacrifices. This seems to have been a problem, since in the later document the offer is made that animals would not be sacrificed, and it is this version that is endorsed by the satrap. This confirms that the Persians responded to the requests and complaints of the local peoples, including those relating to cultic practice, but in all of this there is no indication that the Persian authorities initiated anything themselves, nor did they pay for anything.

The "Passover Papyrus" is also important.[25] The interpretation is made more difficult by its fragmentary nature. Since only the left-hand side is preserved, the exact width of the column can only be

---

19. Dandamaev and Lukonin 1989: 362–66; Tuplin 1987: 149–53; Hornblower 1982: 161–63; Posener 1936: 164–76.

20. See also the essays in Watts 2001.

21. The writings are now all published in Porten and Yardeni 1986–99 (= *TAD* A–D).

22. Two copies of the same letter have been preserved (*TAD* A4.7//A4.8 = *AP* 30//31), one more fragmentary than the other, but most of the text can be reconstructed as a result of the overlap.

23. *TAD* A4.10 = *AP* 33.

24. *TAD* A4.9 = *AP* 32.

25. *TAD* A4.1 = *AP* 21.

guessed at, making reconstruction of the original text somewhat arbitrary. A variety of plausible reconstructions of the lacunae have been made. The word *Passover* does not occur in the extant text, but the subject seems unmistakable because of the content. There are several points to notice about the text. It is not an official Persian decree but a letter from someone called Hananiah to fellow Jews; however, the king and Arsames (Aramaic Aršam), the satrap of Egypt, are invoked, suggesting that the letter might be based on an official directive of some sort. Whatever might have come from the king or satrap, the celebration of the Passover was not a new idea: the word appears a couple of times in the ostraca from Elephantine in a way that suggests that the festival was a regular part of the people's lives.[26]

What was the background of the Passover Papyrus? In light of the intriguing gaps in the text, one might come up with a number of plausible scenarios. One of the most likely is that the letter reflects a permit from the Persian court to continue celebrating the Passover, possibly in the light of local opposition. The local Khnum priest may well have opposed the sacrifice of lambs. Whether the Exodus story was a part of the Passover celebration at this time or, if so, whether the Egyptians knew of it and objected to it, is a matter of speculation, though some commentators have argued this point.[27] But one must keep in mind that this was a few years before the destruction of the Elephantine Jewish temple, and friction between the two temple communities seems to have built up over a period of time. If so, the decree may not have permitted the use of lambs since only leaven is mentioned in the portion of the text preserved, but we cannot be sure. What seems quite unlikely is that the government was primarily trying to tell the Jews how to celebrate one of their festivals or that it was establishing the Jewish religion in some way. Like the other examples of Persian decrees known to us, this was probably a response to a request from the Jews themselves, not a unilateral act on the part of the Persian king. Although the king's name is mentioned, the precise situation was handled by the local officials, the satrap, and especially the Jewish leader Hananiah.

---

26. The word פסח does not occur anywhere in the extant Elephantine Papyri. The word occurs twice in the ostraca, however, in its Aramaic form of פסחא: *TAD* D7.6:9–10; D7.24:5. In both cases, the observance is mentioned in passing in letters, indicating that it was a part of the writers' normal lives.

27. On the subject, see Gruen 1998: 60–63.

The Udjahorresnet inscription originated with an important Egyptian court official and commander of the royal navy under both the Saite and the Persian regimes.[28] At his death he followed wide convention by leaving behind a statue inscribed with a personal testament, including a brief biography. Several points are to be noted about this inscription. First, Udjahorresnet was a high official and important to the king, which explains why he had direct contact with the king. Second, the king was willing to accommodate a personal request about one temple in Egypt; the inference from this is that other temples were not given such special privileges or attention. Third, although the king could have unilaterally initiated the decision to send Udjahorresnet to take charge of the "house of life" (where medicine was studied), this seems unlikely. Even if the inscription does not say so explicitly, the most likely interpretation is that Udjahorresnet himself suggested the idea to the king or that the king was responding to a request from the Egyptian side.

This interpretation is supported by a document on the reverse of the *Demotic Chronicle* in the name of Cambyses that speaks of allotments to the temples in Egypt.[29] It states that former allotments of such things as firewood and animals for offerings, previously distributed to the temples by the ruler, were to be reduced or eliminated altogether. This shows Cambyses reducing the governmental allotment of requirements for the divine offerings. Only three temples were excepted from the general decree on the native temples: at Memphis, Hermopolis, and a third one (reading uncertain).

A statue of Darius I, with an inscription in the languages of Old Persian, Elamite, Babylonian, and Egyptian, was discovered in Susa.[30] The inscription shows the desire of Darius to appear in the traditional image of the kings of Egypt. It, along with the Udjahorresnet inscription, portrays him as concerned about the prosperity of the Egyptian temples. However, this is not the same as exempting the temples from taxes or granting all of them special privileges carte blanche. This can be compared with the Egyptian tradition about Cambyses that made him the destroyer of temples and the Egyptian sacred, even to the point of killing the Apis bull. This is negative propaganda that distorted the

---

28. Lichtheim (1980: 36–41) gives an English translation. For the Egyptian text and a discussion, see Posener 1936: 1–26, 164–75. See also Blenkinsopp 1987.

29. Spiegelberg 1914: 32–33; Griffith 1909: 26–27.

30. For information on this statue, see Kervran et al. 1972. See also the special section in the *Cahiers de la délégation archéologique française en Iran* 4 (1974), especially the articles by F. Vallat 1974a and 1974b.

Persian role.[31] The truth is in between: the Persian conqueror did not suppress native Egyptian worship, but he did take away many of the traditional privileges and bring the temples under the tax regimen. He did occasionally grant special privileges, but these were the exception (e.g., the Temple of Neith, at the request of Udjahorresnet). Darius continued what Cambyses had begun.

The Pherendates letters relate to relations between the satrap of Egypt and the Temple of Khnum.[32] In one the satrap Pherendates gives regulations about the qualities required before someone could be advanced to the office of *lesionis* (an important administrative position in the temple). This might suggest that the Persian government sought to oversee and regulate all cults and temples. Several considerations militate against such an interpretation. First, his initial letter seems to have been a response to one from the Khnum priests relating to a candidate. Second, a letter from the Khnum priests dated some months later simply declares to Pherendates the one whom they had appointed as *lesionis* and makes no reference to the satrap's ruling about whom to appoint. Yet we have no indication that Pheredates saw this as an affront to his authority. Third, it also seems that it was traditional for the Pharaoh or his representative to have the opportunity of veto over anyone about to be appointed *lesionis*. The Pherendates correspondence should evidently be seen in this context. The Persian administration of course always retained the theoretical right to interfere wherever it felt necessary, including into matters of temples and cults. But the exchange of letters in Pherendates' archive does not suggest regular meddling in temple or religious matters.

The Xanthus Trilingual is an inscription in Aramaic, Greek, and Lycian dating to the end of the Persian Period.[33] As an authorization of a cult at Xanthus in Lycia, it is particularly relevant because it shows how the Persian government dealt with the establishment of a local cult. The Lycian and Greek versions differ in small but interesting ways from the Aramaic, being slightly more expansive at several

---

31. The report that he killed the Apis bull by stabbing it to death seems to be only a piece of anti-Cambyses propaganda since records show that the bull alive at the time of his conquest did not die until several years later (Posener 1936: 30–47, 171–75; Brown 1982; Lloyd 1988; though see the recent reassessment of this conclusion by Depuydt 1995).

32. Three letters were originally published by W. Spiegelberg 1928, though it is now likely that his third letter related to a lower official with a similar but slightly different name from Pherendates (Hughes 1984: 75–77). The first two letters, however, are the ones that interest us here. An English translation is found in Porten 1996: 290–91.

33. See the initial publication of the text, with discussion and commentary, in Metzger et al. 1979; see also Teixidor 1978; Lemaire 1995.

points. The Lycian is probably the version representing the request by the townspeople, but the Greek differs little from it. Essentially the local people requested the establishment of a cult of the god Kdwrṣ and donated land for the site. They also pledged an amount for the annual support of the priest and offerings. The satrap is the one to whom the request went, not the king, and the satrap issued the authorization. Not a hint within the inscription suggests that the Persian government provided any support for the cult except to give permission for it to be established. All the expenses, including the donation of land, seem to have been provided by the local community requesting to have the cult established. They seem to have made it free of local taxes but not imperial taxes.

Often cited in this connection is the Gadatas inscription. Voices have been raised questioning its authenticity from the start.[34] Now, the most thorough study argues that it is a forgery from the Hellenistic Period.[35] The arguments appear convincing, which means that this inscription should no longer be used as evidence for imperial support of local cults. Similarly, the inscription of Droaphernes (available only in a Roman-Period copy) has been cited as bearing on Achaemenid imperial religious policy, but it now appears to relate only to the dedication of a local statue.[36]

Some of the Persepolis Treasury Tablets and Persepolis Fortification Tablets mention the payment of rations and support to various priests and cult attendants.[37] One might come to the conclusion that it was general Persian policy to support religion, temples, and the like in its Empire.[38] This was not the case, however, since these most likely relate to official state cults.[39] Heidemarie Koch argues that the Elamite, Iranian, and Babylonian cults headed by the type of priest called a *šaten* actually devoted part of their offerings to Ahura Mazda and only a portion to the native, local gods.[40] As Pierre Briant writes:

---

34. Supporting authenticity have been Meiggs and Lewis 1969: #12 (pp. 20–22); Brandstein and Mayrhofer 1964: 91–98; Wiesehöfer 1987. Opposing it are such individuals as van den Hout 1949: 144–52; Hansen 1986; also apparently P. Frei (in Frei and Koch 1996) since he does not list it among the inscriptions to take into account.

35. Briant 2003.

36. Briant 1998; 2002: 677–78, 999–1000.

37. On these tablets, see Cameron 1948; 1958; 1965; Hallock 1969. For an overview of them, see Cameron 1965, Hallock 1985, Koch 1992 (especially pp. 25–67), and Briant 2002 (especially pp. 422–71).

38. Cf. Williamson 1991.

39. Cameron 1948: 5–9.

40. Koch 1977: 177, 181.

We have no references to Greek, Cappadocian, or Syrian gods. Considering the fact that more than 120 (of the published) Fortification tablets are concerned with priests, gods, and services, it is hard to imagine that the absence of gods other than Iranian, Elamite, and Babylonian deities is due to chance. Nor is there any good reason to believe that the Persians forbade the *kurtaš* [an Elamite term referring to laborers or workers] to honor their traditional gods. However, the available evidence strongly suggests that the administration did not provide grain or wine for their sacrifices. It thus appears justifiable to consider the example of Elamite and Babylonian religious practice a special case.[41]

What can we conclude about Persian policy on religion? We can summarize the main points arising from this brief survey as follows:

1. The alleged support of cults and religion under the Persians is often exaggerated in modern literature. This is in part due to the propaganda of the Persian kings themselves.[42] In actual practice the Persians continued what was already general policy in the Near Eastern empires: to declare their personal piety in their inscriptions—of how they were diligent to obey their god(s) and follow his (their) will (the inscriptions of Babylonian and Assyrian rulers are filled with these—the Persians are hardly unique) and to give precedent to their own state and/or personal royal cults. The Persians had their own cults, including apparently some traditional Elamite and Babylonian cults that were continued under Persian rule.

2. The Persians tolerated local cults as long as they did not threaten insubordination; on the other hand, they would punish or even destroy any local cults that were seen as providing a support for rebellion.[43] Yet little evidence exists that cults generally received state support, as sometimes alleged, which is hardly surprising since temples usually had their own incomes. On the contrary, temples were regulated and taxed, both in goods and services; overall Persian policy was to reduce the income of temples.[44] Apart from the central cults, the Persians occasionally granted special favors (not necessarily permanent) to certain specific cults. But this was for political reasons (such as the cults of certain temples in Egypt, according to a text on the back of the

---

41. Briant 2002: 438.
42. Kuhrt 1983.
43. Dandamaev and Lukonin 1989: 356–60; Briant 2002: 543–49.
44. Tuplin 1987: 149–53; Dandamaev and Lukonin 1989: 362–66; Hornblower 1982: 161–63; Posener 1936: 164–76.

Demotic Chronicle and the Udjahorresnet inscription) and seems very much the exception.[45]

3. If the Persian administration was consulted or asked to intervene in religious matters, they would respond (at least sometimes, from the examples available to us, if possibly not always). But the evidence is that such requests normally went to the local ruler, either the governor or the satrap, not the emperor.

There is still a great deal not known about the administration and the place of religion under Achaemenid rule. This makes it hard to assert a negative (e.g., that the Persians did not do certain things). Nevertheless, this does not absolve us of the historian's responsibility to make the best judgment we can from the extant data. While many questions cannot be answered with certainty, nevertheless, we must weight matters in the light of probability. In the light of present information, it seems likely that the Persians allowed the Jews to carry out their religion, including the building of their temple and the establishment of the priesthood when a petition was made to the appropriate authorities (usually local, not directly to the Persian king). From the evidence available (apart from some admittedly propagandistic passages in later Jewish literature) the Persians would not have provided financial support or other imperial resources or granted tax concessions to the Jerusalem temple.

The Documents

In this section I will go through each document in some detail, looking at the specified linguistic criteria and also the contents that seem relevant to authenticity.

Document 1 (Ezra 1:2–4): Decree of Cyrus

One of the first acts of Cyrus after conquering Babylon was to allow the return of the statues of the various gods to their native cities. In the last days of the Neo-Babylonian empire, Nabonidus had collected many of the divine statues into Babylon.[46] As a part of Cyrus's propaganda to the newly conquered peoples, he had himself proclaimed as the choice of their particular god. In a decree addressed to Babylon, he was the choice of Marduk.[47] In Nippur, however, Cyrus was presented

---

45. For examples from Mesopotamia, see Tuplin 1987: 150.

46. Cf. Beaulieu 1993.

47. Cyrus Cylinder, lines 10–15. For an English translation, see *CoS* 2.315; *ANET*, 315–16. For the text, see Schaudig 2001: 552.

as the choice of Sin according to a tablet from there.[48] A more reliable source is the *Babylonian Chronicles*. One of these confirms that gods were returned, but only the Babylonian gods are specifically mentioned.[49] The Cyrus Cylinder and the *Babylonian Chronicles* thus indicate that Cyrus allowed the restoration of temples and cult statues. In this light, we can take it for granted that some Jews were allowed to return from Babylonia to Judah and that the temple was allowed to be rebuilt.

Ezra 1 goes further than this, however. According to Ezra 1:2–4, soon after the beginning of his reign Cyrus himself issued a decree authorizing—indeed, commanding—the rebuilding of the ruined temple and also allowing the Jews to return to Palestine. This decree had seemed to many to fit the propaganda of the Cyrus Cylinder and the actions related in the *Nabonidus Chronicle*. Nevertheless, the authenticity of this decree has often been questioned. Although it has been defended,[50] a number of commentators have not been convinced.[51] Even if at first blush some have thought the Cyrus Cylinder supported the issue of a specific decree on behalf of the Jews to allow the Jews to return, it must be noted that Cyrus's allowance seems to have been a general policy, not one on behalf of a specific nation. Furthermore, the areas named are limited to Sumer and Akkad, while nothing is said about the other side of the Euphrates, much less the Jews. The propagandistic nature of Cyrus's decrees has been made clear since Bickerman wrote,[52] and we should be careful about taking such pronouncements at face value. The religious policy of the Persians was not that different from the basic practice of the Assyrians and Babylonians before them. They tolerated—but did not promote—the local cults (except the traditional temples in the Persian heartland). It seems very unlikely that Cyrus would have taken the trouble to issue a decree specifically on behalf of a minority ethnic group in the first year of his reign, nor do the parallels cited suggest otherwise.

Cyrus's decree is in Hebrew, whereas the expected scribal language would have been Aramaic. Bickerman suggests that 1:1–4 was an oral message and therefore in the language of the native peoples (Hebrew

---

48. De Vaux 1971: 68–69.

49. *Nabonidus Chronicle* iii 21–22. For text and translation, see Grayson 1975: 110.

50. One of the most important defenders has been Bickerman 1976, but see also Williamson 1985: 6–7, 11–14; Clines 1984: 36–39.

51. E.g., Galling 1964: 61–77; Blenkinsopp 1988: 74–76; Morton Smith 1987: 78, 186 n. 16.

52. Kuhrt 1983.

in this case). The only evidence offered is from the biblical text, however, and these are all examples that could easily be Jewish propaganda (e.g., Esth 1:22; 2:12; 8:9). In addition, the alleged decree, despite its short length, is full of biblical theology. The reference to a prophecy of Jeremiah in 1:1 may not be a part of the decree, though this is not certain, but the decree refers to "Yhwh the God of Israel" (Ezra 1:3). It might be possible that the name *Yhwh* would have been used (even though he is also called "the god of heaven"), but not the term *Israel*. The province was always referred to as *Judah* and the people as *Judahites*.[53] Bickerman defends even this theology,[54] though others accepting the decree are more cautious.[55] A further suspect point is the requirement for the local people (apparently even non-Jews) to provide funds and provisions for anyone who wants to go to Jerusalem to build the temple.[56] What is the likelihood that an official Persian decree would have such statements? On the other hand, they are precisely what we would expect from a Jewish writer inventing a decree to support his theology.[57]

---

53. In the Persian and Greek Periods, there is little evidence for the name *Israel* in extrabiblical sources. The name does not occur among the Elephantine Papyri. It *might* occur once among the Egyptian inscriptions in Greek (in a broken context in what seems to be a synagogue inscription from the Roman Period), but some read *Isdraēl* (Horbury and Noy 1992: #17 [p. 25]). The name also does not occur in the Greek papyri in Egypt either. It occurs only once in Rome but in a late inscription of the third–fourth century C.E. (Noy 1995: #489 [pp. 390–91]), though the significance is puzzling. A woman is referred to as a "proselyte" and a "Jew, Israelite," but it is not clear why the double designation is given. None of the Greek or Roman writers mention Israel until Pompeius Trogus at the turn of the Common Era (apud Justin, *Historiae Philippicae* 36, Epitome 2.3–4; he represents the origin of the Jews as from Damascus, one of whose kings is said to be *Israhel*). Nevertheless, Trogus uses the common term *Jews* for the people of his time, not Israel. The term *Israelite* was apparently used in pre-Christian Greco-Roman sources only to refer to members of a community on Delos associated with the cult on Mt. Gerizim. Two inscriptions, one from about 200 B.C.E. and one from about 100 B.C.E. were written by 'the Israelites in Delos who sent to sacred Argarizein' an offering (οι εν δηλω ισραελειται/ισραηλιται οι απαρχομενοι εις ιερον [αγιον] αργαριζειν [Brunneau 1982; Kraabel 1984]; the mention of Mt. Gerizim [*Argarizein*], although not decisive, is often an indication that this is a Samaritan community [cf. Pummer 1987]). They were not "Jews" but "Israelites," while the Jews are nowhere called "Israelites" at this time according to presently available sources. The obvious conclusion from all this is that use of the term *Israel/ites* for *Judah/ites* is an *internal* development. It would not be used by outsiders, especially the Persian administration.

54. Bickerman 1976: 103–4.

55. Williamson (1985: 9–10) admits this is probably the contribution of the editor.

56. Cf. Blenkinsopp 1988: 75–76.

57. E.g., Williamson (1985: 16) sees an exodus motif here.

In sum, it seems very likely that a general policy of allowing the descendants of deported peoples to return to their homelands and to rebuilt ruined temples was followed, along the lines of the Cyrus Cylinder. But this was a matter of *allowance*, not the subject of a royal edict calling on the community to fund such projects. It is also unlikely that in his very first year of reign, with all that had to be done, Cyrus took the time to issue an edict expressly on behalf of a small ethnic community, in Hebrew and filled with Jewish theology. If the Jews petitioned for the temple to be rebuilt, it would have gone to the local governor or satrap, not the king. There seems little doubt that the Cyrus decree issued not from the Persian chancellory but the desk of a Jewish theologian.

Document 2 (Ezra 4:9[?]–16): Letter to Artaxerxes

The problem with this letter is the confused nature of the text, which makes it difficult to know where it starts. It seems to begin three different times (vv. 8, 9, 11), yet the expected greeting to the king (which should come in either v. 11 or v. 12) is absent.[58] Additionally, the senders label themselves only as "your servant, man of Beyond the River." The collective singular is no problem, but the lack of personal names is without parallel in authentic letters of the Achaemenid Empire. The inner address is often shortened in comparison with the outer address, but the main correspondent is always named.[59] Furthermore, two late forms occur in 4:9 (כנותהון, דהוא). The 1st-common plural suffix on verbs seems to have been -ן until the fourth century, when -נא seems to have become common.[60] The spelling in this letter, although supposedly from the time of Artaxerxes I, shows the later form (4:12, 14, 16). This seems quite important if 4:9 is a part of the text of the letter, but the confused nature of the material makes it difficult to be sure that the verse is a part of the original letter. A further problem is the form מלכים (4:13), which looks suspiciously Hebrew. There are several possible loanwords from Akkadian and Persian, but most of them are not certain or also occur in post-Achaemenid Aramaic texts.[61] The name of a tax בלו (4:13) is probably borrowed from Akkadian and does

---

58. Schwiderski 2000: 376.
59. Schwiderski 2000: 354–57, 375–76.
60. Folmer 1995: §2.10 (pp. 155–61).
61. Ezra 4:9: אפרסתכיא; 4:11: פרשגן; 4:12: חוט, אשיא; 4:13: מ(נ)דה, הלך, אפתם; 4:15: אשתדור. Ezra 4:9 seems to have some proper names, though one or two might be the names of officials: טרפליא, אפרסיא, ארכויא.

not appear to be attested at a later time. The word אריך (4:14) appears most likely to be an Old Persian loanword (from *ārya-ka* 'worthy of an Aryan'), but other derivations have been suggested. Thus, the loanwords are little help in determining authenticity. Finally, the wording of the letter does not look like the courteous phrasing that one would expect from loyal subjects to the emperor; on the contrary, compared to Document 4 this letter sounds rather abrupt and even rude.

Document 3 (Ezra 4:17–22): Reply of Artaxerxes

Two late forms appear in this letter, in 4:17 (כנותהון) and in 4:20 (להון). In addition, several other points suggest that this is either a fictitious document or one that has been worked over by later Jewish scribes. It is doubtful whether the Persian archives would have had any mention of Mesopotamian interaction with Judah or Jerusalem in particular. That question apart, however, 4:20 states that mighty kings who ruled over Jerusalem also ruled over all Abar-Nahara, and tribute was paid to them. This is patently untrue, since no Jewish kings ruled over Abar-Nahara and collected tribute from it, and it is incredible that such information was found in the archives available to the Persians. This portion of the document, at least, looks like Jewish propaganda, pure and simple. Indeed, the term *Abar-Nahara* seems to be used of the local Palestinian region (4:17: "Samaria and the rest of Abar-Nahara"), a strange usage for a Persian-Period document.

The two loanwords (4:17, 22: שלו, פתגמא) are both found in later Aramaic texts. There is one example of a later spelling of the 1st-person plural (4:18: אלינא). Several problems with the epistolary form occur in this letter. In 4:17 only the recipient is named, not the sender, which is unparalleled in official correspondence. One might explain this by the editing of the letter when it was inserted into the book,[62] but the designation of the group addressed has some elements not found in Achaemenid letters (marked by square brackets): [שאר] כנותהון די [יתבין] בשמרין ו[שאר] עבר־נהרה. The king uses the greeting שלם, which is found in Hellenistic Aramaic writings and may have arisen in imitation of the typical Hellenistic epistolary greeting, χαίρειν.[63] Finally, Rehum is designated the בעל־טעם. Schwiderski argues that this is not a title or office;

---

62. Porten (1983: 397) argues that it is omitted because the introductory sentence already named the king. Schwiderski (2000: 357–59, 376–77) notes that this sort of address formula is found mainly in the ostraca; however, he also allows that the omission might be due to editing and is thus not decisive for authenticity.

63. Schwiderski 2000: 364–65, 377–78.

rather it normally designates the one responsible for the letter, but in such cases the בעל־טעם is not mentioned in the address but in the conclusion of the letter.[64] Either the composer of this letter misunderstood the meaning of the term as a title or has misplaced it in the address.

Document 4 (Ezra 5:7–17): Letter of Tattenai

All the grammatical forms in this letter are early: בידהם (5:8), להם (5:9, 10), לכם (5:9), שמההתהם (5:10), בראשהם (5:10). Especially important is the picture presented of Sheshbazzar as someone who not only was governor (פחה) but also began the building of the temple, laying its foundations (5:14–16). This differs from the scenario given in Ezra 1–3, where Sheshbazzar's role is downplayed, nothing is said about his being governor, and the founding of the temple is done by Zerubbabel. It seems to me that this argues in favor at least of a different tradition and also likely for a greater proportion of authentic material in the document, especially when we add in the early nature of the linguistic criteria. Nevertheless, a number of problematic points are present:

- It has already been noted (Document 1) that Cyrus is unlikely to have been concerned about issuing personal decrees with regard to a small province on the edge of the Empire in his first year of rule.
- Also, it is unlikely that the temple vessels from the time of Zedekiah were still in existence to be sent back to Jerusalem. They would probably long since have been melted down for the coffers of the Neo-Babylonian empire. If they had not been, what are the chances that they would have been kept isolated in the records and their identity preserved? They had no special significance for the Babylonians and would just have been booty alongside that taken from many other native peoples. The writer of the document may have had a writing claiming to be a list of such vessels as found in Ezra 1:7–11, however, and assumed that it was authentic.
- Ezra 5:8 refers to the temple as "the house of the great God," which strikes one as the sort of phrase that a Jewish writer might use when dealing with non-Jews rather than the phrase used of a local temple and local deity by a Persian administrator in an official letter.

---

64. Schwiderski 2000: 190–93, 358–59, 377.

- Ezra 5:8 has a loanword אספרנא (apparently from Old Persian *a/usprna* 'the whole, completeness'). The word occurs in the Arsames correspondence[65] but seems not to be used in later Aramaic, though it occurs fairly frequently in Ezra (5:8; 6:8, 12, 13; 7:17, 21, 26). The other Persian loanword (5:17: גנזיא 'treasures'), however, is also known in later Aramaic.

- Several forms in 5:8–12 have the 1st-person plural suffix spelled נא- (the later form rather than the earlier ן-).

- Ezra 5:9 has "elders" as those in charge rather than the governor as should be expected (see discussion on Document 5).

- Ezra 5:9 says that the original city and temple were built by a "king of Israel." As noted above,[66] the people were called "Jews/ Judeans" and the country "Judah"; however, it is possible that the tradition of the builder as Solomon who was king over Israel was sufficient to evoke the name "Israel" here, especially since this information is in a quotation or paraphrase from the Jews themselves.

- Ezra 5:12 has "Nebuchadnezzar" instead of the expected form "Nebuchadrezzar."[67]

- Ezra 5:13 refers to "Cyrus, king of Babylon," yet the title "king of Babylon" was not held by Cyrus in his first year but by Cambyses, only being transferred to Cyrus at the very end of his first year.[68]

- With regard to epistolary style there are a number of problems.[69] The address containing the name of the recipient with ל- is unprecedented in official correspondence of the Achaemenid Period but appears in Hellenistic and Roman times (cf. the use of the dative in Greek correspondence). Nor is the sender named, along with the expected self-designation of "your servant(s)" (the failure of such a self-designation would be unthinkable in a letter to the king). The greeting, שלמא כלא has no parallel in Achaemenid greetings but looks very similar to the Hellenistic πολλὰ χαίρειν. Finally, there is no transition marker (e.g., וכעת) between the prescript and the body of the letter.

---

65. *TAD* 6.13:4 = Driver 1957: #10:4; *KAI* 263.
66. See n. 53 above.
67. Compare the form נבוכדרסר in *KAI* 227 obv. 5.
68. Grabbe 1988: 199–204.
69. Schwiderski 2000: 360, 365–68, 371–73, 378–79.

It appears that, while there is much to be said for authentic material in the letter—indeed, it appears to have the largest such content of all the alleged documents—there is also evidence of intervention by Jewish scribes at some point.

Document 5 (Ezra 6:2–5): Decree of Cyrus

That some sort of decree to allow rebuilding of the tempel was issued by the Persian authorities seems reasonable, especially if Document 4 has a high degree of authentic content. Nevertheless, several points in this decree militate against its trustworthiness.

- Any order permitting the rebuilding of the temple is likely to have come from the local governor or perhaps the satrap but would hardly be a matter with which the Persian king would concern himself.
- In 6:2 we read the later form, דכרנה, when we should expect זכרן;[70] however, it is not clear whether this is a part of the document or only a heading given by the editor/compiler of Ezra 1–6.[71]
- More important is the oddly proportioned temple in only two dimensions which apparently measures about 60 cubits wide by 60 cubits high (ca. 90 feet by 90 feet) but with no length (6:3). The length might have been lost in a textual corruption, but the height is a very unlikely figure.
- The Persians might allow the temple of this local cult to be rebuilt, but the probability is small that the Persian government would pay for the building (6:4).
- Permission for the temple vessels to be returned is not unbelievable, except that it seems odd that the vessels would have been preserved half a century or more after they were looted by the Babylonians (see Document 4).
- The form "Nebuchadnezzar" occurs in 6:5 instead of "Nebuchadrezzar" (see Document 4).
- The way that this document is attached to Document 5 is also problematic (6:5–6).
- In 6:4 נדבכין seems to be a loanword from Akkadian *natbāku(m)*, but the word also appears in later Aramaic.

---

70. This heading with the spelling דכרן is, however, found on one fragmentary Persian document from Elephantine (*TAD* D3.1:1), which is dated to the early fifth century.

71. Unfortunately, Schwiderski does not discuss this document because it has no formal epistolary elements (2000: 1, 343, 352 n. 50).

Thus, if this has a genuine document at the core, it has probably been revised by Jewish scribes and has perhaps also suffered textual damage in transmission.

Document 6 (Ezra 6:6–12): Reply of Darius

Some portions of this letter fit with Document 4. Yet a number of points arouse suspicion:

- The governor (פחה) of Judah is mentioned, a point in favor of authenticity (6:7); however, it is qualified by the phrase 'and elders' (שׂבי יהודיא), while 'elders' alone is used in the next verse (6:8). The mention of "elders" fits very much the bias of the compiler of Ezra, whereas the reference to a governor goes against it.[72]
- The directions to Tattenai to 'get away from' (רחיקין הוו) Jerusalem seem harshly out of character when directed at an official of the king who is simply doing his duty (6:6).
- Ezra 6:8 grandly appropriates money from the royal tribute to pay the expenses of building the temple.
- Ezra 6:9 gives an open-ended permission for the temple personnel to obtain whatever animals and other material they need for offerings just by asking. Even in the unlikely event that the government provided such offerings, the quantity would be specified. Judging from the available documentation, it was not in the nature of the bureaucracy to issue "blank checks."
- In 6:11 an order is redundantly set a second time (despite 6:8).
- Ezra 6:11–12 surprising states a harsh penalty for anyone who attempts to set aside the royal order. Why would the Persian emperor feel the need to make such a statement? How likely is it that his order would be challenged in the first place? Furthermore, how likely would it be that the king would be so solicitious on behalf of the Jews to set such a fierce threat to any possible opposition? It is suspiciously like what the Jews would want the king to say. Furthermore, 6:12 goes on to call on God to overthrow "any king or people" that interferes with the Temple in Jerusalem. Why would the king of Persia make references to "kings" who would threaten the temple? There were few kings remaining in the Empire, and any threat was more likely to come from Persian officials. The pronouncement does not fit the perspective

---

72. See Japhet 1982; 1983.

of the Persian rulers, though it harmonizes well with a Jewish outlook.

- The reference to the God who makes his name to dwell in Jerusalem (6:12) looks like a piece of Jewish theology (cf. Deut 12:11; 14:23; 16:2, 6, 11; 26:2).

- A late form is found in 6:6 (וכנותהון); however, the early form in 6:9 (להם) is interesting. It might be that the decree authorized regular offerings for the king in some form, which seems to be the intent of 6:9–10.

- Finally, this short letter finishes with a *third* order (6:12)—with Darius invoking his own name—to do this quickly, in a statement without parallel in the letters from the epigraphic sources.[73] Is this an emperor writing a letter or a Jewish writer creating the royal backing that he would like to have seen?

- The letter begins without address or prescript, with only a transition marker (כען); such a letter form is exemplied only in ostraca letters but not official correspondence.[74] But if the address and prescript have simply been omitted by the editor, who begins directly with the body of the letter, then the detailed address to "Tettenai, governor of Transeuphrates, Shethar-bozenai and their colleagues, the officials who are in Transeuphrates" is without precedent in the body of official letters.

- The loanword אספרנא, which does not appear to occur in later Aramaic, is found in 6:8, and 12 of the letter; however, it is also found in a framework passage outside the letters (6:13). The word אפרסכין (an official of some sort) in 6:6 is of uncertain derivation, perhaps from Old Persian but perhaps from Akkadian. In 6:8 נכסי is a loanword from Akkadian *nikkassu(m)* 'account, wealth' (also Ezra 7:26) but is also attested in later Aramaic. The word שלו (6:9) is possibly from Akkadian but is also found in later Aramaic. However, in 6:10 ניחוחין is from Hebrew and a very strange loanward to find in a decree supposed to be from Darius the Persian king.

The issuance of an authorization of building seems quite credible (especially if Document 4 contains a high degree of authenticity, as suggested above), but it is likely to have come from the satrap or local governor, rather than the king. The presence of an early grammatical

---

73. Schwiderski 2000: 373.
74. Schwiderski 2000: 361–62, 379.

form may support this interpretation. But if so, the original document seems to have been thoroughly reworked by Jewish scribes. The letter is filled with elements that look as if they would come not from the Persian chancellory but from a Jewish propagandist.

Document 7 (Ezra 7:12–26): Decree of Artaxerxes to Ezra

This decree has often been seen as the most important of the documents and as a major contribution to understanding the history of Judah in the Persian Period. It is also one of the more complex of the supposed Persian documents. The following points should be noted:

- At the beginning of the decree, 7:13 makes the statement that anyone of the "people of Israel and its priests and Levites" who wants to go to Jerusalem has permission to go with Ezra (7:13); 7:15 mentions "the God of Israel whose dwelling is in Jerusalem." Yet foreigners never refer to Judah or its people as "Israel"; these are phrases that would be used by a Jew writing with a theological purpose, not by a scribe (whatever his ethnic affinity) drawing up a document in the Persian chancellory.[75]
- According to 7:14, the king and "his seven counselors" also allow Ezra to regulate[76] (לבקרא על) Judah and Jerusalem by the 'law' (דת) of God in his hand. These "seven counselors" appear in no other document relating to the king in the Persian Period. That the king had counselors can be taken for granted; that he would have shared his authority by issuing decrees or orders in their names as well as his is unthinkable.[77] The king and his counselors also tacitly place themselves under the sovereignty of Yhwh by their generous gift.
- After Ezra is given permission to convey the silver and gold that the king and his counselors have generously offered (7:15), this is followed by "all the silver and gold found in all the satrapy of Babylon," which is in addition to all the gold and silver freely donated by the people and priests (7:16). This money is to be used for purchasing animals, grain, and drink to be offered on the Jerusalem altar (7:17). Whatever money is left over can be used for whatever the priests want, according to God's will (7:18). Finally, any other needs, such as of temple vessels, are to be paid

---

75. See n. 53 above.
76. Steiner (2001) argues that a more appropriate translation would be 'act as overseer over'.
77. Cf. Briant 2002: 128–30; Lewis 1977: 22–23.

from the royal treasury, up to 100 talents of silver (7:19–22). As discussed below, this generosity can be nothing but Jewish propaganda.

- Ezra has considerable political power bestowed on him: according to 7:25–26 he is "to appoint officials and judges to be judging all the people in the region of Ebir-nari, both those who know the law and those who do not," according to the wisdom of the law in his hand (7:25–26). He is to teach those who do not know the law. It is often suggested that this "obviously" refers only to Jews, but such interpretations prefer to apologize for the text rather than read it for what it says.[78] There is no basis in the decree itself for the interpretation that Ezra's authority is limited to Jews. The overt referent is to all the people in the satrapy west of the Euphrates, and the mention of the "law of your God and the law of the king" suggests that not just Jews are being mentioned. The intent of the phrase seems to be that "the law of your God" is treated the same as "the law of the king" (cf. Grabbe 2001b). Any who do not obey are to be punished as appropriate. Ezra has clearly been given some very sweeping powers. The extent of these powers is hinted at in Ezra 8:36, where the orders of the king are handed over to the "satraps and governors of the province Beyond-the-River." In reality, it is unlikely that Ezra would be allowed to impose his own choice of judges and magistrates and also the laws of his god on all of Ebir-nari, especially considering that this region had a powerful satrap who seems to be ignored. Although the power and office of the satrap varied from place to place, time to time, and even individual to individual, satraps were usually members of the royal family with a great deal of independence and power, including military command and troops. It seems rather unlikely that Ezra would be allowed to interfere in the legal and judicial system of the satrapy without

---

78. For example, Williamson (1998: 161) states: Ezra "was expected to teach to Jews in the Levant living outside the province of Judah itself (7:25–6). There is no historical possibility here of any expectation that the whole population of Transeuphrates should come under Jewish law; rather, as a new development, the Persians gave official sanction to the notion that religious allegiance should be allowed some recognition alongside civil responsibility." Fried (2001: 65), however, argues, "According to the plain meaning of the text, Ezra was to appoint judges and magistrates. . . . These judges were to judge all the people of the entire satrapy of Beyond the River. . . . They would adjudicate the cases of Jew and non-Jew alike (those who know the law and those who do not). There is no provision for separate judges for the separate ethnic groups. The same men would judge each person in the satrapy."

some reference to the satrap. Nor is it credible that all "the satraps and governors" would submissively gather in Jerusalem—
hundreds or thousands of *parsang*s from their territories—to receive their orders from Ezra.

- The decree ends with dire threats for anyone who does not obey
  it (7:26). As in 6:11 this seems be an example of overkill, if one
  might use the expression. Of course, the punishment for disobeying the emperor could be drastic, but it hardly needed spelling
  out. This looks like the wishful thinking of a Jewish writer rather
  than an imperial edict.

- When we look at the language, we find a strange situation. The
  early and later forms seem almost to alternate: 7:16 (אלההם); 7:17
  (עליהם ,7:24 ;(ישאלנכון) 7:21 ;(אלהכם) 7:18 ;(ומנחתהון ונסכיהון, אלהכם
  לכם). While the early forms might argue for an actual decree of
  Artaxerxes at the base of 7:12–26, the later forms suggest considerable scribal intervention, in which case it is difficult to say what
  the original decree authorized.

- With regard to the epistolary formula the address takes the form
  of the sender (Artaxerxes) plus -ל followed by the addressee
  (Ezra), but the use of -ל to mark the addressee belongs to the
  Hellenistic–Roman Period.[79] It is possible, however, that a scribal
  error has changed an original -על or -אל to -ל. Although the letter
  has no greeting, it is possible that the king would not have felt
  one was necessary, but it has a mysterious גמרא at the end of the
  prescript just before the transition marker.

- As noted above (on 6:8) the Persian loanword אספרנא (Ezra 7:17,
  21) is found in several passages in Ezra. In 7:23 אדרזדא seems to be
  from Old Persian *drzdra* (= Avestan *zrasda*) 'firm, competent' and
  does not occur in later Aramaic. The other loanwords have
  already been discussed but are also found in post-Achaemenid
  usage.[80]

The first thing that strikes one about this decree is the amount of silver
and gold made available to Ezra. First, gifts of silver and gold come
from the king and his seven counselors (7:15). Then Ezra is allowed to
take all the gold and silver found in the province of Babylonia, along
with the freewill offerings of the people (7:16). To this are added donations of vessels for God's house (7:19). Finally, just in case Ezra runs

---

79. Schwiderski 2000: 362–64, 368–71, 379–80.
80. Ezra 7:24: מדה ,בלו ,הלך. See on Document 2 above.

short of ready cash, he has the modest sum of 100 talents of silver available from the treasury for his "other needs" (7:20–23). By any calculation, there is an enormous amount of wealth freely available to the Jewish community. In addition, the priests and Levites are exempted from tribute (7:24).

At this point, it would be useful to consider the rest of the Ezra story in relation to the Artaxerxes decree. There are a number of descrepancies between the decree and the events in Ezra 8–10.[81] Nevertheless, Ezra 8 exhibits the same spirit of great wealth bestowed on the Jews as the decree of Ezra 7. The gold and silver said to have been donated for the Jerusalem temple amounted to 650 talents of silver, 100 talents of gold, and various expensive vessels for the temple. A talent was usually about 3,000 shekels, the preserved shekel weights being about 10 grams each (a convenient figure, though it might have been a bit heavier, even up to 14 grams; cf. Powell 1992: 6.905–6). A talent was thus approximately 30 kilograms (roughly 65 pounds); 100 talents of gold was about 3 metric tons of gold. In this case, the silver amounted to about 19,500 kilograms or $19\frac{1}{2}$ tons of silver. To this were to be added the 100 silver vessels of a talent each, 20 of gold, and 2 of an exceptionally fine quality of bronze. Leaving out the two bronze vessels, it all adds up to *more than 25 metric tons of silver and gold!*

Ezra and his small band was transporting no less than a king's ransom from Babylon to Judah. According to Herodotus 3.91, the entire satrapy of Ebir-nari produced tribute of only about 350 talents of silver per year. A standard rate of gold to silver in the Persian Empire seems to have been about 13 to 1 (Herodotus 3.95; Bivar 1997: 44). This would make the 120 talents of gold (including the gold vessels) equivalent in silver to 1,560 talents, to make a total equivalent in silver of more than 2,300 talents of silver. Considering that the entire Persian Empire under Darus is said to have yielded 14,560 talents of silver a year, we are expected to believe that a tiny province on the edge of the Empire has had 15 percent of the annual Persian income assigned to it. No wonder that Ezra offers such profuse praise to God at the end of the chapter (7:27–28)! This is all ostensibly done so that sacrifices could be offered

---

81. See the discussion in Grabbe 1994. Janzen (2000) has recognized the problem, but his solution is to reject the decree of Ezra 7 as inauthentic while giving more credence to aspects of Ezra 8–10. His solution cannot be accepted, however, because he overlooks what has been pointed out in some of my publications that he cites: the Ezra narrative in Ezra 8–10 is as problematic and contradictory as Ezra 7. Simply removing Ezra 7 from the equation does not resolve the tensions that run through the whole narrative.

on behalf of the king and his sons, but it hardly takes such vast wealth and a relief of taxes to see that sacrifices were offered for the king daily on the Jerusalem altar. A simple gift of an animal or two per day would have sufficed.[82] It is one thing to supply gifts to the temple; it is quite another to provide such lavish riches for what was, after all, only a very local cult site. This is not the decree of a Persian king but the wishful thinking of a Jewish apologist.

Synthesis of the Study of the Individual Documents

The book of Ezra–Nehemiah is artfully put together, as a number of literary and structural studies have shown.[83] The recent thorough study of Ezra 1–6 by B. Porten demonstrates in detail the skillful literary composition of this section of the book.[84] Yet such artifice, far from proving the authenticity of the documents embedded in it, argues that the author of Ezra 1–6 has also composed or heavily edited the documents to fit his literary patterns. It is not very likely that so many literary parallels between the documents and the framework surrounding them would emerge if the documents had not been edited to create these correspondences. The individual documents have now been analyzed in detail, and several general points arise out of this study. By bringing these points together we get a better picture of the documents themselves and how to evaluate them.

Linguistic Forms

First, the question of language. The Aramaic documents show a mixture of older and younger linguistic elements. The younger linguistic forms dominate the Aramaic narrative as a whole and could simply reflect the date when the documents were composed or revised. The question is how to explain the early forms (speaking primarily of the 2nd- and 3rd-personal plural pronominal suffixes כם- and הם-). Although they tend to appear sporadically, it seems unlikely that they result from scribal archaizing. The distribution of their occurrences tells against such a theory. The most natural explanation is, rather, that

---

82. With regard to relieving the temple personnel from taxes, we do have one such example from Antiochus III, but that was in special circumstances and was only temporary. See Josephus, *Ant.* 12.3.3–4 §§138–46. For an analysis of this decree, see my study (Grabbe 2001a: 139–42).

83. Eskenazi 1988; Grabbe 1998: 94–109.

84. Porten 2002.

there once were Persian-Period documents either (a) whose language and orthography have been updated by scribes or (b) which have been considerably reworked at a later time. Alternative (a) seems unlikely. It might explain the later orthography, such as די instead of זי or the 1st-person plural suffix as נא- instead of ן-, but it does not explain the preservation of older forms alongside the younger, nor does the pattern conform to that of known government documents from the Persian Period. Alternative (b) seems to be the best explanation on the linguistic side; that in some cases Achaemenid-Period documents have been considerably reworked by later scribes. Of course, some of these documents genuinely from the Persian Period could still be Jewish compositions, while those documents without early linguistic features could still be later forgeries.

It might be asked whether the orthography is of any significance since it could be due purely to scribal error or assimilation during generations of copying. Such an explanation might explain a few of the late forms. It is probably not the explanation for the large number of late forms that look more systematic. Nor is it the explanation for the early forms since scribes are more likely to introduce late forms into early texts than the other way round, nor can it explain the pattern of early and late forms found in the documents as a whole. Scribes may make sporadic changes by accident or systematic changes to update texts. They are hardly likely to have created the mixture of early and late forms found in the documents just by the accumulation of occasional assimilations through centuries of copying.

A question to be asked is whether the documents were simply created by the one who wrote the Aramaic narrative in which they occur, as Torrey assumed (1896, 1910). This does not seem to be the case, for two reasons: first, as has long been known, the documents do not fit the narrative into which they have been inserted. You can hardly use the letter of Artaxerxes—of any Artaxerxeses—to stop (or complete [Ezra 6:14]) a building project during the reign of Darius. Second, the narrative has only late forms. The only exception is found in Ezra 5:3–5 which, while not a part of a document, still has several early forms (להם, לכם). Yet this passage is copied almost verbatim from 5:9–10, which is a part of a document. Thus, contrary to Torrey, I have to conclude that the documents came first and that the narrative was only created later by an author who aleady had the documents and inserted them into the narrative. The documents could still be forgeries, of course, but they were probably not composed by the author of the narrative.

Persian and Akkadian Loanwords

This aspect of the investigation was rather disappointing. Genuine documents from the Persian administration (e.g., the Arsames letters) tend to have a significant number of Persian and Akkadian loanwords. And, indeed, a number of Persian and Akkadian loanwords appear in the Ezra documents, as we would expect in authentic documents. We face two problems, however: (1) the derivation of a number of the apparent loanwords is rather uncertain, and (2) many of them appear in later Aramaic. As should be obvious, we cannot use such data to demonstrate authenticity.[85] Unfortunately, most of the words in question fall into one or the other of these categories or both:

אפרסיא	(4:9: uncertain derivation)
אפרסכיא	(5:6; 6:6: uncertain derivation)
אפרסתכיא	(4:9: uncertain derivation)
אפתם	(4:13: uncertain derivation)
אריך	(4:14: uncertain derivation)
ארכויא	(4:9: uncertain derivation)
אשיא	(4:12; 5:16; 6:3: later Aramaic)
אשתדור	(4:15, 19: uncertain derivation; later Aramaic)
גנזיא	(5:17; 6:1; 7:20: later Aramaic)
הלך	(4:13, 20; 7:24: later Aramaic)
חוט	(4:12: later Aramaic)
טרפליא	(4:9: uncertain derivation)
מ(נ)דה	(4:13, 20; 6:8; 7:24: later Aramaic)
נדבכין	(6:4: later Aramaic)
נכסין	(6:8; 7:26: later Aramaic)
פרשגן	(4:11, 23; 5:6; 7:11: uncertain derivation; later Aramaic)
פתגמא	(4:17; 5:7, 11; 6:11: later Aramaic)
שלו	(4:22; 6:9: uncertain derivation; later Aramaic)

This leaves only three loanwords the derivation of which is reasonably certain and that are not attested in later phases of Aramaic:

---

85. Some loanwords that seem to be derived from Old Persian or Akkadian and to have entered Aramaic during Achaemenid times are also attested in later phases of Aramaic. This is unsurprising. For a loanword in the Ezra documents to be also attested in later phases of Aramaic is not necessarily inconsistent with authenticity; however, the only loanwords we can use *to demonstrate* authenticity are those whose derivation is reasonably certain and that ceased to be used beyond Imperial Aramaic.

בלו (4:13, 20; 7:24) comes from Akkadian *biltu*. It does not appear in later Aramaic, but in each case in Ezra it appears in a list of taxes. Two of the other tax terms (4:13, 20; 7:24: הלך; 4:13, 20; 7:24: מ[נ]דה) are attested in later Aramaic, however, suggesting that the nonoccurrence of בלו in later texts might be an accident of preservation.

אספרנא seems fairly certain to be from Persian *a/usprna* and does not so far appear to be attested in the later phases of Aramaic; however, the word is found in several passages in Ezra (5:8; 6:8, 12, 13; 7:17, 21, 26), including the framework narrative (6:13) which, as noted above, seems to be later.

אדרזדא (7:23) seems to be from Old Persian **drzdra* (= Avestan *zrasda*) 'firm, competent' and does not occur in later Aramaic.

If in all the documents only three loanwords could give any argument for authenticity (and two of these may be subject to challenge), we have to accept the fact that this part of the investigation has not taken us very far. This is true, even if we allow for two or three of those loanwords of uncertain derivation to be included here instead of in the list above. All we can say at this point is that the loanwords argue neither decisively for nor against the authenticity of the Ezra documents.

The Epistolary Formulas

A survey of the letters has found major problems with the epistolary features of most of the documents. As Porten has suggested, some of these can be explained by the editing of the documents by the compiler as he inserted them into the narrative framework.[86] This is only a partial explanation, however, and covers only a few of the problems. As already noted above, the epistolary formulas in the Ezra documents have been given their most detailed examination in the extensive work by Dirk Schwiderski.

Schwiderski concludes that the Aramaic letters of Ezra do not agree in certain essential points with the Imperial Aramaic letter formula, but that where differences exist, these are often paralleled from letters of the Hellenistic Period. His explanation is that the letters of Ezra 4–6 are most likely fictive letters originating in the early Hellenistic Period (3rd century B.C.E.).[87] Only in the case of Ezra 7:12–26 are the deviations from the Imperial Aramaic formula too problematic to make a clear case for or against authenticity. This matches the conclusions

---

86. Porten 1978–79: 177–78; 1983; 2003: 54–57.
87. Schwiderski 2000: 381–82.

above about the language of the texts. If there were original texts, they have been heavily edited in the Hellenistic Period.

Jewish Theology

A number of the documents contain elements of Jewish theology. The first point relates to use of the term "Israel" for the Judeans. All the genuine Persian-Period documents refer to 'Jews' and 'Judah' (יהוד, יהודין/יהדיא), yet we find statements to the effect that "the God of Israel is the God who is in Jerusalem" (1:3); that anyone of the "people of Israel and its priests and Levites" who wants to go to Jerusalem has permission to go with Ezra (7:13); and that the king made offerings to the "God of Israel" (7:15). Yet non-Jews never refer to Judah or its people as "Israel"; these are phrases that would be used by a Jew writing with a theological purpose, not by a scribe (whatever his ethnic affinity) drawing up a document in the Persian chancellory.[88]

A further point of theology can be found in the references to "elders" as the Judean leadership. Although they are named in tandem with the governor in one verse (Ezra 6:7), they seem to be the sole leadership in other passages (5:9; 6:8).[89] A further example of theology is found in the phrase "the God who makes his name to dwell there" in Jerusalem (6:12). These are not the words of a Persian king or the Persian chancellory but the Deuteronomic language of a Jewish scribe (cf. Deut 12:5, 11, 21; 14:23, 24; 16:2, 6, 11; 26:2). The language is as inappropriate to a document from the Persian administration as a letter ending with "affectionately yours" from your tax office or from a credit card company beginning with "Hallelujah."

Jewish Propaganda

Finally, we come to what can only be called "Jewish propaganda" in many of the documents. Here I am continually amazed at the contortions scholars will go to in order to defend the indefensible. It is time we confronted some of the absurdities found in what are, after all, supposed to be Persian decrees. The main form taken by this propaganda is the favor alleged to have been bestowed on the Jews by the imperial government: a stream of Persian decrees in support of the

---

88. See n. 53 above.

89. Japhet (1982, 1983) notes that part of the book's theology is a deemphasis on individual leaders (such as the governor) and a particular stress placed on the activities of groups, including the elders.

Jewish community—and not just imperial decrees but *royal* decrees at that—and great wealth lavished on the temple and cult personnel.

Part of the means of getting across this message comes from the framework and arrangement of the material, beginning with Cyrus's decree to build a temple, the temporary adversity that is dispelled by a decree from Darius (following a confirmation of Cyrus's decree), and finally a further decree from Artaxerxes. This all leaves the impression of an Empire that is not just benevolent but positively solicitous on behalf of the Jews. Yet the propaganda is also firmly embedded in a number of the letters themselves. Cyrus *commands* the rebuilding of the temple in Ezra 1:2. In an example of back-handed praise, Jerusalem is credited with having powerful kings in the past who ruled over all of Transeuphrates (Ezra 4:20). The "Aramaic decree of Cyrus" states that the expenses for rebuilding the temple were to be paid from "the king's house," the royal coffers (6:4). This is reinforced by Darius's decree, which also states that the expenses are to come from the king's resources, from the taxes of the region (6:8). It is Artaxerxes' decree in Ezra 7, however, that is the most blatant in the wealth lavished on the temple and cult personnel, as pointed out in detail above.[90]

As noted at the beginning of the essay, the Persians tolerated local shrines and temples, but they also taxed them. Far from contributing funds to them, the administration made sure that nonstate cults paid their way, especially when they had been powerful centers of vested interests in the past.[91] There is little to think that they made an exception in the case of Judah or the Jewish temple. Yet we find that no less than three of the six Aramaic documents, from three separate periods of time, allege that the Persian government financed Jewish activities. One such document just might be credible, two would be hard to swallow, but three demonstrates a literary pattern. The Jews may have been given permission to revive the Jerusalem cult, but it is not likely that they were given imperial funds with which to do it. The fact is that parallel texts and examples give no reason to believe any such thing. To conclude this section, the idea that the Persian administration actually gave financial support to local cults, which one frequently reads in the scholarly literature, is actually based on these very biblical documents with their tendentious claims.

---

90. See pp. 553–555.
91. On the Egyptian cults, see nn. 28–29 above. For examples from Mesopotamia, see Tuplin 1987: 150.

Conclusions

We can summarize the situation as follows:

1. Any Achaemenid documents in Ezra have been subject to extensive scribal intervention. But there is scribal intervention and scribal intervention: the question is whether we have simple—if systematic— updating of orthography and language or a major reworking of older texts. Defenders have often salvaged authenticity by ascribing some inauthentic features to editing and "scribal updating." This can be accepted up to a point, but it cannot become the *deus ex machina* to explain all inauthentic elements. Ironically, the more one appeals to editing to save authenticity, the more one admits that the documents are not original in their present form.

2. Overall, the documents show a mixture of older and earlier linguistic elements. This can be explained in various ways, but the simplest explanation seems to be that any Persian-Period documents have been heavily edited by the later scribes who created the Aramaic narrative into which they inserted the documents. This does not preclude that those documents without any early forms may have been created entirely in the post-Achaemenid Period.

3. A study of the epistolary formulas in the Ezra documents has shown that, overall, they do not agree with those of early texts. Rather, they best match those found in early Hellenistic texts, suggesting this is when they were written or edited. (The one exception is the decree of Ezra 7, where the investigation was inconclusive, while Ezra 1:2–4 and 6:2–5 were not included in Schwiderski's study.) This result fits with the conclusions about the language of the texts. Any original texts from before Alexander have been heavily edited in the Hellenistic Period.

4. Jewish theology is found in most of the documents. References to "Israel," the "elders" as the leadership (with no mention of the governor), "the God who makes his name to dwell" in Jerusalem, and the like are unlikely to be part of official documents from the Persian chancellory. This already indicates intervention from Jewish scribes at some point in the history of the Ezra text.

5. The most blatant problem with the Ezra documents is the amount of propaganda, ranging from imperial financing of the temple and its various projects to the making available of huge sums from the imperial treasury in gifts for the Jerusalem Temple from the Persian emperor personally. All decisions seem to be made by the king himself, with the powerful satrap and the local governor and other officials

ignored. In spite of the credulity of many modern scholars, this state of affairs is not supported by known Persian documents and practices.

I have given some serious reasons why it is unlikely that all the documents are authentic in their present form. Nevertheless, there are also reasons to reject Torrey's and Gunneweg's idea that they are complete fabrications from a later age.[92] Although it is difficult to prove authenticity beyond doubt or to eliminate the possibility of clever forgeries, the hypothesis of complete invention does not seem the best explanation of the data. It is possible that one or two documents are a fabrication, albeit probably fairly early ones, but I suspect that we have some authentic documents that have been reworked by Jewish scribes to a lesser or greater extent. We may also have Achaemenid-Period Jewish writings that were subsequently reworked.

Based on a weighing of probabilities, I suggest that the documents of Ezra fall along a spectrum of authenticity, with some having a greater probability of authenticity or, rather, a larger content of authentic material, even if combined with insertions from later scribes and some having a lower—or even a rather low—probability of being authentic (or having any authentic material). If this is the case, the problem of evaluating them is an acute one. A good example of documents as literary inventions to spice up a narrative can be found in the Greek text of Esther, where various decrees are not just said to be issued, as in the Hebrew text, but are also "quoted" in full (3:1–7; 6:1–24; 8:13). It would be difficult to find a scholar willing to defend these as authentic decrees from a Persian king. One of the best examples of Jewish scribes taking a genuine decree and altering it to fit their own propaganda is found in a passage of Josephus relating to citizenship for Alexandrian Jews.[93] A scribe can doctor up one document consid-

---

92. Torrey 1970: 140–47; Gunneweg 1985: 85–111.

93. See the discussion in Grabbe 1992: 407–8. Josephus quotes a decree allegedly from the Roman Emperor Claudius that states that the Jews have "equal civic rights" with the Greeks (*Ant.* 19.5.2 §§280–85). Fortunately, an authentic decree of Claudius on the subject has been found in the papyri from Egypt (Tcherikover, Fuks, Stern 1957–64: 2.36–55 [text #153]), and it says something quite different, making it clear that most Jews did not have citizenship along with the Greeks. A Jewish scribe seems to have taken this or a similar genuine decree of Claudius and made sufficient changes for the decree to say the opposite of what it actually said. (Pucci Ben Zeev 1998 argues that the decree assigned to Claudius in Josephus is genuine and is not a duplicate of the clearly authentic decree found in the papyri; she makes a reasonable case, but I still have my doubts.) Of course, the Jews were not the only ones to do this; similar falsifications on behalf of interested parties are found throughout history.

erably without changing the overall message, while another may have made only a couple of relatively minor changes yet with the result that the document then says something quite different from the original. After this brief investigation, the most that can be done is to attempt to rank the documents in order of credibility. I would rank Document 4 as having the most authentic material and the Hebrew Cyrus decree of 1:2–4 as having the least, with the others ranging between these two.

> Document 4 (5:7–17): Letter of Tattenai
> Document 7 (7:12–26): Decree of Artaxerxes to Ezra
> Document 5 (6:2–5): (Aramaic) Decree of Cyrus
> Document 6 (6:6–12): Reply of Darius
> Document 2 (4:9(?)–16): Letter to Artaxerxes
> Document 3 (4:17–22): Reply of Artaxerxes
> Document 1 (1:2–4): (Hebrew) Decree of Cyrus
> [NB: highest probability at the top and lowest at the bottom]

Document 4 has only examples of early linguistic forms and also supplies information found nowhere else in Ezra—indeed, information that goes contrary to Ezra 1—that Sheshbazzar was appointed governor. Yet even this letter is not without problems, talking about temple vessels that were likely destroyed long before Sheshbazzar, using an incorrect form of Nebuchadrezzar's name, and mentioning only the elders at one point. One can come up with hypotheses to explain these points and perhaps salvage the document as a genuine Achaemenid document. Yet if the letter most likely to be reliable—or with the most reliable material—has these problems, what about the others?

We can only make decisions on the data we have, not the data we may unearth tomorrow, but this is the nature of scholarship. New discoveries may confound all current theories. A further point is that all theories and arguments of authenticity are matters of probability. Some may find it perfectly believable that Ezra managed to extract more than 25 metric tons of silver from the Persian government or had a slush fund of 100 talents of silver. Most scholars, however, will find this a bit hard to accept. All in all, it seems to me that the compiler of Ezra had available some original Persian documents at least part of the time, but he or a prior tradent worked these over for apologetic or theological purposes or even to support claims made by the Jewish community to the Persian administration. Any use made of these letters must be careful and critical, with thorough supporting arguments.

Bibliography

Batten, Loring W.
  1913   *A Critical and Exegetical Commentary on Ezra and Nehemiah.* International Critical Commentary. Edinburgh: T. & T. Clark.
Beaulieu, Paul-Alain
  1993   An Episode in the Fall of Babylon to the Persians. *JNES* 52: 241–61.
Berger, P.-R.
  1975   Der Kyros-Zylinder mit dem Zusatzfragment BIN II Nr. 32 und die akkadischen Personennamen im Danielbuch. *ZA* 64: 192–234.
Bickerman, Elias J.
  1976   The Edict of Cyrus in Ezra 1. Pp. 72–108 in vol. 1 of *Studies in Jewish and Christian History.* Arbeiten zur Geschichte des antiken Judentums und des Urchristentums 9. Leiden: Brill. [Partial revision of *JBL* 65 (1946) 244–75]
Bivar, A. D. H.
  1985   Achaemenid Coins, Weights and Measures. *CHI* 2: 610–39.
Blenkinsopp, Joseph
  1987   The Mission of Udjahorresnet and Those of Ezra and Nehemiah. *JBL* 106: 409–21.
  1989   *Ezra–Nehemiah.* OTL. London: SCM.
Brandstein, W., and Mayrhofer, M.
  1964   *Handbuch des Altpersischen.* Wiesbaden: Harrassowitz.
Briant, Pierre
  1998   Droaphernès et la statue de Sardes. Pp. 205–26 in *Studies in Persian History: Essays in Memory of David M. Lewis,* ed. Maria Brosius and Amélie Kuhrt. Vol. 11 of *Achaemenid History.* Leiden: Nederlands Instituut voor het Nabije Oosten.
  2002   *From Cyrus to Alexander: A History of the Persian Empire,* trans. Peter T. Daniels. Winona Lake, Indiana: Eisenbrauns. [English translation of *Histoire de l'empire perse de Cyrus à Alexandre.* 2 vols. Achaemenid History 10. Leiden: Nederlands Instituut voor het Nabije Oosten, 1996]
  2003   Histoire et archéologie d'un texte: La *Lettre de Darius à Gadatas* entre Perses, Grecs et Romains. Pp. 107–44 in *Licia e Lidia prima dell'Ellenizzazione: Atti del Convegno internazionale—Roma 11–12 ottobre 1999,* ed. M. Giorgieri, M. Salvini, M.-C. Trémouille, and P. Vannicelli. Monografie Scientifiche: Serie Scienze umane e sociali Consiglio Nazionale delle Ricerche. Rome: CNR.
Brown, Truesdell S.
  1982   Herodotus' Portrait of Cambyses. *Historia* 31: 387–403.
Brunneau, P.
  1982   " 'Les Israélites de Délos' et la juiverie délienne." *Bulletin de correspondance hellenique* 106: 465–504.
Bryce, T. R.
  1983   Political Unity in Lycia during the "Dynastic" Period. *JNES* 42: 31–42.
Cameron, George G.
  1948   *Persepolis Treasury Tablets.* Chicago: University of Chicago Press.

1958   Persepolis Treasury Tablets Old and New. *JNES* 17: 161–76.
1965   New Tablets from the Persepolis Treasury. *JNES* 24: 167–92.
Clines, David J. A.
1984   *Ezra, Nehemiah, Esther.* Century Bible Commentary. London: Marshall, Morgan & Scott / Grand Rapids: Eerdmans.
Cowley, A.
1923   *Aramaic Papyri of the Fifth Century* B.C. Reprinted Osnabrück: Otto Zeller, 1967.
Dandamaev, M. A., and Lukonin, V. G.
1989   *The Culture and Social Institutions of Ancient Iran.* Cambridge: Cambridge University Press.
Depuydt, Leo
1995   Murder in Memphis: The Story of Cambyses's Mortal Wounding of the Apis Bull (ca. 523 B.C.E.). *JNES* 54: 119–26.
Driver, G. R.
1957   *Aramaic Documents of the Fifth Century* B.C. Rev. ed. Oxford: Clarendon.
Eskenazi, Tamara Cohn
1988   *In an Age of Prose: A Literary Approach to Ezra–Nehemiah.* SBLMS 36. Atlanta: Scholars Press.
Fitzmyer, Joseph A.
1979   The Phases of the Aramaic Language. Pp. 57–84 in *A Wandering Aramean: Collected Aramaic Essays.* SBLMS 25. Atlanta: Scholars Press.
Frei, Peter, and Koch, Klaus
1996   *Reichsidee und Reichsorganisation im Perserreich.* 2nd ed. Freiburg: Universitätsverlag / Göttingen: Vandenhoeck & Ruprecht.
Fried, Lisbeth S.
2001   "You Shall Appoint Judges": Ezra's Mission and the Rescript of Artaxerxes. Pp. 63–89 in *Persia and Torah: The Theory of Imperial Authorization of the Pentateuch,* ed. James W. Watts. SBLSymS 17. Atlanta: Society of Biblical Literature.
Galling, Kurt
1964   *Studien zur Geschichte Israels im persischen Zeitalter.* Tübingen: Mohr (Siebeck).
Grabbe, Lester L.
1988   Another Look at the *Gestalt* of "Darius the Mede." *CBQ* 50: 198–213.
1991   Reconstructing History from the Book of Ezra. Pp. 98–107 in *Second Temple Studies: The Persian Period,* ed. Philip R. Davies. JSOTSup 117. Sheffield: JSOT Press.
1992   *Persian and Greek Periods;* and *Roman Period. Judaism from Cyrus to Hadrian.* 2 vols. Minneapolis: Fortress. [British edition in one-volume paperback, London: SCM, 1994]
1994   What Was Ezra's Mission? Pp. 286–99 in *Second Temple Studies,* vol. 2: *Temple Community in the Persian Period,* ed. Tamara C. Eskenazi and Kent H. Richards. JSOTSup 175. Sheffield: JSOT Press.
1998   *Ezra and Nehemiah.* Readings. London: Routledge.
2001a Jewish Historiography and Scripture in the Hellenistic Period. Pp. 129–55 in *Did Moses Speak Attic? Jewish Historiography and Scripture in the*

Hellenistic Period, ed. Lester L. Grabbe. JSOTSup 317 = European Seminar in Historical Methodology 3. Sheffield: Sheffield Academic Press.

2001b The Law of Moses in the Ezra Tradition: More Virtual than Real? Pp. 91–113 in *Persia and Torah: The Theory of Imperial Authorization of the Pentateuch*, ed. James W. Watts. SBLSymS 17. Atlanta: Society of Biblical Literature.

Grayson, A. Kirk
1975 *Assyrian and Babylonian Chronicles*. Texts from Cuneiform Sources 5. Locust Valley, New York: Augustin.

Greenfield, Jonas C.
1974 Standard Literary Aramaic. Pp. 280–89 in *Actes du Premier Congrès international de linguistique sémitique et chamito-sémitique, Paris 16–19 juillet 1969*, ed. A. Caquot and D. Cohen. Janua Linguarum, Series Practica 159. The Hague: Mouton.

Greenfield, Jonas C., and Porten, Bezalel
1982 *The Bisitun Inscription of Darius the Great: Aramaic Version*. Corpus Inscriptionum Iranicarum 1: Inscriptions of Ancient Iran. London: Humphries.

Griffith, F. L.
1909 *Catalogue of the Demotic Papyri in the John Rylands Library, Manchester, with Facsimiles and Complete Translations*. 3 vols. Manchester: University of Manchester Press.

Gruen, Eric S.
1998 *Heritage and Hellenism: The Reinvention of Jewish Tradition*. Hellenistic Culture and Society 30. Berkeley: University of California Press.

Gunneweg, A. H. J.
1985 *Esra*. KAT 19/1. Gütersloh: Mohn.
1987 *Nehemiah*. KAT 19/2. Gütersloh: Mohn.

Hallo, William W. (ed.)
1997–2002 *The Context of Scripture*. 3 vols. Leiden: Brill.

Hallock, Richard T.
1969 *Persepolis Fortification Tablets*. Chicago: University of Chicago Press.
1985 The Evidence of the Persepolis Tablets. Pp. 588–609 in vol. 2 of *CHJ*.

Hansen, O.
1986 The Purported Letter of Darius to Gadatas. *Rheinisches Museum* 129: 95–96.

Horbury, William, and Noy, David
1992 *Jewish Inscriptions of Graeco-Roman Egypt*. Cambridge: Cambridge University Press.

Hornblower, Simon
1982 *Mausolus*. Oxford: Clarendon.

Hout, M. van den
1949 Studies in Early Greek Letter-Writing. *Mnemosyne* (4th series) 2: 19–41, 138–53.

Hughes, G. R.
1984 The So-called Pherendates Correspondence. Pp. 75–86 in *Grammata Demotika: Festschrift für Erich Lüddeckens zum 15. Juni 1983*, ed. H.-J. Thissen and K.-T. Zauzich. Würzburg: Zauzich.

Janzen, David
  2000   The "Mission" of Ezra and the Persian-Period Temple Community. *JBL*
         119: 619–43.
Japhet, Sara
  1982   Sheshbazzar and Zerubbabel against the Background of the Historical
         and Religious Tendencies of Ezra–Nehemiah. *ZAW* 94: 66–98.
  1983   Sheshbazzar and Zerubbabel against the Background of the Historical
         and Religious Tendencies of Ezra–Nehemiah. *ZAW* 95: 218–30.
Kent, Roland G.
  1953   *Old Persian.* 2nd edition. AOS 33. New Haven: American Oriental
         Society.
Kervran, M., et al.
  1972   Une statue de Darius découverte à Suse. *Journal asiatique* 260: 235–66.
Koch, Heidemarie
  1977   *Die religiösen Verhältnisse der Dareioszeit: Untersuchungen an Hand der
         elamischen Persepolistäfelchen.* Göttinger Orientforschungen, 3rd series:
         Iranica 4. Wiesbaden: Harrassowitz.
  1992   *Es kündet Dareios der König . . . : Vom Leben im persischen Großreich.* Kul-
         turgeschichte der antiken Welt 55. Mainz am Rhein: von Zabern.
Koehler, Ludwig, and Baumgartner, Walter (eds.)
  2001   *The Hebrew and Aramaic Lexicon of the Old Testament*, rev. Walter Baum-
         gartner and Johann Jakob Stamm. Translated under the supervision of
         M. E. J. Richardson. Leiden: Brill.
Kraabel, A. T.
  1984   "New Evidence of the Samaritan Diaspora Has Been Found on Delos,"
         BA 47: 44–47.
Kraeling, E. G.
  1953   *The Brooklyn Museum Aramaic Papyri.* New Haven: Yale University
         Press.
Kuhrt, Amélie
  1983   The Cyrus Cylinder and Achaemenid Imperial Policy. *JSOT* 25: 83–97.
Kutscher, E. Y.
  1971   The Hermopolis Papyri. *IOS* 1: 103–19.
Lebram, J. C. H.
  1987   Die Traditionsgeschichte der Ezragestalt und die Frage nach dem his-
         torischen Esra. Pp. 103–38 in *Sources, Structures and Synthesis*, ed. He-
         leen Sancisi-Weerdenburg. Vol. 1 of *Achaemenid History.* Proceeding of
         the Groningen 1983 Achaemenid History Workshop. Leiden: Neder-
         lands Instituut voor het Nabije Oosten.
Lemaire, André
  1995   The Xanthos Trilingual Revisited. Pp. 423–32 in *Solving Riddles and Un-
         tying Knots: Biblical, Epigraphic, and Semitic Studies in Honor of Jonas C.
         Greenfield*, ed. Ziony Zevit, Seymour Gitin, and Michael Sokoloff.
         Winona Lake, Indiana: Eisenbrauns.
Lewis, David M.
  1977   *Sparta and Persia.* Columbia Classical Studies 1. Leiden: Brill.

Lichtheim, Miriam
1980 *The Late Period.* Vol. 3 of *Ancient Egyptian Literature.* Berkeley: University of California Press.
Lloyd, Alan B.
1988 Herodotus on Cambyses: Some Thoughts on Recent Work. Pp. 55–66 in *Method and Theory,* ed. Amélie Kuhrt and Heleen Sancisi-Weerdenburg. Vol. 3 of *Achaemenid History.* Proceeding of the London 1985 Achaemenid History Workshop. Leiden: Nederlands Instituut voor het Nabije Oosten.
Meiggs, Russell, and Lewis, David (eds.)
1969 *A Selection of Greek Historical Inscriptions to the End of the Fifth Century B.C.* Oxford: Clarendon.
Metzger, H., et al.
1979 *La Stèle trilingue du Létôon.* Fouilles de Xanthos 6. Paris: Klincksieck.
Meyer, Eduard
1896 *Die Entstehung des Judenthums.* Halle: Niemeyer. [Reprinted Hildesheim: Olms, 1965.]
Muraoka, Takamitsu, and Porten, Bezalel
1997 *A Grammar of Egyptian Aramaic.* HO 32. Leiden: Brill.
Myers, J. M.
1965 *Ezra, Nehemiah.* AB 14. Garden City, New York: Doubleday.
Noy, David
1995 *The City of Rome.* Vol. 2 of *Jewish Inscriptions of Western Europe.* Cambridge: Cambridge University Press.
Olmstead, A. T.
1933 A Persian Letter in Thucydides. *AJSL* 49: 161ff.
Porten, Bezalel
1978–79 The Documents in the Book of Ezra and the Mission of Ezra. *Shnaton* 3: 174–196 [Hebrew] + xix–xx [English].
1983 The Address Formulae in Aramaic Letters: A New Collation of Cowley 17. *RB* 90: 396–415.
1996 *The Elephantine Papyri in English: Three Millennia of Cross-Cultural Continuity and Change.* Documenta et monumenta Orientis antiqui 22. Leiden: Brill.
2002 Theme and Structure of *Ezra* 1–6: From Literature to History. *Transeuphratène* 23: 27–44.
2003 Elephantine and the Bible. Pp. 51–84 in *Semitic Papyrology in Context: A Climate of Creativity—Papers from a New University Conference Marking the Retirement of Baruch A. Levine,* ed. Lawrence H. Schiffman. Leiden: Brill.
Porten, Bezalel, and Yardeni, Ada
1986–99 *Textbook of Aramaic Documents from Ancient Egypt.* 4 vols. Jerusalem: Hebrew University, Department of the History of the Jewish People.
Posener, G.
1936 *La première domination perse en Egypte: Recueil d'inscriptions hiéroglyphiques.* Bibliothèque d'Étude de l'Institute Français d'Archéologie Orientale 11. Cairo: Institut Français d'Archéologie Orientale.

Powell, Marvin A.
1992 Weights and Measures. Pp. 897–908 in vol. 6 of *ABD*.

Pucci Ben Zeev, Miriam
1998 *Jewish Rights in the Roman World: The Greek and Roman Documents Quoted by Josephus Flavius.* Texte und Studien zum Antiken Judentum 74. Tübingen: Mohr Siebeck.

Pummer, Reinhard
1987 "Αργαριζιν: A Criterion for Samaritan Provenance?" *JSJ* 18: 18–25.

Rudolph, Wilhelm
1949 *Ezra und Nehemia.* HAT 20. Tübingen: Mohr Siebeck.

Schaeder, Hans Heinrich
1930a *Iranische Beiträge I.* Schriften der Königsberger Gelehrten Gesellschaft 6. Halle: Niemeyer.
1930b *Esra der Schreiber.* Beiträge zur historischen Theologie 5. Tübingen: Mohr Siebeck.

Schaudig, Hanspeter
2001 *Die Inschriften Nabonids von Babylon und Kyros' des Großen samt den in ihrem Umfeld entstandenen Tendenzschriften: Textausgabe und Grammatik.* AOAT 256. Münster: Ugarit-Verlag.

Schwiderski, Dirk
2000 *Handbuch des nordwestsemitischen Briefformulars: Ein Beitrag zur Echtheitsfrage der aramäischen Briefe des Esrabuches.* BZAW 295. Berlin: de Gruyter.

Smith, Morton
1987 *Palestinian Parties and Politics That Shaped the Old Testament.* London: SCM. [Corrected reprint of New York: Columbia, 1971]

Spiegelberg, Wilhelm
1914 *Die sogenannte demotische Chronik des Pap. 215 der Bibliothèque Nationale zu Paris: Nebst den auf der Rückseite des Papyrus stehenden Texten.* Demotische Studien 7. Leipzig: Hinrichs.
1928 Drei demotische Schreiben aus der Korrespondenz des Pherendates, des Satrapen Darius' I., mit den Chnum-Priestern von Elephantine. *Sitzungsberichte der preussischen Akademie der Wissenschaften, phil.-hist. Klasse*: 604–22.

Steiner, Richard C.
2001 The *mbqr* at Qumran, the *episkopos* in the Athenian Empire, and the Meaning of *lbqr'* in Ezra 7:14: On the Relation of Ezra's Mission to the Persian Legal Project. *JBL* 120: 623–46.

Tcherikover, V. A.; Fuks, A.; and Stern, M.
1957–64 *Corpus Papyrorum Judaicarum.* 3 vols. Cambridge: Harvard University Press / Jerusalem: Magnes.

Teixidor, Javier
1978 The Aramaic text in the Trilingual Stele from Xanthus. *JNES* 37: 181–85.

Torrey, Charles Cutter
1896 *The Composition and Historical Value of Ezra–Nehemiah.* BZAW 2. Giessen: Ricker.

1970   *Ezra Studies*, ed. with a Prolegomenon by W. F. Stinespring. New York: Ktav. [Original 1910]

Tuplin, Christopher
1987   The Administration of the Achaemenid Empire. Pp. 109–66 in *Coinage and Administration in the Athenian and Persian Empires: The Ninth Oxford Symposium on Coinage and Monetary History*, ed. I. Carradice. BAR International Series 343. Oxford: B.A.R.

Vallat, F.
1974a   Les textes cunéiformes de la statue de Darius. *Cahiers de la délégation archéologique française en Iran* 4: 161–70.
1974b   L'inscription trilingue de Xerxès à la porte de Darius. *Cahiers de la délégation archéologique française en Iran* 4: 171–80.

Vaux, Roland de
1971   The Decrees of Cyrus and Darius on the Rebuilding of the Temple. Pp. 29–57 in *Bible and the Ancient Near East*. London: Darton, Longman & Todd. [Translation from *RB* 46 (1937) 29–57]

Voigtlander, E. N. von
1978   *The Behistun Inscription of Darius the Great: Babylonian Version*. Corpus Inscriptionum Iranicarum 1: Inscriptions of Ancient Iran. London: Humphries.

Watts, James W. (ed.)
2001   *Persia and Torah: The Theory of Imperial Authorization of the Pentateuch*. SBLSymS 17. Atlanta: Society of Biblical Literature.

Weissbach, F. H.
1911   *Die Keilinschriften der Achämeniden*. Vorderasiatische Bibliothek 3. Leipzig: Hinrichs. [Reprinted Leipzig: Zentral-Antiquariat der DDR, 1968]

Widengren, Geo
1977   The Persian Period. Pp. 489–538 in *Israelite and Judaean History*, ed. John Hayes and J. Maxwell Miller. Philadelphia: Fortress.

Wiesehöfer, J.
1987   Zur Frage der Echtheit des Dareios-Briefes an Gadatas. *Reinisches Museum* 130: 396–98.

Williamson, Hugh G. M.
1985   *Ezra, Nehemiah*. WBC 16. Waco, Texas: Word.
1991   Ezra and Nehemiah in the Light of the Texts from Persepolis. *BBR* 1: 41–61.
1998   Judah and the Jews. Pp. 145–63 in *Studies in Persian History: Essays in Memory of David M. Lewis*, ed. Maria Brosius and Amélie Kuhrt. Vol. 11 of *Achaemenid History*. Leiden: Nederlands Instituut voor het Nabije Oosten.

"See, We Are Serving Today" (Nehemiah 9:36): Nehemiah 9 as a Theological Interpretation of the Persian Period

MANFRED OEMING

Heidelberg University

In Ezra and Nehemiah (also in the books of Chronicles), the Persian government is regarded very positively. The Achaemenid kings are—like the Davidic dynasty—the custodians of Israel who have been appointed by Yahweh. It is they who have enabled the building of the Second Temple and the city walls of Jerusalem and the reformation of the community by promulgation of the law.[1]

Wherever these books (like the rest of the Old Testament) speak of the Achaemenids, the general attitude is so warm and positive that the statements have raised suspicions in the minds of many exegetes. They understand these texts to be pointed, pro-Persian propaganda for the Israelite withdrawal of support from contemporary anti-Persian rebel movements.[2] In order for us to answer the question whether these texts are truly mere propaganda, we need to examine them in detail.

Author's note: Translations of quotations from works in other languages are my own.

1. For example, Ezra 1:1ff.: "Now in the first year of Cyrus, king of Persia, in order to fulfill the word of Yahweh by the mouth of Jeremiah, Yahweh stirred up the spirit of Cyrus, king of Persia" (see also 2 Chr 36:22–23); or Neh 2:8: "And the king granted me what I asked, for the gracious hand of my God was upon me" (see also 2:18), or Ezra 7:1, 6: "After this, in the reign of King Artaxerxes of Persia, Ezra son of Seraiah, son of Azariah, son of Hilkiah, . . . this Ezra came up from Babylon. He was a scribe versed in the Law of Moses, which Yahweh, God of Israel, had given. The king granted him everything that he asked, for the hand of Yahweh his God was over him."

2. Albertz 1992: 472: "The missions of Nehemiah (444–432) and Ezra (398?) were also most likely connected to rebel movements. They were a clever strategic move by the Persian government to strengthen the endangered pro-Persian coalition with the aid of high-ranking Judean officials by granting further autonomy and thus ensuring continued loyalty to the Persian Empire: as Persian steward, Nehemiah, and with him the pro-Persian coalition, could take credit for the successful building of the wall and thus the elevation of Judah to a province of equal status."

As in all other instances, Old Testament historiography is, unfortunately, interested neither in political, military, and economic facts nor in a consistent portrayal of the organizational structure and culture of the Persian era. Its entire focus is on the *interpretation* of all events as they are viewed by the God of Israel. The history of Achaemenid rule over Judah and the Judahites is made transparent in light of the actions of Israel's God in history. The portrayal of history becomes an object lesson in theology. The narration of history towers as high as the description of the nature of Yahweh.

Nehemiah 9 is one of the central texts in this context. The meaning of this short narration and long prayer of elaborate, skillful language, full of allusions and citations,[3] is found not merely in poetic-aesthetic considerations[4] or in its historiographic objective but rather in theology. The structure of this passage is clear (see outline).

The origin and date of Nehemiah 9 has been a matter of debate.

1. Based on a few allusions to the situation of the Northern Kingdom shortly after its destruction by the Assyrians (see especially the "kings of Assyria," v. 32), Welch[5] suggested in 1929 that the text was written during the early seventh century. His followers were Rehm and Rendsburg.[6]

2. The complex mixture of traditions, however, seems to indicate a much later period of composition. The most radical position is held by Gunneweg, who considers Nehemiah 9 to be a supplement to the Chronicler's History and "undoubtedly one of the latest texts in the Old Testament."[7] We are thus looking at a spectrum of almost 500 years of potential dates for the composition of this passage.

3. I lean toward a position in the middle—neither 700 nor 170: the most likely date for the Chronistic History still seems to be the

---

3. The evaluation of these texts reveals a profound change in the attitude of Christian OT scholars. For example, because of the multiple citations that he found in Nehemiah 9, Jahn (1909: 134) regarded the text almost a century ago as "a compiled prayer, one of the most feeble products of remorseful postexilic Judaism." Recently, however, R. Rendtorff (1997: 117) expressed admiration, because "these texts show an impressive, independent use of the earlier religious traditions of Israel, a shaping of them into significant new impressive forms that became an integral and important part of our biblical heritage."

4. For a linguistic analysis, compare the commentaries, especially Duggan 2001: 139–233.

5. Welch 1929.

6. Rehm 1957; Rendsburg 1991.

7. Gunneweg 1987: 129.

Outline of Nehemiah 9:
Nehemiah 9 as Compact Theology

vv. 1–5	Narrative framework as introduction
v. 1	fasting in sackcloth and ashes
v. 2	separation from all foreigners
v. 3	one-fourth of the day devoted to the reading of the Torah
vv. 4–5	cry to God led by a Levite
vv. 6–31	The prayer of confession (a short hymnic repetition of the whole Torah; God addressed directly)
v. 6	creation
vv. 7–8	Abraham as God's chosen
vv. 9–11	the Exodus and God's guidance through the Red Sea
v. 12	guidance through the desert
vv. 13–14	revelation at Sinai: Torah as the center of God's acts of salvation
vv. 15–21	perseverance in crisis (God's grace as the central element)
vv. 22–25	gift of the land
vv. 26–31	Israel's rejection of the covenant in spite of prophetic preaching–punishment–cry for help–salvation
vv. 32–37	The thematic goal: the present situation of the Jewish community
v. 32	*"and now"*: the current situation is seen as a problem from "the time of the kings of Assyria"
vv. 34–35	summary of the "sin of the fathers": *they* did not repent and did not serve
vv. 36–37	*"but we* are slaves in the land—under Persian kings—and in great misery"
v. 38 (Neh 10:1)	Conclusion[8]
	Renewal of covenant

---

late Persian era, between 400 and 330, because there are no real references to the Hellenistic Period.

The Interpretation of Verses 1–35

Despite disagreements regarding the date of the text, scholars have been mostly in agreement with regard to its interpretation:

---

8. The versification varies. BHS reads Neh 10:1. Various sources number the verse 9:38, because it contains the final sentence of the prayer. However, it also marks a renewal of the covenant (v. 1, "And because of all this, we make a firm *covenant* in writing, and our princes, Levites, *and* priests seal *it*"). A diachronic separation of prayer and covenant renewal is proposed by Gunneweg.

1. Nehemiah 9 is a psalm with a historical retrospective, analogous to Psalms 78, 105, 106, and 138.[9]
2. It is a compilation by well-educated scribes. K. Schmid summarizes this position well: "The fact that Nehemiah 9 presupposes and uses the historiography of Genesis–2 Kings (as well as other texts) can be seen clearly in its many verbal allusions and in its character as a mixed composition of Priestly and Deuteronomic theologies."[10]
3. Nehemiah 9 is most likely not an account of a concrete historical situation—despite the exact date that appears in 9:1. It also was not composed for liturgical purposes but must instead be regarded as "theological literature"[11] that addresses the reader with a didactic purpose.
4. I would like to push this view further:[12] Nehemiah 9 is a summary of Old Testament teachings on God, synthesizing the traditions about God's actions in history in the Pentateuch and the Deuteronomic History[13] with several prophetic traditions, especially Jeremiah, Ezekiel, Zephaniah, and Zechariah.[14] The prayer of confession takes on the character of a creedal summary.

In contrast to Gerhard von Rad, who understood 10:1[9:38] to be the origin of the tradition,[15] I suggest that this verse is the final part of a very compact summary. Chapter 9 clearly exhibits catechismal elements—that is, it is a kind of "creed" from the Persian Period, a confession of the faith held by the postexilic congregation. The primary intention of the text is twofold: to define the nature of God and to define "true Israel."[16]

The theological character of this "definition" is clear. God's action is of primary importance. The beginning is marked by an indicative statement: God is the source of all life as a gift of grace (v. 6), of bread and water in the desert, of land and political autonomy. God the creator, determiner, liberator, and protector is a gracious God. The primary *Leitwort* defining God's actions is נתן. The "grace-formula"[17] is alluded to

---

9. Cf. Mathias 1993.
10. Schmid 1999: 303.
11. Gunneweg 1987: 129.
12. See Rendtorff (1997: 111), who speaks (with von Rad) of a "historical creed."
13. Schmid 1999: 302–6.
14. The included quotations have been analyzed in detail by Boda 1999.
15. Von Rad 1938.
16. Cf. Oeming 1990.
17. Cf. Dohmen 1996; Scoralick 2002; Michel 2003.

several times in the text, not without reason (v. 17b): "But you are a God of forgiveness, gracious and merciful, slow to anger and abounding in grace, and you did not forsake them." I agree with Mathys: "The central theme of the text is God's loyalty and mercy despite Israel's persistent disobedience."[18] However, the greatest gift was the Torah. It is described in vv. 13–14 in warm, inviting words with three hymnic adjectives: "and you gave them right ordinances and true laws, good statutes and commandments, and you made known your holy sabbath to them and gave them commandments and statutes and a law through your servant Moses."

The second aspect of this creed is also obvious: Israel is Yahweh's partner. Israel is the community of those who have lived their entire history with this God, including all his previous judgments. This is why this community is so aware of the imperative that follows the many rich indicatives. *Because of all this*, Israel must part with all foreign things and commit itself explicitly and in writing to the Torah. Israel may continue to count on the fact that the merciful God will continue to forgive trespasses against his will, but it must also be ready to repent at all times. All of God's punishments result from the stated desire to lead Israel back to the law לַהֲשִׁיבָם אֶל־תּוֹרָתֶךָ. The meaning of history is found in divine pedagogy: God intends to lead out of sin into the living space created by the Torah. Prophecies of judgment are also a part of this historical plan: "Many years you were patient with them, and warned them by your spirit through your prophets; yet they would not listen. Therefore you handed them over to the peoples of the lands" (v. 30).

Nevertheless, because Israel failed to exist in a listening and living relationship with Yahweh, God failed, despite his longsuffering efforts, and cast Israel away into the hands of the peoples of the nations (v. 30b). Now, however, Israel has the opportunity to make a new beginning. They have done penance for the sins of their fathers and ask that God recognize the atoning effect of his punishment: "Now therefore, our God—the great and mighty and awesome God, keeping covenant and steadfast love—do not treat lightly all the hardship (כָּל־הַתְּלָאָה) that has come upon us, upon our kings, our officials, our priests, our prophets, our ancestors, and all your people, since the time of the kings of Assyria until today." Israel asks God for forgiveness in accordance with his nature described in the "grace-formula" so that they may receive a new

---

18. Mathys 1994: 4.

chance to become what they are. This is the point of the entire context of Nehemiah 8ff.

What are the characteristic elements of the theology of this text? First of all, Nehemiah 9 is a summary. It condenses the most important elements of the preexilic and exilic traditions of Judahite teachings on God, synthesizing the traditions from the different sources. I will tell you this much: if you must write a theology of the OT, you should study Nehemiah 9 *intensively.* It is compacted. It is like a ZIP file, and you have to unpack it.

Second, into this penitential prayer, a complete creed has been integrated. In the form of a prayer, the text offers a theology in its entirety. Before the author expresses his wishes to God, he confesses his belief: I believe in the creation of heaven and earth by Adonai (v. 6); I believe that Adonai chose and tested Abraham (vv. 7–8); I believe that Adonai saw the distress of our ancestors in Egypt, heard their cry at the Red Sea, and guided them through the desert; I believe that God revealed his will at Sinai; the Torah is at the center of God's acts of salvation; I believe that Adonai gave the land to Israel; I confess that Israel rejected the covenant again and again, so God punished them; but I also believe that in the middle of his punishing, Adonai heard their cry for help and offered salvation anew. The center of the whole story is the so-called grace formula: "You are a God of forgiveness, gracious and merciful, slow to anger, and abounding in grace, and you have not forsaken them."

The Problems of Verses 36ff.

If the evaluation of the Achaemenid kings in Chronicles, Ezra, and Nehemiah is so positive and if the main lesson learned from Israel's history can be described as "God is merciful and full of grace," how then shall we understand the very negative conclusion of this prayer? If the general evaluation of the Persian kings is so positive, must we consider this passage to be a secondary addition to the book of Nehemiah? This question has been asked by several scholars, and the historic psalm in Nehemiah 9 has frequently been analyzed. In addition to the commentors Gunneweg, Eskenazi, and Williamson, numerous other scholars have dealt with this text, such as Mark Boda, Michael W. Duggan, Maurice Gilbert, Harm van Grol, Hans-Peter Mathys, Judith Newman, Volker Pröbstl, Gary Rendsburg, Rolf Rendtorff, and Klaus Zastrow (see the literature). There are three primary answers offered to these questions.

A. A Solution Based on the History of Tradition

According to this theory, Neh 9:6–37 did not originate in the time Nehemiah but is much older. It reflects the circumstances of the Assyrian epoch some years after the fall of Samaria, about 700 B.C.E. It was implanted in its present context by the final redactor of Nehemiah, who did not realize that it contradicted its new context.[19]

B. A Solution Based on Redactional History

Nehemiah 9 is the product of a later redactor. We can either assume, with Gunneweg, that it is "a post-Chronistic supplement"[20] or, with Kratz, a "large slice," the remains of layers that belonged to the beginning of the Maccabean revolt and reflect the situation around 170 B.C.E.[21]

C. Solutions Based on the Contemporary Historical Context

(1) The text belongs to the middle Persian Period (about 440 B.C.E.) and reveals the real political world view of the lower stratum of the Jewish community. The friendly words concerning the Achaemenid kings are part of political propaganda of the pro-Persian commissioners. In the psalm (and the circles behind the author) we can hear the voice of the people: they hate the strange rulers, especially the taxes. Neh 9:36–37 presents us with the voice of the anti-Persian opposition. The text articulates the true basic attitude of the general population during the economic crisis of the fifth century. It belongs in the context of anti-Persian rebel movements in Egypt and Phoenicia. Ezra and Nehemiah were explicitly sent to pacify such groups (see Albertz).[22]

(2) The Chronicler has messianic hopes and wishes for a new Judean king like David and Solomon (see Neh 13:26).[23]

(3) The statements contained in these final verses are not really negative but must be understood as simple realism: Israel must resign itself to the fact that it is only of subordinate political importance (see, e.g., Galling).[24]

---

19. This is the position of Welch 1929; Rehm 1957; and Rendsburg 1991.

20. Gunneweg 1987: 129: "This long prayer presupposes the Pentateuch, with JE, D, and P; and the other historiographical scriptures of the OT, especially Dtn and Dtr; and belongs therefore to the latest portions of the Old Testament."

21. Kratz 2000: 87–92.

22. Albertz 1993: 457.

23. Im 1985.

24. Galling 1958: 240.

All of these solutions presupposed that the book of Nehemiah contains contradictions. But here I wish to discuss the strengths and weaknesses of the solutions to date. Then I will present a completely new translation with supporting evidence. This fresh understanding will demonstrate that it is possible to interpret the whole book as having inner consistency.

First, a comparison of the strengths and the weaknesses of the above theories looks like this:

A: Strength: By dating the text to the Assyrian period, we can easily understand the expression "kings of Assyria." It also becomes clear why so little is said about the Exile and the Return from Exile. The great *weakness* of theory A, however, is the fact that the contents of Nehemiah 9 must be dated to a later stage of tradition, as Gunneweg, Schmid, Boda, and Duggan have clearly shown. It could not have been preexilic.

B: Strength: The strength of a late date lies in its ability to explain the negative tone of the text. Its *weakness* results from its assumption that the book contradicts itself. We must also ask why the anti-Hellenistic stance was not made more explicit.

C1–3: Strength: The strength of a return to the contemporary historical context lies in the relevance of the text to the religious and political disputes of the mid-fifth century. The narrated time and the actual time do not have to be separated artificially. The *weakness* of this theory, as in the previous cases, is the assumption of contradictions in the book of Nehemiah. Not only are the rebel critics supposed to be silenced but any messianic expectation is supposed be stifled by the memoirs of Nehemiah. It would be a massive self-contradiction if the same mission would also promote national-political hopes or even the expectation of a Messiah.

In my view, C3 is the strongest of the above hypotheses. Israel must resign itself to the present situation and accept Persian rule as God's wise and just pronouncement. However, describing this passage as a *lament* over hard times flies in the face of the beginning of the prayer. The prayer begins with praise and thanksgiving, not resigned hopelessness.

A New Translation and Solution

All these solutions are unconvincing, and consequently I propose a new solution. But first I would like to examine the traditional translation of Neh 9:36–10:1:

35. וְהֵם בְּמַלְכוּתָם וּבְטוּבְךָ הָרָב אֲשֶׁר־נָתַתָּ לָהֶם וּבְאֶרֶץ הָרְחָבָה וְהַשְּׁמֵנָה אֲשֶׁר־נָתַתָּ
לִפְנֵיהֶם לֹא עֲבָדוּךָ וְלֹא־שָׁבוּ מִמַּעַלְלֵיהֶם הָרָעִים:

36. הִנֵּה אֲנַחְנוּ הַיּוֹם עֲבָדִים וְהָאָרֶץ אֲשֶׁר־נָתַתָּה לַאֲבֹתֵינוּ לֶאֱכֹל אֶת־פִּרְיָהּ וְאֶת־טוּבָהּ
הִנֵּה אֲנַחְנוּ עֲבָדִים עָלֶיהָ:

37. וּתְבוּאָתָהּ מַרְבָּה לַמְּלָכִים אֲשֶׁר־נָתַתָּה עָלֵינוּ בְּחַטֹּאותֵינוּ וְעַל גְּוִיֹּתֵינוּ מֹשְׁלִים
וּבִבְהֶמְתֵּנוּ כִּרְצוֹנָם וּבְצָרָה גְדוֹלָה אֲנַחְנוּ:

10:1 וּבְכָל־זֹאת אֲנַחְנוּ כֹּרְתִים אֲמָנָה וְכֹתְבִים וְעַל הֶחָתוּם שָׂרֵינוּ לְוִיֵּנוּ כֹּהֲנֵינוּ:

The semantic fields created by the words of the text must be analyzed in more detail. This reveals several new, surprising interpretations. Five terms especially evidence possible polysemantic usage.

1. עֲבָדִים: Almost all commentaries translate this word 'slaves'. Many scholars understand it negatively; for example, Galling: "And today we must be slaves, and the land that you gave to our fathers to enjoy its fruits and fine products—we remain in it only as slaves!"[25] The semantic field of עבד, however, is much wider.[26]

First, I would like to emphasize that this word carried a specific connotation during the Persian era. The Persepolis inscription and Pseudo-Aristotle indicate that the ancient Persian expression *bandaka* (Greek: δουλοι) was a title of honor for vassals who maintained orderly, positive relations with the king of Persia. "Today we are עֲבָדִים" thus means: "Today we are well-regarded allies of the Persian Empire."

A second meaning of עֲבָדִים should be considered as well. Verse 35a is closely connected to v. 34: "Our fathers did not serve. We today are servants." This connection is usually interpreted as irony: "Because our fathers did not serve, we today are servants." This interpretation is not without alternative nuances, however. The connection can also be described as adversative: "Our fathers refused to serve God; they did not repent—*but* we today are servants (of God)." "We here today" then becomes a statement of contrast to the actions of the fathers and also of pride (despite humility) in one's own actions of faith, which are in continuity with the actions of the patriarchs.

Today, Israel renounces the sin of the fathers. Thus, עֲבָדִים could be a religious title of honor! He who does God's will is an *'ebed*. The people who decisively follow Torah are the *'ăbādîm*. Unfortunately, there is no

---

25. Galling 1958: 238.

26. Lipschits 2002: 157–71. Lipschits states that the title belongs primarily in the context of the royal court. It does not refer to a specific position but indicates a special closeness between certain individuals and the king. By analogy, the term "servant of Yahweh" indicates that an individual is closely connected to God. The terminology of Nehemiah 9 thus means that Judah was in good standing with the Persian government.

possessive "your"; otherwise the situation would be clear. But the group's reference to themselves as "servants" is not an impossibility.[27] We find the absolute use of עבד—without a possessive pronoun or an object—in only two passages. Isa 19:23 states: "In that day shall there be a highway out of Egypt to Assyria, and the Assyrian shall come into Egypt and the Egyptian into Assyria, and the Egyptians shall serve [*no object*] with the Assyrians." Job 36:11 states: "If they obey and serve [omitting *him* or *God*], they shall spend their days in prosperity, and their years in pleasure." Both passages belong historically in the Persian era and witness to the use of the absolute verb עבד as referring to a voluntary and deeply respectful devotion to God. This evidence supports the translation presented here, making it much more than a merely probable rendering of the Hebrew text.

2. Both verses deal with the topic of *land*. Normally, these statements are understood as a lament over the fact that the Israelites must be servants in their own land. This cannot be the only interpretation, however. The land is first and foremost characterized as the land "that God has given": וְהָאָרֶץ אֲשֶׁר־נָתַתָּה לַאֲבֹתֵינוּ לֶאֱכֹל אֶת־פִּרְיָהּ וְאֶת־טוּבָהּ. In this statement, the land is personified and used as the logical subject of the possessive suffixes as well as the verbs: the land produces fruit and various good gifts. Ownership of this land flowing with milk and honey constitutes one element of Israel's identity. The withdrawal of this wonderful gift of ownership (compare v. 34) was, in accordance with good Dtr theology in v. 30b, the direct result of Israel's continued lack of obedience to the Torah. Nevertheless, because God is a merciful God, Israel may *once again* reside in the land. Stated differently: the fact that Israel is once again in the land is a reassuring sign of God's grace.

The words אֲנַחְנוּ עֲבָדִים עָלֶיהָ thus mean: '*We* [emphasized] are servants in *it* [emphasized]'. In this manner, an antithesis is built up around the fathers, who were not 'in it'. At the same time, the statement insists on continuity with the patriarchs (compare vv. 7–8). The fact that the land reproduces (*Hiphil*: וּתְבוּאָתָהּ מַרְבָּה) "her" fruit and good gifts is proof of the return of God's grace. Two translations seem possible, but which meaning is intended? I believe we should interpret the repetition that frames v. 35 as positive emphasis: "Now, we are servants and living in the land that you promised to our forefathers. Look,

---

27. Compare διάκονος in the NT, most often in connection with a possessive suffix or genetive (iof God, of Christ), but at times also as *status absolutus*: 1 Cor 3:5: τί οὖν ἐστιν Ἀπολλῶς τί δέ ἐστιν Παῦλος; διάκονοι δι' ὧν ἐπιστεύσατε, καὶ ἑκάστῳ ὡς ὁ κύριος ἔδωκεν. At Qumran, the term referred to 'angels'.

we are servants in *it*." If we consider the idea of the "empty land" (2 Chr 36:21) the context for the book of Nehemiah (the list of the returning remnant in Nehemiah 7 definitely seems to reflect this context), then the statement in v. 35 has an especially positive ring to it: we rejoice over the fact that we can live in the land promised to our fathers and that we see the promise of an abundant land come true in our lifetime.

3. The word מֹשְׁלִים is normally understood as the description of dictatorial despotism, although this is not always necessarily the case. Joseph's actions in Egypt, for example, are seen as a blessing and described as follows: וְכִי־הוּא מֹשֵׁל בְּכָל־אֶרֶץ מִצְרָיִם. God's own rule is often described with the word מֹשֵׁל (e.g., Ps 66:7–8). Without denying the connotation of stern, rigid rule, we can add the meaning 'benevolent care of a ruler'. By including Gen 4:7 in the discussion, we also adduce the connotation of 'gaining control over evil'. We should not forget either that the kings addressed are the kings that God himself has given! They are kings by the grace of God! An important part of Israelite religion is the interpretation of foreign rule as instituted by God. Thus, the Babylonians in Jeremiah, for example, cannot merely be understood as a "rod of punishment" (see especially the letter to the exiles in Jeremiah 29), but also must be seen as part of God's history of salvation: they ruled in accordance with God's plan. By analogy, the Persians are legitimate rulers and good kings (certainly better than Israel's own kings) in the theology of the book of Nehemiah (especially if one considers the book of Nehemiah to be theologically connected to the book of Chronicles, as I do). I cannot find a hidden allusion to messianic hopes in Neh 9:36. Instead, I take the humble confession of sin meaningfully, as indicated by the genre: a prayer of confession: לַמְּלָכִים אֲשֶׁר־נָתַתָּה עָלֵינוּ בְּחַטֹּאותֵינוּ.

4. Some scholars argue that כִּרְצוֹנָם is always understood as pure despotism. However, this understanding is not transparent here, nor is it obligatory. Barstad states in his article in *ThWAT*: "The noun . . . is best understood as enjoyment, pleasure, delight, favor, kindness, grace, love, agreement, or as intention, will, wish, lust, desire."[28]

5. וּבְצָרָה גְדוֹלָה: What, specifically, is 'our great distress'? Biblical scholarship is divided on the issue. The distress is either seen as the political-economic hardship under Persian rule or as the mixed marriages. The primary argument for the latter view is the parallel in Ezra 9. I do not think the meaning of this term can be ascertained within such narrow boundaries. Heinz-Josef Fabry shows clearly that the term

---

28. *ThWAT* 7.647.

primarily refers to "the distress caused by enemies after one falls away from YHWH."[29] In many cases, God himself is the initiator of this distress. The term also implies crying out to God, for he is a helper in times of distress. The term is thus closely connected to a theology of prayer. Our sins have caused 'narrowness' (צַר), a situation in which only prayer will help.

The semantic fields created by all five terms demonstrate *striking polyvalence*. It is possible to read this constellation *negatively*; this is the way that it is usually read. It is also possible to reverse this understanding and read the constellation *positively*. This positive reading creates a meaning that contrasts with virtually all interpretations of this passage (the parentheses contain clarifying additions):

> (9:35) Even while they were in their kingdom, enjoying your great goodness to them in the spacious and fertile land you gave them, they did not serve you or turn from their evil ways. (36) (But) We, we are today (your) servants, in the land that you promised our fathers. Look, we are (your) servants on it. And it multiplies its fruit for the kings that you (legitimately) placed over us because of the sins of our fathers. They reign over our bodies and over our livestock with benevolent care. Yet we are now in great distress (because we once again are close to rejecting your Torah). (10:1) And because of all this, we (now) make a firm agreement in writing. And on that sealed document are the names of our officials, our Levites, and our priests.

Consequences

If we understand the last three verses in this manner, as a polyvalent description indicative of the contemporary situation, then the book no longer contradicts itself, and this chapter is appropriate to the book's context. Nehemiah 9 then becomes an integral part of the Ezra–Nehemiah composition. In my view (which I cannot spell out in more detail here), the book is an imposing attempt to create a model of a "true Israel" during the mid-Persian Period (ca. 450 B.C.E.). The *sanctuary*, rebuilt in 515, is not the only element in this model. Included in it is also *religious autonomy in relation to Samaria* as well. The *writings* of Moses *and* the Prophets are of equal canonical status; consequently, a creedal statement can (and must) comprise quotations from *both* sources. The small community of approximately 30,000 Judeans[30] creates a group identity partly by building a wall. This *wall* is not just a

---

29. *ThWAT* 6.1118–19.
30. Compare these numbers with Lipschits 2003: 356.

protective measure against political enemies or marauding bands. As Nehemiah's memoirs show, this wall is primarily connected to religious ideas. It has a twofold function: on the one hand, it protects against external religious influences. The wall creates a sacred space, a kind of temenos (compare Psalms 46, 48), and thus protects the "intermixing of the seed" (intermarriage). If foreign women enter the walled area, religious integrity is in danger: outside the wall, nothing is safe.

On the other hand, the wall exerts ethical pressure inward. The statutes of the Torah are valid within the walls, without exception. Whoever lives inside the walls has committed himself/herself to a life in full accordance with the Torah. This is the primary point of Nehemiah 8–10.

Let us return to the beginning of this essay: is a text such as (Ezra and) Nehemiah entirely Persian propaganda? Considering the theological-religious dimension of the text described above, I believe it to be informed by a profound, almost radical piety.[31] Whether this piety is pro-Persian or anti-Persian is not of primary importance. If we reduce Jeremiah's message to the statement that he was pro-Babylonian, then we will not have understood much of what Jeremiah was trying to say. From a Persian point of view, the religion of the pre-Chronistic circle around Ezra and Nehemiah was certainly a positive development. But the people in this circle were most likely not concerned about whether their theology was pro- or anti-Persian. They were concerned with conceiving and realizing a vision of the "true Israel." The coincidence of religious programs and political agendas was not purely accidental. With the rabbinical commentator Melim, we can translate אֲנַחְנוּ הַיּוֹם עֲבָדִים: 'We, we today should serve'.[32]

---

31. The recent thesis by David Janzen (2002: 116–17) argues that the most prominent motif for the actions of Ezra and Nehemiah was religiously motivated *fear*, "a high level of anxiety," and therefore a "desire for purification and separation . . . to a community whose worldview has been shaped by destruction, exile and return. Persian control made it very clear that the central government could institute another exile on a whim. To a group who saw exile as a very real experience, foreign control and military presence could only have increased anxiety. We have seen that in both Ezra 9 and Nehemiah 9 the community members are described as 'slaves', and their tenure in the land as a probationary period. One that God could quickly end. Due to this religious feeling of guilt the community of Nehemiah protects its identity through a wall that separates it from the unclean world surrounding it." I am not convinced by this theory. It explains only some aspects. We have to differentiate between piety and neurosis. The fear of a new exile is not mentioned in the text. This was one reason that some date it to the historical period of the Northern Kingdom.

32. Rabinowitz 1990: 168.

In the historical context of the anti-Persian rebellions in Egypt,[33] Nehemiah 9—like the whole mission of Ezra and Nehemiah—seems to be a part of the pro-Persian propaganda machinery. We must be careful, however, if we analyze the meaning of all the words in vv. 36–37, we can detect ambiguity, at least in every concept:

Traditional translation of Neh 9:36–37	My proposed translation of Neh 9:36–37
Look, today we are slaves, and the land that you gave our fathers to enjoy its fruit and bounty—here we are slaves on it! On account of our sins, it yields its abundant crops to kings whom you have set over us. They rule over our bodies and our beasts as they please, and we are in great distress.	Look, we, we today are serving in the land that you promised our fathers. Look, we, we are (your) servants on it. And it reproduces its fruit for the kings that you (legitimately) placed over us because of the sins (of our fathers). They reign over our bodies and over our livestock with benevolent care. Yet we are now in great distress (because we once again are close to rejecting your Torah).

The semantic fields created by all these terms are strikingly polyvalent. Compare the two different translations: It is possible to read this constellation negatively in an anti-Persian manner, which is the way it is usually read. It is also possible to reverse this understanding to read it positively. The Persians are the patrons of Judah installed by God.

Before the 2003 Heidelberg conference, Nehemiah 9 was for me only a psalm outside the Psalter, a penitential prayer with some historiographical elements (like a few other Psalms, such as 78, 105, 106, and 138). But in light of the historical, political, archaeological and sociological circumstances, this text changed its face. I have determined that it summarizes the whole theological world view of the Judahite community before Ezra. It does *not* exhibit the characteristic elements of the theology of the Chronicler, such as concentrating on the temple, its personnel, and the Davidic dynasty. Neither is the emphasis the Exile or the Return. It is a genuine text from the middle Persian Period that explains history in an impressive creed.

---

33. We know about the anti-Persian activities: in 460 B.C.E. there was an attempt by the Attic-Delphic coalition to conquer Egypt. Artaxerxes I (465–424) was troubled again and again by their aggression. In 459 there was an Egyptian revolt against the Persians with the help of the Greeks. In 458 the Greek army invaded the coast. In 456 Megabyzus was sent to suppress this revolt. In 454 the Greeks retreated from Egypt by land due to an armistice. In 448 the Peace of Callias between the Persians and Athens was concluded.

Bibliography

Albertz, R.
1992 *Religionsgeschichte Israels in alttestamentlicher Zeit.* Das Alte Testament Deutsch: Supplement 8/2. Göttingen: Vandenhoeck & Ruprecht.

Anderson, Carl R.
1987 *The Formation of the Levitical Prayer of Nehemiah 9.* Th.D. dissertation. Dallas Theological Seminary.

Bautch, Richard J.
2003 *Developments in Genre between Post-exilic Penitential Prayers and the Psalms of Communal Lament.* Society of Biblical Literature Archaeology and Biblical Studies 7. Atlanta: Society of Biblical Literature.

Boda, Mark J.
1996 Chiasmus in Ubiquity: Symmetrical Mirages in Nehemiah 9. *Journal for the Study of the Old Testament* 71: 55–70.
1997 Praying the Tradition: The Origin and Use of Tradition in Nehemiah 9. *Tyndale Bulletin* 48: 179–83.
1999 *Praying the Tradition: The Origin and Use of Tradition in Nehemiah 9.* Beihefte zur Zeitschrift für die Alttestamentliche Wissenschaft 277. Berlin: de Gruyter.

Chrostowski, Waldemar
1990 An Examination of Conscience by God's People as Exemplified in Neh 9,6–37. *Biblische Zeitschrift* 34: 253–61.

Dohmen, Christoph
1996 Wenn Texte Texte verändern: Spuren der Kanonisierung der Tora vom Exodusbuch her. Pp. 35–60 in *Die Tora als Kanon für Juden und Christen,* ed. Erich Zenger. Herders biblische Studien 10. Freiburg: Herder.

Duggan, Michael W.
2001 *The Covenant Renewal in Ezra–Nehemiah (Neh 7:72B–10:40). An Exegetical, Literary, and Theological Study.* Society of Biblical Literature Dissertation Series 164. Atlanta: Society of Biblical Literature.

Fensham, Frank C.
1981 Neh. 9 and Pss. 105, 106, 135 and 136: Post-exilic Historical Traditions in Poetic Form. *Journal of Northwest Semitic Languages* 9: 35–51.

Galling, Kurt
1958 *Die Bücher der Chronik, Esra, Nehemia.* Das Alte Testament Deutsch 12. Göttingen: Vandenhoeck & Ruprecht.

Gilbert, Maurice
1981 La place de la Loi dans la prière de Néhémie 9. Pp. 307–16 in *De la Tôrah au Messie: Études d'exégèse et d'herméneutique bibliques offertes à Henri Cazelles pour ses 25 années d'enseignement à l'Institut Catholique de Paris (Octobre 1979),* ed. M. Carrez, J. Doré, and P. Grelot. Paris: Desclée.

Gosse, Bernard
1998 L'Alliance avec Abraham et les relectures de l'histoire d'Israël en Ne 9, Ps 105–106, 135–136 et 1 Ch 16. *Transeuphratène* 15: 123–35.

Grol, Hermanus W. M. van
  1999   'Indeed, Servants We Are': Ezra 9, Nehemiah 9 and 2 Chronicles 12
          Compared. Pp. 209–27 in *The Crisis of Israelite Religion: Transformation
          of Religious Tradition in Exilic and Post-Exilic Times*, ed. B. Becking and
          M. C. A. Korpel. Oudtestamentische Studiën 42. Leiden: Brill.
Gunneweg, Antonius H. J.
  1985   *Esra*. Kommentar zum Alten Testament 19/1. Gütersloh: Gütersloher
          and Mohn.
  1987   *Nehemia*. Kommentar zum Alten Testament 19/2. Gütersloh: Güters-
          loher and Mohn.
Holmgren, Frederick C.
  1992   Faithful Abraham and the $^{\prime a}m\bar{a}n\hat{a}$ Covenant Nehemiah 9,6–10,1. *Zeit-
          schrift für die alttestamentliche Wissenschaft* 104: 249–54.
Im, Tae-Soo
  1985   *Das Davidbild in den Chronikbüchern*. Europäische Hochschulschriften
          23/263. Frankfurt: Peter Lang.
Jahn, G.
  1909   Die Bücher Esra (A und B) und Nehemia, text-kritisch und historisch-
          kritisch untersucht mit Erklärungen der einschlägigen Propheten-
          stellen und einem Anhang über hebräische Eigennamen. Leiden: Brill.
Janzen, David
  2002   Witch-Hunts, Purity and Social Boundaries: The Expulsion of Foreign
          Women in Ezra 9–10. Journal for the Study of the Old Testament Sup-
          plements 350. Sheffield: Sheffield Academic.
Janzen, J. Gerald
  1998   Nehemiah ix and the Aqedah. Pp. 311–14 in *"Lasset uns Brücken bauen
          . . .": Collected Communications to the XVth Congress of the International
          Organization for the Study of the Old Testament, Cambridge 1995*, ed. K.-D.
          Schunck and M. Augustin. Beiträge zur Erforschung des Alten Testa-
          ments und des antiken Judentums 42. Frankfurt: Peter Lang.
Kessler, Rainer
  1996   Das kollektive Schuldbekenntnis im Alten Testament. *Evangelische
          Theologie* 56: 29–43.
Knoppers, Gary N.
  1995   Prayer and Propaganda: Solomon's Dedication of the Temple and the
          Deuteronomist's Program. *Catholic Biblical Quarterly* 57: 229–54.
Kratz, Reinhard G.
  2000   *Die Komposition der erzählenden Bücher des Alten Testaments: Grundwis-
          sen der Bibelkritik*. Uni-Taschenbücher 2157. Göttingen: Vandenhoeck
          & Ruprecht.
Lipschits, Oded
  2002   On the Titles *äbäd hamäläk* and *äbäd JHWH*. *Shnaton* 13: 157–71. [Heb.]
Lipschits, Oded, and Blenkinsopp, Joseph (eds.)
  2003   *Judah and the Judeans in the Neo-Babylonian Period*. Winona Lake, Ind.:
          Eisenbrauns.

Mathias, D.
1993   *Die Geschichtstheologie der Geschichtssummarien in den Psalmen.* Beiträge zur Erforschung des Alten Testaments und des antiken Judentums 35. Frankfurt: Peter Lang.

Mathys, Hans-Peter
1994   *Dichter und Beter: Theologen aus spätalttestamentlicher Zeit.* Orbis Biblicus et Orientalis 132. Freiburg: Universitätsverlag / Göttingen: Vandenhoeck & Ruprecht.

Michel, Andreas
2003   Ist mit der "Gnadenformel" von Ex 34,6(+7) der Schlüssel zu einer Theologie des Alten Testaments gefunden? *Biblische Notizen* 118: 110–23.

Miller, Patrick D.
1995   *They Cried to the Lord: The Form and Theology of Biblical Prayer.* Minneapolis: Fortress.

Newman, Judith H.
1998   Nehemiah 9 and the Scripturalization of Prayer in the Second Temple Period. Pp. 112–23 in *The Function of Scripture in Early Jewish and Christian Tradition*, ed. Craig A. Evans and James A. Sanders. Journal for the Study of the New Testament Supplements 154 = Studies in Scripture in Early Judaism and Christianity 6. Sheffield: Sheffield Academic Press.

Oeming, Manfred
1990   *Das wahre Israel: Die "genealogische Vorhalle" 1 Chronik 1–9.* Beiträge zur Wissenschaft vom Alten und Neuen Testaments 128. Stuttgart: Kohlhammer.

Plöger, Otto
1957   Reden und Gebete im deuteronomistischen und chronistischen Geschichtswerk. Pp. 35–49 in *Festschrift für Günther Dehn zum 75. Geburtstag am 18. April 1957 dargebracht von der Evangelisch-Theologischen Fakultät der Rheinischen Friedrich Wilhelms-Universität zu Bonn*, ed. W. Schneemelcher. Neukirchen-Vluyn: Neukirchener Verlag.

Pröbstl, Volker
1997   *Nehemia 9, Psalm 106 und Psalm 136 und die Rezeption des Pentateuchs.* Göttingen: Cuvillier.

Rabinowitz, Yosef
1990   *Ezra/Nechemia: A New Translation with a Commentary Anthologized from Talmudic, Midrashic and Rabbinic Sources.* Art Scroll Tenach Series. New York: Mesorah.

Rad, Gerhard von
1938   *Das formgeschichtliche Problem des Hexateuchs.* Beiträge zur Wissenschaft vom Alten und Neuen Testaments 78. Stuttgart: Kohlhammer.

Rehm, Martin
1957   Nehemias 9. *Biblische Zeitschrift* 1: 59–69.

Rendsburg, Gary A.
1991   The Northern Origin of Nehemiah 9. *Biblica* 72: 348–66.

Rendtorff, Rolf
1997   Nehemiah 9: An Important Witness of Theological Reflection. Pp. 111–
       17 in *Tehillah le-Moshe: Biblical and Judaic Studies in Honor of Moshe
       Greenberg*, ed. Mordechai Cogan, Barry L. Eichler, and Jeffrey H. Tigay.
       Winona Lake, Ind.: Eisenbrauns = Pp. 265–71 in *Der Text in seiner
       Endgestalt: Schritte auf dem Weg zu einer Theologie des Alten Testaments*.
       Neukirchen-Vluyn: Neukirchener Verlag, 2001.

Rudolph, Wilhelm
1949   *Esra und Nehemia samt 3 Esra*. Handbuch zum Alten Testament 20.
       Tübingen: Mohr-Siebeck.

Schmid, Konrad
1999   *Erzväter und Exodus: Untersuchungen zur doppelten Begründung der Ur-
       sprünge Israels innerhalb der Geschichtsbücher des Alten Testaments*. Wis-
       senschaftliche Monographien zum Alten und Neuen Testament 81.
       Neukirchen-Vluyn: Neukirchener Verlag.

Schwemer, Anna M.
1999   Prophet, Zeuge und Märtyrer: Zur Entstehung des Märtyrerbegriffs
       im frühesten Christentum. *Zeitschrift für Theologie und Kirche* 96: 320–
       50.

Scoralick, Ruth
2000   *Gottes Güte und Gottes Zorn*. Die Gottesprädikationen in Exodus 34,6f
       und ihre intertextuellen Beziehungen zum Zwölfprophetenbuch. Her-
       ders biblische Studien 33. Freiburg: Herder.

Segert, Stanislav
1991   History and Poetry: Poetic Patterns in Nehemiah 9:5–37. Pp. 255–65 in
       Storia e tradizioni di Israele, ed. Daniele Garrone. Brescia: Paideia.

Welch, Adam C.
1929   The Source of Nehemiah IX. *Zeitschrift für die Alttestamentliche Wissen-
       schaft* 47: 130–37.

Williamson, H. G. M.
1988   Structure and Historiography in Nehemiah 9. Pp. 117–31 in *Proceed-
       ings of the Ninth World Congress of Jewish Studies, Panel Sessions: Bible
       Studies and Ancient Near East, Jerusalem, 1988*, ed. M. Goshen-Gottstein.
       Jerusalem: Magnes.

Zastrow, Klaus
1998   *Die drei großen Bußgebete von Esra 9, Nehemia 9 und Daniel 9*. Ph. D. dis-
       sertation. Heidelberg.

Sociolinguistics and the Judean Speech Community in the Achaemenid Empire

FRANK H. POLAK

Tel Aviv University

It is my aim in this essay to place the Late Biblical Hebrew language in sociolinguistic perspective and thus to sketch a social and cultural profile of the community in which texts such as the book of Ezra–Nehemiah were formed.[1] Hence, the angle of this study is slightly different from customary linguistic or philological analysis. The subject matter of sociolinguistics is explained by Dell Hymes (1974: 4):

> What seem variation and deviation from the standpoint of a linguist's analysis may emerge as a structure and a pattern from the standpoint of the communicative economy of the group among whom the analyzed form of speech exists.

Sociolinguistics, then, studies the interaction between the way language is used in communication, the social conditions surrounding the communication process, and the speakers' attitudes to this process.[2] The people who are united by the common networks of communication constitute a *speech community*, a term that may denote a neighborhood, a village or a town, but also a region, an ethnic or religious group, a socioeconomic class, or, in modern times, a nation-state.[3] For this essay

---

1. We will use the following abbreviations: CBH—Classical Biblical Hebrew; LBH—Late Biblical Hebrew; QH—Qumran Hebrew; MH—Middle/Rabbinic Hebrew; BA—Biblical Aramaic; OfA—Official Aramaic. For Papyri: BMAP—Kraeling 1953; CAP—Cowley 1923; DAD—Driver 1965; HP—Bresciani and Kamil 1966; WDSP—Gropp 2001.

2. One notes the title of the introductory essay by Halliday (1964): "The Users and Uses of Language." Fishman (1970: 4) describes sociolinguistics as "the study of the characteristics of language varieties, the characteristics of their functions, and the characteristics of their speakers as these three constantly interact, change, and change one another within a speech community," or, alternatively, as "the interaction between these two aspects of human behavior: use of language and the social organization of behavior" (1971: 217). Fasold (1987: ix, 1) mentions the interrelationship between language variation, communication, and the speaker's definition of the social situation.

3. Hymes (1974: 47, 51) speaks of "a social group" or "the entire organization of linguistic means within it" and defines it as "a community sharing knowledge of rules for

589

this concept is especially appropriate, since in Akkadian, Aramaic, and LBH the terms *lišānu*, לָשֹׁן, and לָשֹׁון can refer to ethnic groups identifiable by their language: וכרוזא קרא בחיל לכון אמרין אמיא עממיא ולשניא (Dan 3:4: Then a herald proclaimed aloud, "You are commanded, O peoples, nations, and languages").[4] A speech community also shares a common culture and thus a common literary background. Special *registers* are formed by different categories of group language according to occupation, rank, and location; such as, for instance, the language of the market or the army, medical parlance, legal phraseology, and so forth.[5] Study of the way language is used in social interaction uncovers much information concerning the societal framework and thus enables us to sketch a social and cultural profile of the speech community.[6]

The sociolinguistic perspective, then, has much to contribute to our understanding of the social and historical background of the biblical text. This angle is particularly suitable for the study of Late Biblical Hebrew,[7] since a characteristic representative of this language state, the book of Ezra–Nehemiah, reflects, like the book of Daniel, a symbiosis of Hebrew and Aramaic[8] and thus a bilingual culture. The study of bilingualism as a social phenomenon is, of course, one of the main branches of sociolinguistics.[9] Moreover, within Ezra–Nehemiah one notes sharp differences between the registers of character speech (quoted discourse attributed to a speaking subject) and discourse in

---

the conduct and interpretation of speech . . . comprising knowledge of at least one form of speech, and knowledge also of its patterns of usage." He focuses on "communities organized as systems of communicative events" and highlights "speech networks" (1974: 17, 50); a similar approach is advocated by Williams 1992: 69–75. Fasold (1987: 43–44, 148; 1990: 40–42) discusses the overlapping of communities, the attitude toward language use, and the nature of a community that uses several languages or language levels in different contexts. More formal definitions are offered by Gumperz, 1971: 114–28; Fishman 1971: 232.

4. So also Zech 8:23 (עשרה אנשים מכל לשנות הגוים); Isa 66:18 (לקבץ את כל הגוים והלשנות); see *HALOT* 1909; *CAD* L 209–15, s.v. *lišānu*, esp. p. 214 (4c).

5. Hymes 1974: 58–59; Halliday 1964: 87–90; Fishman 1971: 235–37; Ferguson 1994. The variety of registers in biblical dialogue is described in Polak 2001: 74–94.

6. The importance of the historical context of language use is underlined by Young 1993: 87–91.

7. A definition of LBH, relative to literary corpus and linguistic development, is offered by Hurvitz 1982: 157–60; 1997a: 307–11; Young 1993: 94–96; Naveh and Greenfield 1984: 119–25.

8. See Sérandour 1996; on Daniel, see Rouillard-Bonraisin 1996.

9. Li 2000; Fasold 1987: 1–146; Fishman 1971: 286–93. In the Semitic sphere, this subject is reviewed by Kaufman 2002; Kapeliuk 2002. Bilingualism among indigenous tribes is studied by Salisbury 1972 (Papuan); Sorensen 1972 (Amazon Indian).

the narrator's voice (Polak 2001: 65–69). Discourse typology is another subject of sociolinguistic research.

From this point of view, then, we will discuss the impact of the administration on language use, and in particular, the status of Hebrew as a written language and as vernacular. Finally, we shall deal with the position of Hebrew as a language of religion.

Bilingualism and Administration

Bilingualism is not a matter of "languages in contact" but of communities in contact and, thus, of political and social structure. The use of Aramaic in the Second Commonwealth is a case in point. It is often assumed that Aramaic was brought to Judea by the returning exiles,[10] who learned it in Babylonia as the dominant language.[11] However, this theory does not explain how Aramaic persisted to such an extent that the Aramaic script almost replaced the Paleo-Hebrew script, and that the Torah was read together with the Targum.[12] If the use of Aramaic were confined to the returning exiles, it could have died out after two generations, in the same way that French was abandoned by the Huguenot refugees in the former Cape Colony.[13] In consequence, it seems more plausible that the position of Aramaic was conditioned by its sociopolitical functions as the imperial language in western Asia[14] and, hence, the language of the administration in the subjugated provinces, such as Yehud.[15] This point has been clear since the discovery of the

---

10. Naveh and Greenfield 1984: 119; Sáenz-Badillos 1993: 112–13.

11. Since the exiles in Babylonia were living together in larger concentrations, such as as *āl-Yahūdu* (Joannès and Lemaire 1999: 20–27; see the contribution by L. E. Pearce in the present volume (pp. 399–411); Zadok 2002: 31–36, 57, 61; Eph'al 1978: 76–83), we may safely assume that they used Hebrew in nonpublic context (so also Lemaire 2003: 38–39; see Vanderhooft 2003b: 220–26; Dandamayev 1984: 338–41; Bickerman 1984: 344–49). Problems of language use in immigrant communities are discussed by, for example, Haugen 1972a, 1972b. On the interplay of different languages in intimate and public discourse see, for example, Fishman 1972; Tanner 1972; Fasold 1987: 183–208.

12. If מפרש meant 'in translation' (Naveh and Greenfield 1984: 117; cf. Ezra 4:18), the first witness to the Targum would be found in the section in which Ezra reads the Torah (Neh 8:8). But this interpretation is rejected, with good reason, by, for example, Williamson 1985: 56, 279.

13. Van Ginneken 1928: 206; Holm 1989: 341–42.

14. Naveh and Greenfield 1984: 117; Porten 1968: 56–58; Folmer 1995: 7–28; Kutscher 1977c; 1997b: 104–29, 135–36, 142–46. On the use of Aramaic in Babylonia see, e.g., Lemaire 2001: 7–14; Zadok 2003: 558–78; Kaufman 1974: 8–10; Naveh 1970: 16–21; Greenfield 2001b; 2001a: 363–64; Gropp 2001: 19–30.

15. Aramaic probably played an important role already during the Babylonian conquest (Lipschits 1999; Zorn 2003: 419, 428–33, 434–39; Kaufman 1974: 9–10, 43 and n. 16 on

Aramaic texts at Elephantine and the Môṣā stamp impressions (Avigad 1958; Zorn, Yellin, and Hayes 1994). Today we can add the Samaria Papyri from Wādi Dâliyeh (Cross 1985; Gropp 2001), the document found at Keteph Jericho (Eshel and Misgav 1988), and the Aramaic documents from Idumean Khirbet-el Qôm/Maqqedā (Eph'al and Naveh 1996; Lemaire 1996; Lemaire 2001: 8 n. 6). The letter that the heads of the Israelite community at Elephantine sent to Bagavahi, the *peḥā* at Jerusalem (CAP 30, 31), is also written in Aramaic, as is the memorandum (זכרן) containing the answer (CAP 32).

The social and cultural consequences of this situation can hardly be overestimated. Because of administrative and social exigencies, the entire Judean community was affected by Aramaic. Real estate contracts, for instance, would be written in Aramaic, as they were in Elephantine and Samaria. Any complaint and judgment would have to be argued before the royal judges. Hence, Aramaic would be the preferred language of all persons doing business with the government,[16] that is to say, probably the entire property-owning and professional part of the population, including even craftsmen.[17] Thus Aramaic developed into the main language in administrative, legal, and commercial contexts (prestige language).[18]

Syntactic analysis of the Aramaic texts in Ezra 4:8–6:12 suggests some differentiation between the administrative language and the popular use of Aramaic. The embedded letters presented as official documents contain examples of a distinctly eastern word order, in

---

p. 10), before the return of the exiles, even though this regime presumably left more room for local autonomy, as argued by Vanderhooft 2003a: 254–55. Betlyon (2003: 269) speaks of a *"laissez-faire* approach" by the administration, which was interested mainly in tribute. On Judean social structure under the Persian administration see, for example, Blenkinsopp 1991.

16. Fasold 1987: 32–54, 147–211; Fishman 1972; Tanner 1972; Blom and Gumperz 2000: 120–23, 126–27; Li, Milroy, and Ching 2000: 206–8.

17. See, e.g., CAP 1, line 3; CAP 8, line 13; 10, lines 13–19; BMAP 1, line 6; 12, line 28. On the widespread use of Aramaic in family correspondence and ostraca in Elephantine and Hermopolis, see Porten 1968: 264–77. The Samaria Papyri concern slave sales and the sale of a house (Gropp 2001: 3–8, 103–8). Contributions by Porten and Yardeni (pp. 457–488) and Lemaire (413–456) to the present volume deal with Aramaic ostraca from Khirbet el-Qôm documenting the delivery of goods to the representatives of the Empire. These details gravely weaken the assumption that the use of Aramaic was largely confined to the Judean upper classes and foreign contacts, as argued by Schaper 1999: 16–17. On minimal literacy among craftsmen in Athens, see Marrou 1956: 72; for ancient Israel, see Young 1998: 245–49, 412–20.

18. Ferguson 1959: 325–40; Fishman 1971: 286–93; Fasold 1987: 34–54; Rendsburg 1990: 1–6.

which the object precedes the verbal predicate, as often found in Egyptian Aramaic documents. This order is especially notable in infinitive clauses.

Infinitive Clauses in OfA Documents from Egypt

CAP 6, lines 6–7   וטענוך לי מומאה למומא ביהו על דבר ארקא זך
And they imposed on you *to swear me an oath by Yahu* on that plot

CAP 26, line 9   עדן הוה אופש[ר]ה למעבד
It is time *to make repairs* (cf. line 3)

DAD III, lines 7–8   אנת שם טעם, סרוש[ית]א
[ז]י פסמשך י[שם] להם טעם למעבד, זכי יתעבד להם
You, give orders that the *punishment* that Psamshek *will order to carry out on them*, that will be carried out on them

Ahiqar 63   [ג]ברן אחרנן מלכא [יש]לח אחרין, פגרה זי אחיקר זנה למחזה
The king will send other men after us *to see the corpse of Ahiqar here*

Since this word order is frequently found in Akkadian texts, it is viewed as a hallmark of Eastern Aramaic.[19] Its use in the official style fits the eastern center of gravity of the Achaemenid administration (Briant 2002: 70–72, 84–93).[20]

Infinitive Clauses in the Letters Embedded in the Text of Ezra

Ezra 4:22[21]   וזהירין הוו שלו למעבד על דנה
Take care *not to be lax* in this matter

---

19. Muraoka and Porten 1998: 308. Although Folmer (1995: 536–39) notes an increase in the use of this construction toward the end of the fifth century (DAD; CAP 31), there is no need to relate it to the later Persian Period, since the SOV order in general is attested in Aramaic of the Neo-Assyrian Period (see p. 595 below). On Kaufman's skepticism, see the next note.

20. Kaufman (1974: 133) prefers to attribute this construction to Persian influence, in view of its low frequency in Neo-Assyrian and Neo-Babylonian texts. However, he admits (n. 96 there) that in NA and NB texts this construction is often found. In this connection we note some instances in inscriptions from the Chaldean Empire (Langdon 1912): Nebuchadnezzar, Text 14, col. II, line 57–col. III, line 5; col. III, lines 11–13) and Nabonidus (Langdon, Nabonidus, Text 3, col. II, lines 6–9; 6, col. I, lines 24–25: *ana šuršud temen, uṣurat bītīšu šullum, papāḫ u šubāti ana šīmat ilūtīšu epēš ūmīšamma utnennišumma* 'I prayed to him daily to establish the foundation stone, to complete the blueprints of his house, to prepare the cella and the residences for his divine canon'; cf. H i, B, col. I, lines 21–23, for which see Gadd 1958). Probably the Aramaic scribes adopted the higher registers of literary Babylonian as standard.

21. In the following excerpts, the rendering is given according to the NJPSV.

Ezra 5:13   כורש מלכא שם טעם בית אלהא דנה לבנא

King Cyrus issued an order *to rebuild this House of God*

Ezra 7:18   ומה די עליך [עלך] ועל אחיך [אחך] ייטב
בשאר כספא ודהבה למעבד, כרעות אלהכם תעבדון

And whatever you wish *to do with the leftover silver and gold, you and your kinsmen* may do, in accord with the will of your God

Thus, the eastern word order of the embedded letters reflects the syntactic register of the imperial administration.[22] The narrator even adopts the official tone for questioning by the authorities:

Ezra 5:3   מן שם לכם טעם ביתא דנה לבנא ואשרנא דנה לשכללה

Who issued orders to you *to rebuild this house and complete its furnishing*?

Word Order in Official Aramaic

In clauses with finite verbs as predicate, one notes the sequence of subject-object-predicate (or modifier-predicate).

DAD VII, lines 1–2[23]   קדמן כזי מצריא מרדו אדין (פ)סמשך פקידא קדמיא
גרדא ונכסיא זילנא [זי] במצרין חסין נטר

Formerly, when the Egyptians rebelled, then Psamshek, the former steward *diligently* guarded *our gardu (servant staff) and property in Egypt*

DAD XIII, line 5   אלהיא שלם ישמו לך

May the Gods grant you *good health*

CAP 30, line 14[24]   ואיש מנדעם באגורא זך לא חבל

And nobody damaged *anything in that Temple*

CAP 31, line 6   וידרנג זך לחיא אגרה שלח על נ[פין] ברה

that wicked Vidranga sent *a letter* to his son Naphaina

Since this word order is usual in Akkadian, it is viewed as an eastern feature in OfA.[25] This inference is now confirmed by recently published Aramaic slave conveyances from Assyria (700–680 B.C.E.):

---

22. Note also Ezra 7:13, 18, compared with the exception in 5:17.

23. Similarly DAD III, line 5; IV, line 3; V, line 8.

24. See also CAP 7, lines 5, 9; 8, line 27; 27, lines 7–8; 30, lines 11–12; 31, lines 4–5, 14, 20–21, 28.

25. See Kutscher 1977a: 58–59; 1977b: 104–7, 110–13. Since this word order is already attested in Aramaic tablets from the Neo-Assyrian Period (Lemaire 2001: 26–33), there is no place for the skepticism of Folmer (1995: 524–26, 533) and Muraoka and Porten (1998: 301–5, 307–8; although in the end they accept the SOV order as an eastern characteristic. Of course, Kutscher (1977b: 106–7) already pointed to Assyrian parallels of such formulas as the opening salutation (e.g., CAP 30, lines 1–2; 31, line 2). Fronting of noun phrases as object/modifier appears frequently in NB royal inscriptions.

מן על מן יתהפך, אורה סוסין חורן יבל לבעל חירן
whoever retracts vis-à-vis the other must bring a span of white horses to
Baʿal Ḥīrān[26]

מן על מן יתהפך, מנה זהב על ברכי אשר ננוה ישם וכספא שלשן למראוה יהב
whoever retracts vis-à-vis the other must place a mina of silver on the
knees of Ishtar (pronounced as /iššar/) of Nineveh, and pay thirty
(shekels of?) silver to his (i.e., the slave's) master[27]

Word Order in the Letters Embedded in Ezra 4–6

This order is also found in some clauses in the letters embedded in
the book of Ezra (Porten 2003: 55–59, 60–61; Grabbe 1998), such as:[28]

Ezra 4:19   והשכחו די קריתא דך מן יומת עלמא על מלכין מתנשאה
And it has been found that this city has *from earliest times* risen *against
kings*

Ezra 6:7[29]   פחת יהודיא ולשבי יהודיא בית אלהא דך יבנון על אתרה
Let the governor of the Jews and the elders of the Jews rebuild *this House
of God* on its site

With regard to word order, then, the style of the embedded letters
fits the eastern nature of OfA as the imperial language of the Achaemenids.[30]

Word Order in the Narrator's Account

By contrast, in the narrative itself most clauses have the object
following the predicate, as was customary in Western Aramaic, for
example,[31]

Ezra 5:2   באדין קמו זרבבל שאלתיאל וישוע בר יוצדק
ושריו למבנא בית אלהא די בירושלם

---

26. Lemaire 2001: 14–15 (text I, lines 6–9; pl. 1). Lemaire (p. 18) notes the Assyrian
parallels to the formula involved and relates אורה to Akkadian *urû* (span horses) and to
Hebrew ארות סוסים (1 Kgs 5:6).

27. Lemaire 2001: 24–28 (text II, lines 5–9; pl. 2); on the Assyrian parallels, see p. 27.
Cf. also text III, lines 60–68 (pp. 33–35).

28. See also Ezra 4:12, according to the MT cantillation signs and in comparison with
4:23.

29. The LXX reads οἱ ἀφηγούμενοι τῶν Ιουδαίων καὶ οἱ πρεσβύτεροι τῶν Ιουδαίων οἶκον
τοῦ θεοῦ ἐκεῖνον οἰκοδομείτωσαν ἐπὶ τοῦ τόπου αὐτοῦ. Kropat (1909: 6) compares Dan 4:33
and the well-known LBH construction; see also Williamson 1985: 72.

30. Kitchen 1965: 75–77; Kutscher 1947; 1977b: 142–46; Folmer 1995: 709–14, 719–20,
744–50.

31. So also 4:17; 6:1, 16. In the quoted discourse of Ezra 6:13 the eastern order would
have been characteristic of the officials of the Empire receiving Darius's orders.

Thereupon Zerubbabel son of Shealtiel and Jeshua son of Jozadak began rebuilding *the House of God in Jerusalem* (infinitive clause)

Ezra 5:5 ועין אלההם הות על שבי יהודיא ולא בטלו המו

But God watched *over the elders of the Jews* and *they* were not stopped (finite verb as predicate)

These preferences suggest a significant contrast between the mostly western nature of the Aramaic history in Ezra 4–6 and the eastern character of the syntax in the embedded letters, reflecting the official style of the Achaemenid Period.[32] The fact that western features prevail in the narrator's account itself, is not less significant.[33] Since the audience addressed by this narrative is the Judean community, we infer that the Aramaic used by this community contained more western features than OfA proper.

The Status of Written Hebrew

In view of the widespread use of OfA in governmental and legal contexts, it obviously was the main language for scribal education in the western parts of the Achaemenid empire.[34] Hence, at the provincial chancery of Yehud, the scribes would have been educated in OfA rather than in Hebrew, which had ceased functioning as the standard language of the Judean bureaucracy when the Chaldean conquest put an end to the Judean Kingdom and its royal court (Young 1993: 89–90).

What were the consequences for the status of written Hebrew?

Aramaisms in the Field of Administration and Commerce

The first and most obvious result of the official status of Aramaic was the adoption of Aramaic language features by scribes writing He-

---

32. The syntactic factor is to be taken into account in any discussion of the status of these letters, as undertaken recently by Schwiderski 2000: 354–62. Contrary to Schwiderski's considerations, the departures from the original formulary, such as the absence of introductory salutations or even the addressee (6:6), are best explained as abbreviations by the narrator. This explanation also holds true for the salutation שלם (Ezra 4:17), probably a curtailed version of a longer formula, for example, שלמכון ישגא (Dan 3:31; cf. CAP 30, lines 1–2). Schwiderski's attribution of this form to Greek influence, in view of the greeting χαίρειν, seems less apt. The title בעל טעם (considered spurious by Schwiderski 2000: 358–59; see Kaufman 1974: 109 n. 390) is now attested in Neo-Babylonian as [LU]*se-pir-ri bēl ṭēmi* (EN *ṭé-e-mu* 'scribe chancellor': Stolper 1989: 285, lines 5–6; see also Zadok 2002: 35–36; Vanderhooft 2003b: 226).

33. The variation in word order in Daniel 2, 4–5 (mainly eastern) and chaps. 3, 6–7 (mainly western or mixed) is analyzed in Polak 1993: 258–60. On language variation in BA, see also Kitchen 1965: 76–77, 79; Folmer 1995: 754–55.

34. Porten 1984: 395–98; on scribal know-how, see Porten 1968: 191–94, 334–43; Gropp 2001: 3–32.

brew, for example, Aramaic lexemes, in particular in the field of government and administration,[35] whereas the use of the corresponding terms of Classical Hebrew decreased.[36] The adoption of Aramaic terminology reflects the social context in which OfA was used most frequently, that is to say, administrative and commercial intercourse.[37]

The adoption of מלכות (for CBH ממלכה, מלוכה) is probably dependent on its use in official documents.[38] Thus one also notes LBH פקודים ('precepts' or 'orders'; Ps 103:18; 119:4).[39] The use of אגרת alongside ספר ('written document' and in particular 'letter') is similar,[40] as is the introduction of נכסים (Josh 22:8; Eccl 5:18; 6:2; 2 Chr 1:11–12) as a term for property (Aramaic נכסין: Ezra 6:28; 7:26) alongside the Hebrew terms רכוש and מִקְנֶה (Hurvitz 1997a: 311–14; Wagner 1966: 84). Additional terms in this context are שלט, מדינה, בירה.[41] The LBH term for request, בַּקָּשָׁה, reflects Aramaic morphology. The verb כנס 'to gather' (the harvest, taxes, laborers) represents the economic side of the administration. The register of commerce includes such terms as קבל 'to receive', replacing Hebrew לקח (Hurvitz 2000c: 181–85). The word קבל in this meaning is now attested in the Aramaic deeds from Samaria from the fourth century B.C.E.[42] The phrase מן העולם (ו)עד העולם (with determination) also fits this administrative/commercial context. Although in Hebrew this idiom represents hymnic language (Ps 106:48, ברוך ה' אלהי ישראל מן העולם

---

35. This logic also applies to the adoption of Persian administrative, legal, and other official terms in BA and LBH, such as, for example, דת, all Persian terms for treasury and archives (גנז), פרדס, פתשגן פתגם (often indicating an official command), and so on (Kitchen 1965: 40–42; Dandamayev 1984: 332–34; Achenbach 2000). Systematic analysis of Esther indicates a large number of loanwords: Wahl 1999.

36. On the other hand, as expected in view of the typology of "languages in contact," Judean Aramaic adopted Hebrew features, as shown by Qumran Aramaic (Fassberg 1992; Qimron 1992b: 119–22).

37. Economic terminology in Qoheleth is analyzed by Seow 1996.

38. See Hurvitz 1972: 79–88; and cf. CAP 6, lines 1–2, ראש מלכותא כזי ארתחשסש מלכא יתב בכרסאה; WDSP 1, line 1.

39. See also Ps 19:9; 103:18; 111:7; 119:15, 56, 134, 159, 168 etc. For the Aramaic equivalents, see Hurvitz 1972: 126–29; Ezra 1:2; 4Q196 (4QTobitᶜar) 14, line 8 פקֹ[ו]די אבוך די פקרך ...] (Tob 6:16; DJD 19.20); 4Q198 (4QTobitᶜar) 1, line 2 [ופקדה ואמר ל[ה (DJD 19.57).

40. For the word אגרת: Esth 9:26, 29; Neh 2:7, 8, 9; 6:5, 17; 1 Chr 9:1; 2 Chr 32:17 (with the meaning 'book', 'record', or 'document': Esth 2:23; Ezra 6:18; Neh 8:1, 3, 5, 8, 18; 9:3; 12:23; 13:1; Dan 1:4, 17; 9:2; 12:1, 4; Eccl 12:12; 1 Chr 9:1; 2 Chr 17:9; 20:34; 35:12). See Hurvitz 2000a: 150–51; Wagner 1966: 19.

41. Kutscher 1982: 52, 75–76; Rosenthal 1963: 57–59; Kaufman 1974: 156; Deroy 1956: 127–31; Schirmer 1926: 19, 39–43; Strang 1970: 122–23, 184–85, 252, 254, 367, 389.

42. The participle מקבל in the declaration that due payment has not been received (passive Pael; cf. Gropp 2001: 41; מקובל אני מרבי מיאשא, *m. Peʾah* 2:6), is attested in a number of slave-sale deeds: WDSP 1, line 8; 2, line 7; 3, line 8; see Gropp 2001: 41–42, 14, 23; Cross 1985: 8, 12.

ועד העולם; and similarly Neh 9:5),[43] it matches the Aramaic phraseology in the deeds from Samaria (לעלמא).[44]

The term חדוה 'joy', 'happiness' occurs in Biblical Aramaic (Ezra 6:16; Hurvitz 1972: 23–24; Wagner 1966: 51) and in LBH (Neh 8:10; 1 Chr 16:27). The root חדי is used in the opening greeting of the letter that the heads of the Israelite community on Elephantine sent to Bagavahi, וחדה ושריר הוי בכל עדן (CAP 30:3; 31:3, 'and be happy and healthy at all times'). Hence this root is also representative of the administrative register.[45]

One of the few characteristic verbs in LBH that does fit an administrative or commercial setting, namely, שבח ('to praise', Ps 106:47)[46] was also used in both Aramaic and CBH. This overlap could be the reason for its frequency in LBH, since bilingualism can bring with it an inclination to use terms that suit both languages.[47]

With regard to syntactic structure, one notes some cases in which the object of the infinitive clause preceded the predicate (as in Aramaic and Akkadian), for example, ובדבר יום ביום להעלות כמצות משה (2 Chr 8:13: *'What was due for each day he sacrificed* according to the commandment of Moses'); בני יהודה וירושלים אתם אמרים לכבש לעבדים ולשפחות לכם (2 Chr 28:10: 'Do you now intend *to subjugate the men and women of Judah and Jerusalem* to be your slaves?');[48] ותכתב אסתר . . . את כל תקף לקים את אגרת הפורים הזאת השנית (Esth 9:29: 'And Esther wrote . . . this second letter of Purim *for the purpose of confirming the authority*'); אתה צויתה פקדיך לשמר מאד (Ps 119:4: 'You have commanded that your precepts be kept diligently').[49] We

---

43. See also the doxology concluding the first segment in Psalms (Ps 41:13); see Hurvitz 1972: 158–59; BA עד עלמא (Dan 2:20) matches LBH עד העולם (Ps 133:3; 1 Chr 17:14 as against 2 Sam 7:16).

44. WDSP 1, line 4 לעלמא מן אחרוהי ולבנוהי לה; 2, line 4; 3, line 4; 5, line 5; see Gropp 2001: 10–11, 31, 38.

45. Muffs (1992: 121–41, 144–51) notes that the lexeme חדוה matches *ḫūd libbi*, used in Babylonian contracts to indicate that the parties undertake the obligations out of their own free will.

46. Hurvitz 1972: 88–91; Wagner 1966: 111. In LBH note also Ps 145:4 (cf. מלכותך, v. 11); 147:12 (cf. כנס, v. 2); Eccl 4:2; 8:15; 1 Chr 16:35; and in CBH: Ps 89:10. Psalm 117 is too short for analysis. For the form ישבחונך (Ps 63:4), compare CBH ישאונך (Ps 91:12).

47. Holm 1988: 96, 187; Deroy 1956: 74–77; Weinreich (1963: 32–34 and n. 15) notes this phenomenon the borrowing of morphemes.

48. Kropat 1909: 59–60. The other two examples given by Kropat are doubtful at best (2 Chr 29:16; 30:17). For the Aramaic usage, see pp. 593–594 above. Talshir (1988: 180) notes that the infinite construct with ל, when used as finite verb, tends to come at the end of the clause, for example, Ezra 3:12; 2 Chr 36:19.

49. In addition, this verse contains LBH פקודים 'commandments', for which see above.

have already seen that constructions of this type pertain to the field of administration because they are often found in official documents.[50]

An additional phenomenon is that Hebrew words may adopt the function of an Aramaic partially-correspondent term.[51] Thus the Hebrew relative particle (אשר) assumes the functions of Aramaic די, which marks the relative clause, like Hebrew אשר, but in addition serves as an introduction to the object clause (like Akkadian *ša*). Because this feature relates to the formation of subordinate clauses and thus mainly to written language, this feature is also characteristic of the administrative register.

The administrative register also contains to some typical LBH features that are not directly related to OfA,[52] such as the use of ל to mark the final item of a list; for example,[53]

Ezra 7:28   ועלי הטה חסד לפני המלך ויועציו ולכל שרי המלך הגברים

and who inclined the king and his counselors and the king's military officers to be favorably disposed toward me

1 Chronicles 29:6   שרי האבות ושרי שבטי ישראל (. . .) ולשרי מלאכת המלך

The officers of the clans and the officers of the tribes of Israel . . . and the supervisors of the king's work

In this connection we must mention the use of the definite article to introduce a relative clause; such as,[54]

Ezra 8:25   תרומת בית אלהינו ההרימו המלך (. . .) וכל ישראל הנמצאים

The contribution to the House of our God which the king (. . .) and all Israel who were present had made

Ezra 10:14   וכל אשר בערינו ההשיב נשים נכריות יבא לעתים מזמנים

And all our townspeople who have brought home foreign women shall appear at scheduled times

---

50. For other examples, see above, pp. 593–594.

51. Many examples of the extension of function and meaning are discussed by Weinreich 1963: 39–40, 47–48.

52. Also note the order of counting: (1) material + (2) unit of measure + (3) numeral—עשרים אלף (3) בתים (2) ויין (1); כרים (2) עשרים אלף (3) ושערים (1) (2 Chr 2:9)—in contrast to the Classical order: (1) numeral + (2) unit of measure + (3) material: עשרים אלף (1) חטים (3) כר (2); שמן כתית (3) כר (2) ועשרים (1) (1 Kgs 5:25); see Talshir 1988: 181; Kropat 1909: 11.

53. So also 1 Chr 28:1; 2 Chr 24:12; 26:14; see Kropat 1909: 6; Talshir 1988: 179.

54. Note Ezra 10:17; 1 Chr 26:28; 29:17 (הנמצאו פה); 2 Chr 29:36 (על ההכין), and see Kropat 1909: 59–60; Talshir 1988: 180. The case of Josh 10:24, ההלכוא אתו, is best explained as a corruption of ההלכים אתו (LXX τοὺς συμπορευομένους αὐτῷ), with the interchange of ם and א.

Because the use of the definite particle to introduce participial clauses is well known, the syntagm at hand is most easily explained as a learned extension of the participial construction.

The Style of Written Language

Because scribal education at this juncture centered on Official Aramaic, Hebrew epistolography and (or more generally, the art of formulating documents in Hebrew) was no longer promoted by the chancery. Consequently, we must assume that these arts were reserved for the most learned of the scribes, such as Ben Sira in the Hellenistic period (Hurvitz 1997b; Joosten 1999).

Hebrew prose in a characteristically learned, scribal style is found in many sections of the book of Ezra–Nehemiah, such as the Hebrew temple-building chronicle (Ezra 1; 3:1–4:7; 6:19–22), the Ezra memoir (Ezra 8:1–10:44), Nehemiah 8, and large parts of the Nehemiah memoir.

One of the typical features of this style is the use of long noun groups, particularly indicating the participants in the action; for instance:[55]

Ezra 3:1 ויקם ⟦ישוע ⟨בן יוצדק⟩ ⟨ואחיו הכהנים⟩⟧ [וזרבבל ⟨בן שאלתיאל⟩ ואחיו⟧] ויבנו את [מזבח ⟨אלהי ישראל⟩] להעלות עליו עלות ככתוב [בתורת ⟨משה ⟨איש האלהים⟩⟩]

Then Jeshua son of Jozadak and his brother priests, and Zerubbabel son of Shealtiel and his brothers set to and built the altar of the God of Israel to offer burnt offerings upon it as is written in the Teaching of Moses, the man of God[56]

Ezra 10:15 אך [⟨יונתן בן עשהאל⟩ ⟨ויחזיה בן תקוה⟩] עמדו על זאת [⟨ומשלם ⟨ושבתי הלוי⟩] עזרם

Only Jonathan son of Asahel and Jahzeiah son of Tikvah remained for this purpose, assisted by Meshullam and Shabbethai, the Levites

The extensive reciting of the participants almost turns into a list. Such detailed specification, though rare in Classical biblical narrative,[57] is the norm in the opening of real estate contracts and other documents from the Achaemenid Period; for instance,

---

55. Noun groups are indicated by angular brackets, for example, ⟨איש חסיד⟩. Larger noun phrases will be marked by square brackets, e.g., [⟨ארבעים יום⟩ ⟨וארבעים לילה⟩]. See also, e.g., Ezra 3:7–9; 4:2–3, 5; 9:1; Neh 1:1; 2:10, 13; 3:1; 4:1; 5:14; 6:1; 8:4, 7; 9:4.

56. Cf. Ezra 5:2: באדין קמו [⟨זרבבל ⟨בר שאלתיאל⟩⟩ ⟨וישוע ⟨בר יוצדק⟩⟩] ושריו למבנא [בית אלהא⟩ די בירושלם]. Note also, e.g., Ezra 4:8, 9, 10, 17, 23; 5:2–3, 6; 6:6, 13, 14, 18.

57. Note also some passages from the late monarchic period (Gen 6:10; 7:13; 14:1–2; 2 Kgs 18:18; 22:12; 23:2, 4; Jer 36:12). Contrast Gen 21:22; 26:26. In NA and NB royal inscriptions, such summaries are often found.

CAP 1, lines 1–4   בי[ו]ם 2 ל[י]רח אפף שנת 27 לדריוש מלכא

אמרת סלואה ברת כניה ויתומה אחתה ליההאור ברת שלומם,

אנחן יהבן לכי פלג מנתא זי יהבו לן דיני מלכא

On the second day of the [m]onth of Epiphi, year 27 (i.e., October 22, 495
B.C.E.) of Darius (i.e., I), said Salluʾā, daughter of Qenāyā, and Yetomā her
sister, to Yehoʾūr, daughter of Šelomam, we give you half the share that
the royal judges . . . allotted to us

CAP 8, lines 1–2   ב 21 לכסלו הו יום 1 למסורע שנת 6 ארתחשמש מלכא

אמר מחסיה בר ידניה יהודי מהחסן ביב בירתא לדגל הומדת

לנשן מבטחיה ברתא לאמר

On the 21st of Kislev, that is day 1 of Mesore, year 6 of Artaxerxes the
King (i.e., 459 B.C.E.), said Maḥsēyā, son of Yedaniā, a Judean, holding
property in the fortress of Elephantine, from the detachment of Hauma-
data, to Dame Mibṭaḥiā, the daughter, as follows

CAP 13, lines 1–2   ב2 לכסלו הו יום 11 לירח מסורע שנת 19 ארתחשסש

מלכא אמר מחמיה בר ידניה ארמי זי סון לדגל וריזת למפטחיה ברתה לאמר

On the 2nd of Kislev, that is day 11 of the month of Mesore, year 19 of
Artaxerxes the King (i.e., November 18, 446 B.C.E.), said Maḥsēyā, son of
Yedaniā, an Aramean of Syene from the detachment of Varyazata, to his
daughter Mipṭaḥiā, as follows

CAP 30, lines 1–4 (407 B.C.E.)   אל מר[א]ן בגוהי פחת יהוד ידניה

וכנותה כהניא זי ביב בירתא, שלם מראן אלהי שמיא ישאל שגיא בכל עדן,

(. . .) וכען עבדך ידניה וכנותה כן אמרין

To our Lord, Bagavahi, governor of Yehud, your servants Yedaniā and
his colleagues, the priests in Elephantine the fortress. May the God of
Heaven be much interested in the welfare of our lord at all times, . . .
And now, your servant Yedaniā and his colleagues speak thus

Detailed specification is characteristic of all documents of this pe-
riod, such as CAP 8 (lines 1–2; 459 B.C.E.); CAP 13 (lines 1–2; 446 B.C.E.)
We also find this styleme in the slave sale deed from Samaria (335
B.C.E.):[58]

בֿ20 לאדר שנת 2 ראש מכלות [ד]ריהוש מלכא בשמר[ין בירתא זי בשמרין

מדינתא] ליהונתן שמה בר שאלה דנה עבד זילה תמים

[חנניה בר בידאל זבן ליהונור בר לנרי בכסף ש35]

On 20 Adar year 2 (i.e., of Arses), accession year of Darius (i.e., III) the
King, in Samar[ia the citadel, which is in Samaria the province] [Ḥā-
nanyā son of Beyadʾel sold] Yehōḥānan, by name, son of Šeʾīlā, a slave of
his, without blemish, [to Yehōnūr, son of Lanēry for 35 silver shekels]

---

58. WDSP 1 (see also Cross 1985: 8); the reconstruction is warranted by the continuation (line 5: הן אנה חנניה בר ב[י]דאל), and a parallel document, WDSP 4, line 1: בשמרין [. . .
(ויהונור [,]ליהונורי] בר לנרי, and lines 3, 5 ב]ירתא זי בשמרין מדינתא].

Thus the detailed enumeration of the participants, which is characteristic of such books as Ezra–Nehemiah, Haggai, and Zechariah, reflects
the administrative register as evidenced by the legal documents of the
Achaemenid Period.[59]

Other characteristics of Hebrew prose in this style include the preference for long clauses with two syntactic arguments or more (35–
50%)[60] and for hypotaxis (25–50%). A relatively large portion of the
hypotactic clauses contain two arguments or more, long noun groups,
and subordinate clauses (complex hypotaxis).[61] These details suggest
that the characteristic biblical prose style of the Achaemenid Period
was at home in the official scribal chancery. The profile of this style is
illustrated by the description of Passover (Ezra 6:19–22). In the tables
below, the three analytical columns at the right indicate (1) the *number
of arguments in independent clauses* (Arg); (2) the *status of subordinate
clauses* (Subordin): attributive (attr), complex hypotaxis (cemb, indicating embedded clauses with two arguments or more, or long noun
groups; or chier, the complex hierarchy of subordination to hypotactic
clauses); and (3) the *number of words per noun group* (Noungr).

(1) *Ezra 6:19–22*		*Arg*	*Subordin*	*Noungr*
v. 19	ויעשו בני הגולה את הפסח בארבעה עשר לחדש הראשון	3	-	2, 3
v. 20	כי הטהרו הכהנים והלוים כאחד	2	-	2
	כלם טהורים	1	-	-
	וישחטו הפסח לכל בני הגולה ולאחיהם הכהנים ולהם	2	-	6
v. 21	ויאכלו בני ישראל (השבים) וכל (הנבדל)	1	-	3
	השבים מהגולה		attr	-
	הנבדל מטמאת גוי הארץ אלהם (לדרש)		cemb	3
	לדרש לה' אלהי ישראל		chier	3
v. 22	ויעשו חג מצות שבעת ימים בשמחה	3	-	2, 2
	כי שמחם ה'	1	-	-

59. The extended noun groups in the epithets found in the Aḥiqar tale from Elephantine have been discussed in Polak 2003: 47.

60. The term *argument* refers to syntactic constituents immediately dependent on the
predicate, for example, subject, object, modifier; but attribute and apposition are counted
under the heading *noun group*. For further details, see Polak 2002: 264–65 (sample from
Neh 8:1–18), and the following note.

61. For detailed analysis of various pericopes, see Polak 1998: 63–68, 71–78, 96–100
(samples from Ezra 4:1–5; 9:1–5; 10:1; 2 Chr 32:1–6, 9, 16–23; Esther 8); 2001: 57–59, 65–69
(samples from Ezra 10:7–14; Esth 4:6–16). In addition, note the remarks of Eskhult 1990:
116–18.

(1) *Ezra 6:19–22*	Arg	Subordin	Noungr
והסב לב מלך אשור עליהם (לחזק)	3	-	3
לחזק ידיהם במלאכת בית האלהים אלהי ישראל	cemb	5	

The second part of the table summarizes these data for the various categories and presents the percentage of each category, relative to the number of clauses:

Total: Argm.	12 Clauses Number	Per 100		Number	Per 100
0 Arg	–	–	Complex Hypot	3	25.00
1 Arg	3	25.00	Noun Groups	11	91.67
0–1 Arg	3	25.00	Long Groups	2	16.67
2+ Arg	5	41.67	Grouped Nouns	34	283.00
Subord	4	33.33			

In this pericope, short clauses (0–1 arguments) compose 25% of the text, whereas long clauses (2–3 arguments) compose almost 42% of the text. One-third of the text consists of subordinate clauses, most of them in complex hypotaxis. Almost all clauses (91%) include a noun group, two of which are long and complicated:

v. 21	בני ישראל השבים מהגולה
v. 21	וכל הנבדל מטמאת גוי הארץ אלהם לדרש לה׳ אלהי ישראל
v. 22	לחזק ידיהם במלאכת בית האלהים אלהי ישראל

The expression כי הטהרו הכהנים והלוים כאחד ('for the priests and Levites had purified themselves to a man',) contains the Aramaism כאחד 'together', like Aramaic כחדה (Dan 2:35: ודהבא באדין דקו כחדה פרזלא חספא נחשא כספא 'Then the iron, the clay, the bronze, the silver, and the gold were crushed together', NKJV).[62] This adverbial also appears in the account of the foundation of the temple:

Ezra 3:9	ויעמד ישוע בניו ואחיו קדמיאל ובניו בני יהודה כאחד
	לנצח על עשה המלאכה בבית האלהים

---

62. See BDB, 25; all passages in which Hebrew כאחד appears are dated to the exilic/postexilic period: Eccl 11:6; Ezra 2:64 (//Neh 7:66); 3:9; 2 Chr 5:13. One notes זאב וטלה ופרה ודב תרעינה;וגר זאב עם כבש . . . ועגל וכפיר ומריא (ימרו) יחדו (Isa 65:25) as against ירעו כאחד יחדו ירבצו ילדיהן (Isa 11:6–7). For the original Hebrew, כאיש אחד, see Num 14:15; Judg 6:16; 20:1, 11; 1 Sam 11:7; 2 Sam 19:15; Ezra 3:1 (Neh 8:1).

Jeshua, his sons and brothers, Kadmiel and his sons, the sons of Judah, together were appointed in charge of those who did the work in the House of God

The legal background of the chancery style is illustrated by the typology of the Convention (אמנה) attributed to Nehemiah's initiative, with its intricate sentence structure and long noun groups:[63]

(2) *Nehemiah 10:29–40*	Arg	Subordin	Noungr
ושאר העם הכהנים הלוים השוערים המשררים הנתינים			12
וכל (הנבדל) נשיהם בניהם ובנתיהם כל (יודע)			
הנבדל מעמי הארצות אל תורת האלהים		cemb	2, 2
יודע		attr	
מבין		attr	
מחזיקים על אחיהם אדיריהם	2		8, 4, 2
ובאים באלה ובשבועה (ללכת) (ולשמור) (ולעשות)	2		2
ללכת בתורת האלהים		cemb	2
אשר נתנה ביד משה עבד האלהים		chier	4
ולשמור		cemb[a]	
ולעשות את כל מצות ה׳ אדנינו ומשפטיו וחקיו		cemb	6
ואשר לא נתן בנתינו לעמי הארץ		cemb	2
ואת בנתיהם לא נקח לבנינו		cemb	
ועמי הארץ (המביאים) לא נקח מהם בשבת וביום קדש	2		2, 3
המביאים את המקחות וכל שבר ביום השבת (למכור)		cemb	2, 3
למכור		chier	
ונטש את השנה השביעית ומשא כל יד	1		4
והעמדנו עלינו מצות (לתת)	2	-	-
לתת עלינו שלשית השקל בשנה לעבדת בית אלהינו		cemb	3, 3, 15
. . . .			
והיה הכהן בן אהרן עם הלוים (בעשר)		2	3
בעשר הלוים		sub	
והלוים יעלו את מעשר המעשר	5	-	2, 2, 2
לבית אלהינו אל הלשכות לבית האוצר			

(v. 29, v. 30, v. 31, v. 32, v. 33, v. 39)

---

63. A similar profile was found for Ezra 2:69–3:7 (22 clauses); 3:8–13 (27 clauses), with very low values for 0–1 Arg (27.27% and 14.81%, respectively); high values for 2+ Arg (50.00%, 37.04%), subordination (22.72% and 48.15%), and noun groups (100.00% and 92.59%).

(2) *Nehemiah 10:29–40*	Arg	Subordin	Noungr
v. 40 כי אל הלשכות יביאו בני ישראל ובני הלוי	3	–	4, 4
את תרומת הדגן התירוש והיצהר			
ושם כלי המקדש והכהנים (המשרתים) והשוערים והמשררים	1		5
המשרתים		attr	
ולא נעזב את בית אלהינו	1		2

a. Counted as such because it is a compound predicate in a series of subordinate infinitive clauses.

Total: Argm.	35 Clauses Number	Per 100		Number	Per 100
0 Arg	–	–	Complex Hypot	17	48.57
1 Arg	4	11.43	Noun Groups	44	125.71
0–1 Arg	4	11.43	Long Groups	13	37.14
2+ Arg	10	28.57	Grouped Nouns	149	425.71
Subord	21	60.00			

The diction of this pericope is even more intricate than that of the preceding segments. The high incidence of complex hypotaxis (48.57% of all clauses) is striking. One also notes the frequency of long noun groups (37.14%; even including groups consisting of 15 nouns) and the large number of grouped nouns (149; in the mean, more than 4 in each clause). In a legal context, such an involute style is only to be expected (Crystal and Davy 1969: 193–217; Polak 2001: 87–89). Aramaic influence is obvious in the use of אשר to introduce an object clause: ואשר לא נתן בנתינו לעמי הארץ (v. 31), like Aramaic די. In the infinitive clause the object precedes the predicate: ואת בכורי בקרינו וצאנינו להביא לבית אלהינו לכהנים (v. 37: 'and to bring *the firstlings of our cattle and flocks* to the House of our God for the priests'). The verb לקח is used in the meaning 'to buy' (v. 32: ועמי הארץ המביאים את המקחות . . . למכור, לא נקח מהם), 'the peoples of the land, who bring their wares . . . , we will not buy from them'); מקחות means 'merchandise'. The term העמיד forms a Hebrew analogue for Aramaic הקים/קים (*Haphel/Pael*, 'to establish a statute'): והעמדנו עלינו מצות לתת עלינו שלשית השקל בשנה (v. 33: 'We also lay on ourselves the obligation to charge ourselves yearly one-third of a shekel', NRSV; cf. Dan 6:8; *HALOT* 1968), comparable with the Aramaic terms לקבל זנה אסרא (זי) הקימו ביניהם ('according to this contract ⟨which⟩ they established between them').[64] These segments illustrate the intricate

---

64. WDSP 1, line 11 (cf. lines 4–5); 3, lines 9–10.

nature of the chancery style under Babylonian and Persian domination and also show to what extent scribal language was dominated by Aramaic. Thus, the diction of LBH prose basically reflects the style of authors–scribes who were educated at the governmental chancery.

The Hebrew Vernacular in the Achaemenid Period

As Official Aramaic became the standard language of the Judean chancery, Hebrew lost its status as the prestige language in governmental and commercial contexts,[65] and spoken Hebrew became the vernacular for the household, one's circle of friends, and informal conversation on more or less private subjects.[66] The memoirs of Ezra and Nehemiah point to the use of Hebrew in popular and religious assemblies but not in government contexts (Ezra 10; Nehemiah 5, 8–9).

The Persistence of the Hebrew Vernacular

The vitality of spoken Hebrew is evidenced by a number of segments in direct discourse in the memoirs of Ezra and Nehemiah (Polak 2001: 65–67). In the account of the assembly that decided on the expulsion of the foreign wives, we hear the voice of the people:[67]

Ezra 10:12b–13[68]   כן / כדבריך [כדבריך ketîb] עלינו לעשות /
אבל העם רב / והעת גשמים / ואין כח לעמוד בחוץ / והמלאכה לא
⟨ליום אחד⟩ / ולא לשנים / כי הרבינו לפשע ⟨בדבר הזה⟩

True. As your demand, we must do. But there are many people, and it is the rainy season; and there is no patience for remaining out in the open. And this is not the work of a day or two, for we have transgressed extensively in this matter.

---

65. Young 1993: 16–21, 74–75, 87; Ferguson 1959. Nehemiah's complaint about the lack of knowledge of "Judahite" (Neh 13:24) would be rather implausible if commercial and administrative business had required the knowledge of Hebrew.

66. Fishman 1971: 236–39, 250–59, 288–93; 1972: 16–23; Fasold 1987: 34–52. A perfect model for the inclusion of more and more Aramaic features of all kinds by speakers of the Hebrew vernacular is provided by Haugen's findings in Norwegian immigrant communities in English-speaking Minnesota (Haugen 1972b).

67. The proposal in Ezra 10:14 appears in formal language, appropriate to the official recommendation. The contrast between this style and the casual diction of the popular response shows that the narrator was quite conscious of the difference between the various registers and their settings.

68. In this notation the forward slash (/) indicates the boundaries between simple clauses, and angular brackets (⟨ ⟩) indicate noun groups (the accumulation of noun groups in a noun complex is indicated by square brackets). Subordinate clauses are indicated by underlining.

Apart from the latter, explanatory sentence, which includes a subordinate clause and a short noun group (לפשע בדבר הזה), all clauses are short and simple, even ואין כח לעמוד בחוץ. This diction fits the cross-cultural typology of spontaneous spoken language, as analyzed by such linguists as Chafe, Halliday, and Miller and Weinert:[69] short simple clauses with only a few arguments, a small number of subordinate clauses, and only a few noun groups.[70] Hence, quoted discourse of this type is to a certain extent representative of the vernacular.[71]

An additional example is found in the account of the reading of the Torah:

(3) Nehemiah 8:9–11[a]	Arg	Subordin	Noungr
היום קדש הוא לה׳ אלהיכם	2		2, 2
אל תתאבלו	-	-	-
ואל תבכו	-	-	-
. . . .			
לכו	-	-	-
אכלו משמנים	1	-	-
ושתו ממתקים	1	-	-
ושלחו מנות (לאין)	2	-	-
לאין נכון לו		sub	
כי קדוש היום לאדנינו	2	-	-
ואל תעצבו	-	-	-
כי חדות ה׳ היא מעזכם	1		2
. . . .			
הסו	-	-	-

---

69. Crystal and Davy 1969: 102–15; Chafe 1985; Halliday 1989; Miller and Weinert, 1998: 14–16, 22–24, 46–49, 72–79, 94–99, 132–33, 139–82, 267–306; Eggins and Slade 1997: 67–115; Biber and Conrad 2001.

70. If כן is not construed as a short clause of assent (Josh 2:4, כן / באו אלי האנשים 'It is true, the men did come to me'; NJPSV; see *HALOT* 482 [I כן]), it must be taken as a proleptic particle, anticipatory of כדבריך. The latter construction exemplifies another feature of the colloquial: fragmented/elliptical syntax (Crystal and Davy 1969: 49–51, 108–14; Miller and Weinert 1998: 22, 23–26, 58–71; Eggins and Slade 1997: 89–95, 106–13).

71. Quoted discourse is always a literary convention that lacks intonation and most of the hallmarks of casual conversation, such as "huh uh," pausing, interruptions, or overlapping speech. According to Page (1973: 4, 6–22) Dickens succeeded in giving the impression of colloquial language by imitating only a few aspects of spoken discourse. Interactional aspects of the structuring of literary dialogue (Shakespeare's *Othello*) have been studied by Coulthard 1985: 182–92.

(3) Nehemiah 8:9–11[a]	Arg	Subordin	Noungr
כי היום קדש	1	-	-
ואל תעצבו	-	-	-

a. My analysis of this pericope disregards statements in the narrator's voice.

Total:	14 Clauses				
Argm.	Number	Per 100		Number	Per 100
0 Arg	6	42.86	Complex Hypot	–	–
1 Arg	4	28.57	Noun Groups	3	21.43
0–1 Arg	10	71.43	Long Groups	–	–
2+ Arg	2	14.29	Grouped Nouns	6	42.86
Subord	1	7.14			

These segments include a number of rare or unique lexemes and structures, for example, ונשב נשים נכריות (Ezra 10:2; so also 10:10, 14, 17–18; Neh 13:23–27),[72] לאין נכון לו (relative clause without introductory particle; Neh 8:9).[73] The origin of the Aramaism חדוה has already been pointed out.[74] Here, it is used together with the obviously literary מעזכם. An additional Aramaism is found in the response to Ezra's exhortation, לעתים מזמנים (Ezra 10:14;[75] also Neh 10:35; 13:31).[76] Thus the quoted discourse in these pericopes suggests an original Hebrew vernacular with some Aramaic coloring.

The tone of the vernacular also stands out in the Nehemiah Memoir. For instance, Nehemiah's address to the magnates contains many characteristics of casual, spoken language:

(4) Nehemiah 5:7–11		Arg	Subordin	Noungr
v. 7	משא איש באחיו אתם נשאים	2		3
	. . . .			

72. Marcus (1998) views the use of הושיב נשים as an Aramaism. But, apart from the Peshiṭta on verses in which the MT uses this idiom, he does not indicate any Aramaic parallel. GB, 323, and HALOT 444–45, point to an Ethiopian parallel; see also Ps 113:9, and note Japhet 1968: 367.

73. See n. 107 below (p. 615).

74. See above, p. 598 and n. 45.

75. The intricate style of the proposed resolution in v. 14 is characteristic of an official tone, whereas a vernacular tone is apparent in the simple clauses of v. 13.

76. Wagner 1966: 49; for the derivation of זמן from Akkadian simānu, see Kaufman 1974: 91–92.

(4) Nehemiah 5:7–11	Arg	Subordin	Noungr
v. 8 אנחנו קנינו את אחינו היהודים (הנמכרים) כדי בנו	3	-	2, 2
הנמכדים לגוים		attr	-
וגם אתם תמכרו את אחיכם	2	-	-
ונמכרו לנו	1	-	-
. . . .			
v. 9 לא טוב הדבד	1	-	-
אשר אתם עשים		attr	-
הלוא ביראת אלהינו תלכו מחדפת הגוים אויבינו	2	-	2, 3
v. 10 וגם אני אחי ונערי נשים בהם כסף ודגן	3	-	2, 2
נעזבה נא את המשא הזה	1	-	2
v. 11[a] השיבו נא להם כהיום שדתיהם כרמיהם	3	-	9
זיתיהם ובתיהם ומאת הכסף והדגן התירוש והיצהר			
אשר אתם נשים בהם		attr	-

a. The noun (אשר אתם נשים בהם . . . הכסף) ומאת should be emended to ומשאת (Rudolph 1949: 130).

Total:	12 Clauses					
Argm.	Number	Per 100			Number	Per 100
0 Arg	–	–	Complex Hypot		–	–
1 Arg	3	25.00	Noun Groups		9	75.00
0–1 Arg	3	25.00	Long Groups		1	8.33
2+ Arg	6	50.00	Grouped Nouns		27	225.00
Subord	3	25.00				

Although the style of Nehemiah's discourse is more cultivated than the casual diction of the preceding segments (note the noun groups in vv. 9b–11), it is less intricate than the style of written language of this period, mainly because complex hypotaxis is not used. No Aramaic features appear. The response to Nehemiah's demands, probably consisting of a series of different answers, has a casual ring: נשיב / ומהם לא נבקש / כן נעשה כאשר אתה אומר ('We shall give them back, and not demand anything of them; we shall do just as you say', v. 12, NJPSV).

Thus, the memoirs of Ezra and Nehemiah reveal an impressive sensitivity to the diction of spontaneous spoken discourse.

The Independence of the Hebrew Vernacular

The independent position of the vernacular is suggested by a number of nonstandard forms that could hardly be ascribed to direct

Aramaic influence. For example, Nehemiah's complaint about the many Judeans who married "Ashdodite, Ammonite, and Moabite women" (Neh 13:23) contains the phrase ואינם מכירים לדבר יהודית ('and they did not know how to speak Judahite'). The use of הכיר to indicate practical ability (German *können*; Latin *posse*) replaces the classical construction of ידע plus infinitive, for example, לא ידעתי דבר ('I don't know how to speak'; Jer 1:6; so also Job 34:33).[77] Another aspect of the interchange of הכיר and ידע is found in 4QMMT (ואנחנו מכירים שבאוו מקצת הברכות והקללות שכתוב בס[פר מו[שה 'we realize that part of the blessings and the curses written in the b[ook of Mo]ses have come true').[78] Both cases are most plausibly explained as hypercorrection. The wording of Nehemiah's comment, then, illustrates the relative independence of spoken Hebrew. The special position of the vernacular between CBH and Aramaic fits the social and cultural context of foreign domination[79] because Hebrew usage was no longer dependent on the standard language of the royal chancery. In this situation, the regional vernaculars (urban as well as rural) began to develop independently.[80]

We should also mention in this context the narrowed use of לקח to indicate 'buying', such as, for instance, ועמי הארץ המביאים את המקחות וכל שבר ביום השבת למכור לא נקח מהם בשבת וביום קדש (Neh 10:32: 'The peoples of the land who bring their wares (המקחות) and all sorts of foodstuff for sale on the sabbath day—we will not buy from them on the sabbath or a holy day'; so also 5:2–3). This narrowing of meaning can hardly be explained in terms of Aramaic influence, for in Aramaic 'buying'/ 'selling' is indicated by זבן (Qal and Pael); לקח occurs in its usual semantic range in the Elephantine documents.[81] Thus, it seems preferable to view the narrow meaning 'to buy' against the background of changes in the field of commerce. In this period coined money gradu-

---

77. So also Exod 36:1; 1 Sam 16:18; 1 Kgs 3:7; 5:20; Isa 7:15; 8:4; 56:11; Amos 3:10; and in LBH: Eccl 4:17; 6:8; 10:15; 2 Chr 2:13.

78. 4Q398, frags. 11–13, lines 3–4 (Qimron and Strugnell 1994: 36).

79. Important evidence for the independence of LBH has been adduced by Talshir 1987; Qimron 1992a, 2000; see also Hurvitz 2000b. Elwolde (1997) highlights the continuity of CBH, LBH, and QH. A sense of continuity perfectly squares with Qimron's analysis of the QH lexicon and Smith's discussion of the use of *wayyiqtol* in LBH and QH (Qimron 1986: 86–97, 105–18; Smith 1991: 59–63).

80. Young 1993: 90–91; Fasold 1987: 216–22, 247–54; Weinreich 1963: 99–103, 108–9; Fishman 1971: 330–36.

81. For instance, CAP 7, lines 6, 9; 8, line 17; 9, lines 9, 11; 10, lines 9, 13, 17; 20, line 6; 27, line 18; 30, line 12; BMAP 7, line 36; 11, line 10; DAD 3, obv. lines 5–8, 9; rev. line 10. With the meaning 'to receive': HP 1, rev. line 9; with the meaning 'to buy': HP 3, rev. line 9.

ally became a common means of payment.[82] Hence, at the important economic centers commercial transactions mainly involved the use of money, although barter or weighing of silver cannot be excluded.[83] It seems, then, that the introduction of money brought with it changes in the perception of the act of payment and thus in terminology, changes that did not pass over the Judean speech community.

Grammatical Features of the Vernacular

Morphological and syntactical distinctions between LBH and the classical language are well known. Some of these changes may reflect the convergence of Aramaic influence and vernacular features, such as the increase in the use of *še* to replace *ʾašer*.[84] But in other cases the vernacular preserves distinctive forms that are not attested in Aramaic or MH.

A characteristic postclassical form is *waʾeqṭĕlā* for first-person *wayyiqṭōl*, for example, ונסעה (8:16), ואשלחה (8:15), ואבינה (8:15), ואקבצה (Ezra 7:28), ונסעה (Neh 1:5), ואתאבלה (9:31), ואמרטה משער ראשי וזקני ואשבה משומם (8:31), ואתנה (2:1, 9), ואצאה (2:13), etc.[85] In other places we find short forms, for instance, ואקרא (Ezra 8:21; similarly 8:32), ונשב (10:2), ואמר (Neh 1:5; 2:3). This use of *waʾeqṭĕlā* is a remarkable extension of the classical functions of the cohortative. Does this imply that the proper use of the cohortative had been forgotten?[86] Some data indicate that such an inference is questionable.

---

82. On the spread of coins along the coast and in Judea, see Stern 2001: 555–70. Judean commercial terminology is related to the terminology of the surrounding areas.

. 83. Meshorer (1998: 33) emphasizes that weighing is implied in the deposition of 'twenty gold bowls worth one thousand darics' (Ezra 8:27).

84. In prose: Ezra 8:20; Jonah 1:7; 4:10; 1 Chr 5:20; 27:27; in poetic or nearly poetic texts: Ps 122:3–4; 123:2; 124:1–2, 6; 129:6–7; 133:2–3; 135:2, 8, 10; 136:23; 137:8–9; 144:15; 146:3, 5; Job 19:29; Cant 1:6–7, 12; 2:7, 17–3:5 and passim; Eccl 1:3, 7, 9–11, 14, 17, and passim; Lam 2:15–16; 4:9; 5:18. In sections that are not obviously postexilic, note the Northern forms: Judg 5:7 (poetic); 6:17; 7:12; 8:26. Many scholars (e.g., Seow 1996: 660–61) attribute this form to a Northern dialect. Rendsburg (1990: 113–18) rejects this theory in view of the paucity of the evidence, preferring to describe it as a colloquialism.

85. Bauer and Leander 1922: 301–2; Bergsträsser 1929: 23.

86. The use of the long form is often explained as a result of the loss of the feeling for the distinction between the cohortative and the short form (*ʾeqṭōl*), for example, Bergsträsser 1929: 50 l (cf. 1918: 11, 13); Kutscher 1974: 39–40, 327. Thus it has been maintained that this form arose in analogy with the jussive forms, which are often identical with the *wayyiqṭol* forms of the second and third person (Kutscher 1974: 39–40; 327; this view is quoted as Müller's theory by Driver 1892: 79–80).

The Cohortative

Quoted discourse in the Nehemiah Memoirs preserves a number of instances of the cohortative such as, for example, Nehemiah's emphatic plea, נעזבה נא את המשא הזה (Neh 5:10, 'let us now abandon those claims!'). In this case the verbal form is followed by the enclitic נא, in keeping with the idiomatic use of this form in proposals.[87] In addition, the long form is used in spoken discourse to indicate purpose, for instance, in the complaint שדתינו וכרמינו ובתינו אנחנו ערבים ונקחה דגן ברעב (Neh 5:3, 'We must pawn our fields, our vineyards, and our homes in order to buy grain to stave off hunger').[88] We encounter the long together with the short form in the prophet's proposal, נועד אל בית האלהים / אל תוך ההיכל / ונסגרה דלתות ההיכל (6:10, "Let us meet in the House of God, inside the sanctuary, and let us shut the doors of the sanctuary").[89] Both forms, then, represent spoken language.[90]

Wĕqāṭal

An additional characteristic of CBH is the use of *wĕqāṭal* to indicate distant/conditional future. This feature stands out in Nehemiah's warning against enslavement, וגם אתם תמכרו את אחיכם ונמכרו לנו (Neh 5:8, 'will you now sell your brothers so that they must be sold back to us?').[91] The classical form also occurs in Nehemiah's deliberations, ומי כמוני אשר יבוא אל ההיכל וחי (6:11, 'Besides, who such as I can go into the sanctuary and live?'). Nehemiah's enemies are likewise represented as using this form, עד אשר נבוא אל תוכם / והרגנום / והשבתנו את המלאכה (4:5, 'before we come upon them and kill them and stop the work', NRSV 4:11). One notes Tobiah's sarcastic remark:[92] גם אשר הם בונים / אם יעלה

---

87. Cf., e.g., אמלטה נא שמה (Isa 5:5); ועתה אודיעה נא אתכם את אשר אני עשה לכרמי (Gen 19:20; so also 33:15; Judg 14:12).

88. Admittedly, some of these quotations reflect fictitious discourse. Sanballat, for instance, probably spoke mostly Aramaic (Neh 3:34–35), as indicated by the Aramaic documents from Wādi Dâliyeh. A purported letter sent by Sanballat includes some obvious Aramaisms, such as the indication of the agentive of the passive predicate by *lamed auctoris*, ועתה ישמע למלך כדברים האלה. Marcus (1998: 108) explains the clauselet היעזבו להם in Sanballat's speech as a calque reflecting Aramaic שבק 'to allow' (following Ehrlich).

89. The forms לכה ונועדה יחדו are put in Sanballat's mouth (Neh 6:2) and therefore hardly bear explanation as high literary usage.

90. On a scale of literariness, the rare verb ועד must rank higher than סגר.

91. So also Neh 2:18, 20; 6:13; Ezra 9:12.

92. In Nehemiah's Memoirs, note 4:5, 16; 6:3, 11, 13. Other examples in LBH prose: Esth 6:9; Dan 1:10; Ezra 9:12 (in religious context, drawing on D; drawing on H: Neh 1:9). One may also find a cohortative in Neh 2:17 (לכו ונבנה את חומת ירושלם), but this form is ambiguous. Since the next verse offers נקום ובנינו, ונבנה could be viewed as simple *yiqṭōl*.

שׁוּעָל / וּפָרַץ חוֹמַת אַבְנֵיהֶם (Neh 3:35, 'Whatever they build, if even a fox goes up on it, he will break down their stone wall', NKJV 4:3). Explanation of the idiomatic use of *wĕqāṭal* as a literary classicism, worthy of leaders and magnates, is hardly likely to account for its use in the mouth of such adversaries as 'Tobiah the Ammonite servant' (2:10).

Thus, at the time that the Memoirs of Ezra and Nehemiah were composed and revised, Hebrew speakers most probably were still conscious of the idiomatic use of *wĕqāṭal* forms and cohortative, even in the vernacular.[93]

Waʾeqṭĕlā: A Vernacular Form

It seems that the characteristics of the vernacular provide the most plausible explanation for the problematic use of the *waʾeqṭĕlā* form. According to Bauer and Leander the cohortative (*Affekt-Aorist*) serves to express emotional involvement.[94] This analysis bears on the use of *waʾeqṭĕlā*, since many linguists, for instance Chafe and Tannen, view involvement as one of the main characteristics of spoken discourse and oral narrative.[95] Because *waʾeqṭĕlā* is peculiar to spoken discourse and first-person narrative, the argument that it expresses the speaker's involvement in his narrative is quite plausible. After all, in many languages, involvement affects morphology and syntax. For instance, in Classical Greek, spoken discourse may use special forms of the demonstrative pronouns and deictic adverbs (*iota demonstrativum*),[96] a feature that is all the more significant because the use of deictics is far more frequent in spoken than in written discourse.[97] Oral narrative in many languages tends to use present tense as a narrative tense (*praesens historicum*), thus representing the narrated events as though they are actually occurring at the time of the narration.[98] Accordingly, the *waʾeqṭĕlā* form is better viewed as a modal indicator of involvement in spoken

---

93. Smith (1991: 26–27, 31–32) tends to ascribe the shifts in LBH to the influence of the vernacular, whereas scribal language preserved the ancient forms as an archaism.

94. Bauer and Leander 1922: 302z (Anm.), preceded by Stickel's analysis as quoted by Driver 1892: 79. This analysis, which is also taken into account by Kutscher (1974: 327), explains a number of cases in which *ʾeqṭĕlā* is paralleled by the perfect; e.g., Ps 77:6; Isa 59:10; expressions of fear are found in Isa 38:10; Jer 4:21; Ps 57:5.

95. Chafe 1982: 35–53; Tannen 1985; 1984: 27–32, 80–87, 144–51; 1989: 9–97, 167–95.

96. LSJ 814b; Dover 1997: 63–64; involvement is highlighted in the discussion of Greek deixis by Humbert 1960: 29–34.

97. Fox 1987: 45–62, 75, 139–43; Miller and Weinert 1998: 140–41, 194, 267–68; Hausendorf 1995.

98. Dover 1997: 67–69; Carnoy 1924: 279–80. For Afrikaans, see van Ginneken 1928: 210–11; for English, Norrick 2000: 12–15.

discourse. Its adoption for written LBH prose is an accolade for the particular expressiveness of the vernacular style. The disappearance of these forms in MH is most plausibly explained by reference to the Aramaic influence on written language and thereby, in the long run, also on the vernacular.

Hebrew as the Language of Religion

Finally, we must deal with the use of Hebrew in a religious context. During and after the Exile, Hebrew retained its status as the preferred language of religious life (Ezra 3:11; 9:6–15; Neh 1:5–11);[99] witness such texts as the book of Lamentations,[100] the Maʿaloth Psalms, and Psalm 137.[101] The language of these texts, however, is not significantly different from other texts in LBH.[102] The book of Ezra–Nehemiah contains a number of prayers, religious admonitions, and descriptions of fasting and prayer that contain many characteristic LBH forms and lexemes:

LBH Lexemes[103]

מלכות

Nehemiah 9:35   והם במלכותם ובטובך הרב . . . לא עבדוך

נשא as a marriage term

Ezra 9:12   (cf. 9:1) בנותיכם אל תתנו לבניהם ובנתיהם אל תשאו לבניכם׃

---

99. Hence the Judean community is better described as bilingual (with spoken and written Hebrew and Aramaic) and diglossic, because the Hebrew vernacular was opposed to (a) OfA and (b) Hebrew as the preferred language for religious purposes. Rabin (1958: 152; followed by Schaper 1999: 16) classifies the Judean community as trilingual.

100. Dobbs-Allsop (1998) notes the mixture of CBH and LBH lexemes in Lamentations and concludes that these poems represent a transitory stage. In our terms, these poems were probably composed by poets who had learned the craft during the monarchy but were writing during the Babylonian domination.

101. Hurvitz 1972: 153–63, 174; 1985; 1997b. On imitation of ancient linguistic models in Ben Sira, see Joosten 1999.

102. The style of scribal language is most obvious in Dan 9:1–4, 20–22, and in Daniel's prayer itself (e.g., vv. 4, 6, 7, 8, 10, 11, 12–13, 15–17, 18). One also notes such stylemes in prophetic sayings: Hag 1:2, 4, 6, 11; 2:2, 3, 4, 5, 6, 12, 15–16, 17, 18–19. In 2:22–23 there is a long series of noun groups. Also note Zech 1:4, 6, 8, 10 (complex subordination), 12, 13–14, 15; 2:2, 4, 8, 12, 16; 4:2, 10, 11–12, 14; 5:3–4; 6:1–3, 5, 6, 7, 10, 11, 14; 7:5, 7, 10, 12; 8:5, 6, 7, 9, 10–13, 14, 15, 19, 20–22, 23.

103. In addition, note גויה meaning 'body' (Neh 9:37; Dan 10:6). The use of this lexeme in Ezek 1:11 and 23 is indicative of the transitional status of this prophet, as shown by Rooker 1990.

עבדות

Ezra 9:8	להאיר עינינו אלהינו ולתתנו מחיה מעט בעבדֵתנו
Ezra 9:9	כי עבדים אנחנו ובעבדתנו לא עזבנו אלהינו
Nehemiah 9:17	ויקשו את ערפם ויתנו ראש לשוב לעבדתם במרים

חדוה (Aramaic)

| Nehemiah 8:10 | כי חדות ה' היא מעזכם |

LBH Syntax[104]

Infinitive negated by אֵין, indicating negated modality: 'it is not possible/ necessary/ permitted to'.[105]

| Ezra 9:15 | הננו לפניך באשמתינו כי אין לעמוד לפניך על זאת |

There are also LBH features in descriptions of fasting and prayer.[106]

Wa'eqtĕlā

Ezra 7:28	ואני התחזקתי (. . .) ואקבצה מישראל ראשים לעלות עמי
Ezra 8:23	ונצומה ונבקשה מאלהינו על זאת ויעתר לנו
Ezra 9:3	וכשמעי את הדבר הזה (. . .) ואמרטה משער ראשי וזקני ואשבה משומם
Ezra 9:5	ובקרעי בגדי ומעילי ואכרעה על ברכי ואפרשה כפי אל ה' אלהי
Ezra 9:6	ואמרה אלהי בשתי ונכלמתי להרים אלהי פני אליך

Qāṭal as the continuation of an infinitive clause, not introduced by ויהי.

| Ezra 9:3 | וכשמעי את הדבר הזה קרעתי את בגדי |
| Nehemiah 8:5 | וכפתחו עמדו כל העם |

Asyndetic relative clauses (no relative pronoun).[107]

| Nehemiah 8:10 | ושלחו מנות לאין נכון לו |

---

104. In Ezra 9:6 one notes the construction כי עונתינו רבו למעלה ראש. BDB 752 refers to 2 Chr 34:4, והחמנים אשר למעלה מעליהם; M. Aboth 2:1, דע מה למעלה ממך. Rudolph (1949: 88) prefers the emendation למעלה מעל הראש (haplography).

105. On this syntagm see Hurvitz 1999; Seow 1996: 663–65; in particular note עליו אין להוסיף וממנו אין לגרע (Eccl 3:14) as against לא תסף עליו ולא תגרע ממנו (Deut 13:1; 4:2); Esth 4:2; 8:8. In religious context one notes: וגם ללוים אין לשאת את המשכן (1 Chr 23:26); אין לשמור למחלקות (2 Chr 5:11). The semantic aspects of this construction are not sufficiently taken into account by Ehrensvärd 1999.

106. Cf. also Dan 9:1, 3–4, 7, 9, 22, 23, 24, 25, 26.

107. So also Ezra 1:5, 6; 1 Chr 29:3; 2 Chr 30:18–19; 31:19 (note Gen 39:4 וכל יש לו) as against v. 5, בכל אשר יש לו; in poetry this construction is expected: Ps 71:8; 74:3). See Kropat 1909: 66–67. Talshir (1988: 180) mentions this construction with כל as antecedent.

אשר for כי

Nehemiah 8:14   וימצאו כתוב בתורה (. . .) אשר ישבו בני ישראל בסכות בחג

העבר קול (Ezra 1:1)

Nehemiah 8:15   ואשר ישמיעו ויעבירו קול בכל עריהם ובירושלם

אלהי השמים (cf. Jonah 1:9; Ezra 1:1; CAP 30–31)

Nehemiah 1:5   ואמר אנא ה' אלהי השמים האל הגדול והנורא

מן העולם עד העולם

Nehemiah 9:5   108 קומו ברכו את ה' אלהיכם מן העולם עד העולם

Thus, in spite of all the effort to preserve the Classical language, Classical and characteristic LBH forms are found side by side. In the Nehemiah narrative we encounter a Classical ויהי clause, followed by _qāṭal_ and a typical _waᵓeqṭĕlā_ form: ויהי כשמעי את הדברים האלה ישבתי ואבכה ואתאבלה ימים (Neh 1:4, 'When I heard these words, I sat and wept, and was in mourning for days'). In short, the use of Classical forms does not signify pure Classical Hebrew.

I readily admit that the language of religion was cultivated by the priests, particularly the temple singers. However, the temple was no longer being sustained by the Judean monarchy but by the local community, according to the agreement attributed to Nehemiah (Neh 10:33–40; 13:4–9, 10–13, 28).[109] Since in the fourth century the high priests Jaddua and Johanan had enough authority to mint coins in their own name,[110] it is clear that the priesthood had far more significant contacts with the administration than commoners.[111] Moreover, ac-

---

108. On this phrase, see Hurvitz 1972: 158–59 and pp. 597–598 above.

109. According to Ezra 6:6–10, the temple service was sustained by Darius; see Weinberg 1992: 111–12, 116–17; Blenkinsopp 1991: 22–27, 39. If we dismiss these claims as spurious (Bedford 2001: 143–48), we still have to take into account that the Judean community needed authoritative backing in the face of satrapal opposition (Bedford 2001: 149–51, 201–2). In that respect it is preferable to assume some imperial support (even though some of the claims of 6:8–6 may be exaggerated). By the same token, we must take into account the consideration that no exiles could leave Babylonia without authorization, thus implying imperial backing (note Bedford 2001: 149). One notes the successful intervention by Bagavahi and Delayah on behalf of the community at Elephantine (CAP 32), who also turned to the high priest. Hence, these officials had enough clout to influence the decisions of Aršama, who was a prominent member of the imperial family.

110. The coin of יוחנן הכהן and its historical implications are analyzed by Barag 1986–87; Schaper 2002, against Bedford 2001: 204–5. On the coin of Jaddua, from the first half of the fourth century, see Spaer 1986–87.

111. The prominent role of the priesthood is indicated by the extent of priestly participation in the reconstruction of the town walls (Neh 3:1, 4, 20–22, 28–29) and the priestly

cording to the testimony of the Ezra Memoir, they were more involved in mixed marriages than other strata in Judean society. Their economic position also implies social and commercial contacts. Thus, we can hardly suppose that the priests would have been able to preserve the language of the preexilic period in general. Characteristic features of LBH are found in the prose attributed to the prime example of a scholarly author-scribe, Ezra himself.

Priests, temple singers, and scholarly scribes, then, did not constitute an isolated elite. The people who expressed their beliefs, hopes, and fears in Hebrew presented themselves as part of the speech community to which they belonged, and participated in the struggle of this community to attain a position of its own in the context of the Empire.

---

connections with the Tobiads (Neh 13:4–7; Ezra 2:60–63). The position of the priesthood in the Ptolemaic and Seleucidic Empires is analyzed by Bickerman 1988: 141–45, 149–54.

Bibliography

Achenbach, R.
    2000   Die Titel der persischen Verwaltungsbeamten in Esra 4,9b [MT*]. *ZAH* 13: 134–44.
Albertz, R., and Becking, B. (eds.)
    2003   *Yahwism after the Exile: Perspectives on Israelite Religion in the Persian Era.* Assen.
Avigad, N.
    1958   New Light on the MṢH Seal Impressions. *IEJ* 8: 113–19.
Barag, D.
    1986–87   A Silver Coin of Yoḥanan the High Priest and the Coinage of Judea in the Fourth Century B.C.E. *Israel Numismatic Journal* 9: 4–21.
Bauer, H., and Leander, P.
    1922   *Historische Grammatik der hebräischen Sprache des Alten Testaments.* Halle.
Becking, B., and Korpel, M. C. A. (eds.)
    1999   *The Crisis of Israelite Religion: Transformation of Religious Tradition in Exilic and Post-Exilic Times.* OTS 42. Leiden.
Bedford, P. R.
    2001   *Temple Restoration in Early Achaemenid Judah.* JSJ Supplements 65. Leiden.
Bergey, R.
    1984   Late Linguistic Features in Esther. *JQR* 75: 66–78.
Bergsträsser, G.
    1918–29   *Hebräische Grammatik.* 2 vols. Leipzig. [repr. Hildesheim, 1962]

Betlyon, J. W.
2003   Neo-Babylonian Military Operations Other Than War in Judah and Jerusalem. Pp. 263–83 in *Judah and the Judeans in the Neo-Babylonian Period*, ed. O. Lipschits and J. Blenkinsopp. Winona Lake, Indiana.
Biber, D., and Conrad, S.
2001   Register Variation: A Corpus Approach. Pp. 175–96 in *The Handbook of Discourse Analysis*, ed. D. Schiffrin, D. Tannen and H. E. Hamilton. Oxford.
Biber, D., and Finegan, E. (eds.)
1994   *Sociolinguistic Perspectives on Register.* New York and Oxford.
Bickerman, E. J.
1984   The Babylonian Captivity. Pp. 342–58 in *The Cambridge History of Judaism. Volume One, Introduction: The Persian Period*, ed. W. D. Davies and L. Finkelstein. Cambridge.
1988   *The Jews in the Greek Age.* Cambridge, Massachusetts.
Blenkinsopp, J.
1991   Temple and Society in Achaemenid Judah. Pp. 22–53 in *Second Temple Studies. 1. Persian Period*, ed. P. R. Davies. JSOTSup 117. Sheffield.
Blom, J.-P., and Gumperz, J. J.
2000   Social Meaning in Linguistic Structure: Code-Switching in Norway. Pp. 111–36 in *The Bilingualism Reader*, ed. Li Wei. London.
Bresciani, E., and Kamil, M.
1966   Le lettere aramaiche di Hermopoli. Pp. 356–428 in *Atti della Accademia Nazionale dei Lincei.* Classe di Scienze Morali, storiche e filologiche 8/12. Rome.
Briant, P.
2002   *From Cyrus to Alexander. A History of the Persian Empire.* Trans. P. T. Daniels. Winona Lake, Indiana.
Briquel-Chaconnet, F. (ed.)
1996   *Mosaïque de langues mosaïque culturel: Le Bilinguisme dans le Proche-Orient ancien.* Paris.
Carnoy, A.
1924   *Manuel de linguistique Grecque.* Louvain and Paris.
Chafe, W. L.
1982   Integration and Involvement in Speaking, Writing and Oral Literature. Pp. 35–53. in *Spoken and Written Language: Exploring Orality and Literacy*, ed. D. Tannen. Norwood, New Jersey.
1985   Linguistic Differences Produced by Differences between Speaking and Writing. Pp. 105–123 in *Literacy, Language and Learning: The Nature and Consequences of Writing and Reading*, ed. D. R. Olson, N. Torrance and A. Hildyard. Cambridge.
1994   *Discourse, Consciousness and Time: The Flow and Displacement of Conscious Experience in Speaking and Writing.* Chicago.
Cook, J. (ed.)
2002   *Bible and Computer—The Stellenbosch AIBI-6 Conference: Proceedings of the Association Internationale Bible et Informatique: "From Alpha to Byte," University of Stellenbosch, 17–21 July, 2000.* Leiden.

Coulthard, M.
1985   *An Introduction to Discourse Analysis.* 2nd ed. London.
Coulthard, M. (ed.)
1994   *Advances in Written Discourse Analysis.* London.
Cowley, A. E.
1923   *Aramaic Papyri of the Fifth Century.* 2nd ed. Oxford.
Cross, F. M.
1985   Samaria Papyrus 1: An Aramaic Slave Conveyance of 335 B.C.E. *ErIsr* 18 (Avigad volume): 7*–17*.
Crystal, D., and Davy, D.
1969   *Investigating English Style.* London.
Dandamayev, M.
1984   Babylonia in the Persian Age. Pp. 326–42 in *The Cambridge History of Judaism, Volume One: Introduction; The Persian Period,* ed. W. D. Davies and L. Finkelstein. Cambridge.
Deroy, L.
1956   *L'emprunt linguistique.* Paris.
Dimant, D., and Rappaport, U. (eds.)
1992   *The Dead Sea Scrolls: Forty Years of Research.* STDJ 10. Jerusalem and Leiden.
Dobbs-Allsop, F. W.
1998   Linguistic Evidence for the Date of Lamentations. *JANES* 26: 1–36.
Dover, K.
1997   *The Evolution of Greek Prose Style.* Oxford.
Driver, G. R.
1965   *Aramaic Documents of the Fifth Century B.C.* 2nd ed. Oxford.
Driver, S. R.
1892   *A Treatise on the Use of the Tenses in Hebrew.* 3rd ed. Oxford.
Eggins, S., and Slade, D.
1997   *Analysing Casual Conversation.* London.
Ehrensvärd, M.
1999   Negating the Infinitive in Biblical Hebrew. *ZAH* 12: 147–63.
Elwolde, J. F.
1997   Developments in Hebrew Vocabulary between Bible and Mishnah. Pp. 17–55 in *The Hebrew of the Dead Sea Scrolls and Ben Sira: Proceedings of a Symposium Held at Leiden University,* ed. T. Muraoka and J. F. Elwolde. STDJ 26. Leiden.
Eph'al, I.
1978   The Western Minorities in Babylonia in the 6th–5th Century B.C.: Maintenance and Cohesion. *Or* 47: 74–90.
1979   Changes in Palestine during the Persian Period in Light of Epigraphic Sources. *IEJ* 48: 106–19.
Eph'al, I., and Naveh, J.
1996   *Aramaic Ostraca of the Fourth Century BC from Idumea.* Jerusalem.
Eshel, H., and Misgav, H.
1988   A Fourth Century B.C.E. Document from Ketef Yeriḥo. *IEJ* 38: 158–76.

Eskhult, M.
  1990 *Studies in Verbal Aspect and Narrative Technique in Biblical Hebrew Prose.* Uppsala.
  2000 Verbal Syntax in Late Biblical Hebrew. Pp. 84–93 in *Diggers at the Well: Proceedings of a Third International Symposium on the Hebrew of the Dead Sea Scrolls and Ben Sira*, ed. T. Muraoka and J. F. Elwolde. STDJ 36. Leiden.

Fasold, R.
  1987 *The Sociolinguistics of Society.* Oxford.
  1990 *The Sociolinguistics of Language.* Oxford.

Fassberg, S. E.
  1992 Hebraisms in the Aramaic Documents from Qumran. Pp. 243–55 in *Studies in Qumran Aramaic*, ed. T. Muraoka. Abr Nahraim Supplement 3. Leuven.
  2001 The Movement of *Qal* to *Pi'el* in Hebrew and the Disappearance of the *Qal* Internal Passive. *HS* 42: 243–55.

Ferguson, C. A.
  1959 Diglossia. *Word* 15: 325–40 [repr. pp. 65–80 in *The Bilingualism Reader*, ed. Li Wei]. London.
  1994 Dialect, Register and Genre: Working Assumptions about Generalization. Pp. 15–30 in *Sociolinguistic Perspectives on Register*, ed. D. Biber and E. Finegan. New York and Oxford.

Fishman, J. A.
  1970 *Sociolinguistics: A Brief Introduction.* Rowley, Massachusetts.
  1971 The Sociology of Language: An Interdisciplinary Social Science Approach to Language in Society. Pp. 217–404 in *Advances in the Sociology of Language, Volume I: Basic Concepts, Theories and Problems; Alternative Approaches*, ed. J. A. Fishman. The Hague.
  1972 The Relationship between Micro- and Macro-Sociolinguistics in the Study of Who Speaks What Language to Whom and When. Pp. 15–32 in *Sociolinguistics*, ed. J. B. Pride and J. Holmes. Harmondsworth.

Folmer, M. L.
  1995 *The Aramaic Language in the Achaemenid Period: A Study in Linguistic Variation.* OLA 68. Leuven.

Fox, B.
  1987 *Discourse Structure and Anaphora: Written and Conversational English.* Cambridge.

Gadd, C. J.
  1958 The Harran Inscriptions of Nabonidus. *AnSt* 8: 35–92.

Ginneken, J. van
  1928 *Handboek der Nederlandsche Taal, Deel I: De Sociologische Structuur der Nederlandsche Taal I.* 2nd ed. Hertogenbosch.

Grabbe, L. L.
  1998 "The Exile" under the Theodolite: Historiography as Triangulation. Pp. 80–100 in *Leading Captivity Captive: 'The Exile' as History and Ideology*, ed. L. L. Grabbe. JSOTSup 278. Sheffield

1999 Israel's Historical Reality after the Exile. Pp. 9–32 in *The Crisis of Israel- ite Religion. Transformations of Religious Tradition in Exilic and Post-Exilic Times*, ed. B. Becking and M. C. A. Korpel. OTS 42. Leiden.

Greenfield, J. C.

2001a Aramaic and its Dialects. Pp. 361–75 in *ʿAl Kanfei Yonah: Collected Stud- ies of Jonas C. Greenfield on Semitic Philology*, ed. S. M. Paul, M. E. Stone and A. Pinnick. 2 vols. Jerusalem.

2001b Babylonian-Aramaic Relationships Pp. 203–213 in *ʿAl Kanfei Yonah. Collected Studies of Jonas C. Greenfield on Semitic Philology*, ed. S. M. Paul, M. E. Stone and A. Pinnick. 2 vols. Jerusalem.

See also Naveh and Greenfield

Gropp, D. M.

2001 *Wady Daliyeh II: The Samaria Papyri from Wady Daliyeh*. Pp. 1–116 in *The Samaria Papyri from Wady Daliyeh and Qumran Cave 4. XXVIII. Miscella- nea, Part 2*, ed. M. Bernstein, M. Brady et al. DJD 28. Oxford.

Gumperz, J. J.

1971 *Language in Social Groups: Essays by John J. Gumperz*, ed. A. S. Dil. Stan- ford.

Halliday, M. A. K.

1964 The Users and Uses of Language. Pp. 75–110 in *The Linguistic Sciences and Language Teaching*, ed. M. A. K. Halliday, A. McIntosh and P. D. Strevens. London.

1989 *Spoken and Written Language*. 2nd. ed. Oxford.

Hanson, P. L.

1964 Paleo-Hebrew Scripts in the Hasmonean Age. *BASOR* 175: 26–42.

Haugen, E.

1972a Language and Migration. Pp. 1–36 in *The Ecology of Language: Essays by Einar Haugen*, ed. A. S. Dil. Stanford.

1972b The Confusion of Tongues. Pp. 110–32 in *The Ecology of Language: Es- says by Einar Haugen*, ed. A. S. Dil. Stanford.

Hausendorf, H.

1995 Deixis and Orality: Explaining Games in Face-to-Face Interaction. Pp. 181–97 in *Aspects of Oral Communication*, ed. U. M. Quasthoff. Re- search in Text Theory 21. Berlin.

Holm, J.

1988–89 *Pidgins and Creoles*. 2 vols. Cambridge Language Surveys. Cam- bridge.

Horbury, W. (ed.)

1999 *Hebrew Study from Ezra to Ben-Yehudah*. Edinburgh.

Humbert, J.

1960 *Syntaxe grecque*. 3rd ed. Paris.

Hurvitz, A.

1972 *The Transition Period in Biblical Hebrew: A Study of Post-exilic Hebrew and its Implications for the Dating of Psalms*. Jerusalem. [Hebrew]

1982 *A Linguistic Study of the Relationship between the Priestly Source and the Book of Ezekiel*. CahRB 20. Paris.

1983   The Hebrew Language in the Persian Era. Pp. 210–23 in *The Return to
        Zion in the Persian Era*, ed. H. Tadmor. The World History of the Jewish
        People 6. Tel Aviv. [Hebrew]
1985   Originals and Imitations in Biblical Poetry: A Comparative Examina-
        tion of 1 Sam 2:1–10 and Ps 113:5–9. Pp. 115–21 in *Biblical and Related
        Studies Presented to Samuel Iwry*, ed. A. Kort and S. Morschauser. Wi-
        nona Lake, Indiana.
1997a   The Historical Quest for "Ancient Israel" and the Linguistic Evidence
        of the Hebrew Bible: Some Methodological Observations. *VT* 47: 301–
        15.
1997b   The Linguistic Status of Ben Sira as a Link between Biblical and Mish-
        naic Hebrew. Pp. 72–86 in *The Hebrew of the Dead Sea Scrolls and Ben
        Sira; Proceedings of a Symposium Held at Leiden University*, ed. T. Mu-
        raoka and J. F. Elwolde. STDJ 26. Leiden.
1999   Further Comments on the Linguistic Profile of Ben Sira: Syntactic Af-
        finities with Late Biblical Hebrew. Pp. 132–45 in *Sirach, Scrolls and
        Sages Proceedings of a Second International Symposium on the Hebrew of
        the Dead Sea Scrolls and Ben Sira*, ed. T. Muraoka and J. F. Elwolde. STDJ
        33. Leiden.
2000a   Can Biblical Texts Be Dated Linguistically? Chronological Perspec-
        tives in the Historical Study of Biblical Hebrew. Pp. 143–60 in *Congress
        Volume Oslo 1998*, ed. A. Lemaire and M. Saebø. VTSup 80. Leiden.
2000b   Was QH a "Spoken" Language? On Some Recent Views and Positions:
        Comments. Pp. 110–14 in *Diggers at the Well: Proceedings of a Third In-
        ternational Symposium on the Hebrew of the Dead Sea Scrolls and Ben Sira*,
        ed. T. Muraoka and J. F. Elwolde. STDJ 36. Leiden.
2000c   Once Again the Linguistic Profile of the Priestly Material in the Pen-
        tateuch and Its Historical Age: A Response to J. Blenkinsopp. *ZAW* 112:
        180–91.
2003   Hebrew and Aramaic in the Biblical Period: The Problem of "Arama-
        isms" in Linguistic Research on the Hebrew Bible. Pp. 24–37 in *Biblical
        Hebrew: Studies in Chronology and Typology*, ed. I. M. Young. JSOTSup
        369. London.
Hymes, D.
1974   *Foundations of Sociolinguistics: An Ethnographic Approach*. Philadelphia.
Izre'el, S. (ed.)
2002   *Semitic Linguistics: The State of the Art at the Turn of the Twenty-First Cen-
        tury*. IOS 20. Winona Lake, Indiana.
Japhet, S.
1968   The Supposed Common Authorship of Chronicles and Ezra–Nehemiah
        Investigated Anew. *VT* 18: 330–71.
Joannès, F., and Lemaire, A.
1999   Trois tablettes cunéiformes à onomastique ouest-sémitique (collection
        Sh. Moussaïeff). *Transeu* 17: 17–33.
Joosten, J.
1999   Pseudo-classicisms in Late Biblical Hebrew. Pp. 146–59 in *Sirach,
        Scrolls and Sages Proceedings of a Second International Symposium on the*

Hebrew of the Dead Sea Scrolls and Ben Sira, ed. T. Muraoka and J. F. Elwolde. STDJ 33. Leiden.

Kapeliuk, O.
2002   Languages in Contact: The Contemporary Semitic World. Pp. 307–40 in *Semitic Linguistics: The State of the Art at the Turn of the Twenty-First Century,* ed. S. Izre'el. IOS 20. Winona Lake, Indiana.

Kaufman, S. A.
1974   *The Akkadian Influences on Aramaic.* Assyriological Studies 19. Chicago.
2002   Languages in Contact: The Ancient Near East. Pp. 297–306 in *Semitic Linguistics: The State of the Art at the Turn of the Twenty-First Century,* ed. S. Izre'el. IOS 20. Winona Lake, Indiana.

Kitchen, K. A.
1965   The Aramaic of Daniel. Pp. 31–79 in D. J. Wiseman et al., *Notes on Some Problems in the Book of Daniel.* London.

Kraeling, E. G.
1953   *The Brooklyn Museum Aramaic Papyri.* New Haven, Connecticut.

Kropat, A.
1909   *Die Syntax des Autors der Chronik verglichen mit der seiner Quellen.* BZAW 16. Giessen.

Kutscher, E. Y.
1947   Biblical Aramaic: Eastern or Western Aramaic. Pp. 123–27 in *World Congress of Jewish Studies: Summer 1947.* Jerusalem. [Hebrew]
1974   *The Language and Linguistic Background of the Isaiah Scroll (1QIsaᵃ).* STDJ 6. Leiden.
1977a   The Hermopolis Papyri. Pp. 53–69 in *Hebrew and Aramaic Studies,* ed. Z. Ben-Hayyim, A. Dotan, G. Sarfatti. Jerusalem.
1977b   Aramaic. Pp. 90–155 in *Hebrew and Aramaic Studies,* ed. Z. Ben-Hayyim, A. Dotan, G. Sarfatti. Jerusalem.
1977c   Two "Passive" Constructions in Aramaic in the Light of Persian. Pp. 70–89 in *Hebrew and Aramaic Studies,* ed. Z. Ben-Hayyim, A. Dotan, G. Sarfatti. Jerusalem.
1982   *A History of the Hebrew Language,* ed. R. Kutscher. Jerusalem and Leiden.

Langdon, S.
1912   *Die neubabylonischen Königsinschriften.* VAB 4. Leipzig.

Lemaire, A.
1996   *Nouvelles inscriptions araméennes d'Idumée au Musée d'Israël.* Transeu-phratène Supplément 3. Paris.
2001   *Nouvelles tablettes araméennes.* Hautes Études Orientales 34. Geneva.
2003   Formation et évolution de l'hébreu ancien. *TsafonL Revue d'études juives du Nord* 45: 29–36.

Lemaire, A., and Saebø, M. (eds.)
2000   *Congress Volume: Oslo, 1998.* VTSup 80. Leiden.

Lindenberger, J. M.
1994   *Ancient Aramaic and Hebrew Letters.* SBLWAW. Atlanta.

Lipschits, O.
1999   The History of the Benjamin Region under Babylonian Rule. *Tel Aviv* 26: 155–90.

Lipschits, O., and Blenkinsopp, J. (eds.)

2003 *Judah and the Judeans in the Neo-Babylonian Period.* Winona Lake, Indiana.

Li Wei

2000 Dimensions of Bilingualism. Pp. 3–25 in *The Bilingualism Reader,* ed. Li Wei. London.

Li Wei; Milroy, L.; and Ching, Pong Sin

2000 A Two-Step Sociolinguistic Analysis of Code-Switching and Language Choice: The Example of a Bilingual Chinese Community in Britain. Pp. 188–209 in *The Bilingualism Reader,* ed. Li Wei. London.

Lubetski, M., et al. (ed.)

2003 *Boundaries of the Ancient Eastern World: A Tribute to Cyrus H. Gordon.* JSOTSup 273. Sheffield.

Marcus, D.

1998 Is the Book of Nehemiah a Translation from Aramaic? Pp. 103–110 in *Boundaries of the Ancient Near Eastern World: A Tribute to Cyrus H. Gordon,* ed. M. Lubetski et al. JSOTSup 273. Sheffield.

Marrou, H. I.

1956 *A History of Education in Antiquity.* New York.

Meshorer, Y.

1998 *Ancient Means of Exchange: Weights and Coins.* Haifa.

Miller, J. E., and Weinert, R.

1998 *Spontaneous Spoken Language: Syntax and Discourse.* Oxford.

Muffs, Y.

1992 *Love and Joy: Law, Language and Religion in Ancient Israel.* New York and Jerusalem.

Muraoka, T.

2000 An Approach to the Morphosyntax and Syntax of Qumran Hebrew. Pp. 193–214 in *Diggers at the Well: Proceedings of a Third International Symposium on the Hebrew of the Dead Sea Scrolls and Ben Sira,* ed. T. Muraoka and J. F. Elwolde. STDJ 36. Leiden.

Muraoka, T. (ed.)

1992 *Studies in Qumran Aramaic.* Abr Nahrain Supplement 3. Leuven.

Muraoka, T., and Elwolde, J. F. (eds.)

1997 *The Hebrew of the Dead Sea Scrolls and Ben Sira: Proceedings of a Symposium Held at Leiden University.* STDJ 26. Leiden.

1999 *Sirach, Scrolls and Sages: Proceedings of a Second International Symposium on the Hebrew of the Dead Sea Scrolls and Ben Sira.* STDJ 33. Leiden.

2000 *Diggers at the Well: Proceedings of a Third International Symposium on the Hebrew of the Dead Sea Scrolls and Ben Sira.* STDJ 36. Leiden.

Muraoka, T., and Porten, B.

1998 *A Grammar of Egyptian Aramaic.* HO 1/32. Leiden.

Naveh, J.

1970 *The Development of the Aramaic Script.* The Israel Academy of Sciences and Humanities: Proceedings 5/1. Jerusalem.

Naveh, J., and Greenfield, J. C.

1984 Hebrew and Aramaic in the Persian Period. Pp. 115–29 in *The Cam-*

bridge History of Judaism. Volume One. Introduction; The Persian Period,
ed. W. D. Davies and L. Finkelstein. Cambridge.

Norrick, N. R.
2000 *Conversational Narrative: Storytelling in Everyday Talk.* Amsterdam.

Olson, D. R.; Torrance, N.; and Hildyard, A. (eds.)
1985 *Literacy, Language and Learning: The Nature and Consequences of Writing and Reading.* Cambridge.

Page, N.
1973 *Speech in the English Novel.* London.

Polak, F. H.
1993 The Daniel Tales in Their Aramaic Literary Milieu Pp. 249–65 in *The Book of Daniel in the Light of New Findings,* ed. A. S. van der Woude. BETL 106. Leuven.
1998 The Oral and the Written: Syntax, Stylistics and the Development of Biblical Prose. *JANES* 26: 59–105.
2001 The Style of the Dialogue in Biblical Prose Narrative. *JANES* 28: 53–95.
2002 Parameters for Stylistic Analysis of Biblical Hebrew Prose Texts. Pp. 261–84 in *Bible and Computer—The Stellenbosch AIBI-6 Conference: Proceedings of the Association Internationale Bible et Informatique: "From Alpha to Byte" University of Stellenbosch 17–21 July, 2000,* ed. J. Cook. Leiden.
2003 Style Is More Than the Person: Sociolinguistics, Literary Culture and the Distinction between Written and Oral Narrative. Pp. 38–103 in *Biblical Hebrew: Studies in Chronology and Typology,* ed. I. M. Young. JSOTSup 369. London.

Porten, B.
1968 *Archives from Elephantine: The Life of an Ancient Jewish Military Colony.* Berkeley.
1984 The Jews in Egypt. Pp. 372–400 in *The Cambridge History of Judaism, Volume One: Introduction; The Persian Period,* ed. W. D. Davies and L. Finkelstein. Cambridge.
2003 Elephantine and the Bible. Pp. 51–84 in *Semitic Papyrology in Context. A Climate of Creativity.* Papers from a New York University Conference Marking the Retirement of Baruch A. Levine, ed. L. A. Schiffman. Leiden.

Porten, B., and Yardeni, A.
1986 *Textbook of Aramaic Documents from Ancient Egypt, Newly Copied, Edited and Translated into Hebrew and English, 1: Letters.* Jerusalem.
1989 *Textbook of Aramaic Documents from Ancient Egypt, Newly Copied, Edited and Translated into Hebrew and English, 2: Contracts.* Jerusalem.

Pride, J. B., and Holmes, J. (ed.)
1972 *Sociolinguistics.* Harmondsworth.

Qimron, E.
1986 *The Hebrew of the Dead Sea Scrolls.* HSM. Atlanta.
1992a Observations on the History of Early Hebrew (1000 B.C.E.–200 C.E.) in the Light of the Dead Sea Documents. Pp. 349–61 in *The Dead Sea Scrolls: Forty Years of Research,* ed. D. Dimant and U. Rappaport. STDJ 10. Jerusalem and Leiden.

1992b Pronominal Suffix כה- in Qumran Aramaic. Pp. 119–22 in *Studies in Qumran Aramaic*, ed. T. Muraoka. Abr Nahraim Supplementa 3. Leuven.
2000 The Nature of DSS Hebrew and Its Relation to BH and MH. Pp. 232–44 in *Diggers at the Well: Proceedings of a Third International Symposium on the Hebrew of the Dead Sea Scrolls and Ben Sira*, ed. T. Muraoka and J. F. Elwolde. STDJ 36. Leiden.

Qimron, E., and Strugnell, J.
1994 *Qumran Cave 4. V: Miqṣat Maʿaśe Ha-Torah*. DJD 10. Oxford.

Rabin, C.
1958 The Historical Background of Qumran Hebrew. Pp. 144–61 in *Aspects of the Dead Sea Scrolls*, ed. C. Rabin and Y. Yadin. Scripta Hierosolymitana 4. Jerusalem.

Rendsburg, G.
1990 *Diglossia in Ancient Hebrew*. AOS 72. New Haven, Connecticut.

Rooker, M. F.
1990 *Biblical Hebrew in Transition: The Language of the Book of Ezekiel*. JSOTSup 90. Sheffield.

Rosenthal, F.
1963 *A Grammar of Biblical Aramaic*. Wiesbaden.

Rouillard-Bonraisin, H.
1996 Problèmes du Bilinguisme en Daniel. Pp. 145–62 in *Mosaïque de Langues Mosaïque Culturel: Le Bilinguisme dans le Proche-Orient Ancien*, ed. F. Briquel-Chaconnet. Paris.

Rudolph, W.
1949 *Esra und Nehemia samt 3. Esra*. HAT 1/20. Tübingen.

Sáenz-Badillos, A.
1993 *A History of the Hebrew Language*. Cambridge.

Salisbury, R. F.
1972 Notes on Bilingualism and Linguistic Change in New Guinea. Pp. 52–64 in *Sociolinguistics*, ed. J. B. Pride and J. Holmes. Harmondsworth.

Schaper, J.
1999 Hebrew and its Study in the Persian Period. Pp. 15–26 in *Hebrew Study from Ezra to Ben-Yehudah*, ed. W. Horbury. Edinburgh.
2002 Numismatik, Epigraphik, alttestamentliche Exegese und die Frage nach der politischen Verfassung des achämenidischen Juda. *ZDPV* 118: 150–68.

Schiffrin, D.; Tannen, D.; and Hamilton, H. E. (eds.)
2001 *The Handbook of Discourse Analysis*. Oxford.

Schirmer, A.
1926 *Deutsche Wortkunde: Eine Kulturgeschichte des deutschen Wortschatzes*. Berlin.

Schwiderski, D.
2000 *Handbuch des nordwestsemitischen Briefformulars*. BZAW 295. Berlin.

Seow, C. L.
1996 Linguistic Evidence and the Dating of Qoheleth. *JBL* 115: 643–66.

Sérandour, A.
  1996   Remarques sur le bilinguisme dans le livre d'Esdras. Pp. 131–44 in
           *Mosaïque de Langues Mosaïque Culturel: Le Bilinguisme dans le Proche-
           Orient Ancien*, ed. F. Briquel-Chaconnet. Paris.
Smith, M. S.
  1991   *The Origins and Development of the* Waw-Consecutive: Northwest Semitic
           Evidence from Ugarit to Qumran. HSS 39. Atlanta.
Sorensen Jr., A. P.
  1972   Multilingualism in the Northwest Amazon. Pp. 78–93 in *Sociolinguis-
           tics*, ed. J. B. Pride and J. Holmes. Harmondsworth.
Spaer, A.
  1986–87 Jaddua the High Priest? *Israel Numismatic Journal* 9: 1–3.
Stern, E.
  2001   *The Assyrian, Babylonian and Persian Periods (732–332 B.C.E.).* Vol. 2 of *Ar-
           cheology and the Land of the Bible.* New York.
Stolper, M.
  1989   The Governor of Babylon and Across-the-River in 486 B.C. *JNES* 48:
           283–305.
Strang, B. M. H.
  1970   *The History of English.* London.
Tadmor, H. (ed.)
  1983   *The Return to Zion in the Persian Era.* WHJP 6. Tel Aviv. [Hebrew]
Talshir, D.
  1987   The Autonomous Status of Late Biblical Hebrew. *Meḥqĕrei Lāšōn* 2–3:
           161–72. [Hebrew]
  1988   A Reinvestigation of the Linguistic Relationship between Chronicles
           and Ezra–Nehemiah. *VT* 38: 165–93.
Tannen, D.
  1984   *Conversational Style: Analyzing Talk among Friends.* Norwood, New
           Jersey.
  1985   Relative Focus on Involvement in Oral and Written Discourse. Pp. 124–
           47 in *Literacy, Language and Learning: The Nature and Consequences of
           Writing and Reading*, ed. D. R. Olson, N. Torrance and A. Hildyard.
           Cambridge.
  1989   *Talking Voices: Repetition, Dialogue, and Imagery in Conversational Dis-
           course.* Cambridge.
Tannen, D. (ed.)
  1982   *Spoken and Written Language: Exploring Orality and Literacy.* Norwood,
           New Jersey.
Tanner, N.
  1972   Speech and Society among the Indonesian Elite: A Case Study of a
           Multilingual Community. Pp. 125–41 in *Sociolinguistics*, ed. J. B. Pride
           and J. Holmes. Harmondsworth.
Thomason, S. G., and Kaufman, T.
  1988   *Language Contact, Creolization, and Genetic Linguistics.* Berkeley.

Vanderhooft, D.

2003a Babylonian Strategies of Imperial Control in the West: Royal Practice and Rhetoric. Pp. 235–62 in *Judah and the Judeans in the Neo-Babylonian Period*, ed. O. Lipschits and J. Blenkinsopp. Winona Lake, Indiana.

2003b New Evidence Pertaining to the Transition from Neo-Babylonian to Achaemenid Administration in Palestine. Pp. 217–35 in *Yahwism after the Exile: Perspectives on Israelite Religion in the Persian Era*, ed. R. Albertz and B. Becking. Assen.

Verheij, A. J. C.

1990 *Verbs and Numbers: A Study of the Frequencies of the Hebrew Verbal Tense Forms in the Books of Samuel, Kings, and Chronicles.* Assen.

Wagner, M.

1966 *Die lexikalischen und grammatikalischen Aramäismen im alttestamentlichen Hebräisch.* BZAW 96. Berlin.

Wahl, H. M.

1999 Die Sprache des hebräischen Esterbuches: Mit Anmerkungen zu seinem historischen und traditionsgeschichtlichen Referenzrahmen. *ZAH* 12: 21–47.

Weinberg, J.

1992 *The Citizen-Temple Community.* JSOTSup 151. Sheffield.

Weinreich, U.

1963 *Languages in Contact: Findings and Problems.* The Hague.

Williams, G.

1992 *Sociolinguistics: A Sociological Critique.* London.

Williamson, H. G. M.

1985 *Ezra, Nehemiah.* WBC 16. Waco, Texas.

Woude, A. S. van der (ed.)

1993 *The Book of Daniel in the Light of New Findings.* BETL 106. Leuven.

Young, I. M.

1993 *Diversity in Pre-exilic Hebrew.* Tübingen.

1995 The "Northernisms" of Israelite Narratives. *ZAH* 8: 63–70.

1998 Israelite Literacy: Interpreting the Evidence. *VT* 48: 239–53, 408–22.

Zadok, R.

1979 *The Jews in Babylonia during the Chaldean and Achaemenid Periods.* Haifa.

2002 *The Earliest Diaspora: Israelites and Judeans in Pre-hellenistic Mesopotamia.* Tel Aviv.

2003 The Representation of Foreigners in Neo- and Late-Babylonian Legal Documents (Eighth through Second Centuries B.C.E.). Pp. 471–589 in *Judah and the Judeans in the Neo-Babylonian Period*, ed. O. Lipschits and J. Blenkinsopp. Winona Lake, Indiana.

Zorn, J. R.

2003 Tell-en-Nasbeh and the Problem of the Material Culture of the Sixth Century. Pp. 413–47 in *Judah and the Judeans in the Neo-Babylonian Period*, ed. O. Lipschits and J. Blenkinsopp. Winona Lake, Indiana.

Zorn, J.; Yellin, J.; and Hayes, J.

1994 The *m(w)ṣh* Stamp Impressions and the Neo-Babylonian Period. *IEJ* 44: 161–83.

Benjamin Traditions Read in the
Early Persian Period

J. BLENKINSOPP

University of Notre Dame, South Bend

The Persistence of Tribal Identity

However and whenever the Israelite tribal system originated, it seems that tribal consciousness persisted into the Neo-Babylonian and Persian Periods and even intensified in the wake of the disasters of the early sixth century B.C.E. The main point of reference is the Benjaminite region, which was the focus of resistance to the war party at the Judean court. After the predictable crushing of the revolt, the administrative center of the southern Palestinian region was established at Mizpah in Benjaminite territory. Gedaliah, appointed by the Babylonian overlords as administrator of the province, perhaps as a puppet king,[1] was therefore probably himself a Benjaminite.[2] In any case, his assassination by Ishmael, a claimant to the Judean royal house (מִזֶּרַע הַמְּלוּכָה, Jer 41:1), signaled the beginning of a period of Benjaminite–Judean hostility

---

1. The absence of a title, supplied gratuitously in modern translations, could be due to embarrassment that Gedaliah was not of the Judean royal line. Use of the verb פקד (*Hiphil*) rather than מלך (*Hiphil*), as in the case of Jehoiakim (2 Kgs 23:34) and Zedekiah (2 Kgs 24:17; Jer 37:1), could be for the same reason. Ishmael, Gedaliah's assassin, is described as one of the king's chief officials (Jer 41:1), and he is listed among the leading figures in Gedaliah's entourage (2 Kgs 25:23; Jer 40:8). The king's daughters resident in Mizpah who were carried off by Ishmael, perhaps as hostages, would more naturally be understood to be the daughters of Gedaliah rather than of Jehoiachin (Jer 41:10). If Jaazaniah, servant of the king *y'znyhw 'bd hmlk*, owner of the fine onyx seal discovered at Tell en-Nasbeh, is the person of the same name listed among Gedaliah's officials (2 Kgs 25:23; cf. Jer 40:8), the royal status of Gedaliah would be confirmed. See W. F. Badè, "The Seal of Jaazaniah," *ZAW* 51 (1933) 150–56. The appointment of client kings in the provinces was not unknown to the Babylonians; see, for example, 2 Kgs 24:17.

2. He was the grandson of Shaphan (2 Kgs 25:22), whose line is traced back to a certain Meshullam (2 Kgs 22:3), a name that, though not uncommon, occurs in Benjaminite lists (Neh 11:7; 1 Chr 9:7–8). Jeremiah, a Benjaminite who owned real estate in the territory of that tribe (Jer 32:1–15), and who was arrested as a deserter when on his way north out of Jerusalem (Jer 37:11–16), was a protegé of Gedaliah (Jer 39:14; 40:5–6).

which continued throughout the first century of Persian rule. The principal biblical sources suggest that by the mid-fifth century the conflict was resolved. The group that responded enthusiastically to the edict of Cyrus, built the temple, and was summoned to resolve the issue of exogamous marriage is referred to as "Judah and Benjamin" (Ezra 1:5; 4:1; 10:9), and by that time Judeans and Benjaminites had settled together in Jerusalem (Neh 11:4, 7–9).[3]

It seems, then, that Judean–Benjaminite hostility was an important factor in Palestinian politics during this poorly documented period. Given the scarcity of contemporaneous documentation, it may therefore be worthwhile to review the biblical texts that incorporate Benjaminite traditions and attest directly or indirectly to Benjaminite–Judean hostility. It is notorious that these texts can rarely if ever be dated with confidence, and this problem must be acknowledged at the outset. But there is broad agreement that the two centuries of Persian rule were decisive for the compilation and redaction of the core material that came to form the biblical canon, and it would be surprising if the political conflicts of that period had left no mark on the texts themselves; quite apart from the possibility that some of these texts may have been composed at that time. This, at any rate, is an approach that merits investigation.

The Location of Rachel's Tomb

The birth of Benjamin and death of Rachel occur in the course of Jacob's journey from Shechem to Hebron via Bethel, Ephrath, and Migdal-Eder, immediately after the second vision at Bethel, when Jacob and his family were a short distance from Ephrath (Gen 35:16–21). At both this point (35:19) and later, when Jacob on his deathbed recalls the death of his wife (48:7), Ephrath is glossed as Bethlehem. The pretext for this scribal clarification is the existence of the similar toponym Ephrathah in the region of Bethlehem. Ephrathah is the name of a Judean phratry (Mic 5:1), the one to which David belonged—he is בֶּן־אִישׁ אֶפְרָתִי (1 Sam 17:12). Elimelech's family, Ruth's in-laws, are also Eph-

---

3. The designation "Judah and Benjamin" is elsewhere restricted to Chronicles (2 Chr 11:1, 3, 10, 12, 23; 14:7; 15:2, 8–9; 25:5; 31:1; 34:9, 32); the expression in 1 Kgs 12:21, 23 is similar but not identical. Benjamin as a personal name is also attested from that time in both biblical (Ezra 10:32; Neh 3:23; 12:34) and nonbiblical texts. On the latter see A. T. Clay, *Business Documents of Murashû Sons of Nippur Dated in the Reign of Darius II (424–404 B.C.* (Philadelphia: Dept. of Archaeology and Palaeontology of the Univ. of Pennsylvania, 904) 148 (##104, 205).

rathites from Bethlehem (Ruth 1:2; cf. 4:11). The LXX adds the names Tekoa and Ephrathah to the Judean town list (Josh 15:59) and identifies the latter with Bethlehem (Θεκω καὶ Εφραθα αὐτη ἐστὶν βηθλεεμ). The Ephrathah–Bethlehem connection is also in evidence in the Chronicler's genealogies of tribal eponyms: in 1 Chr 2:50 the sequence is Ephrathah–Hur–Salma–Bethlehem, while in 1 Chr 4:4 the somewhat abbreviated form is Ephrathah–Hur–Bethlehem.[4] In keeping with this Judean scribal tradition, the site of Rachel's tomb on the road from Jerusalem to Bethlehem has been a popular destination for Jewish and Christian pilgrims since at least the fourth century of the Common Era; perhaps much earlier if Matt 2:18 is drawing on a topographical rather than an exclusively literary tradition.

This tradition notwithstanding, it is certain that the original location of Rachel's burial was in Benjaminite not Judean territory. This is no more than we would expect given the eponymous character of the tradition about Benjamin's birth.[5] However, it is also clearly attested. In the course of his designation as tribal chieftain, Saul was instructed that after leaving Samuel, whose residence was in Benjaminite Ramah, he would encounter two men at Rachel's grave in the territory of Benjamin (1 Sam 10:2).[6] Further confirmation of a Benjaminite location is at hand in the striking image about the sound of weeping coming from Rachel's tomb that could be heard in Ramah (Jer 31:15).

The Judean appropriation of Rachel's grave tradition as a means of enhancing Judah's prestige and furthering its political ascendancy is not an isolated phenomenon. By the time of the Chronicler, the site of Solomon's temple had been identified with the אֶרֶץ הַמּוֹרִיָּה, where Abraham came close to sacrificing Isaac, his son (2 Chr 3:1; Gen 22:2).[7]

---

4. See Sara Japhet, *I and II Chronicles: A Commentary* (OTL; Louisville: Westminster/ John Knox, 1993) 72–73, 82, 87–88, 107–8; Aaron Demsky, "The Clans of Ephrath: Their Territory and History," *TA* 13/14 (1986/1987) 53.

5. I set aside the question whether the birth narrative was elicited by the grave tradition and attached secondarily to it, as suggested, for example, by J. Alberto Soggin, "Die Geburt Benjamins: Genesis XXXV 16–20 (21)," *VT* 11 (1961) 438–39.

6. Ramah, identified with the Arab village er-Rām, was the point of departure for Saul's journey (1 Sam 7:1, 7; 8:4; 15:34; 16:13; 19:18–24; 20:1; 25:1; 28:3). If בְּצֶלְצַח refers to a locality, its whereabouts are unknown, and it should not be emended to צֶלַע, the place of Saul's burial (2 Sam 21:14; cf. Khirbet Salah, Josh 18:28). For alternative attempts to explain the expression, see Diana Edelman, "ZELZAH (PLACE)," *ABD* 6.1073, who opts for an adverbial phrase.

7. The location of the Genesis narrative is not otherwise specified. The context would suggest the Beer-sheba region or "the land of the Philistines" (Gen 21:25–34; 22:19). The Peshitta reads "the land of the Amorites." Joseph Naveh took one of the Khirbet Beit Lei inscriptions to refer to "Moriah the dwelling of Yah," but this reading is no longer accepted

Another example is provided by the history of Kiriath-jearim. Originally a Benjaminite settlement and a member of the Gibeonite tetrapolis within Benjaminite territory together with Beeroth, Chephirah, and Gibeon itself (Josh 9:17; 18:28), it too was absorbed into Judah, and its Judean status is particularly emphasized.[8] It is hardly surprising that the only Gibeonite–Benjaminite settlement to play a role in the vicissitudes of the Ark, therefore in the prehistory of the Jerusalemite Temple, was the one taken over by Judah, and that later tradition represents a priest with a familiar Aaronid name as its custodian (Eleazar in 1 Sam 7:1; cf. Uzzah and Ahio in 2 Sam 6:3). The way in which the resumption of worship in Jerusalem as described in Ezra 1–6 is modeled on narrative traditions about the origins of the First Temple suggests that the transference of the Ark by David from Kiriath-jearim (or "the fields of Jaar," Ps 132:6) to Jerusalem could have served as a model for the restoration of the cultic and political ascendancy of Judah over against Benjamin in the early Persian Period.

To return to the Rachel tomb tradition: What seems to have happened is that the existence of a similar toponym in or near Bethlehem provided the pretext for transferring this tradition from Benjamin to Judah. At one time this was thought to have taken place as early as the establishment of Jeroboam's kingdom, and it was understood as one aspect of Judah's attempt to make good on its claim to Benjaminite territory at that time.[9] But the Benjaminite location of the tradition still held the field at the time of the composition of the account of Saul's rise to power and, even later, when the three lines of verse about Rachel weeping were composed. This Jeremian passage (31:15) cannot be dated earlier than the sixth century B.C.E. If the children whose absence

---

(*IEJ* 13 [1963] 86); cf. A. Lemaire, *RB* 83 (1976) 560–61. Beginning with the Targum, the expression הַר יהוה has been taken to allude to the future temple, but the scene of the Akedah is not the only "mountain of YHWH"; the term occurs also in Num 10:33 and 2 Sam 21:6. In *Gibeon and Israel* (Cambridge: Cambridge University Press, 1972) 57, 124 n. 25, I proposed a connection with the "mountain of YHWH" on which the ritual execution of Saul's descendants took place (2 Sam 21:1–14), perhaps to be identified with the Gibeonite high place.

8. קִרְיַת יְעָרִים לִיהוּדָה (Judg 18:12), קִרְיַת יְעָרִים בִּיהוּדָה (Josh 18:14); קִרְיַת יְעָרִים עִיר בְּנֵי יְהוּדָה (1 Chr 13:6).

9. See, inter alia, Otto Eissfeldt, "Der geschichtliche Hintergrund der Erzählung von Gibeas Schandtat (Richter 19–21)," *Kleine Schriften* (Tübingen: Mohr, 1963) 2.64–80; R. Brinker, *The Influence of Sanctuaries in Early Israel* (Manchester: Manchester University Press, 1946) 145–46. None of the more recent commentators I have read shows much interest in this issue of the transfer of the grave tradition as an ideological issue. Claus Westermann, *Genesis 12–36: A Commentary* (Minneapolis: Augsburg, 1985 [1981]) 554, finds only an "irrelevant gloss" in Gen 35:19.

Rachel is lamenting are Judeans deported by the Babylonians rather than, or in addition to, Israelites deported by the Assyrians, a date subsequent to 586 would be required. In this respect it may be significant that Ramah, where the lamentations were heard, was the staging post for the deportations after the fall of Jerusalem (Jer 40:1).

In summary: in view of the persistence or revival of a distinctly Benjaminite identity in the Neo-Babylonian Period, together with the indications of Judean–Benjaminite hostility referred to above, we should allow for the possibility that the takeover of the grave tradition of the great matriarch was one aspect of the process by which Judean–Jerusalemite hegemony was revalidated during the first century of Persian rule.

The Benjaminite Tribal Oracle (Deuteronomy 33:12)

The compilations of oracles on the twelve tribes in Gen 49:1–28 and Deut 33:1–29 have much in common. Both are described as blessings, though several of the individual units do not sound much like blessings. The Genesis series is arranged according to the tribal matriarchs, with the four sons of the surrogate wives of Jacob situated between Leah's six sons and Rachel's two, concluding therefore with Benjamin. In the Deuteronomy series the compiler made up for the omission of Simeon by the inclusion of Ephraim and Manasseh. Benjamin is here listed fourth, Joseph and Levi are the longest, while Judah is relatively brief and low-key. Both series are compilations of disparate, often cryptic, tribal mottoes that most scholars hold came into existence at different times and under different circumstances. Our present concern is exclusively with the Benjamin sayings and, since the one in Genesis is of a more general and unspecific nature, primarily with the Deuteronomic version (Deut 33:12).[10]

---

10. Setting aside totemic and astrological explanations, the depiction of Benjamin as a wolf has been referred to different epochs and episodes in the history of the tribe beginning with the premonarchic period. Thus, Hans-Jürgen Zobel, *Stammesspruch und Geschichte* (Berlin: Alfred Töpelmann, 1965) 107–8, dates it to about 1200 B.C.E., earlier than the Song of Deborah; Frank Moore Cross and David Noel Freedman, *Studies in Ancient Yahwistic Poetry* (Missoula, Montana: Scholars Press, 1975) 69–70, to the period of the judges; while Claus Westermann, *Genesis 37–50: A Commentary* (Minneapolis: Augsburg, 1986 [1982]) 241 simply states rather gratuitously that the description of the wolf points to an early date. According to Klaus-Dietrich Schunck, *Benjamin: Untersuchungen zur Entstehung und Geschichte eines israelitischen Stammes* (Berlin: Alfred Töpelmann, 1963) 74, it refers to Saul's campaign against the Ammonites in 1 Samuel 11, and John Skinner, *Genesis* (2nd ed.; Edinburgh: T. & T. Clark, 1930) 533–35 also refers it to Saul's military

The Benjamin oracle in Deut 33:12 has a decidedly arcane character, and its decryption is not helped by a fair number of textual problems and prosodic irregularity. It is also the only oracle in which the tribal name does not appear in the saying itself.[11] Its original form can be reconstructed as a prosodically regular poem containing a prefatory note and three verses in trimeter:

לְבִנְיָמִן אָמַר
יְדִיד יָה יִשְׁכֹּן לָבֶטַח
עֶלְיוֹן חֹפֵף עָלָיו
¹²וּבֵין כְּתֵיפָיו שָׁכֵן

The saying may be translated more or less literally as follows:

> Concerning Benjamin he said:
> "The beloved of Yah in safety dwells,
> Elyon hovers over him [all day long],
> and He dwells within his borders."

The oracular saying is constructed in a kind of ring composition with the verb שׁכן in the first and third verse but (on this reading) with contrasting referents. In the first verse the reference is to Benjamin. He is the beloved of Yah (YHWH), and his peace and safety are secured by the presence of the deity, that is, the sanctuary of the deity, within his borders. The verb שׁכן occurs frequently in such sayings, not surprisingly in view of the importance of tribal *Lebensraum*.[13] The expression יִשְׁכֹּן לָבֶטַח, sometimes without the attached preposition, is a conventional way of expressing a sense of religiously-grounded security, almost always associated with a sanctuary as the residence of the deity.[14]

---

prowess. It seems to me that the language about wolves tearing their prey (טרף; cf. Ezek 22:27) and being seen mostly in the early morning and late evening (cf. זְאֵבֵי עֶרֶב 'evening wolves', Zeph 3:3; Hab 1:8) is too vague and conventional to allow for a decision.

11. Schunck, *Benjamin*, 70–72, thinks that this is because it was originally part of the Joseph oracle immediately preceding, but he does not explain why Benjamin would be omitted.

12. *Notes:* The short form of the Tetragrammaton (יָה) is attested in Exod 15:2; Ps 68:19, etc.; cf. Solomon's other name, Jedidiah (יְדִידְיָה), 2 Sam 12:25; I read אֶלְיוֹן for the first of the two occurrences of עָלָיו; cf. the LXX ὁ θεος; one of these two is redundant: The Sam. and Syr. omit the first; the Vulg. and some Hebrew MSS the second; Cross and Freedman, *Studies in Ancient Yahwistic Poetry*, 113–14 read עֵלִי (ʿēlî) in preference to עַל (ʿal) as the name of the deity, as in 1 Sam 2:10 and 2 Sam 23:1, though the MT has עָלָיו in 1 Sam 2:10; כָּל־הַיּוֹם should probably be omitted *metri causa*.

13. Japheth (Gen 9:27), Ishmael (Gen 16:12), Zebulon (Gen 49:13), Israel (Num 23:9; Deut 33:28), Gad (Deut 33:20), and Gilead (Judg 5:17).

14. On the part of Israel (Deut 33:28; Jer 23:6), Jerusalem (Jer 33:16), the psalmist (Ps 16:9), and those who heed the sage's advice (Prov 1:33).

The cultic use of the verb שׁכן in this context is of course well attested[15] and would lead to the conclusion that the third verse alludes not to Benjamin but to the God of Benjamin (אֵל בִּנְיָמִין).[16]

The expression בֵּין כְּתֵיפָיו, literally 'between his shoulders', may seem to be but is not of the same order as 'under the shadow of his/ your wings' (בְּצֵל כְּנָפָיו/כְּנָפֶיךָ), used of divine protection in the hymns (Pss 17:8; 36:8; 57:2; 61:5; 63:8). In the only other occurrence of the expression, we are told that Goliath had a scimitar slung between his shoulders (1 Sam 17:6) but, in addition to this literal, anatomical sense, the term can refer to an architectural feature, for example, a doorpost or the side of a building. It can also be used to indicate a topographical feature, a hillside or a slope, or (given the anatomical basis of the metaphor) two such features opposite each other. For our purpose, the first relevant point to note is that wherever כָּתֵף occurs in biblical texts with this topographical meaning the context always has to do with boundaries, whether of the Philistines (Isa 11:14), Moab (Ezek 25:9), or Israel as a whole (Num 34:11). The second point is that in the boundary lists in Joshua כָּתֵף appears exclusively with reference to the boundary shared by Judah and Benjamin, namely, the southern boundary of Benjaminite territory.[17] The "shoulders" mentioned in the oracle are therefore the boundaries of Benjamin within which dwells the deity in his sanctuary, the deity whose presence is the source of Benjamin's sense of security.

The question now arises regarding the identity of this deity, and it will be at once clear that the identification will be contingent on the dating of the text. Hence a brief look at the literary context of the Benjamin oracle is in order. Most commentators agree that the "Blessing of Moses" has been inserted at a fairly late stage of the compositional history of Deuteronomy, since it interrupts the commissioning of Joshua, which should be followed immediately by the death of Moses.[18] With the possible exception of Levi, the individual components also betray

---

15. With reference to the wilderness sanctuary (Exod 25:8; 29:45, etc.) and Mount Zion (Isa 8:18; Joel 4:17; Ps 74:2, etc. Compare with the substantive מִשְׁכָּן (Exod 25:9; 26:1; Josh 22:19; Ezek 37:27; Ps 26:8, etc.).

16. On these names, see the remarks of D. N. Freedman and M. P. O'Connor, "יהוה, YHWH," *TDOT* 5.502; E. E. Elnes and P. D. Miller, "Elyon," *DDD* 293–99.

17. Josh 15:8, 10, 11 (Judah); Josh 18:12–13, 16, 18–19 (Benjamin).

18. Deut 32:48–52 + 34:1, 7–9; cf. the identical but uninterrupted sequence in Num 27:12–23, though omitting the actual death of Moses. See Martin Noth, *Exodus: A Commentary* (London: SCM, 1966 [1964]) 204, 208; Andrew D. H. Mayes, *Deuteronomy* (London: Oliphants, 1979) 396.

little evidence of the Deuteronom(ist)ic theology and style.[19] The individual units have been inserted into an ancient or archaizing poem celebrating YHWH's victorious progress from his home in the deep south (Sinai, Seir, Mount Paran) and his rule over the tribal assembly (יַחַד שִׁבְטֵי יִשְׂרָאֵל, Deut 33:5b). The sayings themselves are so diverse in length and form as to suggest an equal diversity in origin and background. Not all are necessarily ancient. The Judah saying, for example, seems to presuppose a time when this tribe was isolated from the rest of Israel, beset by enemies, and in need of divine assistance. Several situations during the time of the kingdoms could conceivably serve as background to the saying but if, as proposed above, the Blessing was inserted in the final stages of the composition of Deuteronomy, the situation might be that of Judah in the decades subsequent to the Babylonian conquest.

Let us look at the options. Those who favor an early date, the prestate period or the early monarchy, have several Benjaminite sanctuaries from which to choose. The early status of Jerusalem is not entirely clear. According to the lists in Joshua, the Judah–Benjamin boundary passed south of the "Jebusite shoulder" (כֶּתֶף הַיְבוּסִי, 15:8; 18:16), thus leaving Jebusite territory within the Benjaminite region, and in fact the name יבוס appears as a toponym in the Benjamin settlement list (18:28). But the gloss identifying הַיְבוּסִי or יְבוּס with Jerusalem may be misleading, since we know from the Amarna tablets and the Execration texts that Jebus was not the pre-Israelite name of Jerusalem. The early status of Jerusalem seems to have been a matter of controversy between Judeans and Benjaminites. A Judean source claims that the Benjaminites were unable to drive the Jebusites out of Jerusalem (Judg 1:21), a claim that can be read as an element in the anti-Benjaminite polemic at the beginning and end of Judges, to be discussed in the next section. But in spite of the claim, Jerusalem is assigned to Judah in Josh 15:63, though we are told that it became de facto Israelite (Judean) only from the time of David (2 Sam 5:6–10).[20]

Gilgal features in the narratives about the conquest and the reign of Saul (Josh 3–6; 1 Sam 11:14–15; 13:8–15), and the sanctuary at Gilgal is occasionally condemned alongside Bethel in prophetic diatribe (Amos

---

19. Deut 33:4a תּוֹרָה צִוָּה לָנוּ מֹשֶׁה, does not make a good fit with the context and is generally taken to be an addition; moreover, תּוֹרָה does not occur elsewhere in Deuteronomy as the object of the verb צִוָּה. There is nothing specifically Deuteronom(ist)ic about צִדְקַת יהוה or מִשְׁפָּטָיו in the Gad oracle (33:21b).

20. On the misidentification of Jebus with Jerusalem, see J. Maxwell Miller, "Jebus and Jerusalem: A Case of Mistaken Identity," *ZDPV* 90 (1974) 115–27.

4:4; 5:5; Hos 4:15; 9:15; 12:11). But Gilgal never achieved prominence as a religious center, and the same can be said about Nob, to which the Elide priesthood moved after the Philistines conquest of Shiloh, and where they were exterminated by Saul (1 Samuel 21–22). Since Bethel was originally assigned to Ephraim (Judg 1:22–26), it could be considered a candidate only from the time when it was taken over by Benjamin.[21] We will have to return to Bethel later in our investigation. Coming at the issue from a quite different angle, Alexander Rofé proposed that the sanctuary of Nebo east of the Jordan, sanctified by the presence of the tomb of Moses, was the topographical *Sitz im Leben* of the entire series of oracles.[22]

At the time of the early monarchy, the most important of all these sanctuaries was Gibeon, described as "a great city, like one of the royal cities" (Josh 10:2). More to the point, it is described as 'the greatest high place' (הַבָּמָה הַגְּדוֹלָה) or, in other words, the greatest religious center in the land, and it remained so down into the reign of Solomon (1 Kgs 3:4). Its importance in the pre-Solomonic period has been obscured by anti-Saul polemic apparent throughout the biblical and postbiblical historiographical tradition,[23] but the biblical texts themselves attest that it was the principal religious rival of Jerusalem prior to the building of Solomon's temple (1 Kgs 3:4–16). Its prestige is further enhanced by the Chronicler, according to whom the wilderness sanctuary tended by Zadok together with the altar of burnt offerings was located at Gibeon before the temple was built (1 Chr 16:39; 21:29; 2 Chr 1:3, 13). The tradition is expanded in rabbinic sayings, according to which Shiloh, Nob, and Gibeon were the three divine residences before the Jerusalem Temple was built.[24]

If the option is for an early date and an early sanctuary Gibeon, therefore, must be a leading candidate. However, certain features of the Benjamin oracle suggest a somewhat different approach. As a conventional expression for religious security, יִשְׁכֹּן לָבֶטַח appears in hymnic, prophetic, and aphoristic contexts, not all of which are of early

---

21. Zobel, *Stammesspruch und Geschichte*, 108–12, dates the saying to the time of the Judges, shortly after the composition of the Song of Deborah, and identifies the sanctuary with Bethel.

22. A. Rofé, "Moses' Blessing, the Sanctuary at Nebo, and the Origin of the Levites," in *Studies in Bible and the Ancient Near East: Festschrift S. E. Loewenstamm* (Jerusalem: Rubinstein, 1978) 409–24 [Hebrew with English summary].

23. See my *Gibeon and Israel*, 53–97 and "The Quest for the Historical Saul," in *No Famine in the Land: Studies in Honor of John L. McKenzie* (ed. James W. Flanagan and Anita W. Robinson; Missoula, Montana: Scholars Press, 1975) 75–99.

24. *B. Zebaḥ* 61b; cf. 118b; *b. Yoma* 67b; *b. Meg.* 9b; *b. Soṭah* 16a.

date. Furthermore, in biblical texts other than Deut 33:12 the verb שָׁכַן, referring to a sanctuary as residence of a deity, is limited to the wilderness sanctuary and Mount Zion, the latter as the permanent abode of YHWH. Perhaps, then, the Benjamin saying has appropriated language and ideas traditionally associated with the Jerusalem Temple considered as the source of Judah's security, a major theme in psalms and prophetic texts.[25] In that case, we might consider an allusion to an alternative sanctuary in Benjaminite territory, perhaps at Bethel, during the period from the destruction of Solomon's Temple to the resumption of worship in Jerusalem on the same site.[26] The Benjaminite oracular saying in Deut 33:12 could then be read in the context of well-attested Judean–Benjaminite polemic during that period.[27]

The War of Extermination against Benjamin Led by Judah (Judges 19–21)

The last section of the book of Judges has an account of a war waged by the tribal federation under Judean leadership against Benjamin, a war that came close to exterminating that tribe but ended with its restoration and, with it, the restoration of the twelve-tribal structure. This Judean, anti-Benjaminite narrative theme at the end of the book has its counterpart at the beginning. The oracle solicited at the outset of the conquest of Canaan obliged by assigning leadership to Judah, exactly as in the war of extermination at the end of the book (Judg 1:1–2; cf. 20:18). YHWH was with Judah (1:19), and so Judah succeeded in taking Jerusalem where Benjamin had failed (1:8, 21), a statement contradicted by the account of the capture of the city by David (2 Sam 5:6–10). This no doubt deliberate inclusive literary technique insinuates a

---

25. In psalms, and especially the so-called Psalms of Zion, the theme is often expressed using the verb בטח and related forms (Psalms 27, 46, 48, 61, 76, 84, 87, 122, 125). The temple as a source of confidence (בִּטָּחוֹן) divorced from attention to the moral life is criticized in Jeremiah's temple sermon (Jer 7:1–15), and the same idea may be behind the Rabshakeh's harangue before the walls of Jerusalem, in which the same verb or a related form occurs seven times (2 Kgs 18:19–25 = Isa 36:4–10).

26. For a more detailed presentation of this hypothesis of an alternative Benjaminite sanctuary during this period, see my "Judean Priesthood during the Neo-Babylonian and Early Achaemenid Periods: A Hypothetical Reconstruction," *CBQ* 60 (1998) 25–43; "Bethel in the Neo-Babylonian Period," in *Judah and Judeans in the Neo-Babylonian Period* (ed. Oded Lipschits and Joseph Blenkinsopp; Winona Lake, IN: Eisenbrauns, 2003) 95–109.

27. There may also be a polemical nuance in the epithet יְדִיד used with reference to the Jerusalem Temple (Ps 84:2) and the Judean people (Jer 11:15; Ps 60:7 = 108:7), not to mention Jedidiah (יְדִידְיָה), the other name of Solomon, builder of the temple (2 Sam 12:25). The verb חפף (hapax) also brings to mind the חֻפָּה ('shelter') for Mount Zion of Isa 4:5.

quite different understanding of the conquest tradition from the account of the book of Joshua, in which most of the principal episodes take place in Benjaminite territory.

The campaign described in Judges 19–21 is characterized by hyperbole, fantasy, and no doubt unintentional comedy. As George Foot Moore put it, the account of military expeditions punctuated with religious exercises, weeping, and lamenting is the work of a theocratic scribe who had never handled a more dangerous weapon than an imaginative pen.[28] The campaign was occasioned by a particularly atrocious crime committed by the male inhabitants of Benjaminite Gibeah. The many repetitions and aporias in the telling of the story have predictably given rise to a wide range of hypotheses to explain its composition. Thus, George Foot Moore, author of what is still one of the best commentaries on the book, thought in terms of an old narrative base overlaid with a postexilic *rifacimento*, a kind of midrash with some affinity to narrative in Chronicles, from no earlier than the fourth century B.C.E.[29] Variations on this combination of early and late strands have been and continue to be advanced, and different opinions on the historical character, or at least the historical background, of the events described have been and continue to be based on them.[30]

We are not obliged to assign an early, that is, preexilic, date to the narrative on account of the reference to "the days of Gibeah" in Hosea (9:9; 10:9) since, in the context, the allusion would more naturally be to the appointment of Saul as king (cf. Hos 7:3–7; 8:4; 10:3, 7, 15; 13:10–11). Moreover, Hosea also mentions Gilgal as the site of Israel's "original sin," here too no doubt with reference to Saul (Hos 9:15; cf. 1 Sam 11:14–15). Attempts to identify distinct strands of Priestly (P) and Deuteronomistic (D) material in Judges 19–21 have not enjoyed much success.[31] Expressions of frequent occurrence in these sources (e.g., וַתִּקָּהֵל הָעֵדָה, 20:1, elsewhere only in P contexts) could as well be explained on the hypothesis that, in its present form, the narrative dates

---

28. George Foot Moore, *Judges* (ICC 7; Edinburgh: T. & T. Clark, 1895) 431.

29. Ibid., xxxi, 421–22. For a survey of older commentaries, see pp. 406–8.

30. See, inter alia, G. A. Cooke, *The Book of Judges* (Cambridge: Cambridge University Press, 1913) 171–97; Otto Eissfeldt, "Der geschichtliche Hintergrund der Erzählung von Gibeas Schandtat (Richter 19–21)," *Kleine Schriften zum Alten Testament* (1963 [1935]) 2.64–80; Robert Boling, *Judges* (Garden City, NY: Doubleday, 1975) 278; J. Alberto Soggin, *Judges: A Commentary* (Philadelphia: Westminster, 1981) 278–305; Schunck, *Benjamin*, 57–70.

31. A recent attempt is that of Patrick M. Arnold, *Gibeah: The Search for a Biblical City* (Sheffield: JSOT Press, 1990) 63–69.

to a time later than both P and D. The story of the crime, the campaign, and its aftermath not only incorporates familiar type scenes and topics, which is obvious, but was constructed on the basis of narrative material available in writing at the time of composition or at least of final redaction. The following parallels merit consideration:

(1) The account of the homosexual aggression of the men of Gibeah and its tragic outcome (Judg 19:14–26) appears to draw on the account of the threat of a similar attack on Lot's guests in Sodom (Gen 19:1–11). In both cases the gross breach of the immemorial duty toward guests is contrasted with the exquisite hospitality of, respectively, Abraham toward his three visitors and the Ephraimite resident alien toward the Levite, his female companion, and servant. We might factor in also the somewhat excessive *bonhomie* of the woman's father, who persuaded his guest to stay four nights instead of one, as originally intended (Judg 19:2–9). The two stories run closely parallel: in both cases the guests arrive at sundown, their benefactors urge them not to spend the night in the open (בָּרְחוֹב) and invite them insistently (וַיִּפְצַר־בּוֹ, וַיִּפְצַר־בָּם) to come inside (וַיָּסֻרוּ, סוּרוּ־נָא). In both accounts the guests are to wash their feet, food and drink are prepared, after which the men of the city surround the house and demand to send out the men (man) in order to "know" them (him). The host goes out and tries to reason with them in practically identical words (אַל־אַחַי אַל־תָּרֵעוּ, אַל־נָא אַחַי תָּרֵעוּ), and so on. If these two passages were taken by themselves, apart from their contexts, the question of priority and dependence might be difficult to decide. But Judg 19:14–26 is part of a larger narrative that shows many signs of late composition, or at least late revision, as practically all commentators agree. The overtly ideological character of the incident in Judges also argues for a deliberate reworking of an existing narrative model.

(2) The Levite's action in cutting up the corpse of his female companion has a remarkably close parallel in Saul's summoning of the tribes to a holy war by carving up his oxen and sending the parts around the tribes (1 Sam 11:7). It is precisely the grotesque nature of the Levite's act that practically compels us to derive it from 1 Sam 11:7 rather than the reverse. Since both actions take place in Gibeah, Judg 19:29 may even be a spoof on Saul (admittedly one in execrable taste) in keeping with the relentless hostility toward Saul in the Judean historiographical tradition.[32] The similarity between Saul's summons to

32. On the relation between Judg 19:29 and 1 Sam 11:7, see Moore, *Judges*, 421; Schunck, *Benjamin*, 63–64; Arnold, *Gibeah*, 77–78. G. Wallis, "Eine Parallele zu Richter 19,29ff und 1 Sam 11,5ff aus dem Briefarchiv von Mari," *ZAW* 64 (1952) 57–61, proposed

war to rescue Jabesh-gilead in 1 Sam 11:1–11 and the episode narrated in Judges is not confined to the extraordinary manner in which it was carried out. Not only does Gibeah feature in both, but the numbers are equally fantastic (e.g., 1 Sam 11:8), and in both instances the people have a tendency to weep and lament in between pursuing military action (1 Sam 11:4–5; Judg 20:23, 26; 21:2).

The close ties between Benjamin and Gilead provide a ready explanation for the failure of Jabesh-gilead to attend the plenary session of the קָהָל and the campaign of extermination with which they too were threatened. Gileadites rescued the body of Saul from Beth-shan, cremated it, and buried it in their own territory (1 Sam 31:11–13; 2 Sam 2:2–7; 21:12–14). Gilead probably lay within Saul's kingdom, and it is mentioned first among the territories ruled briefly by Ishbaal, Saul's son (2 Sam 2:9).[33]

(3) The war of extermination waged by Moses against Midian, narrated in a late P strand of the Pentateuch (Numbers 31), may have provided a model for the preemptive strike against Jabesh-gilead for the purpose of securing wives for the surviving Benjaminites (Judg 21:1–14). In each account 12,000 Israelites are chosen for the mission, and in both the only survivors of the general massacre are virgins. Phineas, grandson of Aaron, is involved in both episodes (Judg 20:28; Num 31:6), and the command to kill the remaining women is worded in practically identical fashion in both accounts.[34]

(4) The ambush that eventually put paid to the Benjaminites, described at length in Judg 20:29–48, is close enough in detail to the description of Joshua's tactics leading to the capture and destruction of Ai in Josh 8:10–29 to suggest the possibility of a direct borrowing rather than a variant on a familiar military theme or as the result of oral tradition.

(5) A final and, in this instance, small-scale borrowing may be the specialized military skills of left-handed "sons of the right hand," that is, Benjaminites (20:16), reminiscent of the Historian's account of the left-handed Benjaminite assassin, Ehud (Judg 3:15). The Chronicler is also familiar with ambidextrous Benjaminite warriors (1 Chr 12:21).

---

a Mari parallel in which the head of an executed criminal was sent to reluctant allies to persuade them to mobilize; but the parallel is not so close, because there is no dismemberment.

33. On 1 Sam 11:1–11, see Diana Edelman, "Saul's Rescue of Jabesh-Gilead (1 Sam 11:1–11): Sorting Story from History," *ZAW* 99 (1984) 195–209.

34. וְכָל־אִשָּׁה יֹדַעַת מִשְׁכַּב־זָכָר תַּחֲרִימוּ (Num 31:17); וְכָל־אִשָּׁה יֹדַעַת אִישׁ לְמִשְׁכַּב זָכָר הֲרֹגוּ (Judg 21:11).

Judges 19–21 Reflects Judean–Benjaminite Hostility in the Neo-Babylonian and Early Persian Period

Whatever the prehistory of Judges 19–21, these parallels suggest that the narrative is a relatively late composition. The question therefore arises whether it can be read as reflecting situations and events in the Judean–Benjaminite region in the Neo-Babylonian and early Persian Periods. In Judges 20–21 Mizpah is the place where the tribal league convenes in plenary assembly, decisions affecting all the tribes are taken, oaths sworn, and declarations of war promulgated (Judg 20:1, 3; 21:1, 5, 8); in these respects, therefore, somewhat comparable to the Greek εκκλησια. As in Ezra–Nehemiah, this assembly is referred to as the קָהָל.[35] Presence at its sessions is enjoined under pain of death (Judg 21:5), and in Ezra 10:8 absentees from the Jerusalemite קָהָל are threatened with the social death of ostracism and forfeiture of property. Moreover, both assemblies have a serious issue of exogamous marriage on the agenda, and in both, business is conducted in the presence of YHWH (20:1; 21:5, 8).

In the later, antimonarchic strand of the Deuteronomistic History, Mizpah was an important center of civic and religious activity in the transitional period to the monarchy (1 Sam 7:5–12; 10:17–27).[36] It was also known as a place of prayer (προσευχῆ) as late as the Hasmonean Period (1 Macc 3:46). This last piece of information is of some significance for the present argument, since the language recalls both the account of the anti-Benjaminite war and the situation subsequent to the fall of Jerusalem. Like the confederates in Judges 20–21, Judah Maccabee and his associates assembled at Mizpah for prayer, fasting, penitential rites, and oracular consultation regarding their prospects. Then, like the confederates in Judges 20–21, they went forth into battle strengthened by these religious exercises. The account of the Maccabean assembly at Mizpah following the desecration of the temple by Antiochus IV (1 Macc 3:44–47) therefore seems to provide additional support for a link between the Judges 19–21 and the situation in the Neo-Babylonian and early Persian Period, when Mizpah replaced Jerusalem as administrative center of the region (2 Kgs 25:23; Jer 40:6).

But the confederates also convene three times at Bethel to seek oracular guidance after successive defeats and to offer sacrifice, fast,

---

35. Ezra 2:64; 10:1, 8, 12, 14; Neh 5:13; 7:66; 8:2, 17; 13:1.
36. Note the verbal parallelism between וַיִּשְׁמְעוּ פְלִשְׁתִּים כִּי־הִתְקַבְּצוּ בְנֵי־יִשְׂרָאֵל הַמִּצְפָּתָה (1 Sam 7:7) and וַיִּשְׁמְעוּ בְּנֵי בִנְיָמִן כִּי־עָלוּ בְנֵי־יִשְׂרָאֵל הַמִּצְפָּה (Judg 20:3).

and lament (Judg 20:18–19, 23, 26–28). Then, after annihilating all but 600 of the Benjaminites, they somewhat incongruously returned to Bethel to lament the loss of the tribe they had just all but exterminated and to decide on another campaign of extermination, this time against the Gileadite allies of the Benjaminites (21:2–11). Predictably, the presence in the narrative of two centers, Mizpah and Bethel, has been explained as the result of the conflation of two distinct sources. This is certainly a possibility, though we have seen that the case for a combination of D and P is not very strong, and in any event the final version features both centers.

We have no direct, literary information about Bethel for the period in question and, unfortunately, no reliable archaeological information for the site either. Bethel was reestablished as a religious center by the Assyrians after the conquest of the kingdom of Samaria (2 Kgs 17:24–28), and there is no reason to believe that Josiah's violent decommissioning of the Bethel sanctuary was more lasting in its effects than other examples of his religious zeal (2 Kgs 23:4, 15, 20). Together with other Benjaminite sites, it also survived the Babylonian punitive campaign of 588–586. Those who claim to have found evidence for a destruction level at Beitin (Bethel) date it no earlier than the mid-sixth century, and it could be as much as a century later.[37] If, therefore, it continued in existence between the destruction and rebuilding of the Jerusalem Temple, its ancient prestige as a sanctuary combined with its proximity to the administrative center of the province would have recommended its continued use.

Some Provisional Conclusions

One or two other scraps of information of possible relevance to our theme can be combed out from a close reading of the historical books. A note added to the account of Ishbaal's assassination by two Benjaminite turncoats informs us that the people of Beeroth, one of the four Gibeonite cities, had fled to Gittaim, where they were living as resident aliens at the time of writing (2 Sam 4:3). Gittaim is listed as a Benjaminite settlement in Neh 11:33, and if it is identical with the Gath (not to be confused with Philistine Gath), whose inhabitants were

---

37. See J. L. Kelso, *The Excavation of Bethel (1934–1960)* (Cambridge, MA: American Schools of Oriental Research, 1968) 11, 37, 51; and L. A. Sinclair in the same volume, pp. 75–76. Further details in J. Blenkinsopp, "Bethel in the Neo-Babylonian Period" in *Judah and the Judeans in the Neo-Babylonian Period* (ed. Oded Lipschits and Joseph Blenkinsopp; Winona Lake, IN: Eisenbrauns, 2003) 93–107.

expelled by Benjaminites (1 Chr 8:13), it may point to Benjaminite expansion westward in the postdestruction period. The rebuilding of Ono and Lod by Benjaminites, also reported by the Chronicler (1 Chr 8:12), would point in the same direction.[38] In the same "Benjaminite chapter" of Chronicles (1 Chr 8:6), the transfer of Benjaminites from Geba to Manahath, the latter perhaps located in the Negev, would fit the context of Benjaminite–Judean hostilities, though clearly other explanations are possible.[39]

Brief mention should also be made of the supposition that the rivalry between David and Saul was still a live issue in the early Persian Period.[40] We saw earlier that the Babylonians may have planned to replace the Judean royal house, with its bad reputation for rebellion (cf. Ezra 4:15–16), Gedaliah may have been the designated successor, and this may have led to his assassination by one of the surviving members of the Judean royal house. But evidence for a movement in favor of a descendent of Saul as ruler-designate is lacking, and it does not help that the genealogy of Saul's line in 1 Chr 8:33–40 (cf. 9:39–44) ends well before the Persian Period.[41]

It will be well to repeat that, in the absence of reliable data from other sources, our attempt to extract historically reliable information from uncooperative biblical texts is an exercise in probabilism. The archaeology of the Benjaminite region would in principle provide a valuable control on conclusions drawn from the biblical texts. With the possible exception of limited indications of destruction at Tell el-Fûl, Benjaminite sites escaped punishment at the hands of the Babylonians. If the claim for extensive destruction of Benjaminite sites in the late

---

38. Oded Lipschits, "The History of the Benjamin Region under Babylonian Rule," *TA* 26 (1999) 155–90, argues for Benjaminite expansion in that direction on archaeological grounds.

39. See E. A. Knauf, "Manahath," *ABD* 4.493–94. If, however, וַיַּגְלוּם (*heglîm*) in the same verse is a verbal form in *Hiphil* ('he exiled them') rather than a proper name, the exiling would be the doing of other Benjaminites.

40. Argued by Diana Edelman, "Did Saulite-Davidic Rivalry resurface in early Persian Yehud?" in *The Land That I Will Show You: Essays on the History and Archaeology of the Ancient Near East in Honour of J. Maxwell Miller* (ed. J. Andrew Dearman and M. Patrick Graham; Sheffield: Sheffield Academic Press, 2001) 69–91.

41. This linear genealogy has 15 generations. Calculating the average length of a generation at 25 years and counting from about 1050 B.C.E., the genealogy extends no further than the reign of Manasseh in ca. 665 B.C.E. This calculation is confirmed by the Davidic genealogy in 1 Chr 3:1–24, which has 12 generations from Zedekiah, the last Judean ruler, to the seven sons of Elionai, therefore covering the period from ca. 597 to ca. 297 B.C.E. The genealogy could, of course, be incomplete, but in that case no conclusions could be based on it.

sixth or early fifth century could be sustained, it would be compatible with the thesis of Benjaminite–Judean hostility during the first century of Persian rule.[42] But more recent and cautious evaluations of the scant data available suggest continuity in material culture in the Benjamin-ite region through the first century of Persian rule followed by demo-graphic decline rather than destruction.[43] If this conclusion holds good, it would be compatible with Nehemiah's consolidation of the po-litical quasi autonomy of Judah following his arrival in the province in the twentieth year of Artaxerxes I, therefore 445 B.C.E.

---

42. K.-D. Schunck, "The archaeological record attests to the destruction of numerous Benjaminite towns (Bethel, Gibeon, Gibeah) in the first quarter of the fifth century B.C.E.," in "Benjamin," *ABD* 1.673; see also along the same lines Geo Widengren in John J. Hayes and J. Maxwell Miller (eds.), *Israelite and Judaean History* (Philadelphia: Westmin-ster, 1977) 502, 525–26. More recently and apodictically Ephraim Stern: "The archaeo-logical evidence shows that all these cities in the territory of Benjamin were laid waste in approximately 480 B.C.E. This date is virtually certain, and is based on the date of the Attic pottery uncovered in the excavations of Mizpah, Bethel, Tell el-Fûl, and Gibeon. There is no known event that can account for this destruction." But then he rather spoils the effect by adding "Perhaps these towns were only abandoned for various, unknown internal reasons." See his *Archaeology of the Land of the Bible* (New York: Doubleday, 2001) 2.322–23.

43. See n. 38 above.

The Saul Polemic in the Persian Period

YAIRAH AMIT

Tel Aviv University

Saul, his kingship and his descendants are extensively and in great detail described in the book of Samuel. This book narrates the story of the conflict between the House of Saul and the House of David, setting it in the early days of the Israelite monarchy—that is, the eleventh and tenth centuries B.C.E. Yet echoes of this conflict recur in literary materials from the Persian Period, though the texts describing the divided kingdom do not even hint that the Northern Kingdom of Israel tried to restore the House of Saul to the throne.

In view of these facts, in this essay I focus on two issues:

1. a description of the literary materials of the Persian Period that highlight the role of the House of Saul and thus contribute to the revived polemic between the Houses of Saul and David;
2. the question whether this polemic was purely literary or rested on historical roots.

References to the House of Saul in Persian-Period Materials

The House of Saul keeps recurring in literary materials dating to the early Persian Period and toward its end—namely, the story of The Rape at Gibeah and Its Results (Judges 19–21), the book of Chronicles, and the book of Esther.

The Anti-Saul Polemic in the Story of The Rape at Gibeah and Its Results

As far back as 1869, Güdemann argued that this story was a tendentious polemic against the House of Saul, designed to strengthen the legitimation of David and his dynasty. He suggested that the story was composed during David's rule in Hebron, when a long war was waged by David and his people against the remnants of the House of Saul.[1]

---

1. See Güdemann 1869: 364–65.

Saul himself is not mentioned in the story, but various elements suggest that he is its unspoken target: the conflict is waged between Bethlehem-Judah and the Benjaminite Gibeah (Judges 19), and a number of motifs link the affair to the stories of Saul—for example, the reference to Jabesh-gilead (Judg 21:1–15 vis-à-vis 1 Sam 11; 31:11–13; 2 Sam 21:12; and 1 Chr 10:11–12), or the spreading of information by means of a dismembered body (Judg 19:29 vis-à-vis 1 Sam 11:7).[2]

Many scholars tended to date the composition of the story of Gibeah to an early time,[3] mainly because there are biblical stories describing the conflict between the two royal houses in the early monarchy and during the united kingdom (2 Sam 1–4, 9; 16:1–13; 19:16–31, 41–44; 20:1–22, 21; 1 Kgs 2:8–9, 36–46). But already in 1878, Wellhausen suggested that the story of Gibeah was an ideological postexilic work that did not reflect a historical reality.[4] Additional support for a late date has come from a number of scholars,[5] based on: (1) critical evaluation of later, post-Deuteronomistic editing; (2) stylistic features of a later language; (3) geographical-historical considerations; and (4) literary dependence (intertexuality). According to Edenburg the combination of all these considerations proves that the story was composed during the transition between the late Babylonian and early Persian Periods.[6] This conclusion begs the question: What was an anti-Saul polemic doing in such a relatively late period—or, in other words, what did the Persian Period have to do with Saul? Even if we regard Saul as the archetype of the kings of the Northern Kingdom or an embodiment of the tribe of Benjamin, the question remains: What did the Northern kings or the tribe of Benjamin have to do with the Persian Period?

The question is all the more significant because it is not accidental or unique but arises from even later literary materials of that period, namely, the books of Chronicles and of Esther.

---

2. A list of additional links, already noted in my book: Amit 2000: 179–84; for a previous version, see Amit 1994. These links indicate that Saul was the implied object of the story and that the story belonged to the genre of hidden polemic. On this genre, see Amit 2000; Amit 2003: 135–51 and especially p. 146.

3. For example, Güdemann 1869 and lately O'Connell 1996: 342. For a detailed report, see Edenburg 2003: 26–28.

4. Bleek and Wellhausen 1878: 201–4.

5. See Auld 1984: 252–57; Becker 1990: 294–97; Amit 1994: 38–40; Blenkinsopp 1998: 30–34; idem 2003: 98–99, and lately Edenburg 2003.

6. Cynthia Edenburg (2003: 353), a student of mine and of Nadav Naʾaman, has completed her doctoral dissertation.

Saul in the Book of Chronicles

The book of Chronicles is famously devoted to the history of the House of David and seems to have little use for Saul and his kingship. Yet far from ignoring the reign of Saul, it refers to it even when it could have avoided mentioning it.[7]

Chronicles opens its historical sequence of events with the death of Saul, as the background to the devolution of the monarchy to David (1 Chronicles 10).[8] However, the author is not content to paint a picture of a leadership vacuum needing to be filled but reworks the story in 1 Samuel 31, so that it becomes an anti-Saul document, depicting his death as God's punishment on a leader who strayed. As the chronicler presents it, Saul sinned against God, paid for his enormities, and the crown passed to David: "Saul died for the trespass that he had committed against the Lord in not having fulfilled the command of the Lord; moreover, he had consulted a ghost to seek advice, and did not seek advice of the Lord. So He had him slain and the kingdom transferred to David son of Jesse" (1 Chr 10:13–14).[9] Readers familiar with the book of Samuel would know that Saul inquired of God, but he did not answer him, "either by dreams or by urim or by the prophets" (1 Sam 28:6). Only then, in desperation, did he turn to the woman of Endor who consulted ghosts. In other words, the Chronicler was so keen to defame Saul, that he was willing to deviate from and distort his own sources. Even readers who are not familiar with the book of Samuel cannot miss the Chronicler's blatantly hostile depiction, which emphasizes Saul's guilt in disobeying God and in preferring idolatrous means.[10]

In addition, a comparison between 1 Samuel 31 and 1 Chronicles 10 reveals the systematic and biased attitude of the Chronicler. Not only did he put in anti-Saul conclusions, throughout the story he made

---

7. My detailed article on this subject, "Saul in the Book of Chronicles" will shortly be published.

8. On the genealogies of Saul (1 Chr 8:29–40; 9:35–44) that precede the historical sequence, see pp. 655–656 below. On the question why does the Chronicler begin with the death of Saul, see lately Trotter (1999), who mentions the solutions of Mosis (1973: 17–43); Japhet (1989: 407; 1993: 230), and Zalewski (1989).

9. For an analysis of these two verses that sum up Saul's failures, see Amit 2001: 97–99. See also Zalewski 1989. According to Williamson 1982: 94–96: "These two verses are undoubtedly the Chronicler's own composition." See also Japhet 1993: 229–230, and others.

10. On the significance of the use of the root *mʿl* (מעל) in the book of Chronicles, see already in Mosis 1973: 29–33 and lately in Johnstone 1998: 95–99 and see also Walters 1991, who is influenced by Johnstone's previous work.

changes of nuance and minor details designed to turn the death of Saul into a defamatory document and deprive it of its heroic and tragic effect.[11] A comparison between the two texts reveals the variety of devices used by the Chronicler to diminish Saul's character and his death.[12] For example, in Samuel the burial of Saul and his sons is accompanied by a moving description of the noble action of the men of Jabesh-gilead, who walked all night and risked their lives to remove the bodies of Saul and his sons from the wall of Beth-shan, the Philistine fortress, in order to bring their beloved king back for an honorable burial. By contrast, the Chronicler ignores the Gileadites' night-long march, suggests that the Philistines were only interested in the king's head and armor, and impaled the head in the temple of Dagon (1 Chr 10:9–10). This implies that the Gileadites had merely picked up the bodies of Saul and his sons that had been left on the battlefield and took them to Jabesh (10:11–12)—hardly a heroic act, since the king's skull remained impaled in the Philistine temple. The comparison with the description in 1 Samuel 31 shows that the Chronicler reduces the brave action of the men of Jabesh-gilead to an ordinary one and makes them into lesser figures than the young Amalekite, who went to the battlefield when it was still possible to remove the king's crown and armlet (2 Sam 1:6–10). The devaluation of the heroism of the men of Jabesh-gilead eliminates the quality of solidarity, sacrifice, and valor of Saul's loyal troops and their total commitment to their king.

In the same way, in describing Saul's final defeat, the Chronicler replaces the phrase "as well as all his men" (1 Sam 31:6) with "his entire house" (1 Chr 10:6). Where the author of Samuel sought to emphasize the awesome death of the king and all his warriors, the Chronicler used the occasion to create the impression that all of the House of Saul perished with him, leaving the way open for David's accession.[13]

So the Chronicler's polemic against Saul and his house was an open and direct one, presented at the start of his historical narrative, and its object was to make clear that Saul's death and the transfer of the throne to David were acts of providential historical justice.

---

11. For another inferred motivation, see Josephus, *Ant.* 6.14.4.

12. For a detailed analysis of the comparison between these two chapters, see Amit 1985 and Zalewski 1989.

13. I say "to create the impression" because the Chronicler knows about Saul's descendents; see 1 Chr 8:29–40; 9:35–44. On the other hand, when dealing with genealogies, he provides a setting that shows that these descendents are unfit to inherit the throne: Esh-baal and Merib-baal are associated with Baal worship, and Merib-baal is also lame in both legs.

Not content with this opening, the Chronicler also interpolated a number of other passages, suggesting that Saul's reign was altogether a failure.[14]

The Chronicler does not describe the period when Saul was hunting David down but notes briefly that, before Saul vacated the throne, David hid from him in Ziklag (1 Chr 12:1). He proceeds to relate that at this time David was joined by famous warriors (meaning, men who deserted Saul's army in favor of David), among them "kinsmen of Saul from Benjamin," "armed with the bow and could use both right hand and left hand to sling stones or shoot arrows with the bow" (1 Chr 12:2).[15]

Moreover, the Chronicler mentions Benjaminites who had already left their camp and joined David's in previous stages, when he was still wandering in the desert of Judah (1 Chr 12:17). Thus the Chronicler creates the impression that support for David even in the early stages of his career included the tribe of Benjamin and Saul's nearest associates.[16] While readers of Samuel gain the impression that David was especially good at surviving and that his later loyalty to Achish, son of Maoch, king of Gath (1 Samuel 27; 29) and to some elders of Judah (1 Sam 30:26–31) shows a tinge of treason,[17] the Chronicler's narrative reads like an apologia for David, implying that the various tribes, led by the Benjaminites, gradually joined him, until his camp was "as vast as the army of God" (1 Chr 12:22).[18]

And as if that were not enough, the Chronicler notes that some of those who came to Hebron "to transfer Saul's kingdom to him in accordance with the word of the Lord" (v. 24) were "of the Benjaminites, kinsmen of Saul, 3,000 in their great number, hitherto protecting the interests of the House of Saul" (v. 29). Thus it appears that even some of Saul's own tribe supported the crowning of David.[19]

In these last three passages, the Chronicler does not criticize Saul's period directly but only hints at it. This is not the case in the following passage. Here the criticism of Saul's reign even leaks into his description of the transferring of the Ark from Kiriath-jearim to Jerusalem. The opening of this chapter (13:1–5) consists of a unit without a parallel in the book of Samuel, noting that "throughout the days of Saul we

---

14. See Japhet 1993: 259–61.
15. Compare with Judg 3:15, 21; 20:16; and also with 2 Chr 17:17.
16. See Williamson 1982: 102.
17. See recently Malul 1996.
18. See Japhet 1993: 267.
19. On the small numbers, see Williamson 1982: 111–12.

paid no regard to it [the Ark]" (v. 3). This complements the final statement on the death of Saul (1 Chr 10:13–14), which also uses the verb
drš, implying that: (1) in the time of Saul necromancers and witchcraft
were consulted in preference to seeking God's word;[20] and (2) unlike
Saul, David acted to promote the true and proper worship of God. That
is why his first act after his accession was the conquest of Jerusalem,
followed after by bringing up the Ark.

Biblical literature had to contend with the question: What was
wrong with the first-chosen royal House, and why was it necessary to
replace it with that of David? As we have seen, this contest was waged
in a variety of ways—openly, indirectly, and covertly. The book of
Judges, concluding with the story of the Outrage at Gibeah and its
results, openly attacks the behavior of the tribe of Benjamin and especially of its town Gibeah, and by inference, covertly also Saul. The
author of Samuel has a complex and balanced approach to the human
failings of the kings and is able to depict indirectly Saul's good qualities and David's bad ones.[21] But the author of Chronicles, writing during the Persian Period,[22] a time of political despair, used David and his
dynasty as a symbol of real hope for political freedom.[23] He chose to
create a one-sided story, depicting an almost idealized David, who replaced a sinful failed king.[24]

A question arises that I shall leave open at this point: Why was not
the Chronicler content to use a formulaic text on the replacement of a
reigning dynasty, such as "in order that the Lord might fulfill the
promise that he had made through [such and such] prophet"?[25] Alter-

---

20. It is noteworthy that according to the Masoretic version of 1 Sam 14:18–19 the
Ark was at the camp, and according to 1 Sam 28:3b: "Saul had forbidden [recourse to]
ghosts and familiar spirits in the land."

21. On the delicate balance in the shaping of Saul's character and on his place in the
Deuteronomistic History, see Amit in press.

22. Most scholars are convinced that the book of Chronicles was composed in the 4th
century B.C.E. See, for example, Williamson 1982: 15–16, who speaks of the early 4th century; Japhet 1993: 23–28, who sets it at the century's end.

23. On the question whether the book expresses concrete or eschatological hopes, see
Japhet 1989: 493–504. I find especially persuasive the arguments of Urbach (1975: 658):
"The conception of redemption in Sirach and also in sources close to it in time is realistic.
And is primarily concerned with the supplementation of the deficiencies of Israel's sov-
ereignty, well-being, and prosperity." See also Fishbane (1988: 387): "it appears that a
post-exilic reality is addressed via these prophetic personae of the Chronicler."

24. For a different view, namely, that the Chronicler was not extremely anti-Saul, see
Abramsky 1983: 53–54. See also Abramsky 1977 and especially pp. 379–83.

25. See the way in which the breakup of the unified kingdom is described in 2 Chr
10:15.

natively, why was not the Chronicler satisfied to give a balanced description, like that in the book of Samuel, of the final days of Saul? In other words, Why was it so important for him to depict Saul in a bad light and his reign as a time of turning away from God?

Saul in Esther

We know that Saul is never mentioned by name in the book of Esther. But as many interpreters have noted there are clear allusions to Saul in the text.[26] The association with Saul is worked into Esther by the technique of the hidden polemic.[27]

At the start of the plot, the author hints at a connection between the two protagonists, Mordecai and Esther, and Saul's genealogy: "In the fortress Shushan lived a Jew by the name of Mordecai, son of Jair son of Shimei son of Kish, a Benjaminite" (Esth 2:5). Saul's father was, of course, also a Benjaminite named Kish (1 Sam 9:1). By itself, this clue may be refuted. First, because Mordecai's genealogy is associated with the exile of Jehoiachin and goes back only three generations; second, because, if Mordecai is associated with Jehoiachin, he could not have lived during the reign of Xerxes, or he would have had to be about 120 years old;[28] third, because one of the three names in the genealogy is Jair, which does not appear in Benjaminite genealogies. For these reasons it is difficult to argue an unequivocal link between Kish in Esther and Kish in the book of Samuel. Three generations prior to Jehoiachin or Xerxes take us back to the sixth or the seventh century B.C.E., whereas the action in the book of Samuel takes place hundreds of years earlier. We must therefore look for other clues showing a link between the book of Esther and Saul, son of Kish.

One additional clue is the association of Haman, who is called an "Agagite" in the Masoretic Text (Esth 3:1, 10; 8:3, 5; 9:24), with Agag, the king of Amalek, whom Saul had failed to destroy (1 Sam 15:8, 9, 20,

---

26. Thus, from Josephus (*Ant.* 11.6.1) and the Sages (*Pirqe R. El.* 50; *b. Meg.* 13a; *Esth Rab.* 2:7; and more) to Berlin (2001: xxxviii–xxxix), who emphasizes: "Rabbinic exegesis includes it at various points. In the synagogue, on the Sabbath preceding Purim, Shabbat Zakhor, Deut 25:17–19, and 1 Samuel 15 are read. On the morning of Purim, the reading is Exod 17:8–16, the battle between Israel and Amalek." See also Bush (1996: 378–79).

27. Lately a student of mine, Danit Bar-Or Sabag (in press), has been working on her M.A. thesis on the hidden polemics in Esther. On the allusive character of Esther, see also Abramsky 1983: 46–47 and Berlin 2001: 25, 34, 85, 86.

28. Medieval interpreters solved it by suggesting that the beginning of v. 6 refers to Kish, and he was the one who had been exiled from Jerusalem, not Mordecai. For other solutions, see Abramsky 1977: 371–83; Berlin 2001: 25–26.

32, 33).[29] Calling Haman, the enemy of the Jews, an Agagite, inevitably recalls Agag, king of Amalek, and the Amalekites who hounded the Israelites in the desert, about whom it was said, "Remember what Amalek did to you on your journey. . . . Do not forget!" (Deut 25:17–19).[30]

Besides the clues found in the names of the protagonists, there are clues in the phrasing and motifs. For example, the threat to Vashti to replace her, "Let your majesty bestow her royal state upon *another who is more worthy than she*" (Esth 1:19), recalls Samuel's reproach to Saul: "The Lord has this day torn the kingship over Israel away from you and has given it to *another who is worthier than you*" (1 Sam 15:28).[31] In Samuel the worthier one is David; here it is Esther of the house of Kish. This verbal association and its significance were already noted by the Sages in *Midr. Esth Rab.*, which said: "The language in which the kingship was taken away from her forefather . . . is the language that restored the kingship" (4:9).

A motif-based clue is the reversed attitude toward the spoils. While Saul is described as having disobeyed God and "swooped down upon the spoil" (1 Sam 15:18), the book of Esther reiterates three times that "they did not lay hands on the spoil" (Esth 9:10, 15, 16; see also 8:11).[32]

To summarize, by means of such clues (common devices of the implied polemic) the book of Esther rehabilitates the descendants of Saul: Esther and Mordecai are virtuous; the unfinished business with Amalek is concluded; and Israel did not lay hands on the spoil. As Bahar puts it: "The conclusion is inescapable that the Masoretic form of the book of Esther was composed with an end in mind—to rehabilitate the

---

29. The component "Agagite" does not appear in the shorter Greek version, known as the Alpha-text or A-text, or in L, which is the Lucianic recension; and see Bahar's conclusion (2002: 48–50) about the late reworking of the Masoretic Text. Zadok (1988: 89) thinks that this name is Elamite; and see also Bush (1996: 378–79). According to Berlin (2001: 33–34) the Agagite "is not an ethnic designation that would make any real sense in the Persian empire. By so identifying Haman, the Masoretic Text of Esther makes a clear connection between Haman and the Amalekite king, Agag . . . thereby confirming the connection between Mordecai and King Saul hinted at in Esther 2:5. . . ." See also Abramsky 1983: 48–50; Fox: 362–63, 383–84, 417.

30. See also Exod 17:8–16. Many scholars think that Num 24:7 is faulty according to textual evidence: see, for example, Gray 1903: 366. The Samaritan version and the Septuagint read Gog and thus imply an eschatological meaning (Ezekiel 38–39). But see, for example, Milgrom (1989: 204) and Licht (1995: 36), who interpret this verse as implying to Saul's rival.

31. For example see Berlin 2001: 19.

32. Berlin (2001: 85) emphasizes: "In Esther, the Jews of Persia 'correct' Saul's error . . . this reversal in reference to booty wipes away the sin of the house of Saul. There is now nothing to prevent a complete triumph of the descendants of Saul over the descendants of Agag." See also Fox 1991: 115. Another opinion to Bush 1996: 476–77.

progeny of Saul and thereby provide a legal-theological basis for the right of the House of Saul to a future kingship."[33]

The question arises, if the book of Esther was indeed written, as many scholars suggest, toward the end of the Persian Period,[34] who at that time was concerned to legitimize the House of Saul?

Literary Reality versus Historical Reality

The notion of reviving the kingship of the House of Saul during the Persian or Hellenistic Period seems almost delusional. Even the literature does not show a continuous genealogy of the House of Saul reaching to postexilic times but lists only 12 generations after Saul himself (1 Chr 8:29–40; 9:35–44).[35] In contrast, the genealogical list of the House of David covers 18 generations after David himself (1 Chr 3:10–16), with an additional list of 13 generations (perhaps just 7 or 8, depending on the version and interpretation) after Jehoiachin (3:17–24).[36] The literature, then, offers at least 25 generations after David, of which at least 8 were postexilic after the vassal rule of Davidic kings. This is not the case with the House of Saul, which disappears even before the exile.

Moreover, there is ample, detailed historical material about the descendants of David throughout the time of the united kingdom and the First Temple period quite apart from the lists in Chronicles. This material appear in the books of Samuel and Kings and in the writings of the prophets of the First Temple period that refer to the kings of David's dynasty.[37] In contrast, there is a total blank between what is reported about Saul's offspring—Mephibosheth, son of Jonathan, son of Saul; Mica; and Shimei, son of Gera, mentioned in the time of David and Solomon in connection with the accession (2 Sam 9:1–13; 16:1–13; 19:16; 21:1–14; 1 Kgs 2:8–9, 36–46a)—and the late reference to Mordecai, which links him to Kish and Shimei (Esth 2:5). In other words, where Saul's dynasty is concerned, the reader has almost nothing but the parallel lists in Chronicles (1 Chr 8:29–40, 9:35–44),[38] and even they

---

33. Bahar 2002: 43. See also p. 47. See already Abramsky 1983: 50–51, 55–56, 60–61.

34. See the summary by Berlin (2001: xli–xliii).

35. Abramsky's attempts and efforts (1983: 54) to show that Saul's dynasty continued to the last days of Jerusalem is not convincing.

36. On the genealogy of the Davidic dynasty in biblical sources and the descendants of David in the time of the Second Commonwealth, see Liver 1959: 3–46; and see critical commentaries.

37. See, for example, 1 and 2 Kings; Isa 7:1–17; Jeremiah 21–22, and more.

38. See Williamson 1982: 85–86, 91–92; Abramsky 1977: 371–83; 1983; Japhet 1993: 195–99, 218–19.

do not attempt to bridge the gap between Mica, Saul's great-grandson, and Mordecai, a man of the Persian exile. Thus even in the literary phase (in the books of Chronicles and Esther) no attempt is made to validate Mordecai's connection with Saul's genealogy, and the author of Esther contents himself with hints that serve his implicit polemic.

The fact that there are no hints of remnants of the House of Saul threatening the Davidic dynasty during its rule over Judah surely suggests that, following the division of the kingdom, the House of Saul ceased to be a possible alternative or a source of polemic in Judah. The polemic in the Deuteronomistic literature was openly directed at the Northern Kingdom and its rulers, and these were no longer descended from the House of Saul or members of the tribe of Benjamin.

It has been suggested that an attempt could have been made during the Second Temple period to clear the name of Israel's first monarchy by means of a sympathetic treatment of the House of Saul in Esther. But even a proponent of this suggestion admits that "there is no way of knowing if this idea reflected an existential revival, following the return to Zion, an attempt at rehabilitating the House of Saul, and a popular desire for its restoration or return in some form. And would they really have pinned such hopes on descendants of Kish in their time or times?"[39]

And yet, it should be kept in mind that the late book of Chronicles openly, systematically, and unambiguously sharpens the polemic against the House of Saul. Could this have been a reaction to agitation among the Benjaminites in the early days of the Second Temple, desiring to produce a local leadership?[40] Biblical testimony about the end of the First Temple and the beginning of the Second, as well as the archaeological findings suggest that, after the fall of Jerusalem, Mizpah in Benjamin served as a center of government and that the territory of Benjamin was almost continuously inhabited.[41]

Furthermore, during this period there were several different changes in the power structure. After the failure of Zedekiah's uprising was the Babylonian-appointed Gedaliah, son of Ahikam, son of Shaphan the Jerusalemite (2 Kgs 25:22–26; Jer 40:7–41:18). This appointment ended in assassination, due to the opposition of a Davidic scion,

---

39. Abramsky 1983: 60. Bahar's phrasing (2002) is much more concrete, though he has no new or further evidence.

40. See Bahar 2002: 50 and especially n. 25 with its bibliography.

41. On the status of the land of Benjamin and its administrative center, Mizpah, in this period, see Lipschits 1997: 171–245 ; 1999; Edelman 2001: 74–84; Blenkinsopp 2003: 96.

Ishmael, son of Nethaniah, "of royal descent" (2 Kgs 25:25; Jer 41:1). At the same time Jehoiachin and his sons were held in Babylonia, and, when the Babylonian king Evil-merodach ascended the throne, he improved the situation of Jehoiachin, then in the 37th year of his exile (561 B.C.E.). At this time also the Persian Empire, ruled by Cyrus, replaced Babylonia as the dominant regional power. This period was probably also a low point of the House of David, as shown by the prophecies of the Second Isaiah (40–55), which hardly mention it. In these prophecies Cyrus is God's anointed, the destined liberator, and thereafter "God's servant"—not a scion of the Davidic dynasty.[42] Moreover, in the books of Ezra, Haggai and Zechariah, Sheshbazzar and Zerubabel are not described as descendants of the House of David, and, except for the list in 1 Chr 3:17ff., it is doubtful whether they could be considered legitimate scions of the House of David.[43] Furthermore, Sheshbazzar, who led the returning exiles in the early years, is not mentioned in the description of the construction of the altar (Ezra 3:1–4:5), whereas Zerubabel, credited with the construction, is mostly mentioned together with the high priest, Jeshua, son of Jozadak.[44]

It seems that at such a time of upheaval, and against a background of various changes of power and government and a decline in the prestige of the House of David, a polemic could well arise on the issue of leadership. It is possible that in these circumstances the population of Benjaminite origin hoped to assume the local leadership, a hope that reflected their relative strength in the recovering province of Yehud, as well as their disappointment in the House of David. These expectations were expressed in the literary reference to Saul, the Benjaminite, the first man to assume the kingship over Israel—even though there are doubts if there was a real legitimate heir in that lineage. In such volatile and unstable political circumstances, it was possible to launch an implied polemic against the House of Saul (the affair of the concubine in Gibeah and its results). It is reasonable to assume that this polemic with its hidden significance was launched during the transition from Babylonian to Persian rule by supporters of the Davidic dynasty, because of their opposition to new currents that referred to the Benjaminite option, the House of Saul. The partisans of the Davidic dynasty

---

42. The House of David is mentioned only in Isa 55:3–5, but the passage speaks about the nation as the subject of salvation, and "David's faithful virtues" are referred to as of past time.

43. On the identification of Sheshbazzar with Shenazzar, see Liver 1959: 1–8, 80; but see Berger 1971: 98–100. Japhet (1993: 99) describes the debate as "still ongoing."

44. In Ezra 3:2, Zerubabel is mentioned only after Jeshua, son of Jozadak.

chose to use the technique of the implied polemic, whether because they hesitated to favor openly the scions of their favored but disappointing dynasty, "the fallen booth of David" (Amos 9:11), or because they believed that this technique was a more effective way of changing people's attitudes, since it would not provoke an immediate and obvious resistance to a known figure.

At a later time the strategy visibly changed. The anti-Saul polemic became more open and unambiguous, as may be seen in the book of Chronicles, while the pro-Saul polemic went underground and expressed itself in a covert way in the book of Esther. This reversal shows that the problem of leadership had not gone away. The need to justify support for the Davidic dynasty, which had disappeared after Zerubabel, and the need to find alternatives to the House of David, continued to preoccupy biblical literature during the Persian Period.

We may therefore conclude that the Saul polemic was not a real contest to restore Saul's descendants to the throne. However, it expressed the tensions between the Judeans and the Benjaminites, the disappointment in and disillusionment about the House of David, and a protest against the claim that the Davidic dynasty was the only legitimate option to power.

Bibliography

Abramsky, S.
   1977   *Saul's Kingship and David's Kingship: The Beginning of Kingship in Israel and Its Influence over Generations.* Jerusalem: Shikmonah. [Hebrew]
   1983   Return to the Kingdom of Saul in the Books of Esther and Chronicles. Pp. 30–63 in vol. 1 of *MILET: Everyman's University Studies in Jewish History and Culture,* ed. S. Ettinger, Y. D. Gilat, and S. Safrai. Tel Aviv: Everyman's University Press. [Hebrew]
Amit, Y.
   1985   Three Variations on the Death of Saul: Studies in the Fashioning of the World, in Reliability and in the Tendentiousness of Biblical Narrative. *Beth Mikra* 100: 92–102. [Hebrew]
   1994   Literature in the Service of Politics: Studies in Judges 19–21. Pp. 28–40 in *Politics and Theopolitics in the Bible and Postbiblical Literature,* ed. H. G. Reventlow, Y. Hoffman, and B. Uffenheimer. Journal for the Study of the Old Testament Supplement 171. Sheffield: Sheffield Academic Press.
   2000   *Hidden Polemics in Biblical Narrative,* trans. J. Chipman. Leiden: Brill.
   2001   *Reading Biblical Narratives: Literary Criticism and the Hebrew Bible,* trans. Y. Lotan. Minneapolis: Fortress.

2003   Epoch and Genre: The Sixth Century and the Growth of Hidden Polemics. Pp. 135–51 in *Judah and the Judeans in the Neo-Babylonian Period*, ed. O. Lipschits and J. Blenkinsopp. Winona Lake, Indiana: Eisenbrauns.

In press   The Delicate Balance in the Image of Saul and His Place in the Deuteronomistic History. In *Saul in the Deuteronomistic History*, ed. C. Ehrlic. Tübingen: Mohr Siebeck.

Auld, A. G.
1984   *Joshua, Judges, and Ruth*. Philadelphia: Westminster.

Bahar, S.
2002   Expressions of Sympathy to the clan of King Saul in the Scroll of Esther. *Beth Mikra* 172: 42–53. [Hebrew]

Bar-Or Sabag, D.
In press   *Hidden Polemics in Esther Scroll: The House of Saul and the Absence of God's Name*. M.A. Thesis, Tel Aviv University. [Hebrew]

Becker, U.
1990   *Richterzeit und Königtum*. Beihefte zur Zeitschrift für die alttestamentliche Wissenschaft 192. Berlin: de Gruyter.

Berger, P. R. von
1971   Zu den Namen ששבצר und שנאצר (Esr 1:8, 11; 5:14, 16 bzw. I Chr 3:18). *Zeitschrift für die alttestamentliche Wissenschaft* 83: 98–100.

Berlin, A.
2001   *Esther* אסתר. Jewish Publication Society Bible Commentary. Philadelphia: Jewish Publication Society.

Bleek, F. J.
1878   *Einleitung in das Alte Testament*, ed. J. Wellhausen. 4th ed. Berlin: Reimer. [5th ed. Edited by Erich Zeinger et al. Stuttgart: Kohlhammer, 1995.]

Blenkinsopp, J.
1998   The Judaean Priesthood during the Neo-Babylonian and Achaemenid Periods: A Hypothetical Reconstruction. *Catholic Biblical Quarterly* 60: 25–43.

2003   Bethel in the Neo-Babylonian Period. Pp. 93–107 in *Judah and the Judeans in the Neo-Babylonian Period*, ed. O. Lipschits and J. Blenkinsopp. Winona Lake, Indiana: Eisenbrauns.

Bush, F. W.
1996   *Ruth, Esther*. Word Biblical Commentary. Dallas: Word.

Edenburg, C.
2003   *The Story of the Outrage at Gibeah (Jdg. 19–21): Composition, Sources and Historical Context*. Ph.D. Thesis, Tel Aviv University. [Hebrew]

Edleman, D.
2001   Did Saulide-Davidic Rivalry Resurface in Early Persian Yehud? *The Land That I Will Show You: Essays on the History and Archaeology of the Ancient Near East in Honour of J. Maxwell Miller*, ed. J. A. Derman and M. P. Graham. Journal for the Study of the Old Testament Supplement 343. Sheffield: JSOT Press.

Fishbane, M.
1988   *Biblical Interpretation in Ancient Israel*. Oxford: Clarendon.

Fox, M. V.
1991 *Character and Ideology in the Book of Esther.* Columbia, South Carolina: University of South Carolina Press.

Gray, G. B.
1903 *Numbers.* International Critical Commentary. Edinburgh: T. & T. Clark.

Güdemann, M. G.
1869 Tendenz und Abfassungszeit der letzten Kapitel des Buches der Richter. *Monatsschrift für Geschichte und Wissenschaft des Judentums* 18: 357–68.

Japhet, S.
1989 *The Ideology of the Book of Chronicles and Its Place in Biblical Thought,* trans. A. Barber. Frankfurt am Main: Peter Lang.
1993 *I and II Cronicles: A Commentary.* Old Testament Library. Louisville: Westminster/John Knox.

Johnstone, W.
1998 *Chronicles and Exodus: An Analogy and Its Application.* Journal for the Study of the Old Testament Supplement 275. Sheffield: Sheffield Academic Press.

Josephus, F.
1971 *Jewish Antiquities,* trans. H. St. J. Thackeray and R. Marcus. Loeb Classical Library. Cambridge: Harvard University Press.

Licht, J.
1995 *A Commentary on the Book of Numbers [XXII–XXXVI].* Jerusalem: Magnes. [Hebrew]

Lipschits, O.
1997 *The "Yehud" Province under the Babylonian Rule (586–539 B.C.E.): Historic Reality and Historiographic Conceptions.* Ph.D. Thesis, Tel Aviv University. [Hebrew]

Lipschits, O., and Blenkinsopp, J. (eds.)
2003 *Judah and the Judeans in the Neo-Babylonian Period.* Winona Lake, Indiana: Eisenbrauns.

Liver, J.
1959 *The House of David: From the Fall of the Kingdom of Judah to the Fall of the Second Commonwealth.* Jerusalem: Magnes Press. [Hebrew]

Malul, M.
1996 Was David Involved in the Death of Saul on the Gilboa Mountain? *Revue Biblique* 103–4: 517–45.

Milgrom, J.
1989 *Numbers* במדבר. Jewish Publication Society Torah Commentary. Philadelphia: Jewish Publication Society.

Mosis, R.
1973 *Untersuchungen zur Theologie des chronistischen Geschictswarkes.* Freiburg: Herder.

O'Connell, R. H.
1996 *The Rhetoric of the Book of Judges.* Vetus Testamentum Supplements 63. Leiden: Brill.

Trotter, J. M.
  1999 Reading, Readers and Reading Readers Reading the Account of Saul's
        Death in 1 Chronicles 10. Pp. 294–310 in *The Chronicler as Author: Stud-
        ies in Text and Texture*, ed. M. P. Graham and S. L. McKenzie. Journal for
        the Study of the Old Testament Supplement 263. Sheffield: Sheffield
        Academic Press.
Urbach, E. E.
  1975 *The Sages: Their Concepts and Beliefs,* trans. I. Abrahams. Jerusalem:
        Magnes.
Walters, S. D.
  1991 Saul of Gibeon. *Journal for the Study of the Old Testament* 52: 61–76.
Williamson, H. G. M.
  1982 *1 and 2 Chronicles*. New Century Bible Commentary. London: Morgan
        & Scott.
Zadok, R.
  1988 Haman Son of Hammedatha the Agagite. P. 89 in *Koheleth, Esther Scrolls
        and the Book of Daniel*. Vol. 16b of *World Bible Encyclopedia*. Jerusalem–
        Ramat-Gan: Revivim.
Zalewski, S.
  1989 The Purpose of the Story of the Death of Saul in 1 Chronicles X. *Vetus
        Testamentum* 39: 449–67.

situated itself in between.[4] It was, therefore, not just about the date of P *in abstracto*. The whole debate was (and is until today) motivated by the question of the place of the Law within Judean and Jewish religion: Wellhausen claimed that one could understand Israelite history and culture without the laws embedded in the Priestly source. Against this assertion, August Dillmann[5] and others (on the Protestant side) as well as David Hoffmann as a Jewish scholar tried to prove comprehensively that P predated not only H but also Deuteronomy (D), a literary-historical claim later taken up by Yehezkel Kaufmann, Menahem Haran, and, recently, by Avi Hurvitz, Israel Knohl, and Jacob Milgrom.[6]

---

4. Ibid., 2–6.

5. See the preface of A. Dillmann, *Die Bücher Exodus und Leviticus: Für die zweite Auflage nach Dr. August Knobel neu bearbeitet* (Leipzig: Hirzel, 1880) v–viii.

6. See for example, D. Hoffmann, *Die wichtigsten Instanzen gegen die Graf-Wellhausen'sche Hypothese*, Heft 1 (Jahres-Bericht des Rabbiner Seminars zu Berlin 1902/1903; Berlin: Itzkowski, 1904); idem, Heft 2, Jahres-Bericht des Rabbiner Seminars zu Berlin 1914/1915; idem, *Das Buch Leviticus übersetzt und erklärt*, Erster Halbband: *Lev. I–XVII* (Berlin, 1905); Zweiter Halbband: *Lev. XVII–Ende* (Berlin: Poppelauer, 1906; idem, "Probleme der Pentateuchexegese," *Jeschurun: Monatsschrift für Lehre und Leben im Judentum* (1914ff. [essays in an ongoing sequence]) 1ff.; idem, "Torah und Wissenschaft," *Jeschurun* 7 (1920) 497–505 (see also my "From Mar Samuel to David Hoffmann [1844–1921]: Biographical Mirrorings of an Orthodox Life," *European Association for Jewish Studies Newsletter* 12 [2002] 19–23; idem, "Jewish Bible Scholars in the 19th and Early 20th Century and the Debate on the Hebrew Bible," *LTQ* 37 [2002] 129–44, pp. 136–39); Y. Kaufmann, "Der Kalender und das Alter des Priesterkodex," *VT* 4 (1954) 307–13; idem, "Probleme der israelitisch-jüdischen Religionsgeschichte," *ZAW* 48 (1930) 23–43; 51 (1933) 35–47; idem, *Toledot ha-Emuna ha-Yisra'elit* (3 vols.; Jerusalem: Bialik, 1954) 1.113–42 (= *The Religion of Israel: From Its Beginnings to the Babylonian Exile* [trans. and abridged Moshe Greenberg; Chicago: University of Chicago Press, 1960] 175–211; see also T. M. Krapf, *Die Priesterschrift und die vorexilische Zeit: Yehezkel Kaufmanns vernachlässigter Beitrag zur Geschichte der biblischen Religion* [Freiburg: Universitätsverlag, 1992] 210–78); M. Haran, *Temples and Temple-Service in Ancient Israel: An Inquiry into Biblical Cult Phenomena and the Historical Setting of the Priestly School* (Winona Lake, Ind.: Eisenbrauns, 1985) 1–12, 140–48; A. Hurvitz, "Dating the Priestly Source in Light of the Historical Study of Biblical Hebrew a Century after Wellhausen," *ZAW* 100 (1988) 88–100; idem, "The Evidence of Language in Dating the Priestly Code," *RB* 81 (1974) 24–56; idem, "The Language of the Priestly Source and Its Historical Setting: The Case for an Early Date," in *Proceedings of the Eighth World Congress of Jewish Studies* (1981), Panel Sessions A: *Bible Studies and Hebrew Language* (Jerusalem: World Union of Jewish Studies, 1982) 83–94; idem, "Once Again: The Linguistic Profile of the Priestly Material in the Pentateuch and Its Historical Age. A Response to J. Blenkinsopp," *ZAW* 112 (2000) 180–91; I. Knohl, *The Sanctuary of Silence: The Priestly Torah and the Holiness School* (Minneapolis: Fortress, 1995) esp. pp. 199–200; J. Milgrom, *Leviticus 1–16: A New Translation with Introduction and Commentary* (AB 3; New York: Doubleday, 1991) 1–61; idem, "The Antiquity of the Priestly Source: A Reply to Joseph Blenkinsopp," *ZAW* 111 (1999) 10–22; see in particular the discussions given in J. Blenkinsopp, "An Assessment of the Alleged Preexilic Date of the Priestly Material in the Pentateuch," *ZAW* 108 (1996) 495–518; Otto, "Forschungen," 44–50; see also the

As for today, one can observe a clear rift between Jewish and Christian approaches, Jewish scholars mostly dating P in the preexilic period. More than ever, some kind of consensus about the date of the composition of P, its Sitz im Leben, and its authorship is a long way off.

However, whether one dates P early or late, most scholars interpret the Priestly Code with an immediate correlation between the text and the events described in the text. Although Wellhausen regarded P's depiction of the foundation of the cult and the inauguration of the Aaronid priests in the desert as a merely fictitious (not: fictional!) description,[7] he did try to elicit historical data from the narratives, which, in turn, formed the basis for the interpretation of the texts. In this, the methodological approach toward the biblical text in general and toward the narratives in the Priestly Code in particular has hardly changed until now. Helmut Utzschneider, for example, pinpoints this as follows: "The texts describe the foundation and the construction of a sanctuary in due clarity. This was precisely the task after the destruction of the Temple in Jerusalem, during the time of its reconstruction and the reorganization of its cult."[8]

Yet, even though Utzschneider's study on erection of the tabernacle and ordination of the priests (Exodus 25–40; Leviticus 8–9) combines literary-historical research with literary analysis more comprehensively than any of his predecessors' studies, he nevertheless accepts the premise of a (post)exilic date for P (terminus a quo 586; terminus ad quem 515).[9] He bases this premise primarily on the fact that the texts describe the erection of the tabernacle and the tent (אהל מועד; משכן), and thereby equates the narrative background with a certain period in the history of Judah (i.e., the intermediate period without a temple): an example of exegetical circular reasoning. However, in becoming aware of the exegetical problems linked to this kind of literary-historical exegesis, one can see very clearly that scholars from related disciplines (for

---

outline of the history of the research on the Priestly Code given in H. Utzschneider, *Das Heiligtum und das Gesetz: Studien zur Bedeutung der sinaitischen Heiligtumstexte* (OBO 77; Freiburg: Universitätsverlag, 1988) 22–43.

7. See Wellhausen, *Prolegomena*, 39.

8. Utzschneider, *Heiligtum*, 63 (translation mine).

9. See K. Elliger, "Sinn und Ursprung der priesterlichen Geschichtserzählung," *Kleine Schriften zum Alten Testament* (Munich: Chr Kaiser, 1976) 174–98, pp. 196, 198; Fretheim, "Priestly Document," 313; Otto, "Forschungen," 24, 49–50; E. Zenger and others, *Einleitung in das Alte Testament* (3rd ed.; Stuttgart: Kohlhammer, 1998) 152–53. L. Schmidt (*Studien zur Priesterschrift* [Berlin: de Gruyter, 1993] 259) regards P as even later, presupposing the completion of the Second Temple.

example Mesopotamian and Egyptian language and literature) have to cope with nearly the same problems, as recently shown by the Egyptologist Gerald Moers in his comprehensive study *Fingierte Welten*:

> In most studies in the past the opinion prevailed that one could consider the texts as direct sources of historically or politically significant information, independent of questions of their literary genre or other genre-specific forms of literary representation. . . . With the help of this information, scholars then tried to reconstruct the Egyptian real history with the aim, as kind of a *circulus vitiosus*, of dating the texts based on the historical "realities" extracted from them.[10]

The obvious risk in entering into this circular reasoning is a more likely consequence for a scholar dealing with texts from ancient civilizations (Hebrew, Assyrian, or Egyptian) than for an interpreter of contemporary literature. As a first step in every textual investigation, one must discuss whether the text has *literary* qualities at all,[11] since a text does not gain a literary quality automatically by having oral traditions that were written down at a certain stage in history. With regard to the P texts, contemporary biblical scholars dispute whether their literary disposition is more that of a historical narrative,[12] a collection of (ancient) laws, or *the* prime example of a biblical utopia.[13] However, the

---

10. G. Moers, *Fingierte Welten in der ägyptischen Literatur des 2. Jahrtausends v. Chr Grenzüberschreitung, Reisemotiv und Fiktionalität* (Probleme der Ägyptologie 19; Leiden: Brill, 2001) 3 (translation mine); compare also with idem, "Fiktionalität und Intertextualität als Parameter ägyptologischer Literaturwissenschaft: Perspektiven und Grenzen der Anwendung zeitgenössischer Literaturtheorie," in *Literatur und Politik im pharaonischen und ptolemäischen Ägypten* (ed. J. Assmann and E. Blumenthal; Cairo: Institut Français d'Archéologie Orientale, 1999) 37–52, p. 38.

11. See, e.g., M. Fuhrmann, "Die aristotelische Lehre vom Wirklichkeitsbezug der Dichtung," in *Positionen der Negativität* (ed. H. Weinrich; Munich: Fink, 1975) 519–20; W. Rösler, "Die Entdeckung der Fiktionalität in der Antike," *Poetica* 12 (1980) 283–319; E. L. Bowie, "Lies, Fiction and Slander in Early Greek Poetry," in *Lies and Fiction in the Ancient World* (ed. C. Gill and T. P. Wiseman; Exeter: University of Exeter Press, 1993) 1–37; J. Baines, "Prehistories of Literature: Performance, Fiction, Myth," in *Definitely: Egyptian Literature. Proceedings of the Symposium "Ancient Egyptian Literature: History and Forms"* (ed. G. Moers and F. Kammerzell; Göttingen: Seminar für Ägyptologie und Koptologie, 1999) 17–41.

12. See already M. Noth, *Überlieferungsgeschichte des Pentateuch* (Stuttgart: Kohlhammer, 1948) 7–19 (= idem, *A History of Pentateuchal Traditions: Translated with an Introduction by B. W. Anderson* [Englewood Cliffs, N.J.: Prentice-Hall, 1972] 8–19); Fretheim, "Priestly Document," 314; Elliger, "Sinn und Ursprung," 175, 195–98; N. Lohfink, "Die Priesterschrift und die Geschichte," *Studien zum Pentateuch* (Stuttgart: Katholisches Bibelwerk, 1988) 213–53.

13. See the discussion in E. Blum, *Studien zur Komposition des Pentateuch* (Berlin: de Gruyter, 1990) 303–5 incl. n. 64; Zenger (*Einleitung*, 153) characterizes P as "a critical

methodological problem arising for the exegetical analysis has not been discussed sufficiently: a text regarded as a source for ancient Israelite Law and its development (e.g., Leviticus 1–16) must be treated differently from a text that mirrors (contemporary) topographical data in a narrative on the history of Israelite settlements (e.g., Joshua 13–22) or a text that is a programmatic outline for the restoration of the temple. According to Moers, the common exegetical approach described above represents a kind of historicist reading of the texts that has already answered the question of the literary character of a certain text negatively. In this, Moers sees a methodological gap between a historicist and a literary reading of ancient texts that cannot be bridged easily, because, after all, behind these two opposite ways of interpreting texts lies the basic difference between "fiction" (literary) and "reality" (nonliterary).[14]

One must consider another thing that has received little attention within the broader context of studies dealing with the Priestly Code. Scholars have scrutinized the P texts from genre-specific, traditio-critical, structuralist, and stylistic points of view. Meir Paran, for instance, set up a number of grammatical, phrase logical, and/or syntactic features that he considered characteristic of the style of the Priestly Code (e.g., the use of *inclusio* as in Exod 12:8, often linked to a shift in the tempora: *qāṭal-yiqṭôl* pattern) as well as further rhetorical language figures and stylistic devices (*Parallelismus membrorum*; reduplication).[15] However, the examples mentioned last likewise form a constituent part of poetic language and literature.[16] Two questions therefore arise: first, in what way, if ever, would P be considered part of biblical poetry; and second, if P consists of poetic elements as well as ancient law formulas, what is the relationship between these two literary features. In any case, one can see that most of the studies dedicated to the Priestly Code today remain in the context of introductory investigations and rarely deal with P as *literature*. Except in a few literary studies, P is described

---

utopian contribution to the discussion about the temple not yet completed"; see also K. Koch, "Die Eigenart der priesterschriftlichen Sinaigesetzgebung," *ZTK* 55 (1958) 36–51, p. 51; R. Albertz, *Religionsgeschichte Israels in alttestamentlicher Zeit*, part 2: *Vom Exil bis zu den Makkabäern* (2 vols.; 2nd ed.; Göttingen: Vandenhoeck & Ruprecht, 1996–97) 2.519 n. 105; Knohl, *Sanctuary*, 156.

14. See Moers, *Fingierte Welten*, 4.

15. See M. Paran, *Forms of the Priestly Style in the Pentateuch: Patterns, Linguistic Usages, Syntactic Structures* (Jerusalem: Magnes, 1989) 47–136 [Heb.].

16. See, e.g., J. Kugel, *The Idea of Biblical Poetry: Parallelism and Its History* (New Haven: Yale University Press, 1981) 1–58.

in detail, but the texts are not perceived or appreciated as literature. In the following, therefore, I do not want to repeat the previous debates and add some new ways to rearrange the arguments like a kaleidoscope. On the contrary, I would like to concentrate on literary subject matters, as a kind of *prolegomenon* (sing.!) to a comprehensive study on Priestly texts and literature in the Hebrew Bible, the Qumran texts, and early rabbinic literature.

The characterization of the texts of the Priestly Code as "fiction," a category already introduced by Wellhausen,[17] forms the starting point of our investigation. However, neither Wellhausen nor his successors perceived or used this term literarily, and its connotations were entirely negative. Wellhausen did not differentiate between "fictional" and "fictitious" literature. To him, the Priestly Code as fiction meant over all a splendid faking of the depiction of ancient Israelite cult[18] and, as a corollary, a conscious veiling of the Priestly author(s) and his (their) historical setting, the Second Temple Period.

In contrast, Benno Jacob in 1905 appealed for a nonhistoricist reading of Exodus 25–40. To Jacob, the tabernacle was a systematic but admittedly unhistorical rearrangement of older cultic traditions.[19] In a more literary sense he, too, portrayed the (P-)texts[20] as fiction:

> In all probability, a sanctuary as described here never existed. We do not deny it because the Israelites were missing the necessary materials and skills to erect such a building in the desert. . . . Rather, the whole organism of which the tabernacle is only one part is a fiction. A people Israel, organized and counted as described in the text, never existed. . . . This is the product of an artificial arithmetic.[21]

Unfortunately, Benno Jacob never again wrote about his own classification of the Priestly Code as fictional literature. In view of the desperate situation of the Jewish people at this time, he could not even repeat this expression in his commentary on the book of Exodus in 1944. In

---

17. See above, n. 7; J. Maier (*Das altisraelitische Ladeheiligtum* [Berlin: Alfred Töpelmann, 1965] 81–82) characterizes the whole tradition about the ark in Exod 25:10–22 as *P-Fiktion*; R. Smend (*Die Entstehung des Alten Testaments* [3rd ed.; Stuttgart: Kohlhammer, 1984] 57) underlines P's 'fictitious annal-writing' [*fiktive Annalistik*].

18. See also the characterization of the Priestly account as a "fable" by W. M. L. de Wette, *Beiträge zur Einleitung in das Alte Testament* (2 vols.; Halle, 1806–7; repr. Darmstadt: Wissenschaftliche Buchgesellschaft, 1971) 2.259.

19. See B. Jacob, *Der Pentateuch: Exegetisch-kritische Forschungen* (Leipzig: Veit, 1905) 345.

20. The expression Priestly Code (Priestercodex etc.) is not brought up, although Benno Jacob in *Der Pentateuch* refers only to the texts usually ascribed to this source.

21. Ibid., 342 (translation mine).

addition, only philological-historical research on the Hebrew Bible during that time was considered substantial,[22] and synchronic and literary text analysis was subject to the dictates of historical proof of the unity of the text. Only today does close reading or reader-response criticism rank virtually side by side with literary-historical as *bona fide* approaches to biblical research.

This essay concentrates on the question of the fictional qualities of the Priestly Code. The classification of the Priestly texts as fictional literature presupposes the understanding of the texts as a literary artifact.[23] In addition to discussing the literary function of fiction in general, I will try to develop criteria for the identification of a fictional text. The final section of this essay will focus on a close reading and literary exegesis of selected sections of the description of the erection of the tabernacle and its equipment[24] (focusing on the ארון 'ark', the כפרת 'cover', and the cherubim; Exod 25:10–22). We will see that the Priestly author(s)[25] neither wanted to design an "ideal" or "utopian" outline of a sanctuary and its cult nor wanted to negate the concept of a temple.[26] Even less did they want to contribute to Israel's history. Instead, P designed a "fictional" architecture and fictional equipment, an "impossible possibility" as well as a "possible impossibility." P portrayed a sanctuary that could (and should!) never be built or rebuilt:[27] *ein Denkbild, kein Sehbild.*[28] P gave us an idea about a sanctuary that never

---

22. See, e.g., C. Houtman, *Pentateuch: Die Geschichte seiner Erforschung nebst seiner Auswertung* (Kampen: Kok Pharos, 1994) §§41–58 (= pp. 98–183).

23. Compare also with the characterization by Barthes quoted in T. G. Pavel, *Fictional Worlds* (Cambridge: Harvard University Press, 1986) 5: "The function of narrative is not to 'represent'; it is to constitute a spectacle still very enigmatic for us, but in any case not of a mimetic order. The 'reality' of a sequence lies not in the 'natural' succession of the actions composing it, but in the logic there exposed."

24. In the following referred to as משכן-narrative.

25. I regard P as a source document of its own (see also K. Koch, "P: Kein Redaktor! Erinnerung an zwei Eckdaten der Quellenscheidung," *VT* 37 [1987] 446–67, esp. pp. 456–62, 466; Schmidt, *Priesterschrift*, 1–34; B. J. Schwartz, "The Priestly Account of the Theophany and Lawgiving at Sinai," in *Texts, Temples, and Traditions: A Tribute to Menahem Haran* [ed. M. Fox, V. A. Hurowitz, A. Hurvitz, and others; Winona Lake, Ind.: Eisenbrauns, 1996] 103–34, pp. 105–11; Otto, "Forschungen," 36). For further discussion on this subject, see Blum, *Studien*, 219–85.

26. See Fretheim, "Priestly Document," 321–23.

27. See also the explanations given in V. Fritz, *Tempel und Zelt: Studien zum Tempelbau in Israel und zu dem Zeltheiligtum der Priesterschrift* (Neukirchen-Vluyn: Neukirchener Verlag, 1977) 163; M. Görg, "Keruben in Jerusalem," *BN* 4 (1977) 13–24, p. 22.

28. Ibid., 22; according to Benno Jacob, Exodus 25–31 does not want to provide the reader with technical details, since the text "was not concerned with a *technical description*. It provided guidelines for specific *religious thoughts*" (B. Jacob, *The Second Book of the Bible:*

existed; yet it *did* exist, because he transformed it into literature. Therefore, in the end, I will try to give a preliminary answer to the question
why P wants the reader to imagine such a design: in other words: what
is fictional in P's fiction? Additionally, we will see that the questions
raised by introductory investigations are only applicable to the material
at hand and, therefore, are insufficient for explaining the literary and
theological aims of the entire Priestly Code. The literary quality of the
Priestly Code precludes one-dimensional literary-historical questions.

Fiction and Fictionality

Language is a means by which humans convey their perception of
the world and simultaneously create a certain relationship with it. Extralinguistic experiences are never identical with their linguistic cor-
relative. Although the contents of a documentary find their immediate
equivalent in the described event because the text seeks to describe
any occurrence in the real world as precisely as possible, the moment
of the "real" nevertheless cannot be derived from the language itself
but only from the extralinguistic world. In this case, the creation of a
relationship between the text and the real world begins with the extralinguistic experience.

In order to distinguish a fictional text from an eyewitness report or
a historical account, a reader must be able to discover the pragmatic
signs presented by the author. It is only then that a reader is able to expose a text as fictional. Signs of fiction cannot be drawn from a text on
the semantic level because there are not any linguistic criteria for the
definition of fiction.[29] In most cases, the pragmatic presupposition is
rooted in a collective knowledge or collective memory that has to be
determined differently in every society. In this way, pragmatic signs
presuppose a certain knowledge of historical events, although this cannot be restricted only to history. We know, based only on our previous
historical study, that "Qoheleth" (the 'Preacher') put on the mask of a

---

Exodus [trans. with an introduction by Walter Jacob, in association with Yaacov Elman;
Hoboken, N.J.: Ktav, 1992] 760 = idem, *Das Buch Exodus* [ed. Shlomo Mayer, Joachim
Hahn, and Almuth Jürgensen; Stuttgart: Calwer, 1997] 758).

29. See, e.g., the discussion in H. Weinrich (ed.), *Positionen der Negativität* (Munich:
Fink, 1975) 519–40; R. Warning, "Der inszenierte Diskurs: Bemerkungen zur pragmati-
schen Relation der Fiktion," in *Funktionen des Fiktiven* (ed. D. Henrich and W. Iser; Munich:
Fink, 1983) 183–206, pp. 193–94; R. Ronen, *Possible Worlds in Literary Theory* (Cambridge:
Cambridge University Press, 1994) 36.

king named Qoheleth (son of David, king of Israel [!] in Jerusalem), because there never was a king named Qoheleth who ruled over Israel or Judah. Moreover, as shown by Rüdiger Lux, we know that the ancient readers knew this too.[30] One can say, therefore, that social and cultural features as well as organizational patterns from the real world (such as sociocultural relations, historical knowledge, or literary traditions) necessarily form a constituent element in the fictional text.[31] However, these features do not function like a mirror as a report based on facts would. On the other hand, the "realities" portrayed in the text are not mere fiction. Their admission to the text arises from an 'act of fictionalizing' (*Akt des Fingierens*), which is the foundation for fictional text design.

Above all, the concept of *literary anthropology* as presented by Wolfgang Iser turns out to be a useful tool for the classification of ancient texts as fictional. In his study *Das Fiktive und das Imaginäre*, Iser discusses in particular the communicative function(s) of fiction and its literary use, thereby replacing the conventional literary opposition of "fiction" and "reality" with the triad of "the real"–"the fictional"–"the imaginary" (*Das Reale–das Fiktive–das Imaginäre*).[32] The "act of fictionalizing" embeds "reality" in the text in order to transform the imaginary from a diffuse formation into a well-structured literary form. If the fictional text contains real references without restricting itself to a mere description of the real, then the fictional component is not the closing stage in itself but constitutes the fictional groundwork for a later Imaginary.[33] According to Iser, no organizational pattern or entity from the real world is mirrored 1:1 in the text. Rather, with regard to contents, the opposition of text and historical context forms the starting point.[34] It enables an author to "fictionalize," meaning in a first step the selection of single elements from available reference-rooms.

---

30. See R. Lux, "'Ich, Kohelet, bin König . . .'; Die Fiktion als Schlüssel zur Wirklichkeit in Kohelet 1,12–2,26," *EvT* 50 (1990) 331–42, esp. pp. 335–37.

31. See also Ronen, *Possible Worlds*, 90: "Fictional propositions represent both existents and non-existents: they intermingle denotations of imaginary beings with reference to historical entities."

32. See already W. Iser, *Fingieren als anthropologische Dimension der Literatur* (Konstanz: Universitätsverlag, 1990).

33. See idem, "Akte des Fingierens. Oder: Was ist das Fiktive im fiktionalen Text?" in *Funktionen des Fiktiven* (ed. D. Henrich and W. Iser; Munich: Fink, 1983) 121–51, p. 121; see also idem, *Das Fiktive und das Imaginäre: Perspektiven literarischer Anthropologie* (Frankfurt/M.: Suhrkamp, 1991) 24–51; Moers, *Fingierte Welten*, 19–38.

34. See also Y. M. Lotman, *Die Struktur literarischer Texte* (2nd ed.; Munich: Fink, 1981) 92–121.

These reference-rooms consist of either extratextual units (socio-cultural: norms and traditions) or intertextual entities (intertextually: literary references stemming from any existing textual world).[35] By means of fictionalizing, the author dissolves the elements taken from either extratextual or intertextual reference systems. Simultaneously, a new reference system is established into which these "decontextualized" elements are fit. The decomposition of the individual elements leads to an expansion of their previous semantic or pragmatic realm,[36] because the decomposed elements possess a twofold point of reference: backward toward their former context (which is still to be made out) and forward toward the new reference system.[37] This duplication in regard to content forms what Iser calls the "ambiguity within the fictional text," which to him is a constitutive element in fictional literature.[38] The (historical or theological) context given in the text is exceeded in this manner. The new reference field created by decomposition and (re)-selection represents for the reader a "(textual) world of disorder"[39] because the composition is based on the disintegration of familiar reference systems, which opens up a new dimension of textual understanding hitherto unknown[40] (*Grenzüberschreitung*).[41]

As a first result we may state that the reality represented in the fictional text is not presented for its own sake. Rather, it functions as a reference or means to something that does not exist but will be made imaginable. By means of fictionalizing, the author presents the world in the modus of an 'As-If' (*Als-Ob*),[42] striving for the "irrealization of the real." The fiction gives up any reference to the "natural" world in order to arrange what seems impossible or what remains concealed in reality.[43]

---

35. See Iser, *Das Fiktive und das Imaginäre*, 24–51; Moers, *Fingierte Welten*, 38–79.

36. See Iser, "Akte," 141–43.

37. Moers, *Fingierte Welten*, 57; see also W. Iser, *Der Akt des Lesens: Theorie ästhetischer Wirkung* (4th ed.; Munich: Fink, 1994) 155–61.

38. See also Moers, "Fiktionalität," 40–56.

39. See ibid., 45.

40. See J. Anderegg, *Fiktion und Kommunikation: Ein Beitrag zur Theorie der Prosa* (2nd ed.; Göttingen: Vandenhoeck & Ruprecht, 1977) 33–40; Iser, "Akte," 123–24.

41. See ibid., 148–51; see also M. Oeming, "Bedeutung und Funktionen von 'Fiktionen' in der alttestamentlichen Geschichtsschreibung," *EvT* 44 (1984) 254–66, p. 260.

42. See already A. Assmann, *Die Legitimität der Fiktion. Ein Beitrag zur Geschichte der literarischen Kommunikation* (Munich: Fink, 1980) 9–17; see Iser, "Akte," 149.

43. See Moers, "Fiktionalität," 45.

According to Iser, the intention of a (fictional) text reveals itself by means of the decomposition of the traditional system of reference and the subsequent selection of single elements taken from them. Thus, Iser's approach can be applied especially to the exegesis of ancient texts, because the so-called "genuine intention of the author" leads to solutions more speculative than exegetical even with regard to modern literature.[44] Biblical texts lack basal clues for discovering an author's intention—such as his identity, his sociocultural background, the impetus for the composition of a text, or information about the individual or collective emotional states of the author or group of authors.[45]

With regard to the correlation of single neologisms with their previous reference fields, the exegete can take up conventional exegetical methods: tradition- and genre-criticism likewise deal with the lexemic-lexicographical scrutiny of a certain topos, its contextual setting and changing pragmatic determination, as well as its communicative function in the context at hand. Traditio-historical questions, therefore, can serve as an important tool for determining signs of fiction in a text.

On the other hand, literary criticism has already created a set of parameters for the determination of signs of fiction, which can be applied to the Priestly texts:

1. *Textual frames and dialogues in the text.* Introductions or framing texts provide the setting for the characters and sometimes even create "ideal biographies" (e.g., the תולדת-scheme). In addition, "fictional dialogues" provide the reader with further information on the *dramatis personae.*

2. The *lengthy* quality of the texts as well as a *stereotyped language pattern.*[46] Scholars have often noticed P's repetitive, sometimes even monotonous formulas and ritual style and his long-winded, detailed descriptions of even insignificant details.[47] The Priestly author(s) use(s) them to create an atmospheric density and to overemphasize their claim for literary "reality." Furthermore, the so-called 'formula of order' (כאשר צוה ה') and the "formula of execution" (כן עשׂו/עשׂה) have

---

44. See also Iser, *Das Fiktive und das Imaginäre*, 27.

45. See also C. Suhr, "Zum fiktiven Erzählen in der ägyptischen Literatur," in *Definitely: Egyptian Literature. Proceedings of the Symposium "Ancient Egyptian Literature: History and Forms"* (ed. G. Moers and F. Kammerzell; Göttingen: Seminar für Ägyptologie und Koptologie, 1999) 91–129, p. 90.

46. See also Moers, *Fingierte Welten*, 83 (with n. 264).

47. See already Wellhausen, *Prolegomena*, 7.

to be examined not only regarding their function in structuring the text(s) but also regarding content.[48]

3. *Patterns of time and spatial dimensions.* As already revealed by Yuri M. Lotman (1972),[49] fictional texts show extensive use of expressions of spatial dimensions to symbolize nonspatial relations. P's idiomatic language of repetitive formulas and ritual-style patterns use many terms in the spatial and temporal categories (for example: לפני ה'; מעל; מול; בתוך; מתוך). In particular, the narrative on the erection of the tabernacle illustrates that the pattern of time and spatial dimensions functions as an important means for the literary stylization of personal relations (including the relationship between God and man). Another topic to be mentioned here is that of symbolic measurements and relative orders of magnitude.[50]

4. *Emblematic terms and names.* P uses a variety of emblematic names. It is not by chance that out of all possible choices, Bezaḷel ('in the shade of God'[51]) from Judah and Oholiab the Danite, who bears "tent" (אהל) as a component of his name,[52] are responsible for the manufacture of the tent and the tabernacle (משכן). Furthermore, one might also ask why P presents the Aaronides as the only representatives of the Israelite priesthood, thereby allowing only Aaron and his sons to perform the actual priestly tasks, whereas, in all other biblical (and extrabiblical) documents, the house of Zadok holds this position almost exclusively.[53]

---

48. For a detailed analysis of the "formula of execution" and its derivatives, see also T. Pola, *Die ursprüngliche Priesterschrift: Beobachtungen zur Literarkritik und Traditionsgeschichte von P[g]* (Neukirchen-Vluyn: Neukirchener Verlag, 1995) 116–46; see also Otto, "Forschungen," 21–22.

49. See Lotman, *Struktur*, 311–29; see also Warning, "Der inszenierte Diskurs," 201–2.

50. Many of the aspects mentioned here have already been noticed by Benno Jacob in *Der Pentateuch*. He dedicated a whole chapter to the תולדת-scheme (ibid., 3–56), a chapter to the numbers (ibid., 248–52, 383–90), and wrote a comprehensive treatment of the symbolic meaning of the tabernacle and its equipment (ibid., 256–346).

51. Exod 31:2, 35:30, 36:1–2, 37:1, 38:22; 1 Chr 2:20; 2 Chr 1:5; Ezra 10:30.

52. Exod 31:6–7, 36:2, 38:23; on the name *Oholiab*, see M. Noth, *Die israelitischen Personennamen im Rahmen der gemeinsemitischen Namengebung* (BWANT 3/10; Stuttgart: Kohlhammer, 1928) 158–59; see also the discussion in M. Görg, *Das Zelt der Begegnung: Untersuchungen zur Gestalt der sakralen Zelttraditionen Altisraels* (BBB 27; Bonn: Hanstein, 1967) 39; K. Koch, *Die Priesterschrift: Von Exodus 25 bis Leviticus 16. Eine überlieferungsgeschichtliche und literarkritische Untersuchung* (Göttingen: Vandenhoeck & Ruprecht, 1959) 37.

53. Compare with 2 Sam 8:17, 20:25; 1 Kgs 2:35, 4:2; see Fritz, *Tempel und Zelt*, 154 and n. 182. See already H. Valentin, *Aaron: Eine Studie zur vor-priesterschriftlichen Aaron-Überlieferung* (OBO 18; Freiburg: Universitätsverlag, 1978) esp. pp. 9–25; see also the discussion in Otto, "Aaroniden."

Finally, the term כפרת[54] is restricted to the context of the installation of the sacrificial cult. One has to ask why P introduces a cultic item that in its traditio-historical background holds no immediate antecedent.

5. *Relevant inconsistencies.* The sections on the manufacture of the tent and the tabernacle as well as on the priestly garments show a remarkable number of relevant inconsistencies that cannot (and should not!) be explained by the fact that the Priestly author(s) lacked architectural or formal imagination. Rather, we will see that P literarily ties together cultic objects that are impracticable or even unthinkable in reality.

In the following exegetical application, I will focus especially on the aspects mentioned in items 2, 3, and 5, focusing on stereotyped language-patterns, on patterns of time and spatial dimensions, and on relevant inconsistencies.

The Tabernacle and Its Equipment (Exodus 25–31)

The Dramatis Personae and Their Scope of Actions

In the following, I will outline the *dramatis personae*, their competencies, their activities, and the scope of their actions. Central literary figures are Yahweh on one side and Moses and the Israelites on the other side. Without exception, P sketches them schematically and does not endow them with personal movements, emotional features, or individual traits.[55] The figures put on this "literary chessboard" operate only functionally, their author(s) indicating thereby their effort to depict the scenes from a distance.

One of the most distinctive features of the משכן-narrative is its strict literary correlation with the story of creation (Gen 1:1–2:4a), expressing a clear development with regard to the acting subjects:[56]

---

54. Exod 25:17–22, 26:34, 30:6, 31:7. Except for the P texts in the Pentateuch, this term is taken up only once, in 1 Chr 28:11.

55. See Knohl, *Sanctuary*, 137.

56. See B. Jacob, *Das Buch Genesis: Übersetzt und erklärt* (Berlin, 1934); repr.: *Das erste Buch der Tora: Genesis* (Stuttgart: Calwer, 2000) 67; M. Buber, "Der Mensch von heute und die Jüdische Bibel," in *Die Schrift und ihre Verdeutschung*, ed. M. Buber and F. Rosenzweig; Berlin: Schocken, 1936) 13–45, pp. 40–45; F. Rosenzweig, "Das Formgeheimnis der biblischen Erzählungen," in ibid., 239–61, p. 254; J. Blenkinsopp, "The Structure of P," *CBQ* 38 (1976) 275–92, p. 280; idem, *Prophecy and Canon: A Contribution to the Study of Jewish Origins* (Notre Dame: University of Notre Dame Press, 1977) 54–79, pp. 60–69; Blum, *Studien*, 306.

Gen 1:31:	וירא אלהים את כל אשר עשה והנה טוב מאד	Exod 39:43:	וירא משה את כל המלאכה והנה עשו אתה כאשר צוה ה'
Gen 2:2:	ויכל אלהים ביום השביעי מלאכתו אשר עשה וישבת . . . אשר עשה	Exod 39:32:	ותכל כל עבדת משכן . . . ויעשו בני ישראל ככל אשר צוה ה' את משה כן עשו
Gen 2:3:	ויברך אלהים	Exod 39:43:	ויברך אתם משה
Gen 2:3:	ויקדש אתו . . .	Exod 40:9 (incl. the broader context): . . . את המשכן ואת כל אשר בו וקדשת אתו ואת כל כליו והיה קדש
Gen 3:21:	ויעש ה' אלהים לאדם ולאשתו כתנות עור וילבשם	Lev 8:13 (see also Exod 28:40f.; 29:5, 8; 40:13, 14): ויקרב משה את בני אהרן וילבשם כתנת

This figure shows that in the story of creation P presents God (אלהים) as the only active figure. By contrast, the משכן-narrative introduces Moses as a kind of mediary to pass the orders to the Israelites/BezaPel/Oholiab.[57] 'Speaking' and 'doing' are now actions given to different parties. In the course of the narrative, the Israelites become those who "make," Yahweh remaining in (or even: restricted to) the role of the one who speaks and commands. As in the story of creation, God's commands are carried out immediately and entirely, even *in detail*. In both the narratives, P typifies God as a domineering figure: repeatedly, the משכן-narrative emphasizes that the Israelites execute and complete everything exactly the way he commanded. As a corollary, the משכן-narrative lacks any account comparable with the narratives of discontent and complaining.[58] In addition, P restricts the use of the "formula of order and execution" almost exclusively to the cultic realms (see figure, p. 677). P uses the "formulas of order and execution" outside the cultic narratives only in the flood account (Gen 6:22, 7:5) and in the story of Moses and Aaron in front of Pharaoh (Exod 7:6, 10, 20). With regard to the structure of "command" (God) and "execution" (Israel), P shifts from a broader setting (creation; historical event like the Exodus) into the realm of cult alone. In correspondence to the ongoing textual chronology, Yahweh's commands cover only(!) ritualistic implementations successfully, and in that, P severely restricts Yahweh's power and his scope of action.

This pattern of restraint applies also with regard to God's spatial dimensions mentioned in the texts: the creation narrative does not touch

---

57. Exod 7:2, 25:22, 31:6, 35:10, 38:22; Num 15:23; see Exod 24:16; Lev 1:1; Exod 6:10, 13, 29; 13:1; 14:1; 16:11; 25:1; 30:11, 17ff.

58. Compare with, e.g., Exod 14:10–12, 15:22–27, 16:1–31, 17:1–7; Num 11:4–34, 13:30–14:19, 20:1–13.

The 'Formula of Order' ('כאשר צוה ה)	The 'Formula of Execution' (כן עשׂה ;עשׂו)
Exod 7:6, 10, 20: Moses and Aaron in front of Pharaoh	Gen 6:22, 7:5: Noah and the ark
Exod 12:28, 50: Passover	Exod 7:6: Moses and Aaron in front of Pharaoh
Exod 16:34: Man	Exod 12:28, 50: Passover
Exod 39:1, 5, 7, 21, 26, 29, 31: the Priestly garments	Exod 36:11, 22, 29; 40:16; Num 8:4, 17:26: working on the equipment of the tabernacle
Exod 39:43: completion of the work	Exod 39:42–43: the erection of the tabernacle
Exod 40:19, 21, 23, 25, 27, 29, 32: completion of the building of the tabernacle and its equipment	Num 1:54: the standards and organization of the camp
Lev 8:4, 9, 13, 17, 21, 29; 9:7, 10; 10:15: inauguration of the priests; the sacrifices of ordination	Num 5:4: the treatment of lepers and people having a discharge
Lev 16:34: Yom Kippur	Num 8:20, 22: the Levites
Lev 24:23, 15:36: cultic stoning	Num 9:5: Second Passover
Num 1:19, 2:33; 3:42, 51: military examination	Num 36:10: the daughters of Zelophehad and their marriages
Num 8:3: the lamps	Josh 14:5: the distribution of the land
Num 8:22: the Levites	
Num 17:26: the rod of Aaron	
Num 20:27: Aaron's death	
Num 26:2: military examination	
Num 27:11, 36:10: the daughters of Zelophehad and their marriages	
Num 27:22: Joshua's appointment	
Num 31:7: the campaign against Midian	
Num 31:31, 41, 47: the treatment of the spoils	

the question of *where* (or *from where*) God takes action and, thereby, implies a diffuse divine omnipresence. This changes from Exodus 24 onward: the text gradually specifies God's (i.e., his glory's) location more and more, at first restricting his abode to Mount Sinai (על הר סיני; Exod 24:16) but with his speech already going out 'from the midst of the cloud' (מתוך הענן). In describing Yahweh's location not simply as "on the mountain," but "in the midst of the cloud," P on the one hand seeks to specify God's location and on the other hand making him removed, leaving Moses/the reader with only his voice from out of the cloud, which is not identical with Yahweh.

In correspondence to the precise localization of the presence of God, the text describes Moses' experience on the mountain: since God's glory does not leave the cloud, Moses has to enter 'the midst of the cloud' (בתוך הענן; Exod 24:18). Thus, the opening section of the subsequent account on the foundation of the cultic Law already depicts a constricted locale for God's commands to Moses. The detailed descriptions, beginning with the command to raise a contribution (תרומה; Exod 25:1–9), serve to generate a dense literary atmosphere, as if P also claims to have been on the mountain.[59] Moreover, the phrase . . . וידבר ה׳ אל משה לאמר implies that P was the only "witness" to this conversation; at the same time, this is an "impossible witness," because the description leaves no doubt that there is no space left between God's coming from מתוך הענן and Moses's entering בתוך הענן.

In the course of the account about the command for the construction of the ark (Exod 25:10–22), Yahweh's scope of action is restricted once again. Whereas the introductory passage merely states that the Israelites should make the tabernacle for Yahweh's 'dwelling' among them (ושכנתי בתוכם, Exod 25:8[60]), Exod 25:10–22 puts this in terms that are more concrete by modifying the idea of a vague dwelling into a motif about Yahweh's 'meeting' (יעד* *Niphal*) with Moses and 'speaking' to him (Exod 25:22; 29:42–43; 30:6, 36; Num 17:19[61]). Simultaneously, the text confines Yahweh's spatial extent to an area of 2.5 × 1.5 cubits.[62] P hereby describes Yahweh as constantly retreating to the smallest spot imaginable. Note in particular the accumulation of deictic particles used in Exod 25:22 (and Num 7:89): אשר + מבין שני הכרובים + על הכפרת* על ארון העדות:[63]

> And you shall put the כפרת ['cover'] on top of the ark. . . . There I will meet with you, and from above the cover [מעל הכפרת], from between the two cherubim [מבין שני הכרובים] that are upon the ark of the testimony [אשר על ארון העדות], I will speak with you of all that I will command you for the Israelites. (Exod 25:21–22)

Yahweh's spatial restraint corresponds literally with his renunciation of any execution of his commands: as already mentioned above, Yahweh merely speaks, the power of implementation being reserved for Moses and the Israelites.

In addition, there is another striking facet embedded in the deixis: the motifs of "meeting" and "speaking" are connected with the prepositions ל־ and את (suff.), thereby expressing Yahweh's movement toward Moses, while the preposition מעל simultaneously conveys with-

---

59. See also Suhr ("Zum fiktiven Erzählen," 92), who discusses the difference between the "fictional narrator" and the "(real) author" of a text.

60. Compare also with Exod 29:46; Lev 15:31; Num 5:3.

61. See also Num 7:89.

62. See also *Gen Rab.* 4:4.

63. See already Ramban (Nahmanides) in his commentary, ad loc. (Ramban on Exod 25:21).

drawal. This meaning of מעל can clearly to be seen from the following verses:[64]

מעל

Gen 6:7: the blotting out of man from the face of the land
Gen 8:3 (and 13): the receding of the water from the earth
Gen 17:22: God went up from Abraham
Exod 28:28 // 39:21: the breastpiece may not come loose from the ephod
Exod 40:36; Num 9:17, 10:11: cloud been taken up from over the tabernacle
Lev 4:31: the removing of the fat from the sacrifice of peace offerings
Lev 16:12: the coals of fire from upon the altar
Num 12:10: the withdrawal of the cloud from over the tent
Num 16:26–27: the request for separation from the tents
Num 25:8: the restraining of the plague
Num 25:11: Phinehas turning away God's wrath from Israel

Linguistically, P conveys ambivalence in Yahweh's relationship with humankind (Moses) that fits well in the system of spatial relations used elsewhere in the P source. Exod 25:21–22 is even more significant in this regard because the place where Yahweh wants to meet with Moses (כפרת) is inaccessible to Moses: the ארון (with the כפרת) is behind the curtain (פרכת), and only the high priest is allowed to enter the place 'inside the veil' (מבית לפרכת; Lev 16:2, 12, 15).[65] Nahmanides already noticed that, after the installation of the cult, Yahweh evades an immediate confrontation with Moses.[66]

Even though the כפרת represents a very close space for Yahweh's conversation with Moses, P is at pains to keep a certain amount of distance between Yahweh and the Israelites, as indicated by his use of the preposition לפני (ה'):

לפני ה'

Gen 7:1: Noah as a righteous man before Yahweh
Gen 17:1: Abraham is to walk before Yahweh (not: with him!)
Exod 28:12, 29: the stones on the shoulder pieces of the ephod and the bearing
    of the names before Yahweh
Exod 28:30: the bearing of the Urim und Thummim before Yahweh
Exod 28:38: the gold rosette worn on Aaron's forehead before Yahweh
Exod 29:11: the slaughtering of the bull before Yahweh
Lev 10:2: the death of Nadab and Abihu before Yahweh
Num 26:61: the strange fire before Yahweh
Num 31:5: the atonement before Yahweh

---

64. These are only selected examples.
65. See Haran, *Temples*, 208–21 (see also the plan of the tabernacle, p. 152); see also Milgrom, *Leviticus*, 1–16, 52–57, 1009–84.
66. See Nahmanides' commentary on the phrase וידבר ה' אליו מאהל מועד in Lev 1:1.

One can see very clearly that in the textual progression from Genesis 7, 17 through Exodus 6 and up to Exodus 25 P is pursuing a certain aim in such a way that the spatial dimensions in which humans walk "before Yahweh"[67] get gradually smaller, while simultaneously Yahweh's human counterpart becomes more and more important. The literary figures from Noah to Abraham to Moses/Israelites increasingly gain theological importance, matching the importance of their place in the world and in history. Noah's place is "the world" in a very broad and vague sense, corresponding to Genesis 1–11. Abraham's scope has been delimited to Palestine (ארץ מגורים; Gen 17:8, 28:4ff.) and Egypt. The meeting between Israel and Yahweh can take place only by means of priestly mediation in the cult, its place being the אהל מועד. Israel's meeting with Yahweh takes place within history: however, the meeting place is inside rather than outside, where the space is profane. According to P, the כפרת functions as a symbol for the gradual retreat of Yahweh from the profane toward a consecrated area of 3.75^2 cubits.

Along with Yahweh's different kinds of spatial presence, the Israelites have to move in relation to themselves as well as the outside world. P expresses these relations by means of the prepositions מתוך and בתוך:[68]

מתוך

Exod 12:31: the departure from among the people of Egypt
Exod 28:1: the separation of Aaron and his sons from among the Israelites
Num 3:12; 8:6, 14, 16, 19; 18:6: the taking of the Levites from among the Israelites
Num 4:2, 18: the separation of the Kohathites from among the Levites
Num 16:21, 17:10: the separation of Moses and Aaron from among the congregation
Num 19:20: the cutting off of a person from among the assembly
Num 25:7: Phinehas arises from among the congreation

בתוך

Exod 14:16, 22, 27, 29: Israel enters the midst of the sea
Exod 29:45: Yahweh's dwelling among the Israelites
Lev 16:16: the tent of meeting in the midst of Israel's impurities
Lev 22:32: the sanctification of Yahweh among the Israelites
Num 1:49, 2:33, 26:62 (2x): Levi in the midst of the Israelites
Num 2:17: Levi in the midst of the camp
Num 17:21: the rod of Aaron in the midst of the rods
Num 18:20, 24: Yahweh as Aaron's inheritance in the midst of the Israelites
Num 35:34: Yahweh's dwelling among the Israelites

---

67. Compare also with Exod 40:5: לפני ארון 'before (the) ark'.
68. The lists contain only selected examples.

The division of the Israelites into Aaronides, Levites, and Israel-ites[69] corresponds to the successive spatial separation from Egypt and from the world outside (the camp or even outside the land).[70] Only this movement among themselves as well as in relation to the outside opens up the possibility for Yahweh's dwelling among Israel and for his sanctification.

Of course, scholars have often noted the central role of the (sacrifi-cial) cult and its location within the Priestly Code. According to Mat-thias Köckert, the Law becomes the sphere in which Yahweh reveals himself.[71] Although Köckert is right, his considerations nevertheless convey only some of the implications connected to the idea that Yah-weh reveals himself within the sphere of Law. P's depiction shows that, from the time of the installation of the cult, Israel does not conceive Yahweh's presence independently from the Law; in other words: Yah-weh's presence becomes imaginable *only* within the scope of the cult.

One can say, therefore, that Yahweh's gradual spatial retreat and his presence in the tent of meeting serve as a symbol for his "retreat" from the profane "room" of history. P assigns the execution of the cult to the Israelites alone; there is nothing left for Yahweh to "do." On the other hand, the idea of the "sanctification" of Yahweh indicates that the cul-tic area is the sphere in which Yahweh is in need of Israel: Israel must keep their area clean from all kinds of impurities, because he wants to dwell among them. The "historical way,"[72] having begun with Abra-ham, reaches its final destination with the installation of Israel's cult. Even the oracular system (Urim and Thummim) becomes limited. P depicts Moses' and Aaron's confrontation with Pharaoh/Egypt (Exod 7:6, 10, 20) as the last historical-political event in which Yahweh not only provides Israel with clear instructions (see Exod 7:6) but also in-terferes directly with the course of history. From now on, P uses both the 'formula of order' (כאשר צוה ה') and the 'formula of execution' (עשׂו; כן עשׂה) exclusively in cultic contexts (see Exod 12:28, 50). From the mo-ment that the Israelites become an עדה (Exod 12:3), the "fulfillment of a preestablished plan"[73] cannot take place within the profane area of

---

69. See the order of the camp in Num 2:1–32, 10:11–28.

70. The "separation" of the two subjects Israel and Egypt is a characteristic motif of P; see my "Funktion der 'Verstockung' Pharaos in der Erzählung vom Auszug aus Ägypten (Ex 7–14)," *BN* 93 (1998) 56–76, esp. pp. 71–76.

71. See M. Köckert, "Leben in Gottes Gegenwart: Zum Verständnis des Gesetzes in der priesterschriftlichen Literatur," *JBTh* 4 (1989) 29–61, p. 61.

72. See ibid., 58.

73. See Blenkinsopp, "The Structure of P," 276–77.

history but must be restricted to the cult and the sacrificial service. According to P, only within the cultic sphere can divine order and human implementation correspond meaningfully with one another.[74] P's use of a "divine retreat" from (the realm of) history, the cult, and relationship with humans presages the later pharisaic-rabbinic understanding of the function of the Law. Only by means of Torah(-study) does man gain access to the divine realm.[75] Simultaneously (and sharply formulated), God gains influence and power in his world primarily by means of his people's studying the Torah and fulfilling the Law.

The 'Ark' (ארון), the 'Cover' (כפרת), and the Cherubim

> You shall make[76] an ark of acacia wood; it shall be two and a half cubits long, a cubit and a half wide, and a cubit and a half high. . . . Then you shall make a cover (כפרת) of pure gold; two cubits and a half shall be its length, and a cubit and a half its width. You shall make two cherubim of gold; you shall make them of hammered work, at the two ends of the כפרת. Make one cherub at the one end and one cherub at the other; of one piece with the כפרת you shall make the cherubim at its two ends. The cherubim shall spread out their wings above, overshadowing the כפרת with their wings. They shall face one to another; the faces of the cherubim shall be turned toward the כפרת. You shall put the כפרת on top of the ark; and in the ark, you shall put the testimony that I shall give you. There I will meet with you, and from above the כפרת, from between the two cherubim that are upon the ark of the testimony, I will speak with you of all that I will command you for the Israelites. (Exod 25:10, 17–22)

The משכן-narrative begins with a description of the ark (ארון; Exod 25:10–22), made of acacia wood and overlaid with pure gold. P mentions two functions of the ark: on the one hand, it shall be used as a "container" for the 'testimony' (עדות); on the other hand, it serves as a substructure for the 'cover' (כפרת) with the two cherubim. The text gives equivalent measures for the length and width of the ארון and כפרת.[77] However, the description of the כפרת lacks any details concerning the

---

74. Against the interpretation of Buber, "Mensch," 42 ("Gottes Genosse am Werk der Schöpfung") and E. Zenger, *Gottes Bogen in den Wolken: Untersuchungen zu Komposition und Theologie der priesterschriftlichen Urgeschichte* (Stuttgart: Katholisches Bibelwerk, 1983) 171–72 (see also the discussion in Blum, *Studien*, 310–12), who explain Exodus 25–40 in such a way that man becomes God's partner in the divine work of creation or even completes God's creation.

75. See esp. my "'Sins of the Prophets': Biblical Characters through Rabbinic Lenses," *LTQ* 37 (2002) 197–213, pp. 209–13.

76. Read (with Samaritan and the LXX) ועשית; see also Koch, *Priesterschrift*, 7–8; Fritz, *Tempel und Zelt*, 117 (with n. 29).

77. See Exod 25:10, 17 // 37:11, 6.

third dimension (height),[78] thereby granting it a blurred ambiguity from the very beginning.

The ארון (Akk. *arānu*) as an independent cult object plays an important role, especially in the narrative of the capturing of the ark by the Philistines (1 Samuel 4–6).[79] Traditio-historically, the motif of the ark is connected to the city of Shilo (north of Bethel), an Israelite sanctuary.[80] After the transportation of the ark from Kiriath-jearim into the City of David (2 Samuel 6), the ark gains broader national significance. The ark finds its final destination in the newly built temple of Solomon. 1 Kings 6 assigns a specific role to the representatives of the Northern kingdom, thereby underlining the Israelite origin of the ark. According to the report on the inauguration of Solomon's temple (1 Kgs 8:1–11), the ark serves as a "container" for the two tablets of stone (שני לחות האבנים) put there at Mount Horeb (see also Deut 10:1–5). However, in the context of the architectural composition and interior furnishing of the most Holy Place (דביר), the ark achieves only subordinate significance and disappears almost completely underneath the wings of the massive cherubim. The measurement of the cube-shaped דביר was 20 cubits[3]. Compared with the height of the דביר and the two 10-cubits-high cherubim,[81] the ark, according to the measurements given in Exod 25:10 (a cubit and a half high), seems almost disrespectfully undersized. The cherubim described in 1 Kgs 6:23–28 were made of עצי שמן ('olive wood(?)'/'pine', *Pinus halepensis*[82]) and overlaid (*צפה Piel) with gold. Architecturally, they were in no connection with the ark being placed underneath their wings. The cherubims' function can be determined by

---

78. According to *b. Sukkah* 5a and 5b, the width of the כפרת was one טפח 'handbreadth' (calculated by use of a *gezera shava* [analogy] from Exod 25:25, the rim around the table of acacia wood).

79. 1 Sam 4:3 mentions the ארון ברית 'ark of the covenant'; see also 1 Kgs 6:19; 8:1, 6.

80. See esp. Fritz, *Tempel und Zelt*, 129–39. Fritz assumes the ארון already for the time of Israel's wandering in the desert because the ark as a Canaanite cult object seems improbable to him; see also Fretheim, "Priestly Document," 325–26; M. Noth, *Das 2. Buch Mose: Exodus* (Göttingen: Vandenhoeck & Ruprecht, 1978) 165; Görg, *Zelt*, 123–24 (see also pp. 75–97); Maier, *Ladeheiligtum*, 39–60; B. S. Childs, *Exodus: A Commentary* (6th ed.; London: SCM, 1974, 1987) 530–37.

81. See T. A. Busink, *Der Tempel von Jerusalem: Von Salomo bis Herodes. Eine archäologisch-historische Studie unter Berücksichtigung des westsemitischen Tempelbaus*, vol. 2: *Von Ezechiel bis Middot* (2 vols.; Leiden: Brill, 1970–80) 276–87; see also the illustrations, pp. 167, 198.

82. See O. Keel, *Jahwe-Visionen und Siegelkunst: Eine neue Deutung der Majestätsschilderungen in Jes 6, Ez 1 und 10 und Sach 4. Mit einem Beitrag von A. Gutbub über die vier Winde in Ägypten* (Stuttgart: Katholisches Bibelwerk, 1977) 15 and n. 3, on the basis of his exegesis of Neh 8:15.

the idiom יושב הכרובים (Yahweh of hosts, who is 'enthroned on the cherubim': 1 Sam 4:4[83]) as a throne of cherubim-sphinges.[84] At all events, in short, the traditio-historical background presented here shows that the ארון and cherubim stem from two local, religious-historically completely different contexts of early Israelite cult (cultic traditions from the Northern Kingdom; cherubim tradition from Jerusalem).

One can see at first glance that all of the cultic items mentioned in Exodus 25–31 differ substantially from the items described in 1 Kings 6–8.[85] No object comparable to the כפרת exists at all, and the connection between the ארון and the כפורת is not described in detail. Although the West Semitic root *'rn* meaning 'ark' or '(closed) sarcophagus' already implies a cover,[86] traditional Jewish exegesis has almost always explained the כפורת, too, as a 'cover/lid'.[87] Likewise, the origin and meaning of the term כפורת remain vague.[88] R. Avraham Ibn Ezra[89] refers to the interpretation of Jefet Ben Elis, who understands the expression with reference to Ps 32:1 (כסוי חטאה, the covering of one's sin). Dillmann refers to Lev 9:7; 16:6, 11ff.; Ps 65:4; and Isa 6:7 and understands the term in the sense of a protective covering and the blotting out of one's guilt.[90] However, *כפר Piel in Isa 6:7 implies in particular

---

83. Compare also with 2 Sam 6:2; 2 Kgs 19:15//Isa 37:16.

84. See in particular Keel, *Jahwe-Visionen und Siegelkunst*, 23–36; B. Janowski, "Keruben und Zion: Thesen zur Entstehung der Zionstradition," in *Gottes Gegenwart in Israel: Beiträge zur Theologie des Alten Testaments* (Neukirchen-Vluyn: Neukirchener Verlag, 1993) 247–80, p. 266. I agree with Janowski in his rejection of the thesis presented by Gerhard von Rad (see G. von Rad, "Zelt und Lade," *Gesammelte Studien zum Alten Testament* [3rd ed.; Munich: Chr Kaiser, 1965] 1.109–29; von Rad was followed by J. Jeremias, "Lade und Zion," *Das Königtum Gottes in den Psalmen: Israels Begegnung mit dem kanaanäischen Mythos in den Jahwe-König-Psalmen* [Göttingen: Vandenhoeck & Ruprecht, 1987] 167–82). Von Rad held the view that the ארון-tradition was followed by the Zion-tradition (Yahweh-Melekh-tradition; cf. Ps 47:9, 99:1ff.). It is more likely that the Zion-tradition followed the cherubim-tradition, having survived in the expression ה' יושב הכרובים. In addition, there is no biblical idiom יושב הארון; see also C. L. Seow, "The Designation of the Ark in Priestly Theology," *HAR* 8 (1984) 185–98, p. 190.

85. See already Blum, *Studien*, 303.

86. Compare with the coffin of Joseph mentioned in Gen 50:26.

87. See Rashi (followed by Rashbam), ad loc., who explains כפרת with כסוי 'covering'. According to R. Avraham Ibn Ezra, ad loc. (longer version of his commentary on the book of Exodus), the כפרת is כדמות מכסה 'like a cover' (see R. Sa'adya Gaon, ad loc.).

88. Since the ארון and כפרת in Exod 31:7, 35:12, and 39:35 are referred to as two distinguishable cult objects, it is likely that they do not belong together traditio-historically. Likewise, there is no term כפרת הארון (cstr.).

89. See the shorter version of his commentary on the book of Exodus, ad loc.

90. See Dillmann, *Die Bücher Exodus und Leviticus*, 281, 423–25.

the purification of Isaiah, whose deficient status facing the Holy One is purged away by one of the seraphim, and his anthropological integrity restored in view of the immediate visionary proximity of Yahweh.[91] This denotation could also be applied to the context at hand because the כפורת plays the pivotal role in the process of atonement for the sanctuary on account of the impurities of the Israelites (see Lev 16:14).

P draws a tighter linkage between the כפרת and the cherubim (Exod 25:18–19//Exod 31:7–8), than with the ארון and the כפרת. The cherubim are made 'of hammered work'[92] at the two ends of the כפרת. Although their exact measurement is not given, it is evident that (except for their name) they have nothing in common with their 10-cubits-high wooden predecessors in Solomon's Temple.[93] Furthermore, the cherubim face one another, and they turn their faces toward the כפרת with the ark underneath it. P hereby wants to establish a spatial relationship between the cherubim and the ארון, which these objects lacked in Solomon's Temple, since in the Temple of Jerusalem the ark was placed under the wings of the cherubim, whose outlook was oriented forward, toward the doorway of the דביר.[94] Literarily, P brings together what was not closely related in Israel's cultic past.

P's depiction unquestionably ties together two elements from Israel's cultic traditions (ארון and cherubim), which were known to him from either direct observation or from literary traditions. The question arises, therefore, why P insists on placing these two elements together on the כפרת. What does this mean with regard to the function of these items, and what aim does P achieve with such a portrayal?

---

91. See the explanations on Isa 6:7 given by R. Yosef Qara and R. Yesha'ya ben Eliyah di R. Yeshaya ben Eliyah di Trani; see also Rashi on Isa 28:18, who explains *כפר as קינוח and סילוק דבר 'wiping off' and 'removing' (see also Ibn Ezra on Isa 47:11); see also my *Die unerhörte Prophetie: Kommunikative Strukturen prophetischer Rede im Buch Yesha'yahu* (Arbeiten zur Bibel und ihrer Geschichte 14; Leipzig: Evangelische Verlag, 2003) 50–53.

92. According to Dillmann (*Die Bücher Exodus und Leviticus*, 281), they were hollow.

93. *B. Sukkah* 5a–5b discusses the height of the cherubim. The cherubim in Solomon's Temple reached one-third of the temple's total height (according to 1 Kgs 7:2, the temple's height was 30 cubits, and in 1 Kgs 6:23, the height of the cherubim was 10 cubits). The rabbis applied this spatial relationship to the cherubim in the tabernacle. Ten cubits (= 60 טפחים 'handbreadths') was the length/height of each board (Exod 26:16); subtract 10 (9+1 טפחים for the ארון and כפרת); thus 10 טפחים remain for the cherubim = $\frac{1}{3}$ of the total height of the tabernacle; see also the illustration in the Saperstein edition of *Perush Rashi 'al ha-Tora, The Torah: With Rashi's Commentary Translated, Annotated, and Elucidated* (The Artscroll Series; Shemos/Exodus; 4th ed.; New York, 2002) 326.

94. See Busink, *Der Tempel von Jerusalem*, 1.167.

Regarding the last question, we are dependent solely on the context of the description in the Priestly texts.[95] Essential and spatially central to P's depiction is the כפרת. It is the only cultic item that does not possess any antecedent. Literarily, P "invented" the כפרת in order to assign a new location to the ארון and cherubim. In contrast to an enduring 'seat' on the throne (ישב*), Yahweh's 'meeting' with Moses (יעד* Niphal) at the כפרת conveys an impression of being temporary and selective. P hereby rejects the concept of the cherubim-sphinges throne.[96] However, he creates an intimate relationship between the ark and the idiom יושב הכרובים. The narrative of the capturing of the ark (1 Samuel 4–6) presents the ark as a symbol of a powerful, helpful God (1 Sam 4:3–4[97]); however, the relation between the ark and the יושב הכרובים is not specified.

The fact that the כפרת does not possess any reference object serves as the key to understanding it: just as the כפרת is incomparable, Yahweh's actions—that is, "meeting and speaking from above the כפרת"—are not comparable to any prototype. The only "prototype" mentioned is the תבנית "pattern" of the tabernacle and its furniture (Exod 25:9). Against the traditio-historical background still recognizable, one can say, therefore, that P no longer supports either the concept of the cherubim-sphinges throne or the idea of divine military aid. Yahweh no longer dwells within a sanctuary but in personal-spatial relationships "among" the Israelites (Exod 25:8[98]). At the same time, P takes up the ארון and cherubim as symbols for the Northern and Southern Kingdoms of Israel and Judah. Likewise, the names *Oholiab* (from Dan) and *Bezalʾel* (from Judah) form a link between Northern and Southern Kingdoms.

One can say, therefore, that the כפרת serves as a linkage between the Northern and Southern Kingdoms. P hereby sets up a literary relationship in which the specific ideas are eliminated just as they are still decipherable. In other words: literarily, P goes "back" to historical events (the divided kingdoms) that do not yet exist in the desert.

---

95. The term כפרת is mentioned only in Exodus 25, 26, 30, 31, 35, 37, 39, 40; Leviticus 16; Numbers 7; and 1 Chr 28:11 mentions the בית הכפרת. Ezekiel does not use the term.

96. Against Ramban who understands Exod 25:21 clearly against the background of Yahweh יוטב הכרובים and insists on the concept of God's sitting on his throne.

97. 1 Sam 4:3 (MT): נקחה אלינו משלה את ארון ברית ה' ויבא בקרבנו וישענו מכף איבנו.

98. See also 1 Kgs 6:13.

The Power of Fiction: Preliminary Results

We have found that P applies spatial categories to his theological system, and thus the description of God's location, at least, has clearly proved to be a literary stylization. No one would dare to suggest, historically speaking, whether Yahweh spoke with Moses *from above the* כפרת, *from between the two cherubim*. It is, therefore, quite surprising that, with regard to the manufacture of the tabernacle and the installation of the Aaronide priesthood, scholars repeatedly try to absolve the texts of the stigma of being a "fictional," trying to prove, at least, an imaginary historicity.[99]

Biblical scholars have often noted the above-mentioned conclusion that P extensively alludes to traditio-historical elements from the Northern Kingdom of Israel. Menahem Haran, for example, recognized in P's description of the tent a reference to the sanctuary in Shilo.[100] Jacob Milgrom holds the view that the tabernacle depicted in the Priestly Code was portrayed in reference to a Canaanite model. According to Milgrom, the description of the lamp(s) in Exod 25:31–40//37:14–27 corresponds to archaeological evidences from the Late Bronze Period. In the division of Aaronide priests serving in the sanctuary and Levites serving outside the sanctuary, he saw a Hittite cult formula.[101] Volkmar Fritz asserted in 1977 that at least parts of the Priestly Code were written down by representatives of the priesthood of Bethel.[102]

In view of the question of P's historical environment (*Historischer Ort*) one could, therefore, posit that the Priestly Code was written at a time in the history of Israel/Judah, when at least one of the peoples or their (cultic) representatives strived for a synthesis between Northern and Southern cultic traditions. However, one must also ask when such a problem might have emerged? Alternatively, to ask the other way round: was there a time in the history of Israel and Judah when this matter was *not* an issue? The problem of the relationship between Israel

---

99. See C. Houtman, "Wie fiktiv ist das Zeltheiligtum von Exodus 25–40?" *ZAW* 106 (1994) 107–13; Otto, "Aaroniden," esp. pp. 409–10. It seems that the idea that P's Aaronides are a mere literary fiction seems unbearable to him; therefore, Otto assumes a splitting-off of the Aaronides from the Zadokites in the postexilic period.

100. Haran, *Temples*, 189–92, 260–75; for a different view see, e.g., Knohl, *Sanctuary*, 204–12. Knohl sees in P's description the model of a pre-Hezekian temple.

101. See the extensive discussions in Milgrom, *Leviticus*, 10, 29–32, 134–43.

102. See Fritz, *Tempel und Zelt*, 154–57; Janowski, "Keruben und Zion," 334 with n. 354.

and Judah and their religious and cultic traditions emerged, at the latest, around 733/21 (701), and was an issue at least until the first half of the fifth century. Those who claim that a Priestly school could design an outline for a new tabernacle (not a 'house' בית) only after the Babylonian destruction of the temple overlook the fact that Hosea and Isaiah also reproached the political and cultic representatives and at the same time preached political and theological changes while the political and cultic institutions still existed—and (some of them at their peak!) were working very well. We may as well grant the Priestly representatives the right to form literary theological alternatives. Protestant exegetes in many ways are still following the path of Wellhausen, who held that only the prophets held the power to demand religious innovations, whereas the representatives of the cultic institutions (especially in the Second Temple Period) often enough got stuck halfway in their ritualism.[103]

In studying the literary material, we cannot determine whether priestly refugees (from Bethel?) wrote the Priestly Code after having arrived in Jerusalem 721 or whether the Priestly Code was the work of an exilic/postexilic group of Priestly authors. The fictional quality of P's description makes it evident that he did not simply want to mirror existing conditions or outline a utopian cult. With reference to (former or still existing) cultic institutions and equipment and their consistent traditio-historical defamiliarization and literary disintegration,[104] one can say, therefore, that the Priestly Code establishes a "cult within literature." P introduces the cultic institutions as the only means for a meeting between Yahweh and Israel and thereby transfers them out of the natural ("historical") world into the realm of the text. Fritz discussed whether this change of levels might be characterized a as "spiritualization" of the cultic terms or even the cultic service, meaning that P mirrored the abandoning of the sacrificial service in favor of the

---

103. See Wellhausen, *Prolegomena*, esp. pp. 420–24.

104. According to Koch (*Priesterschrift*, 99), the cultic formulas reached P orally and were written down later on. It was only then that this defamiliarization took place (see also Rösler, "Fiktionalität," 302–12, who ranks the transition from orality to literacy high in the emergence of fictional literature). Koch suggests that, within this "literarization," the older cultic formulas were necessarily dissolved (*zerschrieben*; see also K. Koch, "Alttestamentliche und altorientalische Rituale," in *Die Hebräische Bibel und ihre zweifache Nachgeschichte* [ed. E. Blum, C. Machholz, and E. W. Stegemann; Neukirchen-Vluyn: Neukirchener Verlag, 1990] 75–85, pp. 75–77). Although I agree with Koch with regard to the transition from an oral stage to a literary, I call into question Koch's consideration that this defamiliarization took place unintentionally (see Koch, *Priesterschrift*, 101).

word (liturgy).[105] But there is no reason that this change of paradigms could not have happened before the exilic period. In any case, the individual elements of this "fiction" must be earlier, because only traditio-historically well-known, established objects and persons can later be defamiliarized. Furthermore, the question remains open whether the sacrificial service was "simply" replaced by a preliminary liturgy, or whether the process was not more complicated. To turn the arguments upside down, I am positing that such spiritualization had to have taken place before the loss of the temple and sacrificial cult so that, in the face of these events, later generations could adopt this structure.

By relocating the making of the tabernacle to the time of the wandering in the desert, P largely presents Israel's cult statically and "unhistorically" in order to save the concept of Yahweh's "meeting" with Israel: only within the realm of the cult, can Israel meet with Yahweh. By abandoning the concept of a God "wrapped up" by events in the course of history, Israel no longer meets Yahweh *within* (the course of) history but in spite of and in the face of devastating events. By means of fictionalizing, the Priestly author(s) initiated what I call the "realm of exegesis": The "meeting" from above the כפרת, just like P's ark and cherubim, exist(ed) purely (not: "merely"!) in the text. This realm of exegesis has not only preserved all figures involved in this "theological stage play" but simultaneously has created the realm of a theological future, having Yahweh "dwell" in Israel's literature. In this way, P initiated a *fiction of history*,[106] which turned out to be the most unusual of all the "realities" of the last 2,000 years of Israel's exegetical tradition.

---

105. See Fritz (*Tempel und Zelt,* 153), who followed the ideas of H.-J. Hermisson, *Sprache und Ritus im altisraelitischen Kult: Zur 'Spiritualisierung' der Kultbegriffe im Alten Testament* (WMANT 19; Neukirchen-Vluyn: Neukirchener Verlag, 1965); see also the discussion in Blum, *Studien,* 303–5.

106. See also the definition given in R. Kuhns, "The Cultural Function of Fiction," in *Funktionen des Fiktiven* (ed. D. Henrich and W. Iser; Munich: Fink, 1983) 55–66, esp. 55: "I shall argue that the term 'culture' is usefully defined as 'a tradition of fictional enactments.'"

Index of Authors

691

Index of Scripture

New Testament

Deuterocanonical Literature

Index of Sites and Place-Names

716